THE

PUBLICATIONS

OF THE

SURTEES SOCIETY.

ESTABLISHED IN THE YEAR

M.DCCC.XXXIV.

VOL. LI.

FOR THE YEAR M.DCCC.LXVII.

SYMEONIS DUNELMENSIS

OPERA

ET

COLLECTANEA.

VOL. I.

Published for the Society
BY ANDREWS AND CO., DURHAM.
WHITTAKER AND CO., 13 AVE MARIA LANE;
T. AND W. BOONE, 29 NEW BOND STREET;
BERNARD QUARITCH, 15 PICCADILLY, LONDON.
BLACKWOOD AND SONS, EDINBURGH.

1868.

At a Meeting of the Council of the SURTEES SOCIETY, held in the Castle of Durham, on Tuesday, December the 6th, 1864, Mr. CHEVALLIER in the chair, it was ordered "That a volume of the works of Symeon of Durham should be edited for this Society by Mr. Hodgson Hinde."

JAMES RAINE,
Secretary.

LONDON:
MITCHELL AND HUGHES, PRINTERS, 24 WARDOUR STREET, W.

PREFACE.

Symeon of Durham was a monk in the ecclesiastical establishment with which his name is inseparably connected, and stands thirty-eighth in order on the list of its members, furnished by himself,[a] and substantially corroborated by the entries in the *Liber Vitæ* of the Church of Durham.[b]

The original settlement of the fraternity was at Jarrow, under the auspices of Bishop Walcher, in 1074.[c] From this place they were transferred by his successor, William de St. Carileph, to the conventual buildings which he erected for their reception, within the cathedral precincts of his episcopal city, A.D. 1083.[d] Symeon appears to have been resident in Durham, perhaps as a member of the choir, before the removal of the monastery from Jarrow, as he speaks from his own recollection of the performance of the choral service in the cathedral by the secular clergy, during the episcopate of Bishop Walcher;[e] and it is probable from his position on the monastic roll that he joined the fraternity shortly after their transference to that city.

The number of monks who migrated from Jarrow to Durham was twenty-three,[f] to which it is likely enough that the thirty-

[a] Historia Ecclesiæ Dunelmensis, p. 12; edit. Bedford, 1732.

[b] Surtees Society Publications; 1841; vol. ii., p. 45.

[c] Hist. Dunelm., lib. iii., c. xxi.

[d] Ibid., lib. iv., c. ii.

[e] Ibid., lib. ii., c. vi.

[f] Ibid., lib. iv., c. iii. The number of the monks has been erased from the MS. in the Library of the University at Durham, and does not occur in that in the Public Library of the University of Cambridge, but is preserved in the contemporary MS. in the Cottonian Library, Faustina A. v.

seven enrolled previous to Symeon had been reduced by deaths and removals during an interval of nine or ten years.

Assuming the date of his profession to have been about A.D. 1083, we cannot place that of his birth much later than A.D. 1060, and these dates are consistent with the fact related by himself,[g] and with greater particularity by an historian of the succeeding century, Reginald of Coldingham,[h] that he was present at the exhumation of the remains of St. Cuthbert in 1104, and assisted at the solemnity, being at that period one of the senior monks.

The others who officiated on this solemn occasion were Turgot the Prior; Aldwine the Sub-prior; Leofwine and Wiking; Godwin and Osburn, the sacrists; Henry and William the archdeacons; and Algar, afterwards Prior. Of these, seven were of superior standing to Symeon, and two were his juniors.[i] Symeon was not as yet distinguished by any official designation, but he seems afterwards to have attained the rank of precentor, by which title he is described in the rubrics to his History of the Kings of the Angles and Danes, and also in that prefixed to the copy of his History of the Church of Durham, which is preserved in the Cambridge University Library. His obit was celebrated on the 14th of October by his brethren and successors in the Church of Durham,[j] but we have no information as to the year of his decease.[k] His History of the Kings of the Angles and Danes is brought down to the year 1129, and his account of the archbishops of York must have been written

[g] Hist. Dunelm., lib. i., c. x.

[h] Surtees Society Publications, vol. i., p. 84.

[i] The names of those present are from Reginald, as above. Their order of priority is, from Symeon's own list, as follows:—

Turgot, the Prior (6).	Osburn (24).
Aldwine, Sub-prior (48).	Henry (32).
Leofwin (4).	William (35).
Wiking (17).	Algar (49).
Godwin (11).	Symeon (38).

[j] Ancient obituary published by the Surtees Society, at the end of the Liber Vitæ, p. 146.

[k] Dugdale's Monasticon (by Caley and Ellis), vol. vi., p. 1173. William de St. Barbara, his successor, was as early, if not earlier, than 1138.

about the same time, or perhaps a little later. It is dedicated to Hugh, dean of York, of whose tenure of that dignity we have evidence in 1130 and 1133. Symeon must at that time have been between seventy and eighty, and it is probable that his life did not extend long beyond the period of his literary labours.

Such are the few particulars which are known to us of Symeon of Durham, and even these, although they are derived almost exclusively from his own testimony, have not been accepted without question.

The rubric prefixed to his History of the Kings of the Angles and Danes, in the only existing MS., represents the work as extending from the death of the Venerable Beda to the latter part of the reign of Henry I., an interval, as is erroneously stated, of 429 years. Now Beda died A.D. 737, and the addition of 429 years to this date brings us down to 1166, which has been adopted by one commentator after another as the era of Symeon's authorship, ignoring altogether the facts, that the reign of Henry I. terminated in 1135, and the History is actually carried no farther than 1129. On such grounds Bale asserts that Symeon flourished A.D. 1166, and his assertion has been accepted as conclusive by Selden, who contributed an essay to Twysden's great work, the Decem Scriptores,[l] in which he undertakes to prove that Symeon was not the author of the History of the Church of Durham. Nor was the task a difficult one, assuming his premises to have been correct. We may readily admit that an individual who flourished in 1166 could hardly speak from his own recollection of matters which occurred previous to 1080, the year of Bishop Walcher's death; nay, further, we can hardly identify him with one of the senior brethren of his convent who assisted at the translation of St. Cuthbert in 1104. Either we must reject the authority of Bale, or deprive Symeon of the credit of a work on which his reputation as an historical writer mainly depends, and Selden adopted the latter alternative. But he did more than this.

[l] London, folio, 1652.

Ignoring the real author, he advanced the claims of another person, Symeon's superior, the Prior Turgot. The ingenuity of his argument, and his well-earned reputation for judgment and learning, secured for his opinions general and unhesitating acceptance, nor did any one till the lapse of nearly a century attempt an examination of the basis on which his superstructure was built. At length a new edition of the Durham History, based on a MS. unknown to Twysden, was undertaken by Dr. Bedford,[m] and to this was prefixed a dissertation by Rudd, in which the claims of Symeon were successfully vindicated, and the erroneous computation exposed.

The publication by the Surtees Society of the work of Reginald of Coldingham, in which the presence of Symeon at the disinterment of St. Cuthbert's remains is distinctly affirmed, renders it unnecessary to recapitulate Rudd's arguments here, but they may be read with advantage as a model of close and accurate reasoning, perfectly conclusive, irrespective of the corroborative evidence which has since come to light.

The History of the Church of Durham forms no part of the present publication, being reserved for a second volume, to which it may not be thought inexpedient to prefix both the treatise of Selden and the reply of Rudd, and thus to exhibit a complete view of a discussion which, although now set at rest, has always excited peculiar interest amongst historical enquirers.

Of the voluminous historical materials which have been printed under the name of Symeon of Durham, two only are properly described as his *works,* in the sense in which we apply the term to the production of a modern writer, the *History of the Church of Durham,* and the *Account of the Archbishops of York.* The *History of St. Cuthbert* is only a transcript of an ancient document which has furnished matter for the compilation of the *Durham History;* and the tract on the *Siege of Durham, and the fortunes of Uchtred and his successors, earls of Northumberland,* has apparently been transcribed for a kindred purpose, as many of the details have been incorporated in

[m] London, 8vo, 1732.

the *History of the Kings of the Angles and Danes.* The last-mentioned production occupies an intermediate position between an original composition and a mere transcript, being for the most part a *verbatim* copy or an abridgment of earlier writers, with certain additions, some of which are possibly from the pen of Symeon, whilst others have unquestionably been added by a later hand.

In order to include all these pieces, the title of *Symeonis Opera et Collectanea* has been adopted for the present publication. Under the latter designation a place has also been reserved for the very important *History of the Miracles and Translations of St. Cuthbert,* of which no perfect copy has previously been printed, and which, although it has not hitherto, like his other *Collectanea,* been associated with his name, has yet been used by him to a great extent as an authority, and is more than once referred to by him for additional particulars, which he has thought it unnecessary to repeat.

Besides the works enumerated above, there is in the Cottonian Library a MS. chronicle in the handwriting of the twelfth century, to which is prefixed a rubric in a recent hand, attributing its authorship to Symeon of Durham. The work consists of two parts; the first being an account of the succession of the kings of the principal states of the Anglo-Saxon heptarchy; the second, an abridgment of the latter part of Symeon's *History of the Angles and Danes.* From the second part have been gleaned a few passages of no great importance, which are not derived from Symeon's larger work, but which are here printed with it, care being taken to distinguish them from the original text; the compilation from which they are extracted being distinguished in the notes as *Abbreviatio Symeonis.* The first part, of which several other MSS. exist, is printed entire, under the title, which occurs in one of them, of *Libellus de adventu Saxonum, sive de eorumdem regibus.* It has never been printed, and although it may well be doubted whether Symeon had any connection with its authorship, it contains several matters of novelty and importance which render its publication highly expedient in connection with the other pieces in this volume.

Another tract has been printed by Twysden, consisting of various historical and topographical extracts, which have been inserted in the MS. of the History of the Church of Durham which is preserved in the Cambridge University Library. They bear internal evidence of having been thrown together by the transcriber in the reign of Henry II., and not by Symeon in that of Henry I. As, however, they have been so long associated with his name, they are printed in the Appendix.

The present volume thus contains everything which has at any time been ascribed to the authorship of Symeon, with the exception, already noticed, of his History of the Church of Durham. This has been reserved for future publication, with such kindred and illustrative matter, as, taken in conjunction with the previous volumes of the Surtees Society, will exhaust the ancient literature connected with the Life of St. Cuthbert, and the history of his church.

Having explained the scope of the present undertaking, it remains to lay before the reader a more detailed account of the contents of the volume now presented, and of the MSS. from which they have been derived.

I. *The Passion of St. Ethelbert and St. Ethelred.* This legend is taken from the only existing MS. in which the *History of the Kings of the Angles and Danes* is preserved, being indeed described as part of that work, and placed after the rubric to which reference has already been made. On the ground that it may have been copied from the collections of Symeon it is printed here, but it certainly has no connection with the *History of the Kings,* which is confined, on the testimony of the rubric itself, to transactions "after the death of the Venerable Beda." The legend has moreover an appropriate rubric of its own. We have no information as to the name of the author, but we have distinct proof that it was written long before the age of Symeon. The legend informs us that the bodies of the martyred princes were still deposited at Wakering, whereas we know from Gotscelin that they were removed to

Romsey about the year 990.[a] This narrative is repeated nearly *verbatim* in the Life of Mildreda, which passes under the name of that writer, and is printed in an abbreviated form by Capgrave.

II. *The Succession of the Kings of Northumberland* is also treated in the MS. as part of the History of the Kings of the Angles and Danes, and is connected with the Passion of St. Ethelbert and St. Ethelred by the following sentence : "In the beginning of this work I have accurately set forth the succession of the Kentish kings : I must now set forth that of the kings of the Northumbrians, that we may come to the times of those of whom there is no history, after the death of the venerable priest, Beda." This piece is merely a paraphrase, in very inflated language, of the short Northumbrian chronology which is appended to many MSS. of Beda's Ecclesiastical History.

If the version is by Symeon, it was probably executed in very early life, before his judgment was matured. The phraseology is evidently adopted in imitation of that in which the preceding legend is written, and is even more laboured and ambitious in its style. Its value as an authority is of course nullified by the existence of the original document from which it is paraphrased ; but it is of some interest in consequence of the similarity of its style to that of a version of Asser's Life of Alfred, which is incorporated with the first part of the *History of the Kings*, which points to the inference that both are from the same hand; that if one, then both have been operated upon by Symeon; and that the Kentish legend from which the phraseology is derived, in which both are clothed, must have formed part of the collections of the same writer. The question of the authorship, however, will be more satisfactorily discussed in connection with the more important work which immediately follows.

[a] See Preface to Monumenta Historica Britannica, p. 89. Gotscelin's *Passio beatorum martyrum Etheldredi et Ethelbricti* occurs in MS. Bodl., 285, ff. 116-120 *b*. Of his Life of Mildreda, four early MSS. are described by Mr. Hardy in his Catalogue of Materials for British History, vol. i., p. 376.

III. *History of the Kings of the Angles and Danes.* The only ancient copy of this compilation is contained in a MS. volume in the library of C. C. College, Cambridge,[o] formerly in the possession of Archbishop Parker, of which a minute description will be found in the appendix to this Preface, being the result of a careful examination and collation by the Rev. James Raine. Besides the two pieces which precede the *History of the Kings* in the present volume, there are in the MS., interposed between the rubric and the body of the work, many pages of extracts from the writings of Beda, including a large portion of the *Lives of the Abbats of Jarrow and Wearmouth,* with several Latin poems, one of them of considerable length. As all these are accessible in the collected editions of Beda's works, it has not been thought necessary to reproduce them here, especially as they exhibit no marks of that manipulation to which the Northumbrian chronicle and the version of Asser have been subjected.

The rubric is to the following effect:—"Here begins the History of Symeon of holy and sweet memory, monk and precentor of the Church of Durham, concerning the deeds of the kings of the Angles and Danes, and their incessant wars, rapines, and incendiarisms; from the death of the Venerable priest Beda, nearly to the death of King Henry I., the son of William the Bastard, who conquered England, that is, for a period of four hundred and twenty-nine years and four months."

The inaccuracy of the computation in the last line has been already pointed out, but the rubric altogether is very little to be depended upon, and certainly formed no part of the original work, but must have been added not earlier than the reign of Henry II., previous to whose accession there was no occasion to distinguish his predecessor of the same name, as Henry I. To all the matter previously adverted to it is altogether inapplicable, as the whole of it relates to a period inconsistent with the title, for the most part antecedent to the birth of Beda, and in no case posterior to his death. Leland, who has made

[o] F., v., 139.

extensive extracts from this MS., was fully alive to the inaccuracy of the above description, and has modified the rubric, first, by rejecting the false computation, and, secondly, by discriminating between the *Historia post Bedam*, and the incongruous medley of discordant materials which has been associated with it.[p] The historical matter, to which alone the rubric properly applies, consists of two separate compilations, perfectly distinct and unconnected, but which do between them extend over the interval from the death of Beda to the latter years of Henry I., the first part reaching from the termination of the *Ecclesiastical History*, four years before the death of its author, to the year 957, the second going back to the birth of King Alfred, A.D. 848, and ending in the 30th of Henry I., A.D. 1129.

That the scribe of the Cambridge MS. himself, when he copied the several pieces which he has grouped together under this rubric, did not regard them as portions of an integral whole, is obvious on a reference to Mr. Raine's report. Nay, further, he has not even treated the two chronicles, which we are content to accept as the first and second parts of the *History of the Kings*, as if they were in any way connected. The first, although written with some regard to neatness and regularity, is totally void of ornament, whilst the second is executed with considerable elegance, and adorned with an illuminated initial, which if it were to be found in one only of two parts of the same work, we should at all events expect to find at the commencement of the first and not of the second. The preliminary matter, again, is so carelessly transcribed as in many places to be scarcely legible, replete with erasures and

[p] The rubric as modified by Leland is as follows:—Ex historia Symeonis monachi, precentoris Dunholmensis ecclesiæ, quam scripsit de regibus Anglorum et Danorum a tempore Bedæ usque ad ultimos annos Henrici Primi, regis Angliæ; ita tamen ut ante præscriptam historiæ inchoationem incipiat a genealogia regum Cantianorum et vitam Ethelberti et Ethelredi martyrum, et filiorum Eormenredi, qui fuit filius Eadbaldi, et frater Erconberti regum Cantiæ, scribat et posterea adsuat genealogiam regum Northanhynbrorum, multa interserens de abbatibus, cum Weremutensis tum Gyrovicencis cœnobii, ac etiam de Beda (Collectanea, vol. ii., p. 347: ed. 1774).

interlineations, and, as regards the poetry, abounding with alternative readings, as if it had been taken from a still ruder copy, which could not with certainty be deciphered.

That the rubric was an after-thought, is obvious from the position which it occupies. No space remained for it at the top of the page, which was already occupied by the appropriate rubric of the Legend of the Martyrdom of the two Kentish Princes, and it had to be written at the bottom of the previous page.[q] Mr. Raine does not pronounce with certainty whether the rubric is written by the same hand as the two chronicles, but the writing is of nearly the same period.

PART I.—A.D. 732-957.

As the entire history consists of two somewhat incongruous parts, so the first part is composed of two divisions equally distinct, written at different periods, but both far anterior to the age of Symeon, whatever part he may possibly have taken in reducing them to their present form.

The first division, extending to the commencement of the ninth century, has every appearance of having been written contemporaneously with the events which it records. The second is a paraphrase, somewhat abridged in detail, but much more diffuse in language, of Asser's Life of Alfred, with a few

[q] The work which immediately precedes the miscellaneous matter which is grouped with the History of the Kings in the Cambridge MS. is the little tract on the Siege of Durham, at the foot of which the rubric is written. Next before this is the epistle to Dean Hugh on the archbishops of York, which is unequivocally Symeon's, and in the body of which his name occurs. It is difficult to know what inference to draw from this: whether it induced the rubricist to ascribe to Symeon the matter which follows, and which was previously anonymous, or whether the whole had been transcribed from a copy in the same handwriting, or which could be traced to have belonged to Symeon. The only conclusion at which we can safely arrive is a negative one, that in discrediting the authority of the rubric, we do not necessarily disprove Symeon's connection with any of the works with which his name has been associated, but leave it to be decided on other evidence.

unimportant additions, and some scanty notices by way of continuation, the last of which refers to the year 957.

The first division, although it professes to take up the Anglo-Saxon annals from the death of Beda, really commences where his *Ecclesiastical History* ends, three years earlier. The last chapter of Beda contains, as is well known, what is called a *Recapitulation of the whole work,* but which is in fact a chronological summary of the affairs of Britain, founded for the most part on the previous narrative, but containing some information of considerable importance which does not occur there.[r]

This summary is continued up to and after the death of the author in various existing MSS. for a longer or shorter period. In some it ends with A.D. 735; in others it is carried on to 766, and the chronicle under consideration to a very great extent, though not uniformly, coincides with it up to the later date, differing from it only in the same degree that one copy of the Saxon Chronicle differs from another. From 766 to the commencement of the following century it is of precisely the same character, being to all appearance a series of notes committed to writing whilst the events were fresh in the memory of the authors. We have evidence, at all events, that it was compiled previous to the year of Halfdene's incursion, 875, in which the church of Hexham was destroyed. In an entry under A.D. 788 the author describes it as still existing in his own time, as it stood at the date referred to, in all its pristine splendour; whereas we know that the torches of Halfdene's followers had consumed the woodwork and ornamental fittings, and left nothing but the wreck of its bare and blackened walls.

The copy of these annals in the work before us ends abruptly and imperfectly, the entry under the year 803 breaking off in the middle of a sentence. From this year to 830 is a total blank; then occurs one of a series of notices of the suc-

[r] *Inter alia,* the notice of the foundation of the kingdom of Northumberland by Ida, which has been copied in the Anglo-Saxon Chronicle, and by all our early historians, is found in the "Recapitulatio" only: the very name of Ida does not occur in the body of the Ecclesiastical History.

cession of the archbishops and bishops of Canterbury and the Northern sees; after which we have no indication of any farther portion of these earlier materials, but the second division commences after another interval of nineteen years.

It is not to be wondered at that Symeon's name has been connected with this work, although we have shewn that the original fabric at all events is of much earlier date. Not only does he use it during a long period as the basis of the civil history which is necessarily intermixed with his account of the Church of Durham, but in many instances he adopts the peculiarities of its language. The following instances of identity of expression will be sufficient to shew that the coincidence is not fortuitous, but that he must have written with the book open before him :—

1. Describing the elevation of Egbert, bishop of York, to the archiepiscopal dignity, A.D. 735, the following words are used in the annals, and are adopted by Symeon : "Primus post Paulinum, accepto ab Apostolica sede pallio, genti Northanhymbrorum in archiepiscopatum confirmatus est."[s]

2. Speaking of the death of Balther, the hermit of Tyningham, the words in these annals are : "Viam sanctorum patrum est secutus, migrando ad Eum, Qui se reformavit ad imaginem Filii Sui." Symeon has the same words, with the substitution only of "ingressus est" for "est secutus."[t]

3. In reference to the retirement of King Eadbert to the cloister at York, we read here: "In clericatu Deique Omnipotentis servitio." Symeon has the same words, transposing "Dei" and "Omnipotentis."[u]

4. Under the year 793 Symeon copies with slight verbal alterations, first a minute description of the island and monastery of Lindisfarne; secondly, an account of the prodigies which preceded the destruction of the latter; and, lastly, the particulars of the catastrophe. In this case, if we had had any doubt as to which was the original authority, it would have

[s] Compare p. 13, l. 1, with Hist. Dunelm., ii., 3.
[t] Compare p. 20, l. 9, with Hist. Dunelm., ii., 2.
[u] Compare p. 23, l. 1, with Hist. Dunelm., ii., 3.

been removed by his own express statement that he copied from an earlier writer.[v]

5. The account given in this work of the attack of the Danes on the monastery at the mouth of the Don is copied *verbatim* in the History of the Church of Durham, but in the latter we have an explanation, which was unnecessary in the time of the earlier writer, that *Portus Ecgfridi* was the old name of the estuary at Jarrow at the confluence of the Don with the Tyne.[w]

The number of cases of this kind, of the recurrence of combinations of words which would never spontaneously have presented themselves to two independent writers, might be extended, but the above are the most remarkable. We must not, however, omit to point out one very notable instance in which Symeon has unquestionably derived his materials from the Historia de Gestis Regum, but has assigned motives for the acts detailed, which cannot be gathered from the earlier writer, and are even opposed to the obvious deductions from his text; thus clearly demonstrating that Symeon was not the author of these annals, inasmuch as he was not in all cases able to unravel the intricacies of their narrative. Under the year 750 we read that King Eadbert led Bishop Kynewlf captive to Bamburgh, and afterwards confined him in the church of St. Peter at Lindisfarne. Also that Offa, the son of Aldfrid, although innocent, was compelled to take refuge at the shrine of St. Cuthbert, but was dragged, unarmed and almost dead with hunger, from the church.[x]

The natural inference seems to be that both acts of violence were committed by the king, or with his sanction, but Symeon gives quite a different version, attributing the calamities which befell Offa, in general terms, to the persecution of his enemies, and the punishment of the bishop to Eadbert's displeasure at his connivance or non-interference to prevent such atrocities. Even if the text before us admitted of such an interpretation, we have this serious difficulty to contend with, that Offa so far

[v] Compare p. 31, l. 17, with Hist. Dunelm., ii., 5.

[w] Compare p. 32, l. 38, with Hist. Dunelm., ii., 5.

[x] Compare p. 19, l. 3, with Hist. Dunelm., i.., 2.

from being a connection or ally of the ruling monarch, was the last remaining descendant of an elder and antagonistic branch of the house of Ida. Eadbert followed but the instinct of his race in pursuing the rightful heir to the crown with unrelenting severity, and even tearing him from the sanctuary of the altar, whilst the bishop drew upon himself the anger of his sovereign by admitting the fugitive to this ineffectual asylum.

Not only has Symeon availed himself of these ancient annals in the compilation of his *History of the Church of Durham* up to the year 803, where they terminate imperfectly in our copy, but he seems to have followed an unmutilated text to a much later date, for he gives us the succession of the Northumbrian kings from that period to the disruption of the monarchy in 867,[y] and, after that, the reigns of two petty princes, Ecgbert and Ricsig,[z] whose dominions were limited to the territory north of the Tyne; which particulars are not to be found in the Anglo-Saxon Chronicle, nor, so far as we are aware, in any other authority which existed at the time he wrote. From this date indeed the character of his history is altogether changed. It is no longer a continuous narrative, but a series of unconnected anecdotes and miracles, often separated by considerable intervals of time, and generally traceable, where the matter is historical, to existing sources. The inference seems clear that the authority which had guided him from the close of Beda's History had suddenly failed, nor need we be surprised that it should be so, when we remember that at this precise period, in the reign of Ricsig, the devastations of Halfdene occurred, overwhelming in one common ruin all the monasteries of Northumberland, and that the monks, the only historians of the age, were either slain or hopelessly dispersed. We have seen that in these annals the church of Hexham is represented as existing in its pristine magnificence and integrity, and so it did remain till this calamitous period, but scarcely had the pen dropped from the hand of the writer, when it was reduced to a scorched and blackened ruin.

[y] Hist. Dunelm., ii., 5, 6. [z] Ibid., ii., 6.

The anonymous author of the work for the first time made public in this volume, *De Adventu Saxonum,* has used the same materials up to this date in the Northumbrian portion of his compilation, and they must even have existed in the time of Roger of Wendover, a much more recent author, whose narrative precisely agrees with Symeon's, but is occasionally somewhat fuller in details.

We have traces also of a continuation of the *Historia de Gestis Regum Anglorum,* which is probably the same that is cited by Adam of Bremen, an author referred to by Dr. Lappenbergh, under the title of *Gesta Anglorum,* as his authority for events which occurred half a century later, and which we do not find recorded by any other historian. This continuation was probably not the work of a contemporary, nor is it probable that there ever existed a complete and continuous history of the affairs of Northumberland during the troublous period which intervened between the reign of Ricsig and that of Eric, or Hyric, the last of her Danish rulers. For the earlier portion of this interval there are no other details in the History of the Church of Durham than are to be met with in the ancient History of St. Cuthbert: those in the Libellus de Adventu Saxonum are probably from the Gesta Anglorum, and contain little which is not to be found in the Anglo-Saxon Chronicle.

The importance of the early annals embodied in the *Historia de Gestis Regum Anglorum et Dacorum* has been greatly underrated, in consequence of their having been looked upon as the production of an author of the twelfth century, instead of being, as they unquestionably are, the genuine records of the eighth and ninth; as ancient and authentic as any of the materials which have been incorporated in the Saxon Chronicle for the same period.

The original information which they supply relates more particularly to the kingdom of Northumberland, but is by no means confined to it. The following notices apply to the history of the southern states. Under the year 732 we read of the death of Alric, one of the sons and co-heirs of Wictred, king of Kent, which is unnoticed in the Saxon Chronicle, and erroneously dated by Malmesbury. Swebreht also, king of the East Saxons, whose death is recorded A.D. 738, is noticed by no other author. Again, in 740, we read, "Arwine, the son of Eadulf, was slain." Eadulf was one of the petty kings who ruled in separate districts of Kent at that period, unnoticed by historians, but known to us by a charter bearing his name in the Textus Roffensis. The Northumberland Annals appended to Beda mention his death, without noticing his parentage;[a] by no other historian is any mention made of him. Under the year 749 the following statement occurs in our text, which is not to be met with elsewhere: "Ælfwald, king of the East Angles, died. Hunbeanna[b] and Alberht divided his kingdom between them."

As regards the Fasti of the English Church we have much exclusive information. We find the succession of the bishops of Lindsea,[c] and the names of many bishops of the Mercian sees;[d] notices of the consecration of two bishops of Selsea,[e] and of one of each of the dioceses of Hereford, Sherburn, and Elmham;[f] of the deaths of two bishops of London[g] and one of Rochester,[h] all unnoticed by the Saxon Chronicle, in common with which we have also lists of the archbishops of Canterbury and York, and of the bishops of Lindisfarne, Hexham, and Whitherne.

[a] "Aruuini et Eadbertus interfecti." We have no clue to the identity of Eadbertus, if indeed the reading is correct.

[b] Mr. Thorpe would read Beanna or Beonna, and not *Hun*beanna. See his note to the translation of Lappenberg's *England under the Anglo-Saxon Kings*, vol. i., p. 243 : 1845.

[c] 732 Cynebertus moritur.
733 Aldwig—moritur 750.
750 Aldulfus—moritur 765.

[d] Aldwinus qui et Wor moritur 737.
737 Huita (Lichfield); Totta (Leicester)—moritur 764.
Hemeli (Lichfield) moritur 765.
764 Eadbert (Leicester); 765 Cuthfrid (Lichfield).
786 Aldulfus (Lichfield).

[e] 731 Sigfrid; 767 Alubert—moritur 780.

[f] 736 Cuthbert, Heordwald, Ethelfrid.

[g] Ingwald 745; Hathubert 801.

[h] Aldulf 739.

We have also several details of the history of Scotland during the period of the Pictish predominance, which are either altogether unnoticed elsewhere, or confined to the text before us, and the kindred pages of the Northumberland Annals.

A.D. 744. A battle between the Picts and Britons.

A.D. 756. Eadbert, king of Northumberland, and Unust, king of the Picts, led an army against the city of Alclyde, and there received the submission of the Britons on the first day of August. On the tenth of the same month almost the whole of the army perished, on the route from Ouania to Newburgh.

A.D. 774. Alcred, king of Northumberland, fled with a few companions first to Bamburgh, and afterwards to Cynoht, king of the Picts.[i]

Not less important is the confirmation given to the accuracy of the ancient *Chronicon Pictorum*, by the dates which are here furnished of the decease of Unust, or Ungus,[j] and of Cynoht. The Pictish Chronicle does not give the dates of the accession or deaths of the several kings, but specifies the length of each reign, so that the knowledge of the year of the death of one king enables us to ascertain the dates of the whole series, provided we are assured of the accuracy of the statement of the duration of the intermediate reigns. Now the Irish Annals give the date of Cynoht's death A.D. 775, and the Chronicle furnishes the length of his reign twelve years, and of that of his predecessor, Brude, the immediate successor of Ungus, two years, thus fixing the death of Ungus, A.D. 761. Our Annals not only agree with the Irish Annals in placing the death of Cynoht A.D. 775, but confirm the accuracy of the intermediate computation, by supplying the date of Ungus's death also, which the Irish Annals do not, in this very year 761.

The second division of the first part commences, as has

[i] In our Annals under the year 750, we read, Cuthred rex Occidentalium Saxonum surrexit contra Æthilbaldum regem Merciorum; the Northumberland Annals add, "et Oengusum."

[j] Unust, Pictorum rex, defunctus est. The Northumberland Annals add, "qui regni sui principium usque ad finem facinore cruentum tyrannus carnifex produxit."

been already stated, with an abridged paraphrase of Asser's Life of Alfred, which is continued from the Saxon Chronicle to the end of his reign. The first entry refers to A.D. 802, forty-seven years before Alfred's birth, being a narrative of events at that date, which are introduced by Asser in explanation of a custom to which he has occasion to allude under A.D. 856. These particulars are here inserted in chronological order immediately before the last imperfect items belonging to the first division. These items relate to the series of archbishops of Canterbury and bishops of Lindisfarne, which form part of the earlier work, and two similar entries are inserted in the second part by a more recent hand at the bottom of the page. With these exceptions, there are but four entries between 802 and 887 which are not derived from Asser. Of these, three, under the years 875, 877, and 883, are from the Historia de Sancto Cuthberto, and two of them are interlineations; the fourth, under the year 881, is from an unknown source, which has also been made use of in the second part, under the same date, and is unconnected with English history.[k]

From the death of Alfred there is nothing like a continuous narrative, but a series of unconnected notices extend over a period of fifty-eight years; of these, about forty in all, more than half are taken from the Saxon Chronicle; the others furnish many particulars, chiefly in connection with Northumbrian history, which cannot be traced to any earlier source.

The last entry under the year 957 records the death of Edgar and the accession of Edwin, after whose reign of seventeen years, we are told, "reigned his son Edward, who was slain by the treachery of his step-mother, and rests at Shaftes-

[k] Nam et patres cœnobii sanctissimi Benedicti, (quod Floriacum dicitur,) ipsius reliquias a tumulo, quo locatæ fuerant immensa pulchritudine, secum auferentes hac illacque discurrebant. The words in parentheses are only in the notice in the second part. The locality indicated is Fleurie in Lyonnois, and the particulars are probably from Abbo, who was an inmate of that monastery, and whose Legend of the Passion of St. Edmund is referred to in the second part p. 70, l. 21.

bury; to him succeeded his brother Ethelred, the father of King Edward, whom he had begotten of Emma."

This affords us some clue to the date at which the materials comprised in the first part were put together, certainly not earlier than the reign of Edward the Confessor, whose name is here introduced as king, and there are reasons for supposing that it was not later. Surely if it had been written under any of the succeeding kings of the Norman dynasty some allusion would have been made to that stupendous revolution which overwhelmed the Anglo-Saxon commonwealth on Edward's death. Neither in the list of kings from Edgar to Edward would it have ignored altogether the reigns of Suane, Cnute, Harold and Hardicnute. We can understand the feeling that might still prevail in the reign of Edward the Confessor, which would repudiate the Danish monarchs as usurpers, and exclude them from the regal list; but such a feeling could have no existence after the Conquest. If, again, this genealogical summary had been written after Edward's death, his name would hardly have been brought thus prominently forward without some expression of the fond veneration in which his memory was held by his countrymen in aftertimes. Symeon has occasion to refer to him twice in his History of the Church of Durham, and on both occasions applies the prefix of "the most pious king" (iii. 9, 14). That the same hand was employed in shaping the first and second portions of the first part of the History of the Kings of the Angles and Danes, will scarcely admit of dispute. The same exaggerated style pervades both, founded in each case upon the same model; on the Passion of St. Ethelbert and St. Ethelred; which, with the Genealogy of the Kings of Northumberland, clothed in the same florid paraphrase, seems to have formed the collections of an anonymous student in the reign of Edward the Confessor.

It is true that the same grandiloquent phraseology does not so universally pervade the annals of the eighth century, as the subsequent extracts from Asser; but this is due to the nature of the material to be operated upon. The brief notes of which the annals chiefly consist, were hardly susceptible of this species of ornamentation; but whenever an opportunity presented itself, as in the list of the archbishops of Canterbury, at page 12, we at once detect the finger of the paraphrast of Asser, and the Northumbrian genealogy. The detached sentences which form the continuation are again in the simplest language. We have already pointed out the very few additions which this compiler has inserted in the narrative of Asser. His interpolations in the earlier annals are yet fewer. Two only have been detected, both of which occur at page 18, and are referred to in the notes below (*q* and *u*).—The reference in the former to the Saxon Chronicle is characteristic of a writer who has drawn so much of his additional matter from that source. There can be little doubt that the other is from the same pen; at all events it was not introduced by Symeon, who was himself the author of a History of the Archbishops of York, and well acquainted with the position in their series of the second Wilfrid, whose name has caused so much perplexity in the passage referred to.

There are, however, two interpolations of much greater length which can neither be referred to the reign of Edward the Confessor, nor yet to the pen of Symeon in the following century. These occur at pages 14-17, and 26-28, and consist of Legends respecting the two canonized bishops of Hexham, Acca and Alchmund, not only directly at variance with the statements of Symeon, in his History of the Church of Durham, but obviously introduced for the very purpose of contradicting those statements. Symeon tells us (iii. 7), amongst other meritorious actions of the pious priest Alured, that he employed himself in the collection of the bones of the illustrious Saints, whose remains lay scattered amidst the ruins of the monasteries and churches of Northumberland, a portion of all of which, including relics of Acca and Alchmund, he conveyed to Durham, and deposited in the tomb of St. Cuthbert. The Legends, on the contrary, inform us that the relics remain at Hexham, not a bone absent from its proper place; and all this is accompanied by details well calculated to make a deep impression on a credulous age, and effectually to dispose of the testimony of Symeon, without making any direct reference to it.

Many instances have been adduced in which Symeon has not only derived materials from the earlier portion of the *First Part* of this History, but has even adopted its language. Of the latter portion he has not availed himself to the same extent; but we have proof that it was not unknown to him. It contains a notice of the great battle in which Athelstan defeated the combined forces of the Danes, Scots and Cumbrians, the locality of which it fixes at a place called Wendune. Every other early authority describes it by the name of Brunnanburgh; but Symeon[l] informs us that it was "fought at Weondune," which is also called by another name, "Aet-Brunnanwerc" or "Brunnanbyrig." We may assume then that Symeon had access to the entire collection, which is known to us as the *First Part* of the *History of the Kings of the Angles and Danes;* that in all probability he was the possessor of a copy which it is not unlikely that he had himself transcribed, as a storehouse of materials for the History of the Church of Durham; and the only respects in which his copy appears to have differed from that which we now possess, were, first, that the early annals were continued to the reign of Ricsig, towards the close of the ninth century, instead of ending abruptly at its commencement; and, secondly, that it had not the interpolated legends of Acca and Alchmund.

PART II.—A.D. 848-1129.

This part, as far as the year 1119, is based on the History of Florence of Worcester, of which it exhibits the text somewhat abridged, with certain interpolated passages, many of them of considerable length, but presenting in the aggregate a very small proportionate bulk as compared with the substructure on which they are grafted. The remainder of the narrative from 1119 to 1129 is an original composition.

Between the first part and the second is inserted a series of Legends from William of Malmesbury, which it has not been

[l] Hist. Dunelm., ii., 18.

thought desirable to reproduce, but references are given in the notes, by which they may readily be found in the pages of the original author. The rubricist of the MS. has distinguished by the title of "Recapitulatio" that portion of the second part which extends over the same period, which has been already gone over in the first, although after the death of Alfred they have scarcely anything in common. The remainder is described as "Continuatio."

The History of Florence, in all the copies with which we are acquainted, is made to close with the year 1117, a few months previous to the death of its author; but there is reason to believe[m] that his labours terminated some years earlier. It seems to have been brought down to 1119, probably by the same hand which afterwards continued it to 1141, and to have been at once made public. At all events Symeon commences his continuation at the former date. Amongst the interpolations are two long extracts, the first at p. 74 concerning Johannes Scotus from Malmesbury's Life of Aldhelm; the second at p. 81, explaining the conflicting claims of Harold and William to the crown of England, extracted from Eadmer's *Historia Novorum.*

There are also several notices of Rollo and his successors, Dukes of Normandy, from some authority resembling the Chronicle of Caen.

Ecgbert and Ricsig, who are mentioned by Symeon as reigning beyond the Tyne after the disruption of the Northumbrian monarchy by the Danes, are also noticed here; and the date of the latter's death, and the name of his successor, a second Ecgbert, are also given with other particulars, apparently unknown to Symeon, which have probably been derived from the *Gesta Anglorum,* referred to by Adam of Bremen. Many other particulars are also given from Symeon's *History of the Church of Durham,* and some extracts are made from the brief chronological notes in the first part of the History after the death of Alfred. The extracts from the History of Durham have certainly not been made by Symeon himself, as in many cases

[m] See note *j*, p. 106.

they have been so altered as to differ essentially from his narrative. This applies particularly to the account of the possessions of the church of Lindisfarne at p. 67, and of the settlement of Aldwine and his brethren first at Monkchester and afterwards at Jarrow, at p. 94, as will be seen by a reference to the notes. Appended to the latter narrative is a romantic legend of the life of Turgot, which is unsupported by Symeon or any independent authority.

At p. 79 is a notice of the disastrous battle at Carham, A.D. 1018, of which we have the particulars in the History of the Church of Durham, but here we have a statement utterly uncountenanced by Symeon, that Earl Uchtred was the leader of the Northumbrian forces in the engagement, although we know from Florence, as copied a few pages before, that he had been treacherously slain two years previously.

The most unaccountable discrepancy, however, occurs in the account, at p. 103, of the ceremony of laying the foundation of the new cathedral at Durham, a narrative of which we have also a description in the work of Symeon, which is specially devoted to the honour of his Church.[n] According to him the ceremony was performed by the bishop, William de St. Carileph, and Prior Turgot, assisted only by the monks; whilst in the history before us,[o] Malcolm king of Scotland is represented not merely as being present, but as having taken an active part in the solemnity. The co-operation of a sovereign prince on such an occasion was too memorable an event to have been omitted by an historian so warmly interested, and who could not have been ignorant of it, if there were any truth in the story. Neither were the relations between the parties of so amicable a kind as to induce us to accept the statement as authentic without satisfactory proof. Not many years previously Turgot had been driven from the retirement which he sought amidst the shades of Melrose, hallowed by the memory of his patron Saint, by the unceasing persecutions of the Scottish king.[p]

If we are to believe the very authority on which the state-

[n] Hist. Dunelm., iv., 8. [o] p. 103, l. 39.

[p] Hist. Dunelm., iii., 22.

ment of Malcolm's presence on this occasion rests, his hostility was not confined to the Prior, but extended to the whole church of St. Cuthbert, whose patrimony he had three times invaded and laid waste, on one occasion ravaging the sacred island of Lindisfarne;[q] on another, desolating the entire district from the Tees to Wearmouth;[r] on a third, carrying devastation to the very threshold of the episcopal city itself.[s] Two other invasions of Northumberland are mentioned, not specially directed against the patrimony of the church, and the whole are recapitulated as follows:[t]—

"The first was in King Edward's reign, when Earl Tosti "was on a pilgrimage to Rome.

"The second in King William's, when he ravaged Cleve-"land.

"The third in the same reign, when he advanced to the "Tyne, retiring from thence with great booty, after the slaughter "of the inhabitants, and the conflagration of their residences.

"The fourth in the reign of William the younger, when he "advanced with an immense force to Chester, not far from "Durham, intending to have proceeded yet farther, when, being "confronted by a far inferior force, he was seized with panic, "and returned precipitately.

"The fifth was when, having raised all the forces in his "power, he entered Northumberland for the purpose of a final "desolation, but was cut off with his eldest son Edward near "the river Alne."

The first, second, and fourth are the incursions above referred to. The third and the fifth are alone corroborated by any independent authority.

As regards the first incursion, there is nothing very startling in the fact that Malcolm should have taken advantage of Tosti's absence on a religious errand to invade his province, although they are described, as if in reprobation of the breach of faith, as "sworn brothers."

The second was directed chiefly against the possessions of

[q] p. 80, l. 25; A.D. 1061. [r] p. 87, l. 6; A.D. 1070.
[s] p. 104, l. 21. [t] p. 104, l. 16.

Earl Gospatric, who retaliated by making a raid upon Malcolm's Cumbrian territories, and the mutual exasperation is represented as extreme. All this, unsupported by other testimony, appears little entitled to credit, when opposed not only to the general statements which we have from all quarters of the amity which existed between the two, but more especially to the fact that when Gospatric was shortly afterwards driven from his earldom, he took refuge at the Scottish court, where he was not only hospitably received, but was replaced in his adopted country in a position, both as to rank and estate, little inferior to that which he had held in the land of his birth. We can imagine Malcolm ignoring obligations and violating pledges; we can even believe that circumstances might induce him to be reconciled to a former foe, but it is difficult to account for the bestowal of the wealth and honours which he heaped upon Gospatric, after the mutual injuries which they are here said to have inflicted on each other. There are minor discrepancies and inconsistencies in reference to this invasion which it is difficult to reconcile with known facts, and which at all events prove that the account could not have been written by Symeon. The church of St. Peter at Wearmouth is represented as having been burnt down on this occasion,[u] whereas we learn from Symeon that it had been for ages in ruins, its walls only standing, and the site, both within and without, overgrown by timber and brushwood, which were cut down with much labour a few years later, when the edifice was at last put into a state of repair.[v] The accounts of Malcolm's atrocities so closely resemble those ascribed to his son David I. by the Hexham historians, that, knowing as we do that the former portion of this work had received interpolations from a Hexham pen, it is difficult to resist the conviction that the details now under review have been additions from the same quarter.[w] The absurd story of the number of English slaves that were to be found in almost every Scotch household, which has met with such favourable acceptance with many of

[u] p. 87, l. 21. [v] Hist. Dunelm., iii., 22.

[w] Compare p. 8, l. 2-21, with the Chronicles of Richard and John, Priors of Hexham, published by the Surtees Society, pp. 78, 116.

our historians, rests on the solitary authority of this interpolation. The tale of the meeting of Malcolm with his future queen and her brother and sister at Wearmouth is not merely an idle fable unsupported by other evidence, but it is dated two years after the settlement of all the parties in Scotland. Some of the interpolations undoubtedly contain genuine information, but not always on matters of very great importance; and the examples which have been here given are sufficient to point out that they must not in all cases be received without examination. It has been further shewn that a large portion, at all events, is not due to Symeon. Indeed the rubric is the only evidence we possess that he had any connection with the work at all, and this assigns to him the authorship of the first part as well as the second. As regards the first part, he appears at most to have been only the transcriber of the MS. of an anonymous collector of the time of Edward the Confessor, just as he had transcribed the *Historia Cuthberti* and the tract on the *Siege of Durham,* as materials for his own works. In the same way it is probable that, on the appearance of Florence of Worcester's chronicle, he may have made an abridgment of it, adding to it perhaps from year to year such notices of current events as ultimately formed the continuation as we now have it. Some of the interpolations may also have been his. This is indeed, to a great extent, matter of speculation, but it is as near an approach to certainty as with the limited and somewhat contradictory information in our possession we are ever likely to arrive at.

The last entry in this chronicle refers to the year 1129, which is perfectly consistent with Symeon's age, and with the assumption that the continuation proceeded from his pen. In endeavouring to fix the precise date of its completion, our attention is naturally directed to two lists of the abbats of the religious houses founded at York and Whitby, which are introduced in connection with the account of the re-introduction of monastic institutions into Northumberland A.D. 1074, nearly two centuries after their extermination by the Danes.[x] A com-

[x] p. 94.

parison of these lists, if they had come down to us without alteration or addition, would have given us the information we require with a close approximation to complete accuracy; but we know that it was the almost universal practice of transcribers to continue such lists to their own times, thus obliterating the landmarks of the original authors. This has been done by the transcriber of the Cambridge MS., who brings down the series of abbats of York to Clement, and of Whitby to Richard, whose contemporaneous incumbencies extended from 1161 to 1175, thus fixing the date of transcription between those years, whilst the character of the handwriting, as reported on by Mr. Raine, points to the later rather than the earlier year.

The *Abridgment of Symeon*, however, to which allusion has already been made as existing in the Cottonian Library, presents us with farther information. This MS., which is unquestionably of earlier date than that on which our text is founded, closes the series of York abbats with the name of Godfrey, who was appointed in 1132, and only enjoyed his dignity one year. This date approximates so closely to that at which the chronicle closes, that we are tempted to assume that we have the list without alteration by the epitomist, just as it came out of the author's hands, and that the year 1132 represents the precise date of the compilation; or, even if it is the date of the abridgment, the original work must have been finished between the year 1129, to which the narrative is brought down, and 1132, in which it was epitomized. Unfortunately, however, the *Abbreviatio* extends only to 1119, and the only positive testimony which we derive from it is that certain of the interpolations had been inserted in the text of Florence, and the joint work of Florence and his interpolator had been epitomized as early as 1132. This leads to the inference that in 1132 Symeon's continuation was unknown to the public, or at all events to the epitomist, although carried out in the meantime in the privacy of his cell.

It is well known that the History of Roger Hoveden is based to a great extent upon the *Historia Regum*, and that he has transcribed *verbatim* a large proportion of both the parts. It further appears from the series of abbats in his work, that the MS. from which he transcribed must have been of intermediate date between that used by the editor of the *Abbreviatio*, and the Cambridge MS., written whilst Severinus, the immediate successor of Godfrey, was abbat of St. Mary's at York, which position he held till his death in 1161. The ancient annals in the First Part, which were unquestionably perfect to a much later period, when Symeon compiled his History of the Church of Durham, must already have been mutilated when Hoveden's MS. was transcribed; and the particulars which have been inserted to fill up the gap between the year 801 and the birth of Alfred had already been transposed from their proper place in Asser's biography for that purpose. These particulars are retained by Hoveden, but he makes no farther use of the paraphrase of Asser in our text, nor of the brief notices which follow it.

It does not appear that the MS. from which the *Abbreviatio* was made contained the first part; at all events no use has been made of it, but the two parts must have been united previous to the transcription of the MS. which Hoveden copied, as that unquestionably contained farther additions, which are not in the Cambridge MS. Alured of Beverley also made use of both parts in the compilation of his History, which we know was written about A.D. 1143.[y]

The second part is twice referred to by Fordun,[z] once as an authority for the presence of Malcolm at the foundation of Durham cathedral, when he quotes it as the work of Turgot, and, secondly, for the details of certain events antecedent to the marriage of that king with the princess Margaret, when he describes it anonymously as "an old chronicle." Nowhere does he speak of Symeon as the author, nor does he appear to have been acquainted with Symeon's genuine work, the History of the Church of Durham.

[y] See Hardy's Catalogue of Materials for British History, vol ii., p. 172.

[z] See Fordun's extracts from Turgot in the Appendix to this volume, p. 261, also note *y*, p. 258.

In preparing this edition, it has been determined to omit all that portion of the text which is taken from Florence of Worcester, beyond such sentences or parts of sentences, and passages, as are essential to render the additions intelligible. A sufficient justification for this omission might be found in the inexpediency of re-printing, without serving any object of practical utility, a mass of matter, many times exceeding in bulk the contributions of Symeon, even if credit were given to him for every word which is not directly copied from Florence. It is, indeed, performing for Symeon, or whoever the interpolator may have been, the very operation which has been successfully carried out for Florence himself, whose history, it will be remembered, was originally grafted on Marianus Scotus, just as our text has been grafted on him. But the advantage is much more than negative. To retain the text of Florence is not only useless, but prejudicial. How often do we find our best historians quoting his words as the testimony of Symeon, and even insisting on the conclusive authority of those words on Northern affairs, as proceeding from a Northern source.

To ascertain what passages in the existing edition are really due to the alleged author requires a minute collation with Florence, to which few readers, and not many writers, will submit, and of which the majority do not know the necessity. In order to obviate all difficulty on this head, such portions of Florence as have necessarily been retained in the present edition are distinguished by inverted commas, so that the reader may distinguish the additional matter at a glance.

The same course might perhaps have been pursued with regard to the abridgment of Asser, which forms so large a proportion of the first part, but the cases are not precisely similar. Our text affords one or two new readings of Asser,[a]

[a] At p. 55 an important correction of the printed text is supplied. In the MSS. of Asser we find "*Exancestriam*, quod Brittanice dicitur *Cairwisc*, Latine *Civitas*," the next word being deficient. This has been supplied from Florence, who has *Civitas Exe*. Our text gives the true reading, *Civitas Aquarum*, which is the Latin equivalent for the Saxon *Exanceastre*, and the British *Cairwisc*.

and is besides valuable for the purpose of comparing its style with other portions of the works ascribed to Symeon, with a view to determine some questions bearing upon their authorship. The additions, moreover, are so few that there is no difficulty in distinguishing them, as there is in the case of the additions to Florence, which, although comparatively small in bulk, are considerable in number.

IV. *Epistle to Dean Hugh, concerning the Archbishops of York.* This little piece is contained in the same MS. volume in the Library of C. C. College, Cambridge, from which the *History of the Kings of the Angles and Danes* is taken, but the text adopted in this edition is from another transcript in the Cottonian Library,[b] which, although of comparatively modern date, undoubtedly represents an earlier and more accurate original. It has been collated also with a modern copy amongst the Hale MSS. in the Library of Lincoln's Inn,[c] but this turns out to be only a very faulty transcript of the C. C. volume. The narrative of the Acts of the Archbishops extends only to Oswald, who received the pall from Pope Benedict, A.D. 971, but the names of his successors are given down to Archbishop Thurstan, A.D. 1114-1143. The list is further extended in the Cambridge MS. to Archbishop Roger, whose primacy comprised the interval from 1154 to 1181, thus confirming the date which has already been assigned to the transcription of that volume.

The work consists of two parts, one containing the narrative, the other an epistle addressed to Hugh, dean of York, explaining the scope of the undertaking, and adding some miscellaneous information. There were two deans of York of

In the same page our text has Mucelwudu instead of Selwudu in Asser; the latter being the popular name, the former the Saxon equivalent for *Coitmawr*, or Magna Silva, Selwood Forest. The less material deviations are numerous.

[b] Titus A. xix., a small quarto on paper, of the fifteenth century, written probably by a York scribe, as the same hand occurs in other MSS. connected with Yorkshire in the British Museum. It was probably transcribed at York from the original, or at all events from a copy of earlier date than the Cambridge MS.

[c] MS. Hale, vol. xiii., in a hand of the seventeenth century.

this name in Symeon's time, the first between the years 1090 and 1109, the second from 1130 to 1132. As, however, the latter was also the contemporary of archbishop Thurstan, there can be no doubt that he is the person addressed. In the text followed in the present volume the narrative portion precedes the epistolary; in the C. C. volume the order is reversed. The other variations, which are not very material, are pointed out in the notes. Some of the names have been modernized in the Cotton MS., and Arabic numerals have been substituted for Roman. The latter are restored in the text.

There can be no doubt that we have here a genuine work of Symeon, as it is authenticated by his name in the body of the epistle. It is not, however, a production of much value, as it contains no information which is not to be met with elsewhere. We have notice here of the reigns of Egbert and Ricsig, who are also mentioned in the *History of the Church of Durham,* and whose names are only known to us from the works of Symeon and his followers, and from the other pieces which are contained in this volume. The second Egbert does not occur here, or in the Durham History. In the Cotton MS. Symeon's name is spelt with a *y,* as in his autograph copy of the *History of the Church of Durham,* in the University Library in that city. In the Cambridge MS. it is written in an abbreviated form with an *i,* thus, Sim'.

In the Cotton MS. the successors of Thurstan down to George Neville, 1464-76, are added, not in their proper place in the series of archbishops, but at the end of the epistle, thus giving us the date of the transcription.

V. *History of St. Cuthbert, and of such places and regions as belonged to him of old, and down to the present time.* The latter part of the title, rather than the former, truly expresses the object of this brief but very important contribution to the history of the church of St. Cuthbert. The notices of the Saint are incidental, and no particulars of his life, or details of miracles wrought by him after his decease, are introduced otherwise than in connection with the material advantages which were derived from them. The work is referred to by

Symeon on two occasions as the "ancient cartulary of the Church,"[d] in which are recorded grants and acquisitions, to which he adverts in general terms, but omits the particulars, which he says "it is unnecessary to detail, as they are written "elsewhere." It is, indeed, essentially a cartulary, although in a narrative form, and was probably the only evidence which remained of the original charters, which had perished amidst the desolations of the ninth century, when the house of Lindisfarne was twice burnt, its inmates driven forth, and their lands devastated. The only charter which occurs in diplomatic form is of a period subsequent to the removal of the bishopric to Chester-le-Street, and records the bounty of king Athelstan,[e] the brother and predecessor of Edmund, to whose time the narrative is brought down, and which is no doubt truly described as "nunc temporis" by the writer.

This tract is the earliest authority for the story of the appearance of the Saint to king Alfred in a vision, in which he promises him his protection, and assures him of the success of his arms against the Danes.[f] The legend is copied and embellished by Malmesbury,[g] and is briefly told by Symeon,[h] with this qualification, that "since the particulars are elsewhere "fully detailed, it is not expedient to repeat them here."

Symeon also adopts without acknowledgment the details of the death of Halfdene, of the elevation of Guthred to the throne of Northumberland, and the incidents of his reign;[i] also the ravages of Reinold, or Ragnal, and his lieutenants Scula and Onalafball, between the Tees and Tyne, and the punishment of the latter.[j]

From the History of St. Cuthbert he has also culled the miracle of the three bloody waves, which drove back the bark

[d] Hist. Dunelm., ii., 16, 18.

[e] p. 149, l. 14. The pretended charter of King Ecgfrid, which occurs at the end of the Cambridge MS. of the History of the Church of Durham, is a palpable forgery, as will be explained in the next volume.

[f] p. 144. [g] Gesta Regum Anglorum, ii., 121.

[h] Hist. Dunelm., ii., 10.

[i] Compare the History of St. Cuthbert, pp. 143-4, with Hist. Dunelm., ii., 13.

[j] Compare pp. 147-8 with Hist. Dunelm., ii., 16.

in which it was proposed to convey the body of the Saint to Ireland.[k] On one point there is a remarkable discrepancy between the older authority and Symeon, which cannot be regarded as accidental. The former describes the removal of the body of St. Cuthbert, as well as of king Ceolwulf, to Norham from Lindisfarne by Bishop Ecgfrid;[l] the latter mentions that of Ceolwulf only.[m] The topographical information which we find in the *History of St. Cuthbert* is invaluable, notwithstanding the obsolete, and in very many cases vitiated spelling, which renders it difficult to recognize the local names. This difficulty seems to have existed in the time of Symeon, who has not always attempted to grapple with it. Great pains have been taken to correct the text wherever it can be done with certainty: conjectural emendations are suggested in the notes, where also will be found the modern names and the localities of the places mentioned.

This piece was printed by Twysden from a MS. in the public Library of the University of Cambridge, where it is appended to the *History of the Church of Durham,* in connection with which the MS. will be described in the Preface to the second volume. No other copy was then known to exist. A MS. in the Library of Lincoln's Inn[n] is described by the late Mr. Hunter in a report to the Record Commissioners[o] as bearing a great resemblance to it, but on examination such was not found to be the case, the work in question being merely a biography of the Saint, containing no information of novelty or importance.

Whilst this volume was passing through the press, Mr. Raine discovered a very ancient copy in the Bodleian Library,[p] defective at the commencement, but containing a continuation which brings the history of the property of his church to the reign of

[k] p. 146; Hist. Dunelm., ii., 2.

[l] p. 142, l. 4.

[m] Hist. Dunelm., ii., 5.

[n] Hale MSS., vol. cxiv.

[o] Record Commissioners' Report, 1837; p. 374.

[p] MS. Bodl., 596 (237 *b*), ff. 203-206 *b*, vellum, folio; circa 1080. The tract described in Hardy's Catalogue, vol. i., p. 317, as "Farrago Cartarum ad storiam ecclesiæ Dunelmensis spectantium." It formerly belonged to the onastery of St. Augustine, Canterbury.

Cnute. This MS. agrees very closely with the Cambridge copy, but is less corrupt, and in many places confirms the emendations which I had previously made. Symeon has made free use of the continuation as well as of the former part of the work. At the end of it will be found the narrative of the miraculous discomfiture of the Scottish army in the reign of Guthred, which is alluded to in the History of the Church of Durham, with a reference, as before, to an earlier authority for particulars.[q]

VI. *Saxon Poem on the situation of Durham, and the relics of Saints which are preserved there.* This short piece immediately follows the *History of St. Cuthbert* in the Cambridge MS., which contains the only ancient copy which is known to exist. It is referred to by Symeon in his *History of the Church of Durham,* iii. 7. An earlier MS. was destroyed by the fire in the Cottonian Library in 1731. The poem has been ascribed to Ælfred, a priest of the Church of Durham between the years 1056 and 1071.[r]

VII. *Of the siege of Durham and of the probity of Earl Uchtred.* The only copy of the short narrative which is distinguished by this not very appropriate title is preserved in the C. C. manuscript, in which the *History of the Kings* and other pieces in this volume are also found. It is not attributed to Symeon in the original MS., but his name is an unauthorised addition in a much later hand, probably that of Archbishop Parker. Although it contains considerable information as to the succession of the earls of Northumberland before the Conquest, this seems to be purely incidental, its object being to explain the descent of certain manors alienated by Bishop Aldune on his daughter's marriage, some of which had reverted to the church, whilst others remained in lay hands. This is brought down to a period subsequent to the Conquest, and several names of proprietors occur, which are known to us in connection with the disturbances which prevailed in Northumberland both before and after that event. This tract is also th

[q] p. 152, l. 5; Hist. Dunelm., ii., 13.

[r] See Preface to Lindisfarne Gospels, published by the Surtees Society.

earliest authority for the statement of the transfer of the district of Lothian to the crown of Scotland by Eadulf Cudel, earl of Northumberland. It is, however, of less value historically, than as illustrative of the usages and manners of the times. We find a married bishop portioning his daughter out of the property of his see. We have instances, especially in reference to the Bishop's daughter, of the facility of divorce; and a most remarkable case of deadly feud, continued through three generations. We have a curious notice of the obligation of duelling. Cospatric the son of Archil is distinguished from others of the same name, as the individual who ought to have fought with Waltheof the son of Ailsi. As a mirror of every-day life amongst the influential classes in Northumberland, in the first half of the eleventh century, we have no such instructive document. It belongs to an age prior to Symeon, but he has not made use of it to the extent we might have expected. He details the assistance given by Uchtred to the Bishop in clearing the foundations for his new settlement at Durham, but he passes unnoticed the siege which is here recorded. This was probably owing to the difficulty occasioned by an error in the date, pointed out in the notes, which may in his judgment have cast a doubt on the statement altogether, and on the credibility of the writer.

VIII. *History of the Translations of St. Cuthbert.* This work has been compiled within a short time of the establishment of the monastery of Durham, and has received additions from time to time, until it assumed its present shape. One ancient copy, still extant,[s] contains only the first seven chapters, and we have proof that in its original state it consisted of only six. These six chapters must have been in existence when Symeon composed his *History of the Church of Durham* during the priorate of Turgot, which only extended to the year 1109, as we have ample evidence that it was in his hands whilst he was employed upon that work. On the other hand it is equally certain that the seventh chapter was not written until after the

[s] MS. Harl., 1924.

decease of Ranulph Archbishop of Canterbury,[t] which occurred in 1122. The first four chapters are derived from the History of St. Cuthbert, and are all of them adopted or referred to by Symeon. The first contains the vision of King Alfred; the second the miracle of the three bloody waves; the third the legend of Onalafball, or, as his name is here spelt, Onalafbald; the fourth is the history of the destruction of the Scottish host in the reign of Guthred. To all these Symeon, doubtless, had access in the pages of the earlier authority; but the fifth and sixth are not to be found there, but first occur in the present work. The fifth chapter records the punishment of Barcwith or Barcwid, a soldier of Earl Tosti, for a violation of the sanctity of the monastic precincts, to which Symeon specially refers, as it is "elsewhere detailed more fully."[u] The sixth chapter contains a relation, adopted by Symeon, of the miraculous interposition, by which the monks were enabled to pass the sands between the mainland of Northumberland and the island of Lindisfarne at high tide, when they fled with the body of the Saint to escape the anger of William the Conqueror after the slaughter of Robert Cumin and his men at Durham.[v] The seventh chapter, which forms chapter xviii. of the work as it now stands, is the most interesting of the whole, containing a minute and circumstantial account of the exhumation of the body of St. Cuthbert, A.D. 1104. This is found in all existing MSS. of the Translations of St. Cuthbert, to which indeed it gives name, the bulk of the remainder of the work being taken up with a series of miracles, which although due to the interposition of the Saint, are only occasionally connected with the migrations of his remains. It is printed separately in the *Acta Sanctorum,* and a translation is given by the late Dr. Raine in his *St. Cuthbert,* pp. 75-78.

The eleven intervening chapters, vii. to xvii. inclusive, occur in all the MSS. with the exception noted above; chapters xix and xx. are in the Laud, Arundel, and Gale MSS., xxi. in Arundel and Gale only.

[t] See p. 194, note *s*.

[u] Hist. Dunelm., iii., 11.

[v] Ib., iii., 15.

It is remarkable that there is no reference in this work to the vision which led to Guthred's elevation to the throne of Northumberland, which is related in the *Historia Cuthberti* and repeated by Symeon; and, further, that neither here nor in the *Historia* is there any notice of the miraculous preservation of the copy of the Gospels which was washed overboard on the occasion of the attempted voyage to Ireland with the body of the Saint. That legend rests on the authority of Symeon alone,[w] supported by the evidence of the book itself which is preserved to this day, and exhibits marks which have always been attributed to the effects of this immersion.

The present is not merely the first complete edition of the *Translations of St. Cuthbert,* but, as regards by far the greatest portion of its contents, is the only edition. The compilation which is printed under this title in the *Acta Sanctorum* contains only the first chapter and part of the second,[x] the remainder being made up of many pages from Symeon's *History of the Church of Durham,* and of another work entitled *Relatio de Sancto Cuthberto,* which is to a great extent a plagiarism from Symeon. In many of the MSS. in which the *Translations* occur they are followed by the *Relatio,* and the editor of the *Acta Sanctorum* had met with a volume of this kind in a mutilated state, perfect at the beginning and end but defective in the middle, and thus containing the commencement of the *Translations,* and the conclusion of the *Relatio,* which he has not unnaturally supposed to be portions of the same work. These he has connected together by the insertion of matter equal to twelve closely printed octavo pages from Symeon, and has published the whole under the title of the *History of the Translations of St. Cuthbert.* The same text is reprinted in the *Acta Sanctorum,* and again by Mr. Stevenson in the Appendix to *Beda's Historical Works.* Mr. Stevenson says, "The text here given has necessarily been adopted from the *Acta Sanctorum,* no manuscript copy being known in England." It would

[w] Ib., ii., 12.

[x] Ending with the word *undæ,* p. 164, l. 4. The text of the *Relatio* is taken up at p. 226 in the Appendix to this volume, from the word *tenera* in line 32.

be difficult perhaps to give a more conclusive testimony of the inestimable benefit conferred on historic literature by the publication of Mr. Hardy's *Catalogue of Materials for British History,* than is afforded by the fact that a reference to his pages has directed me to no less than nine MSS., one fragmentary, in various repositories in England, which have been collated for this publication. Of forty-four pages, to which the text extends in the present edition, little more than five are to be found in those which have preceded it, exclusive of the eighteenth chapter, which has been printed, as before stated, as a separate work.

On an analysis of Mr Stevenson's pages, I find twelve occupied by Symeon, fifteen by the *Relatio,* and only between five and six by the work to which alone the title is applicable. The mixture of materials of later date has very much perplexed the consideration of the question of the true age of the *Translations of St. Cuthbert.* The indications contained in the first and second chapters might have been accepted as satisfactory proof that the work had been written before the *History of the Church of Durham,* had there not been evidence even stronger in the latter part of what appeared to be the same narrative, leading to a directly opposite conclusion. Symeon has a long story of what a garrulous old man professed to have seen in a vision, and the particulars, which are of great length, are introduced in the very same words into that portion of the *Relatio* which has been mixed up in former editions with the Translations;[y] but Symeon says that *he himself* had heard them from the mouth of the old man, whereas the *Relatio,* as incorporated in the text of the *Acta Sanctorum,* merely says that *many persons* had heard them. The inference is clear that Symeon, who had the legend at first hand, must have written prior to the author, who only has it on the secondary testimony of others; but this, we now know, applies only to the *Relatio,* and not to the *Translations.* The connection which has thus existed for so long between the *Relatio* and the *Translations* has given to the former an adventitious importance to which it has no inherent

[y] See note *n,* p. 228-9.

claim, and it has been thought desirable to give a place to it in the Appendix, divested of those details which are copied verbatim from Symeon. It has thus been compressed within a moderate space, whilst as ample an opportunity is afforded of referring to it in connection with the matters before us as if it had been printed *in extenso*.

The MSS. from which our text has been formed are

1. MS. Harl. 1924, a small quarto on vellum of the twelfth century. This manuscript contains only the first six chapters, and the eighteenth.

2. MS. Cotton, Nero A. ii., also on vellum, of the twelfth century, in duodecimo, ends abruptly in the middle of chapter xviii., but it contains, besides, the *Relatio de Sancto Cuthberto*.

3. MS. Bodl., Laud 491, a small thick quarto volume with some rich illustrations, written between 1160 and 1186; in single columns; a very fine MS., belonging originally to "Leo Pylkynton," prebendary of Durham, whose autograph it bears. It contains Beda's Life of St. Cuthbert, after which is a rubric "Explicit liber de Vita et Miraculis beatissimi patris," etc. Then come two chapters of St. Cuthbert's miracles from Beda's Ecclesiastical History (i., 31, 32), which also precede the *Translations* in the two former MSS. The *Liber de Translationibus* extends to twenty chapters, and is followed by the *Relatio*. The text of this MS. is more correct than that of either of the preceding, but they very nearly coincide in those chapters which they have in common.

4. MS. Arundel 332, a very fine MS. on vellum, of the thirteenth century, in octavo, agrees generally with the foregoing, but has one additional miracle, which forms chapter xxi. of the present edition.

5. MS. Gale, O. iii., 55, a volume which has been very kindly entrusted to the care of the Society by the Master and Fellows of Trinity College, Cambridge. It contains the twenty chapters, and is a MS. of great value and antiquity, having probably been written at Durham in the twelfth century. It subsequently belonged to the Priory of Holy Island. A full description of this MS. is given in the Appendix to the Preface.

In accuracy it is perhaps superior to all the rest, and the text of the tractate *De Translationibus* is mainly derived from it.

Besides these, the following MSS. have been examined :—

6. MS. Bodl., Digby 59, agrees substantially with MS. Laud, 491, but the chapters are somewhat differently arranged, the fourth chapter being placed before the first. It contains twenty chapters in all, after which are several chapters from Symeon. It is in small octavo, written circa 1200, and contains Sir Kenelm Digby's autograph, "*Vindica te tibi; Ken. Digby.*"

7. MS. Fairfax, 6: folio, double columns, a large and fine MS., containing all the Durham Historians; in a hand of the fifteenth century. At the beginning is this line with the Christian name of the transcriber,

"Nomen scriptoris est Petrus plenus amoris."

It contains the two chapters from Beda, with twenty of the Translations as in Laud.

8. MS. Cotton, Titus A. ii., a fine old book of the fourteenth century from the Durham Scriptorium, affords no additional matter.

9. MS. Dec. et Capit. Ebor., xvi., i., 12, a well-known volume which has been much used by the Surtees Society. It is of the fourteenth century, and contains chapters xviii. to xxi. inclusive.

10. MS. Bodl., 514, a thin quarto in the old sheepskin binding, written circa 1200, has belonged to the abbey of Jervaux in Yorkshire, and bears the inscription "*Liber Sanctæ Mariæ de Jorevalle;*" also the name of the grantee of the abbey lands, "Arthur Darcy." It contains only a fragment of the *Translations*, three or four pages of chapter xviii.

All the above MSS., with the exception of No. 9, are noticed by Mr. Hardy. There is also a copy of the twenty chapters c the *Translations* without any distinctive title, with numerou other miracles from Beda, Symeon, and other known sources, i the "Lawson MS., the property of Sir John Lawson of Brough Bart." A minute description of the volume, by Mr. Longstaffe will be found in the Archæologia Æliana, vol. ii., part i., octavc series. This MS. has been largely used by the northern historical writers. It is a small delicately finished volume in a hand of the twelfth century, with many interesting illuminations. Mr. Longstaffe suggests that these chapters, which were not known to him under any distinguishing title, may have been the work of Symeon written previous to the History of the Church of Durham, and afterwards freely drawn upon as materials for his more ambitious volume. The same idea has occurred to Mr. Hardy, who offers also an alternative theory, that, if Turgot did write anything relative to the church of St. Cuthbert, this may have been his work. Either hypothesis is worthy of consideration, with this limitation, that Turgot's connection with the work can only have extended to the first six chapters, as the eighteenth chapter, which was originally the seventh, must, as has been already explained, have been written after his death. Symeon, on the other hand, was as well qualified as Turgot to have described the circumstances detailed in the eighteenth chapter, which relate to the disinterment of St. Cuthbert's remains, at which ceremony both were present, whilst the former only was alive at the date when the narrative was composed.—The intermediate chapters between the sixth and the eighteenth could scarcely have been written by, or even known to Symeon, or he would have made use of them, as he has of those which precede them, whenever they come within the period to which his history is limited.

IX. *The Arrival of the Saxons and the Succession of their Kings.* In noticing the *Abbreviatio Symeonis,* attention has already been directed to this little work, which is prefixed to it in the only MS. of that abridgment which is known to exist,[z] in which both are jointly attributed to Symeon of Durham. We have, however, ample ground for treating this Anglo-Saxon history as a separate production, entirely distinct from the *Abbreviatio,* of which it is unnecessary to speak farther in this place. Of the Anglo-Saxon History we have three copies in which it stands unconnected with any other work. These are

[z] MS. Cotton, Caligula, viii.

MS. Cotton, Domitian, viii.,[a] MS. liii. 11, in the Library of Magdalen College, Oxford;[b] and MS. B., xi. 35, in the Library of the Dean and Chapter of Durham.[c]

We will first describe the contents as we find them in the Cotton MS., prefixed to the *Abbreviatio Symeonis*.[d] This copy, like all the others, commences with a long extract from Nennius, containing the description of Britain, with other particulars, which have been omitted in the present volume. The proper contents are as follow. First, the genealogies of the royal families of Kent, Mercia, Wessex, Bernicia and Deira, from Woden downwards. Next follows an account of the settlement in Britain of the Saxons, Angles and Jutes, and then the succession of the kings of all the states of the Heptarchy, Sussex excepted, in the following order: 1. Kings of Kent; 2. Of East Anglia; 3. Of Essex; 4. Of Mercia; 5. Of Wessex; 6. Kings of Bernicia, and, subsequently, of Northumberland; 7. Earls of Northumberland; 8. Kings of Deira.

To these is appended a list of the founders of the several kingdoms; and then an enumeration in the order of their succession of the archbishops of Canterbury and York; and the bishops of Lindisfarne, and, afterwards, of Durham. Then follows the *Abbreviatio Symeonis*.

[a] Vellum, quarto, thirteenth century.

[b] Quarto, not later than the beginning of the reign of Stephen. At the commencement, in a hand of the beginning of the sixteenth century, is written, "Chronicon monachi cujusdam Dunelmensis."

[c] See Mr. Longstaffe's description of this MS. in Appendix to Preface.

[d] The following description is from Mr. Walbran's report:—"The characters of the MS. refer it to the middle of the twelfth century. The handwriting is of the larger bold character of the period, with plain painted capital letters, with the exception of two, which have a little foliation. The text commences without any leading rubric. At the head of the first page is written in a hand of the seventeenth century, perhaps that of Sir Robert Cotton, whose signature is at the foot, *Chronicon Symeonis monachi Dunelmensis*. After a page and a half of introductory matter from Nennius is a curious illuminated head of Woden, crowned, with the heads of six of his sons disposed around, with genealogies below each. Thus under the head of a grave-looking personage, with yellow curly hair and a long beard, wearing a pyramidal cap, is written, 'Woden genuit Beldei,'" etc. The MS. is on vellum, and in quarto.

The series of the kings of Wessex, and their descendants, kings of England, is brought down to the reign of Henry I., who is also mentioned in the account of the earls of Northumberland as the reigning sovereign, who then held the earldom in his own hands.

The list of archbishops of Canterbury is brought down to William A.D. 1122-36; of York, to Henry Murdac 1147-53; and of the bishops of Durham, to William 1143-53; which shews that this, although the earliest copy extant, is only a transcript of an earlier original, and that the York and Durham lists have been extended to the transcriber's own time.

In MS. Domitian A. viii., although probably transcribed a century later, the lists terminate at an earlier period, having been left without additions as they came from the pen of the original compiler in the reign of Henry I.

William, as in the other list, occupies the throne of Canterbury, but Thurstan, A.D. 1114-39, occurs as archbishop of York, and Ralph Flambard, 1099-1128, as bishop of Durham. This fixes the date of the original work between the years 1122 and 1128, which is of course quite consistent with the alleged authorship of Symeon.

The two MSS., as regards the Saxon history, coincide except in a very few particulars. MS. Domitian has no rubrics to the sections, and there are some variations in the arrangement. The kings of Deira immediately follow those of Bernicia and Northumberland. Then come the archbishops and bishops, and, last of all, the earls of Northumberland.

To the text of this MS. is appended a list of the counties in England, classed under the three divisions of Denelaga, Merchenelaga, and Westsexanelaga, which, as it does not occur in the other MSS., and has no apparent connection with the work, is not inserted here, but will be found in the Appendix,[e] with other matter of a similar kind.

The Magdalen MS. is of the reign of Stephen, to which not only the lists of prelates, but the narrative itself, is brought

[e] See Appendix, p. 221-2, note *w*.

down. We are thus enabled to determine its date to within a year. Stephen, we are told, continued to hold the earldom of Northumberland in his own hands, as his predecessors William II. and Henry had done before him. This could not have been written later than A.D. 1139, in which year the earldom was once more severed from the crown of England, and conferred on Henry, son of David, king of Scotland: neither could it have been written earlier than the previous year, 1138, in which Geoffrey Rufus, who occurs as bishop of Durham, was appointed to that see.

The only additional particulars supplied by this MS. relate to Robert de Mowbray, earl of Northumberland, who, in opposition to other authorities, is said to have ended his life in the monastery of St. Albans, to which he had been a munificent benefactor. From this intimation we may conjecture that this transcript was made either at Tynemouth, a cell of St. Albans founded by this earl Robert, or at the parent establishment.

That the monks of St. Albans were in possession of a copy is unquestionable, as it has been used extensively by historians connected with their house. The series of the earlier kings of the heptarchy, as given by Wallingford, is copied *verbatim* from this source,[f] and many subsequent notices are derived from it. Several remarkable instances will also be pointed out of the obligations of Roger de Wendover, who stands at the head of the great chroniclers of St. Albans, to this work.

The arrangement to the end of the fourth section is the same as in MS. Caligula, but no rubrics are prefixed to the accounts of the kings of Kent and East Anglia. The later sections follow in the following order :—

5. Archbishops of Canterbury and York.
6. Kings of Mercia.
7. Kings of Essex.
8. Bishops of Durham.
9. Kings of Wessex.
10. Kings of Bernicia and Northumberland.

[f] The termination of Wallingford's series of the kings of the heptarchy is pointed out in the notes as regards each state.

11. Earls of Northumberland, without rubric.
12. Kings of Deira.

The orthography of the personal names differs considerably in this manuscript from MS. Caligula.

The Durham MS. is much more recent than any of the others, the history being brought down to the reign of Henry II. Lists of the bishops of many other sees are added. The states of the heptarchy are taken in the following order:—1. Kent; 2. East Anglia; 3. Essex; 4. Mercia; 5. Deira and Bernicia, with those kings who reigned over both provinces; 6. Wessex, and kings of England. As regards the first four and the last, the transcriber abandons the text of MS. Caligula, and copies the genealogies of Florence of Worcester. In the Northumbrian series he combines all that he can find in either authority down to Eiric, the son of Harold, adding, "Deinceps per comites procurata est (provincia) usque ad tempora Normannorum," but he gives no account of these earls, as in the other MSS. Mr. Longstaffe's account of this MS., and of the volume in which it is contained, will be found in the Appendix to the Preface.

Although the compilation before us has no pretensions to an earlier origin than the reign of Henry I., it possesses a higher value than would otherwise attach to it, in consequence of being derived from authorities which no longer exist, and of which it may be looked upon as the sole exponent. This remark applies more particularly to that portion which relates to the Northumbrian states, which contains many particulars which are not to be met with elsewhere.

The series of the successors of Ida previous to the reign of Ethelfrith, whilst it presents the same names which are included in others of our most authentic lists, gives a different order of succession, and so reconciles them with the Saxon Chronicle and Malmesbury, which, although they do not enumerate the names of the others, agree in making Ethelric the immediate predecessor of Ethelfrith. This series is copied by Wallingford, and was only known to us from his chronicle, previous to the examination of the present work. It will be found under his name contrasted with other ancient authorities, in note *g*, p. 9, of this volume.

From Ethelfrith to Ceolwulf, Beda and the ancient Northumbrian chronology appended to his works are the authorities followed. The ancient annals which are incorporated in the *Historia Regum Anglorum* are then taken up, and form the basis of the narrative, not merely to the period where they abruptly cease in the *Historia Regum* A.D. 802, but as far as they are used by Symeon in the *Historia Dunelmensis* to the reign of Ricsig A.D. 873-6. The length of this king's reign, which is not given in that work, is here stated to have been three years, which is also the term assigned to him in the second part of the *Historia Regum*. There is an apparent discrepancy between the two authorities as to the reign of his successor, Egbert II., who is here said to have reigned two years,[g] *i. e.*, to the year 878. In the second part of the *Historia Regum* he is spoken of as if he were still alive on the accession of Guthred to the throne of the southern province, as there stated, A.D. 883. The words are, *Regnavit (Guthredus) super Eboracum; Egbert vero super Northimbros.* The sense, however, in which they were intended to be used might merely be, Guthred had the seat of his government at York, (whereas) Egbert only reigned over the Northumbrians (beyond the Tyne). Our authority, again, gives to Guthred a reign of fourteen years, whereas the *Historia Regum* places his death A.D. 894; but Ethelwerd, a much earlier and better authority, mentions his death and burial at York two years later, A.D. 896, which would be in the fourteenth year of his reign; or, if we compute it from the death of his predecessor, Halfdene, we have fourteen years complete. The following table of Northumbrian chronology, from the slaughter of the two kings, Osbert and Ella, A.D. 867, to the death of Guthred, is compiled from the several works in this volume, with the above correction from Ethelwerd:—

[g] This statement is copied in the little Northumbrian Chronicle printed amongst the Excerpta Historica et Topographica in the Appendix, p. 219, l. 30.

ULTRA TYNAM.		SUPER EBORACUM.	
Egbertus....	867-873	Interregnum, sub Danis	867-875
Ricsig......	873-876	Halfdene	875-882
Egbertus II.	876-878	Guthred	882-3-896

Neither the *Liber de Adventu Saxonum*, nor the *Historia Regum*, give us any intimation of the state of affairs in Northumberland on the death of Guthred; but Symeon, in his *History of the Church of Durham*, informs us that Alfred took the government into his own hands.[h] Even then indeed the Danes had leaders of their own, whom they dignified with the title of kings, but their authority seems to have been personal rather than territorial. Each could command the services of an organized host of his countrymen wherever the prospect of plunder tempted him; but they reigned over no particular locality; and we hear of them now in Northumberland, and now in Essex, Mercia, or East Anglia. When, on the accession of Edward the Elder to the throne of England, his cousin Ethelwald fled into Northumberland, he was received by these petty *reguli*, and acknowledged as "king and prince of the kings." Such is the statement of Henry of Huntingdon, an historian well informed on northern affairs, who further explains that the "Danish kings reigned in a confused manner, sometimes two, sometimes three, at the same time."

Ethelwald was slain A.D. 905, and the following year we find "king Edward from necessity concluded a peace with the army both of East Anglia and of Northumberland," over which these *reguli* now held command, freed from the control of any superior.

In 911, "the army among the Northumbrians broke the peace," and being defeated by the forces of king Edward, two of their kings, Eowils and Halfdene, were slain. Florence of Worcester, by a strange mistake, confounds this Halfdene with his namesake, who was the scourge of the previous generation, and assigns to him a reign of twenty-six years, but the actual interval from Halfdene's accession to the year 911 is not

[h] Hist. Dunelm., ii., 14.

twenty-six, but thirty-six years. He then tells us that Regnold reigned ten years, and his brother Sihtric *a few* years, after whom came his son Guthferth, who was expelled by Athelstan A.D. 926. This chronology is framed on the assumption that Regnold succeeded immediately on the death of Eowils and Halfdene, placing the termination of his reign A.D. 921, and allowing five years for the reigns of Sihtric and Guthferth. But Regnold was engaged in Ireland long after 911,[i] and his connection with Northumberland commenced with the incursion in which he besieged and took York, which is fixed by the Saxon Chronicle A.D. 923, by the *Historia Regum* 919.[j] In 924 he made submission to Edward the Elder, and the following year he was expelled. The Saxon Chronicle allows only one year for the reign of Sihtric, placing his death in 926, and the expulsion of Guthferth in 927. It is remarkable that the *Liber de Adventu Saxonum* makes no mention of Regnold at all, nor does it from this period furnish us with a single name or an incident of Northumbrian history down to the expulsion of Eiric, the last king of that province, with which we are not acquainted from other sources. The *Historia Regum,* on the other hand, whilst following for the most part the authority of the Saxon Chronicle, gives important details from some independent authority,[k] probably, as has been suggested, from a continuation of those annals on which the earlier portion of it is altogether based.[l]

[i] In 915 Regnold and Sihtric landed in Ireland; one at Kildare, the other at Waterford. From this time they appear from the Irish Annals to have exercised a joint authority until A.D. 918, when their brother Guthferth, or Godfrey, made himself master of Dublin, and assumed the chief command, which he retained till his death A.D. 932.

[j] The latter was probably the true date, as the events of Regnold's reign, as recorded in the Historia Cuthberti, the Historia Regum, the Pictish Chronicle, and other authorities, would scarcely have been compressed within a period of two years.

[k] See pp. 62-6 of this volume.

[l] We have traces in Roger of Wendover of the existence of some such work even in his time, from which he gives particulars not to be met with either in the tract before us, in the History of the Church of Durham, or in any other extant authority. He mentions, for instance, the usurpation of Redwulf in the

On the abolition of kingly government in Northumberland, the administration was committed to a succession of earls, some of whom presided over the whole district, whilst at other times it was divided into two provinces. As regards the country north of the Tyne, which had formed the kingdom of the two Egberts and Ricsig, this form of government had existed ever since the death of Guthred. The rulers, indeed, were during the former period known as dukes, instead of earls, but under both, as regarded the Northern province, the government was hereditary in the same family. Ethelward mentions the death of Eadulf, duke of Bamburgh, A.D. 912, and he is spoken of in the *Historia Cuthberti* as the friend of king Alfred.[m] In the same way his son Aldred is described as the friend of king Edward,[n] and his name, Aldred of Bamburgh, occurs in the pages of our general historians, amongst the petty princes who did homage to Edward in 924, and to Athelstan in 926. Aldred had a brother Uchtred,[o] a name of constant recurrence, as is also that of his father Eadulf, amongst the earls who succeeded to his power.

Of these earls we have two lists, both obviously derived from the same authorities, amongst which the tract *De*

fourth year of Ethelred, the son of Eanred, A.D. 844, an event which has escaped the notice of all our other historians, but which is confirmed by the existence of coins bearing the name of the usurper, which have been found with others of the same period at Hexham and elsewhere. Again, although in this tract, as well as in the Historia Regum, we have the date of king Ricsig's death, Wendover alone tells us that it was caused by distress of mind induced by the devastations of Halfdene, who had overrun his kingdom, and parcelled out his lands amongst his followers. Again, we learn from the Historia Regum that Eiric, the last Danish king of Northumberland, was slain by Maccus, the son of Anlaf. Wendover gives much fuller particulars. Besides, supplying the date A.D. 750, two years after Eiric's expulsion, he informs us that he was slain through the treachery of earl Osulf by Macon, the consul, with his son Henry and his brother Reginald, in a solitary region called Stainmore. This Maccus, or Macon, lord of Man and the Isles, the "arch-pirate" of Malmesbury, occurs twenty years afterwards in the list of princes who performed an act of homage to king Edgar on the river Dee, near Chester. Further instances of the exclusive information preserved by Wendover will occur under the earls of Northumberland.

[m] p. 147, l. 25. [n] ibid., l. 24.

[o] ibid., l. 31.

Obsessione Dunelmi, in the present volume,[p] is not the least important. One list follows the series of kings of Northumberland in the *Libellus de Adventu Saxonum*, the other is introduced, somewhat out of place, under the year 1072, in the *Historia Regum*.[q]

In both Osulf is represented as the first earl of the two provinces of Northumberland in the reign of Edred. In the *Historia Regum* we are told that, in the reign of Edgar, Oslac was associated with him, to whom he resigned the province of York, retaining only the district north of the Tyne. According to the *Libellus*, Osulf was succeeded in due course by Oslac in York, and by Eadulf Yvilcild in all the country from the Tees to the Frith of Forth (Myreforth). "These two earls," it is added, "with Elfsius, bishop of the see of St. Cuthbert, presented Kyneth, king of the Scots, to king Edgar, who, when he had done homage, gave him Lothian, and dismissed him with great honour." We can scarcely suppose that Eadulf Yvilcild is a fictitious character, introduced for the purpose of playing a part in the transfer of Lothian to the Scotch, which might with equal propriety have been assigned to Osulf or Waltheof.[r] Neither is there any reason to doubt the perfect

[p] p. 154.

[q] This is evidently not the place which the list originally occupied, as a reference is made two years earlier, A.D. 1070, to a statement contained in it respecting earl Gospatric, "qui, *ut supradictum est*," etc. In Hoveden's Annals, which are to a great extent a mere copy from the Historia Regum, it is placed under A.D. 953, which should undoubtedly have been its position in the latter work, in which we find under the previous year, "Defecerunt hic reges Northanhymbrorum; et deinceps ipsa provincia administrata est per comites" (p. 66).

[r] Until the examination of the *Libellus de Adventu Saxonum*, the earliest known authority for this account of the cession of Lothian was Roger of Wendover, and as no mention of any earl Eadulf earlier than Eadulf Cudel occurred in any list then known, it was assumed that Eadulf had been written by mistake for Waltheof, senior, the father of earl Uchtred. See p. 90, note *c*, and p. 212, note *h*. Wendover's account, again, gives further particulars which are not elsewhere to be found:—"Bishop Alfsey and earl Eadulf conducted Kenneth, king of Scotland, to king Edgar, who made him many presents of his royal bounty. He gave him, moreover, the whole district called Laudian in the native tongue, on this condition, that every year, on certain festivals, when the king and his successors wore the crown, he should come to court, and

bona fides of the narrative of this transaction, written, be it remembered, at a period long prior to any dispute as to the relations between England and Scotland. On the other hand, it is not difficult to account for the author of the *Historia Regum* not merely omitting this incident, but leaving out the name of Eadulf Yvilcild altogether, under the impression that his authority had confounded it with that of Eadulf Cudel, to whom the cession of Lothian is imputed by another authority, the tract *De Obsessione Dunelmi.*

There is in fact no inconsistency between the two statements. Nothing is more probable than that the province now ceded was reclaimed by Uchtred, the most powerful of all the Northumbrian earls, and was again wrested from the grasp of his unwarlike brother and successor Eadulf Cudel. Some particulars occur in the *Historia Regum* which are not in the *Libellus,* but these are generally to be found in the tract *De Obsessione Dunelmi,* with the exception of the account of the death of Eadulf Rus, the assassin of bishop Walcher, by the hands of a woman; his burial at Jedburgh; and the subsequent disturbance of his remains by prior Turgot.

Appendix, No. I. *Historical and Topographical Extracts.* These extracts have been printed amongst Symeon's works by Twysden, from the MS. of the History of the Church of Durham, in the Public Library of the University of Cambridge,[s] and have also found a place in the English translation of that author in the *Church Historians of England,* where they are

celebrate the festival with the other nobles. The king gave him besides many mansions on the road, that he and his successors might find entertainment in going and returning; and these houses continued to belong to the kings of Scotland until the time of Henry II."

[s] MS. F. f., i., 27. The History commences at folio 122 with the *Apologia Symeonis;* next follows the Preface, then the Capitula extending to the middle of folio 128. These extracts occur without any interval, extending from the middle of f. 128 to the bottom of f. 130 *b.*

entitled *Chronicle of the Angles,* by which designation they are once referred to in a note in the present volume.[t]

The first extract is taken verbatim from William of Malmesbury, and a reference has been given in a note to the original, as it has not been thought necessary to reprint it entire. Then follows a series of notices of Northumbrian history, the materials of which have been brought together from a variety of sources. These have been printed with references to the original authorities.

The third part, which is of somewhat greater interest, contains an account of the several Bishops' sees in England, with a list of the counties arranged under the heads of Westsaxenalaga, Denelaga and Merchenelaga. Another copy of it exists in MS. Norf., Arundel 222, and has been printed by Gale in the *Scriptores* xv., under the title of *De partitione provinciæ in schiras et episcopatus, et regna.* A collation of the two copies has resulted in a greatly amended text. A third copy occurs at the commencement of the *Chronicon Monasterii de Hida* (a totally distinct work from the Liber de Hida) MS. Cotton, Domit. A. xiv. The date of the compilation is during the reign of Henry II., whose grandfather is referred to as *Henry I.* This is also the date of the Cambridge MS. The other copies are more recent, the Cotton MS. being of the fourteenth century, the Arundel of the fifteenth. The portion of the latter to which the conclusion of the title, *Partitio in regna,* refers is merely an extract from Malmesbury's History of the Kings of England,[u] and this also is to be found in another part of the Cambridge volume.[v]

Appendix, No. II. *A brief Relation of the Life of St. Cuthbert.* This piece consists of two parts, of which the first contains a short notice of the life of St. Cuthbert, which although it contains little, if any, original information, is perhaps entitled to be preserved amongst the numerous memorials of the saint. The second part contains a number of miracles, almost exclusively derived from Symeon's History of the Church of

[t] p. 73, note *l*. [u] i., 6. [v] Folio 215.

Durham. Of these it has for the most part been considered sufficient to give the title and initial line. They would have been omitted altogether, but for their connection with the publication of the *Translations of St. Cuthbert,* with which, as we have seen, they have been mixed up. The portion which has been mistaken for the conclusion of the *Translations,* commences with the word "*tenera*" at the bottom of p. 226. The last chapter, which contains an enumeration of the possessions of the church founded at Lindisfarne, and ultimately established at Durham, is printed entire for the purpose of comparison with other documents of the same class, none of which altogether correspond.

Of the MSS. which contain the *Translations* of St. Cuthbert, four also contain this *Relation;* MSS. Nero and Titus in the Cottonian Library, Laud in the Bodleian, and Gale in that of Trinity College, Cambridge, all which have been examined for the present edition. Mr. Hardy refers to another, MS. Sloane, 1772, vellum, quarto, twelfth century.

Appendix, No. III. *Life of Margaret Queen of Scotland,* attributed to Turgot, Prior of Durham. It has been thought desirable to bring together in this collection everything which has been ascribed to the pen of Turgot, as bearing upon the question of his alleged authorship of the History of the Church of Durham.

Of the Life of Queen Margaret but one copy exists in manuscript in this kingdom, in a folio volume on vellum, in double columns, of the latter part of the twelfth century, Cotton, Tiberius, D. iii., which was much injured by the great fire in the British Museum. It was long supposed to have been rendered altogether useless for the purpose of reference, but has been repaired and restored so successfully, that, with comparatively trifling exceptions, where the tops of the leaves have been consumed, the whole of the contents can be decyphered by painful study.

It contains a collection of the Lives of British Saints, in which the Life of St. Margaret immediately follows the Legend of the "Passion of the holy martyrs, Primus and Felicianus," and has this rubric, "Incipit Translatio et Vita Sanctæ Margaretæ reginæ Scottorum." It is printed in the *Acta Sanctorum*, and again by Pinkerton in his lives of the Scottish Saints. An abridgment exists in the MS. Cotton, Tiberius E. i., a folio in double columns, also injured by fire. It extends only to four and a half pages, and is of the beginning of the fourteenth century. At the foot of the pages is a pedigree of the descendants of king Malcolm.

This abridgment has been printed by Capgrave with the addition of a section from Aelred of Rievaulx, and has been reprinted by Surius. Pinkerton's collection contains the abridgment, as well as the more extended biography. Both works have been carefully collated with the MSS. by Mr. Raine for the present edition; all variations between the original and the abridgment are pointed out; and those passages which have been rendered illegible by the fire have been supplied from Pinkerton. These are distinguished by brackets, the portions between which represent the amount of injury sustained.

The writer, in his dedication to Matilda, queen of England, the daughter of Queen Margaret, gives only the initial letter of his name, describing himself as "T. servus servorum S. Cuthberti," from which we gather that he was at the time of writing it a monk of Durham. He writes in a great measure from his own knowledge, and details the particulars of an interview with the queen not long before her death. From an expression which she uses in addressing him, "Ego posthac in hac vita diu non subsistam: *tu autem non parvo post me tempore vives,*" it is probable that the author was not then an old man. He was not present at her death, but gives an account of it from the narration of the priest who attended her, and who afterwards became, like himself, a monk of Durham. Fordun twice quotes the work as the production of Turgot,[w] and it is probably on his authority that Capgrave in his edition of the abridgment represents the conversation referred to above, as having taken place between the queen and Turgot, whom he describes as her

[w] See the passages in italics in extract iv., p. 258, and extract v., pp. 259-60.

confessor. This is evidently a misconception. There is nothing in the original biography to lead to the belief that the writer conversed with the queen otherwise than as a confidential friend. That he was her confessor in no way appears; and if we identify him with Turgot, the assumption is preposterous. His avocations at Durham, where he held the responsible position of Prior more than five years previous to Margaret's death, are altogether inconsistent with such an idea. There is indeed no *primâ facie* reason to doubt that a Prior of Durham might be a visitor at the Scotch court, or that his station and character would commend him to the confidence of the queen.

There are, however, circumstances peculiar to Turgot, which render it unlikely that he was either the guest of Malcolm, or the author of such encomiums upon him as are contained in the work.

We know of one previous visit which he paid to Scotland in company with Aldwine, his predecessor in the priorate, when they were driven from Melrose by the persecutions of Malcolm.[x] The same consideration, which makes us doubt the probability of the attendance of the latter at the ceremony of the foundation of Durham cathedral, makes us hesitate to believe that Turgot would voluntarily throw himself upon his hospitality. It is too much to say that either statement is necessarily untrue, but it is strange that, if true, both should remain unrecorded by the contemporary historian of the church of Durham.

The question is further complicated by the existence of a second claimant, Theodericus, whose name is inserted instead of the initial T., in the Acta Sanctorum, the text of which is derived from a foreign MS., with the age and character of which we are unacquainted.[y]

In the list of the monks of Durham we meet with one of

[x] Sed cum regi Scottorum Malcolmo, ad quem locus iste (Mailrosense monasterium) pertinebat, eorum (Aldwini scilicet et Turgoti) ibi conversatio innotuisset, graves ab illo injurias et persecutiones pertulerunt, pro eo quod Evangelicum præceptum servantes, jurare illi fidelitatem noluerunt (Hist. Dunelm., iii., 22).

[y] "Codex Valcellensis, in Hannoniæ monasterio."

this name; but here again a difficulty arises from the lowness of his position on the roll, where he stands the hundred and thirty-first in order. If the transcriber of the MS. had no better ground than the occurrence of the initial T. in Theoderic for selecting him as the author, there are no less than five other monks whose names equally satisfy this condition, and who precede Theoderic in the date of their profession. Turkil stands eighth, just two below Turgot, and Thurstan seventy-sixth, being thirty-eight below Symeon. There are two of the name of Thomas who stand eighty-third and eighty-sixth, and another called Turold, eighty-ninth. Even the last of these, although apparently too low on the roll, stands earlier by forty-two than Theoderic. But for the objection stated above, the claims of Turgot would unquestionably be superior to those of any other, whilst those of Theoderic, except so far as the authority of the MS. supports them, are inferior to all. If Theoderic really was the author, and as such, the friend and confidant of queen Margaret, we can only reconcile the fact with his position on the roll by supposing that he entered the monastery in extreme old age many years afterwards.

Pinkerton's volume, of which only one hundred copies were printed, has become so scarce as to be even more difficult of access than the voluminous Acta Sanctorum from which it was taken, and a new edition of this tract has long been a desideratum.

Appendix, No. IV. *Fordun's Extracts from Turgot.* Of these extracts, a few words in the fourth,[z] and nearly the whole of the fifth[a] are from the Life of Queen Margaret, printed above, which is there referred to as "The Legend of the Life of the Blessed Queen."[b] By far the greater part of the remainder is from the *Genealogy of the Kings of England* by Aelred of Rievaulx, as will be seen by a reference to the notes. The part which is unaccounted for is probably taken from some other work of the same author, whose writings are very numerous, and some are not now known to exist. Amongst others a Life

[z] p. 258, l. 13-14, 16-17. [a] p. 259, l. 10. [b] p. 259, l. 8.

of Queen Margaret is ascribed to him by our early bibliographers. It is even probable that the portions which were originally in the Life ascribed to Turgot, may have been found by Fordun incorporated in the Biography of Aelred, and that on this ground he has ascribed not merely the Life but the Genealogy, and perhaps other works of Aelred, which were collected in the same volume, to Turgot.

The object, however, of publishing the Life of Queen Margaret, and the extracts from Fordun in this volume, is not so much to determine the authorship, as to shew that even supposing them to have been all written by Turgot, there is nothing in them in any way akin to the History of the Church of Durham, or which can in any way advance his claim to the authorship of the work.

A curious account of Turgot's early life will be found in the *Historia Regum*, at page 95, but it seems to be rather legendary than historical, and is probably one of the later additions, subsequent to the time of Symeon. At all events it receives no sanction from his History of the Church of Durham, in which, if authentic, it would probably have found a place. At page 91 we have an instance of the exercise of his jurisdiction, most likely in his archidiaconal capacity, at Jedburgh, which like Melrose was an ancient possession of the church of St. Cuthbert within the dominions of king Malcolm.

His tenure of the priorate was unmarked by any important events, if we except the rebuilding of the church of St. Cuthbert, a work more immediately due to the bishop, but to which he contributed his assistance, and the translation of St. Cuthbert's remains. His subsequent career as Bishop of St. Andrew's was as unsatisfactory as his earlier experience of the same country during his residence at Melrose.

The only complete edition of the works usually ascribed to Symeon of Durham is contained in the *Historiæ Anglicanæ Scriptores Decem*, published by Sir Roger Twysden in 1652, in a bulky volume of 1,500 folio pages, 136 of which, printed, with the exception of a few pages at the commencement, in double columns, are devoted to Symeon. Amongst the contents are several other works of great interest, whilst others are of inferior value.

The editorial labours in respect to this publication have been performed in a manner much more creditable than in the case of the majority of the early editions of our mediæval historians. The text generally is tolerably correct, and the mistakes which occur are much more frequently due to the transcriber of the MS. than to the editor of the printed volume. This especially applies to the frequent errors in the orthography of proper names, in most cases originating in the substitution of one Saxon character for another of nearly similar form.

No attempt has been made by Twysden to ascertain the authorship of the several pieces, or to discriminate between those which are really the productions of Symeon, and those of older date which have been mixed with them. Prefixed to the volume indeed is Selden's essay already referred to, which seeks to award to another pen the merit of the *History of the Church of Durham*; but this, if an exception, is an unfortunate one. Neither has the text in any case been illustrated by such notes as are absolutely essential to the general reader.

The MSS. used by Twysden are contained in two folio volumes, both of which were formerly the property of archbishop Parker, by whose liberality one was consigned to the Public Library at Cambridge, the other to that of C. C. College in the same University. Of both these volumes we have already spoken. From the MS. in the Public Library Twysden has printed the *History of the Church of Durham*, with the *Historical and Topographical Extracts* printed at p. 217 of the present volume; the *Continuation* of the above History; and the *Historia de Sancto Cuthberto*, with certain charters and illustrative documents appended to it and to the *Continuation*. From the C. C. manuscript he has printed the two *Tracts on the archbishops of York, and on the siege of Durham*; and the *History of the Kings of the Angles and Danes*, including under that title not only the two pieces which precede it in this volume, but the long extracts from Beda above referred to.

Besides the two Cambridge MSS. he used others, which will be described in the second volume, on the *History of the Church of Durham,* but none as regards the works in the present volume.

In 1732 an admirable edition of the *History of the Church of Durham,* which we have previously had occasion to notice in connection with Rudd's reply to Selden which is prefixed to it, was published by Dr. Bedford in a small octavo volume. This edition is based on a MS. now in the Library of the University of Durham, which was unknown to Twysden and Selden, and which will be fully described in the Preface to the second volume.

The only other portion of any of the reputed works of Symeon which has hitherto been published is contained in the solitary volume of the Monumenta Historica Britannica. This is limited to the *First Part* of the *Historia Regum,* with such portions of the original matter in the second part as refer to the period antecedent to the Norman Conquest. Of the merits of this publication under the editorship of the late Mr. Petrie, it is unnecessary to speak, but it contains only a small portion of the works of Symeon, and is incorporated in a volume of colossal size.

Seeing, then, that the text of the *Decem Scriptores* is capable of considerable amendment, and is unaccompanied by such explanatory notes and elucidations as historical readers are accustomed to meet with, the Council of the Surtees Society resolved to place the *Works of Symeon of Durham* on their list of intended publications.

To this resolution the existence of a small portion of one of the works in the Monumenta Britannica constituted no objection, but it was doubtful whether the existence of Bedford's edition might not render it expedient to exclude the *History of the Church of Durham* from the proposed publication. The increasing scarcity of that volume, and the growing demand for works of this class, tends year by year to diminish any hesitation which might exist on the subject, but it has been determined in the first instance to confine the publication to the first volume of Symeon's works, leaving the *History of the Church of Durham* as material for a second.

The Editor agreed, at the request of the Council, to undertake the supervision of the first volume only, but he trusts ere long to see the second also completed under an editor more conversant than himself with tasks of this nature.

He was only induced to incur the responsibility to this extent by the kind offer of the Rev. James Raine, the able and indefatigable Secretary of the Society, to relieve him altogether from the task of collating MSS., and to assist him in the correction of the press.

The task of collation, which was expected to be chiefly confined to the Cambridge MSS., has been much more onerous. As regards the works in the former edition, a second MS. of the tract on the archbishops of York required attention, whilst the discovery of another and most important MS. of the *Historia de Sancto Cuthberto* is due to Mr. Raine's research.

The additional matter which has been inserted involved greatly increased labour, a large share of which devolved upon the same kind friend.

Seven of the MSS. of the *Translations of St. Cuthbert*, several of them containing also the *Relatio*, and a mass of extraneous matter, have been examined and collated by him; also the MSS. of the Life of St. Margaret, and the abridgment of the same, both of which required peculiar attention, in consequence of the injuries which they had sustained from fire.

He also made a very minute collation of the *Liber de Adventu Saxonum*, in the Library of Magdalen College, Oxford, with the transcript which I had obtained from the British Museum. All this involved repeated journeys to London, Oxford, and Cambridge.

I am also indebted to Mr. Raine for the references which appear in the notes not only to the endless quotations from the Holy Scriptures, but to verses taken from Boethius, Sedulius, and Aldhelm, as well as to the writings of Baronius relative to councils and other ecclesiastical matters.

I have further to discharge a pleasing duty in acknowledging my obligations to other friends.

To Joseph Burtt, Esq., Assistant-Keeper of the Public Records, for the pains which he took in collating the Hale MS. of the tract on the archbishops of York, with the Cambridge transcript, and also in examining a work in the same collection, which was supposed to resemble the *Historia Cuthberti,* and sending me numerous extracts which shewed the fallacy of that view. The same gentleman kindly superintended the transcription of two MSS. of the Translations of St. Cuthbert in the British Museum, and of the MS. Caligula A. viii. of the *Liber de Adventu Saxonum.*

To Mr. Walbran, so favourably known to the members of the Surtees Society by his volume of the Memorials of Fountains Abbey, and other works, for an elaborate report on the volume in the British Museum containing the *Liber de Adventu Saxonum* and the *Abbreviatio Symeonis,* and for his examination of a second MS. of the former work in the same repository. I should have printed Mr. Walbran's report *in extenso,* if I had not been induced by the great importance of the work to which it refers, to include it in this collection, thus rendering a detailed account unnecessary.

To Mr. Longstaffe I am indebted for a minute description of a MS. volume of historical materials in the Library of the dean and chapter of Durham, containing, *inter alia,* a transcript of the same work, *De Adventu Saxonum,* with numerous interpolations and additions, from which he furnished me with copious extracts.

In addition to the printed works of Symeon in the editions to which I have referred, I have not failed to avail myself of the information contained in the preface and notes to Mr. Stevenson's translation, published in the Church Historians of England.

I cannot forbear expressing my obligations to two works of national importance, the Monumenta Historica Britannica, which will remain a monument to all ages of the learning, judgment, and industry of the late Mr. Petrie, and to the

Catalogue of the Materials for British History, by his friend and coadjutor Mr. Duffus Hardy, the present chief of the Record establishment. Of the value of the latter I have already adduced a striking instance. Of the former I will only say that, irrespective of the erudition which is so eminently displayed in the preface and notes, I have in numerous cases derived assistance and information from a glance at the lucid and comprehensive *Index Rerum*, which I could only have obtained otherwise by a toilsome search through many volumes.

It will be observed that I have invariably spelt the name of my author *Symeon*, instead of *Simeon*, the orthography adopted by Twysden on the authority of the Cambridge MS. In this I am supported by the list of monks in the autograph copy of the History of the Church of Durham, and by the spelling of the name in the Liber Vitæ, and the ancient Obituary of that church. The same orthography also prevails in Reginald's Miracles of St. Cuthbert, and in the Cotton MS. of the Archbishops of York, and is adopted by Leland.

I. H. H.

APPENDIX TO PREFACE.

PART I.

A Description of the MS. of Symeon, MS. C. C. C., F. v. 139, sm. folio, written in double column, *sæc.* xii *exeunte.*

It was given by archbishop Parker to the College.

The MS. contains at the commencement a rough list of its contents, made in the fifteenth century, so that archbishop Parker has not altered the position of any of the portions of the volume, as he did in many other cases.

On the title are the following lines:—

"Divitiis plena, genetrix quoque, Virgo serena,
Sint procul obscæna mortis mihi, mater amæna."

Below this are two short extracts from "Ge(nnad)ius Massiliensis in libro de Illustribus Viris."

Foll. 2 *a*, 17 *b*. *Rubric.* "Incipit Historia omnimoda" (cum bona chronica ejusdem).

Incipit. "Mundum sine initio."

Explicit. "Per lumen scientiæ ad gloriam et honorem perducat."

This consists of sacred and profane history in the shape of notes, and a list of the Popes.

Foll. 18 *a*, 36 *b*. *Rubric.* "Incipiunt Chronica abbatis Prumiensis monasterii, ubi Lotharius imperator ad conversionem venit."

Incipit. "Anno imperii Octaviani Cæsaris xlii."

Explicit. "Ex quo vulnere eadem nocte extinguitur."

It ends with the year 1002, and contains little of importance. See Martene et Durand, Ampl. Coll., iv., 517.

Foll. 37 *a*, 47 *a*. *Rubric.* "Incipit historia piæ memoriæ Prioris Ricardi Haugustaldensis ecclesiæ de gestis regis Stephani et de bello Standardii."

Printed by Twysden and the Surtees Society. This begins with a large letter illuminated in red and green.

Foll. 47 *a*, 49 *b*. *Rubric.* "Incipit Cronica ab Adam usque ad Henricum."

Incipit. "Adam cxxx ann' genuit Seth."

Explicit. "Qui autem post hunc regnaturus sit posteritas videbit."

See Memorials of Hexham, i., pref., cxlv. It is in the same hand as the preceding.

Foll. 49 *b*, 51 *a*. *Rubric.* "Incipit epistola Simeonis monachi ecclesiæ Sancti Cuthberti Dunelmi ad Hugonem decanum Eboracensem de archiepiscopis Eboraci."

Printed by Twysden and in this volume. In the same hand.

Foll. 51 *a*, 52 *b*. *Rubric.* "De Obsessione Dunelmi et de probitate Ucthredi comitis." Archbishop Parker has added several other words which appear in Twysden.

Printed by Twysden and the Surtees Society. In the same hand.

Fol. 52 *b*. The rubric at the commencement of Symeon's Historia Regum, p. 11 of this volume, is at the foot of the page. Fol. 53 *a* begins with another rubric in a rather different character, "Incipit passio Sanctorum Æthelberti atque Ethelredi regiæ stirpis puerorum" (p. 1). The concurrence of the two rubrics is most peculiar, and I know of no other instance.

The Historia Regum ends with folio 77 *b*.

Fol. 78 *a*. A capital letter in red and green, like that at the commencement of Richard of Hexham; and then begins the Recapitulatio in the same hand which wrote the notice of earl Uchtred and the preceding tractates.

Foll. 78 *a*, 130 *b*.

Incipit. "Anno ab incarnatione Domini DCCCXLVIII."

All this is written in one good and uniform hand.

Fol. 130 *b*. *Rubric.* "Incipit historia Johannis Prioris Haugustaldensis ecclesiæ xxv annorum." Printed by Twysden and the Surtees Society. In the same hand. The sequence of this Chronicle is broken by the following insertions :—

(Fol. 132 *b*. *Rubric*. "Incipit descriptio Serlonis monachi, fratris Radulfi abbatis de Parcho, de bello inter regem Scotiæ et barones Angliæ." In verse. Printed by Twysden.

Fol. 133 *a*. *Rubric*. "Quomodo a paucissimis interfectus sit Sumerledus Cicebi, ʒe king, cum suo immenso exercitu."

Incipit. "David rege mortis lege clauso in sarcofago."

Explicit. "Et honori et decori Kentegerni tribuit."

An interesting and unpublished poem. I gave a transcript of it to the late Mr. Joseph Robertson for publication in the proceedings of one of the Scottish clubs.

Foll. 133 *b*, 137 *a*. *Rubric*. "Incipit descriptio viri venerabilis Æthelredi abbatis Rievallis de bello inter regem Scottiæ et barones Angliæ apud Standardum juxta Alvertoniam."

This begins with a red and green letter, as other preceding tracts, and is in the same hand.

Rubric at end. "Explicit descriptio Æthelredi abbatis; incipit descriptio prædicti Prioris Haugustaldensis ecclesiæ."

Printed by Twysden.)

Foll. 137 *a*, 146 *a*. John of Hexham begins again with the words, "Eodem anno mortuus est Petrus Leo."

Foll. 146 *a*, 148 *b*. *Rubric*. "Explicit opus Johannis Prioris xxv annorum; incipit de quodam miraculo mirabili."

The story of the Nun of Watton, printed by Twysden.

Archbishop Parker has added to the rubric, "Autore Aluredo abbate Rievallensi," and Twysden has printed it so.

In the same hand.

Foll. 149 *a*, 157 *a*. *Rubric*. "Quomodo et a quibus cœnobium Sanctæ Mariæ Eboraci fundatum sit, et quantas invidorum perturbationes impulsa sustinuerit, sed, Dei protegente gratia, magis ac magis aucta et multiplicata fuerit."

Incipit. "Quamvis sancta et una et universalis ecclesia."

Explicit. "Per Christum Dominum nostrum. Amen."

Written by abbat Stephen, and continued, afterwards, by Simon de Warwick. Noticed by Leland and Dugdale. Copied by me. In another hand, also of the twelfth century, perhaps a little later.

f

Included with this there is archbishop Thurstan's letter about the secession of the monks of St. Mary's Abbey to Fountains, which has been collated for the Memorials of Fountains Abbey, vol. i.

The rubric at the beginning is, "Quomodo Funtanense cœnobium sumpsit exordium."

Foll. 157 *a*, 159 *a*. *Rubric*. "De Vita et Conversatione Gereberti papæ."

Incipit. "De Johanne qui et Gerebertus dictus est."

Explicit. "In aqua aspectum intuentium fallere."

Foll. 159 *a*, 160 *a*. *Rubric*. "Visio Karoli Imperatoris."

Incipit. "In nomine Dei summi, regis regum."

Explicit. "Sine fine, in sæcula sæculorum. Amen."

Foll. 160 *a*. *Rubric*. "Visio Sancti Maurilii."

Incipit. "Sanctus Maurilius."

Explicit. "Elevatum est."

Foll. 160 *a*, *b*. *Rubric*. "De an(n)ulo statuæ."

Incipit. "Verum ut Romam revertar."

Explicit. "Ad memoriam posteris transmittendum."

The well-known mediæval story.

Foll. 161 *a*—164 *a*. A curious story about a York merchant of the name of Arnulf and the Saxon king Elle who had committed a rape upon his wife.

Incipit. "Domino et patri venerabili atque amando."

Explicit. "Residuum vitæ meæ in dolore peragam."

Printed by Mr. Petrie, and also by the Caxton Society.

Foll. 164 *a b*. *Rubric*. "De eo quod Eboracensis ecclesia nullum dominium super Scottos habere debet."

Incipit. "De Eboracensis ecclesiæ primatu."

Explicit. "Ipsa in suum sola optinet."

Copied. Of little value.

Fol. 164 *b*. *Rubric*. "Visio cujusdam clerici de gloria regis Malcolmi, cui, ad singula interrogata super statu suo, in hunc sensum respondit."

Incipit. "Cur sic, care, taces? Pro me loquitur mea vita."

Explicit. "In cœlestes thesauros intulerunt mella."

Copied by me. Unpublished.

Fol. 165 *a*, is a blank leaf on which is written in a fifteenth century hand the speech of the men of Galloway at the battle of the Standard—as given by Aelred.

Foll. 165 *b*—175 *b*. *Rubric.* "Incipit eulogium brevissimum Britanniæ insulæ quod Ninnius Elvodugi discipulus congregavit."

I have omitted to copy the first and last words of this and the next tract.

This MS. of Nennius has many curious interpolations and additions.

Foll. 175 *b*—178. *Rubric.* "Vita sanctissimi atque doctissimi viri Gildæ incipit."

On the fly leaves, at the end, are a few genealogical and historical notes of no value, and in a late hand.

Some of the tracts at the end of the volume are of a later date than their predecessors, but I should say that there is nothing later than the reign of king John.

The date of the Corpus MS. is probably about 1180. It is later than the MS. of Symeon in Bishop Cosin's library at Durham, as well as inferior to it in execution. The Corpus MS. of Symeon is done by the same hand that wrote the History of the Church of Hexham by Prior Richard, which is in the Cambridge University Library, and probably by the same hand that wrote Symeon's History of the Church of Durham, Beda's Ecclesiastical History, and Ethelwold's account of the abbats of Lindisfarne, which occur in the same volume. These three are better executed than the others, and, if not by the same hand, have at all events been written in the same place.

The date of the rubric at the beginning is perhaps a little later than the MS., but not much. From the allusion in it to Henry I. it is obvious that the writer knew of Henry II., who became king in 1154.

The Historia Regum is carelessly written in several hands and inks. The portion arranged under years is tolerably evenly done, and by one hand probably. The extracts about Ethelbert and Ethelred, the genealogy of the kings, the notices of Benedict and Ceolfrid, the poetical extracts from Beda, and that from

Malmesbury, are in various hands. The poem of Beda is full of interlineations, other words being inserted with the word *vel* before them. The word *vel* occurs in other places throughout the first part of the MS., shewing that it was regarded as subject to correction. There are also many interpolations (given between the lines), not noticed as such in the printed text, which have evidently been done by a north country hand. I regard the greater part of this as Symeon's own notes and extracts, out of which the chronicle from 848 downwards was constructed and perhaps designed to be extended upwards. The scribe found them with the completed portion (*i. e.* from 848 downwards), and copied the whole. He has shewn his estimate of Part No. 2, by copying it carefully and neatly. The First Part he has treated as a set of Notes, as he found it. Even the chronological part is carelessly written, and he has probably added largely to the whole, intending perhaps to make something orderly of it. He probably inserted the accounts of Acca and Alchmund, and secured copies of the Passion of Ethelbert, etc.

The Recapitulatio begins in 848 (Twysden, col. 137), with a carefully made letter in green and red, evidently intended to mark the commencement of a work. It is carefully and neatly written throughout in the same set and orderly hand which wrote foll. 37-52, and which goes on afterwards. In this part there are occasional erasures, and words put between the lines, or in the margin, or at the foot of the page.

Of these the greater number, especially the marginal references relating to northern bishops and persons, are in a coarse hand, which appear in other parts of the MS., *i. e.* in Part No. 1, John of Hexham, and the account of St. Mary's abbey, and especially in Nennius. The references, etc., to the archbishops of York, the bishops of Hexham, Chester and Lindisfarne, are all of them in this hand. The erasures relate generally to northern matters. The writing is probably very early thirteenth century, if not somewhat earlier. The remainder of the marginal references are by the scribe himself, and are in a small neat hand.

Archbishop Parker sometimes puts in the margin of the MS. extracts from other chronicles—of no value.

At the end of the MS. of Symeon a seventeenth century hand has put "Liber vero impressus est amplior in nonnullis quæ hic desunt."

The members of the Surtees Society are under great obligations to the Master and Fellows of C. C. C. Cambridge, for allowing them access to this invaluable MS., and to the Rev. W. M. Snell for his courteous assistance.

APPENDIX TO PREFACE.

PART II.

A Description of MS. B. ii., 35, in the Library of the dean and chapter of Durham. By W. H. D. Longstaffe, Esq.

A collection of MSS. of various dates, paged 1, 3, 5, etc., on the right; left hand unpaged, but counting as pages.

Since Rudd's Catalogue was published, the volume has been re-bound, and now presents, as noticed in Dr. Raine's St. Cuthbert, 121, at the end, Sedbruke's list of the Durham relics.

For tracts 1, 2, 3, see Rudd's Catalogue. No. 3 is believed to be the Historia Anglorum presented by bishop Carileph.

Tract No. 4 is, I believe, the Life of Beda, a translation of which appears in the Church Historians of England, Beda, xxxix. This, with No. 3, "Beda de Gestis Anglorum" (the Ecclesiastical History), and No. 5, his Lives of the Abbats, are in the same early hand, with occasional initials—in which animals entwine. Mr. Stevenson thinks that the Life was written by an author who lived on the south side of the Humber, before the translation of Beda's bones in 1104. The Durham MS. possesses an interest as an early Northumbrian MS., especially with regard to the only passage of which I took a note, in reference to the claims of Monkton:—"Erat autem territorii Gyrwensis haud grandi oriundus viculo. Non longe inde lapsurus in oceanum —— amnis Tina præterfluit." The date of the historian's birth is given as 677.

Tract No. 5, Beda's Lives of the Abbats. See above.

No. 6, p. 235. A MS. of Nennius. See Rudd, who ascribes it to the commencement of the twelfth century, *vide* Hardy's Catalogue, i., 325. It is Stevenson's N., and Petrie's C.; Hardy gives it to cent. 12, Stevenson to cent. 13. My examination not relating to it specially, I speak with deference, but to my eye it seemed earlier than the documents of the time of bishop Pudsey, to which my attention was directed.

Notwithstanding Stevenson's note, xxviii., the MS. requires careful collation. It has not the genealogies, and, in some respects, may not be of a high order; but its northern character deserves attention. It has the miracles.

In Arthur's battles the MS. reads Glem, or Glein: Duglas: Bassas: C*a*llidonis: Guinon: Ribroit.

At the end of Stevenson's, § 56, the MS. proceeds thus:—

"Usque ad tempus quo Ida regnavit, qui fuit filius Eobba, ipse primus [fuit rex *added in a hand contemporary, or nearly so*]. Prima civitas Britanniæ ipsa *in Beornica*ꝺ[a] *est* quæ vocatur *Cair Guorthigirn*." Then the remaining twenty-five cities are enumerated thus:—

Cair Muncip, Cair Meiguod, Cair Ebroauc, Cair Caratauc, Cair Mauchguid, Cair Caint, Cair Peris, Cair Legion, Cair Legeint, Cair Guent, Cair Lerion, Cair Pensa vel Coit, Cair Guintiug, Cair Lualid, Cair Colum, Cair Custeint, Cair Grauth, Cair Lunden, Cair Guoricon, Cair Legion Guar iuuc, Cair Brito, Cair Drotchoi, Cair Urnach, Cair Celeimon, Cair Luit Coit.

Then comes what stands in Stevenson as the preceding sentence, "Hæc sunt nomina," etc.

[a] This mark ꝺ refers to a separate slip bound into the MS. of much the same date, beginning "Ida filius Eobba tenuit regiones, etc., arcem," etc., as in Stevenson's note 14, on his p. 52. After all, whether the copyist did not thoroughly misunderstand his original, and whether "in Beornica" does not properly belong to the "fuit rex" of his interlineation.

I believe that the above are correctly copied, but I cannot speak always with confidence as to the letters *u* and *n*.

Tract No. 7, p. 251, is in a minute and beautiful hand. As to this, and tracts 8 and 9, see Rudd.

Tract No. 10 is in a hand of the twelfth century. There is no rubric, but the text, where not otherwise noted, corresponds with the *Libellus de Adventu Saxonum, et de regibus eorundem*, MS. Cotton., Caligula A. viii.

p. 257. Portraits of Adam and Woden (but not of Woden's sons). Descent from Adam to Woden, with origin of nations.

At each side of Woden are genealogies of his sons. Thus, "Woden genuit Wegdā, qui genuit Sigegarū, qui gen. Sweabdegū, qui gen. Sigegeat, qui gen. Seabaldū, qui gen. Westerflacne, qui gen. Wilglis, qui gen. Uscfrea, qui gen. Yffa, qui gen. Ella Deirorum. Woden gen. Beldeig, qui gen. Brond, qui gen. Freothegarum, etc. Woden gen. Beldeig, qui gen. Brond, qui gen. Benoc, qui gen. Aloc, qui gen. Angenwitz, qui gen. Inguui, qui gen. Esam, qui gen. Eoppam, qui gen. Ida, a quo reges Northanhimbrorum (Berniciorum)." Before what I have given are the descents of Hengest and Penda. Then commences without heading or rubric, "Britannia a quodam consule Romano Bruto," etc.

p. 258. The MS. proceeds with three columns each (except as to this introductory matter), with a margin in which the names of kings and notes are placed. In col. 2 the introductory matter ends, and we have a rubric, "Regnum Cantuariorum. Genealogia regum Cantuariorum" (from the genealogies of Florence of Worcester).

p. 259. Two rubrics, "Regnum Orientalium Anglorum. Gen*e*logia Regum Orientalium Anglorum." "Regnum Orientalium Saxonum. Genealogia Regum Orientalium Saxonum" (also from Florence).

p. 260. Rubric, "De Regno Mertiorum. Genealogia Regum Mertiorum." (The chapter is from the genealogies of Florence of Worcester.)

p. 261. Rubrics. "De Regnis Deiorum et Berniciorum. Genealogia Regum Deiræ—Genealogia Regum Berniciorum et quorundam Regum qui pariter super Deiram et Berniciam regnaverunt." This is a combination of the information contained in Florence and in the Libellus de Adventu Saxonum, containing

I. Account of Ida, his sons, and the length of his reign from Florence.

II. His landing at Flamborough from the Libellus.

III. Ella of Deira, with the contemporary kings of Bernicia from Florence, the name of Hussa being interlined from the Libellus, above that of Theodulfus.

IV. To the death of Osbryht and Ella A.D. 867, from Florence.

V. Kings *usque Tinam* from Florence and *ultra Tinam* from the Libellus.

VI. Guthred's reign of fourteen years *super totam Northumbriam* from the Libellus.

VII. Reigns of Danish kings from Sihtric to Eric, or Eiric, from the Libellus. "Deinceps per comites procurata est provincia, usque ad tempora Normannorum."

p. 262. "*Rubric.* De Regnis West-Saxonum, Anglorum, et eorum qui super Angliam monarchiam adepti sunt. Genealogia Regum West Saxonum, Anglorum, et eorum qui super totam Angliam regnaverunt." This chapter is from Florence's Genealogies.

p. 263. The West Saxon history ends with Henry II. The last sentence is, "Duxit vero uxorem Alienoram, reginam Franciæ, filiam ducis Aquitaniæ." Rest of page blank.

p. 265. Rubric at top of page which is of two columns, with names in the margins. "Cantia. Nomina archiepiscoporum Dorobernensis ecclesiæ." Ends with "xxxviii. Thomas."

p. 267. Rubrics. "Rovecestria. Nomina episcoporum Rofensis ecclesiæ," ending "xxvi. Waltherus." East Saxonia. "Nomina episcoporum Lundoniensis ecclesiæ," ending "xxxix. Gilebertus ab Hereford translatus episcopus."

pp. 268, 269, 270 and part of 271. The various sees. See Rudd's list.

pp. 271-4. "Quo tempore gens Northanh' cum suo rege

Ædwino," etc. No rubric. A sort of summary of the beginnings of the Christian religion in Northumbria, running into the archbishops of York, ending with the death of Turstin, 1140. In double columns.

p. 275. A history of the bishops of Lindisfarne and Durham, without rubric. Continues to p. 278 in double columns. Bamburgh is called "Bebburch," and so in the previous article, p. 271, it is called "Bebboria."

Begins "Aidanus. Hic a Sancto Oswaldo rege, secundo anno imperii sui, anno ab inc. Domini. Dc° xxx° v°, in Lindisfarnensi insula sedem episcopalem suscepit."

p. 275. Beda's bones "translata, in sepulchro Sancti Cuthberti sunt locata."

Ecgredus. "Hic ecclesiam in Norham ædificans, translato illuc corpore Sancti Ceowlfi regis, in ejus honore, Sancti Petri, et beati Cuthberti, eam dedicavit, et villam ipsam cum duabus Geddewordis, atque ecclesiam de Geinforde cum villa, et Ileclif et Wigeclif, et Billigham, quas ipse ædificavit, et quicquid ad *eas* pertinet a flumine Teisa usque Weor, Sancto Cuthberto contulit."

"Applicante tandem ob hyemandum rege Danorum Haldene ad Tinam fluvium circa Thomemuthe."

p. 276. "Facto rege Gutdredo beati Cuthberti præcepto, sedatis procellis, sedes episcopalis in Cuneacestre restauratur." No mention of Tyne and Tees or Wear.

"Cnut Rex Sancto Cuthberto Staindropeschyre dedit."

p. 277. Walcher's murder "ad Gatesheued, quod est Capud capræ."

Foundation of the Priory by St. Carileph. "Ipseque cartis propriis hæc omnia ecclesiæ imperpetuum confirmavit."

"Rex Willelmus II.—dedit episcopatum Rannulfo, qui vocabatur Capellanus regis propter quandam excellentiam familiaritatis."

The history not very minute.

p. 278. The history ends in 1154 with "Rex et Scottorum inclitus David eodem anno apud Karlel ix k. Junii obiit."

Lists of the archbishops of York (ending with Roger de

Ponte), Hexham, Ripon, Carlisle, Lindisfarne (ending "Will. secundus.") Whitherne.

The bishops of Dunelm beginning "Hugo" are continued by later hands.

A genealogy from Adam of the English and Scottish kings. The English end thus:—

"Mathild' imperatrix
Henricus filius ejus
Henricus filius hujus."

The Scottish thus:—

"Malcolmus rex filius Henrici
Willelmus rex frater ejus."

p. 281. Index to Beda. Vide Rudd.

APPENDIX TO PREFACE.

PART III.

A Description of MS. Gale, O. iii. 55, Trin. Coll., Cambridge, ff. 69, including two fly leaves. 8vo. Sæc. xii exeunte.

Fol. 2 *a*. Reliquiæ in eccl. Dunelm. *Inc.* "De veste Domini nostri." *Expl.* "Ossa sanctarum virginum xj millium Coloniæ." [Printed in Hist. Dunelm. Script. Tres, appendix, ccccxxvj-xxx, from a more perfect MS. at York].

Fol. 2 *b*. Nomina episcoporum Lindisfarnensis et Dunelmensis ecclesiæ. *Inc.* "Aidan." *Exp.* "Willelmus." [A later hand has added the years of the reign of Wm. de St. Barbara, and the name of his successor, "Hugo" Pudsey.]

Fol. 3 *a*. A draft of an acknowledgment from Thomas Dawtre, Prior "de Fenkell," of the receipt of an annual pension of 20s. out of the mills of Embleton, paid by Wm. Swan, receiver of the lordship of Embleton for Henry (IV.). Dated at Finchale, July 28. [Dawtre was Prior of Finchale from 1405 to 1411. See Priory of Finchale, xxviii, 158-163.]

Foll. 3 *b*, 25 *b*. Beda's Life of St. Cuthbert. *Inc.* "Epistola Venerabilis Bedæ presbyteri." *Expl.* "Explicit liber de vita et miraculis beatissimi patris Cuthberti." [A list of the chapters. The prologue addressed to bishop Eadfrid; and then the life of the Saint in forty-six chapters, as printed in Smith's edition of Beda, pp. 227-264. The dedication of Beda's Metrical Life of the Saint, addressed to John the Priest, is also given.]

After which are the words in a sixteenth century hand,

"Jhesus be my speyd. Amen." J. H. C.

"Symon Garstell."

Fol. 4 *a*. The name, "Thomas Hersley," occurs, sæc. xvi.

Fol. 4 *b*.

"I pray God off my behalffe
Have mercy off the sowll off Johne Cauff;
Had not dethe cummyt lyke a wyly foxe,
Johne had levyt wylsse he had benne an old old oxe."
(Sæc. xvi.)

"Liber de Vita et Miraculis Sanctorum Cuthberti præsulis, Oswaldi martiris, et Aydani episcopi in Insula Sacra ex dono domini Henrici Dalton, Prioris ejusdem, anno Domini 1513."

Fol. 5 *a*. "Liber domini W. Ellvyt ex dono .... quondam Prioris Dunelm." Sæc. xv.

Foll. 25-6. The miracles wrought upon "Beadothegn" and "Suthbertus," which constitute chapters xxxi. and xxxii. in the fourth book of Beda's Ecclesiastical History. In nearly all the MSS. in which the treatise De Translationibus occurs, these two chapters form the connecting link between that tractate and Beda's Life of Cuthbert.

Fol. 26 *a*. "Excerpta de Vita et Miraculis Sancti Cuthberti." [This is the "Brevis Relatio" as printed pp. 223-233, in this volume. The chapters from i. to xxix. inclusive run in the same order as in our text. Then comes cap. xxxvi., Visio Bosonis: after this follows abruptly the *Historia Translationum*].

Foll. 30 *a*—46 *a*. The "Historia Translationum" as printed in this volume.

Fol. 46 *b*. The "Brevis Relatio" begins again with a chapter, "Quomodo in loco ubi prius jacuerat miracula coruscare et infirmi sanitatem cœperunt recuperare" (Hist. Dunelm., iii., 3). After this the chapters run on thus, according to the numbering of our text, xxx., xxxv., xxxiv., xxxi., xxxii., xxxiii., xxxvi. After these there follows an Indulgence granted in behalf of the church of Durham by Pope Anastasius IV. (This will be printed in the Appendix to the History of the Church of Durham.) Then follows chapter xxxviii. of our text of the "Brevis Relatio."

Foll. 50 *a*—54 *b*. The service on the Deposition of St. Cuthbert with musical notes *Inc.* "Tertia decima kal. Aprilis depositio Sancti Cuthberti. *Officium.* Statuto ei Dominus. *Oratio.*"

Expl. "Ut per ea veniam mereamur peccatorum et cælestis gratiæ donis reficiamur. Per —"

Foll. 57 *a*—58 *b*. *Rubr.* "Quomodo Willelmus episcopus et regia et Apostolica auctoritate fretus clericos incontinentes de Dunelmensi ecclesia eliminavit et monacos induxit." (Symeon's Hist. Dunelm. iv., 1, abridged). After this come some other extracts, chiefly from Symeon, relating to these changes at Durham, ending with the letter of Bishop St. Carileph to the monks, which constitutes the sixth chapter of the fourth book of Symeon's History.

Foll. 59 *a*—*b*. A Hymn to the Blessed Virgin, with musical notes, beginning:—"Salve regina misericordiæ, vitæ dulcedo et spes nostra," and ending abruptly "O dulcis Maria." At the end of it are four lines of a short prayer to the Virgin. After this is some writing in a sixteenth century hand, including a quotation from the Eclogues of Virgil.

"Who so wolde faine doy well,
The dewille's workes lete him expell;
Flee from sinne and lette pase vice,
So thowe shall winne Paradise.
"Humfrey Radclyff."

Foll. 60 *a b*. Several short prayers forming part of the

service, *In Natale Oswaldi,* followed by part of a hymn, with musical notes, beginning thus,

"Regis Oswaldi inclita
Christo canamus merita."

Foll. 61 *a*—66 *a*. The life and miracles of St. Oswald.

Incipit. "Successores Eadwini regis Anglorum in apostasiam corruentes."

Explicit. "Cujus precibus et meritis mereamur a peccatis emundari et prope tua cum illo beatitudine ditari. Amen."

In thirteen chapters, eleven of which are taken almost *verbatim* from Beda. The two last are new, and will be printed in Vol. II.

Foll. 66 *b*—68 *b*. The life of St. Aidan.

Incipit. "Est insula quæ vocatur Hii."

Explicit. "Futuram cum sancta ecclesia credebat."

[Derived altogether from Beda].

After this there are three pages containing hymns to St. Oswald, with musical notes.

"Regalis ostro sanguinis
Lux purpuratur præcluis."

With several fragments of a service in honour of that Saint.

TABLE OF CONTENTS.

APPENDIX.

SYMEONIS DUNELMENSIS

HISTORIA REGUM.

INCIPIT PASSIO SANCTORUM ETHELBERTI[a] ATQUE ETHELREDI, REGIÆ STIRPIS PUERORUM.[b]

Anno ab incarnatione Dominica DC.XVJ, qui est xxj ex quo sanctissimus Augustinus cum sociis ad prædicandum missus est, Æthelbert rex Cantuariorum, post regnum temporale quod l. et vj annis gloriosissime tenuerat, æterna cælestis regni subiit gaudia. Erat autem idem rex filius Irmirici, cujus pater Octa, cujus pater Oiric, cujus pater Hengest, qui cum filio suo Oisc a Wirtigerno rege invitatus Britanniam primus intravit, ut Beda[c] luculento describit sermone. Eadbaldus vero, filius Æthelbyrhti, regni gubernacula suscepit, qui genuit duos filios Eormenredum atque Erconbyrhtum. Eadbaldus rex, transiens ex hac vita, Erconberto sceptra dereliquit imperii. Hic, primus regum Anglorum, in toto regno suo idola relinqui ac destrui præcepit; simul et jejunium quadraginta dierum observari principali auctoritate jussit; cui natus est filius nomine Ecbertus. Natique sunt Eormenredo Æthelbertus atque Æthelredus; quorum vitam et passionis triumphum in exordio nostræ historiæ placet inserere, et gloriam sanctitatis eorum demonstrare.

Erat namque rex Æthelbyrhtus perfectus in imperio glo-

[a] This legend is printed by Twysden and also by Mr. Petrie from the C. C. C. manuscript, as an integral part of Symeon's Gesta Regum, but is evidently the production of a much earlier period. Mr. Petrie calls attention to the fact that the remains of the two martyrs are described as still deposited at Wakering, although we learn from Gotscelin, who wrote an account of their passion A.D. 1090, that they had been removed to Ramsey a century before that period. See Mon. Hist., preface, p. 89. Portions of Gotscelin's narrative are also obviously derived from the present work. This legend and the genealogy of the Northumbrian kings must be regarded as prefatory to Symeon's work, and on that account these are given in this place, as they are not devoid of novelty and interest. The notices of the abbats of Wearmouth and two poems by Beda have been omitted.

[b] This heading is in red letters.

[c] Eccl. Hist., i., xiv.

riosæ potestatis, qui, delectatus summopere verbis Divinæ agnitionis, tinctus est baptismate salutis. Cujus studio vel sagaci auxilio ubique ecclesiarum Dei diffusus est status, et rerum suarum collatione fidelium roboratus extitit conventus. Unde regni monarchia solertissime pro sibi illato posse disposita, vocante (sequi enim inter omnia fecerat) justi Remuneratoris clementia, carnalibus privatur, et ad ardua ætheris cum Sanctis regnaturus sustollitur. Huic vero in regiminis sumministratione succedit filius Eadbaldus, sicut superius præfati sumus, de quo procreantur bini regalis stirpis filii, Eormenredus et Erconbyrhtus, quorum junior imperialis principatum regni, patre disponente, suscepit. Post autem Erconbyrhti decessum, filius ipsius, nomine Ecgbyrhtus, illud potenter gubernavit. Eormenredus vero major absque imperii dominio in hujus caducalis vitæ permansit volubili stadio: cui justo ex justissima conjuge nati sunt filii duo, qui nutriti in herili cælestis Regis palatio, multimodis sunt ditati æternæ gloriæ munere Regio; quorum unus onomate nituit Æthelredus, alter vero vocabulo fulsit Æthelbyrhtus. Namque in eorum natali sanctissimo, cuncti, ut remur, lætati sunt beatorum spirituum ordines in cælo, quia quos in terris destinari conspiciebant, ipsos fortiores post hujus vitæ gravia certamina ad se redituros videbant. Gavisa est telluris sublimitas, se ornari sentiens duplicis doni gratia; et quia ex nimio mulctatur contrariorum infortunio, se semper sperat immeliorari tali subsidio. Gratulatur insuper et mater sancta ecclesia, dum sui tanto Sponsi illustratur dotalicio, quo et meritorum luce melius resplendeat, et semper in sanctioris rectissimum æquitatis culmen crescat. Hujus nempe præcellentis doctrinæ utero traditi, ut sine accuratis disciplinæ magistralis loquamur eloquentiis, primo omnium in serenissimo sanctæ meditationis illius sacrario, nitido salutaris aquæ sunt abluti baptisterio, in cujus puri septem gradibus liquoris septem sunt sortiti dona Spiritus Sancti, episcopali benedictione perfusi, et sancto crismate delibuti. Quibus undique decentissime fulti, vivere studuerunt virgines et corpore sancto tenerrimi, septenis dierum curriculis, ut, septem septies augmentatis et monade supposito, singularis in præsenti vita adquirerent fructum jubilei, hoc est annum æternæ felicitatis. Hoc deinde insignium illustri cura virtutum duplicato corpore et anima, post peractum vitæ cursum, fructum caperent centesimum sacratissimis virginibus consecratum. Egregia namque insignes forma sanctitatis, aptissimis devincti caritatis radiis, cernuæ locupletes humilitatis officiis, inevincibilis ter beati patientiæ titulis, largis pro posse fungentes elemosinarum studiis, indeficientis præcordialibus orationis compti privilegiis, et plurimis Patris spirituum debriantur bonitatum speculis. Quia ergo plantaria virtutum naturaliter eis insita pro nostra capacitate prælibavimus, nunc brevi notationis serie aggredi temptamus, qualiter ad gaudia cælestis patriæ per coronam martyrii vocantur.

Igitur utrisque eorum parentibus ab hujus vitæ miseria decedentibus cum adhuc juvenilis potirentur imbecillitate ætatis, Ecgberhto regi germano consobrino suo sunt traditi, qualiter et solertis prudentiæ educarentur exercitiis, et humanæ infirmitatis sustentarentur solatiis. Talibus vero piorum conaminibus non defuere iniquæ venena jaculationis, quæ semper adversus filios Dei per filios diffidentiæ telis invidiæ armatur. In regali namque palatio *homo* quidam *peccati* et *filius* inventus est *perditionis*,[d] membrum diaboli necnon domus zabuli, qui sæculi vanis tumidus pompis, munificentiaque regali redimitus, *nec Deum timebat nec hominem reverebatur*. Hic cum principe cum pro nimia ambitione honoris super omnes consiliis frueretur, tum pro fætido humanæ levitatis favore in vanum tollebatur, Aman super Mardocheum ignicomis mortiferæ vexationis furcis stimulabatur, quibus ipse postmodum insperate vinctus suspenderetur. Vocabatur porro convenienti sibi nomine Thunur, quod Latina interpretatione sonat tonitrus. Furiis namque teterrimorum spirituum morbidis indesinenter vexabatur, quorum horridis fragoribus in inferni tartarum demergeretur. Videns ergo felices quos supra-taxavimus vivere feliciter, sordidarum scabenti deturpatus meditationum prurigine, in cœnoso mentis impiæ volutabro cœpit cogitare, quibus adinventionum ruderibus eos neci posset tradere. Unde canino dente apud plurimos aulicorum eorum præconia præsumebat rodere, vecordique in calumpnia ipsorum duci talia proferre. "Cum, rex serenissime, strenua mente, solerti opere, perspicacis sensus valitudine, ac vigorabili tui potentatus lance, largissima regnorum tuæ majestati subjacentium sinuamina prudentissimo æquitatis disponantur libramine, est quam pretiosum, ut non tantum stabili nunc virga regni recte moderetur, sceptrumque orbis status gubernetur, quam pulcherrime tuæ propagini prospiciat incolume pacis decus. Non enim tantum tui cura sollicitationum nebulis agitareris, nisi clarissimorum tuæ dignitatis successurorum speciebus natorum optimis delectareris. Quapropter operæ pretium ducimus, ut semita tranquillitatis eis prospera redimatur, quo et respublica ipsis successura nullo turbinum fluctu quatiatur, nullis discordiarum angoribus vacilletur. Cuncta eis bonis omnibus exuberans arrideat felicitas, lætitiæ pleniter inditis perseverabilis

[d] 2 Thess. ii. 3; St. John xvii. 12. The passage below is from St. Luke xviii. 2.

affluat jocunditas! Videre autem videor, ut magna hujus salubritatis oriatur penes te injuria, quia nutris cum diligentia qui aliquando sibi usurpare præsument tui regni fastigia, mutabunt quæ diligenter eis exhibes talia, in tui tuorumque posterorum inutilia. Ex assistentibus tuæ celsitudinis loquor Æthelredo et Æthelbyrhto tyrunculis, qui magis in augmento tuæ liberorumque crescunt dampnationis quam cujuslibet tuæ provectionis. Ergo perquisita directi ominis scientiola qua æqua promoveatur in eos rationis sententiola; consultum communis crederem esse utilitatis tuæ, ut aut eos in longinquum dirigi exilium jubeas regionis, aut citissime tradi mihi sinas jugulis." Rege hæc dissimulante, utraque se nolle denegante, illo tamen obnixe ut fieri permitteret stimulante, et hoc sæpius repetente, dum tepide et non argute prohibuit, audaciæ temeritatem ut perderentur intulit. O quam subdola semper in insontes perfidorum calliditas! O quam immitis fraudulentorum in innocentes sævitia! Nulla lenis gratissima pietatis cura, non eis ulla mansuetudinis intersunt viscera. Sola quæ meditantur acerba, quæ portant venenis similia. Quid plura? mortifera idem in se-ipsum armatur pestifer turbo nequitia, qua absente regis præsentia manus nisus est extendere in Deo cernua innocentum colla.

Hac igitur invidi persecutoris insectatione martyres Christi coronati sunt palma victoriæ, et, a Christo suscepti, in prædio perennis vitæ lætantur cum angelis cælestis patriæ. Pretiosa vero tantarum membra agonistarum jussit inhonestis subselliorum locis humo contegi regalium, credens latere diu cunctis quod peregerat stupidæ commentum perversitatis nequitia scelesti interemptoris. Porro nullo eis indulto fletus suspirio, nullo decem cordarum reboante officio, non hymnorum pulcherrimo Ambrosiano titulo, nec Gregoriano potitis dulcis armoniæ organo; non defuere summæ Deitatis tamen multiplicis virtutis exennia.

Etenim intempesta noctis quiete visa est Divinitus corusca super aulam palatii regis fulsisse luminis columpna, quæ illustratione insolita plures turbavit ex regis familia. Dantesque fragorem clamoris in admiratione nimia expergefactus est rex, et hoc minime cognoscens surrexit a stratus sui cubiculo, et iter paravit ad nocturnales matutinorum hymnos. Cum digressus a domo, videt orbem novi splendoris incanduisse albedine, cujus procreatio diffluebat a præfato lucis mirabili solio. Enimvero tam recentis stupefactus intuitu, mentis agitari cœpit sollicitus rex cogitationibus, et ubi essent quos pridie præviderat, et de confabulatione perdendorum martyrum quam minister iniquitatis cum eo jamdudum habuerat, movebatur siquidem meditatione acerrima. Tunc celerrime ascito tanti criminis auctore sciscitatur qua forent propinqui sui positi regionis longinquitate, quorum non fruebatur præsentiæ inclita pulchritudine. Iniquissimo sane surdas his punctionibus aures præbente carnifice, atque Cain voce superbo mentis supercilio se nescire turpiore grunniente, minaci vultu, quippe ut perterritus Divinæ lucis claritate, ei fertur talia inculcavisse; "Tu mihi plurima de eis semper sermocinatus es bonis contraria, tu de eorum exilio mala, tu de internicione nefaria, tu adversus eos multa mordebaris insania. Tibi pleniter enarrare nostræ sollertiæ oportet, nequissime, qualiter inveniantur quos gravi insectabaris odii zelo, corrupta mente." Ad hæc ille furcifer sentina malitiæ fætidus: "Sub tuæ," inquit, "mortua eorum jacent cadavera loco sedis domus." Princeps quid ageret? Perculsus namque timoris ingenti turbine, quia in parte torquebatur mordaci macula alis conscientiæ, dum fortiter non restitit bonitatis hosti; et quia vindicare nequibat quod peractum injuste fuerat, stupens inhærebat, in quantumque poterat pœnitebat. Aurora itaque diei terris illucescente, convocatis quibus ad præsens innitebatur comitibus, regnique sui principibus cum episcopis, in quibus supereminebat archipræsul Dorovernensis multæ beatitatis vir, vocabulo Deus-dedit, ad locum præfatorum innocentum concitus pergit, terram suffossorio avellit, corporaque sanctissima indecenter jugulata ac inhoneste condita detegit. Heu quam surda aure tunc mentis constitit si non flevit, cum filios avunculi sui innocentes perditos conspexit! Heu quam ferreo usus est pectore si dum propinquos carnis suæ felici sanguinis vidit tinctos rubore, non tangitur cordis dolore! Heu quam gravi lacrimarum potuit suffundi imbre, dum tantæ nobilitatis flores inclitos tam futili vidit traditos sepulturæ!

Igitur cum hominum exequiis etiam non defuerunt magnalia perpetuæ Deitatis. Coronatos namque in regni æternitatis solio etiam hic visitare dignatur miro potentiæ Suæ miraculo. Talia gerebantur in villa regali quæ vulgari dicitur Easterige pronunciatione. Cum ergo sanctorum pretiosissima innocentum corpora terræ secreto forent superstatuta feretro, propositum est ut, delata in urbem Cantiæ, Christi sepelirentur in monasterio; et moveri non quiverunt ab illo in quo statuta fuerant loco. Propositum est ut ad Sancti Augustini ferrentur ecclesiam, siquidem levari nequiverunt. Ad plurima quoque et honorabilia portare decreverunt loca et tumbis appositarum manuum deficiebant brachia. Tandem salubri reperto consilio, ut ad famossissimum gestarentur monasterium, Wacrinense vocitatum, tam citissimæ agilitatis insperato levantur officio, ut nihil oneris videretur in gestamine diu desiderato. Quo cum perventum fuisset, cum pulcherrimis hymnorum cantilenis, lenibusque psalmorum melodiis, multis resonantibus choris et jubilationum cymbalis, suscipiuntur, tradunturque principalem retro aram sepulturæ decenti. Hic multis annorum curriculis eis positis, Excelsus Dominus, *Qui humilia respicit et alta a longe cognoscit,*[d] eos creberrimis ditare miraculis voluit; de quibus duo posterorum notitiæ nunc propalare præsenti sermone [statuo].

Accidit ut quidam alterius bonis cæcatus ovem cujusdam pauperis tolleret secretius, quam gestans in humeris, ligatis pedibus, deferre gliscebat secus arcisterium sanctorum martyrum, sed non potuit. Portari ibidem potuit, sed dehinc vehi non valuit. Reus itaque hujus sceleris continuo frustratur flatu vitali, prosterniturque mortuus, humi ovem viventem habens in manibus, eo insequente cui furtum fuerat illatum. Recipit innocens proprium, dimittit reum morte præventum subitanea sanctorum ultione innocentum. Continuo currens ad ædituum sciscitatur si peremerit latronem illum; a nullo mortali didicit jugulatum; acceptaque licentia reportandi quod suum fuerat, lætus et hilaris revertitur in sua, Deo ac Sanctis Ejus multas gratias agens.

Igitur quoniam passiones sanctorum martyrum, prout potuimus, strictim prælibavimus, restat quomodo Divina ultio super iniquissimum judicem, piissimæ necis eorum auctorem, pervenerit, breviter tangamus. Fuerat eis ex paterno maternoque soror procreata semine, Eormenburga vel Domneva nomine, quam habebat in conjugium copulationis legitimæ rex Merciorum, Mearwoldus nomine, quam Ecgberhtus rex ad se, misso legationis suæ gerulo, disposuit vocare. Quæ veniens, suscipitur ab omnibus primatibus illius regionis, uti dignum erat, honorabili perspicuæ ambitionis dignitate. Decernens itaque eam honorare, ut quodcunque vellet honestatis sibi competentis in potestatis suæ ditione rogaret, et sine mora acciperet, sancta mulier humili responsione subinfert, ut tantum terræ illi concederet quantum cerva quam sibi nutrierat, in una die Divino instinctu pede peragraret. Rex vero gratanter continuo jubet in crastinum præparari comitum agmen, quo fretus, navibus ad insulam Tened dictam faceret callem. Quo positi, ipsaque cum cerva insulam navigio ingressa, viam cerva lustrandi arripit, a principeque et Christi famula cum plebe militari insequitur equis. Jam ex parte quamplurima circumita, nefandus carnifex turbatur invidia, et quasi pro fidelitate regis, cui nihil remanere videbatur ex ipsius vastitate amæna, cœpit, quasi in viis ejus compatiens, garrire talia, "Cum cuncta peragas perspicacis pru-

[d] Psalm cxxxviii. 6.

dentiæ gubernaculo, quare hoc brutum animal, sicut aliquid magni gerat, sequeris incessu devotissimo?" His dictis, Deitatis summis perculsus jaculis, ex sonipede ruit. Continuo suscipitur cum armis equoque nimis nimiumque infelix Thunor novo terræ hiatu, ac nimio terrore rex cum omnibus suis commilitonibus correptus, operiri concite jubet horrendo lapidum acervo ipsius corpus, anima perenni servata incendio, baratri cœnosis ignibus, de quibus dictum est pœnis, "Transibunt animæ de pœnis nivium ad calorem nimium." Qui locus a transeuntibus Thunerhleaw vocatur, talique vocabulo potitur. Talibus stupidæ mortis officiis insano lanista utente, ac pro deliciis tormentorum pœnas luente, prædicta fera, quantum Divina voluntas concessit, eis comitantibus iter fecit, et sic gradum fixit mirantibus cunctis. Rex quod spoponderat viso territus miraculo fecit, manu propria formavit, sicque domum rediit.

Mulier vero, sanctæ virtutis amica, ac Deo valde electa, in hac insula ecclesiam almæ Dei genitricis Mariæ perpetuæ Virginis, in memoria innocentum Christi martyrum, fratrum suorum, constituit, filiamque suam bonæ indolis virginem, Mildrydam appellatam, ecclesiasticis in transmarinis partibus disciplinis eruditam, postmodum ibi constituit, cum septuaginta sanctimonialibus a sancto archiepiscopo Deus-dedit consecratis, inibique congregavit. Ibi ergo beatæ genitrix Mildrithæ post excursum plurimorum annorum, post exhibitionem bonarum virtutum, post ædificationem plurimarum mentium virorum et virginum quas in Christo confortavit cum lampade justitiæ, a Christo meruit audire, *Surge, propera, amica mea, veni de Libano, veni, coronaberis.*[e] Cujus anima ad cæli deducta palatium, a Christo percipit immarescibilia victoriæ dona, cum Eo Sanctisque Ejus regnatura in perenni gloria. Sane in monasterii regimine succedit inclita ejus soboles, quam educaverat decentissime nobilis et in Christi servitio non deficiens Mildrytha prædicta, sanctissima virgo, multa fulgens miraculorum gratia.

Unde unum narramus miraculum, quod sine dubio confirmat quia fecerat ei Dominus plurima quæ sunt mortalibus inedicibilia. Quadam namque temporis serie, lassescentibus membris pro nimia laboris diuturnitate, quiescebat in lectulo, modico gravata sopore: cui astitit angelus Domini in columbæ specie residens in ejus capite, ut eam tueretur a malignorum spirituum illusione. Hæc beata virgo, sicut ejus felix genetrix, bona relinquens sequacibus vestigia, Omnipotente spirituum Patre ejus animam sumente, terra plorante, cælo gaudente, vivit in

[e] Cantic. ii. 10; iv. 8.

æterna beatitudine; sacratissimo ipsius corpore in templo beatæ Dei genitricis Mariæ, perpetuæ virginis, digniter in condigno loco tradito sepulturæ. Præterea dum spurcissimi persecutoris piorum martyrum subitum mortis interitum statuimus describere, postmodum inflleximus oculos ad veneranda sororis neptisque eorum gesta, quibus insimul *Christus fuit vivere, et mori lucrum*;[f] cujus gratia ad alia narranda, Eo succurrente, est properandum, retinentes ordinem narrationum.

[f] Phil. i. 21.

GENEALOGIA REGUM NORTHANHYMBRORUM.

In exordio hujus operis genealogiam regum Cantuariorum strictim prælibavimus; nunc Northanhymbrorum libet demonstrare, ut ad eorum tempora valeamus pervenire, de quibus non est narratum post obitum reverendissimi sacerdotis Bedæ.[g]

[g] This paragraph refers to the preceding legend, which seems to have been the model on which the style of the Northumbrian Genealogy was formed. This latter piece is of no value as an original authority, being a mere paraphrase in very bombastic language of the "Brief Northumbrian Chronology," printed in the Monumenta Historica, page 290, with a few additions subsequent to the introduction of Christianity from the Ecclesiastical History of Beda. The sequence of the successors of Ida is the same in both lists; and although there is some discrepancy in the length of the several reigns, the summation of the whole is the same in each. Where differences occur, the Northumbrian Chronology seems the better authority, confirmed as it is by the genealogy appended to Nennius. The following table will explain the variations.

GENEALOGY.		CHRONOLOGY.		NENNIUS.	
Ida.........	11	Ida.........	12	Ida.........	12
Glappa......	1	Glappa......	1	(omitted)....	1
Adda......	8	Adda........	8	Adda.......	8
Ethelric.....	7	Ethelric.....	4	Ethelric.....	4
Theodoric....	4	Theodoric....	7	Theodoric...	7
Frithwald....	7	Frithwald....	6	Frithwald....	6
Hussa......	7	Hussa.......	7	Hussa.......	7
	45		45		45

Florence of Worcester has a distinct list, not only differing in the length and sequence of the reigns, but introducing a new name, Theolwulf, and omitting Hussa. Wallingford has framed a list from those several authorities, adopting the order in which the names occur in Florence; but taking the length of the reigns from the Northumberland Chronology, and giving a place to Hussa instead of Theolwulf. Hussa indeed is noticed with too great particularity, not merely in the Genealogy, but in the narrative of Nennius, to allow of the omission of his name; whilst the general accuracy of the succession of the kings, as recorded by Florence, is corroborated by the Saxon Chronicle; which, although it omits two others, expressly mentions Ethelric as the immediate predecessor of Ethelfrith. As this is a matter of some interest in Northumbrian history, I subjoin the series of Florence and the composite list of Wallingford.

FLORENCE OF WORCESTER.		WALLINGFORD.	
Ida.........	11	Ida.........	12
Adda.......	7	Adda.......	8
Glappa......	5	Glappa......	1
Theolwulf...	1	Hussa......	6
Frithwulf....	7	Frithwulf....	7
Theodoric...	7	Theodoric...	7
Ethelric....	7	Ethelric.....	4

Of these Adda, Ethelric, and Theodric, were sons of Ida; and our three first cited authorities seem to have misled us by placing them in the order of their birth, rather than in that of their succession to the throne.

Ida rex annis regnavit xj, quo abstracto, Glappa j regnavit anno, quem secutus Adda, viij annis tenuit regni fastigia. Illo vero penetrante ima pro meritis, Æthelric regnum adeptus est terrenum, quod tenuit vij annis. Is, secreta inferni visitans, Theoderico imperia dereliquit, qui bis binis annis regnum tenens, regnum simul perdidit et vitam,

> "Tendens in externas ire tenebras,
> Quo pressus gravidis colla catenis,
> Cogitur nunc miserum cernere regnum."[h]

Post hunc Frithwold adeptus est sceptrum regni vij annis, qui subtractus a sæculo monarchiam regni dereliquit regi Husso. Ipse vero vij annis jura imperii tenens, didicit per se verum esse quod sequitur,

> "Mors spernit altam gloriam,
> Involvit humile pariter et celsum caput,
> Æquatque summis infima."

Octavus in regno refulsit Æthelfryth fortissimus regum, qui, xx et viij annis regno potitus, vita et regno est privatus. Huic successit Edwinus rex, qui fidem Christianitatis percipiens, rex et martyr cælos penetravit pro meritis, xvij annis regnum conservans cum honore summæ potestatis. Oswaldus vero post hunc regnum Northanhymbrorum Christianissimus suscepit, quod et viij annis tenuit: qui supernæ civitatis gaudia petens, et cæli secreta scandens,[i] regnum post ipsum Oswius rex suscepit ad tuendum xx et viij annis. Quo ablato ab imis ad supera, Ecfrido commisit terrena imperia, qui regnum xv annis tenuit. Quo a Pictis interfecto, quia injuste vastaverat Hiberniam,[i] regnavit pro eo Alfridus, frater ejus, xix annis. Quo occiso, Cöenredus regni gubernacula suscepit xj annis. Cui in regnum successit Osricus xj annis. Osrico vero successit Ceolwlfus frater Cöenredi viij annis. Huic Beda historiographus Anglorum Historiam destinavit.

[h] Boethius de Consol. Philosoph., i., 3, 25, 27. Several words, however, are altered. The two short sentences before may be written like verse, but they do not occur in Boethius. The passage below comes from the same author, ii., 12-14.

[i] These four words are interlined.

INCIPIT HISTORIA[k] SANCTÆ ET SUAVIS MEMORIÆ SYMEONIS MONACHI ET PRÆCENTORIS ECCLESIÆ SANCTI CUTHBERTI DUNELMI DE REGIBUS ANGLORUM ET DACORUM, ET CREBERRIMIS BELLIS, RAPINIS ET INCENDIIS EORUM; POST OBITUM VENERABILIS BEDÆ PRESBYTERI FERE USQUE AD OBITUM REGIS PRIMI HENRICI FILII WILLELMI NOTHI QUI ANGLIAM ADQUISIVIT[l] [id est ccccxxix annorum et iiij mensium].

DCCXXXII.[m]

Anno ab incarnatione Domini DCC.xxxij, ut præfati sumus, Berthwaldus archiepiscopus est defunctus. Eodem anno Tatwine est consecratus archiepiscopus nonus Dorovernensis ecclesiæ, Ethilbaldo rege Merciorum quintum-decimum agente annum imperii.[n] Ipso quoque anno Ceolwlfus rex captus, attonsus, et remissus est in regnum.[o] Erat vero miro[p] studio imbutus, ut Beda testatur in exordio sui proëmii veridicus. Acca episcopus eodem anno de sua sede est fugatus,[q] et Cyneberht Lindisfarorum[r] ecclesiæ antistes obiit. Ipso autem anno Alric et Esc cum aliis plurimis occisi sunt die x kal. Septembris, v feria.[s]

[k] This Colophon is in red letters.

[l] In the MS. this rubric is placed at the commencement of the collection, preceding the separate title of the Passion of Ethelbert and Ethelred, to which, however, and the intermediate pieces, it has no reference whatever. It is here prefixed to the historical narrative to which it refers, commencing with events immediately preceding the death of Beda. The concluding words, "id est cccc.xxix annorum et iiij mensium," which have been shewn in the Preface to be inaccurate, have been put within brackets.

[m] The following note is inserted in a hand of the seventeenth century in the C. C. C. manuscript in this place: "Historia Simeonis Dunelmensis monachi, sed desunt folia nonnulla. Debuerat possuisse immediate post titulum operis ante passionem Ethelberti et Ethelredi," thus recognizing the applicability of the title to this part of the collection only.

[n] This is copied from the Recapitulation at the end of Beda's Ecclesiastical History. Some of the following statements are taken from the ancient Northumbrian Annals at the end of certain MSS. of Beda, which are printed in the Monumenta Historica, pp. 288-9. These are referred to in the following notes by the initials N. A.; the Saxon Chronicle by S. C. Notices which occur only in Symeon are distinguished by the letter S.

[o] N. A., sub anno 731.

[p] Parker has inserted the word *Scripturarum*, which is printed by Twysden.

[q] N. A. 731, S. C. 733.

[r] Lindissæ interlined.

[s] S.-Alric is probably the same person who is mentioned by Beda (Mon. Hist., p. 282) as the youngest son of Wictred king of Kent, and who on the death of his

DCCXXXIII.

Anno DCC.xxxiij Tatwine archiepiscopus, accepto ab Apostolica auctoritate pallio, ordinavit Alwig et Sigfrid episcopos.[t] Eclipsis facta est solis xix kal. Septembris, circa horam diei tertiam, ita ut pene totus orbis solis quasi nigerrimo et horrendo scuto videretur esse coopertus.[u]

DCCXXXIV.

Anno DCC.xxxiiij luna sanguineo rubore est perfusa, quasi hora integra, ij kal. Februarii circa gallicantum. Dehinc nigredine subsequente ad lucem propriam est reversa.[v]

Eodem anno Tatwine archiepiscopus nonus Dorovernensis civitatis in Cantia obiit die iij kal. Augusti.[w] Primus ipsius civitatis episcopus erat Augustinus, gloriosus doctor totius regni, ac egregius fundator Christianitatis.[x] Qui, ad supernæ civitatis gaudia sublevatus, sceptra tanti fastigii dereliquit Laurentio. Is pro meritis supernis allectus civibus, dispensationem catholicæ ecclesiæ commendavit Mellito episcopo. Mellitus denique post laborum suorum certamina, tanquam miles emeritus, cælestium donorum consecutus est præmia. Post eum quarto in loco Justus succedit, qui in Domino Deo confisus ad montem virtutum secundum nominis sui palmam transmigravit victoriosus. Secutus est ipsum Honorius, hoc est honore plenus, qui officium sibi commissum bene ministrans, poli culmina conscendit pro meritis. Deus-dedit cathedram ascendit sexto in loco, qui patrum secutus vestigia, hæres factus est in cælesti curia. Deinde Theodorus doctissimus[y] exurgens, septimum locum gloriose exornavit. Berthwaldus octavo succedit loco; quem secutus est Tatwine episcopus, sicut præfati sumus.

Eodem anno ordinatus est Friothuberht Haugustaldensis ecclesiæ episcopus sub die vj idus Septembris.[z]

DCCXXXV.

Anno DCC.xxxv Nothelmus archiepiscopus ordinatus[a] est, et

father, A.D. 725, was left one of the heirs to his kingdom with his brothers Edilbert and Edbert.

It is true that Malmesbury tells us that Alric reigned thirty-four years, Edilbert eleven, and Edbert twenty-three; but we have on the other hand the much higher authority of the Saxon Chronicle, which, agreeing with Malmesbury as to the length of Edbert's reign, assigns the longer period of thirty-four years not to Alric but to Edelbert, making no mention of the date of Alric's death, or the length of his reign. Esc is mentioned by no other writer.

[t] S. [u] N. A., S. C. [v] N. A., S. C. [w] N. A., S. C.

[x] Interlined are the words, which Twysden prints unnecessarily, "*Vel Christianæ fidei et religionis.*"

[y] Interlined. [z] N. A., 735.

Egberhtus Eboraci antistes, primus post Paulinum, accepto ab Apostolica sede pallio, genti Northanhymbrorum in archiepiscopatum confirmatus[a] est.[b] Beda doctor obiit in Gyruum.[c]

DCCXXXVI.

Anno DCC.xxxvj Nothelmus, pallio a Romano pontifice suscepto,[d] ordinavit tres episcopos; Cuthbertum, videlicet, Heordwaldum et Æthelfridum.[e]

DCCXXXVII.

Anno DCC.xxxvij Aldwine, qui et Wor, episcopus defunctus est; et pro eo Hwitta et Totta Mercis et Midil-Anglis sunt consecrati antistites.[f] Eodem anno regnum Northanhymbrorum Celwlfus dimisit, et monachus apud Lindisfarnensem insulam factus est, et pro eo[g] Eadberht, filius patrui ejus, successit.

DCCXXXVIII.

Anno DCC.xxxviij Swebriht, Orientalium Saxonum rex, obiit.[h]

DCCXXXIX.

Anno DCC.xxxix Ethelheard, rex Occidentalium Saxonum, defunctus est,[i] et pro eo Cuthred, frater ejus, rex constituitur.

Ipso quoque anno Nothelm archiepiscopus post annos iiij accepti episcopatus diem *(sic)* obiit in pace,[j] et Aldulf Hrofensis ecclesiæ episcopus diem clausit ultimum.[k]

DCCXL.

Anno DCC.xl Æthelwald, Lindisfarnensis ecclesiæ antistes, migravit ad Dominum, et Kynewlf in episcopatum subrogatus est.[l]

[a] *Ordinatus* interlined. [b] N. A., S. C.

[c] N. A., S. C., 734. [d] S. C.

[e] S.-Cuthbert was bishop of Hereford; Hereward of Shirburn; "Ethelfrid of Elmham." *Petrie.*

[f] S.-Aldwin, bishop of Litchfield. His see extended over the whole of Mercia, including the Mid-Angles. On the division of the diocese Hwitha was placed at Litchfield; Totta at Leicester. *Florence of Worcester, Appendix.*

[g] The words from *Celwlfus* to *eo* are at the foot of the page in a somewhat later hand. A blank is left in the text as if there had been an omission or an erasure. The relationship between Ceolwulf and Eadbert is not given in N. A., but is supplied by S. C.; whence we learn that Ceolwulf was the son of Cutha, son of Cuthwin, son of Ledwold, son of Egwold, son of Aldelm, son of Ocea, son of Ida; and that Eadbert was the son of Eata, son of Ledwold.

[h] S.

[i] N. A., 739, S. C. 741. The latter describes Cuthred as the *kinsman* of his predecessor.

[j] N. A., 739, S. C. 741. [k] S. [l] N. A., 737, S. C. 739.

Eodem vero anno reverendæ memoriæ Acca episcopus sublevatus est in regionem viventium.[m] Erat ipse beatus strenuissimus actu, et coram Deo et hominibus magnificus. In ecclesiasticæ quoque institutionis regulis sollertissimus extiterat, et usque dum præmia piæ devotionis capiat existere non desistit, utpote qui a pueritia in clero sanctissimi atque Deo dilecti Bosa, Eboracensis episcopi, nutritus atque eruditus est. Deinde ad Wilfridum episcopum spe melioris propositi adveniens, omnem in ejus obsequio usque ad obitum ejus explevit ætatem. Cum quo etiam Romam veniens, multa illic quæ in patria nequiverat ecclesiæ sanctæ instituta utilia didicit, et suis subjectis tradidit. Sustollitur Sanctus de præsenti sæculo xiij kal. Novembris; cujus perducitur spiritus ab Angelis ad bravium supernæ felicitatis; corpus vero ejus ad orientalem plagam extra parietem ecclesiæ Haugustaldensis, quam xxiiij annis pontificali rexit dignitate, sepultum est; duæque cruces lapideæ mirabili cælatura decoratæ positæ sunt, una ad caput, alia ad pedes ejus. In quarum una, quæ scilicet ad caput est, literis insculptum est, quod in eodem loco sepultus sit. De quo loco post annos plusquam ccc depositionis suæ a quodam presbytero Divina revelatione translatus est, ac in ecclesia intra feretrum condigno honore positus est. Ubi usque hodie in magna veneratione habetur. Ob cujus sanctitatis meritum omnibus demonstrandum casula et tunica et sudarium, quæ cum sanctissimo ejus corpore in terra posita erant, non solum speciem sed etiam fortitudinem pristinam usque in hodiernum diem servant. Inventa est etiam super pectus ejus tabula lignea in modum altaris facta, ex duobus lignis clavis argenteis conjuncta, sculptaque est in illa scriptura hæc: *Almæ Trinitati, Agiæ Sophiæ, Sanctæ Mariæ.* Utrum vero reliquiæ in ea positæ fuerint, vel qua de causa cum eo in terra posita sit ignoratur. Attamen absque rationabili devotionis causa, summæ venerationis cultu cum sancto ejus corpore nequaquam esse condita creditur. Vestimenta vero ejus prædicta fratres ejusdem Hagustaldensis ecclesiæ aliquotiens populo monstrare solent, a quo cum omni devotione deosculantur.

Plurima vero miracula de Sancto Acca etiam vulgo narrantur, quæ omnia scripto explicare perlongum est. Aliquam tamen de illis memoriæ[n] breviter commendare libet, videlicet quam mirabiliter ac terribiliter adversarios suos, pacem ecclesiæ in qua requiescit infringere temptantes, vel ipsam ecclesiam funditus evertere molientes, crebro coercuerit, et qualiter re-

[m] S. C. 737. The legend of Acca is undoubtedly an interpolation, and certainly not the work of Symeon. See Preface.

[n] An interlineation.

liquias de corpore suo furtim auferre volentibus sæpius obstiterit. Fuit frater quidam in præfata Hagustaldensi ecclesia, Aldredus nomine, qui nunc in Christo requiescit, vir veracissimus et morum probitate conspicuus, sed et in Scripturis Sanctis bene eruditus, qui tale miraculum de Sancto Acca in semetipso patratum fratribus ejusdem ecclesiæ narrare solebat. Cum ipse adhuc esset adolescens, nutrireturque in domo fratris sui, cujusdam presbyteri qui sæpe-fatam Hagustaldensem regebat ecclesiam, antequam donatione venerabilis memoriæ Thomæ Secundi, Eboracensis archiepiscopi, canonicis regularibus qui ibidem usque hodie Deo serviunt tradita esset, placuit eidem fratri suo ossa reverenda Sancti Accæ adhuc cum pulvere corporis mixta separare, separatimque in theca quam in hoc paraverat recondere. Prolatas ergo venerabiles reliquias super altare Sancti Michaelis in australi porticu ecclesiæ situm deposuit, ibique ossa de pulvere collegit et in syndone munda involuta in theca recondidit, et dum eam in chorum, ubi stare debebat, deferret, porticum illam cum reliquiis quæ remanserant, prædicto fratri suo tuendam delegavit. Qui solus ibi remanens cœpit inter se cogitare, quia magno munere etiam præcelsa quælibet ecclesia se ditatam crederet, si vel unum de ossibus tam gloriosi confessoris haberet. Proposuit ergo ad altare accedere, et perquirere si forte aliquid de minutis ossibus in pulvere relictum invenire posset, quod penes se reponens alicui ecclesiæ ad honorem Dei et Sancti Accæ donaret. Sed id reverenter perpetrare non ausus, prius humi procumbens septem pœnitentiales psalmos devote cantavit, Deum exorans quatinus tale furtum Ei non displiceret, quod non sacrilega mente sed piæ devotionis et venerationis gratia facere cogitabat. Post hanc orationem se erigens, quod proposuerat explere temptabat. Cumque ostio interioris porticus, in qua erant venerandæ reliquiæ, appropinquasset, ecce! subito calor quidam, quasi ignis vaporantis de ore clibani ardentis, ei obvius fuit, eumque magno timore perculsum retroire coegit. Ille vero credens hoc ei ideo contigisse, quod cum minori devotione quam deberet tantam rem assequi vellet, solo tenus iterum prostratus, multo uberiores et devotiores preces quam antea fecerat Domino fudit, quatinus quod devote desiderabat digne adipisci valeret. Post aliquantum itaque intervallum surgens, cum timore et reverentia magna ad ostium porticus accessit, sed multo ardentiore calore quam antea de illa egrediente, repercussus est. Quo facto intelligens non esse voluntatem Dei ut aliquid de reliquiis Sancti Accæ furtim asportaret, tertio id temptare non ausus est.

Sed et aliud miraculum de eodem Deo dilecto confessore non est silentio prætereundum, quod multi qui usque hodie supersunt per reliquias ejus patratum esse testantur. Cum venisset ad præfatam Hagustaldensem ecclesiam quidam canonicus regularis et sacerdos, scilicet Edricus, qui illuc primus canonicorum a viro venerabili Thoma archiepiscopo missus est, invenit acervum de terra congestum juxta majus altare quod infra cancellos ecclesiæ erat, quem inde auferre volens, effodere eum cœpit. De quo cum aliquam partem fodisset, reperit thecam ligneam non admodum magnam. Quam aperiens, invenit duo sigilla plumbea, insculptis literis quid intus continerent intimantia. In quorum altero scriptum erat, quod de Sancto Acca reliquiæ intro haberentur. Mox ergo illud confringens, invenit pulverem cineri simillimum, nonnullaque ossa de sancto ejus corpore pulveri immixta, quæ inde tollens in honestiori theca reposuit. Erat tunc temporis paupercula quædam sanctimonialis femina in ipsa villa, quam prædictus frater pro simplicitate ejus et innocentia vitæ oppido diligebat. Ista multo tempore extiterat cæca, ita ut ad ecclesiam, et ubicumque necesse ire habebat, semper ab alio duceretur. Quadam die repente venit in cor fratris præfati talis cogitatio, ut unum de ossibus illis quæ nuper invenerat, in aqua benedicta abluere deberet, mulierique de ipso lavacro dare, ut inde oculos suos lavaret, si forte Deus, meritis sancti confessoris sui Accæ intercedentibus, lumen oculorum hoc venerando lavacro ei restituere dignaretur. Fecitque ille quod Divino instinctu ammonitus, sicut postea claruit, faciendum cogitaverat. Abluensque unum de ossibus in aqua benedicta, mulieri dedit, præcipiens ei quatinus de illa oculos suos lavaret. Quæ cum ita fecisset, quasi post duarum horarum spatium per merita et intercessiones Sancti Accæ visum recepit.

Fuit alter quidam homo pauper in eadem villa cujus guttur intercutaneo morbo in tantum intumuerat, ut nec loqui nec manducare posset. In cujus ore cum idem frater de ipsa aqua parum infudisset, repente post unius horæ spatium disrupta est cutis ex inferiori parte tumoris, sicque exeunte tumore sanatus est.

Qualiter vero Malcolmus rex Scottorum ab invasione pacisque violatione ecclesiæ Hagustaldensis, Sancto Acca cæterisque Sanctis qui in ea requiescunt, meritorum suorum præsidiis illam conservantibus coercitus sit, silentio tegere nimis impium est. Licet enim vulgo etiam notissimum sit, tamen ne penitus cum tempore a memoria hominum transeat, notitiæ posterorum scripto tradendum est. Malcolmus igitur rex Scottorum, homo scilicet ferocissimus mentemque bestialem gerens, Northumbrensem provinciam crebra irruptione misere devastare solebat, plurimosque de illa viros et mulieres captivos in Scotiam deducere. Qui cum quadam vice cum numerosiore solito exercitu fines provinciæ illius, eam devastaturus, ingressus fuisset, provinciales ejus adventum audientes, fere omnes ad ecclesiam Hagustaldensem, cum rebus suis quas secum portare poterant, sub protectione Sanctorum in illa quiescentium confugerunt. Quod ut Malcolmus comperit, proposuit illo pergere, omnesque qui eo confugerant exspoliare, ipsamque ecclesiam funditus evertere. Quod audiens presbyter ejusdem ecclesiæ, porrexit obviam ei, ammonuitque illum ne tantum nefas in Sanctos Dei, ecclesiæ illius patronos, committere præsumeret. At ille, ejus spernens monita, eum a se cum injuria projecit. Qui ad ecclesiam festinato rediens, omnes qui ibidem confugerant in commune exhortatus est, gloriosos Sanctos Dei, sub quorum præsidium confugerant, instanter deprecari, quatinus illos solita pietate sua a tam immani hoste Scottisque bestiis crudelioribus protegere dignarentur. Et fecerunt ita. Nocte vero sequenti cum idem presbyter præ tristitia in soporem decidisset, apparuit ei vir quidam vultu et habitu venerandus, qui ab eo sciscitabatur, quasi ignorans, causam tantæ tristitiæ. Cumque pro hostium imminentium sævitia se pavere respondisset, ait illi, "Ne timeas, quoniam, antequam illucescat, rete meum in fluvium mittam, per quod omnino Scottorum transitus impedietur." Hæc cum dixisset evanuit. Mane autem facto, inventus est amnis qui Tyna dicitur, absque pluviarum inundatione et ventorum violentia, in tantum excrevisse, ut absque navis[o] amminiculo minime transiri posset. Præterea eadem nocte et die sequenti tanta repente nebula accidit, ut maxima pars exercitus supradicti regis per tenebras dispersa a se invicem dilaberetur, ita ut plures ad aquilonem, multi ad orientem, nonnulli quoque ad meridiem, aperte miraculo Divino confusi, per intercessionem Sanctorum Hagustaldensis ecclesiæ cum magna festinatione tenderent. Rex vero Malcolmus cum illa particula exercitus sui quæ cum eo remanserat veniens, omnem transmeandi copiam sibi negatam vidit. Resedit ergo supra ripam fluminis, exspectare volens donec aqua diminueretur ut transire posset. Sed cum tribus diebus expectasset, aquamque absque omni pluviæ amministratione cotidie magis ac magis crescere videret, tam evidenti miraculo perterritus, cum magna festinatione recessit: sicque ab ejus crudelitate omnes qui ad præfatam Hagustaldensem ecclesiam confugerant, meritis Sanctorum in illa requiescentium erepti sunt.

Sed nunc ad historicam narrationem prætermissam redeamus. Ipso vero anno quo Sanctus Acca episcopus ad cælestia mi-

[o] This word is interlined.

gravit, Arwine filius Eadulfi[p] occisus est, die x kal. Jan., feria vij. Refert Historia vel Cronica hujus patriæ, quod eodem anno Cuthberht undecimus Dorovernensis ecclesiæ archiepiscopatum susceperit.[q] At vero post Aldulfum Hrofensis ecclesiæ Dun sacerdotium assumpsit.

DCCXLI.

Anno DCC.xlj monasterium in Eboraca civitate succensum est ix kal. Maii, feria prima.[r]

DCCXLIV.

Anno DCC.xliv factum est prælium inter Pictos et Brittones.[s]

DCCXLV.

Anno DCC.xlv visi sunt in aëre ictus ignei quales numquam ante mortales illius ævi viderunt; et ipsi pene per totam noctem visi sunt, kal. scilicet Januarii.[t]

Eodem quoque anno, ut quidam refert, dominus Wilfridus Secundus, Eboracæ civitatis episcopus, migravit ad Dominum iij kal. Maii.[u] Nos vero dicimus quod priusquam Beda suam Historiam explicuisset, translatus sit ille primus Wilfridus ex hoc mundo ad celsitudinem æternæ visionis. Ipsis quoque diebus Lundoniæ civitatis episcopus, nomine Ingwald, de Egypto hujus sæculi translatus est.[v] Eadem tempestate antistes in Wiccum defunctus est.[w] Etiam anno eodem Herebald abbas obiit. His temporibus floruit sanctus anachorita Guthlacus.[x]

[p] "Aruuini et Eadbertus interfecti."—N. A.

[q] The reference to the Saxon Chronicle in this place is unaccountable, as the accession of archbishop Cuthbert is equally recorded in the Northumbrian Annals. The next entry of the death of Aldulf, bishop of Hereford, and the appointment of Dun, is in the Saxon Chronicle only.

[r] "This year York was burned."—S. C. [s] S.

[t] "Stars were seen to shoot rapidly."—S. C.

[u] N. A., S. C. The words "*secundus*" above, and "*ille primus*" lower down, are interlined. Mr. Petrie supposes the individual referred to, to have been Wilfrid, bishop of Worcester, not Wilfrid "the second," or "the younger" bishop of York (Mon. Hist., pp. 288, 329). This mistake has originated in the assumption that when Egbert succeeded Wilfrid A.D. 732, the vacancy was occasioned by the death of the latter; but such was not the case. Wilfrid resigned his see, and spent his last years in retirement, as appears from Alcuin's poem on the archbishops of York. See Raine's Lives of the Archbishops of York, vol. i., p. 93. Wilfrid, bishop of Worcester, however, does appear to have died the same year, and his death to be recorded in the text below as "antistes in Wiccum."

[v] N. A. [w] S. C.

[x] S. The last sentence an interlineation.

DCCXLIX.

Anno DCC.xlix Ælfwald rex Orientalium Anglorum defunctus est, regnumque Hunbeanna et Alberht sibi diviserunt.[y]

DCCL.

Anno DCC.l Eadberht rex Kyniwlfum episcopum in urbem Bebbam captivum adduxerat, basilicamque beati Petri obsidere fecit in Lyndisfarnea.[z] Offa filius Alfridi quoque [ad] reliquias Sancti Cuthberti pontificis innocens coactitie accurrebat, pene defunctus fame de ecclesia sine armis abstractus est.[a] Eodem anno Alwih episcopus translatus est ad alterius vitæ contemplationem, et Aldulf diaconus ejus ordinatur in episcopum. Cuthred autem rex Occidentalium Saxonum surrexit contra Æthilbaldum regem Merciorum.[b]

DCCLII.

Anno ab incarnatione Dominica DCC.lij eclypsis lunæ facta est pridie kal. Augusti.[c] Quia mentio facta est de hac re, libet ignorantibus pandere quid sit eclypsis, id est deliquium vel defectus lunæ. Eclypsis lunæ est quotiens in umbram terræ luna incurrit, non enim suum lumen habere dicitur, sed a sole illuminari putatur. Eclypsis lunæ non nisi plena id est xv erit. Defectus solis nunquam nisi ortu lunæ fieri solet. Certum est, inquit Plinius, defectum solis non nisi novissima, id est xxx, primave fieri luna, quod coitum vocant.[d] Omnibus autem annis fieri utriusque sideris defectus statutis diebus, horis, sub terra. Nec tamen cum superne fiunt ubique cerni possunt, aliquando propter nebulam, sæpius globo terræ obstante convexitatibus mundi. Eclypsis solis est quotiens luna xxx ad eandem lineam qua sol vehitur pervenit, eique se objiciens solem obscurat. Nam deficere nobis sol videtur dum illi orbis lunæ opponitur.

DCCLIV.

Anno DCC.liv Bonifacius, archiepiscopus (qui et Winfridus) Francorum, martyrio coronatus est cum quinquaginta tribus.[e]

[y] S.

[z] Respecting the dedication of the cathedral church of Lindisfarne to St. Peter by archbishop Theodore, see Beda, Mon. Hist., p. 199.

[a] S. These particulars of the captivity of bishop Kyniwolf, and the outrage on Offa, are given with some variations in Symeon's History of the Church of Durham. See Preface to this volume.

[b] N. A. add after *Æthilbaldum Regem*, et Oengusum.

[c] N. A.

[d] Nat. Hist., ii., c. xiii.—In margin, *Lata obc'. . . apud Eboracum.*

[e] N. A.

DCCLV.

Anno DCC.lv Cuthred, rex Occidentalium Saxonum, obiit, cujus regni sceptra Sigberht accepit.[f]

DCCLVI.

Anno ab incarnatione Dominica DCC.lvj Eadberht rex, xviij anno regni sui, et Unust rex Pictorum duxerunt exercitum ad urbem Alcluth.[g] Ibique Brittones in deditionem receperunt, prima die mensis Augusti. Decima autem die ejusdem mensis interiit exercitus pene omnis quem duxit de Ouania ad Niwanbirig,[h] id est ad Novam Civitatem.

Eodem anno Balthere anachorita[i] viam sanctorum patrum est secutus, migrando ad Eum Qui se reformavit ad imaginem Filii Sui.

Luna autem xv sanguineo rubore superducta viij kal. Decembris, xv ætate, id est plena luna. Sicque paulatim decrescentibus tenebris ad lucem pristinam pervenit. Nam mirabiliter ipsam lunam sequente lucida stella et pertranseunte, tanto spatio eam antecedebat illuminata, quanto sequebatur antequam esset obscurata.[j]

DCCLVII.

Anno DCC.lvij Æthelbald rex Merciorum a suis tutoribus fraudulenter interfectus est. Eodem vero anno Merci bellum inter se civile inierunt. Bearnred in fugam verso, Offa rex victor extitit.[k]

DCCLVIII.

Anno DCC.lviij Eadberht rex Northymbrorum sponte contulit filio suo regnum sibi a Deo collatum, nomine Osulfo, qui uno anno regnum tenuit, amisit, perdidit. Quia occisus

[f] S. C.

[g] Erroneously written *Alcwith* in the MS. Immediately below is another mistake in the MS. text, the words *inde conditionem* being written instead of *in deditionem*. The correct reading is interlined.

[h] *Niwanbirig* is no doubt Newburgh on the Tay. There is a small lake in Glen-Turret, in the parish of Monivaird in Strathearne, Perthshire, called Loch Ouan, which may be the Ouania of the text, as it lies on a practicable route between the Clyde and the Tay. This word has been printed *Ouoma* by Twysden and Petrie. Hoveden has *Ouama*, or rather *Deouama*, by running the preposition into the proper name.

[i] "In Tiningaham." *Symeon, Hist. Ecclesiæ Dunelm.*

[j] N. A. notice this eclipse; also one of the sun the same month.

[k] N. A., S. C.

est nequiter a sua familia[l] juxta Mechil Wongtune ix kal. Augusti.

DCCLIX.

Anno DCC.lix Ethelwald, qui et Moll dictus erat, regnare incipit nonas Augusti. Cujus tertio anno inchoante, gravissimum juxta Eldunum secus Melros[m] gestum est bellum octavo idus Augusti, in quo cecidit Oswine post triduum, prima feria. Ethelwald vero rex, qui Moll est nominatus, victoriam sumpsit in bello. Ipso quoque anno Unust, Pictorum rex, defunctus est.[n]

DCCLXII.

Anno DCC.lxij Ethelwald, rex præfatus, accepit reginam Etheldrytham kal. Novembris in Cateracta.[o]

DCCLXIV.

Anno DCC.lxiv nix ingens gelu ligata omnibus retro sæculis incomparabilis, a principio hiemis pene usque ad medium veris terram oppressit.[p] Cujus vi arbores oleraque magna ex parte aruerunt, ac marina animalia multa inventa sunt mortua.

Eodem quoque anno Ceolwlf, quondam rex, tunc Domini nostri Jesu Christi servus monachusque, obiit. Huic vero regi Beda historiographus veridicus direxit epistolam, sic inchoando. *Gloriosissimo regi Ceolwlfo Beda famulus Christi et presbyter. Historiam gentis Anglorum quam nuper edideram, libentissime tibi desideranti, rex, et prius ad legendum et nunc scribendum, ac plenius ex tempore meditaturum transmitto.* Anno eodem multæ urbes monasteriaque atque villæ per diversa loca, necnon et regna, repentino igne vastatæ sunt, verbi gratia Stretburg, Venta civitas, Homwic, Londonia civitas, Eboraca civitas, Donacester, aliaque multa loca illa plaga concussit,[q] ut illud

[l] "A ministris suis," N. A.; "by his household," S. C. Neither authority mentions the locality. Mechil Wongton was probably Weighton between York and Beverley, the prefix Mechil (Great) being applied to it, as that of Market is in modern times, to distinguish it from another place of the same name.

[m] *Secus Melros* is an interlineation; Eildon, near Melrose, being the locality intended. The Saxon Chronicle calls the place Edwine's cliffe (query, Edinburgh, which occurs in early writings as Edwine's burgh). N. A. give no details, beyond the words, "Ouuini occisus est." Huntingdon has these particulars: "Mol rex Nordhumbriæ interfecit Oswine, fortissimum ducum suorum, qui committens prælium erga dominum suum apud Eadwinesclive, jure gentium spreto, jure Dei occisus est." Wendover describes Oswine as "gravissimum ducem."

[n] "Anno 761, Oengus Pictorum Rex obit, qui regni sui principium usque ad finem facinore cruentum tyrannus carnifex produxit."—N. A.

[o] S. [p] A.D. 761, S. C. [q] S.

impleretur quod scriptum est, *Erit terræ motus.*[r] Eodem anno Frehelm presbyter et abbas obiit, et episcopus Merciorum gentis nomine Totta defunctus est. Et Eadberht pro eo ordinatus est episcopus. His quoque temporibus Frithwald episcopus Candidæ-casæ ex hoc sæculo migravit, pro quo Pectwine in loco illius episcopus subrogatur.

DCCLXV.

Anno DCC.lxv ignei ictus in aëre visi sunt, quales quondam apparuerunt tempore nocturno kal. Januarii, ut superius prænotavimus. Eodem anno Ethelwald regnum Northanhymbrorum amisit in Winchanheale[s] tertio kal. Novembris. Cui Alcred, prosapia Idæ regis exortus, ut quidam dicunt, successit in regnum. Quo anno Hemeli, Merciorum episcopus, obiit, cujus vice Cuthfrid ordinatus est episcopus in Liccetfeldan. Eademque tempestate Bregwine, archiepiscopus Cantiæ civitatis, ex hac vita subtractus est, cui Lamberht successit vice regiminis. Aldulf quoque antistes in Lindisse eodem anno hanc vitam dereliquit, aliamque petivit. Post quem Ceolwlf electus et consecratus est.

DCCLXVI.

Anno DCC.lxvj Ecgberht, archiepiscopus Eboracæ civitatis, in pace Christi requievit xiij kal. Decembris, xxxiv anno episcopatus sui; et Frithuberht, Hagustaldensis ecclesiæ antistes, eodem anno de hac mortali carne migravit ad veræ lucis perennitatem x kal. Januarii, episcopatus sui anno xxxij.[t]

DCCLXVII.

Anno DCC.lxvij Alberht Eboracæ civitatis, et Alchmund Hagustaldensis ecclesiæ ordinati sunt episcopi viij kal. Maii. Eodem tempore Aluberht ad Ealdsexos ordinatus est episcopus, et Ceolwlf in Lindissi antistes consecratus est. Ipso quoque anno Etha anachorita feliciter in Cric obiit, qui locus distat ab Eboraca civitate x miliariis.

[r] St. Matt. xxiv. 7, etc.

[s] Winchanheal, or as it occurs A.D. 787, Wincahala (for Pincahala is a mere mistranscription, arising from the similarity of the Saxon types of P and W), is identified by Wendover with Finchale, near Durham.

[t] N. A., S. C. The Northumberland Annals have only been preserved to this year, but the writer of this Chronicle must have been in possession of similar materials to the close of the eighth century, as his narrative diverges more and more from the Saxon Chronicle, and is henceforth chiefly occupied with details of Northern affairs which are unnoticed by that authority.

DCCLXVIII.

Anno DCC.lxviij Eadberht, quondam rex tunc autem clericus, decimo anno amissionis regni sui in clericatu Deique Omnipotentis servitio apud Eboracum[u] feliciter spiritum emisit ad superos xiij kal. Septembris. Eodem anno Pipin rex Francorum mortuus est,[v] et Hadwine ordinatus est episcopus ad Machni: atque Alcred rex eodem tempore accepit reginam Osgearn.

DCCLXIX.

Anno DCC.lxix Ceteracte succensa est ab Earnredo tyranno, et ipse infelix eodem anno incendio periit Dei judicio.[w]

DCCLXXI.

Anno DCC.lxxj Sibald abbas obiit, et Egric, (presbyter?) et lector, de hoc instabilis vitæ cursu migravit ad consortium electorum, quo percipit epinicion[x] perpetuum.

His diebus Offa rex Merciorum Hestingorum gentem armis subegerat. Eodem quoque anno Karlmon, famosissimus rex Francorum, subita præventus infirmitate, defunctus est. Sed et frater ejus Karl, cum dimidium prius patris obtinuit[y] principatum, totius regni monarchiam et Francorum fastigium populorum dehinc est indeptus invicta fortitudine.

DCCLXXII.

Anno DCC.lxxij Pictel dux et Swithulf abbas obierunt in Domino. Carl quoque Francorum rex, collecta manu valida, et bellicosis suæ majestatis viris conjunctis, Saxonum gentem est ingressus. Multisque ex principibus ac nobilibus viris suis amissis, in sua se recepit.

[u] The words, "*Quondam rex, tunc autem clericus;*" also the words, "*apud Eboracum,*" are interlineations.

[v] Symeon in his History of the Church of Durham asserts, on I know not what authority, that a friendly intercourse subsisted between Pepin and Eadbert king of Northumberland.

[w] No mention occurs elsewhere of "Earnred tyrannus," which suggests the question whether the person intended is not "Bearnred tyrannus," who usurped the throne of Mercia A.D. 755—757. It is true that certain historians assert that the latter was defeated and slain by Offa in the latter year; but our earliest authorities (which are followed in the present text), the Northumbrian Annals and the Saxon Chronicle, merely record his expulsion. The destruction of Catterick is not noticed elsewhere.

[x] "*i. e., triumphum*" is an interlineation, as is the word "*famosissimus*" a little further down.

[y] "*Vel obtinuisset,*" interlined.

DCCLXXIII.

Anno ab incarnatione Dominica DCC.lxxiij Hadwinus, Migensis ecclesiæ antistes, sublatus est, et Leuthfriht pro eo est subrogatus episcopus. Wlfhaeth[z] quoque hoc anno, abbas Beverlacensis, diem Domini videre desideravit, cui et concessum est, quem subsecutus est. Eodem tempore Alberht, Eboracæ antistes ecclesiæ, pallii ministerium ab Adriano papa sibi directum accepit.

DCCLXXIV.

Anno DCC.lxxiv Eaddwlf dux ex hujus vitæ naufragio subtrahitur, et eodem tempore Alcredus rex, consilio et consensu suorum omnium, regiæ familiæ ac principum destitutus societate, exilio imperii mutavit majestatem. Primo in urbem Bebban, postea ad regem Pictorum nomine Cynoht, cum paucis fugæ comitibus secessit.[a] Bebba vero civitas urbs est munitissima,[b] non admodum magna, sed quasi duorum vel trium agrorum spatium, habens unum introitum cavatum, et gradibus miro modo exaltatum. Habet in summitate montis ecclesiam præpulchre factam, in qua est scrinium speciosum et pretiosum.[c] In quo involuta pallio jacet dextera manus Sancti Oswaldi regis incorrupta, sicut narrat Beda historiographus hujus gentis. Est in occidente et in summitate ipsius civitatis fons miro cavatus opere, dulcis ad potandum, et purissimus ad videndum.

Ethelredus quoque, filius Ethelwaldi, pro eo regnum suscepit: qui tanto honore coronatus vix quinque annos tenuit, veluti declarat subsequens sermo scriptoris.

Eadem tempestate Karl, Francorum rex invictissimus, nobilissimam Longobardorum urbem, Ticinam, longa obsidione vexatam, simul cum ipso rege Desiderio ac totius Italiæ imperio, cepit.

DCCLXXV.

Anno DCC.lxxv rex Pictorum Cynoth ex voragine hujus cænulentis vitæ eripitur, et Eadwlf dux per insidias fraudulenter captus, post spatium exigui temporis occiditur, sepelitur, obliviscitur. Ebbi quoque abbas vectigal morti dedit, egrediens et pergens ad Eum Qui mortuus vitam perpetuam concedit.

[z] In the margin, "*Wlfach obiit abbas.*"

[a] "*Vel se concessit,*" interlined. The Saxon Chronicle and Huntingdon give further details. The latter says, "Northumbri fugaverunt regem eorum Alred ab Eoverwic in hebdomada Paschæ, et eligerunt sibi Edelred filium Mol, qui regnavit annos iiij."

[b] In the margin, "*De civitate Bebba.*" See Beda, iii., 6.

[c] "*Et pretiosum,*" interlined.

Karl[d] denique rex, ut præfati sumus, bellicosissimus Francorum, cum omni exercitus sui virtute vallatus, confortatus, glorificatus, gentem Saxonum est ingressus centuriatibus atque legionibus stipatus, quam magnis et inedicibilibus regionem præliis gravissimis[e] vastavit, igne ferroque debacchans, quia erat consternatus animo.[f] Urbes denique duas Sigeburht et Aresburht,[g] atque provinciam Bohweri, olim a Francia oppressam, suo potenter adjecit summo imperio.

DCCLXXVII.

Anno DCC.lxxvij Pechtwine, episcopus Candidæ-casæ, xiij kal. Octobris migravit ex hoc sæculo ad æternæ salutis gaudium, qui eidem ecclesiæ xiiij annis præfuit. Cui Æthelbyrht successit.

DCCLXXVIII.

Anno iiij Ethelredi regis, scilicet anno DCC.lxxviij, tres duces, Aldwlf videlicet, Cynwlf et Ecga, eodem rege præcipiente, fraude necati sunt ab Ethelbaldo et Heardberhto principibus kal. Octobris.[h] Quid gestum sit anno DCC.lxxix sequens declarabit sermo.

DCCLXXIX.

Anno igitur DCC.lxxix Ethelredo expulso de regali solio et in exilium fugato, cogitur *mœstos inire modos, miserasque* habere *querelas*.[i] Elfwald vero filius Oswlfi, Ethelredo expulso, regnum Northanhymbrorum suscepit, tenuitque x annis. Erat enim iste rex pius et justus, ut sequens demonstrabit articulus.

DCCLXXX.

Anno DCC.lxxx Osbald et Athelheard duces; congregato exercitu, Bearn, patricium[j] Elfwaldi regis, in Seletune succenderunt ix kal. Januarii. Eodem anno Alberht archiepiscopus

[d] "*Vel quoque*," interlined.
[e] "*Gravissimis*," interlined.
[f] "*Vel efferatus*," interlined.
[g] "*Et Aresburht*," interlined.
[h] The Saxon Chronicle says, "Æthelbald and Heardberht slew three high-reeves; Ealwulf the son of Bosa at King's-Cliffe, and Cynewulf and Egga at Helathirn." Huntingdon and Wendover, differing from our text, say that the assailants were in rebellion against king Ethelred. The deaths of Cynewulf and Egga took place in a great battle "apud Hilathurnum;" Aldwulf, Ealwulf or Aidulf, is described as "primatem" or "principem exercitus regis;" and Wendover renders the King's-Cliffe, or Cyningen-Cliffe of the Saxon Chronicle, "Cunesclive," which nearly resembles the present orthography of Conniscliffe, a village on the Tees.
[i] Boethius de Consol., i., 2; iii., 9.
[j] Huntingdon and Wendover call Bearn the king's justiciary, and represent him as "rigidior æquo."

ex hac luce migravit ad æternæ lucis perennitatem, Eanbaldo, se adhuc vivente, ad eandem sedem ordinato. Cymwlf quoque episcopus eodem anno, relictis sæcularibus curis, Higbaldo gubernacula ecclesiæ cum electione totius familiæ commisit. Eodem etiam anno Eanbald episcopus pallium ab Apostolica sede sibi directum accepit; qui eo suscepto[j] in episcopatum solenniter est confirmatus.

DCCLXXXI.

Anno DCC.lxxxj Hibaldus consecratus est episcopus.[k] Alchmundus Hagustaldensis ecclesiæ præsul, eximiæ religionis et magnarum vir virtutum, postquam xiij annis sublimiter præfatam rexisset ecclesiam, regnante gloriosissimo Northanhymbrorum rege Elfwaldo, anno iij regni ejus, vij idus Septembris huic vitæ modum fecit; qui pro meritis æternæ beatitudinis est particeps factus. Sepultus vero est juxta prædecessorem suum reverendæ memoriæ Sanctum Accam episcopum. De quo loco post annos plusquam CCL. Divina revelatione translatus est hoc modo.[l] Tempore illo fuit quidam dregmo in territorio Hagustaldensis ecclesiæ, Deum valde timens, et elemosinarum operibus, prout facultas sibi suppeditabat, haud segniter deditus, ac per omnia a comprovincialium moribus vita discordans. Erat enim miræ simplicitatis et innocentiæ homo, ac erga Sanctos Dei devotionis et venerationis immensæ. Quapropter eum omnes vicini sui in magno honore habebant, illumque verum Dei cultorem appellabant. Huic itaque quadam nocte in stratu suo quiescenti apparuit quidam vir pontificali infula decoratus, virgamque pastoralem in manu tenens. Cum qua eum pulsans, sic ait illi, "Surge, vade et dic Ælfredo filio Westueor, presbytero Dunelmensis ecclesiæ, quatinus plebe coadunata territorii Haugustaldensis, transferat corpus meum de loco illo ubi sepultus sum, ac intra ecclesiam in honestiori loco reponat. Dignum est enim illos venerationem ab omnibus in terris accipere, quos Rex Regum dignatus est in cælis stola gloriæ et immortalitatis induere." Quem cum ille interrogasset, "Domine, tu quis es?" Ille respondit, "Ego sum Alchmundus, ecclesiæ Haugustaldensis episcopus, qui eidem loco quartus post beatum Wilfredum gratia Dei præfui. Corpus vero meum juxta prædecessorem meum venerandæ memoriæ Sanctum Accam episcopum positum est. Ad quod transferendum tu quoque cum presbytero simul adesto." Hæc cum dixisset, disparuit. Mane autem facto, homo ille cum magna festinatione ad præfatum presbyterum porrexit,

[j] "*Vel accepto*," interlined.
[k] This sentence is at the foot of the page.
[l] The legend of Alchmund, like that of Acca, is an interpolation.

quicquid vidisset, quodve mandatum ei deferre jussus esset, per ordinem ei indicavit. Qui lætus admodum effectus, convocavit plurimam populi multitudinem, rem notam eis faciens, diemque statuit quo venerabiles reliquias transferrent. Die ergo statuta presbyter præfatus ad sepulcrum accedens, illud a terra denudari præcepit. Quod cum factum esset, adjuvante se viro illo cui revelatio facta fuerat, populorum turbis hinc inde stantibus, veneranda ossa de tumulo collegit, lintheoque involuta ac in scrinio recondita super feretrum collocavit. Et quia pro tantæ veneratione diei sacro-sanctas hostias Domino offerendi hora transierat, posuerunt eum nocte illa in porticu Sancti Petri ad orientalem plagam ipsius ecclesiæ Haugustaldensis, sequenti die cum canticis, et hymnis, et missarum solemniis in ecclesiam illum transferre statuentes.

Nocte vero illa prædictus sacerdos excubias circa venerabiles reliquias cum clericis suis celebrans, cæteris alto somno depressis, accedens ipse scrinium aperuit, unumque de minutis ossibus, partem videlicet digiti unius, clanculo auferens penes se reposuit, cupiens illud ecclesiæ Sancti Cuthberti Dunelmensi ad honorem Dei et Sancti Alchmundi conferre. Luce itaque terris reddita, ad transferendum corpus almificum plurima populi multitudo convenit. Cumque jam hora tertia appropinquaret, jubente presbytero, manus apponentes feretrum levare conati sunt, sed illud movere minime valebant. Repulsis igitur his qui primi accesserant, judicatisque quasi indignis tanti patris reliquias suis humeris deferre, accesserunt alii, qui sicut et priores casso labore defecerunt. Deinde aliis et aliis se ingerentibus, a nullo penitus moveri valebat. Animo vero consternati, seseque mutuo intuentes, omnes qui aderant mirabantur rei novitatem stupentes. Tunc sacerdos illius reatus[m] se ipsum causam esse nesciens, exhortatus est omnes Deum deprecari, quatinus illis revelare dignaretur pro qua culpa hoc eis contigisset. Et factum est. Illis autem in ecclesia pernoctantibus, Deumque pro jam dicto negotio exorantibus, apparuit iterum Sanctus Alchmundus eidem homini, cui prius apparuerat intra, forte tunc infra ecclesiam irruente subito sopore prægravato, et cum aliquantum severo vultu ait ad eum, "Quid est quod facere voluistis? Putastis membris desectum me in ecclesiam referre, in qua Deo et Sancto Andreæ Apostolo Ejus integro corpore et spiritu servivi? Surge ergo, et contestare coram omni populo ut corpori meo citius restituatur quod inconsulte inde ablatum est, alioquin me de loco in quo nunc sum nullatenus movere poteritis." Et cum hæc dixisset,

[m] This word is an interlineation.

ostendit ei manum suam medietate unius digiti carentem. Facta autem die, vir ille in medio populi astans, quid sibi nocte illa revelatum fuisset universis propalavit, vehementi verborum invectione mulctari dignum esse indicans quicumque hoc facere præsumpsisset. Tunc sacerdos se deprehensum cernens, in medium prosiluit, et qua de causa quave intentione hoc perpetrasset omnibus patefecit: restituensque Sancto Alchmundo quod pie devotionis gratia ei abstulerat, congrua satisfactione veniam illico impetravit. Et accedentes clerici qui aderant, absque ulla vi levaverunt eum, ac in ecclesia transtulerunt iiij nonas Augusti, ubi usque hodie a fidelibus condigno honore veneratur, ad laudem et honorem domini nostri Jesu Christi. Tilberhtus namque Sanctus[n] pro eo in episcopatum subrogatur, consecratur, elevaturque in solio episcopalis cathedræ in loco qui appellatur Wulfeswelle, hoc est Fons Lupi. Actum est hoc vj nonas Octobris.

DCCLXXXIII.

Anno DCC.lxxxiij, qui est annus quintus Elfwaldi regis, Werburhg quondam regina Merciorum, tunc vero abbatissa, defuncta est, semper cum Christo, ut credi fas est, victura. Ipso quoque tempore Kymwlf episcopus, de quo supra-diximus, anno pontificatus sui quadragesimo, dereliquit terrestria; qui ad supernam feliciter migravit patriam.

DCCLXXXVI.

Anno DCC.lxxxvj, qui est annus Elfwaldi regis octavus, Botwne, venerabilis abbas Ripensis ecclesiæ, in conspectu astantium fratrum ergastulum hujus laboriosæ vitæ deseruit, mercedem jubilei anni percipiendo. Ipso quoque obeunte, Alberht pro eo abbas præelectus et consecratus est. Eodem anno Aldulf consecratus episcopus ab Eanbaldo archiepiscopo, Tilberhtoque, et Hygbaldo præsulibus, in monasterio quod dicitur Et-Corabrige,[o] multisque muneribus ac donis ditatus, honorifice ad suam ecclesiam est remissus.

His diebus Ricthryth, regina dudum, jam tunc abbatissa, optata percepit munera alterius vitæ, deferens coram sacris obtutibus Domini oleum cum lampadibus. Ea tempestate Kynwlf, Occidentalium Saxonum rex, a perfido tyranno Kynheardo lugubri interfectus est morte, et ille crudelis interemptor ab Osredo duce in ultione domini sui immisericorditer interemptus est, regnumque Occidentalium Saxonum Brihtric accepit.

[n] An interlineation.

[o] Corbridge on the Tyne, close to Hexham.

Tempore illo legati ab Apostolica sede a domino Adriano papa ad Britanniam directi sunt, in quibus venerabilis episcopus Georgius primatum tenuit; qui antiquam inter nos amicitiam et fidem catholicam quam Sanctus Gregorius papa per beatum Augustinum docuit innovantes, honorifice suscepti sunt a regibus et a præsulibus vel primatibus[p] hujus patriæ, et in pace domum reversi sunt cum magnis donis, ut justum erat.

DCCLXXXVII.

Anno DCC.lxxxvij synodus congregata est in Winchala[q] iiij non. Septembris. In quo tempore Alberht abbas Hripensis ex rapidis flatibus hujus sæculi spiritum emisit ad superos æternæ felicitatis jubilos. Mox vero, ablato ipso, Sigred ordinatur pro eo.

DCCLXXXVIII.

Anno DCC.lxxxviij Ælfwaldus rex, conjuratione facta ab ejus patricio, Sicgan nomine, miserabili occisus est morte ix kal. Octobris in loco qui dicitur[r] Scythles-cester juxta Murum. Corpus vero eximii regis ad Hehstealdesige cum magnis monachorum cuneis et clericorum cantilenis perlatum est, et in ecclesia sanctissimi Andreæ Apostoli honorifice sepultum est, quam construxit dignissimus pater Wilfridus archiepiscopus ad laudis præconium supradicti Apostoli. Præcellit opus ipsius cœnobii cætera ædificia in gente Anglorum, licet multa sint et inedicibilia in plerisque locis; sed in eo loco longitudines latitudinesque atque pulchritudines excellunt.[s] In quo cœnobio sunt parietes variis coloribus exornati, et historiæ depictæ, sicut supradictus Wilfridus episcopus instituit. Verumetiam dominus Acca, qui post ipsum illum locum gubernavit, glorioso compsit ornatu. Sepulto rege, ut prædiximus, regnavit Osred filius Alcredi regis, nepos ejus,[t] pro eo unum annum. In loco vero quo Ælfwaldus rex justus[u] interfectus est, cælitus lux emissa dicitur videri a plurimis. Constructa est ibidem ecclesia a fidelibus illius loci, atque in honore Dei et Sanctorum Cuthberti episcopi et Oswaldi regis et martyris consecrata.

[p] "*Vel primatibus*," interlined, and "*sive a principibus*," in the text.

[q] Written in error Pinchala in the MS. See a note under A.D. 765.

[r] *Qui dicitur* interlined. Scythles-cester is probably Chesters near Chollerford. Cester, Chester, or Chesters always denotes the site of a Roman station. This Chesters is on the line of the Roman wall, the Murus referred to in the text, and, save Corbridge, is by much the nearest station to Hexham. No trace of the prefix Scythles is to be found either within memory or in record.

[s] In the margin *De Hextildissaham*. This description of the Church of Hexham must have been written previous to the destruction of the original structure by the Danes, A.D. 875.

[t] The words "*nepos ejus*" are interlineations.

[u] "*Justus*" interlined.

DCCXC.

Anno DCC.XC Ethelredus de exilio liberatus est et iterum per gratiam Christi regni solio est subtronizatus. Osredus autem rex dolo suorum principum circumventus et captus ac regno privatus, attonsus est in Eboraca civitate, et postea necessitate coactus exilium petit. Cujus anno secundo Eardulf dux captus est et ad Ripun perductus, ibique occidi[v] jussus extra portam monasterii a rege præfato. Cujus corpus fratres cum Gregorianis concentibus ad ecclesiam portantes, et in tentorio foris ponentes, post mediam noctem vivus est in ecclesia inventus.

Eodem anno Badwlf ad Candidam-casam ordinatur episcopus in loco qui dicitur Hearrahalch, quod interpretari potest Locus Dominorum. Anno vero priore Ethelberht episcopus, sua sede relicta, Sancto[w] Tilberhto episcopo jam obeunte, prædictus præsul episcopatum Haugustaldensis ecclesiæ accepit in propriam dominationem.

DCCXCI.

Anno DCC.XCj filii Elfwaldi regis ab Eboraca civitate vi abstracti, et de ecclesia principali per promissa fallaciæ abducti, miserabiliter sunt perempti ab Ethelredo rege in Wonwaldremere,[x] quorum nomina Oelf et Oelfwine fuere.

Eo quoque anno Lamberhtus, Dorovernensis ecclesiæ archiepiscopus, ex hac lucis tenebrositate transmigravit ad veræ lucis beatitudinem. Abbas vero Ethelherdus Hludensis monasterii ad eandem sedem est electus et ordinatus episcopus.

DCCXCII.

Anno DCC.XCij Karolus rex Francorum misit sinodalem librum ad Britanniam sibi a Constantinopoli directum. In quo libro, heu, pro dolor! multa inconvenientia et veræ fidei contraria reperientes, maxime quod pene omnium orientalium doctorum non minus quam trescentorum vel eo amplius episcoporum unanima assertione confirmantium imagines adorare debere, quod omnino ecclesia Dei execratur. Contra quod scripsit Albinus epistolam ex auctoritate Divinarum scripturarum mirabiliter affirmatam, illamque cum eodem libro, et persona episcoporum ac principum nostrorum, regi Francorum attulit.[y]

Ipso denique anno Osredus de exilio sacramentis et fide

[v] *Occidi, vel occisus est,* interlined.
[w] *Sancto,* an interlineation.
[x] Winandermere, or Windermere.
[y] For an account of this controversy the reader must look in Baronius, xiii., ed. Pagi. Albinus is, of course, Alcuin.

quorundam principum clam de Eufania venit, ibique, deficientibus ab eo suis militibus, captus est a rege præfato,[z] atque eo jubente occisus in loco qui dicitur Aynburg[a] xviij kal. Octobris. Corpus vero ejus ad ostium Tyni fluminis perlatum est, et in basilica ejusdem eximii cœnobii sepultum.

Eodem anno Ethelred rex accepit reginam Elfledam, filiam Offæ regis Merciorum, iij kal. Octob. apud Cateractam.[b]

DCCXCIII.

Anno DCC.xciij, qui est annus Ethelredi regis quartus, dira prodigia miseram Anglorum terruere gentem. Siquidem fulmina abominanda, et dracones per aëra, igneique ictus sæpe vibrare[c] et volitare videbantur; quæ scilicet signa famem magnam, et multorum hominum stragem pessimam atque inedicibilem, quæ subsecuta est, demonstravere.

Ipso quoque anno Sicga dux, qui interemit Elfwaldum regem, interiit propria nece: cujus corpus ad insulam Lindisfarnensem perlatum est ix kal. Maii.

Lindisfarnensis insula[d] magna est per ambitum, verbi gratia viij vel amplius miliariis se extendens. In qua est nobile monasterium quo eximius Cuthbertus antistes positus erat cum aliis præsulibus qui ejus successores dignissimi extiterant. De quibus dici congruenter[e] potest quod canitur, *Corpora Sanctorum in pace sepulta sunt.*[f] Lindis dicitur flumen quod excurrit in mare, duorum pedum latitudinem habens, quando ledon fuerit, id est, minor æstus, et videri potest: quando vero malina fuerit, id est, major æstus maris, tunc nequit lindis videri. Æstus oceani lunam sequitur, tanquam ejus aspiratione retrorsum trahatur in accessum, ejusque impulsu retracto refundatur. Qui quotidie bis affluere et remeare unius semper horæ dodrante et semiuncia, quæ est dimidia, transmissa videtur, ut Beda testatur. Sicut enim luna quatuor punctis spatio quotidie

[z] *Scilicet Etheldredo* interlined.

[a] The locality of this catastrophe is not mentioned by any other early historian, nor is the locality of Aynburg known.

[b] The Saxon Chronicle says, "King Æthelred took a new wife," and Huntingdon adds, "suâ relictâ." Wendover says, "Rex Northanhumbrorum Ethelredus, propriâ relictâ uxore, novam duxit, unde a propriâ gente interfectus est." His death was attended by prodigies; "orbiculi visi sunt circa solem significantes fortasse multorum regum et nobilium mortem."

[c] *Crebrescere* in the margin.

[d] In the margin, *Descriptio Lindisfarnensis insulæ.* This description and the accompanying narrative of the atrocities then perpetrated, and the portents by which they were preceded, is copied by Symeon into his History of the Church of Durham, book ii., c. v. See Beda, iii., 3, and Alcuini Opp., ed. 1777, i., 11, 19-20.

[e] *Vel convenienter* in the margin.

[f] Eccl. xliv. 14.

tardius oriri, tardius occidere, quod pridie orta est vel occiderat, solet: ita etiam maris uterque æstus, sive diurnus sit et nocturnus, seu matutinus et vespertinus, ejusdem pene temporis intervallo tardius quotidie venire, tardius redire non desinit. Punctus, vero, quinta pars est horæ. Quinque enim puncti horam faciunt. De concordia maris et lunæ sic quidam cecinit rhetor, id est, Aldelmus præsul,

"Nunc ego cum pelago fatis communibus insto,
Tempora reciprocis convolvens menstrua cælis.
Ut mihi luciflua decrescit gloria formæ,
Sic augmenta latex[g] cumulato gurgite perdit."[h]

Farne autem insula, qua beatissimus Cuthbertus heremiticam duxit vitam, non tanta est ut Lindisfarne; sed est posita in mare, magnis exturbata fluctibus diebus et noctibus.

His strictim dictis, ad ordinem revertamur narrationis. Eodem sane anno Pagani ab aquilonali climate navali exercitu, ut aculeati crabones, Britanniam venientes, hac illacque ut dirissimi lupi discurrentes, prædantes, mordentes, interficientes non solum jumenta, oves et boves, verum etiam sacerdotes, Levitasque, chorosque monachorum atque sanctimonialium, veniunt, ut præfati sumus, ad Lindisfarnensem ecclesiam; miserabili prædatione vastant cuncta, calcant sancta pollutis vestigiis, altaria suffodiunt, et omnia thesauraria sanctæ ecclesiæ rapiunt. Quosdam e fratribus interficiunt, nonnullos secum vinctos assumunt, perplurimos opprobriis vexatos nudos projiciunt, aliquos in mare demergunt. Apte de illis dicitur quod sequitur.[i]

"Fortuna vices premit insontes,
Debita sceleri noxia pœna.
At perversi resident celso
Mores solio, sanctaque calcant
Injusta vice colla nocentes.
Latet obscuris condita virtus
Clara tenebris, justusque tulit
Crimen iniqui."[j]

Illis vero recedentibus, et de præda vel malis[k] actibus gratulantibus, quid eis fortuna sequentis anni advexit stilus fidelis demonstrabit.

DCCXCIV.

Anno DCC.XCIV prædicti Pagani portum Ecgfridi regis vas-

[g] *i. e.*, "*mare*" interlined.

[h] These lines occur in the Liber Ænigmatum of St. Aldhelm, and are used of the moon. *Cælis* ought to be *Cyclis*. *Opera S. Aldhelmi, ed. Giles*, 250.

[i] *Vel quibus recte illud aptari potest*, in the margin.

[j] Boethius de Consol. Philosoph., i., 29—36. The MS. has *more* and *justos*. Twysden disarranges the lines.

[k] "*Pravis*" interlined.

tantes, monasterium ad ostium Doni amnis[l] prædarunt. Sed Sanctus Cuthbertus non sine punitione eos sinebat abire. Princeps quoque[m] eorum ibidem crudeli nece occisus est ab Anglis, et, post exigui temporis spatium, vis tempestatis eorum naves quassavit, perdidit, contrivit; et perplurimos mare operuit. Nonnulli itaque ad littus sunt ejecti, et mox interfecti absque misericordia. Et recte illis hæc contigerunt, quoniam se non lædentes graviter læserunt.

His diebus Colcu, presbyter et lector, ex hac luce migravit ad Dominum, (a) Quo percipit laudem felicitatis pro laboribus terrenis. Ea tempestate Ethelheard, quondam dux tunc autem clericus, in Eboraca civitate defunctus est kal. Augusti.

Adrianus papa venerandus eodem anno sublevatus est ad Dei visionem vij kal. Januarii; qui sedit annos xxvj, menses x, dies xij. Est quoque in ecclesia Sancti principis Apostolorum Petri sepultus, et super sepulcrum platoma[n] parieti infixa, gesta bonorum ejus aureis literis et versibus scripta. Hoc marmor ibi Karolus rex, ob amorem et memoriam prædicti patris, facere jussit, regali fretus diademate.

DCCXCV.

Anno DCC.XCV idem rex fortissimus[o] Karolus cum manu valida Hunnorum gentem armis vastando subegerat, *(sic)* eorum principe fugato, et ipsius exercitu superato vel perempto, sublatis inde xv plaustris auro argentoque palliisque olosericis pretiosis repletis, quorum quodque quatuor trahebant boves. Quæ omnia idem rex, propter victoriam a Domino sibi concessam, Christi ecclesiis atque pauperibus dividere præcepit, grates Deo referens cum omnibus secum pugnantibus.

DCCXCVI.

Anno DCC.XCVJ, qui est annus vij Ethelredi regis, Alric, quondam dux tunc clericus, in Eboraca civitate defunctus est. Et paulo post, id est v kal. Aprilis, eclypsis lunæ facta est inter gallicinium et auroram.

Eodem vero anno Ethelredus rex occisus est apud Cobre

[l] Symeon, in his Durham History, describes this occurrence at the Portus Ecgfridi, of which he adds, "hoc est Gyruum," or Jarrow, situated at the confluence of the rivulet Don with the Tyne (book ii., c. v.). Leland has the following apposite note (Collectanea, vol. i., p. 328);—"Portus Ecfridi sinus, qui a Tina ad Girwi penetrat. Penetrabat et interius usque ad Hilton, pene 3 pas. millibus super Girwi, quo antiquitus et naviculæ pervenerunt. Fluviolus hunc sinum intrat."

[m] *Quippe* interlined.

[n] *Vel marmor* interlined.

[o] *Fortissimus* is an interlineation.

xiiij kal. Maii, anno vij regni sui :[p] Osbald vero patricius a quibusdam ipsius gentis principibus in regnum est constitutus, et post xxvij dies omni regiæ familiæ ac principum est societate destitutus, fugatusque, et de regno expulsus, atque ad insulam Lindisfarnensem cum paucis secessit; et inde ad regem Pictorum cum quibusdam e fratribus navigio pervenit. Eardulf enim, de quo supra-diximus, filius Eardulfi, de exilio vocatus, regni infulis est sublimatus, et in Eboraca, in ecclesia Sancti Petri, ad altare beati Apostoli Pauli, ubi illa gens primum perceperat gratiam baptismi, consecratus est, vij kal. Junii. Et non multo post, id est, vij kal. Augusti, Offa rex potentissimus[q] Merciorum, postquam xxxix annos regnavit, defunctus est; cui successit in regno filius ejus Ecgferth, qui eodem anno, morte superveniente, debitum neci invitus concessit. Coenvulf quoque, pater Sancti Kenelmi martyris,[r] dehinc diadema regni Merciorum suscepit gloriose, tenuitque invicta virtute potenti vigore sui potentatus. Ipso quoque anno Ceolwlf in Lindisse vitæ hujus tempora contempsit, futuri sæculi consolationem expectans.

Et paulo post, id est iiij idus Augusti, Eanbaldus archiepiscopus obiit in monasterio quod dicitur Etclete, corpusque ejus magno comitante agmine ad Eboracam civitatem portantes, in ecclesia beati Petri Apostoli sepultum est honorifice. Statim vero alter Eanbaldus, ejusdem ecclesiæ presbyter, in episcopatum est electus, convenientibus ad ordinationem ejus Ethelberto et Hygbaldo atque Badwlfo episcopis, in monasterio quod dicitur Sochasburg,[s] xviij kal. Septembris, die Dominica.

DCCXCVII.

Anno DCC.xcvij Eanbaldus ille posterior, accepto ab Apostolica sede pallio, in archiepiscopatum genti Northanhymbrorum solemniter confirmatus est vj idus Septembris, qua die celebratur solemnitas,[t] de qua poeta ait,

> "Splendet honore dies, est in quo virgo Maria
> Stirpe David regis procedens edita mundo."

Eodem anno Ethelbertus, Augustaldensis[u] episcopus, defunctus est xvij kal. Novembris, in loco qui dicitur Bartun; cujus corpus ad Hestaldesige est perlatum, et venerabiliter a fratribus ipsius cœnobii sepultum. Electus vero est pro eo Headred in

[p] These four words are interlined. Oobre is probably Corbridge.
[q] *Potentissimus* is interlined.
[r] These four words are interlined.
[s] Sockburn on the Tees.
[t] *Id est nativitas Sanctæ Mariæ* interlined.
[u] This word is an insertion.

episcopatum, et post excursum paucorum dierum, hoc est iij kal. Novembris, ab Eanbaldo archiepiscopo et Hygbaldo episcopo spirituali honore ordinatus est in loco qui nuncupatur Wduforda.

DCCXCVIII.

Anno DCC.xcviij conjuratione facta ab interfectoribus Ethel-dredi regis, Wada dux in illa conjuratione cum eis bellum inierunt *(sic)* contra Eardwlfum regem in loco qui appellatur ab Anglis Billingahoth juxta Walalege; et, ex utraque parte plurimis interfectis, Wada dux cum suis in fugam versus est, et Eardwlfus rex victoriam regaliter sumpsit ex inimicis.[v] Eodem anno Lundonia igne repentino cum magna hominum multitudine consumpta est. His tempestatibus Kenwlf, rex Merciorum, cum omni exercitus sui virtute provinciam Cantuariorum ingressus, miserabili prædatione pene usque ad internicionem potenter vastavit. Captus est eodem tempore Eadberht rex Cantuariorum, cujus oculos præcepit avelli rex Merciorum, et manus immisericorditer præcidi, præ superbia et fraude ipsorum. Deinde Domini suffragio potitus, adjecit imperium ipsius regni suo imperio, imponens sibi coronam in capite, sceptrumque in manu.

Eodem quoque anno, qui est annus iij Cenwlfi prædicti regis, synodo congregata in loco qui appellatur Wincanhalth,[w] præsidente Eanbaldo archiepiscopo aliisque quamplurimis principalibus et ecclesiasticis[x] viris, multa de utilitate sanctæ Dei ecclesiæ gentisque Northanhymbrorum omniumque provinciarum consiliati sunt, et de observatione Paschalis festi, et judiciorum divinorum atque sæcularium, quæ in diebus justorum regum et ducum bonorum atque sanctorum episcoporum, aliorumque sapientium, monachorum scilicet atque clericorum,[y] quorum prudentia, et justitia, atque divinis artibus status regni Northanhymbrorum suaviter et inedicibiliter redolebat his temporibus. Rationabili vero consilio providebant, ut de honore ecclesiarum Dei servorumque Ejus necessitatibus disputarent, et servitium Domini augerent, ut pro his mercedem æternæ retributionis bonam perciperent. Præcepit dominus antistes Ean-

[v] The Saxon Chronicle says that Alric son of Headfearht fell in this engagement. Walalege is certainly Whalley in Lancashire. There is a mountain near Blackburn called Billinge or Billange, and Billingahoth is supposed by Whitaker to be the village of Langs (quasi Billangs), which lies between Blackburn and Whalley.

[w] Written with a *P* in the MS.

[x] These three words are at the foot of the page.

[y] These two words are interlined.

baldus recitari quinque synodorum fidem, de quibus in Historia Anglorum[z] sic habetur.[a]

Suscipimus sanctas et universales quinque synodos beatorum et Deo acceptabilium Patrum, sicut præsentis libri continet textus. Glorificamus sane et adoramus atque veneramur Dominum nostrum Jhesum Christum, sicut isti glorificaverunt, nihil addentes vel subtrahentes. Et anathematizamus corde et ore quos anathematizaverunt prædicti Patres, glorificantes Deum Patrem omnipotentem sine initio, et Filium Ejus unigenitum ex Patre generatum ante sæcula, et Spiritum Sanctum procedentem ex Patre et Filio inenarrabiliter, sicut prædicaverunt hi, quos supra memoravimus, sancti Apostoli, et Prophetæ, et Doctores, et nos credimus, propter quod et locuti sumus. Hos itaque prædictos Patres nos pie atque orthodoxe juxta Divinitus inspiratam doctrinam eorum professi credimus constanter, et confitemur secundum sanctos Patres proprie et veraciter Patrem, et Filium, et Spiritum Sanctum, Trinitatem in Unitate consubstantialem, et Unitatem in Trinitate, hoc est, unum Deum in tribus subsistentibus personis consubstantialibus, æqualis gloriæ et honoris.

His dictis et confirmatis reversi sunt ad propria, laudantes Deum pro omnibus beneficiis Suis.

Hujus fidei integritatem sic alibi esse descriptam legimus, per quam salvari speramus, sicut cæteri justi confidebant.

"Cum Pater in Verbo sit semper et in Patre Verbum,
Sitque unus Verbi Spiritus atque Patris:
Sic de Personis tribus est tibi non dubitandum,
Unum ut tota fide confiteare Deum."

Et infra.

"Corde Patris genitum creat et regit omnia Verbum,
Nec tamen est aliquid quod sine Patre gerat.
Unus enim amborum motus, ratio una, voluntas,
Par virtus, idem spiritus, unus amor."

Et juxta.

"Sic magnus Deus est de Se, valet, et manet in Se,
Cui summum et proprium est semper id esse quod est.
Splendet enim verum vero de lumine lumen,
Ut genitum agnoscens noverit ingenitum.

"Una trium Deitas, una est essentia ab uno;
Idem est cum Verbi Spiritus atque Patris.
Nullum opus abjunctum, nulla est non æqua potestas:
In cunctis unum sunt tria principium."

[z] See Beda, iv., 7. Eanbald's synod reasserted and confirmed the resolutions of the synod at Hatfield under the presidency of archbishop Theodore in A.D. 680. This quotation varies somewhat from the original in Beda.

[a] *Vel scribitur* interlined.

De orthodoxa fide hæc pertractantes ad historiæ nostræ narrationem redeamus.

DCCXCIX.

Anno DCC.xcix naves plurimæ in mari Britannico vi tempestatis quassatæ sunt atque concussæ vel collisæ, et cum magna multitudine hominum sunt dimersæ. Eodem anno Brorda Merciorum princeps, qui et Hildegils vocatur, defunctus est. Abbas vero, vocitatus More, a Tilthegno,[b] præfecto suo, lugubri morte interemptus est. Moll quoque dux, paulo post, jussione urgente Eardwlfi regis, occisus est. Ipso quoque tempore Osbald, quondam dux et patricius et ad tempus rex, tunc vero abbas, diem suscepit ultimum, cujus corpus in ecclesia Eboracæ civitatis sepultum est. Aldred vero dux, interfector Etheldredi regis, a Thorhtmundo duce in ultionem domini sui ejusdem regis interfectus est. Quid gestum sit eodem anno referre libet.

Romani quoque inter se dissecabantur, et magnam dissensionem habebant, in qua Leonem papam sanctissimum apprehenderunt ligaveruntque; cujus lingua inter maxillas duriter protracta, et in gutture crudeliter extensa, præcisa est ab ipsis.[c] Eruerunt et oculos prædicti pontificis radicitus; quæ res cunctis cernentibus crudele spectaculum est factum. Dehinc absque ulla humanitate semivivum eum relinquentes, inconsulte domum reversi sunt. Sed Magnus Conditor orbis ex alto cuncta intuens, Quem, quia respicit omnia solus, verum possumus dicere solem, non sic Suum contempsit fidelem famulum. Omnipotens igitur Dominus, post pauci temporis interstitium, sic eum salutifero sanavit antidoto, ut postmodum videre clare et loqui posset, prorsus ab eo expellens caligines oculorum, et concedens ei pristinæ sanitatis linguam, ut penitissima[d] edere verba prædicationis valuisset, et omnia officia honorifice implere.

"Cesset inscitiæ[e] nubilus error,
Cessent profecto mira videri"

universa opera Domini. Hoc miraculum repente diffusum est per cardines quadrati orbis, ad gloriam et laudem Christi no-

[b] Twysden has this in one word, *Atilthegno.*

[c] There is a full account of this barbarous deed in Baronius, xiii., 344, *et seqq.*, ed. Pagi.

[d] *Vel profundissima* interlined.

[e] *Vel ignorantiæ* interlined. This quotation comes from Boethius de Consol. Philosoph., iv., 11-12; but in that author the first line runs as follows:—

"Cedat inscìti nubilus error."

The words in the preceding sentence from *Magnus* to *Solem* are adapted from the same author, v., 6-13.

minis, ut ab omnibus ubique prædicetur et laudetur, quia *mirabilis* est *Deus in Sanctis suis*.[f]

DCCC.

Anno DCCC Heardred, Haugustaldensis ecclesiæ præsul, anno tertio episcopatus sui, regiminis diem vidit extremum; pro quo Eanbryth electus est et ordinatus episcopus in loco qui dicitur Apud-Cettingaham. Eodem anno Alhmund, filius Alcredi regis, ut dicunt quidam, a tutoribus Eardwlfi regis est apprehensus, ejusque jussione cum suis profugis occisus est.

Tempore quoque eodem ante natale Domini, ix kal. Januarii, ventus ingens, ab Africo vel a Favonio exurgens, suo inenarrabili flatu urbes, multæ domus, ac villæ perplurimæ per diversa loca sunt destructæ et ad solum dirutæ: arbores quoque innumeræ radicitus evulsæ, et ad terram prostratæ sunt. Quo anno inundatio maris ultra terminos suos profluxit, illud secum obliviscens quod dicit Psalmus, *Terminum posuisti quem non transgredientur*.[g] Facta est et magna pecorum strages in locis diversis.

Karolus quoque eximiæ virtutis, rex Francorum, paulo ante, ipso anno, cum magna exercitus sui multitudine Romuleæ urbis mœnia ingreditur, ibique per aliquot menses demoratus est,[h] locaque sancta frequenti visitatione adorat, ditat, exornat munere regali. Præcipue vero ecclesiam beati Petri Apostoli, necnon et Sancti Pauli, donis exornavit regalibus, auro scilicet et argento gemmisque pretiosis. Leonem quoque venerabilem papam magnifice muneravit, ejusque adversarios dispersit, quosdam extinxit vel exilio damnavit, nonnullos interfecit qui contra eum impie conjurationem promoverunt. His atque aliis quamplurimis rebus ordinatis, ipse armipotens imperator quæ ad honorem et correptionem ecclesiarum Christi Christianorumque populorum pertinebant, in die natalis Domini nostri Jesu Christi ingreditur cum ducibus et magistratibus et militibus in ecclesiam sanctissimi principis Apostolorum Petri, in qua a domino Leone papa purpura regaliter induitur; cui corona aurea capiti imponitur, et regale sceptrum in manibus datur. Hanc dignitatem ipso die meruit ab omni populo percipere, ut imperator totius orbis appellaretur et esset. Eo quoque tempore legati Græcorum, cum magnis muneribus a Constantinopoli directi, ad eum veniebant, rogantes ut illorum susciperet regnum et imperium. Similiter legati ab Hierosolimis a Christianis populis ibi manentibus missi, Romamque venientes, vexillum

[f] Psalm lxviii. 35. [g] Psalm civ. 9.

[h] There is a full account of all these events in Baronius, xiii., 354, et *seqq.*

argenteum inter alia munera regi ferentes, clavesque locorum sanctorum Dominicæ resurrectionis aliorumque ei optulerunt, obnixe flagitantes ipsorum esse susceptorem et defensorem. Rogabant eum ut Christianæ religioni subdita sancta cœnobia conservaret, regeret ac defenderet, et contra insurgentes gentes exurgeret bellica virtute et regali majestate. Annuit benignissimus rex beatis precibus qui ad se confluxerant, et non solum se paratum esse ad devincendos inimicos in terra, verum etiam in mari, si necessitas compulisset. Intellexit beatas fore respublicas, si eas vel studiosi sapientiæ regerent, vel si earum rectores studere sapientiæ contigisset. Is ad urbem Ravennam perveniens, ad Aquas deinde porrexit, de his omnibus cum suis optimatibus tractaturus.

DCCCI.

Anno DCCC.j Edwine, qui et Eda[i] dictus est, quondam dux Northanhymbrorum, tunc vero per gratiam Salvatoris mundi abbas in Dei servitio roboratus, velut miles emeritus diem clausit ultimum in conspectu fratrum xviij kal. Februarii. Sepultus est quoque in monasterio suo quod appellatur Et-Gegenforda[j] honorifice in ecclesia.

His temporibus Eardulf rex Northanhymbrorum duxit exercitum contra Kenwlfum regem Merciorum propter susceptionem inimicorum ejus. Qui et ipse congregans exercitum secum aliarum promovit auxilia provinciarum plurima, longa inter eos expeditione facta. Tandem cum consilio episcoporum ac principum Anglorum ex utraque parte pacem inierunt per gratiam regis Anglorum. Factaque firmissimæ pacis concordia inter eos, quam sub jurejurando in evangelio Christi ambo reges confirmaverunt, Deum testem atque fidejussorem interponentes, ut in diebus eorum, quamdiu vita potirentur præsenti et regni essent infulis suffulti, pax firma veraque inter eos amicitia inconcussa et inviolata persisteret. Contigit in illis esse completum quod legitur,

"Gratius astra nitent, ubi notus
Desinit imbriferos dare sonos;
Lucifer ut tenebras pepulerit,
Pulchra dies roseos agit equos."[k]

Astra splendebant gratius; hoc est, principes gaudebant profusius dum reges pacem dabant inter se clementius. Notus

[i] Probably identical with Wada, whose rebellion against Ethelred, the son of Mol, and defeat near Whalley, are recorded above, A.D. 798.

[j] Gainford on the Tees, where some interesting remains of an early ecclesiastical settlement have been recently discovered.

[k] Boethius de Consol. Philosoph., iii., 7-10.

ventus est calidus, qui solet imbriferos dare sonos. Ut dies roseos agit equos; id est, totius regni status exultabat dum serena redierunt tempora illius ævi mortalibus, gratia Domini largiente, Qui tempestatibus et coruscis præstat quietudinis serenitatem :

"Et numeris elementa ligat, ut frigora flammis,
Arida conveniant liquidis, ne purior ignis
Evolet, aut mersas deducant pondera terras."[l]

Eodem anno Hathuberht, Lundoniæ civitatis antistes, vitæ hujus contempsit tempora. Et, paulo post, magna pars vici ipsius repentino igne consumpta est.

DCCCII.

Anno DCCC.ij[m] ab incarnatione Dominica Brychtric, Occidentalium (Saxonum) rex, qui eidem genti x et vij annis nobilissime præfuit, defunctus est; cujus imperium et regnum post eum Ecgberht, ex regali illius gentis prosapia, suscepit ac tenuit. Rex autem Brichtric Occidentalium Saxonum accepit sibi in conjugium[n] Earburgam, quæ erat filia regis Merciorum, nomine Offa, qui vallum magnum inter Britanniam atque Merciam, id est de mari usque ad mare facere imperavit. Cumque filia regis esset multis suffulta honoribus, miris se extollebat ambitionibus, quæ more paterno tyrannice vivere cœpit, et omnem hominem execrari. Sicque, ut omnibus esset perosa, non solum ducibus et magistratibus, verum etiam cunctis populis, omnes religiosos viros ad regem semper accusare non cessavit, et ita maledicta virum suum constrinxit blanditiis, ut illos quos accusare cœpit, aut vita aut regno privaret; et si a rege impetrare non posset, veneno eos clam disperdere[o] non distulit. Erat eodem tempore quidam prædives adolescens, præamabilis[p] regi prædicto et carus; quem cum accusare vellet ad regem et minime præ-

[l] Boethius, iii., 10-12.

[m] The death of Beorhtric, or Brichtric, is referred by the Saxon Chronicle and Florence to A.D. 800. The account which follows of the misdeeds of Eadburga is copied from Asser's Life of Alfred, where it is related on the authority of Alfred himself, in explanation of the custom of the West Saxon kings to exclude their consorts from sitting beside them on the throne. The narrative is introduced by Asser under A.D. 856, when the custom was relaxed on the marriage of Ethelwulf with Judith the daughter of Charles king of France. The story is also to be found in Florence with slight omissions, and variations of language. A comparison of the text before us with the other versions, shews that it has been derived direct from Asser, and not through the medium of Florence. Bouquet, in his collection of French annals, derives the story from Asser and not from any national source.

[n] *Vel in matrimonium* interlined.

[o] *Vel necare* interlined.

[p] *Vel valde amabilis* interlined.

valeret; veneno ipsum ipsa malevola necavit.[q] De quo veneno cum ipse rex inscienter gustasset, periit. Neque etiam illa venenum regi proposuerat dare sed puero, quem princeps ducum præoccupans, ambo necis poculum biberunt, ambo gustu amarissimo perierunt. Quo ex hoc sæculo[r] perempto, venefica illa nequissima timore perterrita[s] fugiendo ultra mare est egressa, cum innumerabilibus thesauris, regem adiens Francorum famosissimum Karolum. Ad quem cum ante solarium astaret et regi deferret munera pretiosa, sic est eam affatus. "Elige, Eadburg, quem velis, me aut filium meum qui mecum in solario astat." At illa sine deliberatione stulte respondit, dicens, "Si mihi optio daretur, filium tuum magis eligerem quam te, quia junior esse videtur." Cui rex Carolus ita respondisse fertur, "Si me eligeres, haberes filium meum, sed quia illum elegisti, nec me nec illum propitium habebis." Contulit tamen illi propter improbitatem ejus optimum monasterium, in quo deposito sæculari habitu, sub specie hypocrissima indumento sanctimonialium assumpto, perpaucis fungebatur annis: sicut enim execrabilis[t] et flebilis ipsa nequiter et irrationabiliter in propria vixit regione: ita multo nequius, miserabilius, et irrationabilius in terra aliena vixisse deprehenditur.

"Æstas (ut quidam ait) Cererem fervida siccat,
Remeat pomis gravis autumnus,
Hiemem defluus irrigat imber:"[u]

Sed hujus pessimæ reginæ mentem nec pulchritudo æstatis, nec algor hiemis valuit a libidine cohibere. Namque interstitio[v] peracto, dum quæ sancta erant exerceret, ut quidam æstimabant, a quodam suæ propriæ gentis ignobili viro constuprata est.

"Cedat inscitiæ nubilus error,
Cessent profecto mira videri:"[w]

Mulierem, inquit, in adulterio deprehensam. Nihil itaque est quod admirere, *nihil occultum quod non sciatur.*[x] Post hæc, præcipiente magno Carolo imperatore, projecta est cum magno mentis tædio et angore[y] a suo sancto monasterio: quæ in paupertate et miseria vitæ suæ tempora vituperabiliter ad finem perduxit. Quæ ad ultimum uno servulo comitata, cotidie mendicans per domos et per civitates atque castella, in Pavia miserabiliter obiit.[z]

[q] *Vel extinxit* interlined. [r] *Vel scelere* interlined.

[s] The words from *venefica* to *perterrita* are at the foot of the page.

[t] An interlineation: so are the words *nequiter et, nequius, et irrationabilius,* in the course of the next few lines.

[u] Boethius de Consol. Philosoph., iv., 27-9.

[v] *Vel parvo tempore* interlined. [w] Quoted before, p. 37.

[x] St. Luke xii. 2. [y] *et angore* interlined.

[z] The narrative of Asser is followed to this point; but the language employed

Defuncto rege glorioso Brychtrico, Occidentalis regni suscepit post ipsius obitum regnum et imperium Ecgberht rex, qui, ex regali illius gentis prosapia exortus, diadema totius regni capiti imposuit maximo sceptro redimitus. Erat enim strenuissimus vir et potens, multaque regna suo subjecit imperio. Regnavit annis xxxvj.[z] Et Ecgberhto successit Ethelwlfus filius ejus potentissimus.[a] Cui successit filius ejus Ethelbaldus. Deinde frater suus Ethebyrtus. Post quem frater suus Ethelredus. Post hunc frater eorum Elfredus. Denique Ethelwlf habuit ex conjuge sua nobili[b] iiij filios, scilicet Ethelbaldum et Ethelbirtum et Etelredum et Alfredum,[c] qui omnes sibi invicem in regnum successerunt.

DCCCIII.

Anno DCCC.iij Hibaldus episcopus obiit, et Egbertus[d] . . . .
. . . .

DCCCXXX.

Anno DCCC.XXX Celnodus ei successit et consecratus est episcopus; et Felgildus abbas obiit; et Egredus episcopus factus est.

DCCCXLVI.

Anno DCCC.xlvj Eanbertus episcopatum suscepit.[e]

DCCCXLIX.

Anno Dominicæ incarnationis DCCC.xlix exortum est lumen

is more vituperative and the quotations are interpolated. What follows seems to have been part of the original narrative, which has been interrupted by the introduction of the story of Eadburga from Asser.

[z] The words from *erat enim* are at the foot of the page.

[a] This word is an interlineation.

[b] The words *ex conjuge sua nobili* are interlined.

[c] These words are crowded together at the foot of the page. So also are the events of the next three years. There is evidently a break in the MS. here. With the year 849 it goes on with a fresh page in a neater and more orderly hand.

[d] This sentence is incomplete; and there appears to have been a considerable hiatus in the text from which the C. C. C. manuscript has been copied (see Petrie, Mon. Hist., p. 673). Twysden has attempted an amendment by transferring the words "ei successit" from the next paragraph in the MS. to the end of the present, and has thus completed the first sentence, and has also got rid of the anomaly which the text in its mutilated state presents, of making Celnod appear to have been the successor of Egbert, whereas the former was archbishop of Canterbury, the latter bishop of Lindisfarne. He still, however, leaves an interval of twenty-seven years unaccounted for; during which two archbishops occupied the see of Canterbury, and one bishop, Heathured, succeeded to that of Lindisfarne, all of whom probably appeared in their proper order in the MS. previous to its mutilation. An attempt has been made to supply the omission as regards Heathured, by an insertion in the C. C. C. manuscript; but this has been made erroneously under the year 891, instead of 819. Refer to A.D. 891, below.

[e] This entry is inserted at the bottom of the page in the MS.

e tenebris. Elfredus rex Anglorum natus est in regali villa quæ ab Anglis Wanetinge appellatur: cujus genealogia tali serie contexitur. Elfred rex filius erat Ethelwlfi regis, qui fuit Egberhti, qui fuit Alhmundi, qui fuit Affa, qui fuit Eoppa, qui fuit Ingild. Ingild et Ine fratres fuerunt. Ine rex famosissimus erat per totius fines gentis Anglorum, qui Occidentalium regionum regna regaliter regebat; et, peractis in regno plurimis annis, Romam porrexit, relinquens patriam et regnum præsens ut cum Christo possideret æternum, quod ei concessit Divinæ majestatis imperium. Hii fuerunt filii Coenredi, qui fuit Ceolwold, qui fuit Cuda, qui fuit Cutherwine, qui fuit Ceawlm, qui fuit Cinric, qui fuit Creoda, qui fuit Cerdic, qui fuit Elesa, qui fuit Gewis, a quo Britones totam illam gentem Gewis nominant, qui fuit Brand, qui fuit Belde, qui fuit Woden, qui fuit Frithuwald, qui fuit Frealaf, qui fuit Frithenulf, qui fuit Geta, quem jamdudum Pagani pro Deo venerabantur. Cujus Sedulius, poeta insignis, mentionem faciens in Pascali carmine, ita exorsus est.

"Cum sua Gentiles studeant figmenta poetæ
Grandisonis pompare modis tragicoque boatu
Ridiculove Getæ seu qualibet arte canendi,"[f] *et cætera.*

Qui Geta fuit Cetwa, qui fuit Beaw, qui fuit Seldwa, qui fuit Heremod, qui fuit Itermod, qui fuit Hatra, qui fuit Wala, qui fuit Bedwig, qui fuit Sem, qui fuit Noe, qui fuit Lamech, qui fuit Matusalem, qui fuit Enoch, qui fuit Malaleel, qui fuit Canaan, qui fuit Enos, qui fuit Seth, qui fuit Adam primi hominis. Mater vero regis Elfredi Osburg appellata est, quæ erat religiosa nimium femina nobilisque ingenio, quam nobilitatem exornavit prudentia mentis. Erat quoque pater ejus Oslac vocitatus, qui fuit pincerna Ethelwlfi regis devotus atque fidelissimus. Ortus enim fuit de Gothis et Jutis de semine Stuph et Wihtgar duorum fratrum.[g]

His sic prælibatis jam pro posse susceptum exequamur negotium suscepti operis.

DCCCLI.

Anno Dominicæ incarnationis DCCC.lj, nativitatis Elfredi iij, Ceorl comes pugnavit contra Danos, et Christiani victoriam de inimicis adepti sunt. Dani quoque hiemaverunt in insula quæ vocatur Scepige, id est Insula Ovium. Eodem anno magnus

[f] These are the first three lines of the Paschale Opus of Sedulius. Cf. Opp. Poet. Lat., Lond. 1713, ii., 1660.

[g] The whole of the paragraph to this point is taken from Asser, where the quotation from Sedulius is extended to ten lines. The genealogy, both in the present text and in Asser, is replete with inaccuracies, which it is unnecessary to point out in detail. A more accurate version will be found in the Saxon Chronicle and in Florence of Worcester. Mon. Hist., p. 348., *ib.*, p. 549.

exercitus Paganorum venit cum trecentis quinquaginta navibus in ostium Tamensis fluminis. Qui Doroberniam, id est Cantuariorum civitatem, depopulati sunt, et Berhtulfum Merciorum regem cum omni exercitu suo, qui ad præliandum contra illos venerat, in fugam verterunt. Post hæc audaciores Dani effecti, exercitus omnis ipsorum ad Suhtrige est congregatus. Quod audiens bellipotens Ethelwlfus rex Saxonum, congregavit et ipse exercitum copiosum, et filius suus Ethelbaldus cum eo in loco qui dicitur Aclea, id est, in Campo Quercus. Cumque decus Angligenæ gentis armis splendesceret resultantibus, diutissime pugnaverunt Angli cum Danis, fortiter repugnantes quia viderunt atrociter regem bellare ipsorum, ideo fortiores hostibus facti sunt in bello. Cumque diutissime viriliter decertarent, et acerrime animoseque ex utraque parte pugnatum esset, maxima pars Paganæ multitudinis funditus deleta atque occisa est, ita ut nunquam in aliqua regione in una die ante nec post tanti occubuerunt in morte. Christiani vero ipso die victoriam honorifice tenuerunt, et loco funeris dominati sunt, grates reddentes Domino in hymnis et confessionibus.[h]

DCCCLII.

Anno Dominicæ incarnationis DCCC.lij Ethelstanus rex et Alchere[i] comes magnum Paganorum exercitum invenerunt in Cantia in loco qui dicitur Et-Sandwic, quem ibidem, Deo auxilium concedente, prope occiderunt, et ex navibus eorum novem rapuerunt: cæteri per fugam terrore perculsi fugerunt.

DCCCLIII.

Anno Dominicæ incarnationis DCCC.liij, nativitatis Elfredi v, Burhred[j] Merciorum rex per nuncios deprecatus est Ethelwlfum, Occidentalium Saxonum regem, ut ei auxilium conferret, quo mediterraneos Brittones, qui inter Merciam et mare occidentale habitabant, dominio suo subdere posset, qui contra eum frequenter reluctabantur. Rex autem Ethelwlf, legatione ejus accepta, exercitum movit, stipendia[k] distribuit, cum Burhredo rege intrepidus ad bellum exiit. Mox ut ingressus est ad gentem illam devastandam, cepit, occidit, subdiditque regi Burhredo, qui gratias agens dimisit eum cum gaudio ad propria remeare. Eodem anno Ethelwlfus rex filium suum Elfredum, cum magno nobilium militum agmine constipatum, Romam

[h] This section is from Asser.
[i] Asser, from whom this section is also taken, writes the name Ealhere.
[j] This paragraph is from Asser, who writes this name Burgred.
[k] *Vel spolia* interlined.

transmisit. Quo tempore beatus papa Leo Apostolicæ sedi præerat; qui præfatum infantem ordinans unxit in regem, et in filium adoptionis sibimet accipiens confirmavit, et ad patriam atque ad patrem cum benedictione Sancti Petri Apostoli direxit. Ea tempestate Alchere comes et Wada cum Cantuariis et Suthrigiis contra Paganorum exercitum duriter pugnavit in insula quæ Saxonica lingua Tened dicitur, Britannico sermone Ruim appellatur. Primitus Christiani victoriam habuerunt, sed, prolongato diu prælio, ex utraque parte plurimi corruerunt, multique in flumine suffocati sunt et occisi, inedicibilis multitudo. Duces vero prædicti ambo ibidem occubuerunt pro gentis suæ liberatione. Ethelwlfus rex gloriosæ potestatis ipso anno post festivitatem sanctæ resurrectionis Christi, filiam suam Burhredo regi Merciorum tradidit cum magna gloria, ut regibus mos est, in villa quæ dicitur Et-Cippanhama, quo nuptiis peractis reginæ præcepit nominis dignitatem.

DCCCLIV.

Anno Dominicæ incarnationis DCCC.liiij Wlfhere archiepiscopus pallium suscepit, et Eardulf suscepit episcopatum Lindisfarnensem.

DCCCLV.

Anno DCCC.lv, nativitatis præfati regis vij, Paganorum exercitus tota hieme in insula Scepige hiemaverunt. Quo tempore Ethelwlfus rex decimavit totum regni sui imperium pro redemptione animæ suæ et antecessorum suorum. Ipso vero anno cum magno honore ad limina principis Apostolorum profectus est, habens secum Elfredum, eo quod illum magis diligeret quam cæteros. Susceptus est rex Anglorum ab Apostolico viro decenter: quo moratus est anno integro, orationibus et elemosinis insistens diligenter. Eo quoque ad patriam revertente, filio suo Ethelbaldo et Scirburnensi Ealhastano episcopo et plurimis aliis perosus erat. Vixit ergo Ethelwlfus rex clementissimus annis duobus postquam Romuleas adire sedes cepit. Qui inter alia præsentis vitæ bona et studia regalis operis, de suo transitu præmeditatus est, ne filii sui post obitum suæ vitæ disceptarent, epistolam satis eleganti compositione composuit, quæ omnia quæ sui juris erant distribuit. Per omnem hæreditatem suæ terræ semper in decem mansis unum pauperem aut indigenam vel peregrinum cibo et potu sive vestimento jussit adjuvari vel pasci, pro se et pro omnibus successoribus suis. Romam quoque pro redemptione animæ suæ trescentas mancusas[1] portari præcepit, centum ad limina Sancti Petri spe-

[1] *Mancusa in se continet triginta denarios,* in the margin.

cialiter ad emendum oleum, et centum ad honorem Sancti Pauli, centum universali papæ Apostolico. Defuncto igitur Ethelulfo rege glorioso, filius ejus Ethelbald contra Jesu Christi interdictum et Christianorum traditionem, ac contra omnium Paganorum consuetudinem thorum patris sui ascendens, Juditham, Karoli Francorum regis filiam, cum magna infamia in matrimonium duxit, effrænisque duobus et dimidio annis Occidentalium Saxonum post nobilissimi patris sui obitum imperii gubernacula rexit.[m]

DCCCLX.

Anno DCCC.lx, nativitatis Elfredi clitonis insignis xij, Ethelbald defunctus est atque in Scireburna sepultus. Quo ablato e sæculo, Ethelbyrht ipsius frater has provincias suo regno adjunxit, hoc est Cantiam et Suthrigam, Suthsexam quoque cum omnibus villis et territoriis, ut justum erat. In ipsius quoque regni statu magnus Paganorum exercitus de mari adveniens Wintoniam civitatem hostiliter invadens depopulatus est. Exercitus vero prædictus cum reverteretur cum ingenti præda ad naves, Osric, dignissimus dux Hantunnensium, cum suis populis advenit, et Ethelwlf comes insignis cum Bearrocensibus viriliter occurrit cum immenso exercitu, consertoque prælio Pagani passim trucidantur ab Anglis suffultis a spiritibus angelicis. Cumque diutius hostes dirissimi stare nequirent præ vulneribus, cadebat crudeliter perplurima multitudo, alii per latibula densarum veprium se abdentes, nonnulli muliebriter fugam arripientes. Angli vero loco funeris fortuna arridente dominati sunt. Ethelbyrht itaque rex quinque annis regnum sibi commissum pacifice et amabiliter atque honorabiliter gubernavit; qui cum magno suorum principum, episcoporum, omniumque populorum dolore viam universitatis adiit, relinquens terreni regni monarchiam alterius cœpit esse particeps. Sepultus est igitur juxta fratrem suum in Sciréburnan, quo expectat consolationem futuræ resurrectionis.[n]

DCCCLXIV.

Anno DCCC.lxiiij Pagani hiemaverunt in insula quæ appellatur Tened, quæ circumdatur undique maris flumine. Qui firmum cum Cantuariis pepigerunt fœdus, quibus Cantuarii pecuniam pro fœdere servato reddere promiserunt. Interea tamen Dani vulpino more noctu clam castris erumpentes, fœdereque dirupto,

[m] The events here recorded under the year 855, but which really occupied that and the four following years, are taken from Asser.

[n] Wholly from Asser.

et promissionem pecuniæ spernentes, paucis diebus extiterunt quieti. Sed, o nefas! totam orientalem plagam Cantiæ gentis depopulati sunt. Sciebant majorem pecuniam se furtiva præda quam pace adepturos, quod et factum est.[o]

DCCCLXVI.

Sequenti vero anno, hoc est DCCC.lxvj, nativitatis autem Elfredi xviij, Ethelred, frater Ethelbyrti regis, Occidentalium Saxonum regni gubernacula suscepit. Eodem anno magna Paganorum classis de Danubia Britanniæ fines introiit, et sic ad regnum Orientalium Anglorum, quod Saxonico dicitur eloquio East-Engle, hiemavit, ibique ipse copiosus exercitus equestris factus est, equitantes et discurrentes hac illac, prædam diripientes enormem, non parcentes viris, vel feminis, vel viduis, nec virginibus.

His diebus Elfredus clito jugi meditatione cœpit Divinis imbui doctrinis, qui miro patris matrisque amore supra omnes fratres suos ab ipsis diligebatur cunabulis. Crescente denique illo corpore in puerili ætate, forma cæteris suis fratribus decentior videbatur, vultuque insignis renitebat et verbis refulsit egregiis. Cervino quoque desiderio æstuabat sui cordis penetralia suffundi, et thalamum pectoris sacris literis imbui. Sed, pro dolor! parentum ac nutritorum incuria illiteratus permansit usque ad duodecimum suæ ætatis annum. Saxonica quoque poëmata gloriosus adolescens et futurus rex die noctuque discere studuit, eratque docilis, in arte venatoria industris, in omni peritia incomparabilis. Cum ergo quadam die ejus dignissima genitrix sibi et fratribus suis quendam Saxonicum poëmaticæ artis librum ostenderet, ait eis, "Quisquis, carissimi filii, vestrum istum potuerit codicem citius discere, dabo ei ipsum." At ille, Divina inspiratione instinctus, et pulchritudine principalis literæ exhilaratus, ita matri respondit. "Verene," sic ait matri suæ, "dabis?" Ad hæc illa arridens et gaudens atque affirmans, "Dabo," inquit, "dabo." Mox autem tulit librum de manu suæ genitricis, magistrum adiit, libellum ostendit, et legit præceptore ostendente. Post spatium non longi temporis venit ante præsentiam dilectæ matris, librumque memoriter recitavit. Ipsa vero grates immensas reddit Salvatoris gratiæ, agnoscens gratiam Dei esse in mente juvenis. Post hæc inflammatus Divini amoris desiderio psalmos perplurimos, cursumque diurnum, id est celebrationes horarum, didicit ipse devotus, quos in uno volumine congregatos die noctuque in sinu suo inseparabiliter portabat. O felix hominum genus! O rex

[o] From Asser.

prudens! gestas Gestantem, sapientiæ claves vehis; sapientiam diligis, sapiens eris, *faciens judicium et justitiam in terris*.[p] O clerici, attendite et videte regem in sinu librum deferre die noctuque; vos vero nec legem Dei scitis nec scire vultis. Præcipue idem, rex factus, lugebat filium suum, id est animum, quod liberalibus non fuerat artibus instructus.[q]

DCCCLXVII.

Anno DCCC.lxvij, nativitatis Elfredi regis xix, prædictus Paganorum exercitus de Orientalibus Anglis ad Eboracam civitatem migravit, quæ in aquilonali ripa Humbrensis fluminis sita est. Eodem tempore maxima inter Northanhymbrorum populos discordia erat succensa, et apte, quia qui odium diligit odium inveniet. His diebus Northanhymbrorum gens legitimum suæ gentis regem, Osbryht vocitatum onomate, de regno hostiliter expulerunt, et tyrannum quendam nomine Alla super apicem regni constituerunt; venientibus super regnum Paganis, consilio Divino et optimatum adminiculo discordia illa sedata est. Rex vero Osbryht et Alla, adunatis viribus, congregatoque exercitu, Eboracum adeunt oppidum. Quibus advenientibus classica multitudo confestim fugam arripiunt; quorum fugam et pavorem Christiani cernentes, fortiores ipsis inventi sunt. Pugnatum est satis crudeliter ex utraque parte, quo ambo reges occubuerunt. Reliqui vero qui evaserunt pacem cum Danis pepigerunt.

Ipso autem anno Ealhstan, Scireburnensis ecclesiæ episcopus, viam et vitam deseruit temporalis sæculi, postquam episcopatum per annos quinquaginta honorabiliter rexerat: qui in pace ecclesiæ requiescit, sepultus decenter in sede sui episcopatus.[r]

DCCCLXVIII.

Anno DCCC.lxviij, Elfredi regis xx, uxorem accepit de Mercia, nobilem scilicet genere, filiam Ethelredi Gainorum comitis, qui cognominabatur ab Anglis Mucel, eo quod erat corpore magnus et prudentia grandævus. Ea tempestate prædictus Paganorum exercitus Northanhymbros reliquit, Snotingaham pessimo adventu visitavit et adiit, quæ civitas Britannico sermone Tiguocobauc[s] interpretatur, Latina interpretatione Speluncarum Domus dicitur. Quo in loco hospites insidiosi eodem anno hiemavere, quorum adventus omnibus populis satis erat ingratus. Audiens

[p] Jer. xxiii. 5. [q] Asser. [r] Asser.

[s] This word, written in the MS. Tignocebanc, is corrected, and its significance restored from the text of Asser.

autem eorum adventum armipotens rex Merciorum, Burhred appellatus, et omnes optimates, consilium habuit cum suis comitibus et commilitonibus et omni populo sibi subjecto, qualiter inimicos bellica virtute exuperaret sive de regno expelleret. Direxit et nuncios veloci cursu ad Elfredum insignissimæ virtutis virum, et ad Ethelredum fratrem ejus, ut ei fraternum ostenderent adminiculum quo possent victrici fortitudine eos debellare. Quod ipsi, quasi intrepidi leones, agere non distulerunt. Tunc incitus Elfredus rapidis cœpit præceptis exercitum congregare, illud corde tenus recordans. "Nunquam dives agit qui trepidus gemens sese credit egentem." Nequaquam potens vir agit quod desiderat qui trepidus constat, et qui se putat egentem, id est miserum, si agat quod optat viriliter decertando. Frater ejus, simili succensus furore, usque ad Snotingaham perveniunt parati adversus temptamina stare. Pagani vero munitione arcis muniti bellum promittunt, acies struunt, numerosum exercitum ostendunt, sed tremebundi claris cernentes visibus Christianum populum in centenis et millenis millibus adversariis resistere, sacris ducibus exhortantibus. Tandem per gratiam Omnipotentis Domini cessavit ventus turbinis, sedata sunt corda iniquorum, pacem rogantes et fœdus a Christianis, ac si ipsi tali, propitio Christo, mente exorarent,

"Rapidos, Rector, comprime fluctus,
Et quo cælum regis immensum
Firma stabiles fœdere terras."[s]

Facta est inter reges et Paganos pax, et segregati ab invicem, sicut oves ab hædis sequestrantur.[t]

DCCCLXIX.

Anno DCCC.lxix, ætatis vero Elfredi xxj, præfatus exercitus rursum ad gentem Northanhymbrorum profectus est, ibique anno integro permansit[u] debacchans et insaniens, occidens et perdens perplurimos viros ac mulieres.

DCCCLXX.

Sequenti vero anno dum solis jubar mundi perlustraret orbes, et annus advenisset DCCC.lxx ab incarnatione Domini,

[s] Boethius, i., 46-8.

[t] S. Matt. xxv. 32.
The facts here detailed are all from Asser, but the narrative is spun out with verbiage and quotations, which are not in the original.

[u] Up to this point is Asser's; the remainder, apparently, an unauthorized addition.

tunc refulsit tempus quo Elfred rex vicesimum primum habuit annum. Danorum vero enormis multitudo, et, ut ita dicam, legionum catervæ congregatæ sunt, ita ut multa viderentur millia affore, et sicut de mille in viginti myriadas excrevissent. Pervenit dehinc per Merciam in Orientales Anglos, et in civitate quæ dicitur Theoford intrepidus hyemavit. Rex autem Eadmundus ipsis temporibus regnavit super omnia regna Orientalium Anglorum, vir sanctus et justus, sicut finis ejus sanctissimæ vitæ probavit eventus. Eodem vero anno rex prædictus contra ipsum exercitum atrociter et viriliter cum suis pugnavit. Sed quia misericors Deus eum præscivit per martyrii coronam ad cælestis gloriæ coronam pervenire, ibidem gloriose occubuit. De cujus passionis honore libet aliqua historiæ nostræ inserere, ut sciant et agnoscant filii hominum quam terribilis est Christus filius Dei in consiliis hominum, et quam glorioso triumpho exornat quos hic passionis titulo excruciat, ut illud impleatur, *Non coronatur quis nisi legitime certaverit.*[v] Rex autem Eadmundus imperium Orientalium Anglorum suscepit devotus, quod et tenuit dextra forti potentiæ, Deum Omnipotentem semper adorans ac glorificans pro omnibus bonis suis quibus usus fuerat. Eodem anno quo rex et martyr insignis per coronam martyrii supernæ felicitatis gaudia subiit, Ceolnoth, archiepiscopus Doroberniæ civitatis, viam veritatis adiit: qui in eadem civitate est sepultus a clericis.[w]

DCCCLXXI.

Anno Dominicæ incarnationis DCCC.lxxj, nativitatis Elfredi gloriosi regis Saxonum xxij, exosæ memoriæ Paganorum exercitus Orientales Anglos deseruit: qui regnum Occidentalium Saxonum adiit, veniens ad villam regiam quæ dicitur Et Redingum, in meridianam Tamensis fluminis ripam, in illa plaga quæ nuncupatur ab incolis ipsius patriæ Bearroc-scire. Tertio vero die quo ibi advenerunt inimici Anglorum, comites eorum cum magna multitudine in parte illius fluminis equitaverunt, prædamque immensæ multitudinis acceperunt. Quidam autem ex ipsis vallum inter Tamense et Kenetan flumina facere studuerunt; sed consilium eorum et opus Danorum dissipatum est per auxilium angelorum, ut impleretur in eis illud scolastici;

"Quamvis se Tyrio superbit ostro,
Comet et niveis [caput] lapillis,
Invisus tamen omnibus pollet."[x]

[v] 2 Tim. ii. 5.

[w] This account is altogether from Asser, but is here amplified to thrice its original bulk.

[x] From Boethius de Consol., iii., 1-3, 7-8, with some variations.

Et aliud:

"Quis illos igitur putet beatos,
Quos miseri tribuunt, honores?"

Cumque perversi raptores viriliter operibus desudarent, advenit protinus Ethelwlf, Bearrocensis regionis incliti vigoris dux, cum suis agminibus centuriatus, et trilicis toracis circumdatus. Cernens autem multitudinem barbarorum princeps Christianorum populorum, dixit suis, "Horum numerosus est exercitus, sed tamen est spernendus. Qui si aliquando contra nos aciem struens valentior incubuerit, noster quidam dux, qui Christus est, fortior illis est. Obviant denique Christiani Danis confidentes in tuitione Christi nominis," Dux præfatus suos hortatur præcipue ut resisterent adversariis, constitutus cum suis inclitis legionibus in loco qui appellatur Englafeld. Ubi dimicatum est satis atroci bello, quo ex utraque parte ceciderunt vulnerati multi et occubuerunt. Occubuit ibidem quidam princeps Danorum cum magna multitudine sui exercitus; cæteris fuga elapsis, Christiani victoriæ palmam adepti sunt, et loco funeris dominati sunt.

His ita peractis, post, bis binis dierum curriculis expletis, rex præpotens Etheredus ac frater ejus Elfred, adunatis exercitibus copiosis, ut regum est potestas et virtus, ad Readingum venerunt, desiderantes aut gloriose vivere in regno, aut in bello occumbere pro Christo. Cumque armipotens rex Ethelred cum fratre dilectissimo ad portam arcis pervenissent, cædendo et prosternendo hostes ante et retro, Pagani e contra cædebant hostica rabie resistentes. Sed heu, pro dolor! victoriam eo die inimici Anglorum assumebant. Æthelwlfus, quoque, Bearrocensis, qui prius ut leo fremuit in bello, tunc cum cæteris fidelibus occubuit in Christo. Quo dolore et verecundia Anglorum populus commotus, auxilium implorabant angelorum, ut eis dignarentur impendere adminiculum Divini adjutorii. Iterum enimvero post quatuor dies contra præfatos inimicos exercitum commovent, arma arripiunt, statuunt legiones in loco qui dicitur Ecscesdun, quod Latine Mons Fraxini potest reverenter interpretari. Ibi autem totis viribus et plena voluntate ad prælium prodeunt viri famosi ad bella fortissimi.

Dani quoque, ut sunt astuti, in duas se turmas dividentes, viriliter pugnare cum suis. Habebant et ipsi duos reges multosque duces, qui, cauta ratione utentes, mediam partem exercitus duobus regibus concedebant, dimidiam vero omnibus ducibus. Quod Angli cernentes constituunt et ipsi duas turmas, et machinas, et machinatorum propugnacula. Ælfred autem rex promptissime cum suis legionibus procedit ad bellum, sciens

E 2

proculdubio non in multitudine hominum affore victoriam, sed Dei in miseratione et misericordia. Rex, quoque, Ethelred in tentorio erat in oratione constitutus, missam et quæ Dei sunt sollicite audiendo. Quæ sancta mysteria regi et Christiano populo multum proficiebant, uti in sequentibus ostendetur.

Decreverant ergo Christiani populi et Angli devotissime audacter committere contra inimicos bellum, et, ut Ethelred rex, fortissimus principum, contra legiones dimicaret cum suis myriadis, unus videlicet rex Anglorum contra duos Danorum. Ælfred vero rex cum suis ducibus et commilitonibus, satrapis et populis, debuit contra omnes Paganorum duces belli sortem sumere, ut decretum est. Quibus res publica utrisque regibus et populis sat satis bene complacuit. Quibus ita firmiter ab utraque parte dispositis, cum rex Ethelred in oratione diutius moraretur, et Pagani parati ad locum diri certaminis citius advenissent, Elfred, tunc secundus in regno, non potuit hostiles diutius acies sufferre, nisi eos aut bello superaret aut morte. Repente vero consternatus animo irruit super aggregatas multitudines Danorum cum sacris agminibus Anglorum: venit autem rex præcinctus armis et orationibus, qui intuitus exercitum fratris satis eleganter esse ordinatum, quasi Judas bellicosus processit ad bellum. Dimicatum est virili intentione ab utrisque partibus, quo in loco ceciderunt quinquageni et centeni necnon milleni. Qui pro patriis legibus et patria ceciderunt, perducti sunt, ut credi libet, ad patriam æternæ felicitatis. Alii vero ad eum perducti sunt, de quo dictum est, "Ipse est caput omnis injustitiæ." Reges autem non solum verbis populum constantem hortabantur, verum etiam armis hostes bellica virtute prosternebant. Tandem Dani, videntes suorum corruisse sociorum agmina, turbati sunt, admirati sunt, commoti sunt, timorque immensus apprehendit eos. Erant enim Divino perculsi Dani timore infra cordis cubicula, impetus Anglorum diutius non ferentes in ipso concilio. Qui opprobriosam arripientes fugam, laxatis gladiis dextras dederunt, pacemque petierunt. Extendentes reges gladios vix sedaverunt populum bellicantem. Fugerunt hac illac ignobile vulgus, quos per totius diei horas Angligenus persecutus est populus. Multa millia prostrata sunt in illa die; quorum interitum pii reges cernentes, gloriam dixerunt Deo immensam Qui eis talem ipso die contulit victoriæ palmam. Cecidit quoque ibi Bergsecg[y] rex et hi duces cum eo, dux Sidroc veteranus comes, de quo illud aptatur, *Inveterate dierum malorum.*[z] Corruit ibidem dux Sidroc junior, atque Osbern dux militiæ, duxque Frana, duxque Harald cum suis

[y] Bægsceg—*Asser*. [z] Daniel xiii. 52.

agminibus; qui latam et spatiosam viam arripientes descenderunt in profundum laci. *Viam disciplinæ nescierunt, nec intellexerunt semitas ejus: a facie illorum longe facta est.*[a]

Bello peracto glorioso, reges et omnis populus immenso repletus est tripudio, videntes Danorum fugam et Anglorum constantiam. Post quatuordecim dierum excursum, rex Ethelred præstantissimus, ignorans annum jubilei habere remissionem, adjutus fidelissimo auxilio fratris sui, coadunavit exercitum, congregavit spolia, divisitque arma et dona perplurima suis commilitonibus. Sciebant pro certo ipsi principes populorum beatas fore respublicas, si eas vel studiosi sapientiæ regerent, vel si earum rectores studere sapientiæ contigisset. Congregati sunt rursum ad bellum Angli atque Dani, quibus cum durissimum esset illatum robur, Pagani victoriam prope assumpserunt.

Eodem vero anno rex Ethelred, plenus ætate et perfectus in bonitate, post perpetrationem insignium bellorum, futuræ vitæ et perpetui regni felicitatem cœpit videre cum Rege sæculorum in terra viventium. Subtracto ab hoc sæculo rege prædicto, mox Elfredus a ducibus et a præsulibus totius gentis eligitur, et non solum ab ipsis verum etiam ab omni populo adoratur ut eis præesset *ad faciendam vindictam in nationibus, increpationes in populis.*[b] Adepto regni gubernaculo totius gentis semper bellicosus refulsit, et victor in omnibus bellis, fortuna arridente Christoque faciente. Rebellavit contra eum prædictus exercitus satis acerrime, qui Anglorum intuentes austeritatem, et suam cognoscentes imbecillitatem, terga in fugam verterunt. Sed, proh dolor! per audacitatem persequentium reversi, rursum ad prælium sunt provocati, capientes victoriæ munus, et loco funeris sunt dominati. Ipso quoque anno Saxones cum eisdem Paganis pacis concordiam pepigerunt, ea ratione ut ab eis discederent.[c]

DCCCLXXII.

Anno Dominicæ incarnationis DCCC.lxxij, nativitatis Elfredi regis xxiij, præfatus Paganorum exercitus Londoniam adiit, ibique hiemavit; cum quo Mercii pacem pepigerunt.[d]

DCCCLXXIII.

Anno DCCC.lxxiij, nativitatis autem Elfredi regis Anglorum[e] xxiiij, sæpe-memoratus exercitus Londoniam deserens, ad

[a] Baruch, iii., 20, 21. [b] Psalm cxlix. 7.
[c] All this is taken from Asser, but is very diffusely paraphrased.
[d] Asser. [e] This word is interlined.

Northanhymbrorum regionem profectus est, ibique hiemavit, cum quo iterum Mercii pacem pepigerunt.[e]

DCCCLXXIV.

Anno Dominicæ incarnationis DCCC.lxxiiij, nativitatis autem Elfredi regis Anglorum xxv, supra-memoratus exercitus Lindissem provinciam deseruit, Merciam adiit, et in Hripadun hiemavit. Burhredum quoque, Merciorum regem, de regno depulerunt, et ad Romam exire compulerunt xxij regni sui anno. Qui, postquam Romam adierat, non diu vixit sæculo, quoniam pervenit ad Eum Qui est vera vita, sepultusque honorifice est in ecclesia Sanctæ Mariæ genitricisque Domini nostri Jesu Christi, semper virginis, expectans Ejus adventum secundum, quando bonis justa præmia largiter concedit, malis dira dispensat supplicia. Dani quoque, post hujus expulsionem, regnum Merciorum suo dominio subdiderunt. Commendaverunt illud cuidam militi ipsius gentis, nomine Ceolwlfo, ea ratione ut, quando vellent, rursum absque dolo, absque malo haberent.

DCCCLXXV.

Anno Dominicæ incarnationis DCCC.lxxv, nativitatis autem Elfredi regis xxvj, prædictus exercitus Repadun deseruit, seseque in duas partes divisit. Una pars cum Haldene ad regionem Northanhymbrorum secessit, et eam vastavit,[f] et hiemavit juxta flumen quod dicitur Tine, et totam gentem suo dominatui subdidit, et Pictos atque Stretduccenses depopulati sunt.

Eardulfus episcopus et abbas Eadredus de Lindisfarnensi insula corpus Sancti Cuthberti tollentes, per ix annos ante faciem barbarorum de loco ad locum fugientes, cum illo thesauro discurrerunt. Altera quoque pars ipsius classis cum Gutthrum et Oscytel et Amund, regibus Paganorum, ad locum qui dicitur Grantabric pervenit, ibique hyemavit. Rex vero Elfred, navali prœlio confortatus, sex naves invenit in mari, cum quibus fortiter debellans, unam cepit; cæteri fugerunt timore perculsi.[g]

DCCCLXXVI.

Anno Dominicæ incarnationis DCCC.lxxvj, nativitatis autem Elfredi regis xxvij, præfatus exercitus nocte de Grantabric exiens, castellum quod dicitur Werham intravit. Quorum subitum adventum rex Saxonum prænoscens, fœdus cum eis

[e] Asser.
[f] This and the two preceding words are interlineations.
[g] Asser.

pepigit, ea conditione ut ab ejus regno discederent, obsides accipiendo. Ipsi vero, more solito obsides et juramenta non servantes, nocte quadam, fœdere dirupto, ad Exancestriam diverterunt, quod Brittannice dicitur Cairwisc, Latine, Civitas Aquarum.[h]

DCCCLXXVII.

Anno Dominicæ incarnationis DCCC.lxxvij, nativitatis autem Elfredi xxvij, exercitus ipse nefandus Exancester dereliquit, Cippanham regiam villam adiit, ibique hiemavit. Ælfred vero rex his diebus magnas sustinuit tribulationes et inquietam vitam agebat.[i] Rex Elfredus, apto confortatus oraculo per Sanctum Cuthbertum, contra Danos pugnavit, et sic, quo ipse Sanctus jusserat tempore et loco, victoria potitus est, semperque deinceps hostibus terribilis et invincibilis erat, Sanctumque Cuthbertum præcipue honori habuerat.[j] Qualiter hostes vicerit paulo post hic legitur.

Eodem denique anno Inguar et Healfdene cum bis denis ac ternis navibus, de Demetica regione, in qua hiemaverant, egressi ut lupi feroces, post multas ibi Christianorum strages patratas, post combustiones cœnobiorum, ad Domnaniam enavigaverunt, et ibi a regis ministris fortissimis cum mille ducentis viris occisi sunt ante arcem Cynwith,[k] quia in eadem arce perplurimi regis famuli, ut dictum est, se concluserant causa refugii. Rex autem Elfred, in Domino Deo confisus, cum paucis agminibus stipatus, fecit arcem in loco qui appellatur Ethelingalge, in quo habitans cum suis commilitonibus hostes frequenter infatigabiliter contrivit ab arce. Hoc egit tempore resurrectionis Domini nostri Jesu Christi. Qui egressus ab arce, viribusque susceptis, post, septem videlicet septimanis dierum et monade, hoc est quinquaginta diebus suppletis, venit ad petram Ecgberti, quæ est in orientali parte saltus qui Anglico eloquio dicitur Mucelwudu,[l] Latine vero Magna Silva, Britannico more Coitmawr. Ibi ergo obviaverunt regi dilectissimo omnes accolæ Sumortunenses ac Wiltunenses, necnon Huntunenses, visoque lætati sunt immenso cordis tripudio, quasi redivivum ipsum suscipientes. Post ter-

[h] Asser. [i] *vel ducebat* interlined.

[j] This reference to the protection afforded by St. Cuthbert to King Alfred is not in Asser. See Symeon's History of the Church of Durham, book ii., c. 10.

[k] Cynuit—Asser.

[l] Mucelwudu is written in the MS. Mucelpurlu, the scribe having fallen into the general error of confounding the Gothic *m* with the letter *p*. This mistake is complicated by the *d* having been written so as to resemble the letters *r l*. There is no doubt as to the name really intended as it occurs both in Asser, and in the "Recapitulation" in the present compilation. Coit-Maur, again, by the same confusion of *w* and *p*, has been written Coit-Mapur.

tium vero diem venit cum immenso exercitu ad locum qui dicitur Ederderandun,[m] quo juxta immensas Paganorum phalanges invenit paratas cum densa multitudine ad bellum. Exorto solis jubare limpidissimo, rex et omne decus suæ plebis induerunt se bellicis ornatibus, scilicet trilici toraca fidei, spei, charitatisque Dei. Hi exurgentes a solo audacter provocabant incelebres ad bellum, de clementia Conditoris sperantes securi, ac vallo muniti astantis regis, cujus vultus ut angeli splendentis refulsit. Commiserunt ergo bellum per longa tempora diei utrique populi, quorum voces et collisiones armorum per longa terrarum spatia audita sunt.

Cernens igitur Speculator insignis desuper penetral Sui terreni regis desiderium, concessit ei angelicæ potestatis suffragium. Is denique potitus victoria hostes suos prostravit, gratias reddens summo Salvatori cum cordis lætitia. Cumque ibidem rex cum suis legionibus arrideret, inimici qui remanserant ipsius magnis ejulatibus deflerent, ob famis et frigoris austeritatem atque tanti regis timorem, rogant pacis clementiam qui eam semper impugnabant. Promittunt obsides, et juramenta in dextris extendunt. Auscultans hæc omnia rex, suatim motus clementia concedit cuncta petita. Rex vero ipsorum, Gutthrum onomate, Christianum se velle fore testatus est: qui sub manu piissimi regis in baptismatis purgatione regaliter susceptus est. Tinctns est idem Guderum baptismate salutis cum aliis viris electis xxx, quem rex Saxonum in filium adoptionis accepit. Qui, postquam baptizatus est, duodenis noctibus cum ipso mansit in magna gloria; cui Spiritualis Pater multa et inedicibilia largitus est dona, ac omnibus qui Christianitatis fidem perceperunt.[n]

DCCCLXXIX.

Anno Dominicæ incarnationis DCCC.lxxix., nativitatis Elfredi regis xxviij, prædictus Paganorum exercitus de Cippanham, ut promiserat, consurgens Cirencestre adiit, quæ Britannico appellatur elogio Cairceri, ibique per unius anni cursum mansit. Ipso quoque anno immensus venit Paganorum exercitus de ultramarinis climatibus in Tamensi fluvio: qui adunatus est supradicto cuneo, complices effecti, quod pravorum est. Eclypsis inter nonam et vesperam facta est eodem anno.[o]

[m] Ethandum—Asser.

[n] With the exception indicated above, all these details are from Asser, but placed by him in the preceding year.

[o] Asser.

DCCCLXXX.

Anno Dominicæ incarnationis DCCC.lxxx, nativitatis autem Elfredi regis gloriosi xxix, sæpe-memoratus Paganorum exercitus a Cirencestre egressus ad Orientales accessit Anglos;[p] ipsam regionem dividentes inhabitare cœperunt. Pagani qui in Fulanhame hiemaverant, Britannicam deseruerunt insulam, Franciamque visitare cœperunt pessima agnitione, quo uno anno permanserunt.[q]

DCCCLXXXI.

Anno Dominicæ incarnationis DCCC.lxxxj, nativitatis autem Elfredi regis xxx, præfatus exercitus equis ascensis in Francorum finibus devenit, quod mirabile videri potest quod visibiles hostes contra tam fortem bellicosumque populum auderent insurgere. At tunc feroces Franci invicta fortitudine a castellis, et oppidis, et civitatibus atque turribus viriliter progredientes, more leonum succensi sunt ira, videntes nefarias sceleratorum potestates emergere, gaudio lætitiaque exultare malos, jacere bonos terrore prostratos, innocuos flere, nocentes exultare. Inito consilio prudenti audaces Franci bellum iniere durissimum cum Paganis. Finito prælio Franci cum triumpho reversi sunt. Pagani equis acquisitis hac illac equitabant.[r] His diebus plurima in eadem gente monasteria concussa sunt ac desolata. Nam et fratres cœnobii sanctissimi Benedicti, ipsius reliquias a tumulo quo locata fuerant immensa pulchritudine secum auferentes, hac illac discurrebant.

DCCCLXXXII.

Anno Dominicæ incarnationis DCCC.lxxxij, nativitatis autem Elfredi gloriosi regis xxxj, Paganorum exercitus suas naves per flumen quod dicitur Mese in Francigenæ gentis regionem pertraxit, et ibi hiemavit uno anno. Eodem denique anno, Elfred rex Saxonum, audacissimus ducum, navali prœlio suffultus, contra Paganicas naves in mari congressus est. Ex quibus ipse equilocus duas potenti virtute naves exuperavit, occisis omnibus qui in eis erant. His exuperatis principum princeps grates reddidit dignas sospitatis Auctori. Quid deinde gestum sit referre libet. Principes duarum navium post hæc cum omnibus sociis valde vulneravit, qui, depositis enerviter armis, curvis poplitibus precibusque supplicibus dedere se regi magno, quamdiu scintillula vitalis caloris eis arrideret.

[p] An interlineation. [q] Asser.
[r] From Asser up to this point.

DCCCLXXXIII.

Sequenti anno, hoc est DCCC.lxxxiij, nativitatis vero Elfredi famosissimi regis xxxij, ipse nec nominandus exercitus naves suas per flumen quod appellatur Scald pertraxit, ibique uno mansit anno.[s]

Guthred ex servo factus est rex, et sedes episcopalis in Cunkecestra restauratur.[t]

DCCCLXXXIV.

Anno Dominicæ incarnationis DCCC.lxxxiiij, nativitatis denique Elfredi famosissimi regis xxxiij, indignissimus exercitus in duas se turmas segregavit. Una quidem in orientalem Franciam porrexit, altera ad Britanniam veniens Cantiam adiit quæ Rofecestrer dicitur. Ante hujus portam castellum Pagani fecerunt, nec tamen civitatem expugnare potuerunt, quia cives illius civitatis se viriliter defenderunt, quoadusque defensor totius regni, Elfred rex, cum magno exercitu supervenit. Adveniente subito rege, ad naves suas Dani confestim confugiunt concussi terrore, relicta sua arce et equis quos de Francia secum adduxerant, necnon captivis quos de Francia de eadem gente ceperant.

Eodem tempore et anno ipse armipotens rex classem suam de Cantia plenam bellatoribus in Orientales direxit Anglos. Cumque ad ostium Sture fluminis adveniret, confestim tredecim naves paratæ ad bellum Paganorum obviaverunt eis, qui hinc inde acriter pugnantes, Pagani omnes occisi, omnesque naves cum omni pecunia eorum captæ sunt. Qui autem fugere poterant ex Danis, catervatim congregavere undique naves, consertoque navali prœlio cum Anglis ubi dormiebant somno inerti, occisi sunt, inermis multitudo: quibus illud aptatur congruenter quod legitur, "multi claudunt visus cum aspicere deberent."

Ipso nempe anno magnus exercitus Paganorum de Germania in regionem antiquorum Saxonum supervenit, contra quos adunatis undique bellicis viris, id est, Saxones atque Frixones, viriliter atque fortiter pugnavere: in quibus duobus bellis Christiani populi, Divinæ pietatis clementia concedente, victoriam habuere.

Ea tempestate sanctissimæ memoriæ præsul Marinus universitatis viam arripuit transmittendo spiritum unde prius venerat. Is denique scolam Saxonum in Romana urbe pro

[s] From Asser to this point.

[t] The whole of this sentence is an interlineation. See Symeon's History of the Church of Durham, book ii., c. 13.

amoris affectu benignissimi regis Elfredi constituit ab omni tributo [liberam], qui etiam multa dona ipsi transmisit; inter quæ dedit illi partem sanctissimæ crucis in qua Dominus noster Jhesus Christus pro universali hominum salute pependit. Nati sunt ergo regi filii et filiæ satis perspicui ac decoræ formæ, quorum quarumque nomina hic sunt deflorata, Eadward et Ethelward, Ethelfled et Ethelgifu, atque Elfthrid. Eadward vero filius regis, et Ealthrid, soror ejus, semper in curia regis cum magna nutritorum atque nutricum diligentia sunt nutriti. Nam et psalmos, et Saxonicos libros et carmina studiose didicere. Æthelward itaque, junior filius ejus, ludis literariæ disciplinæ subditus emicuit cum plurimis militum puerulis, nobilibus scilicet et ignobilibus. Æthelfled, soror eorum, Eadredo Merciorum principi in matrimonio copulata est; soror quoque ipsorum Ethelgyfa monasticæ vitæ ferulis subjuncta est.

His temporibus fideliter glorioseque regimine rexit ecclesiam Christi Plegmundus archiepiscopus, qui venerandus vir sapientiæ fructibus renidebat, præditus bis binis columpnis, justitiæ, videlicet, prudentiæ, temperantiæ, fortitudinis. Warfridus vero regni sceptra Wigornensis civitatulæ eodem tempore purpurabat devotissimo cordis ingenio. Qui, imperio regis jussus atque expetitus, librum Dialogorum Gregorii in Saxonicam linguam evertit, aliquando sensum ex sensu elegantissime interpretatus est. Æthelstanum quoque et Werwlfum, sacerdotes insignes de Mercia, ad se invitarat, eo quod hi præstantius atque perfusius in Divinæ legis eruditione pollebant: Hos præcipuo amoris honore dilexit, honoravit; quorum doctrina et eruditione magnificatus est rex pacificus super omnes reges terræ.[u]

DCCCLXXXVI.

Anno Dominicæ incarnationis DCCC.lxxxvj, nativitatis vero Elfredi regis gloriosi xxxv, nec nominandus exercitus Danorum iterum in occidentalium Francorum regionem venit, qui applicuerunt in flumine quod Signe dicitur. Parisium quoque civitatem adiit ibique hiemavit: transitum pontis civibus prohibuit. Sed Deo adminiculum veri auxilii concedente, et civibus viriliter se protegentibus, munitionem irrumpere non potuit. Eodem tempore rex Anglorum, post incendia urbium stragesque populorum, Londoniam, permaximam civitatem, honorifice restauravit et habitabilem fecit, quam Ethelredo, præcipuo duci Merciorum, commendavit servandam. Omnes vero Angli et Saxones qui prius ubi erant dispersi cum Paganis aut a captivitate liberati

[u] All this is from Asser.

venerunt sponte ad regis præsentiam, sponte se suo domino inclinantes. Ipse autem, ut erat clementissimæ mentis, cunctis indulsit patrocinium suæ benignitatis.[v]

DCCCLXXXVII.

Anno Dominicæ incarnationis DCCC.lxxxvij, nativitatis autem Elfredi incliti regis xxxvj, supradictus exercitus Parisium civitatem relinquens venit ad Sigene, deinde ad ostium fluminis quod Materre nominatur, exhinc ad locum qui Cazendest,[w] villa regia, pervenerunt: in quo loco etiam hiemaverunt integro anno. Sequente vero anno in ostio fluminis quod appellatur Jona intraverunt, non sine magno regionis dampno, et illic morati sunt uno anno. Ipso denique tempore Elfredus rex Saxonum, Divino instinctus munere, legere et interpretari sacros apices potuit. Erat itaque multis tribulationibus hujus mundi afflictus, quamvis in regia foret potestate constitutus. Nam etiam de Jerosolima ab El(ia) patriarcha epistolas et dona illi diversa directa vidimus et legimus. Qualiter dilatavit regni sui imperia, et renovavit urbium mœnia, atque civitatum munitiones roboravit quæ erant dirutæ, et quæ non erant fecit, quis urbana facundia suffultus possit labiis exultationis edicere? Sancta quoque loca qualiter ditavit ornamentis et regalibus donis quis enunciet? Perturbatus erat frequenter animo contra principes et pentecomarchos et omne genus perversorum, quoniam ipsi noluerunt eum sequi in studiis quibus ipse desudabat. Sed tamen ille solus, Divino suffultus amminiculo, regni gubernacula, velut præcipuus gubernator navim suam, hoc est, vitam suæ gloriosæ mentis ad portum pacifici paradisi studuit transferre. Solebat frequenti memoria hoc retinere quod canitur,

"Quisquis volet perennem
Cautus ponere sedem,
Stabilisque nec sonori
Sterni flatibus Euri."[x]

Et infra:—

"Quam [vis] tenet ruinis,
[Hujus sæculi status]
Miscens æquora ventus;
Tu conditus quieti,
Felix robore valli,
Duces serenus ævum,
Ridens ætheris iras."

Hæc spirituali indagine secum rex piissimæ mentis revolvens,

[v] Asser. [w] Caziei, *Asser*. Chezy.
[x] Boethius, ii., 1—4; 17-21. The line, "Hujus sæculi status," does not occur in the edition of Boethius published in 1680.

inedicibilibus bonitatum fructuum actibus redolebat. Diebus solempnibus festis quanta munera suis episcopis et ducibus atque militibus contulit, quis enarret? Tunc pauperes jubilando exultabant; tunc orphani et viduæ nimio gaudio cordis applaudebant. Noverat illud scholastici. *Tunc est pretiosa pecunia cum translata fuerit in alios; largiendi usu desinet possideri.*[y] Cœpit denique assidue non solum episcopos ætherea claritate nitentes admonere, ut populi delicta corrigerent, et vulgarem stultitiam castigando acrius coercerent; et non solum pastores admonuit populorum, verumetiam ducibus et dilectissimis ministris præcepit, ut semet-ipsos ad communem totius regni utilitatem sapientissime suppeditarent.

Fecerat idem rex monasterium præpulchrum in loco qui dicitur Ethelingaige, in cujus occidentali limite arx munitissima, præfati regis imperio et operatione, consita est. In quo cœnobio diversi generis monachos undique congregavit et in eodem loco collocavit. Aliud quoque constituit monasterium juxta orientalem portam civitatis quæ Sceftesburg appellatur, satis habitationi sanctimonialium habile, in quo filiam suam Ethelgyfu, devotam Deo virginem, abbatissam constituit. Tanta enim dona et possessiones ambobus concessit monasteriis, ut sufficeret eis ad victum et ad vestitum quamdiu vita comes afforet.

His quæ supra retulimus pleniter firmiterque peractis, sæpenominatus rex Elfredus solito suo more intra suæ mentis thalamum cœpit sagaci ingenio pertractare, et pertractando ruminare illud quod in Divinis scriptum est literis. "*Si,*" inquit, "*recte offeras, et recte non dividas, peccasti.*" Et illud medullitus est præmeditatus quod ait Salomon sapientissimus regum: *Cor sane regis in manu Domini est Omnipotentis.*[z] Censum quoque suum trifarie divisit, ita ut istic libet prætitulari. Primæ partis sectionem sui census, bellatoribus annualiter largitus est. Secundam, operatoribus quos ex multis gentibus aggregaverat. Tertiam, advenis undique ad se venientibus; sciens illud cordetenus, *hilarem datorem diligit Deus.*[a] Erat enimvero in multis et in multifariis tribulationum stimulis constitutus quamvis in regia esset potestate subtronizatus.[b]

DCCCLXXXVIII.

Anno Dominicæ incarnationis DCCC.lxxxviij Beocca princeps

[y] Boethius, ii., argumentum.

[z] Prov. xxi. 1.

[a] Cor. ix. 7.

[b] The particulars detailed in this section are still from Asser, and are treated in the same style of loose paraphrase. The quotations are not in Asser. His Life of Alfred does not extend beyond this year (A.D. 887).

Romam detulit eleemosynam regis Ælfredi. Illo itinere obiit Ethelsuith, soror ejusdem regis, et sepulta est in Pavia.[c]

DCCCXC.

Anno DCCC.XC Beornhelm abbas elemosinam regis Elfredi et Occidentalium Saxonum Romam pertulit. Eodem anno Guthrum rex Northanhymbrorum obiit. Hunc, sicut superius legitur, rex Ælfredus elevavit de baptismate, et vocavit eum Ethelstan. Quo anno præfatus exercitus a Sigene perrexit Sanlaudan, quod est situm inter Britanniam et Galliam. Sed a Brittonibus in fugam versi, plures in amne proximo submersi sunt.[d]

DCCCXCI.

Anno DCCC.xcj Heathured suscepit episcopatum.[e]

DCCCXCII.

Anno DCCC.xcij Eboracensis episcopus, Wlfhere, obiit anno sui archiepiscopatus xxxix.[f]

DCCCXCIII.

Anno DCCC.xciij Orientales Saxones et Northumbrenses obsides dederunt, et juraverunt regi Elfredo fidelitatem contra prædictos Paganos qui jam in Angliam reversi fuerant.[g]

DCCCXCIV.

Anno DCCC.xciiij exercitus prædictus qui obsedit Exancestre vastavit omnia circa Cissacestre. Sed non multo post ab his qui erant in civitate in fugam versi sunt, multi occisi, et multæ ex navibus eorum captæ.[h] Hoc anno Guthred rex obiit.

[c] This is from the Saxon Chronicle, but not through the medium of Florence of Worcester, who also copied from the Chronicle. Two matters of detail are mentioned, which are omitted by Florence; that Alfred's sister died on her journey to Rome; and that she was buried at Pavia.

[d] This also is from the Saxon Chronicle, where Godrum or Guthrum is described as the "Northern King," which is here mistranslated Rex Northanhymbrorum. Florence correctly renders it Rex Northmannicus, as Guthrum was king of the northmen of East Anglia.

[e] This sentence is at the foot of the page, and the entry is altogether misplaced. Heathured became bishop of Lindisfarne in 819, not in 891.

[f] The death of the Archbishop is noticed under the year 893, in the MS. Latin version of the Saxon Chronicle, Domitian, A. viii., 2. The notice here, however, is probably derived from some list of the Archbishops to which the compiler, no doubt, had access.

[g] This is a fragmentary extract from the Saxon Chronicle.

[h] From the Saxon Chronicle to this point.

DCCCXCIX.

Anno DCCC.xcix Elfredus rex obiit cum regnasset annis xxviij cui filius Edwardus successit, diligenter a patre admonitus ut præcipue Sanctum Cuthbertum honoraret. Eardulfus quoque episcopus in Cunceceastre obiit, quo corpus Sancti Cuthberti transtulerat, cum quo per ix annos ante Paganorum exercitum multo cum labore et penuria de loco ad locum fugerat. Huic Cuthbertus in episcopatum successit.[i]

DCCCC.

Anno DCCCC Ethelbald ordinatus est in episcopatum Eboracensis ecclesiæ.

DCCCCI.

Anno DCCCC.j Osbrith regno pulsus est.

DCCCCII.

Anno DCCCC.ij Brehtsig occisus est.

DCCCCVI.

Anno DCCCC.vj rex Edwardus, necessitate compulsus, pacem firmavit cum Orientalibus Anglis et Northhymbrensibus.[j]

DCCCCX.

Anno DCCCC.x Angli et Dani pugnaverunt apud Teontanbole. Rex Edwardus Londoniam et Oxnaforda et quæ ad eam pertinent suscepit: quo anno multa piratarum manus circa Sabrinam flumen crudeliter vastando grassata est, sed ibi citius tota pene interiit.

DCCCCXII.

Anno DCCCC.xij Reingwald rex et Oter comes et Oswl Cracabam irruperunt et vastaverunt Dunbline.

DCCCCXIV.

Anno DCCCC.xiv Niel rex occisus est a fratre Sihtrico.[k]

DCCCCXIX.

Anno DCCCC.xix rex Inguald irrupit Eboracum.[l]

[i] See the ancient Historia de Sancto Cuthberto, which will be printed in the present volume; also Hist. Eccl. Dunelm., book ii., chap. xxx., etc.

[j] Saxon Chronicle. [k] Saxon Chronicle.

[l] Saxon Chronicle, A.D. 921, which, however, is in error in describing Niel and Sihtric as brothers. Compare Annals of the Four Masters.

DCCCCXX.

Anno DCCCC.XX rex Sihtricus infregit Devennport.

DCCCCXXIII.

Anno DCCCC.XXIIJ Edwardus rex mortuus est, relinquens imperium filio suo Ethelstano.[m]

DCCCCXXV.

Anno DCCCC.XXV Wigredus episcopus consecratur ad episcopatum Sancti Cuthberti.

DCCCCXXVII.

Anno DCCCC.XXVIJ Ethelstanus rex de regno Brittonum Gudfridum regem fugavit.[n]

DCCCCXXXIII.

Anno DCCCC.XXXIIJ rex Ethelstanus jussit Eadwinum fratrem suum submergi in mare.[o]

DCCCCXXXIV.

Anno DCCCC.XXXIIIJ rex Ethelstanus cum multo exercitu Scotiam tendens, ad sepulcrum Sancti Cuthberti venit, illius patrocinio se suumque iter commendavit, multa ac diversa dona, quæ regem decerent, ei optulit et terras, æterno igni contradens cruciandos quicunque ei aliquid ex his subtraxerint. Deinde hostes subegit: Scotiam usque Dunfoeder et Wertermorum terrestri exercitu vastavit, navali vero usque Catenes depopulatus est.[p]

DCCCCXXXVII.

Anno DCCCC.XXXVIJ Ethelstanus rex, apud Wendune[q] pugnavit, regemque Onlafum cum DC et XV navibus, Constantinum quoque regem Scottorum, et regem Cumbrorum, eum omni eorum multitudine in fugam vertit.

DCCCCXXXIX.

Anno DCCCC.XXXIX Æthelstanus rex obiit, cui frater suus Edmundus in regnum successit; quo anno rex Onlaf primo venit Eboracum, deinde ad austrum tendens, Hamtonam obsedit.

[m] S. C., anno 923. This year king Regwold won York.

[n] Saxon Chronicle.

[o] This year Ædwin the etheling was drowned at sea, S. C.

[p] This year king Ethelstan went into Scotland as well with a land army as a fleet, and ravaged a great part of it, S. C. See also *Historia de Sancto Cuthberto.*

[q] "Weondune, quod alio nomine Ætbrunnanwere vel Brunnanbyrig appellatur" (Symeon, *Hist. Eccles. Dunelm.*, lib. ii., c. 18).

Sed nihil ibi proficiens, vertit exercitum ad Tameweorde, et, vastatis omnibus per circuitum, dum rediens ad Legraceastre perveniret, occurrit ei rex Edmundus cum exercitu. Nec erat pugna difficilis, quoniam duo archiepiscopi Odo et Wlstan placatis alterutrum regibus pugnam sedaverant. Pace itaque facta, terminus utriusque regni erat Wetlinga-strete. Edmundus ad australem plagam, Onlaf ad aquilonalem regnum tenuerunt.[r]

DCCCCXLI.

Anno DCCCC.xlj Olilaf, vastata ecclesia Sancti Balteri et incensa Tiningaham, mox periit. Unde Eboracenses Lindisfarnensem insulam depopulati sunt, et multos occiderunt. Filius vero Sihtrici, nomine Onlaf, regnavit super Northanhymbros.[s]

DCCCCXLIII.

Anno DCCCC.xliij Northumbri regem suum Onlaf de regno expulerunt.[s]

DCCCCXLV.

Anno DCCCC.xlv Edmundus rex, expulsis duobus regibus, regnum optinuit Northanhymbrorum.[t]

DCCCCXLVIII.

Anno DCCCC.xlviij Edmundus rex occisus est et frater ejus Edredus regnum suscepit, cultor justitiæ et pietatis. Moxque Northumbriam circuiens totam possedit,[u] sed post juratam ei fidelitatem Northymbrenses quendam Danum, Eiricum, præfaciunt regem.

DCCCCL.

Anno DCCCC.l Eadredus rex, vastata Northymbria, cum jam rediret, Northymbrenses erumpentes extremos exercitus regis peremerunt. Statuit rex reducto exercitu provinciam penitus delere,[v] sed indigenæ, abjecto quem constituerant rege, Eadredum citius muneribus placarunt.[w]

DCCCCLI.

Anno DCCCC.lj Owel, rex Brittonum, obiit.[x]

[r] Many particulars are here related which are not in the Saxon Chronicle. The latter authority places the death of Athelstan A.D. 940, and the siege of Tamworth by Anlaf A.D. 943.

These particulars are not from the Saxon Chronicle.

[t] Saxon Chronicle, A.D. 944.

[u] S. C., A.D. 946.

[v] This word is interlined.

[w] S. C., A.D. 948.

[x] Higuel rex Brittonum obiit. A.D. 950. *Annales Cambriæ*—A.D. 948, *Chronicle of the Princes of Wales. Monumenta Historica*, pp. 837, 847.

DCCCCLII.

Anno DCCCC.lij defecerunt hic reges Northanhymbrorum; et deinceps ipsa provincia administrata est per comites.

DCCCCLIII.

Anno DCCCC.liij comes Osulf suscepit comitatum Northanhymbrorum.

DCCCCLV.

Anno DCCCC.lv, Eadredo rege defuncto, successit Eadwinus filius Edmundi qui ante eum regnavit.[y]

DCCCCLVI.

Anno DCCCC.lvj beatus Dunstanus abbas ab Eadwino expellitur.[z]

DCCCCLVII.

Anno DCCCC.lvij, mortuo Eadwino, frater ejus Eadgarus successit in regnum, qui magnæ devotionis extitit erga Dei cultum, ideoque in pace et honore servientibus sibi octo regibus regnum tenuit xvij annis. Post quem filius ejus Eadwardus regnavit, qui, dolo novercæ suæ interfectus, Scestoniæ requiescit. Cui successit frater suus Ethelredus, pater Eadwardi regis, quem susceperat ex Emma.

[y] Saxon Chronicle.

[z] Saxon Chronicle.

SEQUITUR RECAPITULATIO SUPERIORUM DE REGE ELFREDO.

DEINDE SUCCESSIO REGUM PER ORDINEM, QUI ET QUALITER AD REGNUM PERVENERUNT ANGLORUM.[a]

DCCCXLVIII.

"Anno[b] ab incarnatione Domini DCCC.xlviij Anglo-Saxonum "rex, Elfredus, in illa plaga quæ nominatur Barrocscire nas-"citur."[c]

DCCCLIV.

Anno DCCC.liiij, nativitatis regis Elfredi vj, Wlfere, regnante rege Osberto super Northimbros, suscepto pallio, confirmatus est in archiepiscopatum Eboracensem; et Eardulfus suscepit episcopatum Lindisfarnensem, quo pertinebant Lugubalia, id est Luel (nunc dicitur Carleil), et Northam,[d] quæ

[a] The words, "de Historia Willelmi Malmesbiriæ," are here added in red ink in the MS., but do not apply to the "Recapitulatio," or the "Successio Regum," which are derived mainly from Florence of Worcester, and in no part from the Historia of Malmesbury, but to certain extracts from the latter, which have been interpolated in a hand somewhat more recent than the text. These extracts have been omitted, but may be consulted in the original by the aid of the following references to the edition of William of Malmesbury, published by the English Historical Society under the editorship of Mr. Duffus Hardy:—

I. Vision of King Edgar, book ii., sections 154, 155; vol. i., pp. 248-251.
II. Vision of Bishop Brihtwold, book ii., section 221; vol. i., pp. 374-375.
III. Prodigy significant of the union of England and Normandy, book ii., sect. 207; vol. i., p. 358.
IV. Vision of Edward the Confessor, book ii., section 226; vol. i., pp. 380-381.

[b] The initial A is an illuminated letter in green and gold in the MS.

[c] Here follows a genealogy similar to that at pp. 42-3, taken from Florence of Worcester. For reasons assigned in the Preface, it has not been considered necessary to reprint any portion of the "Recapitulatio," which is copied either from Asser, as paraphrased in the former part of the present work, or from Florence of Worcester, or any portion of the "Successio Regum," which is derived from Florence, except in cases where it is intermixed with additions from other sources, which would not be intelligible without it. Such extracts from Asser and Florence are distinguished by inverted commas.

[d] Norham.

antiquitus Ubbanford dicebatur. Omnes quoque ecclesiæ ab aqua quæ vocatur Tweda usque Tinam Australem, et ultra desertum ad occidentem, pertinebant illo tempore ad præfatam ecclesiam; et hæ mansiones Carnham[e] et Culterham,[f] et duæ Geddewrd[g] ad australem plagam Tevietæ, quas Ecgredus episcopus condidit: et Mailros, et Tigbrethingham[h] et Eoriercorn[i] ad occidentalem partem, Edwinesburch[j] et Pefferham, et Aldham, et Tinningaham,[k] et Coldingaham,[l] et Tillemuthe,[m] et Northam supradictam. Werthewurd[n] quoque ipsius ecclesiæ possessio erat, donante rege Ceolwlfo, cum omnibus appenditiis suis. Hanc enim mansionem ipse rex, abrenuntians mundo, secum ecclesiæ Lindisfarnensi contulit, in qua monachus effectus cælesti regno militavit. Cujus corpus postea delatum in ecclesiam supradictæ villæ Northam multis ibidem, ut fertur ab habitatoribus ipsius loci, claruit miraculis. Hoc rege, jam monacho facto, efficiente, data est Lindisfarnensis ecclesiæ monachis licentia bibendi vinum vel cerevisiam: ante illud tempus non nisi lac vel aquam bibere solebant, secundum antiquam traditionem Sancti Aidani, primi ejusdem ecclesiæ antistitis et monachi, qui cum illo de Scotia venientes, ibidem, donante rege Oswaldo, mansionem acceperant, et cum magna districtione futuræ vitæ servientes degere gaudebant. Præterea memoratus Ecgredus episcopus, ædificans ecclesiam in loco qui dicitur Geinforde, donavit eam Sancto Cuthberto. Condidit etiam Billingeham in Heorternysse[o] et duas alias villas, Ileclife et Wilegeclife,[p] ad australem plagam fluminis Taise, quas Sancto Cuthberto ad victum sibi servientium dedit: similiter et Wudecestre, et Hwitingeham, et Eadulfingaham, Egwiluingeham,[q] donante rege Ceolwlfo, antiquitus S. Cuthberti fuerunt.[r]

[e] Carham on the Tweed.

[f] Holm-Cultram in Cumberland. [g] Jedworth, or Jedburgh.

[h] Query, Tigbrechingham, from the error of the transcriber, of constant occurrence, in mistaking *c* for *t*, as below Werthewurd has been written for Werchewurd. Tig-Breich would signify a habitation on the Breich, a small river which for some distance separates the counties of Linlithgow and Edinburgh, in which the two places mentioned immediately afterwards are situated.

[i] Abercorn. [j] Edinburgh.

[k] Tynningham and Aldham are in the consolidated parish of Whitekirk and Tynningham, in East Lothian. There is no modern village of Pefferham, but the locality is sufficiently indicated by the course of the Peffer rivulet, which runs through the parish. [l] Coldingham in Berwickshire.

[m] Tillmouth, at the confluence of the rivers Till and Tweed, between Norham and Berwick. [n] Warkworth in Northumberland.

[o] Billingham in Hartness, a district of the county of Durham, of which Hartlepool is the capital. [p] Cliffe and Wycliffe.

[q] Woodhorn, Whittingham, Edlingham, and Eglingham are villages and parishes in Northumberland.

[r] This list of the possessions of the church of St. Cuthbert enumerates several which are not mentioned as such, either in Symeon's History of the Church of

DCCCLXVI.

"Anno DCCC.lxvj Ethelred, regis Ethelberti frater, Occiden-"talium Saxonum regni gubernacula suscepit. Eodem anno "magna Paganorum classis," ducibus rege Haldano, Inguar et Hubba[s] "de Danubia Britanniam advenit, et in regno Occi-"dentalium Saxonum—hiemavit."

DCCCLXVII.

"Anno DCCC.lxvij prædictus Paganorum exercitus de Orien-"talibus Anglis ad Eboracam civitatem migravit, quæ in aqui-"loni ripa Humbræ fluminis sita est," omniaque vastaverunt usque Tinemutham.[t] "Eo tempore maxima inter Northumbros "discordia diabolico instinctu orta fuerat, *etc.* Nam Northumbri "eo tempore legitimum regem suum, Osbryth nomine, regno "expulerant, et tyrannum quendam, Ella nomine, non de regali "prosapia progenitum, super regni apicem constituerant. Sed "advenientibus Paganis, consilio Divino et optimatum admini-

Durham, or in the ancient Historia de Sancto Cuthberto. Carham is mentioned in the Historia as the gift of king Ecgfrid. Symeon does not specify it by name, but after mentioning Carlisle, and other endowments not here recorded, he says, "Grants of other lands were also made which it would be tedious and unnecessary to detail," and refers to the charters of the church (book i., c. ix.). Holm-Cultram is not mentioned by either authority, but it may be remarked that the churches both at this place and at Carham are dedicated to St. Cuthbert.

Abercorn, Tigbrechingham, and Edinburgh were probably the ancient possessions of the Abbey of "Abercurnig," noticed by Beda, but whether that establishment was a dependency of Lindisfarne, or whether its possessions were transferred on its extinction to the church of St. Cuthbert, does not appear.

Pefferham, Tynningham, and Aldham were included in the original grant of lands to the see of Lindisfarne, one section of which comprised the whole county of East Lothian from Lammermoor to the mouth of the Esk, near Musselburgh, within a few miles of Edinburgh. All this, says the Historia, belonged to the monastery of St. Balther at Tynningham.

Coldingham is mentioned at a very early period both by Beda and Symeon as the seat of a religious establishment presided over by Ebba, the sister of king Oswald, but there is no reason to suppose that it was originally dependent on Lindisfarne (Hist. Eccl., iv., 19; iv., 25. Hist. Dunelm., ii., 7).

[s] Halfdene, Inguar, and Ubba occur as the Danish leaders at a later period, but are not named so early by any other historian. The two latter are mentioned in the Saxon Chronicle as the chiefs of the party who slew Edmund, king of East Anglia, in 870, and Bagsecg and Halfdene are described as "the heathen kings" the following year, in which Bagsecg was slain with several earls. At that period the three brothers mentioned above appear to have directed all the proceedings of the invaders. The mistake seems to have originated in attributing to this particular year a list of Danish chieftains in the History of the Church of Durham (book ii., cap. vi.), which refers to the whole expedition, and not to the year 876 only, at the head of which these names are found, introduced by the words, "His temporibus."

[t] See History of the Church of Durham, book ii., c. vi., where we are told that the barbarians did not on this occasion proceed farther than the mouth of the Tyne, from whence they returned to York.

"culo, pro communi utilitate discordia illa aliquantulum sedata "est. Osbryth et Ella adunatis viribus congregatoque exer- "citu Eboracum oppidum adeunt. Quibus advenientibus, Pa- "gani fugam arripiunt, et intra urbis mænia se defendere pro- "curant. Quorum fugam et pavorem Christiani cernentes, intra "urbis mænia eos persequi, et murum frangere instituunt. "Quod et fecerunt. Non enim tunc adhuc illa civitas firmos "et stabilitos muros illis temporibus habebat. Cumque Chris- "tiani murum, ut proposuerant, fregissent, eorumque magna "pars in civitatem simul cum Paganis intrassent, Pagani, do- "lore et necessitate compulsi, super eos atrociter irrumpunt, "cædunt, fugant, prosternunt intus et extra." Hoc factum est xij kal. Aprilis,[u] feria vj ante Dominicam Palmarum.[v] "Illic "maxima ex parte omnes Northumbrensium cæsi, occisis duobus "regibus, deleti occubuerunt: reliqui vero qui evaserunt pacem "cum Paganis pepigerunt." Quibus peractis, prædicti Pagani sub suo dominio regem Egbertum præfecerunt. Egbertus vero regnavit post hæc super Northumbros ultra Tine sex annis.[w]

DCCCLXX.

"Anno DCCC.lxx—sanctissimus Orientalium-Anglorum rex, "Eadmundus," ut in sua legitur Passione, "ab Inguaro rege "paganissimo, indictione ij, xij kal. Decembris, die Dominico, "martyrizatus est." Cum quo et Humbertus episcopus occiditur.[x]

DCCCLXXII.

Anno DCCC.lxxij—Northumbri suum regem Egbertum et suum archiepiscopum Wlfere expulerunt.[y]

DCCCLXXIII.

"Anno DCCC.lxxiij sæpe-memoratus exercitus Lundoniam "deserens, in Northanhymbrorum regione porrexit, et ibi hie- "mavit in pago, quæ dicitur Lindesig," apud Torchasiam:[z] "cum quo iterum Mercii pacem pepigerunt."

[u] This date is from the History of the Church of Durham, ii., 6.

[v] In sancto die Palmarum (Hist. de S. Cuthberto).

[w] Hist. Dunelm., ii., 6.

[x] The narrative within inverted commas is from Florence. The reference to the Passion, by which is meant the Legend of the Passion of St. Edmund by Abbo, is not in Florence. The statement of the death of Bishop Humbert is from the History of the Church of Durham, ii., 6.

[y] Hist. Dunelm., ii., 6.

[z] The Saxon Chronicle says the Danish winter quarters were at Torksea in Lindsea. Asser and Florence mention Lindsea only, and the Chronicle of St. Neot's, which generally repeats Asser, has Torksea only. The first part of this work omits both, whilst Huntingdon has the words as they stand in our text.

Egbertus rex Northanhymbrorum moriens, successorem habuit Ricsig, qui regnavit tribus annis; et Wlfere in suum archiepiscopatum receptus est.[a]

DCCCLXXV.

"Anno DCCC.lxxv supra-memoratus exercitus, Reopedune de-"serens, in duas se divisit turmas. Cujus altera pars cum "Halfdene in regione Northanhymbrorum porrexit, et totam "Northymbrorum regionem suo dominio subdidit," ac omnia monasteria destruxit.[b] Eardulfus, episcopus Lindisfarnensis, et abbas Eadredus corpus Sancti Cuthberti de insula Lindisfarnensi tollentes, per septem annos passim vagabantur.

DCCCLXXVI.

Anno DCCC.lxxvj—rex Ricsig Northanhymbrorum moritur et secundus Egbertus regnat super Northumbros ultra amnem Tyne.[c] Rollo, primus Normannorum dux, qui et Rodbertus, cum suis Normanniam penetravit xv kal. Decembris.[d]

DCCCLXXVII.

"Anno DCCC.lxxvij—Elfredus vero rex his diebus magnas "sustinuit tribulationes et inquietam vitam agebat." Tandem, apto confortatus oraculo per Sanctum Cuthbertum, contra Danos pugnavit, et quo ipse Sanctus jusserat tempore et loco victoria potitus est, semperque deinceps hostibus terribilis et invincibilis erat, Sanctumque Cuthbertum præcipue honori habebat. Qualiter hostes vicerit paulo post hic legitur.[e]

"Eodem denique anno" Ingwar et Halfdene reges, "cum

[a] Symeon's History of the Archbishops of York. From the History of the Church of Durham it would appear that Ricsig was raised to the throne on the expulsion of Egbert. This computation fixes the commencement of his reign a year later.

[b] These four words are an insertion in the MS. Respecting the destruction of the monasteries, and the wanderings of Eardulf and Eadred with the body of the Saint, see History of the Church of Durham, ii., 10.

[c] There is no mention of this second Egbert either in the History of the Church of Durham or of the Archbishops of York. His name occurs, with those of his two predecessors, in the brief chronicle prefixed to the Cambridge MS. of the History of the Church of Durham, but the length of the several reigns does not correspond in the two authorities. See note below under A.D. 883.

[d] This is the first of a series of entries respecting the dukes of Normandy, which have been taken from some source resembling, but not quite identical with, the Chronicle of Caen. In the margin of the MS. are these words, *De Rollone primo Normannorum duce. Hic genere Dacus, postea baptizatur, Rodbertus vocatus est.*

[e] Respecting St. Cuthbert's appearance to King Alfred, see History of the Church of Durham, ii., 10. The original authority for this legend is the Historia de Sancto Cuthberto.

"bis denis ac ternis navibus de Demetica regione, in qua hie-"maverant, egressi, ut lupi feroces, post multas tibi strages "Christianorum patratas, post combustiones cœnobiorum, ad "Domnaniam enavigaverunt, et ibi a ministris regis Elfredi "fortissimis cum mille ducentis viris occisi sunt ante arcem "Cymwth."[f]

Rex Elfredus—venit ad petram Ecgberti, quæ est in orientali parte saltus qui Anglico eloquio dicitur Mucel-Wudu,[g] Latine vero Magna Silva, Britannico more Coitmawr.

DCCCLXXVIII.

"Anno DCCC.lxxviij Paganorum rex Guthrum, cum xxx "electissimis de exercitu suo viris, ad Elfredum regem in loco "qui dicitur Aarl pervenit, quem rex in filium adoptionis sus-"cipiens, de fonte sacri baptismatis elimavit," multisque muneribus ditavit, eique post interfectionem Sancti Eadmundi East-Angliam tradidit.[h]

DCCCLXXXI.

"Anno DCCC.lxxxj Paganorum exercitus, invadens Franciam, "bellum iniit cum indigenis." His diebus plurima in eadem gente monasteria concussa sunt et desolata. Nam et fratres cœnobii sanctissimi Benedicti, quod Floriacum dicitur, ipsius reliquias a tumulo, quo locata fuerant immensa pulchritudine, secum auferentes hac illacque discurrebant.[i]

DCCCLXXXIII.

Anno DCCC.lxxxiij præfatus Paganorum exercitus, occupans Cundoth,[j] ibidem per annum grassatur. Exercitus vero qui, ducente rege Halfdene, Northumbriam invaserat, pereunte Dei

[f] Asser, from whom this paragraph is taken, has, "Frater Hinguari et Halfdene," in which he is followed by Florence. Ubba, the brother of Inguar and Halfdene, was the person who lost his life on this occasion. The two others reappear A.D. 883.

[g] Selwood Forest. This reading is peculiar to this work. Asser has Seludu. Mucel-wudu is, however, the true equivalent for Magna Silva (Mickle Wood). The name occurs twice, and is written on one occasion Mucel-Pudu, on the other still more corruptly, Mucel-Purlu. From the same confusion between the Anglo-Saxon *P* and *W*, Coitmawr is on both occasions written Coitmapur.

[h] The last ten words are neither in Asser, Florence, nor the first part of the Historia Regum. The death of St. Edmund, which is here referred to as if it occurred subsequent to the baptism of Guthrum, really took place, and has already been recorded in these pages, seven years previously.

[i] This account of the destruction of the French monasteries, and the removal of the relics of St. Benedict, is not derived from Asser or Florence, but is found in the first part of this work, with the exception of the words, "quod Floriacum dicitur," which do not occur there. The notice of the wanderings of the relics of a saint would have a peculiar charm to the monks of Durham.

[j] Candath—*Florence;* Cundath—*Saxon Chronicle;* Cundoht—*Asser.*

judicio ipso tyranno, sine duce remanserat, occiso, sicut supradictum est, ipso Halfdene et Inguar cum xxiij navibus apud Domnaniam a ministris Elfredi regis.[k] Jam subactis sibi indigenis terræ, dominium usurpavit, ibique manere paravit, et vastatas Northumbriæ provincias incolere. Tunc Sanctus Cuthbertus abbati Eadredo (qui pro eo quod in Luel habitavit Lulisc cognominabatur) assistens, per visionem præcepit, ut episcopo et omni exercitui Anglorum atque Danorum diceret, quatinus Guthredum filium Hardecnut, quem Dani vendiderant in servum cuidam viduæ apud Hwitinghaham, dato pretio, redimerent; et redemptum sibi in regem levarent; regnavitque super Eboracum; Egbert vero super Northimbros.[l] Quod factum est tredecimo anno regni Ælfredi regis. Guthredo[m] itaque ex servo omnium consensu in regem promoto, sedes episcopalis, quæ prius erat in Lindisfarnensi insula, instauratur in Cestre, quæ antiquitus vocabatur Cunecestre, post septem annos transmigrationis ex insula Lindisfarnensi. Est autem locus ille inter Dunelmum et Extoldesam, sex millibus passuum distans a Dunelmo. Tunc et legem pacis, quam ipse Sanctus Cuthbertus per prædictum abbatem mandaverat, ut scilicet quicunque ad corpus illius confugerit, pacem a nullo infringendam per xxxvij dies habeat, tam rex Guthredus quam rex Alfredus perpetuo conservandam confirmarunt. Quam si quisquam quoquo modo violaverit, sicut pacem regis fractam, nonaginta sex libris multandum censuerunt. Ad hoc, in augmentum prioris episcopatus, totam inter Tyne et Teisam præfati duo reges omni consensu Sancto Cuthberto terram perpetuo possidendam addiderunt. Quicunque autem hæc statuta quocumque ingenio infringere temptaverit, hunc infernalibus pœnis tradendum perpetuo anathemate dampnarunt. Jam enim multo ante defecerat episcopatus Hagustaldensis ecclesiæ.

[k] This refers to the erroneous account of the deaths of Inguar and Halfdene given above, A.D. 877. See note under that year. Symeon, in his History of the Church of Durham, gives an account of the death of Halfdene, the particulars of which are derived from the Historia de Sancto Cuthberto, and fixes the date immediately previous to the elevation of Guthred to the throne, instead of interposing an interregnum of five years, as in Asser.

[l] If Egbert II. still lived, he must have been in the seventh or eighth year of his reign, whereas the Chronica Anglorum prefixed to the History of the Church of Durham assigns him a reign of only two years.

[m] *Guthredus ex servo factus est rex. His temporibus sedes episcopalis Lindisfarnensis insulæ usque ad Cunecestriam transmutata est.* In the margin. The same words are interpolated into part i., but without any particulars. The details in this section are taken from the History of the Church of Durham, ii., 13, the original source being the Historia de Sancto Cuthberto.

DCCCLXXXIV.

"Anno DCCC.lxxxiiij, Marinus papa scolam Saxonum in "Roma morantium pro amore et deprecatione Elfredi regis ab "omni tributo et telone(o) liberavit benigne; qui etiam multa "dona prædicto regi transmisit. Inter quæ dedit ei non par- "vam illius sanctæ crucis partem in qua Dominus noster Jhesus "Christus pro hominum salute pependit. Eadem tempestate "idem præsul sanctissimus viam universitatis adiit, transmit- "tendo spiritum ad Deum Qui dedit illum. Prædictus Paga- "norum exercitus, per flumen Suune adiens Embenum, ibi per "annum grassatur."[n]

Hujus regis Alfredi tempore venit Angliam Johannes Scottus, vir perspicacis ingenii et multæ facundiæ, qui dudum relicta patria Franciam ad Karolum Calvum transierat. A quo magna dignatione susceptus, familiarium partium habebatur; transigebatque cum eo tam seria quam joca, individuusque comes et mensæ, et cubiculi. Erat multæ facetiæ ingenuique leporis, quorum exempla hodieque constant, ut sunt ista. Assederat ad mensam contra regem ad aliam mensæ partem. Procedentibus poculis consumptisque ferculis, Karolus, fronte hilarior, post quædam alia, cum vidisset Johannem quiddam fecisse quod Gallicanam comitatem offenderet, urbane increpuit et dixit, "Quid distat inter Sottum et Scottum?" Retulit ille solempne convitium in auctorem, et respondit, "Hæc mensa tantum." Quid hoc dicto facetius? Interrogaverat rex de differenti morum studio, respondit Johannes de loci distante spatio. Nec vero rex commotus est, quia, miraculo scientiæ ipsius captus, adversus magistrum nec dicto insurgere vellet, sic enim eum usitate vocabat. Item cum regi convivanti minister patinam obtulisset, quæ duos pisces prægrandes adjecto uno minusculo contineret, dedit ille magistro, ut accumbentibus duobus juxta se clericis departiretur. Erant illi giganteæ molis, ipse perexilis corporis. Tum qui semper aliquid honesti comminiscebatur, ut lætitiam convivantium excitaret, retentis sibi duobus majoribus, unam minorem duobus distribuit. Arguenti iniquitatem partitionis regi, "Immo," inquit, "bene feci et æque. Nam hic est unus parvus," de se dicens, "et duo grandes," pisces tangens. Itemque ad eos conversus, "Hic sunt duo magni," clericos innuens, "et unus exiguus," piscem nihilominus tangens. Caroli ergo rogatu Ierarchiam Dionysii Areopagitæ in Latinum de Græco, verbum e verbo transtulit. Quo fit ut vix intelligatur Latina litera, quæ volubilitate magis Græca quam

[n] To this point is from Florence. The long narrative which follows respecting Johannes Scotus is from the Life of Aldhelm by William of Malmesbury.

positione construitur nostra. Composuit etiam librum, quem Peri Physion Merimnoi,[o] id est, de Naturæ Divisione, titulavit, propter perplexitatem quarundam quæstionum solvendam bene utilem, si tamen ignoscatur ei in quibusdam, quibus a Latinorum tramite deviavit, dum in Græcos acriter oculos intendit. Quare et hæreticus putatus est, scripsitque contra eum quidam Florus.[p] Sunt enim revera in libro Peri Physion perplurima quæ, nisi diligenter discutiantur, a fide Catholicorum abhorrentia videantur. Hujus opinionis particeps fuisse cognoscitur Nicholaus papa, qui ait in epistola ad Karolum.

Relatum est Apostolatui nostro, quod opus beati Dionysii Areopagitæ, quod de divinis nominibus, vel cælestibus ordinibus Græco descripsit eloquio, quidam vester Johannes, genere Scottus, nuper in Latinum transtulerit. Quod juxta morem nobis mitti, et nostro judicio debuit approbari; præsertim cum idem Johannes, licet multæ scientiæ esse prædicetur, olim non sane sapere in quibusdam frequenti rumore dicatur. Propter hanc ergo infamiam tæduit eum Franciæ, venitque ad regem Elfredum. Cujus munificentia illectus et magisterio ejus, ut ex scriptis regis intelligitur, Melduni[q] resedit. Ubi post aliquot annos, a pueris quos docebat graphiis foratus animam exuit, tormento gravi et acerbo, ut dum iniquitas valida et manus infirma sæpe frustraretur et sæpe impeteret, amaram mortem obiret. Jacuit aliquamdiu inhonora sepultura in beati Laurentii ecclesia, quæ fuerat nefandæ necis[r] conscia. Sed ubi Divinus favor multis noctibus super eum lucem indulsit igneam, ammoniti monachi in majorem transtulerunt ecclesiam, et ad sinistram altaris posuerunt.

DCCCLXXXVIII.

"Anno DCCC.lxxxvij duo monasteria construit nobilia, unum monachorum in loco qui dicitur Ethelingaige," id est Nobilium Insula.

DCCCXCII.

Anno DCCC.xcij Wlfere archiepiscopus Eboracensis obiit, anno sui archiepiscopatus xxxix.[s]

[o] Περὶ φυσίων μέριμνοι, or Libri Quinque de Naturis, printed at Oxford in 1681. See Oudinus, ii., 235.

[p] This is Florus of Lyons, a writer of some repute. There is much about him and his works in Oudinus, and in a book of a writer of much greater merit, the Vetera Analecta of Mabillon.

[q] *Scilicet Melmesbiria* interlined.

[r] *Cædis* interlined.

[s] This is also in the first part. Asser's history closes A.D. 887, and henceforth the Historia Regum is founded on Florence of Worcester. Every notice, which is either original, or derived from any other authority, will be found extracted.

DCCCXCIV.

Anno DCCC.xciiij Guthred, rex Northymbrorum, obiit. Pagani qui Northymbriam incoluere cum Ælfredo rege pacem juramentis stabiliere.[t]

DCCCXCVIII.

Anno DCCC.xcviij Rollo, primus Normannorum dux, cum exercitu suo Carnotensem civitatem obsedit. Sed episcopus ejusdem urbis, Waltelinus, Ricardum Burgundiæ ducem, et Ebalum, Pictavensem comitem, in suum advocans auxilium, tunicam Sanctæ Mariæ in manibus ferens, Rollonem ducem Divino nutu fugavit, et civitatem liberavit. Æthelbald archiepiscopus Eboracensis ordinatus.[u]

DCCCXCIX.

Anno DCCC.xcix Ærdulfus, episcopus Lindisfarnensis, obiit, cui Cuthdred successit. Pulsus est etiam Osbrit a regno.[v]

DCCCC.

Anno Domini DCCCC Ethelbald archiepiscopus Eboracensis ordinatur.[w]

DCCCCVI.

Anno DCCCC.vj Rollo, qui et Robertus, primus dux Normannorum, decessit. Cui Willelmus, filius ejus, Longa-spata successit.

DCCCCXIII.

Anno DCCCC.xiij Tilredus episcopatum suscepit.[x]

DCCCCXX.

Anno DCCCC.xx Rex Northanhymbrorum Sihtricus occidit Niellum fratrem suum et infregit Devenport.[y]

DCCCCXXV.

Anno DCCCC.xxv Wigred episcopus Lindisfarnensis consecratur.

[t] The death of Guthred is recorded in the first part; also in the History of the Church of Durham, where Symeon adds that after his decease Alfred added the province of the East Angles and also of the Northumbrians to his paternal kingdom of the West Saxons.

[u] This is an error. See note below under A.D. 900.

[v] The expulsion of Osbrit is also recorded in the first part, A.D. 901.

[w] The ordination of Ethelbald is stated above to have taken place A.D. 898, but the correct date is A.D. 900. See Symeon's History of the Archbishops of York.

[x] Of Lindisfarne. This notice is inserted in the MS. at the foot of the page.

[y] The death of Niel is assigned in the first part to A.D. 914, and the storming of Devonport to 920. See note to first part, A.D. 914.

DCCCCXXXIII.

Anno DCCCC.xxxiij rex Æthelstanus jussit fratrem suum Ædwinum in mare submergi.[z]

DCCCCXXXIV.

"Anno DCCCC.xxxiiij strenuus rex Anglorum Æthelstanus, "quia rex Scottorum Constantinus fœdus, quod cum eo pe-"pigerat, disrupit, classica manu pervalida et equestri exercitu "non modico, ad Scotiam proficiscitur." Qui prius sepulchrum Sancti Cuthberti adiens, eumque terrarum et aliarum rerum regali donatione honorans, Scotiam usque Dunfoeder et Wertermorum terrestri exercitu vastavit, navali vero usque Cathenes maxima ex parte depopulatur.[a] *

DCCCCXLI.

Anno DCCCC.xlj Ricardus vetus suscepit comitatum Normanniæ et tenuit lij annis. Fuit ipse filius Willelmi comitis, cujus frater fuit Rollo primus Normannorum dux. Wigredus episcopus obiit, et Uctredus successit.[b]

DCCCCXLVIII.

Anno DCCCC.xlix Aldredus, qui post Uchtredum fuit episcopus, obiit, et Ailsi ei successit.[c]

DCCCCXLIX.

Anno DCCCC.xlix Wlstanus, Eboracensis archiepiscopus, proceresque Northymbrenses omnes in villa quæ dicitur Taddenesscylf egregio regi Anglorum Edredo fidelitatem juraverunt.[d]

DCCCCLI.

Anno DCCCC.lj Owel, rex Brittonum, obiit.[e]

[z] From the first part. See note under this year (933).

[a] See the Historia de Sancto Cuthberto, and the History of the Church of Durham. The details of Athelstane's expedition, his visit to Durham, and his gifts to St. Cuthbert, are also recorded in the first part of the Historia Regum.

[b] This sentence is an insertion in an old hand.

[c] This sentence occurs at the foot of the page in an old hand.

[d] The following curious note occurs in the margin of the MS. :—*Taddenes-scylf erat tunc villa regia quæ nunc vocatur Puntfrait Romane, Anglice vero Kirkebi.* It seems probable, however, that Taddenes-scylf is Tadcaster, and not Pontefract.

[e] From the first part.

SYMEONIS DUNELMENSIS

HISTORIÆ CONTINUATIO.[f]

DCCCCLXVIII.

Anno DCCCC.lxviij Aldredus episcopus apud Sanctum Cuthbertum in Cuneacestre vita decessit; cui Elfsius in episcopatum successit.

DCCCCXCIV.

Anno DCCCC.xciiij Ricardus Primus, dux Normannorum, obiit, cujus filius Ricardus uno anno successit. Post quem frater ejusdem Rodbertus.

DCCCCXCV.

Anno DCCCC.xcv Aldunus episcopus transtulit de Cestre in Dunholm corpus Sancti Cuthberti.

M.

"Anno ab incarnatione Domini millesimo Danorum classis "præfata hoc anno Normanniam petit," *etc.*, et sequenti anno, ad Angliam reversa, pejora prioribus egit.

MII.

"Anno M.ij Emmam, Saxonice Elfgivam vocatam, ducis Nor-"mannorum Primi Ricardi filiam, rex Egelredus duxit uxorem" de qua idem rex Eadwardum regem, necnon Alfredum, Godwini comitis longo post tempore dolis interemptum, procreavit.

MXIII.

"Anno M.xiij rex Egelredus reginam Emmam," cum thesauris, "Normanniam ad suum fratrem, Secundum Ricardum

[f] With the year 957 the *Recapitulatio* ends, and we take up the History where it ended in the first part. The writer, however, merely copies Florence till he reaches the year 968. The rule that was laid down in the note to p. 67 is still adhered to.

"Normannorum comitem, et filios suos Eadwardum et Ælfredum "cum magistro illorum Ælfhuno Londinensi episcopo, et Al- "sium Medeshamstudensem[g] abbatem naviter misit. Ipse vero "cum Danica classe, quæ in Tamensi (flumine) jacebat in loco "qui Grenewic nominatur, aliquantisper mansit; et post, ad "insulam Vectam devectus, nativitatem Domini in illa cele- "bravit. Qua peracta, Normanniam devehitur, et a Ricardo "comite honorifice suscipitur," cum quo Rothomagi omne in- colatus sui exegit tempus cum magnis opum apparatibus.

MXIV.

"Anno M.xiiij Suanus tyrannus,—magno cruciatus tormento, "iij non. Februarii miserabili morte vitam finivit," et apud Eboracum sepultus est.[h]

MXVII.

"Anno M.xvij rex Canutus totius Angliæ suscepit impe- "rium" et xix annis potenter tenuit.—"Mense Julio rex Ca- "nutus derelictam regis Egelredi reginam Emmam in conjugium "recepit," ex qua genuit Ardecnutum regem, et filiam Gunildam, quæ nupsit Henrico Romanorum imperatori.

MXVIII.

Anno M.xviij Aldunus episcopus Dunholmensis obiit. Ingens bellum apud Carrum[i] gestum est inter Scottos et Anglos, inter Huctredum filium Waldef, comitem Northymbrorum, et Malcolmum filium Cyneth, regem Scottorum. Cum quo fuit Eugenius Calvus, rex Lutinensium.

[g] Sc. *Burh* interlined.

[h] The legendary account of the death of Suane by the spear of St. Edmund, the immunities of whose privileged territory he had ventured to violate, are copied at length from Florence. The words, *et apud Eboracum sepultus est*, are at the foot of the page.

[i] An account of this battle at Carham on the Tweed, and of the death of Aldwine, will be found in Symeon's History of the Church of Durham, book iii., c. v., but he does not there mention Uchtred as the leader of the Northumbrians, which is a palpable error. Florence of Worcester, in a passage which has been transferred to the text of the Historia Regum, narrates the death of Earl Uchtred two years before this date. He was succeeded by his brother, Eadulf Cudel, whose indolence and cowardice were as conspicuous as the opposite qualities in his predecessor. The cession of Lothian to Malcolm, which is imputed to him as the opprobrium of his government, was the natural consequence of this grievous defeat.

Eugenius, who is described as king of the Lutinenses, is no doubt the Welsh prince Owain, whose death occurs in the Welsh chronicles about this time, Eugenius being the Latin form used by the mediæval chroniclers, both of the Welsh Owen, and the Scottish Eogan.

MXXX.

"Anno M.xxx Sanctus Olavus, quem Canutus rex expu-"lerat," rex et martyr, Haroldi regis Norreganorum filius, in Norrega injuste "perimitur a Norreganis."

MXXXII.

"Anno M.xxxij ecclesia Sancti Eadmundi regis et martyris "hoc anno dedicata est," in qua rex Canutus monachos posuit, ejectis presbyteris. Ignis multis in locis per Angliam desævit. Ælfsige, Wintoniensis episcopus, obiit: Ælfwinus, presbyter regis, successit.

MXXXIV.

Anno M.xxxiiij Malcolm rex Scottorum obiit, cui Machethad successit.

MXLII.

Anno M.xlij—Eadmundus episcopus obiit, cui Edredus per pecuniam in episcopatum successit, et decimo mense moritur.

MXLIII.

Anno M.xliij, defuncto Eadmundo, Egelricus suscepit episcopatum Dunelmensem, Siwardo administrante comitatum Northanhymbrorum.

MLIII.

"Anno M.liij Godwinus comes vita decessit" xvij kal. Maii.

MLIV.

"Anno M.liiij in festivitate Sancti Kenelmi" mortuo Godwino Winchelcumbensi abbati, Aldredus Wigornensis "episcopus "Godricum," Godmanni regis capellani filium, "loco ejus ab-"batem constituit."

MLIX.

Anno M.lix Kinsi Eboracensis episcopus, et Egelwinus Dunelmensis episcopus, et Tosti comes Eboraci deduxerunt regem Malcolmum ad regem Eadwardum.[j]

MLXI.

"Anno M.lxj Aldredus Eboracensis archiepiscopus cum "Tostio comite Romam ivit, et a Nicholao papa pallium sus-"cepit." Interim rex Scottorum Malcolmus sui conjurati

[j] This sentence is added at the foot of the page in a coarse hand.

fratris, scilicet comitis Tostii, comitatum ferociter depopulatus est, violata pace Sancti Cuthberti in Lindisfarnensi insula.

MLXV.

Anno M.lxv—jussu regis Morcarus Northumbris est præelectus[k] comes.

MLXVI.

"Anno M.lxvj—Haroldus Harvager, rex Norreganorum, "pater sancti regis Olavi, in ostio Tinæ fluminis improvise "applicuit. Ad quem comes Tostius, ut prius condixerat, sua "cum classe venit, et citato cursu ostium Humbræ fluminis "intraverunt, et sic adversus cursum Usæ fluminis navigantes, "in loco qui Richale dicitur, applicuerunt" et Eboracum gravi pugna obtinuerunt. "Quod ubi regi Haroldo innotuit, versus "Northymbriam expeditionem propere movit. Sed priusquam "rex illuc veniret, duo germani comites, videlicet Edwinus "et Morkarus, cum ingenti exercitu, in vigilia S. Matthei apos- "toli, feria iiij, in boriali ripa Use fluminis, juxta Eboracum," apud Fulford, "cum Norreganis prœlium commisere, et in "primo belli impetu viriliter pugnantes multos prostraverunt. "At postquam diu certatum est, Angli Norreganorum impetum "non ferentes, haud sine parvo detrimento suorum terga dedere: "multoque plures ex illis in fluvio demersi fuere, quam in acie "cecidere. Norregani vero loco dominantur funeris, et, obsi- "dibus cl de Eboraca sumptis, ad naves repedarunt, relictis in "ea de suis cl[l] obsidibus," *etc.*

"Interea dum hæc agerentur, et rex omnes inimicos suos "autumaret detritos fuisse, nuntiatum est ei Willelmum," consobrinum regis Eadwardi, et "comitem gentis Normannicæ, cum "innumera multitudine equitum, fundibalariorum, sagittariorum "peditumque advenisse, utpote qui de tota Gallia sibi fortes "auxiliarios conduxerat, et in loco qui Pevenesea dicitur suam "classem appulisse."

Ut[m] autem sciatur origo causæ qua Willelmus Angliam bello appetiit, breviter quæ paulo ante gesta sunt repetantur. Orto inter regem Eadwardum et comitem Godwinum gravi, ut supra-dictum est, discidio, exul ab Anglia cum suis omnibus Comes expellitur. Cui postmodum gratiam regis requirenti ut ei repatriare liceret, nullo modo rex concordari voluit, nisi primo, quibus sibi securitas pararetur, obsides haberet. Qua de causa Wlnothus, filius ipsius Godwini, et Hacun, filius

[k] On the expulsion of Tosti from the earldom.

[l] The battle was at Water-Fulford, near York.

[m] This account of the conflicting claims of Harold and William is copied from Eadmer, Hist. Nov., pp. 4, 5; ed. Selden.

Suani, filii sui, obsides dantur, ac in Normanniam Willelmo Bastard, comiti, filio Rodberti filii Ricardi fratris matris suæ, custodiendi destinantur. Elapso dehinc tempore, cum jam Godwinus comes esset mortuus, Haroldus filius ejus petiit a rege ire Normanniam, et fratrem suum atque nepotem, qui obsides ibidem tenebantur, liberare, et liberatos secum patriam reducere. Cui rex, "Hoc," inquit, "non fiet per me, verum-"tamen ne videar te velle impedire, permitto ut eas quo vis, et "experiaris quid possis: præsentio tamen te in nihil aliud ten-"dere, nisi in detrimentum totius Anglici regni et opprobrium "tui. Nec enim ita novi Comitem mentis expertem ut eos "aliquatenus velit concedere tibi, si non præscierit in hoc "magnum proficuum sui." Ascendit itaque Haroldus navem, quæ tempestate valida ejecta cum omnibus quæ secum ferebat in Pontivum fluvium, qui Maia vocatur, a domino terræ illius pro ritu loci captivitati illius addicitur. Constrictus ergo Haroldus quemlibet ex vulgo promissa mercede illectum clam ad comitem Normanniæ dirigit exponere quid illi contigerit. Hoc ille audito, protinus festinato per nuntios mandat domino Pontivi, Haroldum cum suis ab omni calumnia liberum sibi quantoci(ti)us mitti, si pristina illius amicitia amodo, sicut hucusque, vellet potiri. Sed cum ille hominem dimittere nollet, iterum a Willelmo in mandato accepit se necessario Haroldum missurum, alioquin certissimum sciret, Willelmum Normanniæ comitem armatum pro eo abducendo cum suis usque novissimum quadrantem Pontivum quantoci(ti)us adi-turum. Talibus ille minis exterritus, mittit virum cum sociis, qui a Willelmo multum honorifice suscipitur, et audito cur patria exierit, bene quidem rem processuram si in ipso non remaneret Willelmus, respondit. Tenuit ergo virum aliquot diebus circa se, satisque humanum se ac familiarem illi exhi-buit, ut hujusmodi re animum ejus in suos conatus alliceret. Cui tandem aperuit quod in mente habuit. Dicebat itaque regem Eadwardum, quando secum juvene olim juvenis in Nor-mannia demoraretur, sibi interposita fide sua pollicitum fuisse, quia si rex Angliæ foret, jus regni in illum jure hæreditario post se transferret. Et subdens ait, "Tu quoque, si mihi te "in hoc ipso amminiculaturum spoponderis, et insuper cas-"tellum Dofris cum puteo aquæ ad opus meum te facturum, "sororemque tuam quam uni de principibus meis dem uxorem, "te ad me, tempore quo nobis conveniet, destinaturum, necne "filiam meam te in conjugem accepturum promiseris, tunc et "modo nepotem tuum, et cum in Angliam regnaturus venero, "fratrem tuum incolumem recipies. In quo regno, si tuo "favore fuero confirmatus, spondeo quia omnia quod a me "rationabiliter tibi petieris obtinebis." Sensit Haroldus periculum undique, nec intellexit qua evaderet nisi in omnibus voluntati Willelmi acquiesceret. Acquievit itaque. At ille, ut omnia rata forent, prolatis Sanctorum reliquiis, ad hæc Haroldum perduxit, quatinus super illas jurando testaretur, se cuncta quæ convenerant inter eos opere completurum. His ita gestis, Haroldus recepto nepote reversus est patriam. Ubi vero quid acciderit, quid egerit regi percunctanti narravit, "Nonne dixi tibi," ait, "me Willelmum nosse, et in illo "itinere tuo plurima mala huic regno contingere posse? Mag"nas in hoc tuo facto calamitates præsentio genti nostræ ven"turas, quas concedat mihi, quæso, pietas superna ne diebus "meis veniant." In brevi post hæc obiit rex Eadwardus, et juxta quod ipse ante mortem statuerat, in regnum ei successit Haroldus. Cui Willelmus mandavit, ut, quamvis violata fide cætera non servasset, si tamen filiam suam duceret uxorem leviter ferret, alioquin se promissam regni successionem armis sibi vindicaturum proculdubio sciret. At ipse, nec illud quidem facere se velle, nec hoc formidare, dixit. Unde Willelmus indignatus, magna spe vincendi ex hac Haroldi injustitia est animatus. Parata igitur classe non modica cum nongentis navibus[n] Angliam petit, consertoque gravi prælio, Haroldus in acie concidit, et Willelmus victor regnum optinuit. De quo prœlio testantur adhuc Franci qui interfuerunt, quoniam, licet varius casus hinc inde extiterit, tamen tanta strages ac fuga Normannorum fuit, ut victoria qua potiti sunt, vere et absque dubio Dei judicio sit ascribenda, Qui puniendo scelus perjurii ostendit Se non Deum volentem iniquitatem.[o]

MLXVII.

"Anno M.lxvij Wlsius Dorkecestrensis," qui et Lincolniensis, "episcopus decessit Wintoniæ, sed sepultus est Dork"estre."

MLXVIII.

Anno M.lxviij duo papæ in Roma facti sunt, id est episcopus Parmensis qui expulsus est, et episcopus de Luca, qui papa permansit.

MLXIX.

Anno M.lxix cœnobium Sancti Germani de Selebi sumpsit exordium.[p] Misit rex Willelmus Northymbris ad aquilonalem plagam Tine comitem Rodbertum, cognomento Cumin, tertio

[n] These three words are inserted at the foot of the page.

[o] Psalm v. 5.

[p] Added in an old hand at the foot of the page.

regni sui anno. At illi omnes in unam coacti sententiam, ne alienigenæ dominio subderentur, statuerunt, aut illum interficere, aut ipsi simul omnes in ore gladii cadere. Cui appropinquanti Dunelmensis episcopus Agelwinus occurrens, insidias sibi præcavere præmonuit; sed ille neminem hoc audere æstimans despexit ammonentem.[p] Dunelmum cum multa militum manu ingressus permisit suos hostiliter ubique agere, occisis etiam nonnullis ecclesiæ rusticis; susceptus est autem ab episcopo cum omni humanitate et honore. At Northymbri, tota nocte festinantes Dunelmum, summa vi diluculo per portas irrumpunt, et socios comitis imparatos ubique locorum interficiunt. Atrociter nimis res geritur, prostratis per domos et plateas militibus, domum episcopi, in qua comes fuerat susceptus, aggrediuntur pugnantes, sed, cum non ferrent jacula defendentium, domum cum inhabitantibus concremaverunt. Tanta fuit interfectorum multitudo, ut omnia pene urbis loca replerentur cruore. Nam de septingentis hominibus nemo præter unum evasit.[q] Hæc cædes facta est v kal. Februarii, feria iiij. "Quo anno, ante nativitatem Sanctæ Mariæ, Suani, "regis Danorum filii, Haroldus, Canutus, et patruus eorum "Osbernus comes," et episcopus eorum Christianus, "comesque "Turkillus cc et xl navibus de Danubia venientes, in ostio "Humbre fluminis applicuerunt. Ubi eis clito Eadgarus, "comes Waldevus, et Marlessvein, multique alii, cum classe "quam paraverant, occurrerunt." Affuit et Cospatricus comes cum totis viribus Northymbrorum,[r] unanimiter omnes contra Normannos congregati. De quorum omnium "adventu Eboracensis archiepiscopus Aldredus valde tristis effectus, in mag-"nam decidit infirmitatem,[s] et decimo anno sui archiepiscopatus, "iij idus Septembris, feria vj, ut Deum rogaverat, vitam finivit; "et in ecclesia Sancti Petri est sepultus. Octavo post hunc "die, scilicet xiij kal. Octobris, Sabbato, Normanni qui "castella custodiebant, timentes ne domus quæ prope cas-"tella erant, adjumenta Danis ad implendas fossas castellorum "essent, igne eas succendere cœperunt, Qui nimis excrescens "totam civitatem invasit, monasteriumque Sancti Petri cum "ipsa consumpit. Sed ultione Divina citissime vindicatum est

[p] This word is an insertion.

[q] This atrocity is noticed in the Saxon Chronicle, and also by Ordericus Vitalis, who calls the earl Robert de Comines. The details, however, are derived from the History of the Church of Durham, book iii., c. xv.

[r] The presence of Gospatric with the men of Northumberland is mentioned in the Saxon Chronicle, but not noticed by Florence. The former authority also speaks of Bishop Christian accompanying an expedition the following year under the command of Suane himself, but does not name him on the present occasion.

[s] *Obiit Aldredus Eboracensis archiepiscopus.* In margine.

"in eis gravissime. Nam priusquam tota civitas esset com-"busta, Danica classis supervenit feria ij," et hinc Dani, illinc Northymbrani expugnantes "castella eadem die infre-"gerunt. Et plus tribus millibus ex Normannis trucidatis, "Willelmo Malet," qui tunc vicecomitatum gerebat, "cum sua "conjuge et duobus liberis," et Gileberto de Gant "aliisque "perpaucis vitæ reservatis, naves Dani cum innumeris ma-"nubiis," suasque sedes repetierunt Northymbri. "Quod ubi "regi Willelmo innotuit, exercitu mox congregato, in North-"ymbriam efferato properavit animo, eamque per totam hiemem "devastare, hominesque trucidare, et multa alia non cessabat "agere. Interea nuntiis ad Danicum comitem Osbernum "missis, spopondit se clanculo daturum illi non modicæ sum-"mam pecuniæ, et permissurum licenter exercitui suo victum "circa ripas maris rapere, ea tamen interposita conditione, ut "sine pugna discederet peracta hieme. Ille autem, auri ar-"gentique cupidus, non sine magno dedecore sui petitis con-"cessit."

"Normannis Angliam vastantibus, in Northimbria et in "quibusdam aliis provinciis anno præcedenti, sed præsenti et "subsequenti fere per totam Angliam, maxime per Northym-"briam, et per contiguas illi provincias, adeo fames prævaluit, "ut homines humanas, equinas, caninas, et catinas carnes," et quicquid usus abhorret, cogente inedia comederent: alii vero in servitutem perpetuam sese venderent, dummodo qualitercumque miserabilem vitam sustentarent: alii extra patriam profecturi in exilium, medio itinere deficientes, animas emiserunt. Erat horror ad intuendum per domos, plateas et itinera cadavera humana dissolvi, et tabescentia putredine cum fætore horrendo scaturire vermibus. Neque enim supererat qui ea humo cooperiret, omnibus vel extinctis gladio et fame, vel propter famem paternum solum relinquentibus. Interea ita terra cultore destituta, lata ubique solitudo patebat per novem annos. Inter Eboracum et Dunelmum nusquam villa inhabitata, bestiarum tantum et latronum latibula magno itinerantibus fuere timori. Cum hæc Eboraci circum circaque rex ageret, Agelwinus Dunelmensis episcopus et optimates populi,[t] timentes ne, propter occisionem et Comitis, et Normannorum apud Eboracum, gladius regis innocentes æque ut nocentes pari clade involveret, unanimi consilio tollentes sancti patris Cuthberti incorruptum corpus, fugam ineunt iij idus Decembris, feria vj. Primam mansionem habuerunt in Girvum, secundam in Betlingetun, tertiam in

[t] This account of the retreat of Bishop Egelwine to Holy Island is from the History of the Church of Durham, iii., 15.

Tuggahala, quartam in Healande. Sed circa vesperam, cum plenum undique mare advenientibus prohiberet ingressum, ecce! subito sui recessu liberum præstitit introitum, ita ut nec festinantes aliquanto tardius sequerentur fluctus marini, nec tardantes aliquanto citius præcurrerent. Cum autem terram attigissent, ecce! refluum mare sicut ante totas arenas operuerat. Interea regis exercitus etiam per loca quæque inter Tesam et Tine diffusus, vacuis ubique domibus solam invenit solitudinem, indigenis fugæ præsidium quærentibus, vel per silvas et abrupta montium latitantibus. Tunc et ecclesia Sancti Pauli in Girvum flammis est consumpta; Dunelmensis ecclesia, omni custodia et ecclesiastico servitio destituta, spelunca erat pauperum et debilium, et ægrotantium, qui, cum fugere non poterant, illuc declinantes fame ac morbo deficiebant. Instante vere, redeunte ad Suthymbriam rege, Agelwinus episcopus cum omni populo, transactis in Ealande tribus mensibus et aliquot diebus, regreditur cum thesauro sancti corporis, dispositis in redeundo quas habuerant in exeundo mansionibus, atque viij kal. Aprilis, expurgata prius ab omni contaminatione ecclesia, ac pontificalibus officiis, et benedictione reconciliata, cum hymnis et laudibus intrantes sacrum suo in loco corpus reponunt.

MLXX.

Ægelwinus episcopus, rediens de fuga, perpetuam animo meditabatur fugam. Videns namque res Anglorum undique turbari, exteræ gentis, cujus nec linguam, nec mores noverat, grave sibi metuens dominium, decrevit episcopatu dimisso quaqua posset advena sibi providere. Itaque navis ei præparata rebus necessariis impositis prosperum expectabat ventum in portu Weremuthensi. Fuerant ibidem eo tempore et aliæ naves nonnullæ,[u] quarum ductores erant clito Eadgarus cum matre

[u] The narrative of events which follow is unsupported by any independent authority, but is cited, "e vetusta chronica," by Fordun, vol. i., p. 264. The retreat of Edgar with his mother and sisters into Scotland took place at least two years earlier. The Saxon Chronicle places it in the summer of 1067, and adds, "Then it was that king Malcolm desired to have Margaret to wife," and after some hesitation on the part of the princess and her relatives, "the marriage was now fulfilled."

The mutual injuries again inflicted on each other by Malcolm and Earl Gospatric seem inconsistent with the hospitality and protection which the latter had received at the Scottish Court, still more with the renewal of that protection the following year, and the extraordinary favours afterwards bestowed by the Scottish king on the exiled earl. Neither is there the slightest reason to suppose that the church of St. Peter at Wearmouth had ever been restored since the destruction of the monastery by the Danes in the ninth century. At all events the accounts given of it in the History of the Church of Durham, iii., 22, A.D. 1075, when the site was overgrown not only with brambles and thorns, but with forest trees, is altogether inconsistent with the assumption that it was in a state of repair only five years previous.

Agatha et duabus sororibus Margareta et Cristina, Siward, Barn, Marlessuein, Alfwinus filius Normanni, et alii quamplures, qui post expugnationem castellorum Eboraci, Danis in sua revertentibus, quoniam eis auxilio fuerant, indignationem regis sibi metuerant, Scotiam ire profugi parabant, ibique navigationem prosperam præstolabantur. Per idem tempus infinita Scottorum multitudo, ducente Malcolmo rege per Cumbreland traducta, versus orientem divertens, universam Tesedale et ejus finitima loca ultra citraque feroci vastavit depopulatione. Ubi autem ventum est ad locum qui dicitur Anglice Hundredeskelde,[v] Latine autem Centum Fontes, trucidatis ibidem quibusdam gentis Anglicæ nobilibus, rex parte exercitus retenta, partem per viam qua venerant cum infinita præda domum remisit. Hac scilicet calliditate ut cum totus hostis putaretur abiisse, miseros indigenas qui sese suaque propter hostilem metum latibulis quibus poterant tute conservaverant, secure in villas suas domosque regressos, ipse subito præoccuparet incursu improvisos. Quod et factum est. Nam depopulata Clyvelande ex parte, repentina depopulatione occupat Heortternysse, indeque per terras Sancti Cuthberti ferociter discurrens, omnes omnibus rebus, nonnullos etiam ipsis privat animabus. Tunc et ecclesiam Sancti Petri, Apostolorum principis, in Weremuthe, flamma suorum, ipso inspectante, consumpsit. Alias quoque ecclesias cum his qui in eas confugerant concremavit. Ubi cum circa ripas fluminis equitaret, deque altiori loco suorum crudelia in miseros Anglos facinora prospiciens, tali spectaculo animos et oculos pasceret, nuntiatum est illi clitonem Eadgarum suasque sorores regiæ stirpis puellas decoras, pluresque alios prædivites de suis sedibus profugos in illum portum applicuisse navibus. Datis ergo dextris venientes ad se benigne alloquitur, eisque cum suis omnibus regni sui habitationem quamdiu vellent cum pace donavit firmissima. Inter has Scottorum vastationes ac rapinas, Gospatricus comes (qui, ut supradictum est, a rege Willelmo comitatum Northanhymbrorum pretio assecutus fuerat)[w] accitis auxiliatoribus strenuis atroci depopulatione Cumbreland invadit. Peracta cæde et incendio cum magna præda revertitur, seque cum sociis in munitionem Babbanburch firmissimam conclusit. Ex qua sæpius prorumpens, vires hostium debilitavit. Erat enim eo tempore Cumbreland sub regis Mal-

[v] This is perhaps Hunderthwaite, near Romaldkirk. Keld is close by.

[w] This statement respecting the purchase of the earldom by Gospatric is given in an account of the earls of Northumberland, which is inserted not before, but after, the present passage, under the year 1072. The same history of the earls of Northumberland occurs in Hoveden's Annals, which are to a great extent copied from the two parts of the Historia Regum, under the year 953.

colmi[x] dominio, non jure possessa sed violenter subjugata. Auditis ille (cum adhuc flamma suorum ardentem Sancti Petri ecclesiam spectaret) quæ Cospatricus in suos fecerat, vix præ furore se-ipsum ferens, jussit suis, ut nulli Anglicæ gentis ulterius parcerent, sed omnes vel necando in terram funderent, vel captivando sub jugum perpetuæ servitutis abducerent. Qua licentia accepta, miseria etiam erat videre quæ in Anglos faciebant: senes et vetulæ alii gladiis obtruncantur, alii ut porci ad esum destinati lanceis confodiuntur. Rapti ab uberibus matrum parvuli in altum aëra projiciuntur, unde recidentes lancearum acuminibus excipiuntur hastilibus confertim solo infixis; hac crudelitate pro ludorum spectaculo delectabantur bestiis crudeliores Scotti. Sic innocens ætas cælum ascensuras, inter cælum pendens et terram, emittit animas. Juvenes vero et juvenculæ, et quicumque operibus ac laboribus idonei videbantur, ante faciem hostium vincti compelluntur, ut perpetuo exilio in servos et ancillas redigantur. Horum quædam dum, plusquam vires ferrent, currendo ante ora compellentium fatigarentur, illico ruentes in terram, eundem locum casus et mortis habebant. Hæc Malcolmus considerans, nullis miserorum lacrimis, nullis gemitibus flectebatur ad misericordiam, sed potius jussit ut amplius perurgerentur eundo. Repleta est ergo Scotia servis et ancillis Anglici generis, ita ut etiam usque hodie nulla non dico villula, sed nec domuncula sine his valeat inveniri.

Reverso Scotiam Malcolmo, Ægelwinum episcopum versus Coloniam incipientem navigare, mox ventus surgens contrarius in Scotiam reppulit. Quo etiam clitonem Eadgarum cum sociis supra-nominatis prospero pervexit cursu. Cujus Eadgari sororem Margaretam rex Malcolmus, consensu propinquorum illius, matrimonio sibi junxit, feminam regali prosapia nobilem, sed prudentia et religione multo nobiliorem. Cujus studio et industria rex ipse, deposita morum barbarie, factus est honestior atque civilior. Ex qua sex filios suscepit, Eadwardum, Eadmundum, Eadgarum regem, et Alexandrum regem, Ethelredum, David regem,[y] et duas filias, Mahtildam Anglorum reginam, et Mariam quam Eustachius comes Bononiæ in conjugium accepit.

MLXXI.

"Anno M.lxxj—comites Edwinus et Morkarus, quia rex

[x] There is no ground for this assertion. Cumberland was a dependency of the Scottish Crown at all events from the year 945, when it was overrun by Edmund, king of England, and by him transferred to the king of Scotland. During the usurpation of the Scottish Crown by Macbeth, it was held by Malcolm or his father (for on this point historians differ), whose possession up to this time had been undisputed.

[y] *Origo David regis Scotiæ.* In margine.

"Willelmus eos in custodiam ponere voluit, latenter e curia ejus "fugerunt, et aliquamdiu contra illum rebellaverunt. Verum "ubi quod cœperunt, sibi non prospere cessisse viderunt, Ed-"winus regem Scottorum Malcolmum adire decrevit, sed in "ipso itinere, a suis insidias perpessus, occiditur; Morkarus "vero et Herewardus, vir strenuissimus, cum multis aliis Heli "insulam navigio petierunt, in ea hiemare volentes." Agelwinus quoque Dunelmensis episcopus et Siwardus, cognomento Barn, de Scottia renavigantes illo advenerant: "sed hoc audito "rex cum buthsecarlis in orientali plaga insulæ omnem illis "exitum obstruxit, et pontem in occidentali trium (?) miliari-"orum longum fieri jussit. At illi, ubi se viderunt sic esse "inclusos, repugnare desistebant, et omnes, excepto Herewardo, "qui per paludes cum paucis evasit, regi se dedebant. Qui "mox episcopum Agelwinum, Abbandoniam missum, in custo-"dia posuit, ubi in ipsa hieme vitam finivit. Comitem vero "cæterosque per Angliam divisos partim custodiæ mancipavit, "partim manibus truncatis vel oculis erutis abire permisit." Walcherum vero Dunelmensi ecclesiæ rex præfecit episcopum, de clero Leodicensis ecclesiæ. Invitatus namque ab ipso rege venerat ad illum, prosapia clarus, honestus moribus, Divinæ ac sæcularis scientiæ gratia præditus. Quem Eilaf huscarl, apud regem præpollens honore, cum aliis principalibus viris perduxit Eboracum, ubi jussu regis occurrens comes Cospatricus suscepit pontificem perducendum usque Dunelmum: venit autem in ecclesiam suæ sedis media Quadragesima.

MLXXII.

"Anno M.lxxij, post Assumptionem Sanctæ Mariæ, rex Wil-"lelmus, habens in comitatu suo Edricum cognomento Silvati-"cum, cum navali et equestri exercitu Scotiam profectus est ut "eam suæ subjugaret ditioni." Graviter namque rex Scottorum Malcolmus eum offenderat, quia, ut supradictum est, anno præterito regni sui terminos atrociter depopulatus fuerat. Sed ubi rex Anglorum Scotiam intraverat, "rex Malcolmus ei in "loco qui dicitur Abernithi occurrit, et homo suus devenit." Rediens autem inde Willelmus Cospatricum comitatus honore privavit, imponens illi quod consilio et auxilio affuisset eis qui Comitem cum suis in Dunelmo peremerant, licet ipse ibidem præsens non fuisset; et quia in parte hostium fuisset cum Normanni apud Eboracum necarentur.[z]

Sed hic paulatim redeamus ad superiora, gratia comitum

[z] If we are to credit Ordericus Vitalis, these offences had been already condoned. At all events the king had accepted the submission of Gospatric A.D. 1069 (Ordericus, apud Duchesne, p. 515).

Northymbrensium, quatinus statu regum Northanthymbrorum deficiente, a quibus cœperit provincia illa amministrari Comitibus agnoscatur. Ultimus regum provinciæ illius fuit Eiricus quem Northymbrenses, violata fide quam regi Eadredo juraverant, sibi regem fecerunt. Quare offensus rex jussit ut tota provincia funditus vastaretur. Illico Northymbrenses, expulso rege suo atque occiso a Maccus filio Anlafi, juramentis et muneribus placaverunt regem Eadredum, commissa provincia Osulfo comiti.[a] Qui postea, regnante Eadgaro, socium accepit Oslacum. Deinde Osulfus ad aquilonalem plagam Tinæ, Oslac vero super Eboracum et ejus fines curas amministrabat.[b] His successit Walthef Senior,[c] qui successorem habuit filium Uhtredum. Is,

[a] Wendover says that King Yric was slain on a certain waste called "Steinmor," with his son Henry and brother Reginald, "a Macone consule," through the treachery of Earl Osulf, and then King Eadred reigned in those parts (vol. i., pp. 402-3). From the way in which he is mentioned as "Osulf comes," it is probable that he was already in possession of the earldom of Bamburgh, or Northumberland beyond the Tyne, by hereditary right, in succession to the kings and dukes who had held the government from the period when the district south of the Tyne was overrun by the Danes A.D. 867. At all events the Northern earldom continued to descend in his family, whilst that of Yorkshire was bestowed at pleasure by the kings of England; and amongst his descendants we find the recurrence of the same names which prevailed amongst his immediate predecessors,—Eadulf, Aldred, and Uchtred, as also Usulf.

[b] According to the Saxon Chronicle, Oslac, "the great earl," was banished from England A.D. 975.

"Oslac from this land
O'er rolling waters,
Over the gannet's bath
Hoary-haired hero,
Wise and word-skilled,
Over the waters' throng,
O'er the whale's domain,
Of home bereaved."

Mon. Hist., p. 397.

[c] Wendover calls him Eadulf. Under the same year 975 he says: "Bishop Alfsy and Earl Eadulf conducted Kenneth, king of Scotland, to King Edgar, who made him many presents of his royal bounty. He gave him, moreover, the whole district called Laudian (Lothian) in the native tongue, on this condition, that every year, on certain festivals, when the king and his successors should wear the crown, he should come to court, and celebrate the festival with the other nobles. The king gave him besides many mansions on the road, that he and his successors might find entertainment in going and returning; and these houses continued to belong to the kings of Scotland till the time of Henry II." (vol. i., p. 416). This statement is scouted by Chalmers as resting on the testimony of Matthew of Westminster (cited on one occasion by mistake as William of Malmesbury), but is at least worthy of consideration, when traced to the respectable authority of Roger of Wendover. With Waltheof commences the list of Northumbrian earls in Symeon's little tract, De Obsessione Dunelmi, which furnishes some of the particulars which follow in the present text, with much which has not been transferred to it. A comparison of the two authorities furnishes a very complete history of the official earls of Northumberland, respecting whom we have few particulars elsewhere.

cum regnante Agelredo rex Canutus hostiliter invaderet Northymbriam, necessitate compulsus se cum suis ad Canutum contulit; factoque juramento et obsidibus datis, peremptus est a quodam Dano prædivite Thurebrando, cognomento Hold, permittente Canuto. In cujus locum frater ejus Eadulf Cutel substituitur. Reliquerat autem comes Uhtredus tres filios, Aldredum, Eadulfum, Cospatricum, quorum duo primi Comites fuerunt Northymbrorum, alter post alterum. Tertius vero sine Comitatus honore habuit filium Uhtredum, cujus filius erat Eadulfus cognomento Rus, qui postea ducem se exhibuit eorum qui Walcherum episcopum occiderunt, ipseque dicitur sua illum interfecisse manu: sed mox et ipse, a femina occisus, sepultus est in ecclesia apud Geddewerde; sed post a Turgoto, quondam Priore Dunelmensis ecclesiæ et archidiacono, talis inde spurcitia projecta. Post Eadulfum Cudel Aldredus, filius præfati comitis Uhtredi, suscepto comitatu in vindictam patris occisi homicidam Thurebrandum occidit. Cujus Thurebrandi filius Carl et præfatus comes Aldredus, dum vitæ suæ invicem insidiarentur, tandem repacificantur: sed non multo post Aldredus, nil mali suspicans, dolo in silva quæ Risewde vocatur, a Carl conjurato sibi fratre occiditur. Post fratris interitum Ealdulfus comes efficitur Northymbrensium, qui, cum superbia extolleretur, Brittones satis atrociter devastavit: sed tertio post anno, cum ad Hardecanutum reconciliandus in pace venisset, interfectus est a Siwardo, qui post illum totius provinciæ Northanhymbrorum, id est ab Humbra usque Tuedam, comitatum habuit. Cui mortuo successit Tosti. Quo, propter graves injurias quas intulerat, a Northymbrensibus de Anglia expulso, ducatus illius Morkaro committitur a rege Eadwardo, et postmodum a rege Willelmo. Morkarus vero, quoniam alias gravibus negotiis impeditus fuerat, comitatum ultra Tynam tradidit Osulfo, adolescenti filio præfati comitis Eadulfi. Capto postmodum et custodiæ mancipato Morkaro, rex Willelmus comitatum Osulfi commisit Copsio qui erat partis Tostii comitis, viro consiliario et prudenti.[d] Pulsus a Copsio de comitatu Osulfus, in fame et egestate silvis latitans et montibus, tandem, collectis quos eadem necessitas compulerat sociis, Copsium in Nyweburne convivantem concludit.

[d] Morcar, although for some time honourably treated by William, does not appear to have been allowed by him to retain the earldom of Northumberland, which was committed to the charge of Copsi in the month of February, 1067, in the interval between the coronation and the king's departure to the continent (Ordericus Vitalis, iv., 1, 3, pp. 506, seqq.). Copsi, as well as Tosti, occur as benefactors in the History of the Church of Durham, iii., 12, 14. The rebellion of Edwin and Morcar did not occur till the year after the death of Copsi (Ordericus, p. 511), and the imprisonment of the latter was two years later, and for a subsequent offence.

Qui inter tumultuantes turbas lapsus dum lateret in ecclesia proditus, incendio ecclesiæ compellitur usque ad ostium procedere, ubi in ipso ostio manibus Osulfi detruncatur, quinta ebdomada commissi comitatus iiij idus Martii. Mox sequenti autumno, et ipse Osulfus, cum in obvii sibi latronis lanceam præceps irrueret, illico confossus interiit. Quo mortuo, Cospatricus, filius Maldredi filii Crinani, Willelmum regem adiens, multa emptum pecunia adeptus est comitatum Northymbrensium.[e] Nam ex materno sanguine attinebat ad eum honor illius comitatus. Erat enim ex matre Algitha, filia Uhtredi comitis, quam habuit ex Algiva filia Agelredi regis. Hanc Algitham pater dedit in conjugium Maldredo filio Crinani. Tenuit autem comitatum donec rex causis ex supradictis ei auferret. Fugiens ergo ad Malcolmum non multo post Flandriam navigio petit. Cui post aliquantum tempus Scottiam reverso, donavit ei rex supradictus Dunbar cum adjacentibus terris in Lodoneio, ut ex his, donec lætiora redirent tempora, se suosque procuraret.[f] Iste Cospatricus est pater Dolfini, Walthevi et Cospatrici.[g] Post Cospatricum datus est comitatus Walthevo Siwardi comitis filio. Quo postmodum capto, commissa est cura comitatus Walchero episcopo usque in diem occisionis suæ. Inde rex dedit illum honorem Albrio. Quo in rebus difficilibus parum valente, patriamque reverso, idem rex Rodberto de Mulbreio[h] dedit comitatum

[e] Gospatric purchased the earldom in the autumn or winter of 1067. In 1068 he fled to Scotland, having probably been implicated in the rebellion of Edwin and Morcar. Robert Cumin, whose murder is recorded A.D. 1069, was no doubt intended to supersede him. After Cumin's death, notwithstanding that he was concerned in the insurrection at York in conjunction with the Danish invasion, the same year, the king accepted his submission, and allowed him to retain his government (Reconciliati sunt Guallevus præsens, et *Caius-Patricius* absens, sacramento per legatos exhibito. Ordericus, p. 515). This was in 1070; and in 1071 he was deputed to meet Walcher, the newly-appointed bishop of Durham, at York, to conduct him from thence to his episcopal residence. All this time, however, he was indebted less to his sovereign's indulgence than to the strength of his own position, with the impregnable castle of Bamburgh to fall back upon. For no sooner was William in a position to enforce obedience at the head of a powerful army on his return from Scotland, than he deprived him of his earldom on the very charges which had been previously condoned.

[f] This took place A.D. 1072, within two years of the ravages committed by Gospatric on the territories of the Scottish king, and the deadly exasperation of the latter, as detailed above. See note *u*, p. 86.

[g] Dolfin was lord of Carlisle, from which he was driven out, A.D. 1092, by William Rufus, who restored the city and built the castle. Waldeve was lord of Allerdale, in Cumberland, and Gospatric, of Beanley, in Northumberland, both by grants from Henry I.

[h] Dugdale makes Geoffrey, Bishop of Coutances, Mowbray's uncle, his predecessor in the earldom, but, as it appears, on insufficient grounds. Geoffrey was a witness to the foundation charter of the abbey of St. Mary of York, and is described in the chronicle of that house as having so attested it "eo tempore, quo Northymbrorum consulatum regebat." He probably only acted as deputy

Northymbrensem, sed eo capto rex Junior Willelmus, hodieque rex Henricus Northymbriam in sua tenet manu.

His, ob notitiam personarum, per excessum interpositis, ad continuandam interrupti ordinis seriem stilus revertatur. Dejecto ab honore Cospatrico, Waltheovus in comitatum sustollitur, ei ex patris ac matris prosapia debitum. Fuerat enim Siwardi comitis filius ex filia quondam comitis Aldredi Ælfleda.

Eodem tempore, scilicet quo rex reversus de Scotia fuerat, in Dunelmo castellum condidit, ubi se cum suis episcopus tute ab incursantibus habere potuisset. Fuerunt autem amicissimi sibique mutuo acclines Walcherus episcopus et Waltheovus comes. Unde una cum episcopo et in synodo presbyterorum residens, humiliter et obedienter prosequebatur quicquid pro corrigenda in suo comitatu Christianitate statutum ab episcopo fuisset.

MLXXIII.

Anno M.lxxiii. In hoc anno omnia juxta cursum solis et lunæ habentur sicut in anno xv Tiberii, in quo baptizatus est Dominus, id est dies baptismatis viij idus Januarii, die Dominico Epiphaniæ et ij feria, initium jejunii ejus xl diebus. A baptismate itaque Domini in anno quinto decimo Tiberii hucusque sunt revoluti duo magni cicli, hoc est mille lxiiij anni.—Comes Waltheovus, missa manu valida Northymbrensium, necem avi sui Aldredi comitis crudeliter ulciscitur, siquidem filios Carl qui eum occidi fecerat, apud Seteringetun simul convivantes gladius insidiantium consumpsit.

MLXXIV.

Anno M.lxxiiij Hildebrandus, qui et Gregorius, Romanus archidiaconus, papa est electus et factus. Iste papa synodo celebrata, ex decreto Sancti Petri Apostoli et Sancti Clementis, aliorumque Sanctorum patrum et banno interdixit clericis, maxime Divino ministerio consecratis, uxores habere, vel cum mulieribus habitare, nisi quas Nicena synodus vel alii canones exceperunt.[i] Decrevit quoque, sub sententia Sancti Petri, ut cum Simone Mago damnaretur non solum emptor et venditor cujuscumque officii, ut puta episcopatus, abbatiæ, præpositura,

for his nephew, as Morel did afterwards. At all events we know in the case of two charters to which the names of Mowbray and his uncle are both attached, that the former signs as Earl of Northumberland, the latter simply as Bishop of Coutances (Appendix in Hist. Dunelm., Scriptores Tres, pp. v, xvi). See also a judicial document in the same collection, p. liii, in which Waltheof is described as the third earl in order previous to Earl Robert de Mowbray.

[i] See Baronius under the year 1075, etc.

decaniæ vel decimationis ecclesiæ, sed et quicunque consentiret eis. Dominus enim dixit, *Gratis accepistis, gratis date.*[j]

Tres de provincia Merciorum monachi pauperes spiritu, Divinitus missi in provinciam Northanhymbrorum, venerunt Eboracum, petentes ab Hugone filio Baldrici, qui tunc vicecomitatum gerebat, ut eis ducem itineris inveniret, usque locum qui Munekeceastre, id est Monachorum Civitas, appellatur, qui nunc Novum-castellum nominatur.[k] Quo per conductum venientes, ad tempus ibidem morati, cum nullum antiquæ servorum Christi ibi congregationis reperirent vestigium, diverterunt ad Girvum, ubi ruinis vix ostendentibus quid antiquitus fuerint, monachorum cum semirutis ecclesiis visebantur ædificia multa, episcopo Walchero summa cum gratulatione illos suscipiente, et necessaria præbente. Horum nomina fuerunt. Prior eorum ætate et moribus erat Aldwinus, secundus Ealfwinus, tertius Rinfridus. Ex his tribus tria in regione Northymbrorum instaurata sunt monasteria. Unum Dunelmi apud patris Cuthberti sacrum et incorruptum corpus, in honorem Sanctæ Mariæ virginis. Aliud Eboraci in honorem ejusdem Dei genitricis Mariæ, ubi de ecclesiola factum nobile cœnobium. Primum abbatem habuit Stephanum; secundum Ricardum; tertium Gaufridum;[l] quartum Severinum; quintum Clementem, qui et in præsenti. Tertium autem in loco qui quondam Streneshald, id est Sinus Fari, nunc Witebi appellatur. Ibi sedit primus abbas Willelmus, ij Nicholaus,[m] iij Benedictus, iiij Ricardus,[n] qui nunc superest. Denique postquam sævissima Paganorum devastatio gladio ac flamma ecclesias ac monasteria in cineres redegerat, deficiente pene Christianitate, vix aliquæ ecclesiæ, et hæ virgis fœnoque contextæ, sed nulla uspiam

[j] St. Matt. x. 8.

[k] This narrative is mainly derived from the History of the Church of Durham, with some additions and occasional variations. It does not appear from the Durham History that the pilgrims specially directed their steps to Monkchester, or indeed knew anything of it. Their information respecting the ancient monasteries was from Beda, who makes no mention of Monkchester, for the identification of which, with Newcastle-upon-Tyne, we are also indebted to the present work, supported by other authorities of somewhat more recent date. But for this, we might rather have been disposed to ascribe the name of Monkchester to the *Chester* at Wallsend immediately opposite to Jarrow, where the monks afterwards settled, on the north bank of the Tyne, and equally, with the site of Newcastle under the jurisdiction of the earls of Northumberland, as Wallsend became the property of the monks, which Newcastle never was.

[l] *Qui in præsenti.* Abbreviatio. MS. Cott. Calig. A. viii. Hoveden's list ends with Severinus.

[m] *Modo Nicholaus.* Abbreviatio. MS. Cott. Calig. A. viii. Hoveden's list ends with Benedict.

[n] Richard died in 1175, having been abbat for twenty-six years (Charlton's Whitby, 143). Clement is said to have been abbat of St. Mary's, York, from 1161 to 1184. See Preface.

monasteria per cc annos reædificabantur, tepescente paulatim fidei religione, cultu vero religionis penitus deficiente; monachorum nomen erat provincialibus inauditum. In stuporem vertebantur cum quemlibet monachilis habitus et vitæ forte conspicerent. Sed prædictis tribus viris inter illos habitare incipientibus, incipiebant et ipsi de bestiali vita mores in melius commutare, illi ad restauranda sancta loca opem inpendere, ipsi per se semirutas ecclesias restaurare et renovare, vel etiam in quibus antea non erant locis novas ædificare; multi de sæculari vita etiam in monachilem militiam concurrere. Sed hic pauci ex comprovincialibus: plures vero de remotis Angliæ partibus fama illorum acciti eis adjungebantur unanimes. Horum Turgotus erat unus, postea Scottorum episcopus. Is[o] prosapiam trahens de genere Anglorum non infimo, unus erat inter alios qui, nuper subjugata Normannis Anglia, obsides pro tota Lindesia in Lindicolino castro custodiebantur. Ille pecunia emolliens custodiam, cum magno suorum periculo fugit clanculo ad Norwegenses, qui tunc apud Grimesbi navem mercatoriam usque Norwegiam oneraverant. In qua navi etiam legati Willelmi regis Norwegiam mittendi subvectionem sibi paraverant: jamque navis illa totis avolans velis terras aspectibus subtraxerat, cum ecce! fugitivus obses regis ab inferioribus navis partibus, ubi Norwegenses eum absconderant, in medium erumpens, legatos eorumque socios in stuporem vertit. Nam ubique locorum perquisitus fuerat, etiam in navi eadem exactores regis scrutinia fecerant, sed calliditas abscondentium delusit oculos perscrutantium. Itaque legati instabant, ut, depositis velis navem cum fugitivo regis ad Angliam quoquo modo reflecterent. Norwegenses acrius repugnabant ut cæpta velificatio prospero navem cursu in an' *(sic)* perferret. Fit partium altercatio, ita ut adversus se invicem armarentur: sed, quod major vis erat Norwegensium, citius compressa est audacia legatorum, quantoque magis terræ propinquabant, tanto magis illis se humiliabant. Veniens autem illo juvenis fugitivus quam honeste se et caste agebat, nobilibus et optimatibus gratus apparebat. Pervenit et ad notitiam regis Olavi; qui quoniam valde religiosus erat, sacros codices inter manus tractare, et litteras inter regni curas sæpe consuevit addiscere; sæpe etiam sacerdoti ad altare assistere, et induentem vestimenta sacra adjuvare, aquam manibus fundere, et cætera hujusmodi devota peragere. Audito itaque quod clericus de Anglia venisset, quod magnum tunc temporis videbatur, eum ad discendos Psalmos quasi magistrum

[o] This account of the position and early life of Turgot is not from the Durham History, nor is it supported by any earlier authority.

sibi exhibuit. Inter hæc satis superque abundabat rebus, regis virorumque nobilium largitate, proaffluentibus. Compungebatur sæpe animus illius ad contemptum mundi, et, ubi poterat, convivia lætantium declinans solitariis delectatur in lacrimis, orans Deum ut eum dirigeret in viam salutis. Sed quia religiosa desideria dum differuntur sæpe mutantur, ab illo statu paulatim animus defluebat, quem jocunditas sæculi ex successu rerum ad se trahebat. Sed quia invitatus sponte venire noluit, quandoque compulsus domum cælestis Patrisfamilias intravit. Post aliquot namque annos patriam cum multa pecunia renavigabat, sed medio in mari navi prævalida tempestate dissoluta, rerum omnium jacturam pereuntibus sociis sustulit, solam vitam cum quinque vel sex aliis vix cum multo labore servavit. Veniens Dunelmum ad orationem, Walchero episcopo omnia circa se acta exposuit, et quia monachilis propositi animum gereret indicavit. Quod episcopus satis hilariter suscepit, mittensque ad Aldwinum,[p] de quo supradictum est, "Hunc," inquit, "filium meum precor et jubeo suscipias, atque monachili habitu "indutum viam quoque monachilem servare doceas." Quem susceptum ille regulariter probavit, et probato monachicum quandoque habitum tradidit, atque ita verbo informavit et exemplo, ut eidem defuncto, jubente Willelmo episcopo, in Dunelmensis ecclesiæ succederet Prioratum, quem per xx annos strenue amministravit, xij diebus minus; anno enim episcopatus Rannulfi, qui Willelmo successit, viij, impetrante Alexandro rege Scottorum, ab Henrico rege Anglorum assumitur ad episcopatum ecclesiæ Sancti Andreæ in Scottia; in qua est sedes primatis totius gentis Scottorum. Sed per annum et eo amplius dilata est ejus ordinatio propter dissensiones Eboracensis ecclesiæ atque ecclesiæ Sancti Andreæ Scotiæ.[q] Illa

[p] We learn from the Durham History that Turgot entered the monastery of Jarrow under the auspices of Bishop Walcher, but the particulars of his recommendation are not there set forth, as in the text before us.

[q] Respecting these delays, see Eadmer, Hist. Novorum. To obviate the difficulty arising from the non-consecration of the archbishop of York, the bishop of Durham, Ranulf Flambard, proposed that Turgot should be consecrated by himself in the presence of the archbishop elect of York, associating with himself for that purpose the bishops of Scotland and the Orkneys, and he pressed this arrangement upon the archbishop of Canterbury through the medium of a special messenger, Escolland, one of the barons of his bishopric. To this proposal Anselm returned a positive refusal. "Nec debet, nec potest canonice fieri ab eodem electo archiepiscopo, nec ab alio per illum, priusquam ipse fiat archiepiscopus canonica consecratione. Quapropter, nec consulo nec concedo, immo interdico, ne fiat ante consecrationem ejusdem electi archiepiscopi, nisi a me, si forte hoc necessitas exegerit" (Eadmer, p. 97). The consecration, in fact, did not take place till after Anselm's death, when the archbishop elect of York, under the pressure of the king's commands, made those concessions to the authority of his successor which he had resolutely refused to make to Anselm himself.

namque ordinationem et subjectionem primatis Scottorum sibi ex quodam quasi jure exigit, ista vero e diverso affirmat ex nullo antiquitatis vel consuetudinis jure aliquid se debere. Sed ne diutius pastore [viduata] vacillaret ecclesia, rogatus a rege Scottorum, rex Henricus præcepit, ut Eboracensis archiepiscopus, Thomas junior, hunc sine ulla subjectionis exactione consecraret, salva utriusque ecclesiæ auctoritate, ut postea ubi, et quando, et a quibus ratio exigeretur, debitus finis controversiam utriusque partis dirimeret. Veniens ergo sic consecratus Scotiam, cum causis emergentibus digne non posset episcopale officium exercere, Romam ire disposuit, ubi consilio et judicio domini papæ Paschalis vitam suam transigeret. Sed ne id ad effectum perduceret, invalescentibus inter ipsum et regem causis, præ angustia spiritus decidit in melancholiam. Unde accepta licentia remorandi ad tempus Dunelmi propter infirmitatem, vigilia Apostolorum Petri et Pauli venit ad Weremutham, ubi quondam ab Aldwino habitum monachi susceperat; ubi mane, ut poterat, missa celebrata, ad Sanctum Cuthbertum proficiscitur, ibique in lectum decidens, modo lentis, modo nimiis præparatur febribus ad exitum, et hoc per duos menses et quatuor dies.[r] Instante autem hora exitus, cum diceret, sicut poterat, orando, *In pace factus est locus ejus et habitatio ejus in Syon;* et *Laudate Dominum in Sanctis Ejus*,[s] intra manus fratrum suorum animam exhalavit ij kal. Aprilis, feria tertia,[t] hora tertia, anno episcopatus ejus viij transacto et duobus mensibus et x diebus, impetrato munere a Deo quod sedulo rogaverat, ut apud sacrum Cuthberti corpus animam redderet. Sepultus est autem in capitulo. Cujus corpus interpositum corpus Walcheri episcopi habet ad austrum, Willelmi episcopi ad aquilonem. Obiit autem anno ab Incarnatione Dominica M.C.XV.

His per excessum dictis revertatur ad ordinem intermissum stilus.

[r] Hugh the Chantor mentions a visit which Thurstan, archbishop of York, paid to Turgot on his death-bed. See Fasti Ebor., i., 172.

[s] Psalm lxxv. 3; cl. 1.

[t] In a letter from Alexander, king of Scotland, to the archbishop of Canterbury, announcing the death of Turgot, and asking advice as to the appointment of a successor, he says, "11 kl. Septembr. migravit a sæculo, unde valde contristamur, tanto solatio destituti." This date differs by some months from that given in the text. The expression of sorrow also, apparently sincere, evinces a better feeling than is here represented between the king and his bishop (Eadmer, p. 117). It is remarkable that there is no reference in the work before us to the residence of Aldwine and Turgot at Melrose, and to their ill treatment by king Malcolm, as detailed in the History of the Church of Durham.

MLXXV.

Anno M.lxxv dum clerici magis eligerent anathemati subjacere quam uxoribus carere, Hiltibrandus papa, ut per alios, si posset, eos castigaret, præcepit ut nullus audiret missam conjugati presbyteri,[u] sic.

Gregorius papa, (qui et Hiltibrandus,) *servorum Dei servus, per totum Italicum regnum et Teutonicum debitam Sancto Petro obedientiam exhibentibus, Apostolicam benedictionem. Si qui sunt presbyteri, diaconi, subdiaconi, qui jacent in crimine fornicationis, interdicimus eis ex parte Omnipotentis Dei et auctoritate Sancti Petri introitum ecclesiæ usque dum emendent et pæniteant: si qui autem in peccato suo perseverare maluerint, nullus vestrum officium eorum auscultare præsumat, quia benedictio illorum vertitur in maledictionem, et oratio in peccatum, testante Domino per Prophetam,* Maledicam, *inquit,* benedictionibus vestris.[v]

Waltheovus Comes decapitatur.[w] Post quem cura comitatus committitur Walchero episcopo.

MLXXVI.

Anno M.lxxvj rex Danorum, Suanus, bene literis imbutus, obiit; cui filius suus Haroldus successit.

MLXXVIII.

Anno M.lxxviij fundata est abbatia sanctæ Mariæ Eboraci.[x]

MLXXX.

"Anno M.lxxx Dunholmensis episcopus Walcherus, genere "Lotaringus, in loco qui dicitur ad Caput Capræ,[y] ij idus Maii, "feria v., a Northymbrensibus est occisus, in ultionem necis

[u] Baronius must be consulted for an account of this controversy.

[v] Malachi ii. 2.

[w] These words are in the margin in the MS., opposite to the details of Waltheof's treason and execution, which are copied from Florence.

[x] The whole of this paragraph, save the date, is a marginal note in an old hand.

[y] Twysden has inserted Gotesheued in the text. The word Goteshead occurs in the margin in a hand of the seventeenth century. This account, with trifling exceptions, which are indicated by the absence of inverted commas, is copied from Florence of Worcester. It is much more detailed than that given in the History of the Church of Durham, which, however, supplies some particulars not given here, as the names of two of the ringleaders, Waltheof and Eadulf. Of the latter, called Eadulf Rus, further information is supplied above, in the account of the earls of Northumberland under the year 1072. The statements in the Durham History are written in a more apologetic spirit, as regards the provocations offered by the bishop, who is compared to Eli, as suffering for the faults of others.

"Ligulfi, nobilis generosique ministri. Hic itaque vir late per "Angliam possessiones multas ex hæreditario jure possedit. "Sed quia ubique locorum Normanni incessanter ea tempestate "operam dabant suæ feritati, cum suis omnibus ad Dunholme "se contulit, quia Sanctum Cuthbertum corde sincero dilexit." Habuit autem in conjugio Algitham filiam Aldredi comitis, ex qua procreavit filios Uhthredum et Morekarum. Hujus Algithæ soror fuit Elfleda, mater Waltheovi comitis. Unde ipse comes consobrinum suum parvulum, prædictum Morkarum, Deo nutriendum monachis in Girva dedit. Quo tempore ipse comes erat apud Tinemuthe, quem locum simul cum prædicto parvulo ipsis monachis commisit disponendum. Cujus pater Ligulfus ab episcopo "in tantum diligebatur, ut absque illius consilio "majores sæcularium negotiorum causas nullatenus agere vellet "aut disponere. Ob quam rem suus capellanus Leobwinus, "quem in tantum exaltaverat, ut in episcopatu et in comitatu "fere nil sine illius arbitrio agitaretur, invidiæ stimulis succen-"sus, et propter suam potentiam tedis superbiæ nimis inflatus, "se contra prædictum virum arroganter erexit; quapropter non-"nulla ejus judicia atque consilia floccipendebat, omnibusque "modis annullare sudabat. Frequenter etiam coram episcopo, "non sine minis cum eo litigans, illum verbis probosis sæpius "ad iracundiam provocabat. Quadam itaque die cum idem vir "Ligulfus, ab episcopo vocatus ad consilium, legalia quæque et "recta decerneret, obstinatius ei Leobwinus obstitit, et loquelis "illum contumeliosis exacerbavit. Sed quia ille respondit ei "durius solito, de placiti loco discessit illico, et evocans ad se "Gilebertum, cui præsul, quia suus propinquus erat, comitatum "Northymbriensium sub se regendum commiserat, ut se vindi-"caret obnixe rogavit; et Ligulfum quam citius posset morti "tradere maturaret. Ille autem confestim iniquis petitionibus "acquiescens, suis et episcopi et ejusdem Leobswini militibus "in unum coadunatis, ad villam, ubi tunc Ligulfus morabatur, "nocte quadam perrexit, ac illum cum sua familia fere tota in "domo propria injuste peremit. Quo cognito, graviter antistes "ex corde suspiravit intimo, et capicio de capite extracto, et in "terram projecto, Leobwino, qui tunc præsens aderat, tristis "dixit continuo. 'Tuis, Leobwine, factionibus dolosis acta "'sunt hæc et insiliis stolidissimis. Idcirco volo te scire pro "'certo, quia et me, et te, omnemque familiam meam tuæ lin-"'guæ peremisti gladio.' Hoc dicto, in castellum se proripuit "festinato, confestimque nuntiis per totam Northymbriam mis-"sis, omnibus nuntiari curavit, se necis Liulfi conscium non "fuisse, quin potius ejus occisorem Gilebertum, omnesque socios "ejus de Northymbria penitus exlegasse, ac paratum fore semet

H 2

"ipsum purgare secundum judicium pontificale. Deinde missis "intercurrentibus, ille parentesque occisorum, pace adinvicem "data et accepta, locum et diem quo convenire et inter se "pacem firmiorem facere possent statuere. Quo adveniente, "loco constituto in unum convenere. Verum cum illis episco-"pus sub divo placitare noluit, sed in ecclesiam quæ ibi erat, "cum suis clericis ac honorabilioribus militibus intravit. Et "consilio habito, semel et iterum de suis quos voluit pro pace "facienda foras ad eos misit. At illi nequaquam petitis adqui-"escebant, qui Liulfum illius jussione peremptum fuisse pro "certo credebant. Nam Gilebertum ejusque socios nocte post "necem propinqui sui proxima, non solum in domum suam "Leobwinus familiariter et amicabiliter suscepit, verumetiam "episcopus ipse illum, ut prius, in suam gratiam familiamque "recepit. Unde omnes qui [ex] parte antistitis foris inventi "sunt, primitus occiderunt, paucis fuga reservatis. Quo viso, "ut hostium furori satisfaceret, propinquum suum præfatum "Gilebertum, cujus anima quærebatur, præsul de ecclesia jussit "exire. Quem egredientem milites repugnaturi e vestigio sunt "secuti. Sed mox ab hostibus undique gladiis et lanceis appe-"titi, in momento sunt perempti. Duobus tamen Anglicis mi-"nistris propter consanguinitatem pepercerunt. Leofwinum "quoque Dunelmensem decanum, quia sæpius episcopo adversus "illos multa dederat insilia, et clericos alios, statim ut egressi "sunt, occiderunt. Episcopus autem, ut intellexit illorum furo-"rem nulla ratione iri mitigatum quivisse, nisi caput et auctor "totius illius calamitatis occideretur Leobwinus, rogavit illum "egredi foras. Sed cum penitus ut egrederetur ab illo extor-"quere nequiret, ad ecclesiæ januas ipsemet accessit, sibique "vitam concedi poposcit. Quibus renuentibus, caput suæ "clamidis limbo co-operiens foras exivit, et mox inimicorum "gladiis percussus occubuit. Deinde Leobwinum egredi jus-"serunt. Quo nolente, ecclesiæ tecto parietibusque ignem "imposuere. At ille potius ustulatione quam occisione vitam "eligens finire, flammas aliquamdiu sustulit. Sed cum semi-"ustus esset exilivit, et frustatim concisus nequitiæ suæ "pœnas exsolvendo, miser interiit. Ob quorum detestandæ "necis vindictam, rex Willelmus eodem anno devastavit North-"ymbriam;" misso illuc Odone Baiocensi episcopo cum multa militari manu. Quo anno idem rex Willelmus autumnali tempore Rodbertum filium suum Scotiam contra Malcolmum misit. Sed cum pervenisset ad Egglesbreth, nullo confecto negotio reversus, Castellum Novum super flumen Tyne condidit.

"Willelmus suscepit episcopatum Dunelmensem v idus No-

"vembris, sed iiij nonas Januarii a Thoma Eboracensi archi-"episcopo consecratur" apud Gloecestre.

Henricus imperator Hiltibrandum papam in Pentecosten Mogontiæ decernit deponendum, et Wibertum, Ravennæ urbis episcopum, in natali Sancti Johannis Baptistæ pro eo fecit papam.

MLXXXI.

Anno M.lxxxj Henricus rex hostiliter Romam adversus Hiltibrandum papam adiit, oppugnans eam, non tamen intravit.

MLXXXII.

Anno M.lxxxij multis homicidiis et prædationibus inter Henricum regem et Hiltibrandum papam actis, in nocte Palmarum multi sunt occisi.

MLXXXIII.

Anno M.lxxxiij, Henricus rex urbem Romæ infregit et cepit, Wibertum in sede apostolica constituit. Hiltibrandus vero Beneventum adiit, ubi usque ad obitum suum deguit. Henricus autem in Teutonicam patriam rediit. Hoc anno monachi primum in Dunelmum convenerunt, (jubente Guillelmo rege majore, vij kal Junii, feria vj.)[z]

MLXXXIV.

Anno M.lxxxiiij Hiltibrandus, qui et Gregorius, papa obiit.

MLXXXVI.

"Anno M.lxxxvj.—Willelmus rex fecit describi omnem "Angliam, quantum terræ quisque baronum suorum possidebat, "quot feudatos milites, quot carucas, quot villanos,[a] quot "animalia, immo quantum vivæ pecuniæ quisquis possidebat in "omni regno suo."

MLXXXVII.

Anno M.lxxxvij.—Hoc anno reliquiæ Sancti Nicholai de Mirrea in Barensem transferuntur civitatem. Aldwinus Prior Dunelmensis decessit.

MLXXXVIII.

"Anno M.lxxxviij.—Hoc anno inter primates Angliæ orta "est discordia. Pars etenim nobilium Normannorum favebat

[z] The words within parentheses are from the Abbreviatio, MS. Cott. Calig., A. viii. In the margin are the words, *Monachi in Dunelmia.*

[a] In the Abbreviatio in MS. Cotton, Caligula, A. viii., these words are added, "et longitudinem et latitudinem silvarum et pratorum."

"regi Willelmo; sed minima: pars vero altera favebat Rodberto "comiti Normannorum, et maxima, cupiens hunc sibi asciscere "in regnum; fratrem vero ejus aut fratri tradere vivum, aut "regno privare peremptum. Hujus execrandæ rei principes "extiterunt Odo episcopus Baiocensis, qui et erat comes Cantua-"riensis, et Goffridus episcopus Constantinensis, et Rodbertus "comes Moritunensis, et Rogerus comes Scrobbesbyriensis," et excellentiores principes totius Angliæ, excepto Lanfranco archiepiscopo. "Execrabile hoc factum tractaverunt clam in "Quadragesima, statimque post Pascha" cœpit quisque circa se vastare, rapere, omnia deprædare, castella munire fosso et victu. "Goffridus episcopus Constantinensis et Rodbertus de Mulbrei "iverunt Brycstoue, ubi habebant castrum fortissimum, et "omnia devastabant usque locum qui vocatur Bathan."[b] Proceresque de Hereforda et de Scrobbesbyria cum multitudine Walensium perrexerunt usque Wigornam, omnia ante se vastantes, et igne consumentes. Cogitaverunt etiam quod castrum et ecclesiam vellent accipere, quod videlicet castrum tunc temporis commendatum erat Wlstano venerabili episcopo. Quando episcopus ista audivit, valde contristatur, et cogitans quid consilii inde haberet, vertit se ad Deum suum, et rogat ut respiciat ecclesiam Suam et populum Suum ab hostibus oppressum. Hæc eo meditante, familia ejus exiliit de castro, et acceperunt et occiderunt ex eis quingentos viros, et alios in fugam verterunt. Rogerus Bigot intravit castrum de Northwic, et omnes vicit in malum. Odo episcopus, per quem ista mala cœperunt, perrexit Cantiam, et villas regias vastavit, necnon et omnium qui regi fidem tenuerunt terras depopulatus est, et castrum Hrofense obfirmavit. Hoc audito, rex fecit convocare Anglos, et ostendit eis traditionem Normannorum, et rogavit ut sibi auxilio essent, eo tenore, ut si in hac necessitate sibi fideles existerent, meliorem legem quam vellent eligere, eis concederet, et omnem injustum scottum interdixit, et concessit omnibus silvas suas et venationem. Sed quicquid promisit, parvo tempore custodivit. Angli tamen fideliter eum juvabant. Congregavit igitur rex exercitum ut iret Hrovecestram, ubi putabat Odonem episcopum esse. Venientes autem ad Tonebryge invenerunt castrum obfirmatum contra regem. Sed viriliter Angli insilientes in illud, destruxerunt totum castrum, et qui intus erant in manus regi dederunt. His ita actis, rex cum exercitu vertit iter versus castrum de Peveneseia, jam enim Odo

[b] To this point the narrative is chiefly from Florence; the remainder, although to some extent recording the same events, is neither identical in details nor as to the order in which events are placed, and many particulars are added.

episcopus recessit a Rovecestria, et intrabat castrum illud. Quem rex secutus, obsidebat castrum per sex integras septimanas cum magno exercitu. Dum hæc fiunt in Anglia, Rodbertus comes Normanniæ congregat magnum exercitum, et parat eum in Angliam mittere, mox secuturus, quasi de Anglia per Odonem episcopum et cæteros qui ex sua parte ibi erant securus. Sed rex Willelmus jam mare munierat suis piratis, qui venientes in Angliam tot occiderunt et in mare merserunt, ut nullus sit hominum qui sciat numerum pereuntium. Interim, dum hæc fiunt in mare, Odo episcopus et qui cum eo erant, fame coacti, reddentes castrum de Pevenesea promiserunt cum jurejurando se Angliam exituros, nec amplius intraturos nisi rege Willelmo præcipiente, castrum quoque Hrofense ante reddituros. Sed cum venisset Hrouecestre cum hominibus regis, qui ex parte regis deberent castrum recipere, statim cum eisdem ab his qui in castello erant ponitur in vinculis. Quidam asserebant hoc factum esse calliditate episcopi. In hoc certe castro erant strenui milites, et pene tota nobilitas Normanniæ. Erat ibi Eustachius juvenis, Boloniensis comes, et multi nobiles Flandrenses. His itaque a rege auditis, venit cum exercitu Hrouecestram, et obsedit civitatem; et, parvo peracto spatio, hi qui intus fuerunt se reddiderunt, et cum dedecore ejecti sunt de Anglia, et ita episcopus, qui fere fuit secundus rex Angliæ, honorem amisit irrecuperabiliter. Sed episcopus veniens Normanniam statim a Rodberto comite totius provinciæ curam suscepit. Cujus ordinem causæ libellus in hoc descriptus aperte ostendit. Etiam Dunholmensis episcopus, Willelmus, viij anno sui episcopatus, et multi alii, de Anglia exierunt.

MXCI.

"Anno M.xcj—mense Maio, rex Scottorum Malcholmus cum "magno exercitu Northymbriam invasit, si successus succes-"sisset ulterius processurus, et vim Angliæ incolis illaturus. "Noluit Deus, et ideo ab incepto est impeditus. Quo rex "audito, cum fratre suo Rodberto rediit Angliam mense "Augusti. Nec multo post cum classe non modica et equestri "exercitu Scottiam profectus est, ut Malcolmum debellaret." Veniens Dunelmum, episcopum Willelmum restituit in sedem suam, ipso post annos tres die quo eam reliquit, scilicet tertio idus Septembris.

MXCIII.

Anno M.xciij. Ecclesia nova Dunelmi est incepta tertio idus Augusti feria quinta, episcopo Willelmo et Malcholmo rege Scottorum,[c] et Turgoto Priore ponentibus primos in fundamento lapides.

"Comes Scrobbesbyriensis Rogerus, et Wido abbas Sancti "Augustini, et Paulus abbas monasterii Sancti Albani decesse-"runt." Iste Paulus contra interdictum monachorum Dunelmensium ecclesiam de Tynemuthe quam ipsi possederant, per violentiam Rodberti comitis ingressus, tactus ibidem infirmitate, rediens in itinere, in Seteringtun juxta Eboracum moritur. "Rex Scottorum Malcholmus et primogenitus filius ejus Ead-"wardus cum multis aliis, in Northymbria die festivitatis Sancti "Bricii, a militibus Rodberti Northimbrorum comitis occisi "sunt."[d] In cujus morte justitia judicantis Dei aperte consideratur, ut videlicet in illa provincia cum suis interiret, quam sæpe ipse vastare avaritia stimulante consuevit, quinquies[e] namque illam atroci depopulatione attrivit, et miseros indigenas in servitutem redigendos abduxit captivos. Semel Eadwardo regnante, quando Tosti comes Eboracensis profectus Romam fuerat. Iterum regnante Willelmo, quando etiam Clivelandam depopulatus est. Tertio regnante eodem rege Willelmo usque Tynam progressus, post cædes hominum et concremationes locorum multa cum præda revertitur. Quarto, regnante Willelmo Juniore, cum suis copiis infinitis usque Ceastram, non longe a Dunelmo sitam, pervenit, animo intendens ulterius progredi. Sed adunata contra eum militari manu non multa, metu ipso citius revertitur. Quinto, cum omni quo potuit exercitu in ultimam deducturus desolationem, Northymbriam invasit, sed juxta flumen Alne perimitur cum primogenito suo Eadwardo, quem hæredem regni post se disposuerat. Exercitus illius vel gladiis confoditur, vel qui gladios fugerunt inundatione fluminum, quæ tunc pluviis hiemalibus plus solito excreverant, absorti sunt. Corpus vero regis, cum suorum nullus remaneret qui terra illud cooperiret, duo ex indigenis carro impositum in Tynemuthe sepelierunt. Sicque factum est ut ubi multos vita

[c] There is no mention of Malcolm's presence on this memorable occasion, in the work in which of all others we should have expected to have found it recorded, if such had been the fact, in Symeon's History of the Church of Durham. See Preface. Fordun mentions his presence, and cites Turgot as his authority. In no case, however, do Fordun's quotations from Turgot bear any resemblance to the History of the Church of Durham, or advance the claim made on his behalf to the authorship of the work in opposition to Symeon.

[d] Malcolmus rex Scottorum in Northymbria occisus est. *In margine.*

[e] Respecting these five alleged incursions into Northumberland, see Preface. These paragraphs about the death and expeditions of Malcolm are quoted in the letter of R. de Durham, a monk of Kelso, to the Prior of Tynemouth. The monk says that he got it "in Danorum Historia" (Memorials of Hexham, i., app., xv).

et rebus et libertate privaverat, ibidem ipse Dei judicio vitam simul cum rebus amitteret.

MXCVII.

Anno M.xcvij Cisterciense cœnobium sumpsit exordium.[f]

MCI.

Anno M.cj Henricus rex tenuit curiam suam Londoniæ in nativitate Domini, ubi interfuit Ludowicus electus rex Francorum,[g] (et ad mensam sedebat ad dexteram regis, inter regem scilicet Henricum et Anselmum archiepiscopum.)

"Comes Normannorum Rodbertus, equitum, sagittariorum, "et peditum non parvam congregans multitudinem" (applicuit in loco qui Portesmuthe dicitur; ibique in rivaria de Walmesford figi tentoria præcepit. Rex autem ejus adventum apud Hastinges expectans, cum comitem venisse audisset, cum exercitu suo maximo per Surriam venit ad Auwltum ubi et ipse sua tentoria figi fecit. Ibique mediantibus utrorum baronibus, locuti sunt adinvicem rex et comes, concordiaque inter eos prolocuta, venerunt Guintoniam secunda die Augusti, et ibi sacramento et affidatione inter eos facta, redditæ sunt unicuique baronum utrorum terræ.[h])

MCII.

"Anno M.cij.—Anselmus archiepiscopus tenuit magnum con- "cilium de his quæ ad Christianitatem pertinent.—In hoc con- "cilio plures abbates Francigenæ et Angli sunt depositi, et "honoribus privati, quos injuste acquisierunt, aut in eis in- "honeste vixerunt."—Presbyteris quoque concubinæ interdictæ sunt. Unde plures eorum ostia ecclesiarum obseraverunt, omittentes omnia officia ecclesiastica.

MCIII.

Anno M.ciij (natus est Guilelmus, filius R. comitis, die Sanctorum Crispini et Crispiani, in turre Rothomanensium.[i])

MCIV.

"Anno M.ciiij—Corpus Sancti Cuthberti episcopi, ob quo-

[f] This sentence is inserted in a coarse hand.

[g] The words from hence to the end of the sentence are from the Abbreviatio, MS. Cott. Caligula, A. viii.

[h] The words within inverted commas are from Florence, the remainder of the paragraph is from the Abbreviatio, MS. Cott. Caligula, A. viii. It has been thought needless to repeat the words of Florence, which they abridge or supplement.

[i] This sentence is from the Abbreviatio, MS. Cott. Caligula, viii. A.

"rundam incredulitatem abbatum, pontificante Rannulfo epis-"copo, ostensum est, et a Radulfo Sagiensi abbate, postmodum "Hrofensi episcopo," et deinde Cantuariensi archiepiscopo, "et "a fratribus Dunelmensis ecclesiæ certo indicio incorruptum "inventum est," et ita flexilibus artubus, ut magis dormienti quam mortuo similis videretur, "præsente Alexandro comite, postea Scottorum rege"[j] et multis aliis, post annos depositionis suæ cccc et xviij, et v menses, et xij dies, qui est annus quintus Henrici regis, et episcopatus Ranulfi sextus. Ab origine mundi fuerunt transacti v^{m}cccviij.

MCVI.

"Anno M.cvj.—Facta est nimis execrabilis contentio inter "Henricum imperatorem Romanorum et filium ejus Henricum." Et eodem anno mortuus est idem imperator, cum l annis regnasset; cui successit filius ejus Henricus.[k]

MCVII.

"Anno M.cvii.—Willelmus Wintoniensi, Herefordensi Rei-"nelmus, Searesberiensi Rogerus, Willelmus Execestrensi, et "Urbanus Glamorgacensi ecclesiæ, quæ in Walonia est, electi "episcopi, simul Cantuariam venerunt; et in die Dominica, "quæ fuit iij idus Augusti, pariter ab Anselmo consecrati sunt, "ministrantibus sibi in hoc officio suffraganeis ipsius sedis." Gerardus etiam, Eboracensis archiepiscopus, eorum consecrationi, rogatu Anselmi, interfuit.—(Turgotus, Dunelmensis ecclesiæ Prior, ad episcopatum Scottorum eligitur.[l])

MCX.

"Anno M.cx. Rex Anglorum, Henricus, filiam suam Hen-"rico imperatori in conjugem dedit," et misit eam a Dovere usque ad Witsand in initio Quadragesimæ quod fuit iiij idus Aprilis.

MCXII.

Anno M.cxij.—Thomas archiepiscopus Hagustaldensem ecclesiam pene in solitudinem redactam, et in portionem cujusdam præbendæ ecclesiæ Eboracensi datam doluit. Hanc ut honestaret frequentia religiosorum, kalend. Novembris posuit in ea

[j] On a comparison of the text of Florence with this passage, it would appear that the former must have been written between the years 1108 and 1114, during which period Ralph held the bishopric of Rochester. He was advanced to the archbishopric of Canterbury on the 26th of April in the latter year. Alexander became king of Scotland on the death of his brother Edgar, January 8th, 1107.

[k] In the margin, Obiit imperator Henricus. Successit filius ejus Henricus.

[l] This sentence is from the Abbreviatio, MS. Cott. Caligula, A. viii.

canonicos regulares, quibus præfuit primus Prior Aschatillus, canonicus de Hunteduna, vir omnibus amabilis.

MCXIII.

Anno M.cxiij monachi Tironenses in Angliam venerunt x annos antequam Savinienses venerunt in Angliam.[m] Monachi Tironenses in terra David regis Scotiæ apud Seleschirche venerunt, et ibi per annos xv manserunt.[n]

MCXIV.

"Anno M.cxiiij Thomas Eboracensis archiepiscopus," vir eximiæ religionis, "vj kal Martii, feria iij, obiit."[o] Qui cum cæteris sanctarum virtutum operibus, etiam in virginitatis puritate perrexit ad Dominum. Quanta vero morum probitate et vitæ innocentis puritate ante episcopatum et in episcopatu enituerit, nullis humanis verbis digne explicari posse arbitror.

MCXV.

Anno M.cxv.—Turgotus,[p] quondam Dunelmensis ecclesiæ Prior, nunc autem episcopus Scottorum, rediens Dunelmum, ibidem vitam finivit.

MCXVI.

"Anno M.cxvj.—Conventio optimatum et baronum totius "Angliæ apud Searesberiam xiiij kal. Aprilis facta est. Qui in "præsentia regis Henrici homagium filio suo Willelmo fecerunt, "et fidelitatem ei juraverunt. Habita est ibi causa de querela "quæ inter archiepiscopum Cantuariensem Radulfum et elec- "tum pontificem Eboracensem Turstinum per integrum annum "versata fuerat. Hic electus cum ab ipso pontifice moneretur, "ut ecclesiæ Cantuariensi faceret quod debebat, et benedictio- "nem suam ecclesiastico more susciperet, respondit. Bene- "dictionem quidem se libenter suscipere velle, sed professionem "quam exigebat nulla ratione facturum" præter quam beatus papa Gregorius constituit. Nam ipse talem legem inter duos archiepiscopos Angliæ posuit, sed et Honorius papa VI. post eum similiter, ut neuter alteri subjectionis professionem faceret, nisi tantum ut qui prior ordinatus esset quamdiu viveret prior haberetur: quod proprium est servorum Dei, ut vera humilitate

[m] This sentence, with the exception of the date, is at the foot of the page.

[n] This sentence is in the MS. at the end of the annals of the preceding year.

[o] In the margin—Obiit secundus Thomas Eboracensis archiepiscopus: post quem Turstinus eligitur.

[p] The Abbreviatio, MS. Cotton Caligula, A. viii., has "Monachus et Prior Dunelmensis."

sibi invicem acclines sint, et nullus super alium primatus ambitionem exercere velit, sicut Dominus noster veræ humilitatis prædicator et amator, discipulos Suos de hac re litigantes redarguens, dixit eis, *Qui major est vestrum erit omnium minister.*[r] Nullus siquidem post beatum Augustinum (qui non tam archiepiscopus quam Apostolus Anglorum dicendus est) archiepiscoporum Cantuariensium primatum totius Angliæ sibi vindicare præsumpsit usque ad Theodorum archipræsulem, cui propter singularem in ecclesiastica disciplina sollertiam omnes Angliæ episcopi subjici consenserunt, sicut Beda in Ecclesiastica Historia Anglorum testatur, ita scribens de eo. "Is primus in archiepiscopis cui omnes Britanniæ episcopi manus dare consenserunt."[s] Quamobrem Turstinus nullam aliam subjectionis professionem Cantuariensi pontifici facere voluit, nisi quam beatus papa Gregorius instituit. "Rex autem Henricus ubi "advertit Turstinum in sua" sententia "stare, aperte protestatus "est, illum aut morem antecessorum suorum tam in professione "facienda quam in aliis dignitati ecclesiæ Cantuariensis ex "antiquo jure competentibus executurum, aut episcopatu Ebor-"acensi cum benedictione funditus cariturum. His auditis, "ille sui cordis consilio impræmeditatius credens, renunciavit "pontificatui, spondens regi et archiepiscopo se dum viveret "illum non reclamaturum, nec aliquam calumniam inde motu-"rum, quicunque substitutus fuisset."

MCXVII.

Anno M.cxvij.—In kal. Decembris extiterunt nimia tonitrua et fulgura: quæ secuta sunt magna pluviarum inundatio et grandinis congelatio; et iij idus Decembris luna quasi sanguinea et postea obtenebrata apparuit.

MCXVIII.[t]

"Anno M.cxviii.—Præfatus papa Gelasius per mare Burgundiam venit, et adventus ejus mox toti Galliæ innotuit." Cujus in Gallias missa hæc est epistola.

[r] St. Matt. xx. 27; xxiii. 11. St. Mark x. 4.

[s] Slightly varied from Beda, iv., 2.

[t] At this date the work of Florence of Worcester is made to end, and that of his Continuator to commence, on the authority of a rubric in one of the best MSS. The rubric itself, however, is an insertion in a recent hand, and the only real ground for fixing the conclusion of the original chronicle at this point seems to be, that the death of the author took place in the ensuing year. It is quite as probable, however, that Florence discontinued his labours at a somewhat earlier period. We have indeed some ground for supposing that he did not continue or revise his chronicle to within four years or upwards of this period. (See note under A.D. 1104.) The author of the Gesta Regum continues to borrow largely from the Continuator down to 1119, after which he no longer resorts to him, and it is probable that the work, as given to the public at that time, ex-

Gelasius episcopus, servorum Dei servus, venerabilibus fratribus, archiepiscopis, episcopis, abbatibus, clericis, principibus et cæteris per Galliam fidelibus, salutem et Apostolicam benedictionem. Quia vos Romanæ ecclesiæ membra estis, quæ in ea nuper acta sunt dilectioni vestræ significare curavimus. Siquidem post electionem nostram dominus Imperator furtive et inopinata velocitate Romam veniens, nos egredi compulit. Pacem postea minis et terroribus postulavit, dicens se facturum quæ posset ubi nos ei juramento pacis certitudinem faceremus. Ad quæ nos ista respondimus. De controversia quæ inter ecclesiam et regnum est, vel conventioni vel justitiæ libenter acquiescimus loco et tempore competenti, videlicet, vel Mediolani vel Cremonæ in proxima Beati Lucæ festivitate, et fratrum nostrorum judicio vel consilio, qui a Deo sunt judices in ecclesia constituti, et sine quibus hæc causa tractari non potest. Et quoniam dominus Imperator a nobis securitatem quærit, nos verbo et scripto ista promittimus, nisi ipse interim impediat: alias enim securitates promittere nec honestas ecclesiæ, nec consuetudo est. Ille enim, die videlicet post electionem nostram quadragesimo quarto, Bracarensem episcopum, anno præterito a domino prædecessore nostro Paschali papa in concilio Beneventi excommunicatum, in matris ecclesiæ invasionem ingessit. Qui etiam dum per manus nostras olim pallium accepisset, eidem domino nostro et catholicis successoribus ejus, quorum primus ego sum, fidelitatem juravit. In hoc tanto facinore nullum de Romano clero, Deo gratias, Imperator socium habuit. Sed Guibertini soli, Romanus de Sancto Marcello, Centius qui dicebatur Sancti Grisogoni, et Euzo qui per Daciam multo tempore debacchatus est, tam infamem gloriam celebrarunt. Vestræ igitur experientiæ litterarum præsentium præcepto mandamus, ut super his communi per Dei gratiam deliberatione tractantes, ad matris ecclesiæ ultionem communibus præstante Deo auxiliis, sicut oportere cognoscitis, accingamini. Data Caitæ, xvij *kal. Februarii.*[u]

His discurrentibus per provincias litteris, excitati potentes quique cum mediocribus occurrere Apostolico; et certatim parabant interesse concilio quod ipse disposuit se media Quadragesima Remis celebraturum.

tended no farther. Supposing Florence to have brought down his work to the period indicated in the note referred to, A.D. 1108-14, it was natural that the brethren of his house, by whom his merits were so highly appreciated, should be anxious after his death to present the fruits of his labours to the world, and equally natural that they should add to them a continuation up to the period of publication.

[u] This epistle is from Eadmer, with slight verbal variations, as is also the following paragraph, p. 122, ed. Selden. The letter is given in Baronius, who derives it from William of Malmesbury. It is printed in several places.

MCXIX.

Anno M.CXIX. Gelasius papa apud Cluniacum obiit, ibidemque sepelitur.[v] In cujus locum cardinales aliique Romani, qui eum illuc secuti fuerant, Guidonem Viennensem archiepiscopum substituunt, eumque Calixtum nominant. Dumque in Burgundia hæc geruntur, Apostolatus Romanæ ecclesiæ a supradicto Gregorio amministratur. Super his duobus ita in papatum sullimatis orbis concussus in studia partium dividitur, atque aliis hunc, aliis istum favore prosequentibus, gravi ecclesia scandalo percellitur.[w]

"Calixtus papa xiij kal. Novembris generale concilium "instituit Remis. Ad hoc concilium multiplex factus est "archiepiscoporum, episcoporum, abbatum et principum diver-"sarum provinciarum concursus, cum clericorum et laicorum "plebium numerosa multitudine."[x] Numeratæ sunt ibi personarum pastoralium virgæ cccc.xxiiij. Inter quos et Turstinus Eboracensis ecclesiæ archiepiscopus electus, vix quandoque licentia a rege impetrata, propter suum proficiscitur negotium. Præmiserat autem rex legatum suum ad Apostolicum, quatinus inter alia et hoc ei diceretur, ne Eboracensem electum aut ipse consecraret, aut ab alio nisi ab archiepiscopo Cantuariensi, uti moris esse solebat, sacrari aut juberet aut permitteret. Ad hoc Apostolicus; "Ne putet, inquit, rex me de negotio de quo agit "secus acturum quam ratio exigit. Nec enim me ad hoc mea "fert voluntas, ut Cantuariensis ecclesiæ justam dignitatem "humiliem." Sed mane facto Dominici diei præcedentis diem præstituti concilii, Turstino ad benedictionem pontificatus parato, legati Cantuariensis archiepiscopi præsumptuose calumniati sunt consecrationem Eboracensis archiepiscopi a Cantuariensi debere fieri archipræsule. Ad quod Apostolicus: "Nullam, inquit, injustitiam ecclesiæ Cantuariensi facere vo-"lumus, sed salva illius dignitate, quod proposuimus, exe-"quemur." Consecratus est itaque ab Apostolico.[y] Postera die residentibus ordine in concilio ecclesiasticorum graduum personis, assidente quoque rege Francorum Ludowico multisque aliis principalibus viris, ex consensu cunctorum renovantur patrum statuta de statuendis, et recisa de recidendis, quorum hic sunt quinque capitula.

Quæ sanctorum patrum sanctionibus de pravitate symonica stabilita sunt, nos quoque Sancti Spiritus judicio et auctoritate

[v] Obiit Gelasius papa. *In margine.*

[w] Eadmer, p. 123.

[x] From this point no further use is made of the Continuation of Florence of Worcester.

[y] Hic consecratus est Turstinus Eboracensis archiepiscopus. *In margine.* All the above is from Eadmer, pp. 124-5.

sedis Apostolicæ confirmamus. Si quis ergo vendiderit aut emerit, vel per se vel per quamlibet submissam personam, episcopatum, abbatiam, decanatum, archidiaconatum, presbyteratum, præposituram, præbendam, altaria, vel quælibet ecclesiastica beneficia, promotiones, ordinationes, consecrationes, dedicationes ecclesiarum, clericalem tonsuram, sedes in choro, aut quælibet ecclesiastica officia, et vendens et emens dignitatis et officii sui ac beneficii periculo subjaceat. Quod nisi resipuerit, anathematis mucrone perfossus ab ecclesia Dei quam læsit modis omnibus abscidatur.

Episcopatuum, abbatiarum aut quarumlibet ecclesiasticarum possessionum investituram per manum laicam fieri penitus prohibemus. Quicunque igitur laicorum deinceps investire præsumpserit, anathematis ultioni subjaceat. Porro qui investitus fuerit, honore quo investitus est absque spe recuperationis omnimodis careat.

Universas ecclesiarum possessiones quæ liberalitate regum, largitione principum, vel oblatione quorumlibet fidelium eis concessæ sunt, inconcussas inperpetuum et inviolatas esse decernimus. Quod si quis eas abstulerit, aut invaserit, aut potestate tyrannica detinuerit, juxta illud beati Symmachi capitulum anathemate perpetuo feriatur.

Nullus episcopus, nullus presbyter, nullus omnino de clero ecclesiasticas dignitates, vel beneficia, cuilibet, et quasi jure hæreditario, derelinquat. Illud etiam adjicientes præcipimus, ut pro baptismatis, crismatis, olei sacri et sepulturæ acceptione et infirmorum visitatione vel unctione nullum omnino pretium exigatur.

Presbyteris, diaconibus, et subdiaconibus concubinarum et uxorum contubernia prorsus interdicimus. Si qui autem hujusmodi reperti fuerint, ecclesiasticis et officiis priventur et beneficiis. Sane si neque immunditiam suam correxerint, communione careant Christiana.[z]

Hæc concilii decreta imperatori Henrico, cum non longe abesset ex concilio, primum per honestas personas, ad ultimum per ipsum Apostolicum mandantur, ut ante separationem Concilii notum esset, utrum ecclesiis per regnum et singulas quasque sibi subjectas provincias consentiat Canonicas Electiones, videlicet, ut episcopi et abbates eligantur ab ecclesia, et liberas consecrationes, ut, ubi, et a quibus oporteat electi consecrentur; et Investituram Ecclesiarum, ut per investituram pastoralis virgæ

[z] Baronius gives these decrees from Roger Hoveden. It is a singular fact that the foreign church historians should have come to the English chroniclers for so many of the decrees of their own councils, as well as for the bulls of the Popes.

et annuli per ostium Christum ingrediantur; et Investituram Rerum Ecclesiasticarum, ut de rebus ad ecclesias pertinentibus nihil omnino sibi laicalis exigat persona. Ad hæc ille respondit, nihil in his se prætermissurum, quod sui juris esse suorum sibi contulit antiqua consuetudo progenitorum. Quandoque tamen flexus auctoritate generalis concilii, tria illa priora concessit, ultimum vero, scilicet Investituram Rerum Ecclesiasticarum, concedere noluit. Quapropter reverso ad concilium papa, excommunicandus decernitur. Quod cum quidam in concilio ægre ferrent, sententiam protulit Apostolicus, ut, qui in hoc scandalizentur, exeuntes a fratrum consortio separarentur: proposito de illis septuaginta exemplo, qui cum de carne Domini manducanda et sanguine bibendo scandalizarentur, retro abierunt, et jam cum Illo non ambulabant. "Et quoniam," inquit, "*qui non colligit cum Domino spargit, et qui non est cum Eo* "*adversus Illum est*,[a] illam inconsutilem tunicam desuper con-"textam, scilicet sanctam ecclesiam, qui nobiscum sentiendo "indiscissam servare nolunt, dissentiendo a nobis discindere "contendunt." Talia sermocinante Apostolico, illico omnes in eundem cum cæteris consensum reducti, in imperatorem Henricum excommunicationis sententiam jaculantur.[b] Tandem post dies aliquot dissoluto concilio, offensus rex Anglorum Turstino archiepiscopo, quod præter consensum suum se ab Apostolico consecrari fecisset, interdixit ei reditum in omnem suæ dominationis locum.

Post hæc papa Calixtus Gisortium venit; quo ad ejus colloquium rex Anglorum occurrit. Acta sunt multa inter illos, quorum gratia par erat tantas convenisse personas. Inter quæ rex a papa impetravit, ut omnes consuetudines quas pater suus in Normannia et in Anglia habuerat sibi concederet, et maxime ut neminem aliquando legati officio in Anglia fungi permitteret,[c] si non ipse, aliqua præcipua querela exigente quæ ab episcopis regni sui terminari non posset, hoc fieri a papa postularet. Quibus omnibus pro statu temporis definitis, papa rogat regem Turstino amicum fieri, eumque pontificatui ad quem ipsum sacraverat pro amore suo restitui. At rex hoc se dum viveret

[a] St. Matt. xii. 30 with alterations.

[b] All which follows as to the controversy between the Pope and King Henry relative to the consecration of the archbishop, to the words, "Turstinus remansit in Gallia," is copied from Eadmer, pp. 125-6. Symeon seems to have been unacquainted with the history of this controversy by Hugh the Chantor; if he had read it, he would perhaps have given the York view, and not that of Canterbury.

[c] The Abbreviatio, MS. Cott. Caligula, viii. A., ends at this point, the following words being introduced after "permitteret:" "De primo Saxonum vel Normannorum adventu sive de eorundem regibus libellus explicit."

non facturum in sua fide spopondisse confessus est. Ait, "Ego "Apostolicus sum, et si feceris quod postulo ab hac fidei spon- "sione te absolvam. Tractabo de hoc," ait, "et quod consilii "mei tenor invenerit tibi notificabo." Hinc a papa recessit. Cui per internuncios de negotio ita respondit. "Pro amore "vestro qui tantopere postulatis, ea conditione Turstinum ad- "mitto in pontificatum, ut subjectionem quam prædecessores "ejus fecerant ecclesiæ Cantuariensi faciat, aliter me regnante "Eboracensi ecclesiæ non præsidebit." His ita gestis, abeunte Apostolico, Turstinus remansit in Gallia.

Willelmus, filius regis Henrici et Mahtildis reginæ accepit uxorem filiam comitis Andegavensium.

MCXX.

Anno M.CXX, rex Anglorum Henricus et rex Francorum Ludowicus, post multa suarum partium detrimenta, die præstituta ineunt colloquia. Quo ex consensu concordiæ peracto, jussu regis Henrici, filius ejus Willelmus, facto regi Francorum hominio, Normanniæ sub illo suscipit principatum. Ita redeuntibus in pacem regibus, tota tumultuantis Normanniæ seditio comprimitur, et qui contra dominum suum Henricum regem arma levaverant, curvata sub ejus dominium cervice, redeunt; et quoniam in concordia regum facienda archiepiscopus Turstinus vigilantem se ac diligentem exhibuit, hac sui efficacia proniorem ad sese recipiendum regis animum inflexit. Ad hoc epistola Apostolici ad regem jam parantem redire in Angliam directa,[d] Turstinum archiepiscopum suscipere, et in suam præcepit ecclesiam omni postposita excusatione restituere. Sed ad hoc præceptum quid potissimum respondeat rex distulit donec redisset in Angliam; ubi, congregato concilio, quid facto opus esset maturius perquireret. Normanniæ principes, jubente rege, filio suo Willelmo, jam tunc xviij annorum, hominium faciunt, et fidelitatis securitatem sacramentis affirmant. Itaque rex omnibus qui contra se insurrexerant vel devictis vel repacificatis, cunctisque ad votum prospere peractis, quinto profectionis suæ anno necdum completo, lætior solito, in Angliam multo [navigio] revehitur. Delegaverat autem filio cunctoque illius comitatui navem qua nulla in tota classe videbatur melior, sed ut eventus ostendit, nulla infelicior. Patre namque præeunte, paulo tardius sed infelicius sequebatur filius. Nave quippe non longe a terra in ipso velificationis impetu super scopulos in ipso exitu delata ac dissoluta, filius regis cum omnibus qui secum erant interiit vj kal. Decembris, feria v,

[d] Eadmer, p. 136.

noctis initio apud Barbafflot.[e] Mane facto, thesaurus regis qui in navi fuerat invenitur per arenas, corpora vero pereuntium nulla. Perierunt cum filio regis frater suus Ricardus nothus comes, cum filia regis quæ fuerat uxor Rotronis, et Ricardus comes Cestrensis cum uxore sua nepte regis, sorore Theobaldi comitis, nepotis regis. Periit et Othoel magister filii regis, et Goffridus Ridel, et Rodbertus Malduit, et Willelmus Bigot, multique alii principales viri. Nobiles quoque feminæ quamplures cum regiis pueris non paucis, militaris numeri cxl et nautarum l cum tribus gubernatoribus navis. Solus quidam macellarius tabula naufragii pendens evasit. Rex vero prospero cursu Angliam attingens, alium portum intrasse putabat filium, sed die tertio de illius interitu tristi perturbatur nuncio. Et quidem primo subito casu veluti pusillanimis deficiebat; sed mox, dissimulato dolore, regios animos ex contemptu resumpsit fortunæ. Illum quippe solum ex legitimo conjugio susceptum regni post se hæredem constituerat.

MCXXI.

Anno M.CXXJ, concilio totius Angliæ ante Purificationem Sanctæ Mariæ apud Winderesoram adunato, Henricus rex filiam Godefridi ducis Luvaniæ, Adelinam, matrimonio sibi junxit.[f] Ricardus capellanus regis ad Herefordensis, et Rodbertus Peccator, alius capellanus, ad Coventrensis ecclesiæ præsulatum eligitur. Herbertus elemosynarius Westmonasterii Sancti Petri [in abbatem] ejusdem loci eligitur. Edmerus, Cantuariensis ecclesiæ monachus, præcedenti anno electus ad episcopatum ecclesiæ Sancti Andreæ gentis Scottorum, deposita intentione regendi episcopatum, revertitur ad locum suum.[g] Guillelmus de Campellis, Catalawensis episcopus, viij diebus ante exitum suscepto habitu monachico vita decedit xv kal. Februarii. Eodem anno Henricus rex facto longa terræ intercisione fossato a Torkeseie usque Lincolniam per derivationem Trentæ fluminis fecit iter navium. Rannulfus Dunelmensis episcopus murum incepit a boreali parte cancelli ecclesiæ, et perduxit ad arcem usque castelli. Tunc et castellum apud Northam incepit, super ripam Twedæ, in loco qui Ethamesforda dicitur.[h]

[e] Filii regis H. in mari perierunt. *In margine.*

[f] Eadmer, p. 136.

[g] See Eadmer, pp. 130-5, for a full account of the circumstances of his election to the see of St. Andrew's, and his subsequent resignation.

[h] A fuller account of this bishop's works is given in the Continuation to Symeon's History of the Church of Durham, chap. i., p. 258; ed. Bedford.

Monachi Dunelmenses facta de ecclesia quæ est in Tynemutha proclamatione in capitulo Sancti Petri Eboraci, præsentibus episcopis Turstino prædicto, Ranulfo Dunelmensi et Homo Sancti Ebroini, aliisque multis, hanc sui juris fuisse conquesti sunt ex concessione Waltheofi comitis, quando consobrinum suum, scilicet materteræ suæ filium, Morkarum puerum parvulum, eis ad nutriendum Deo in Gyrwensi monasterio contradidit.[i] Quem sic eis in ipsa ecclesia de Tynemutha commendatum, inde ad Gyrvum navigio ipsi monachi perducentes, diligenter nutrire, et in Dei servitium educare studuerunt. Ab hoc, inquiunt, tempore nostri fratres monachi Gyrwenses curam illius loci susceptam gesserunt, Ædmundo ac postmodum Eadredo monachis illorum, ipsi ecclesiæ deservientibus, cum presbytero Elwaldo, qui et canonicus Dunelmensis ecclesiæ fuerat, unde et ad Dunelmum, quotiens suæ vicis ebdomada imminebat, ad celebrandas per ebdomadam missas transire consueverat. Wlmarum quoque, nostræ congregationis monachum, aliosque per vices fratres qui ibidem officia Divina peragerent, illuc de Girwa transmissos meminimus. Ossa Sancti Oswini etiam ut placuit, pro tempore ad se in Gyrvum fratres nostri transtulerunt, indeque in priorem locum, cum voluerunt, reportarunt. Postremo cum Albrius honorem Comitatus suscepisset, ipse quoque nobis in Dunelmum translatis, eundem locum donavit. Unde mox ex capituli totius sententia monachus noster Turchillus illuc mittitur, qui, renovato ecclesiæ ipsius culmine, per multum tempus habitavit ibidem, donec postea a Rodberto de Mulbreio comite, propter odium quod contra episcopum Willelmum habuerat, per ministros ipsius comitis Gumerum et Rodbertum Taca violenter expelleretur. Non multo post abbas monasterii Sancti Albani, Paulus, prædictam ecclesiam a Comite impetravit; quam visurus cum venisset Eboracum, Turgotus, qui tunc Dunelmensis ecclesiæ Prioratum gerebat, missis illuc monachis et clericis, in præsentia archiepiscopi Thomæ Senioris, multarumque magnæ reverentiæ personarum, canonica illum auctoritate prohibuit, ne locum juris ecclesiæ Dunelmensis sibi usurparet, et sic sacrorum canonum et fraternæ caritatis violator existeret. At ille indigna respondens, illud prohibitum nihili pendit. Sed cum illo pervenisset, correptus infirmitate, dum rediret, non longe ab Eboraco in Seterintun vitam terminavit. Taliter ecclesiam de Tynemutha amisimus.

Hæc querimonia facta Eboraci, media ferme Quadragesima, replicatur paulo post in ebdomada Paschali, feria iv, idus Aprilis,

[i] See above under the year 1080; also Symeon's History of the Church of Durham, iv., 4; also Charters and other Documents appended to the Three Durham Historians, No. ix., No. x., and No. xxxvii., pp. xviii, xix, liii.

Dunelmi coram magno conventu principalium virorum, qui tunc forte propter negotia quædam illuc confluxerunt, scilicet Rodbertus de Brys, Alanus de Perceio, Walterus Espec, Forno filius Sig'.[j] Rodbertus de Wituila, Odardus vicecomes Northymbrensium, cum majoribus ejusdem comitatus, aliique quamplures. Coram horum frequentia cum suas monachi depromerent querelas, ecce, Harnoldus de Perceio, vir genere et divitiis notus, et in veritate asserenda constans, exurgens, in testimonium veritatis affirmabat coram omnibus, et audisse se et vidisse comitis pœnitentiam super hanc injuriam quam Sancto Cuthberto violenter irrogaverat. Cum, inquit, captus Comes in loco quem Sancto Cuthberto abstulerat, propter inflicta sibi vulnera in feretro delatus esset Dunelmum, rogavit ut sibi liceret ad orandum ecclesiam intrare. Quod cum sibi a baronibus non permitteretur, in lacrimas resolutus, et ad ecclesiam respiciens cum gemitu, ait. "O Sancte Cuthberte, juste has "calamitates patior, quia in te et in tuos peccavi. Hæc est tua "super meam vitæ nequitiam vindicta. Precor te, Sancte Dei, "miserere mei." His auditis, omnes injuste actum esse contra Dunelmensem ecclesiam dicebant: et licet res in præsenti corrigi nequiverit, tamen prudenter hanc calumniam pro futuro tempore coram tot virorum frequentia factam asserebant.

Epistola[k] Calixti papæ super Turstinum directa ad regem Henricum et Radulfum Cantuariensem archiepiscopum, ipsi episcopale atque sacerdotale interdicit officium, et tam in matrice Cantuariensi quam Eboracensi ecclesiis cum suis parochiis, Divina omnia officia celebrari, cum sepultura mortuorum prohibet, præter baptisma infantum et pœnitentias morientium, nisi infra unum mensem post acceptionem ipsius epistolæ Turstinus sine exactione professionis in suam restituatur ecclesiam Quare a rege revocatus in Angliam, mox in suum reducitur archiepiscopatum.

Hoc anno, peracto Paschali festo, Calixtus papa cum multa manu ab Urbe digressus tamdiu Sutrinam civitatem obsedit, donec et Burdinum et locum ipsum cepisset: sic epistola subdita planius edocet.

Calixtus episcopus, servus servorum Dei, dilectis fratribus et filiis, archiepiscopis, episcopis, abbatibus, prioribus, et cæteris tam clericis quam laicis beati Petri fidelibus per Gallias constitutis, salutem et Apostolicam benedictionem. Quia derelinquit populus Domini legem Ejus et in judiciis Ejus non ambulat, visitat *Dominus* in virga iniquitates eorum, et in verberibus peccata

[j] This should be *Lig'*, and not *Sig'*. Forno, the son of Ligulf, Liolf, or Lyulf, was the grantee of the barony of Greystok in Cumberland.

[k] This letter is in the Life of Thurstan by Hugh the Chantor.

eorum.[l] *Paternæ tamen conservans viscera pietatis, de Sua confidentes misericordia non relinquit. Diu siquidem peccatis exigentibus per illud Teutonicorum regis idolum, Burdinum videlicet, fideles ecclesiæ conturbati sunt, et alii quidem capti, alii usque ad mortem carceris maceratione afflicti sunt. Nuper autem festis Paschalibus celebratis, cum peregrinorum et pauperum clamores nos ferre penitus non possemus, cum ecclesiæ fidelibus ab Urbe digressi sumus, et tamdiu Sutrinam civitatem obsedimus, donec Divina potentia et supradictum ecclesiæ inimicum Burdinum, qui diabolo nidum ibidem fecerat, et locum ipsum in nostram omnino tradidit potestatem. Rogamus itaque caritatem vestram, ut pro tantis beneficiis una nobiscum Regi Regum gratias referatis, et in catholicæ matris ecclesiæ obedientia et servitio constantissime maneatis, retributionem debitam in præsenti et in futuro ab Omnipotente Domino per Ejus gratiam recepturi. Rogamus etiam ut has litteras nostras alter alteri præsentari, omni remota negligentia, faciatis. Data Sutrii, vj kal. Maii.*[m]

Uxor quondam Willelmi, summersi filii regis Henrici, filia Fulconis comitis Andegavensis, rogante patre, remittitur patriam a rege. Filii regis Walanorum, audita summersione Ricardi comitis Cestrensis, incensis duobus castellis, multisque interfectis, quædam in illo comitatu loca graviter depopulati sunt. Unde rex indignatus de tota Anglia producto exercitu infinito ad devastandam Waloniam intendit, sed cum ad Snauedun pervenisset, rex Walanorum muneribus et obsidibus petitis regi Anglorum pacato reconciliatur, moxque exercitus domum remittitur.[n]

MCXXII.

Anno MC.xxij, in vigilia Natalis Domini, ventus validus et insolitus non solum domos, sed etiam turres dejecit lapideas.[o] Turstinus archiepiscopus exigens a Johanne Glasguensi episcopo professionem et subjectionem, cum hoc ille facere nollet, eum suspendit ab officio episcopali. Mox ille Romam proficiscitur, ubi cum sese in causa sua non videret procedere, Jerosolymam profectus, per aliquot ibidem menses benigno patriarchæ hospitio demoratur, ejusque sæpius vices in pontificali ministerio exequitur.[p]

[l] Psalm lxxxix. 32.

[m] This letter is in Baronius, and is derived from English sources.

[n] The words from *regi* to the end of the sentence are inserted in a coarse hand.

[o] This sentence, with the exception of the date, is added at the foot of the page in a coarse hand.

[p] See Fasti Ebor., i., pp. 197-8, for an account of the bishop of Glasgow and this claim.

Abbas Cluniacensis, Pontius, qui Divinitus ad regimen monasterii est assumptus, vir ut fertur optimæ conversationis, a sibi commissa congregatione criminatus apud Apostolicum Calixtum, libentissime accepit ab illo regimine deponi: ordinato autem in ejus locum alio abbate, illico sese ultro expurgans sacramento, ante sacrum corpus beati Petri accusatores falsa sibi objecisse convicit. Graviter tulit Apostolicus tantum virum inconsulte sine culpa depositum, moxque præcepit, ut sua auctoritate recepta ad pristinum monasterii sui regimen reverteretur. At ille respondit ipsam mortem se malle eligere quam Cluniacensis monasterii curam repetere. Hinc, dolente etiam Apostolico, Jerosolimam profectus, honorifice magno cunctorum gaudio excipitur: ubi supra portam quæ dicitur Aurea, sibi faciens mansionem, secretam in Divina contemplatione gaudet ducere vitam. Porro qui pro eo fuerat abbas surrogatus, non multo post ut Cluniacum venit mortuus est. Pontius vero, legatariis et litteris ab Apostolico missis, jubetur redire ad gubernationem monasterii sui. Sed nullo modo a sua singulari poterat abstrahi conversatione.[q]

Sibilla regina Scottorum, filia Henrici regis, subita morte decedit iiij idus Julii.

Calixtus papa et Henricus imperator, discurrentibus inter illos maturis et fidelibus viris, post longas dissensiones et rerum detrimenta, in pacem et concordiam redierunt, sicut literæ per regna et provincias directæ contestantur; quarum exemplaria hic in præsenti subduntur.

Ego Kalixtus episcopus, servus servorum Dei, tibi, dilecto filio, Henrico Dei gratia Romanorum imperatori Augusto concedo electiones episcoporum et abbatum Teutonici regni, qui ad regnum pertinent, in præsentia tua fieri absque symonia et omni violentia, ut, si qua inter partes discordia emerserit, metropolitani et provincialium judicio vel consilio, saniori parti assensum et auxilium præbeas. Electus autem regalia a te accipiat, et quæ ex his jure tibi debet faciat. Ex aliis vero partibus imperii consecratus, infra sex menses regalia per sceptrum a te recipiat, et quæ ex his jure tibi debet faciat, exceptis omnibus quæ ad ecclesiam Romanam pertinere noscuntur. De quibus vero querimoniam mihi feceris et auxilium postulaveris, secundum officii mei debitum, auxilium præstabo. Do tibi veram pacem et omnibus qui in parte tua sunt vel fuerunt tempore hujus discordiæ.

In nomine Sanctæ et Individuæ Trinitatis, ego Henricus Dei gratia Romanorum imperator Augustus, pro amore Dei et sanctæ Romanæ ecclesiæ et domni Kalixti papæ, et pro remedio animæ

[q] For a long account of this matter, see Baronius, sub anno 1125; pp. 359-60, 380-2. See also the Letters, etc., of Peter the Venerable.

meæ, dimitto Deo et sanctis Dei Apostolis Petro et Paulo, sanctæque Catholicæ ecclesiæ omnem investituram per annulum et baculum, et concedo in omnibus ecclesiis quæ in regno vel in imperio meo sunt canonicam fieri electionem et liberam consecrationem. Possessiones et regalia beati Petri quæ a principio hujus discordiæ usque hodiernam diem, sive tempore patris mei, sive etiam meo ablata sunt, quæ habeo, eidem sanctæ ecclesiæ Romanæ restituo. Quæ autem non habeo, ut restituantur fideliter juvabo. Possessiones etiam omnium aliarum ecclesiarum et principum, et aliorum tam clericorum quam laicorum, quæ in werra ista amissæ sunt, consilio principum vel justitia, quæ habeo reddam, quæ non habeo ut reddantur fideliter juvabo. Et do veram pacem domno papæ Kalixto, et sanctæ Romanæ ecclesiæ, et omnibus qui in parte ipsius sunt vel fuerunt, et in quibus sancta Romana ecclesia auxilium postulaverit fideliter juvabo. Et de quibus mihi fecerit querimoniam, debitam sibi justitiam faciam. Hæc omnia acta sunt consensu et consilio principum quorum nomina subscripta sunt; Alberti Moguntiensis archiepiscopi, Frederici Coloniensis archiepiscopi, Brunonis Treverensis archiepiscopi, Ardvini Ratisbonensis episcopi, Ottonis Banemburgensis episcopi, Brunonis Spirensis episcopi, et aliæ multæ ecclesiasticæ personæ ac sæculares. (Sic).[r]

Hac concordia per gentes et populos ubique divulgata, mittuntur etiam litteræ ab Apostolico omnibus archiepiscopis (et) episcopis per regiones et provincias, ut, omni excusatione postposita, festinent occurrere ad concilium quod domnus Apostolicus Romæ celebraturus erat xv kal. Aprilis.

Hoc anno rex Henricus, post festum Sancti Michaelis Northymbranas intrans regiones, ab Eboraco divertit versus mare occidentale, consideraturus civitatem antiquam quæ lingua Brittonum Cairlel dicitur, quæ nunc Carleol Anglice, Latine vero Lugubalia appellatur, quam data pecunia castello et turribus præcepit muniri.[s] Hinc rediens Eboracum, post graves civium et comprovincialium implacitationes, reversus est Suthymbriam.

Radulfus Cantuariensis archiepiscopus obiit xiij kal. Octobris.[t]

[r] For these letters, see Baronius, ed. Pagi, sub anno 1122; pp. 357-8. The names of the witnesses to the emperor's concession are given very inaccurately by Symeon.

[s] Carlisle had recently come into the possession of the Crown by the surrender of Ranulf de Meschines, who received in exchange the earldom of Chester on the death of its last possessor, earl Richard, who perished at sea on the night of the 26th of November, 1122, in company with the king's only son, prince William, and many other persons of distinction, on their passage from Normandy to England; as detailed above.

[t] Obiit Radulfus Cantuariensis archiepiscopus. *In margine.*

MCXXIII.

Anno M.cxxiij. Stephanus comes Bononicensis, postea rex Angliæ, dedit abbati Gaufrido Savinniensi villam, scilicet Tulket, in provincia quæ vocatur Agmundernes, super ripam fluminis Ribble, ad abbatiam construendam ordinis sui, tempore Kalixti papæ; et ibi fere per tres annos permanserunt.[u]

Rex Jerusalem, Baldewinus Secundus, apud Antiocham dolo a Paganis capitur, et tribus fere annis tenetur sub custodia.

Comes Andegavensium, Fulco, reposcit a rege Anglorum Henrico terras, urbes, et castella quæ in dotem fuerant data filiæ ipsius comitis, quando eam filius regis, qui jam summersus est, acceperat uxorem. Quod cum rex non libenter annueret, aliam filiam suam dedit uxorem Willelmo filio Rodberti comitis Normannorum, fratris regis, promittens juveni auxilium, ut quacumque in parte paterni honoris fieret hæres. Rex autem, ne quid adversi ex hoc sibi pararetur, habito cum suis apud Wdestoc, quod Latine dicitur Silvarum Locus, consilio, filium suum nothum Rodbertum et comitem Cestrensem Rannulfum, cum multa militari manu transmisit in Normanniam, propter locorum custodias.

Johannes Bathoniensis episcopus in die Natalis Domini, subito post prandium dolore cordis correptus, sequenti die moritur. Non multo post, id est tertio die post Epiphaniam, Rodbertus Bloet, Lincolniensis episcopus, cum seorsum a cæteris rex et ipse incolumis equitantes colloquerentur consilio, subito quasi moriens decidit equo. Quem cadentem dum rex exciperet, undique accuritur, et episcopus jam nihil loqui prævalens, ad hospitium deportatus postera die moritur.

Deinde cum apud Glawornam in Purificatione Sanctæ Mariæ curiam suam rex teneret, ex præcepto regis initur a majoribus Angliæ consilium de constituendo ad ecclesiam Cantuariensem archiepiscopo. Sed cum ad hanc diversas diversi personas eligerent, dissensio innexuit moram electioni. Prior namque Cantuariensis ecclesiæ cum honestioribus personis aderat, qui electionem ecclesiæ super quasdam ex ordine monachico personas convenisse nuntiabant, quarum quæcumque regi et ejus consilio placeret, eam ecclesiæ præfici postulabant. At episcopis totius Angliæ, qui omnes fuerant ex clericali ordine, reclamantibus nolle se monachum habere primatem, cum æque probos et idoneos ad ecclesiasticum regimen haberent clericos, responderunt legati Cantuariensium. "A tempore," inquiunt, "Sancti Augustini, qui utique monachus hujus ecclesiæ primus

[u] The sentence ending here, with the exception of the date, is added at the foot of the page in a coarse hand.

fuerat præsul, ad regimen illius usque in præsens semper monachi eligebantur pontifices. Deinceps quoque annuente Deo consuetudo servabitur antiqua." Sed rege favente episcopis ut non monachi eligerentur, quatuor clerici proponuntur in medio, ut in quemcunque illorum electio Cantuariensium conveniat, is ex præcepto regis ad archiepiscopatum ascendat. Ergo quoniam antiquum electionis morem eis servare non licuit, necessitate impellente, ad unum illorum quatuor clericorum se conferunt, scilicet Willelmum de Curbellio, quem modestæ vitæ virum ac litteris bene eruditum familiarem habuerant, utpote cum venerandæ memoriæ archiepiscopo Anselmo sæpissime ac familiariter conversatum. Fuerat autem primo Dunelmensis ecclesiæ episcopi Rannulfi clericus, postea, meliorandæ vitæ gratia, apud Cice regularis canonicus effectus, tandem ad archiepiscopatum promovetur. Electus est itaque a monachis : cui dum Turstinus Eboracensis archiepiscopus secundum consuetudinem offerret ut eum ipsum ordinaret; "Si me," inquit, "ut primatem totius Angliæ volueris ordinare, libenter me manibus vestris inclinabo, sin autem, inconsulte contra morem antiquum nolo ordinari." Qui non multo post, id est v kal. Martii, jubente rege, consecratus est Cantuariæ a suis suffraganeis. Statimque postea tam ipse quam Turstinus Romam proficiscuntur, quisque pro sua causa acturus. Rex autem misit Bernardum episcopum de Sancto David, et abbatem monasterii Sancti Eadmundi Anselmum, nepotem Anselmi archiepiscopi, et Polochinum abbatem Glastoniensem fratrem Radulfi archiepiscopi, cum Willelmo archiepiscopo, et in sua legatione ad Apostolicum, et ut ipsius archiepiscopi si quid adversi oboriretur parti adessent. Interea Johannes Glasguensis episcopus ab Apostolico revocatus ab Jerosolymis Romam, præcipitur redire ad suum episcopatum. Godefridus capellanus reginæ, qui cum illa de Teutonia venerat in Angliam, a rege Henrico eligitur episcopus ad ecclesiam Bathoniensem, et Alexander, nepos Rogeri Salesberiensis episcopi, ad Lincolniensem ecclesiam.

Celebratum est Romæ concilium ccc episcoporum xv kal. Aprilis, præsidente papa Calixto Secundo. Renovata sunt ibi statuta majorum de agendis et prohibendis: Quorum capitula scire volentibus subscripta inveniuntur.

Sanctorum patrum exempla sequentes, et officii nostri debito innovantes, ordinari quemquam per pecuniam in ecclesia Dei vel promoveri auctoritate sedis Apostolicæ modis omnibus prohibemus. Si quis vero in ecclesia ordinationem vel promotionem taliter adquisierit, acquisita careat prorsus dignitate.

A suis episcopis excommunicatos, ab aliis episcopis, abbatibus et clericis in communionem recipi proculdubio prohibemus.

Nullus in episcopum nisi canonice electum consecret, quod etsi præsumptum fuerit, et consecratus et consecrator absque recuperationis spe deponatur.

Nullus omnino archidiaconus aut archipresbyter, sive præpositus, vel decanus, animaram curam vel præbendas ecclesiæ sine judicio vel consensu episcopi alicui tribuat. Immo, sicut sanctis canonibus constitutum est, animarum cura et rerum ecclesiasticarum dispensatio in episcopi judicio et potestate permaneat. Si quis vero contra hoc facere, aut potestatem quæ ad episcopum pertinet sibi vindicare præsumpserit, ab ecclesiæ liminibus arceatur.

Ordinationes quæ a Burdino hæresiarcha, postquam a Romana ecclesia est damnatus, quæque etiam a (p)seudo-episcopis per eum postea ordinatis factæ sunt, nos esse irritas judicamus. Nullus etiam in præpositum, nullus in archipresbyterum, nullus in decanum nisi presbyter, nullus in archidiaconum nisi diaconus ordinetur.

Presbyteris, diaconibus, et subdiaconibus concubinarum et uxorum contubernia penitus interdicimus, et aliarum mulierum cohabitationem præter quas Nicena synodus propter solas necessitudines habitare permisit, videlicet matrem, sororem, amitam vel materteram, aut alias hujusmodi, de quibus nulla juste valeat oriri suspicio.

Præterea juxta beatissimi Papæ Stephani sanctionem statuimus, ut laici, quamvis religiosi sint, nullam tamen de ecclesiasticis rebus aliquid disponendi habeant facultatem; sed secundum Apostolorum canones omnium ecclesiasticorum negotiorum curam episcopus habeat, et ea, velut Deo contemplante, dispenset. Si quis ergo principum vel aliorum laicorum dispositionem seu donationem rerum sive possessionum ecclesiasticarum sibi vindicaverit, ut sacrilegus judicetur.

Conjunctiones consanguineorum fieri prohibemus, quoniam eas et Divinæ et sæculi prohibent leges. Leges enim Divinæ hoc agentes et eos qui ex eis prodeunt non solum ejiciunt, sed etiam maledictos appellant. Leges vero sæculi infames tales vocant, et ab hæreditate repellunt. Nos itaque, patres nostros sequentes, infamia eos notamus, et infames esse censemus.

Eis qui Jerosolimam proficiscuntur, et ad Christianam gentem defendendam et tyrannidem infidelium destruendam efficaciter auxilium suum præbuerint, suorum peccatorum remissionem concedimus, et domos, familias, atque omnia bona eorum in beati Petri et Romanæ ecclesiæ protectionem, sicut a domino nostro Urbano Papa statutum fuit, suscipimus. Quicunque ergo ea distrahere vel auferre, quamdiu in via illa morantur, præsumpserint, excommunicationis ultione plectantur. Eos autem qui vel pro

Jerosolimitano, vel pro Hispanico itinere cruces sibi in vestibus posuisse noscuntur et postea dimisisse, cruces iterate assumere et viam instanti Pascha usque ad proximum sequens Pascha perficere Apostolica auctoritate præcipimus, alioquin extunc eos ab ecclesiæ introitu sequestramus, et in omnibus terris eorum Divina officia, præter infantum baptisma et morientium pænitentias, interdicimus.

Quicunque monetam falsam se sciente fecerit, aut studiose expenderit, tanquam maledictus, et pauperum oppressor virorum, et turbator civitatis a fidelium consortio separetur.

Si quis Romipetas et peregrinos Apostolorum limina et aliorum Sanctorum oratoria visitantes capere, seu rebus quas ferunt spoliare, et mercatores novis teloneorum et pedaticorum exactionibus molestare temptaverit, donec satisfecerit communione careat Christiana.[v]

His synodalibus decretis subscriptis et confirmatis, imperatorem Henricum per legatos suos et scripta, secundum præmissum scriptorum tenorem promittentem se sanctæ Romanæ ecclesiæ justa servaturum, generalis concilii sententia ab excommunicationis absolvit vinculo, quo in Remensi concilio fuerat ligatus.

Peracto Concilio, memorati duo Anglorum archiepiscopi ingrediuntur Romam. Sed Eboracensis prævenit Cantuariensem. Paucis post diebus Cantuariensis superveniens difficilem ad pallii impetrationem habuit accessum, impeditus ex his quæ sibi ibidem opposita fuerant; scilicet, Quod in curia quæ a cruore dicitur, ibi enim sanguinum judicia fiunt, sit electus; Quod non communi consensu ecclesiæ Cantuariensis sit ad ejus regimen promotus; Quod se ab Eboracensi archiepiscopo Turstino, sicut mos antiquus exigebat, non passus sit ordinari; Quod primus ex ordine clericali monachis ejusdem ecclesiæ consenserit præponi; Augustinus enim monachus omnes suos successores usque ipsum Willelmum habuit monachos. Sed his objectionibus tandem gratia Imperatoris præfati et Henrici regis Anglorum, qui per legatos suos strenni intercessores erant, repressis, suscepto sollemniter pallio, querebatur in audientia totius senatus Romanæ ecclesiæ Cantuariensem ecclesiam a sua dignitate per surreptionem archiepiscopi Eboracensis degeneratam, quæ a primo ejusdem episcopo Augustino usque ad Radulfum, qui ante ipsum Willelmum fuerat, totius Angliæ primatum gerebat, quem nunc obnixe orabat ecclesiæ, cui et antiqua consuetudo et servata per tot annos privilegiorum auc-

[v] For an account of the decrees of this Council, see Baronius, ed. Pagi, sub anno 1122; pp. 355-6. Symeon, it will be seen, ascribes the Council to the year 1123.

toritas hunc concesserat. Ad hoc Turstinus ex consulto respondit, se ad Concilium, licet occurrere non potuerit, Romam evocatum, nec tunc congruenter posse respondere ad quod non fuerat summonitus; præsertim cum Eboracensis ecclesiæ ibidem privilegia secum non haberet, sine quibus ratio non permitteret disceptandi inde suscipere negotium. Quapropter infectis negotiis utrique redeunt domum, quos ex jussu domini papæ legati Romanæ ecclesiæ secuturi essent in Angliam; quibus præsentibus, congregato totius Angliæ concilio, memoratis archiepiscopis ecclesiarum suarum privilegia propalantibus, sua utrique parti decernente justitia reformarentur jura. Willelmus electum Lincolniensis ecclesiæ, Alexandrum, et electum Bathoniensis Godefridum consecravit Cantuariæ.

Rex Henricus hoc anno, proximo post Dominicam Pentecostes, ij feria, transfretavit in Normanniam, ut si quid adversi per Willelmum, fratris sui filium, oboriretur, sicut jam futurum ei nunciabatur, ipse regia reprimeret virtute. Interjectis autem non omnino iiij mensibus, Galerannus comes de Mellant et sui omnes, relicto rege, castella sua munientes, ea contra regem tenuerunt. Rex vero convocato exercitu, oppido comitis quod Brionne vocatur combusto, turrem solam quam capere non valuit relinquens, aliud ejus oppidum, scilicet Pontem Audomari, quod vulgo vocatur Puntaldemer, flammis combussit, omnibus in circuitu per xx et eo amplius miliaria vastatis et incensis, ut hostes quid mali facerent non invenirent. Castellum autem illius oppidi septies viginti milites per vij ebdomadas obsessi contra regis exercitum defenderunt. Videns autem rex se non ut disposuerat proficere, ligneam turrim quam Berfreit vocant erexit. Qua ad castellum arte deducta, desuper præliatores sagittas et ingentes lapidum moles super inclusos jaciebant. Altitudine xxiiij pedum super murum præsidii eminebat machina, unde sagittarii et alabastarii præliabantur. Obsessi non valentes ulterius ferre vires desuper pugnantium, deditione facta exierunt: quos rex quemque quo voluit abire permisit. Milites vero quos rex de Minori Britannia conduxerat, incenso oppido prædicto, terram suffodientes, invenerunt in cistis multa quæ cives, prævidentes periculum, in subterraneis recondiderant, aurum, argentum, vestes pretiosas, pallia, piper, gingiberum, et alia hujusmodi. Quæ universa sibi tollentes abierunt. Habitatores autem illius oppidi, reconciliato sibi rege, cum jam ruinas oppidi cœpissent reædificare, Comes præfatus subito quicquid fuerat igne injecto in favillas vertit. Præter supradictos et alii procerum nonnulli discedentes a rege suas munitiones contra illum ope firmiori et numero pugnatorum instaurant. Quarum quasdam rex vi aggrediens recepit, quasdam vero velut inexpugnabiles reliquit. Crebras irruptiones a Willelmo, sui fratris filio, sustinuit, qui plus Fulconis Andegavensium comitis, soceri sui, viribus nitebatur quam propriis. Rex autem magis suorum suspectus est proditionem, quam extraneorum expavit incursus. Ob istiusmodi dissensiones et rerum difficultates, gravibus Anglia est attrita exactionibus pecuniarum, quæ ad negotia regis peragenda omni populo indicebantur. Teodulfus Wigornensis episcopus, et Radulfus Cicestrensis episcopus obierunt. Habitum est concilium[w] apud Bituricas v idus Decembris.

MCXXIV.

Anno M.cxxiiij. Alexander rex Scottorum obiit vij kal. Maii, cum regnasset xviij annis, et tribus mensibus. Cui frater ejus David succedens, regnum quod frater suus laboriosissime tenuit, mox ille sine contradictione susceptum quaquaversum inclinum sibi et quietum tenuit. Ipso autem anno Alexander, iiij ante suam mortem mensibus, in episcopatum ecclesiæ Sancti Andreæ, quæ in Scotia est, fecit eligi Rodbertum priorem canonicorum regularium apud Sconam. Sed ejus ordinatio multo est tempore dilata propter subjectionem debitam quam ab illo secundum consuetudinem exigebat Turstinus Eboracensis archiepiscopus. Scotti autem e contra dicebant stulta garrulitate, hoc nulla debere fieri auctoritate vel consuetudine.

Comes de Mellant prædictus, dum passim inconsulte castella quæ contra regem munierat circumiret, captus ab insidiantibus cum suis non paucis diligenti arctatur custodia. Calixtus papa idus Decembris obiit, pro quo Ostiensis episcopus, mutato juxta morem priorum de Lamberto in Honorium nomine, in papatum substituitur.[x]

Magna fuit per Angliam fames, ut passim per urbes, per villas, et viarum transitus exanimata miserabili horrore cadavera inhumata resolverentur in tabem.

MCXXV.

Anno M.cxxv. Imperator Henricus, cum imperasset xx annis, sine filiis obiit.[y] Unde tres a primatibus regni sunt propositi, ut quilibet eorum eligeretur in regnum. Lipoldus sororius Imperatoris defuncti, et nepos ejus Fretherícus, et Lotharius dux Saxonum. Lipoldus opponens senectutem et filiorum numerum, ne per illos si ipse promoveretur in regnum regni fieret divisio, a se repulit imperium. Fretherícus, cum

[w] "Nihil ejus superest." Pagi, apud Baronium.

[x] Visio de Hon' deest. *In margine.*

[y] Obiit Henricus imperator. Successit Lotharius Dux Saxonum. *In margine.*

se velut regni hæredem ex debito ingereret, eo magis abjicitur quo ejus avunculus omnibus exosus habebatur. Lotharius vero concorditer ab omnibus eligitur. Quod ipse quasi ratiocinando et etiam lacrimando dum niteretur repellere, apud Aquasgrani unctus in regem, Frethericum magna vi sese impugnantem bello fugavit, et ejus quasdam munitiones cepit. Is magno moderamine et justitia disposuit regnum et imperium.

Imperatrix, defuncto marito, amissis quibusdam quas in dotem acceperat munitionibus, ad patrem rediit in Normannia.

Johannes Cremensis, accepta ab Apostolico super Britanniam legatione, cum diu in Normannia retentus esset a rege, tandem permissus in Angliam transvehitur, et ab ecclesiis honorifice excipitur, juxta quod ipse commendatitias in hoc ipsum ad illas ab Apostolico acceperat litteras, quarum inferius exemplaria hic ponuntur.

Honorius episcopus, servus servorum Dei, dilecto filio Johanni presbytero-cardinali, Apostolicæ sedis legato, salutem et Apostolicam benedictionem. Quemadmodum bonorum filiorum est subjecta devotionis humilitate patribus obedire, ita patrum interest benigne caritatis affectu filiis providere. Curam igitur et sollicitudinem tibi a prædecessore nostro felicis memoriæ papa Calyxto in Angliæ regno commissam providentiæ dilectionis tuæ committimus. Obsecramus autem in Domino, ut, tanquam sapiens et discretus Romanæ ecclesiæ filius, quæ ad honorem Dei et sedis Apostolicæ pertinent honestatem studiosius opereris. Data Laterani idibus Aprilis.

Honorius episcopus, servus servorum Dei, dilectis fratribus et filiis, archiepiscopis, episcopis, abbatibus, proceribus, et cæteris, tam clericis quam laicis, per Angliam constitutis, salutem et Apostolicam benedictionem. Quamvis in extremis terrarum positos, ad Petri tamen Apostoli curam Christianæ fidei vos facit universalitas pertinere. Cum enim Petro dictum est, Pasce oves meas, pasce agnos meos,[z] *profecto nulla ovium, nullus agnorum exceptus est ad Christi consortium pertinentium qui non Petri commissus sit pastioni : speciali præter hoc sorte regnum Angliæ beato Petro et Romanæ ecclesiæ pertinere sanctissimi patris nostri Gregorii papæ auctoritas, et beati Augustini prædicatio manifestat. Hoc igitur dispositionis debito provocamur vobis scilicet longe positis sollicitiore diligentia providere. Quamobrem carissimum filium nostrum Johannem, cardinalem sanctæ Romanæ ecclesiæ sacerdotem, in partem nostræ sollicitudinis et vigilantiæ evocantes, vices ei nostras in partibus vestris commisimus. Qui nimirum de ecclesiarum correctione ac stabilitate,*

[z] St. John xxi. 15, 16.

de religionis augmento, et de cæteris quæ probanda vel improbanda visa fuerint, cum vestræ dilectionis auxilio, cooperantibus sanctorum Apostolorum patrociniis, pertractabit. Rogamus ergo vos, et monemus, atque præcipimus, ut eum, tanquam Sancti Petri vicarium, reverenter suscipiatis, humiliter audiatis, atque ad ipsius vocationem synodales cum eo conventus sollemniter celebretis, quatenus per ipsius et vestram industriam in regno vestro quæ corrigenda sunt corrigantur, quæ firmanda sunt Sancto inspirante Spiritu firmentur. Data Laterani, ij idus Aprilis.

Super Scotiæ quoque regnum idem Johannes legati suscepit officium, Apostolico super hoc regi ipsius gentis has litteras mittente.

Honorius episcopus, servus servorum Dei, dilecto filio David illustri Scottorum regi salutem et Apostolicam benedictionem. Oportet devotos et humiles beati Petri filios quæ ad honorem sanctæ Romanæ ecclesiæ spectare cognoverint attentius operari. Unde nobilitati tuæ rogando mandamus, ut dilectum filium nostrum Johannem cardinalem, cui vices nostras in partibus illis commisimus, reverenter suscipias et honores. Episcopos etiam terræ tuæ, cum ab eo vocati fuerint, ad concilium suum facias convenire. Controversia quæ inter Turstinum Eboracensem archiepiscopum, et episcopos terræ tuæ diu agitata est, eidem legato nostro diligentius indagandam discutiendamque committimus, finitam vero sententiam Apostolicæ sedis judicio reservamus. Data Laterani, idibus Aprilis.

Hac auctoritate Johannes prædictus circuiens Angliam, etiam ad regem Scottorum David pervenit apud fluvium Twedam, qui Northymbriam et Loidam disterminat, in loco qui Rochesburh nominatur.[a] Ubi officio legationis peracto, rediens apud Londoniam celebravit concilium, quod de capitulis subter annexis habetur in hunc modum.

MCXXVI.

Anno ab incarnatione Dominica M.cxxvj, pontificatus autem domni papæ Honorii Secundi anno primo, regnante piissimo et glorioso Henrico Anglorum rege, Willelmi magni filio, anno vero regni ipsius xxv, celebrata est synodus[b] Lundoniæ in ecclesia

[a] Rochesburh, now Roxburgh, had grown into importance under the fostering care of David, earl of Cumberland, previous to his accession to the Scottish throne in 1124, and was henceforth numbered amongst the royal residences in Scotland. Some remains of the castle may yet be seen, but not a vestige of the ancient borough.

[b] Baronius derives his copy of the acts of this Synod from William of Malmesbury. Pagi mentions the letters of Honorius, which he seems to have known through Symeon. He also charges him with making a mistake as to the date of the Synod or Council, which should be, he says, 1125 and 1126, and not 1126 only.

beati Petri Apostolorum principis apud Westmonasterium, mense Septembri, nona die ejusdem mensis, ubi post multarum discussionem causarum promulgata sunt hæc capitula et ab omnibus confirmata, numero xvij. Præfuit autem illi synodo Johannes de Crema, sanctæ Romanæ et Apostolicæ ecclesiæ de titulo Sancti Grisogoni presbyter-cardinalis, et prædicti domni papæ Honorii in Angliam legatus, cum Turstino Eboracensi, et Willelmo Cantuariensi archiepiscopis, et cum episcopis diversarum provinciarum numero xx, et abbatibus circiter xl, et cum innumera cleri et populi multitudine.

Sanctorum patrum vestigiis inhærentes quemquam in ecclesia per pecuniam ordinari auctoritate Apostolica prohibemus.

Interdicimus etiam ut pro crismate, pro oleo, pro baptismate, pro pænitentia, pro visitatione infirmorum seu unctione, pro communione corporis Christi, pro sepultura nullum omnino pretium exigatur.

Statuimus præterea, et Apostolica auctoritate decernimus, ut in consecrationibus episcoporum vel abbatum benedictionibus, seu in dedicationibus ecclesiarum, non cappa, non tapete, non manutergium, non baccinia, et nil omnino per violentiam, nisi sponte oblatum fuerit, penitus exigatur.

Nullus abbas, nullus Prior, nullus omnino monachus, vel clericus ecclesiam, sive decimam, seu quælibet beneficia ecclesiastica de dono vel manu laici, sine proprii episcopi auctoritate et assensu, suscipiat. Quod si præsumptum fuerit, irrita erit donatio hujusmodi, et ipse canonicæ ultioni subjacebit.

Sancimus præterea ne quis ecclesiam sibi sive præbendam paterna vendicet hæreditate, aut successorem sibi in aliquo ecclesiastico constituat beneficio. Quod si præsumptum fuerit, nullas vires habere permittimus, dicentes, cum Psalmista, Deus meus, pone illos ut rotam qui dixernnt, hæreditate possideamus sanctuarium Dei.[c]

Adjicientes quoque, statuimus ut clerici qui ecclesias seu beneficia habeant ecclesiarum, et ordinari quo liberius vivant subterfugiunt, cum ab episcopis invitati fuerint, si ad ordines promoveri contempserint, ecclesiis simul et beneficiis earum priventur.

Nullus in decanum, nullus in Priorem nisi presbyter, nullus in archidiaconum nisi diaconus promoveatur.

Nullus in presbyterum, nullus in diaconum nisi ad certum titulum ordinetur: Qui vero absolute fuerit ordinatus, sumpta careat dignitate.

Nullus abbas, nullus omnino clericus vel laicus quemquam per episcopum in ecclesia ordinatum absque proprii episcopi

[c] Psalm lxxxiii. 12-13.

judicio præsumat ejicere. Qui autem secus facere præsumpserit, excommunicationi subjaceat.

Nullus episcoporum alterius parochianum ordinare vel judicare præsumat; unusquisque enim suo domino stat aut cadit,[d] *nec tenetur aliquis sententia a suo non judice prolata.*

Nemo excommunicatum alterius præsumat in communionem suscipere: quod qui scienter fecerit, et ipse communione careat Christiana.

Præcipimus etiam ne uni personæ in ecclesia archidiaconatus aut diversi tribuantur honores.

Presbyteris, diaconibus, subdiaconibus, canonicis, uxorum, concubinarum, et omnium omnino feminarum contubernia auctoritate Apostolica inhibemus, præter matrem, aut sororem, vel amitam, sive illas mulieres quæ omnino careant suspicione. Qui decreti hujus violator extiterit, confessus vel convictus, ruinam proprii ordinis patiatur.

Usuram et turpe lucrum clericis omnimodis prohibemus. Qui vero super crimine tali confessus fuerit aut convictus, a proprio gradu dejiciatur.

Sortilegos, ariolos, et auguria quæque sectantes, eisque consentientes excommunicari præcipimus, perpetuaque damnamus infamia.

Inter consanguineos seu affinitate propinquos usque ad septimam generationem matrimonia contrahi prohibemus: si qui vero aliter conjuncti fuerint, seperentur.

Interdicimus etiam ut viri proprias uxores de consanguinitate impetentes, et testes quos adducunt, non suscipiantur, sed prisca patrum in omnibus servetur auctoritas.

His taliter sinodali decreto confirmatis, Johannem Romam revertentem comitantur, ab ipso evocati, Turstinus Eboracensis archiepiscopus, et Willelmus Cantuariensis, de suis causis in Apostolica audientia acturi.

Monetarii totius Angliæ principales deprehensi adulterinos, scilicet non puros, ex argento fecisse denarios, jussu regis simul Wintoniæ congregati omnes una die, amputatis dextris, evirantur.

MCXXVII.

Anno M.CXXVIJ. Henricus rex cum filia Imperatrice iij idus Septembris rediit in Angliam. Turstinus Eboracensis, et Willelmus Cantuariensis archiepiscopi redeunt Roma. Willelmus quidem legatus Apostolici per Angliam, sed Turstinus in statu quo fuerat revertitur.

[d] Ep. ad Rom. xiv. 4.

MCXXVIII.

Anno M.cxxviij mutata est abbatia de Selechirche ad Kelchou juxta Rochesburc, et fundata est ecclesia Sanctæ Mariæ prædictis monachis Tironensibus, ubi eam pius rex David magnis muneribus ditavit, multis ornamentis ornavit, prædiis et possessionibus amplis nobiliter dotavit.[e]

Rex Anglorum Henricus tenuit curiam suam apud Windere-soram in Nativitate Domini. Transiit inde Lundoniam, ubi, in Circumcisione Domini, jubente illo, archiepiscopi, episcopi, abbates, rexque Scottorum David, comites et barones totius Angliæ juraverunt, ut, filiæ suæ Imperatrici fide servata, regnum Angliæ hæreditario jure post eum servarent, nisi ipse moriens filium de legitimo matrimonio sui hæredem relinqueret. Reginæ quoque juraverunt, ut quæcunque rex illi donasset, rata semper custodirent ac immutata.

Carlo comes Flandrensis in Quadragesima, dum missam audiens in oratione procumberet, circumventus ab insidiantibus morte præventus est, antequam mortem inferentes nosse poterat. Cui fratruelis regis Henrici Willelmus, filius scilicet Rodberti fratris ejus, in comitatus honorem successit, Ludowici regis Francorum adjutus quam maximo auxilio. Antea quidem Fulco Andegavensium comes prædicto juveni suam desponsaverat filiam, sed propter consanguinitatem quam rex Henricus eis inesse jurari fecerat, divortio facto, timentem insidias regis Anglorum, patrui scilicet sui, juvenem rex Francorum suscipiens, data sibi in conjugium sorore reginæ affinitate sibi associavit, et ob id in prædictum comitatum sustulit, jure sibi a parte matris paternæ attinentem. Siquidem Baldwini, Flandrensium comitis filiam, rex Willelmus duxerat, ex qua Willelmum et Henricum reges procreavit, et Rodbertum comitem Normannorum, cujus filius erat Willelmus prædictus. Rex Henricus intendens animum ad obtinendum comitatum præfatum, quasi hæreditario sibi jure debitum, a nepote, sicut jam diximus, est præventus. Quare ne quid adversi ex nepote sibi aboriretur, comitis Andegavensium, cui prius fuerat inimicus, expetiit amicitias, cupiens filiam suam quondam Imperatricem filio ejus matrimonio jungere. Quod ubi tandem utrisque complacuisset, præmissam filiam in Normanniam ipse, paulo post, vij kal. Septembris, subsecutus est, remque ad effectum perduxit, eo tenore, ut regi, de legitima conjuge hæredem non habenti, mortuo gener illius in regnum succederet.

[e] This sentence, excepting the date, is added at the foot of the page in a coarse hand.

MCXXVIII.

Anno M.cxxviij prædictus comes Flandrensis bis in una septimana congrediens cum hostibus parva manu superavit plurimos. Sed paulo post obsidens castellum sibi repugnantium, dum successu vincendi insolens crebrius victos fugientesque repeteret, vulneratus lætaliter in confinio brachii et manus, triduo supervivens, moritur vj kal. Augusti.[f] Cujus, ex placito regis Francorum, rex Henricus hæres ex debito consanguinitatis factus, comitatum sub se disponendum tradidit Theodoro, lineam affinitatis ducenti ex comitibus Flandrensium.[g]

Rannulfus Dunelmensis episcopus, peractis in episcopatu xxix annis, et tribus mensibus, et vij diebus, finem fecit vitæ non. Septembris.

MCXXIX.

Anno M.cxxix. Willelmus Gifard Wintoniensis episcopus obiit. Rex Henricus absoluto de captione comite de Mellant Gualaranno, cunctisque sibi quæ sua fuerant præter munitiones redditis, redintegrata inter se et regem Francorum concordia, accepto Flandrensium comitatu, filia quoque sua ex Imperatrice comiti Andegavensium copulata, omnibusque quaquaversum hostibus vel victis vel repacificatis, arridente sibi undique prosperitate, multo navigio idus Julii in Angliam est reversus. Fluxerant dies pauci, cum ecce! nunciatur regi filiam suam a marito repudiatam, abjectamque sine honore paucis admodum comitibus redisse Rothomagum. Quæ res animos regis acriter perturbavit. Post festum autem Sancti Michaelis, comitantibus archiepiscopis, episcopis, abbatibus, et pene totius Angliæ primatibus, venit Wintoniam, ibique filio sororis suæ Henrico, qui apud Cluniacum ab infantia nutritus erat monachus, Wintoniensis ecclesiæ dedit episcopatum, adjuncta ei in augmentum honoris abbatia Glastoniæ, quam prius ad procurationem sui a rege acceperat. Datus est et episcopatus Conventrensis, qui et Cestrensis, Rogerio nepoti Goffridi Dedintun, qui, ut dignior tanto esset honore, tribus hunc marcarum millibus promeruit. Ordinati sunt autem xv kal. Decembris Cantuariæ a Willelmo ejusdem ecclesiæ archiepiscopo.

Explicit Historia suavis et sanctæ memoriæ Symeonis monachi et præcentoris ecclesiæ Sancti Cuthberti Dunelmi annorum cccc.xxix *et mensium quatuor.*[h]

[f] Obiit Willelmus comes Flandrensis. *In margine.*
[g] The words from *Theodoro* are added in the margin in a coarse hand.
[h] In red letters.

INCIPIT

EPISTOLA SYMEONIS,

MONACHI ECCLESIÆ SANCTI CUTHBERTI DUNELMI, AD HUGONEM DECANUM EBORACENSEM DE

ARCHIEPISCOPIS EBORACI.[i]

DCXXVII.[j]

Anno ab incarnatione Domini DC.xxvij, rex Eadwinus prædicante Paulino baptizatus est. Qui Paulinus per sex annos continuos verbum Dei in Northumbrorum provincia prædicabat: deinde,[k] occiso rege, Cantiam, unde venerat, rediit. Ipse Eboracensis primus præsul ab Honorio papa pallium acceperat, ordinatus a Justo archiepiscopo. Recedente Paulino, Eboracensis ecclesia[l] proprium non habuit episcopum, sed Lindisfarnensis ecclesiæ præsules Aidanus, Finanus, Colmannus et Tuda totius Northumbrorum provinciæ administraverunt pontificatum. Tertio anno episcopatus Colmanni, qui est tricesimus annus pontificatus Scottorum in Anglia, finito conflictu de observantia Paschali, missus est Wylfridus ab Al(c)frido rege in Gallias ut ordinaretur episcopus.[m] Quo adhuc transmarinis

[i] This rubric is from the C. C. C. MS. There is no rubric in the Cotton MS., nor is it probable that any such was prefixed to the original epistle. The orthography of Symeon's name is here altered from the Cambridge MS., where it is spelt with *i* instead of *y*, in conformity with the text of the body of the epistle in the Cotton MS. The Cotton MS., although long posterior in date to that at Cambridge, has been copied from a better text, and is on that account more trustworthy than the other.

[j] This little tract consists of two parts; a narrative of the succession and proceedings of the prelates of the see of York, and an explanatory letter from Symeon to Dean Hugh. The narrative portion is here placed first, as it is in the Cotton MS. In the C. C. C. MS. the order is reversed, and precedence is given to the letter.

[k] After *deinde* the Cambridge MS. has Anno enim DCXXXIIJ.

[l] Per triginta annos, C.

[m] C. adds cum esset annorum circiter triginta.

(in partibus)[n] demorante, consecratus est in episcopatum Eboracensis ecclesiæ[o] Ceadda; et, tribus annis sublimiter regens ecclesiam, dehinc ad monasterium suum in Lestingaen secessit, accipiente Wylfrido pontificatum totius Northymbrorum provinciæ. Interea, mortuo rege Oswino, successit filius ejus Egfridus in regnum. Qui post beatam Etheldridam, quam nomine tenus conjugem primo duxerat, Ermenburgam sortitus est in matrimonium. In cujus corde malignus hostis sibi hospitium fecerat, ubi odiorum et invidiæ contra beatum Wylfridum conficiens fomenta, per linguam mulieris incendit animum regis usque[p] expulsionem pontificis. Sed quia rex pontificem de sua sede præter consensum Theodori archiepiscopi pellere nequibat, mandavit archiepiscopo ut adesset. Auditis quas accusatores finxerant causis, pulsus est ab episcopatu Wylfridus anno ab incarnatione Domini DC.lxxviij, qui est annus sui episcopatus duodecimus, et per decennium exulavit. Secundo anno regni[q] Aldfridi, qui post fratrem Egfridum regnavit, sedem et episcopatum recepit. Sed post quinque annos denuo, accusatus ab eodem rege et plurimis episcopis, præsulatu pulsus est. Tertio decimo secundæ expulsionis suæ anno Haugustaldensem[r] recepit episcopatum, beato Johanne jam pro defuncto Bosan Eboraci substituto. Quatuor post hæc annis supervixit beatus Wylfridus, habens in episcopatu xlv annos. Post quem suscepit præsulatum Haugustaldensis ecclesiæ venerabilis ejus presbiter Acca.[s] Beatus vero Johannes, cum majore senectute minus episcopatui administrando sufficeret, ordinato in episcopatum Eboracensis ecclesiæ Wylfrido presbitero suo, ipse ad monasterium suum, quod in silva Deirorum (est), secessit, ibique in pace vitam terminavit: mansit autem in episcopatu xxxiij annis. At Wylfridus, peractis sui episcopatus xv annis, successorem[t] habuit Egbertum, virum de regio semine nobilem et industrium. Qui post Paulinum primus ab Apostolica sede accepit pallium, septimo anno regni Ceolwlfi regis, centesimo tertio anno post decessum Paulini, hoc est anno Dominicæ incarnationis DCC.xxxv, quo anno venerabilis doctor Beda obiit in Gyrvum. Porro archiepiscopus Egbertus, xxxij anno accepti episcopatus de-

[n] Added from C.

[o] C. here inserts jubente rege Oswino, and after *Ceadda* the words vir sanctus.

[p] Ad expulsionem usque, C.

[q] Alkfridi, MS. Cotton.

[r] Hagustaldensis ecclesiæ, C.

[s] The Cotton MS. has Eata. Acca, the correct reading is substituted from the C. C. C. MS.

[t] Symeon does not inform us whether the vacancy was caused by the death or resignation of Wilfrid. On this point see Hist. de Gestis Regum, sub anno 745, and the note thereon.

functus, successorem habuit Albertum, qui septimo accepti episcopatus anno ab Adriano papa acceperat pallium, septimo anno[u] Alredi regis. Quo videlicet Alberto xiiij anno sui præsulatus obeunte, Eanbaldus ordinatur pro illo, anno Dominicæ incarnationis DCC.lxxx, regnante Aelfwaldo. Anno autem Dominicæ incarnationis DCC.xcvj Eanbaldus xvij sui archiepiscopatus anno moriens, alterum Eanbaldum, qui ejusdem ecclesiæ presbiter fuerat, successorem reliquit, regnante rege Eardulfo.[v] Post Eanbaldum Wlsius rexit archiepiscopatum, Eanredo regnante: moriens autem Wlsius, Wymundum habuit successorem, præfato rege regnante. Cui xvj episcopatus sui anno morienti, Wlfere successit in archiepiscopatum. His temporibus infinita barbarorum manus,[w] navibus adducta in Angliam, ferro et igne omnia vastaverunt. Eboracum veniens oppugnabat civitatem, vastantes *(sic)* omnia per circuitum. Paulo ante adventum illorum Northymbrani expulerant regem suum, substituto in regnum Anna,[x] quodam regii seminis extraneo. Sed instante necessitate revocaverunt expulsum, et tam ille quam alius qui pro eo substitutus fuerat, adunatis[y] totis viribus Northanymbrorum, apud Eboracum bello contra hostes agentes, non sine magna inimicorum strage utrique reges pene cum suis omnibus perierunt.[z] Reliquis qui superfuerant Pagani præfecerunt sub dominio suo regem Egbertum, reconciliatis ab eis hostibus. Inter has[a] strages remotius se agebat apud Hatyngham—episcopus. Hac tempestate passus est[b] martyr Eadmundus. Post septem annos Northumbrani, uno conspirantes consilio, regem suum Egbertum cum episcopo Wlfere de finibus suis propulerunt, et quendam Richsig in regnum substituunt.[c] Deinde post annum Egberto

[u] Alcredi, C. [v] Osredo, C. Osred died in 790.

[w] C. here inserts Inguar, scilicet, et Ubba, et Haldana, cum omni exercitu Danorum et Noraganorum. [x] Ella, C. [y] Coadunatis, C.

[z] C. omits the last seven words, and reads *bella* for *bello*.

[a] C. reads this sentence thus: "Inter has strages remotius se agebat episcopus Wlferius apud Addingeham;" and then interpolates the following description of the place: "In occidentali parte Eboraci in valle quæ vocatur Hwerverdale, super ripam fluminis Hwerf, inter Oteleiam et castellum de Scipetun."

[b] C. adds *Sanctus* before *Martyr*.

[c] C. has restituunt—an obvious error. The date of Egbert's accession is given in Hist. de Gestis Regum, A.D. 867. According to the same authority, he was expelled after a reign of six years, and died the year following. Ricsig's accession is dated from the expulsion of his predecessor A.D. 872, and three years are assigned to his reign. According to the little chronicle interpolated into the Cambridge MS. of the History of the Church of Durham, Egbert reigned six years, Ricsig two, and a second Egbert two years (see Appendix, No. I., to this volume). According to Hist. de Gestis Regum, however, Egbert II. was still reigning over Northumberland, beyond the Tyne, when Guthred ascended the throne of Southern Northumberland at York A.D. 833, eight or nine years after the death of Ricsig. Symeon does not notice this second Egbert, either in the present work or in the History of the Church of Durham.

rege defuncto in sedem suam et ecclesiam revertitur episcopus. Qui xlvij accepti episcopatus anno vita discedens Athelbaldum habuit successorem, anno incarnationis DCCCC.[d] Athelbaldus vero quarto postquam acceperat pontificatum anno pallium accepit regnante Edwardo, filio Elfridi regis. Defuncto autem Athelbaldo successit Lothewardus: post quem Wlstan rexit ecclesiam regnante Edredo[e] fratre Adelstani regis. Cui successit Oscytellus, et per sexdecim annos ecclesiam regens habuit successorem Athelwoldum,[f] regnante Eadgaro regis Edmundi filio. Sed cum idem Athelwoldus quietiorem vitam magis diligeret, Oswaldus suscepit ecclesiæ regimen anno incarnationis Domini DCCCC.lxxj; sequenti igitur[g] anno Romam veniens a papa Benedicto pallium accepit. Post Oswaldum isti sibi ordine successerunt, Adulfus,[h] Wlstanus, Aluricus, Kynsius, Aldredus, Thomas, Gerardus, Thomas, Turstinus.

Hæc,[i] charissime pater et domine, Hugo ecclesiæ Sancti Petri decane, Ego, Symeon,[j] servorum S. Cuthberti servulus, sicut in veteribus libris hinc et inde invenire potui, de successione pontificum Eboracensis ecclesiæ breviter annotavi. Jussa vestræ paternitatis utinam tam efficaciter prosecutus quam libenter! Præterea quod vos scire delectat, istos virtutum viros simul contemporaneos in ecclesia fuisse legimus Northymbrorum, Wylfridum, qui ætatis septuaginta annos habuit, episcopatus autem xlv; Ceadda, Bosan, Eatan, Cuthbertum, Johannem, præclaræ sanctitatis pontifices. Præter hos, ejusdem temporis erat beatus Benedictus, constructor monasteriorum Petri et Pauli in Wermouth et in Girvum, idem nutritor ab infantia et abbas venerabilis Bedæ presbiteri, doctoris. Hilda quoque abbatissa hoc tempore claruit.

Ut autem aliquanto latius nobis noster Beda innotescat, natus est anno ab incarnatione Domini DC septuagesimo septimo, anno, qui est nonus annus adventus Theodori in Britanniam, uno anno ante expulsionem beati Wylfridi primam,[k] Sancto

[d] C. inserts Dominicæ.

[e] C. has Ealdredo fratre Ethelstani regis, and, afterwards, this addition, "Obiit autem DCCCCLV Dominicæ incarnationis anno."

[f] C. reads Aedwaldum, and at the end of the sentence adds another, "Obiit DCCCCLXX Dominicæ incarnationis anno."

[g] C. reads autem for igitur, and omits magis in the preceding line.

[h] C. reads Aldulfus and Aelfricus in this list, and adds Willelmus, Henricus, Rogerus.

[i] In the Cambridge MS. this letter comes first.

[j] C. reads Sim'. The orthography of the Cotton MS., *Symeon*, is confirmed by the authority of the Durham MS. of the history of that church, supposed by Dr. Bedford to have been the autograph of Symeon, where we find the author's name so written in the list of monks.

[k] C. reads uno anno post primam expulsionem, etc.

Cuthberto tunc solitariam vitam agente. Natus est autem in territorio monasterii præfati, et cum esset septem annorum, traditus est a parentibus præfato beato Benedicto abbati,[l] atque, ut ipse de se testatur, omnem usque ad finem vitæ in ejusdem monasterii habitatione peregit ætatem. Videtur autem quibusdam incredibile, quod in extremo mundi angulo vir qui nunquam maria transfretaverit ob addiscendam sapientiam, scolas philosophorum non frequentaverit, tanta eruditione clareat, tanta librorum compositione ubique mundo innotescat: sed hoc non esse mirandum ipse docet, qui, inter DC beatæ vitæ et mirabilis scientiæ monachos enutritus, quicquid scientiæ singuli habuerant, omne hoc ipse in unum sui cordis vasculum, Spiritu Sancto illuminante, contraxerat. Habuerat præ oculis et copiam omnis generis librorum, quos abbas suus Benedictus, inter alia diversa ornamenta, donatione Apostolicorum, Vitaliani, et Agathonis, in monasterium contulerat. Præterea et erat eo tempore quo magna scientiæ studia floruerant in Anglia, quando Theodorus archiepiscopus et Adrianus abbas, peragrata insula, quaquaversum Anglorum gentes commorabantur, scolas sacrarum simul et sæcularium literarum instituebant, ut quicunque cuperent erudiri, haberent inpromptu magistros qui docerent. Unde ipse Beda loquens de his: "Indicio est, inquit, quod "usque hodie supersunt de eorum discipulis qui Latinam "Græcamque linguam æque ut propriam in qua nati sunt "norunt."[m] Ab his eorum discipulis prudens institutus adolescens in lege Domini meditabatur die ac nocte, ut etiam suos doctores ipse doctior supergrederetur. Ostendit ipse quod nec Franciam, nec Italiam, nec Græciam discendi gratia adierit, dicens ubi et a quibus quæ scripserat didicerit. Scribit enim in libro primo Expositionis super Cantica Canticorum, "In hoc "opere lectorem admoneo, ne me superfluum judicet qui de "natura arborum sive herbarum aromaticarum, quæ in hoc "volumine plurimæ continentur, juxta quod in literis antiquorum "didici latius explicare voluerim; feci namque hoc non arro"gantiæ studendo, sed meæ meorumque imperitiæ consulendo, "qui longe extra orbem, hoc est, in insula maris oceani nati "sumus et nutriti: et quæ in primis partibus orbis, Arabia dico, "et Judæa, India, et Ægipto geruntur, non nisi per eorum qui "interfuere scripta nosse valemus."[n] Anno ætatis suæ quinquagesimo nono languescens, die Ascensionis Dominicæ, cum jam exitus ejus instaret, cœpit in oratione dicere Anthifanam,[o] "O rex gloriæ! Domine virtutum," etc., usque in finem. Ad-

[l] C. has præfato abbati Benedicto.

[m] Eccl. Hist., iv., 2.

[n] Beda, Opp., ed. 1612, iv., 721.

[o] Antiphonam, C.

junctaque laude Sanctæ Trinitatis, Gloria Patri, et Filio, et Spiritui Sancto, cum nominatione Spiritus Sancti, suum emisit spiritum, anno Dominicæ incarnationis DCC.XXXV, qui est septimus annus Ceolwlfi regis, ad quem nuper ediderat Historiam Gentis Anglorum. Sepultus est eodem in loco quo conversatus, scilicet in Girvum : sed postea ossa illius ad corpus Sancti Cuthberti sunt translata.

INCIPIT

HISTORIA DE SANCTO CUTHBERTO,

ET DE COMMEMORATIONE LOCORUM REGIONUMQUE EJUS PRISCÆ POSSESSIONIS, A PRIMORDIO USQUE NUNC TEMPORIS.[p]

In nomine Dei summi! De Sancto Cuthberto, et de commemoratione locorum regionumque ejus priscæ possessionis, a primordio usque nunc temporis, hoc modo incipit.

In prima sua juventute, quando Sanctus Cuthbertus erat vigilans super pecora domini sui prope aquam quæ vocatur Leder, in spiritu orabat ad Dominum, sicut ei mos erat semper ab infantia sua, et semper ei fuit, quamdiu vixit cum hominibus. Erat autem etiam sibi mos semper intrare in frigidissimam aquam secreto, et suo solo consilio. Et hoc primum fuit miraculum sibi Divinitus ostensum, quod cum, dormientibus sociis suis, super pecora vigilaret, et in modum crucis positus oraret, vidit animam beati Aidani, Lindisfarnensis episcopi, ab angelis in cælum deferri. Et statim, mane facto, noluit amplius custodire pecora, sed domino suo reddidit, et ad monasterium quod Meilros vocatur ivit, et ad pedes sancti abbatis Bosili cum magna devotione cecidit, et ei quicquid viderat de anima beati episcopi diligenter indicavit: et statim, tonso et coronato capite, monachus effectus est, et postea theoricam actualemque vitam usque in finem vitæ suæ bene custodivit. Tunc sanctus abbas Boisil statim notam fecit regi Osvingio sanctam visionem beati Cuthberti, et quod plenus esset Spiritu Sancto. Tunc rex et omnes meliores Angli dederunt Sancto Cuthberto omnem hanc terram quæ jacet juxta fluvium Bolbenda,[q] cum his villis, Sugariple,[r] et,

[p] The text followed in the earlier part of this tractate is that used by Twysden, the MS. in the Public Library at Cambridge, no other copy being known of any authority.

[q] The Beaumont, or Bowmont, rises on the confines of England and Scotland, and after its confluence with the College, assumes the name of Glen, celebrated in connection with the ministrations of Paulinus.

[r] Sowerhopeshill (or shiel), on one of the loftiest mountains in the Cheviot range, on the boundary line between the two realms, "an exceeding high and

Hesterhoh,[s] et Gistatatun et Waquirtun, et Cliftun,[t] et Scerbedle,[u] et Colwela, et Eltherburna,[v] et Thornburnum, et Scocadūn,[w] et Gatha'n,[x] et Minethrum.[y] Et ipse sanctus abbas sub testimonio ipsius regis monasterium Melros cum omnibus suis appenditiis, ut haberet illud proprium post diem obitus sui. Quo mortuo idem Sanctus Cuthbertus post eum abbas extitit, et diu ibi vixit, verbum Dei evangelizans, et multitudinem magnam baptizans. Tandem disponens arctius vivere, inde exivit, et in quandam remotam insulam nomine Pharne[z] se contulit, et ibi per novem annos se quasi in carcere conclusit pugnans contra humani generis hostem, ne mens sua a Deo averteretur: et ibi erat cum eo Spiritus Sanctus, sicut nunc est, et semper erit. In hac eadem insula diu moratus est Sanctus Aidanus episcopus tempore Pendæ regis filii Wybbindi, quibus successit rex Osvingius. Eodem tempore defunctus rex Oswegius est, et regnavit pro eo filius ejus Egfridus. Quo regnante Theodorus archiepiscopus[a] Eboracensis et omnis populus communi consilio, et una concordia, Sanctum Cuthbertum fieri episcopum apud Helstaldesham acclamaverunt. Ille vero omnibus modis renitebatur, se peccatorem, et episcopatu indignum asserens, et se in sua insula arctissime concludens exemplo beati Gregorii papæ, qui cum peteretur episcopus a Romanis, fugit, et non nisi per vim rediit, secundum illud Evangelicum, *Omnis qui se exaltat humiliabitur, et qui se humiliat exaltabitur.*[b] Tunc rex Ecgfridus, et archiepiscopus Theodorus, et omnis populus, congregata synodo, communi consilio decreverunt, ut eum, vellet nollet, de insula educerent, et in episcopatu subrogarent. Quod et factum est. Raptus enim a populo juxta Eboracam civitatem ad villam quæ vocatur Alna[c] deductus. Ubi, accepto ab omnibus fidelitatis sacramento, ad Eboracam civitatem honori-

pointed hill, on the top of which is a natural rock, on which are many thousand tons of stones, collected, and laid in circles. It rises for a mile at forty-five degrees elevation from its base" (*Companion to Armstrong's Map of Northumberland*, 1769).

[s] Hesteroth, or Hesterheugh, the hill above Kirk-Yetholm, between the Beaumont and Halter-burn.

[t] Gateshaw, Whitton, and Clifton, all in the parish of Morbattle, Roxburghshire.

[u] Scerbedle should be Merbedle, now Morbattle.

[v] Halterburn, in the parish of Yetholm.

[w] Shotton, in the parish of Kirknewton, Northumberland.

[x] Yetholm, or Yetham, in Roxburghshire.

[y] Mindrim, in the parish of Carham, Northumberland.

[z] Farne.

[a] Theodore had the charge of the Northern church during an interregnum. Hence his name of archbishop.

[b] Luke xiv. 11.

[c] Alne, near Easingwold. Symeon confounds this place with the river Aln in Northumberland, *Hist. Dunelm.*, i., 9.

fice est perductus, et in ecclesia beati Petri Apostoli a Theodoro archiepiscopo est ordinatus. In qua ordinatione fuerunt septem episcopi, Ceadde et Cedde, et quatuor alii sancti episcopi. Eadem die Eata episcopus Lindisfarnensis, et Sanctus Cuthbertus, communi consilio Ecgfridi regis, et archiepiscopi et illorum septem episcoporum, et omnium majorum, sedes suas commutaverunt. Sicque Eata apud Helstaldesham sedit; sanctus vero Cuthbertus propter priorem conversationem Lindisfarnensem cathedram obtinuit.

Et hic est Lindisfarnensis terræ terminus; a fluvio Tweoda usque ad Warnamunde,[d] et inde superius usque ad illum locum ubi hæc aqua quæ vocatur Warned[d] oritur juxta montem Hybberndune;[e] et ab illo monte usque ad fluvium qui vocatur Bromic,[f] et inde usque ad fluvium qui vocatur Till:[g] et tota terra quæ jacet ex utraque parte ipsius fluminis Bromic, usque ad illum locum ubi oritur. Et illa terra ultra Tweoda, ab illo loco ubi oritur fluvius Edre[h] ab aquilone, usque ad illum locum ubi cadit in Tweoda, et tota terra quæ jacet inter istum fluvium Edre, et alterum fluvium qui vocatur Leder versus occidentem; et tota terra quæ jacet ab orientali parte istius aquæ, quæ vocatur Leder,[i] usque ad illum locum ubi cadit in fluvium Tweoda versus austrum: et tota terra quæ pertinet ad monasterium Sancti Balthere quod vocatur Tinningaham[j] a Lombormore usque ad Escemuthe.

Et rex Ecgfridus et Theodorus archiepiscopus dederunt Sancto Cuthberto in Eboraca civitate totam terram quæ jacet a muro ecclesiæ Sancti Petri, usque ad magnam portam versus occidentem, et a muro ecclesiæ Sancti Petri, usque ad murum civitatis versus austrum.[k] Dederunt etiam ei villam quæ vocatur

[d] Warnmouth and Warne. In both names the transcriber has corruptly substituted *ph* for *w*, a mistake which is corrected in the text. Leland, following another authority in describing these boundaries, has spelt the names correctly, *Collectanea*, vol. i., p. 366; ed. 1770.

[e] Hebburn Bell, a lofty hill in the parish of Chillingham.

[f] The Bremish.

[g] Till and Bremish are the same river; Bremish being applied to the upper part of its course, Till to the lower, where it unites with the Glen. Their joint waters are discharged into the Tweed at Tillmouth, in the parish of Norham.

[h] The name of this river is preserved in its two branches, the Black-Adder, and White-Adder, whose united streams enter the Tweed a little above Berwick.

[i] The Leader falls into the Tweed below Melrose.

[j] Tynningham is a short distance north of Dunbar, on the estuary of the little river Tyne. The territory granted with it, from the Lammermuir Hills to the mouth of the Esk at Musselburgh, includes the whole country of East Lothian.

[k] There is still a church in York dedicated to St. Cuthbert. His church also possessed the rectories of All Saints' Pavement and St. Peter the Little, in the same city.

Creca,[l] et tria milliaria in circuitu ipsius villæ, ut ibi mansionem haberet, quotiens ad Eboracam civitatem iret, vel inde rediret. Et ibi Sanctus Cuthbertus congregationem monachorum posuit, et abbatem ordinavit. Et quia videbatur parva terra, adjecit civitatem quæ vocatur Luel, quæ habet in circuitu quindecim milliaria, et in eadem civitate posuit congregationem sanctimonialium, et abbatissam ordinavit, et scolas constituit. Postquam vero Sanctus Cuthbertus suscitavit puerum a mortuis in villa quæ vocatur Exanforda, dedit ei rex Ecgfridus terram quæ vocatur Cartmel et omnes Britannos cum eo, et villam illam quæ vocatur Suthgedluit, et quicquid ad eam pertinet. Hæc omnia sibi a Sancto Cuthberto commissa bonus abbas Cineferth filius Cygincg sapienter ordinavit, sicut voluit.

Ea tempestate pugnavit Egfrid rex contra regem Merciorum Wulfhere filium Pendici, et cæso exercitu illius ipsum vicit, et in fugam, uno tantum comitante puerulo, convertit. Et hoc obtinuit per auxilium Sancti Wilfrithi, qui cum eo fuit, maxime vero per orationes Sancti Cuthberti qui absens erat. Post hoc bellum dedit Ecgfridus rex Sancto Cuthberto Carrum, et quicquid ad eam pertinet. Et habuit eum in summa veneratione quamdiu vixit, ipse et tota sua cognatio, donec eo defuncto venerunt Scaldingi, et Eboracam civitatem fregerunt, et terram vastaverunt.

Post hoc successit in regnum Ceolwulf filius Cuthwining, qui etiam se Sancto Cuthberto subdidit, et dimisso regno cum uxore pro amore Dei se cum magno thesauro ad monasterium Lindisfarnense contulit, barbam deposuit, coronam accepit, et S. Cuthberto villam nomine Werceworthe cum suis appenditiis[m] dedit. Et hi sunt termini istius villæ. Ab aqua quæ vocatur Lina,[n] usque ad Cocwuda, et inde usque ad civitatem quæ vocatur Brincewele, et a Cocwuda usque Hafodscelfe versus orientem, et ab Alna usque in dimidiam viam inter Cocwud et Alna.

[l] Crayke, near Easingwold, a village on a commanding eminence, which towers above the country formerly occupied by the forest of Galtres.

[m] After this word the text is taken from the Oxford MS., which is earlier in date and more accurate than that preserved at Cambridge.

[n] The Line is a small stream which falls into the sea, ten miles south of Warkworth. The rivers Coquet and Aln are well known. Hafodscelfe is Hauxley, a rocky headland stretching seaward S.E. of the Coquet. Brincewell, I have no doubt, is Brinkburn, not merely from similarity of name, but from the mention in connection with it of the ancient "via" or "street" between the Coquet and Aln, which crosses the former river near Brinkburn. We have thus the bounds of the ancient territory of Warkworth: on the south the Line from the sea to its source, on the confines of Coquet-dale, and so to Brinkburn: on the north a line drawn from the (mouth of the) Aln to the "street" midway between the Coquet and Aln, and so following the "street" to Brinkburn; thus including the entire valley from Brinkburn on the west, and to Hauxley on the east.

Hoc tempore obiit Sanctus Cuthbertus, et successit Ezred episcopus, qui transportavit quandam ecclesiam olim factam a beato Aidano tempore Oswaldi regis de Lindisfarnensi insula ad Northham, ibique eam re-ædificavit, et illuc corpus Sancti Cuthberti et Ceolwulfi regis transtulit; ipsamque villam sancto Confessori dedit cum duabus aliis villis, Gedwearde, et altera Gedwearde, et quicquid ad eas pertinet, a Duna[o] usque ad Tefegedmuthe, et inde ad Wiltuna, et inde ultra montem versus austrum. Postea idem sanctus episcopus Ecgred ædificavit ecclesiam apud villam quæ vocatur Gegnford, et dedit eam Sancto Cuthberto, et quicquid ad eam pertinet, a flumine Tese usque ad Weor, et a via quæ vocatur Deorestrete[p] usque ad montem versus occidentem. Et ultra fluvium Tese tria milliaria versus austrum: et sex versus occidentem. Et idem episcopus ædificavit duas villas, Ileclif, et Wigeclif ultra Tese, et Billingham in Heorternesse,[q] et dedit eas Sancto Cuthberto.

Post hæc Osberhtus rex abstulit Sancto Cuthberto duas villas Werceworthe et Tyllemuthe. Sed post spatium unius anni eripuit Deus ab eo vitam et regnum. Cui successit rex Elle, qui bene promisit sancto Confessori, sed male egit: nam abstulit ab eo Billingham, et Ileclif, et Wigeclif, et Creca, et ideo ira Dei et sancti Confessoris accensa est super eum. Nam Ubba dux Fresciorum cum magno Danorum exercitu in regnum ejus venit, et in sancto die Palmarum apud Eboracam civitatem applicuit. Quod cum audisset Elle, qui tunc propter odium Sancti Cuthberti in Creca morabatur, cum magna superbia surrexit, exercitum cum fratre suo Osberhto[r] congregavit, in hostem irruit: sed mox ira Dei et sancti Confessoris perterritus, cæso exercitu fugit et corruit, vitamque et regnum perdidit, sicut olim contigit Sauli regi filio Cis, qui cum bene promisisset Deo et Samuheli prophetæ, mentitus est, et male egit: et idcirco in pugna contra Philisteos cum filio suo Jonathan, et melioribus filiorum Israel cecidit. Idcirco caveant reges et principes, ne mentiantur, et ne quid auferant Sancto Cuthberto, nec consentiant auferentibus. Quia, ut ait Sanctus Paulus, *Non solum peccant qui faciunt, sed qui consentiunt.*[s]

[o] Instead of *a Duna*, as in the MS., Twysden has printed *adunaque*, not perceiving that Duna is a proper name. The Dunion is the name of a very remarkable hill near Jedburgh, from whence a line is drawn to the Teviot at Jedmouth (Tefy-Gedmouth), and so up that river to Wilton, immediately opposite to the town of Hawick.

[p] This is the earliest mention by any mediæval writer of Deorstrete, the great Roman thoroughfare through the county of Durham, from south to north.

[q] Heorternœsyre. *MS. Cambridge.*

[r] Osbert and Ella are not represented as brothers by any other authority. On the contrary, Osbert is spoken of as a legitimate sovereign, Ella as a usurper, "non de regali prosapia."

[s] Rom. i. 32.

Priusquam Scaldingi venirent in Anglicam terram dederunt Ceolwlfus rex et episcopus Esred Sancto Cuthberto quatuor villas, scilicet Wudacestre, et Hwitincham, et Eadwulfincham, et Ecgwulfincham, et ecclesias harum villarum consecravit idem episcopus.

Occiso igitur Elle et fratre ejus Osberto, nullus de cognatione eorum regnavit, obtinente hoc apud Deum Sancto Cuthberto, in quem multum peccaverant, quia Scaldingi omnes prope Anglos in meridiana, et in aquilonari parte occiderunt, ecclesias fregerunt et spoliaverunt. Igitur Halfdene rex Danorum in Tinam intravit, et usque Wircesforde[t] navigavit, omnia vastans, et contra Sanctum Cuthbertum crudeliter peccans. Sed mox ira Dei et Sancti Confessoris super eum venit. Nam adeo cœpit insanire ac fætere, quod totus eum exercitus suus a se expulit, et longe in mare fugavit, nec postea comparuit.

Eo tempore Sanctus Cuthbertus apparuit in nocte sancto abbati de Luercestre,[u] nomine Eaddred, talia ei firmiter injungens: "Vade," inquit, "super Tinam ad exercitum Danorum, "et dic eis ut si volunt mihi obedientes esse, ostendant tibi "emptitium quendam puerum cujusdam viduæ, nomine Guth-"red, filium Hardacnut, et summo mane da tu, et totus exercitus, "pro eo pretium viduæ. Et hora tertia super pretium: hora "vero secta duc eum ante totam multitudinem, ut eum regem "eligant. Hora vero nona duc eum cum toto exercitu super "montem qui vocatur Oswigedune, et ibi pone in brachio dextro "armillam auream, et sic eum omnes regem constituant. Dic "etiam ei postquam rex effectus fuerit, ut det mihi totam ter-"ram inter Tinam et Wirram, et quicunque ad me confugerit, "vel pro homicidio, vel pro aliqua necessitate, habeat pacem "per triginta septem dies et noctes." Hac visione certus, et rationabili beati Confessoris præcepto roboratus, ad barbarum exercitum sanctus ille abbas confidenter properavit, a quo honorifice exceptus eo ordine quo sibi injunctum fuerat fideliter executus est. Nam et puerum illum invenit, redemit, et magno totius multitudinis favore, regem constituit, terram et pacem

[t] This *ford* can scarcely have been on the Tyne, but probably on its then navigable tributory, the Don, which was crossed by a ford on the only ancient line of road in the district. That district was called Werehale, or *Wyr*hale, whence perhaps *Wyr*cesford. See Charter of Bishop Carileph, *Hist. Dunelm. Scriptores*, iii., p. xxiv; also *Surtees' Durham*, vol. ii., p. 59, and note. Mr. Longstaffe, in his map of Saxon Durham, designates the district (inter Tyne et Wear) "Werewickshire." Fordun, in his Scoto-Chronicon, transcribing an earlier authority, speaks of the district at the mouth of the Wear, as Wervicam.

[u] Probably a corruption of De Luel-cestre. Symeon says that Eadred was called Luliso from the city of Luel (Carlisle), where he received his education in the monastery founded by St. Cuthbert, of which he afterwards became abbat (Hist. Dunelm., ii., 6). Twysden has Delvercestre.

accepit. Tunc Eardulfus episcopus detulit ad illum exercitum, et ad illum montem corpus Sancti Cuthberti, super quod juravit ipse rex et totus exercitus pacem et fidelitatem, donec viverent; et hoc jusjurandum bene servaverunt.

Igitur exercitus ille quem Ubba dux Fresonum, et Healfdena rex Danorum in Anglicam terram adduxit, in tres partes divisus est: una Eboracam civitatem re-ædificavit, terram in circuitu coluit, et ibi remansit. Alia vero quæ terram Merciorum occupavit; et tertia, quæ terram Australium Saxonum invasit, per tres annos multa mala egerunt, omnesque regii generis interfecerunt, præter solum Elfredum patrem Eadvardi regis, qui his tribus annis in Glestigiensi palude latuit, in magna penuria. Quadam igitur die cum totam familiam suam misisset piscatum, præter uxorem, et unum familiarem ministrum, peregrinus quidam affuit, ad eum intravit, cibum petiit. Quod cum ex humana condescensione ei caritative largiri præcepisset, et nihil ibi esse ad totum diurnum victum, præter unum panem, et parum vini a ministro didicisset, Deo gratias egit, et utriusque medietatem ei libenter impertiri jussit. Quod cum minister devote implevisset, et de gratiarum actione illius domino suos retulisset, illuc citissime reversus, panem quidem et vinum integrum reperit: illum vero non invenit, nec quomodo per paludes illas venisset, vel redisset, maxime cum ibi navis non esset, investigare potuit. Super hoc autem non parum admirante Elfredo, et cogitante, ecce! hora diei nona reversa est piscatu familia, cum tribus navibus omnino plenis piscibus, asserentes plus illa die cepisse, quam tribus annis quibus morati sunt in palude. Lætus igitur, et de hoc eventu sollicitus, diem istum lætius et abundantius solito transegit. Factaque nocte cum uxore sua dormitum ivit. Illa vero somno occupata, dum Elfredus de diurno eventu sollicitus vigilaret, ecce! lumen magnum, sicut sol, refulsit, et in ipso lumine senex sacerdos infulatus, nigris quidem capillis, habens in dextera manu Evangeli textum auro gemmisque ornatum, apparuit, et sic eum vigilantem cum his verbis benedixit. Et ab eo diligenter inquisitus quis esset, et quomodo nominaretur, "Care," inquit, "Elfrede, lætus esto: ego sum ille cui hodie "cibum præbuisti caritative, vocor autem Cuthbertus, Christi "miles. Esto robustus, et attende diligenter et læto animo "quod tibi dixero: nam ego deinceps ero scutum tuum, et "amicus tuus, et defensor filiorum tuorum. Et nunc dicam "quid tibi post hoc sit agendum. Surge summo diluculo, sona "fortiter cornu tribus vicibus, ut inimici tui audiant et expavescant, et circa horam nonam habebis quingentos armatos: et "hoc signo credas, quod post septem dies habebis Dei dono et "meo auxilio totum hujus terræ exercitum apud montem As-

"sandune in auxilio tuo paratum. Sicque contra hostes tuos "pugnabis, et sine dubio eos superabis. Post hæc esto lætus et "robustus, sine timore, quia Deus tradidit inimicos tuos in "manibus tuis, et totam istam terram, et regnum hæreditarium "tibi et filiis tuis, et filiis filiorum tuorum. Esto fidelis mihi, "et populo meo, quia tibi et filiis tuis data est tota Albion. "Esto justus, quia tu es electus rex totius Britanniæ. Sit tibi "Deus misericors, et ego sic tibi ero amicus tuus, ut nullus "adversarius adversum te possit prævalere." Et hæc omnia acta sunt secundum hoc quod Spiritus Sanctus dixit per os David prophetæ, *Dominus a dextris tuis confregit in die iræ Suæ reges.*[v] Et alibi. *De fructu ventris tui ponam super sedem tuam.*[w] Tunc Elfredus gratias egit Deo, et Sancto Cuthberto propter misericordiam eorum et perpetuum auxilium, secundum hoc quod dixit Deus ad David per os Samuelis prophetæ. *Juravit Dominus et non pœnitebit Eum.*[x] Et alibi. *Filii tui, et filii filiorum tuorum sedebunt super sedem tuam.*[y] Sic visitavit, confortavit, docuit, juvit iste sanctus Confessor Christi Cuthbertus Elfredum, sicut olim, ut in Anglica Historia legitur,[z] Sanctus Petrus Eadwino regi pagano crucem auream dextra gestans apparuit, se Petrum principem esse Apostolorum asseruit, coronam ostendit, et ut paganismum relinqueret, præcepit; et sic eum ubique victorem futurum prædixit, sicut etiam Samuel David regi fecit. Deinceps Elfredus rex fuit fortis, et lætus, quia sciebat se ubique fore victorem, quamdiu viveret, per donum Dei, et auxilium patroni sui Sancti Cuthberti. Itaque facto mane surrexit, ad terram navigavit, cornu suo tribus vicibus signum dedit, quo sonitu omnes amici ejus sunt exaltati: inimici vero humiliati. Itaque, secundum verbum Dei, circa nonam ipsius diei horam, congregatis ad eum quingentis de melioribus et carioribus amicis suis, publice narravit quid præcedenti nocte vidisset, et a sancto Confessore audisset, et qualiter ab eo confortatus esset. Asseruit etiam illis quod per donum Dei, et auxilium Sancti Cuthberti, cui deinceps deberent merito obedire, hostes vincerent, et terram hæreditario jure obtinerent. Ammonuit etiam eos, ut, secundum doctrinam beati Cuthberti, fugerent avaritiam, invidiam, longam iram, adulteria, perjuria, homicidia, et omnia mala; ut essent Deo fideles, patientes, humiles, hospitales, elemosinarii, misericordes, modesti; et ut haberent inter se sanctam fidem, et justitiam, et veritatem. Ammonuit etiam filium suum Eadwardum, qui ibi erat, quod si vellet esse fidelis Deo et Sancto Cuthberto, non ei esset

[v] Ps. cix. 5. [w] Ps. cxxxi. 11. [x] Ps. cix. 4. [y] Psalm cxxxi. 12.
[z] Beda, Hist., ii., 12. It is not, however, said there that the visitant was St. Peter.

timendum de inimicis suis. Tunc, secundum verbum viri Dei, Elfredus in hostes irruit, eosque superavit, et regnum Brytanniæ accepit, sancteque et juste omnibus in commune bonus, pauperibus et divitibus, bonis et malis, amicis et inimicis, secundum Evangelicum præceptum. His et aliis quamplurimis virtutibus insignitus, postquam intellexit finem vitæ sibi adesse, diu regnans, et bona confectus senectute, vocavit hunc eundem filium suum Eadwardum, et per eum transmisit Sancto Cuthberto duas armillas, et aureum thuribulum, monuitque eum diligenter, ut amaret Deum, et Sanctum Cuthbertum, et speraret in eis, sicut et ipse semper speravit, et adhuc maxime sperabat. Igitur antequam Deus hunc fidelem Sibi regem de hac vita vocaret, addita sunt quædam prædia ecclesiæ sancti Confessoris. Nam Ethred, supradictus abbas, emit a præfato rege Guthred, et a Danorum exercitu, qui sibi sub eo terram diviserant, has villas, Seletun,[a] Horetun,[b] duas Geodene,[c] Holum,[d] Hotun,[e] Twilingatun,[f] et eas Sancto Cuthberto contulit.

Eodem quoque tempore bonus episcopus Eardulfus et abbas Eadred tulerunt corpus Sancti Cuthberti de Lindisfarnensi insula, et cum eo erraverunt in terra, portantes illud de loco in locum, per septem annos; et tandem pervenerunt ad fluvium qui vocatur Derunt-muthe,[g] et illud ibi in navi posuerunt, ut sic per proximum mare in Hyberniam transveherent. Tunc omnis populus ejus, qui eum diu erat secutus, dolens quod eripiebatur pius eorum patronus, stans in littore, flebat et ululabat, eo quod et ipsi relinquebantur captivi, et captivus eorum abducebatur dominus. Tunc Deus magnum miraculum ostendit pro amore dilecti Sui Confessoris: Orta siquidem in mari horribili tempestate, maximæ tres undæ in navim ceciderunt, et statim, mirabile dictu, aqua illa in sanguinem est conversa. Quo viso, episcopus et abbas ad pedes sancti viri ceciderunt, et, timore perterriti, ad littus quantocitius sunt reversi, et sanctum illud corpus ad Crecam detulerunt; et ibi a bono abbate, nomine Geve, caritative excepti, quatuor mensibus manserunt; et inde sanctum corpus ad Cunceceastre transtulerunt. Eo tempore obiit rex Elfredus, et Eardulfus episcopus. Tunc Eadwardus, diu sapienter a patre edoctus, in regnum successit, et illud sapienter rexit; et Cutheardus episcopalem cathedram apud Cunceceastre accepit.

Eodem tempore Cuthardus, episcopus fidelis, emit de pecunia

[a] Monkhesleden. [b] Horden.
[c] The two Edens, Castle Eden and Little Eden.
[d] Hulam, in the parish of Hesleden.
[e] Hutton, in the same parish.
[f] Willington, in the parish of Brancepeth.
[g] Derwentmouth, at Workington, in Cumberland.

Sancti Cuthberti villam quæ vocatur Ceddesfeld,[h] et quicquid ad eam pertinet, præter quod tenebant tres homines, Aculf, Ethelbyriht, Frithlaf. Super hoc tamen habuit episcopus sacam et socnam. Emit etiam idem episcopus de pecunia Sancti Cuthberti villam quæ vocatur Bedlingtun, cum suis appenditiis, Nedertun,[i] Grubba,[j] Twisle,[k] Cebbingtun,[l] Sliceburne,[m] Cammes.[n] Tempore ejusdem Eadwardi regis Tilred abbas de Hefresham villam quæ vocatur Iodene Australis[o] emit. Cujus dimidiam partem dedit Sancto Cuthberto, ut esset frater in ejus monasterio; alteram apud Northam, ut ibi abbas esset. Eodem tempore Bernardus presbiter dedit villam suam, nomine Twinlingatun, Sancto Cuthberto, ut esset frater in ejus monasterio. His diebus Elfred filius Birihtulfinci, fugiens piratas, venit ultra montes versus occidentem, et quæsivit misericordiam Sancti Cuthberti et episcopi Cutheardi, ut præstarent sibi aliquas terras. Tunc episcopus Cutheardus pro caritate Dei et amore Sancti Cuthberti, præstitit illi has villas, Esingtun, Seletun, Thorep,[p] Horedene, Iodene, duas Sceottun,[q] Iodene Australem, Holum, Hotun, Twinlingtun, Billingham, cum suis appenditiis, Scurufatun. Has omnes villas, sicut dixi, præstitit episcopus Elfredo, ut sibi et congregationi fidelis esset, et de his plenum servitium redderet. Quod et fideliter fecit, donec Regenwaldus rex venit cum magna multitudine navium, occupavitque terram Aldredi filii Eadulfi,[r] qui erat dilectus regi Eadwhardo, sicut et pater suus Eadulfus dilectus fuit regi Elfredo. Fugatus igitur Eldredus in Scottiam ivit, Constantini regis auxilium quæsivit, illum contra Regenwaldum regem apud Corebricge in prælium adduxit. In quo prælio, nescio quo peccato agente, paganus rex vicit, Constantinum fugavit, Scottos fudit, Elfredum Sancti Cuthberti fidelem, et omnes meliores Anglos interfecit, præter Ealdredum, et fratrem ejus Uhtred.

Quibus fugatis et tota terra superata, divisit villas Sancti Cuthberti, et alteram partem versus austrum dedit cuidam

[h] This should be Seggefeld (hodie Sedgefield), according to Leland.

[i] Netherton, in the parish of Bedlington.

[j] This name is written Gurb' in Leland (*Collectanea*, xi., p. 373). Gubeon, in the parish of Morpeth.

[k] Twizle also in the parish of Morpeth: all the rest are in the parish of Bedlington.

[l] Choppington. The Cambridge MS. has Bedbington. [m] Sleekburn.

[n] Camboise; written Commer in the Cambridge MS. Cammes in Leland, which accords with the vulgar pronunciation of the name at this day.

[o] Castle Eden.

[p] Thorp, in the parish of Hesleden. In the Camb. MS. it is written Worew.

[q] Seaton. Scurufatun below is Sheraton, in the parish of Hesleden.

[r] The death of Eadulf, or Adulf, duke of Bamburgh, is recorded by Ethelward A.D. 912. The scene of Ealred's defeat is placed by the *Chronicon Pictorum* at Tyne-Moore, hodie Corbridge-Fell.

potenti militi suo qui vocabatur Scula, a villa quæ vocatur Iodene, usque ad Billingham. Alteram vero partem dedit cuidam qui vocabatur Onalafball, a Iodene, usque ad fluvium Weorram. Et hic filius diaboli inimicus fuit, quibuscunque modis potuit, Deo et Sancto Cuthberto. Quadam itaque die, cum, plenus immundo spiritu, cum furore intrasset ecclesiam beati Confessoris, adstante episcopo Cuthheardo et tota congregatione, "Quid," inquit, "in me potest homo iste mortuus "Cuthbertus, cujus minæ quotidie opponuntur? Juro per "Deos meos potentes, Thor et Othan, quod ab hac hora inimi-"cissimus ero omnibus vobis." Cumque episcopus et tota congregatio genua flecterent ante Deum et Sanctum Cuthbertum, et harum minarum vindictam, sicut scriptum est, *Mihi vindicta, et Ego retribuam,*[s] ab eis expeterent, conversus ille filius diaboli cum magna superbia et indignatione voluit egredi. Sed cum alterum pedem posuisset jam extra limen, sensit quasi ferrum in altero pede sibi altius infixum. Quo dolore diabolicum ejus cor transfigente, corruit, suamque peccatricem animam diabolus in infernum trusit. Sanctus vero Cuthbertus, sicut justum erat, terram suam recepit.

Tempore supradicti Eadwardi regis, dedit Wulfheardus filius Hwetreddinci[t] Sancto Cuthberto villam quæ vocatur Bynnewalle. Eodem tempore Edred filius Rixinci equitavit versus occidentem ultra montes, et interfecit Eardulfum principem, ejusque uxorem rapuit, contra pacem et voluntatem populi, et ad patrocinium Sancti Cuthberti confugit. Et ibi tribus annis mansit, cum pace colens terram sibi a Cuthardo episcopo et a congregatione præstitam; a Cunceceastre, usque ad Dyrwente fluvium, et inde usque ad Werram versus austrum, et inde usque ad viam quæ vocatur Deorestrete in occidentali et australi parte, et villam super Tese, quæ vocatur Geagenforda, et quicquid ad eam pertinet. Hanc terram idem Edred cum fidelitate Sancti Cuthberti tenuit, et censum fideliter reddidit, donec supradictus Regenwaldus rex, congregato iterum exercitu, apud Corebrygce pugnavit, ipsumque Edred, et maximam Anglorum multitudinem interfecit; et, victor effectus, totam illam terram quam Edred tenuerat Sancto Cuthberto abstulit, et dedit Esbrido filio Edred, et fratri suo Eltano comiti, qui in hoc prælio robusti bellatores fuerunt. Tandem ipse maledictus rex cum filiis et amicis suis periit, nihilque de his quæ Sancto Confessori abstulerat secum præter peccatum tulit.

Eo tempore Eadwardus rex, plenus dierum et confectus

[s] Heb. x. 30.

[t] The Cambridge MS. reads Hwæorddinci. Bynnewalle is probably Benwell on the Tyne.

bona senectute, filium suum Ethelstanum vocavit, eique regnum suum tradidit, et ut Sanctum Cuthbertum diligeret, et supra omnes Sanctos honoraret, diligenter inculcavit; notificans ei qualiter patri suo regi Elfredo in paupertate et in exilio misericorditer subvenisset; et qualiter eum contra omnes hostes viriliter juvisset; et quomodo sibimetipsi in omnibus necessitatibus suis evidentissime promptissimus semper adjutor fuisset. Qua ammonitione facta feliciter obiit.

Igitur Ethelstanus rex magnum exercitum de australi parte eduxit, et versus aquilonarem plagam in Scottiam illum secum trahens ad oratorium Sancti Cuthberti divertit, eique regia munera dedit, et inde hoc subscriptum testamentum composuit, et ad caput Sancti Cuthberti posuit.[u]

In nomine Domini nostri Jhesu Christi. Ego Ethelstanus rex do Sancto Cuthberto hunc textum Evangeliorum,[v] ij casulas, et j albam, et j stolam cum manipulo, et j cingulum, et iij altaris cooperimenta, et j calicem argenteum, et ij patenas, alteram auro paratam, alteram Græco opere fabrefactam, et j turribulum argenteum, et j crucem auro et ebore artificiose paratam, et j regium pilleum auro textum, et ij tabulas auro et argento fabrefactas, et ij candelabra argentea auro parata, et j missale, et ij Evangeliorum textus auro et argento ornatos, et j Sancti Cuthberti Vitam metrice et prosaice scriptam,[w] et vij pallia, et iij cortinas, et iij tapetia, et ij coppas argenteas cum cooperculis, et iiij magnas campanas, et iij cornua auro et argento fabrefacta, et ij vexilla, et j lanceam, et ij armillas aureas, et meam villam dilectam[x] Wiremuthe Australem cum suis appendentiis, id est, Westun,[y] Uffertun,[z] Sylceswurthe,[a] duas Reofhoppas,[b] Byrdene,[c] Seham, Setun,[d] Daltun, Daldene, Heseldene.[e] Hæc omnia do

[u] At the beginning of this deed, in the Cambridge MS., is the rubric, *Carta regis Ethelstani.* There is a copy of this charter-will in MS. Cotton, Claudius D. iv., 21-2, a MS. of the fifteenth century. It occurs also at p. 93 *b* of the same MS., and is said to be taken "Ex libro Prioris; et concordat cum libro magni altaris." The passage relating to Edmund is said to be "Ex libro magni altaris." Neither it, nor the will of Athelstan, is in the Liber Vitæ, and some other book is no doubt meant. The variations between the Cottonian MS. and our text are trifling.

[v] This book was in the Cottonian Library, Otho B. ix, and was most unfortunately destroyed in the fire.

[w] No doubt, the Life by Beda.

[x] *Dilectam* ought probably to be *dictam*.

[y] The Cambridge MS. has Wertun. Westoe, near South Shields, is the place meant.

[z] Offerton, in the parish of Houghton-le-Spring.

[a] Silksworth, in the parish of Bishop-Wearmouth.

[b] Ryhope, in the same parish.

[c] Burdon, in the same parish.

[d] Seaham and Seaton, in the parish of Seaham.

[e] Dalton, Dalden, and *Cold* Hesleden, in the parish of Dalton. In the Cottonian MS. these places are as follows: Wermuthe Australem, Westun, Wffertun, Silceswurthe, duas Reofhoppas, Byrdene, Saetone, Daltone, Daldene, Hesildene.

sub Dei et Sancti Cuthberti testimonio, ut si quis inde aliquid abstulerit, damnetur in die judicii cum Juda traditore, et trudatur in ignem æternum, qui paratus est diabolo et angelis ejus.[f]

Implevit etiam prædictas coppas pecunia optima, et, jussu ipsius, obtulit totus exercitus ejus Sancto Cuthberto xij hundred, et eo amplius.

Fratrem vero suum Eadmundum de sanctitate et fideli patrocinio sancti Confessoris diligenter prius edoctum fraterne commonuit, ut si quid sinistri sibi in hac expeditione eveniret, corpus suum Sancto Cuthberto referret, et ei illud in die judicii Deo repræsentandum commendaret. Post hæc abiit, feliciter pugnavit, prospere rediit, sapienter multis annis postea regnavit, tandem feliciter obiit. Eo defuncto, Eadmundus frater ejus in regnum successit, magnum rursus exercitum congregavit, et in Scottiam properavit. In eundo tamen ad oratorium Sancti Cuthberti divertit, ante sepulcrum ejus genua flexit, preces fudit, se et suos Deo et sancto Confessori commendavit: exercitus sexaginta libras obtulit: ipse vero manu propria ij armillas aureas, et ij pallia Græca supra sanctum corpus posuit: pacem vero et legem, quam unquam habuit, meliorem, omni terræ Sancti Cuthberti dedit, datam confirmavit: et factus quasi alter Abraham, qui properans in hostes panem et vinum Melchisede(c)h obtulit, finita oratione, multotiens se et totum exercitum beato Confessori commendans, abiit.[g]

In nomine Dei Summi et Individuæ Trinitatis, Ego, Styr filius Ulfi,[h] *impetravi a domino meo Ethelredo rege ut daret Sancto Cuthberto villam quæ vocatur Dearthingtun, cum saca et socna; et ego emi propria pecunia et dedi Sancto Cuthberto iiij carrucatas terræ in Cingcesclife, et iiij in Cocertune, et iiij in Halhtune, et iij in Northmannabi, et ij in Ceattune, cum saca et socna, et ij in Lummalea;*[i] *sub testimonio Ethelredi regis et*

[f] Instead of "Hæc omnia do," the following words occur in the Cottonian MS.: "Has villas, quas malorum malignitas ab ecclesia multo ante tempore abstulerat, reddo." The text at the end comes from St. Matt. xxv. 41.

[g] The Cambridge MS. ends here, and the Saxon Poem on Durham follows. The new matter which is now given is only to be found in the Oxford MS., in which the Poem does not appear at all.

[h] Respecting Styr, the son of Ulf, see the next piece, *De Obsessione Dunelmi.*

[i] Dearthington, spelt by Symeon Dearnington, is Darlington, in which parish are Cockerton and Newton. Cingcesclife is Coniscliffe; and Halhtune, Haughton-le-Skerne; Ceathune is Seaton, in the parish of Stranton; Northmannaby is Normanby, on the opposite side of the Tees; and Lummalea is Lumley, in the parish of Chester-le-street. Both Symeon (Hist. Eccl. Dunelm., book iii., c. iv.) and the anonymous writer, De Episcopis Lindisfarnensibus, from which copious extracts are given by Leland (Collectanea, vol. i., pp. 365-386), notice the grant of Darlington. Symeon says, "He added other lands, which are recorded elsewhere," clearly referring to the work before us. Leland's authority mentions the localities of the other lands except Lumley, which he omits.

Elfrici archiepiscopi Eboracensis, et Alduni episcopi Lindispharnensis, et Alfwoldi abbatis qui sub episcopo erat, et illorum omnium principum qui ea die in Eboraca civitate cum rege fuerunt. Quod si quis de his aliquid Sancti Confessoris abstulerit, recipiat hanc maledictionem in die judicii, Discedite a Me, maledicti, in ignem æternum.[j]

Item Snaculf filius Cytel[k] dedit hanc terram Sancto Cuthberto, Brydbyrig, Mordun, et Socceburg, et Grisebi,[l] cum saca et socna.

Hæ sunt terræ quas Aldhun episcopus et tota congregatio Sancti Cuthberti præstitit his tribus, Ethred eorle, et Northman eorle, et Uhtred eorle,[m] Gegenford, Queorningtun, Sliddewesse, Bereford, Stretford, Lyrtingtun, Marawuda, Stantun, Stretlea, Cletlinga, Langadun, Mortun, Persebrigce, Alclit ij, Copland, Weardseatle, Bynceastre, Cuthbertestun, Thiccelea, Ediscum, Wudutun, Hunewic, Newatun, Healme.[n] Quicumque de his aliquid abstulerit Sancto Cuthberto pereat in die judicii.

Item Cnut rex dedit Sancto Cuthberto[o] tempore Eadmundi episcopi, sicut ipsemet tenuit, cum saca et socna, villam quæ vocatur Standropa cum suis appenditiis, Cnapatun, Scottun, Raby, Wacarfeld, Efenwuda, Alclit, Luteringtun, Elledun,

[j] St. Matt. xxv. 41.

[k] Spelt Cykel both in Symeon and Leland.

[l] Bradbury and Mordon are in the parish of Sedgefield: Socceburg is Sockburn on the Tees. Grisebi is Girsby, on the Yorkshire side of the Tees, opposite Sockburn. The names occur both in Symeon and in Leland's excerpts (p. 377). The latter adds Grisebridge.

[m] Leland has, *Nomina terrarum quas episcopi Lindis. et Concestren., tempore necessitatis, ad tempus, comitibus Northumbr. præstabant, et vix unquam receperant.* The names occur in the Durham copy of Symeon, but not in the C. C. MS. From both texts we learn that certain lands which had been given in pledge by bishop Aldune to the earls of the Northumbrians, were lost altogether to the church by the violence of their successors. Ethred and Northman nowhere occur as earls *of Northumberland,* nor are they so described in our text. They were probably Danes, who exercised authority during the usurpation of Sweyn, to whom earl Uchtred refused his allegiance, as we know their countryman Yric did under Cnut.

[n] The above manors lie as follows:—Stretford, or Startforth, Lartington, and Cotherston (Cuthbertestun), on the south of the Tees; Worsall (Weardseatle), on the same side, but much lower down. All the rest are in Durham. Gainford (Geganford), Cleatlam (Cletlingha), Langton (Langadun), Morton, and Piercebridge are in Gainford parish: Marwood (Marawuda), Stainton, and Streatlam, in the chapelry of Barnard Castle: Sledwitch (Sliddewesse), in the chapelry of Whorlton: Barford (Bereford) is on the Yorkshire side of the Tees, opposite to Gainford. Queornington is Quarrington, in the parish of Kelloe. All the rest are in Auckland and its dependent chapelries: the two Aucklands (Alclit), Binchester, Thickley, Hunwick, Helmington, Newton-Cap, Witton-le-Wear (Wuduton), Escomb (Ediscum), and Copeland in West Auckland township.

[o] The particulars of both Cnut's grants are given both by Symeon and in Leland.

Ingeltun, Thiccelea et Middeltun.[p] Quisquis aliquid de his a Sancto Cuthberto averterit, avertatur Deus ab illo. Item Cnut rex dedit Sancto Cuthberto tempore Eadmundi episcopi Bromtun cum saca et socna.

Hoc est Dei et Sancti Cuthberti miraculum[q] valde animadvertendum et magnificandum, quod aliquando Scotti cum innumerabili multitudine Tuidam fluvium transierunt, et terram Sancti Cuthberti vastaverunt, et Lindisfarnense monasterium, nunquam prius violatum, spoliaverunt. Quo audito, Guthreth rex pro vindicta sancti Confessoris illuc parva admodum manu properavit, eisque jam extrema parte diei in loco qui dicitur Mundingedene[r] occurrit. Et ideo bellum non est inceptum. Nocte vero subsecuta cum rex Guthred multum perterritus et anxiatus eo quod ipse parvissimum, hostes vero, qui jam in manibus erant, maximum haberent exercitum, et sic nec pugnare nec posset fugere, præ nimia et varia cura obdormisset, ecce! miles Christi Cuthbertus ei manifeste apparuit et nimis exanimatum his verbis animavit. "Ne timeas," inquit, "quia ego "tecum sum, neque diffidas paucitati militum, quia hostes mei " adhuc vivi jam coram Deo sunt mortui, nec poterunt tibi re- " sistere qui pacem Dei et meam non timuerunt violare. Facto " mane, surge velociter, irrue in eos confidenter, quia mox in " primo conflictu terra aperietur et vivos in infernum demittet." His dictis abscessit, rex vero evigilavit. Exiliens itaque exercitum convocavit, omnia hæc omnibus publice narravit, moxque facto mane in hostes irruit; sed, secundum viri Dei verbum, eos mox in primo conflictu vivos, terra dehiscente absorptos, non invenit, renovato ibi mirabiliter antiquo miraculo, quando *Aperta est terra et deglutivit Dathan, et operuit super congregationem Abyron.*[s]

[p] Staindrop, Shotton, Raby, Wackerfield and Ingleton in Staindrop parish, as also is " Cnapatun," which Hutchinson identifies with Snotterton, or which may be Keverston. The remainder are in Auckland parish, viz.: Auckland, Eldon, Thickley, Middleton, Lutterington, and Evenwood. The two last are in the chapelry of St. Helen's. Bromtun, which occurs two lines lower, is Brompton, near Northallerton.

[q] Until the discovery of the Bodleian MS., the Translatio Cuthberti was our earliest authority for this miracle. The MS. in question carries us back at least one hundred years, from the twelfth century to the eleventh. The writer has fallen into a strange mistake, in describing the monastery of Lindisfarne as inviolate in the reign of Guthred. It was destroyed and abandoned seven years before his accession, and this was the second violation which it had suffered. Symeon mentions the miracle, but refers for particulars to a known authority, either the present work or the Translatio Sancti Cuthberti.

[r] In another MS., from which Leland has made extracts (Collectanea, vol. i., p. 329), Mundingdene is said to be one mile south of Norham. See the account of this miracle in the Translatio Cuthberti in the present volume.

[s] Psalm cvi. 17.

DE SITU DUNELMI,

ET DE SANCTORUM RELIQUIIS QUÆ IBIDEM CONTINENTUR CARMEN COMPOSITUM.[t]

Is ðeos burch breome geond Breotenrice
steppa gestaðolad, stanas ymbutan
wundrum gewæxen. Weor ymbeornað
ea yðum stronge, ⁊ ðerinne wunað
feola fisca kyn on floda gemonge.
⁊ ðær gewexen is wuda, wæstern micel.
winnað in ðem wycum wilda deor monige
in deope dalum, deora ungerum.
Is in ðere byri eac bearnum gecyðed
ðe arfesta eadig Cuðberch, ⁊ ðes clene cyninges heofud
Osuualdes, Engle [h]leo, ⁊ Aidan biscop,
Eadberch ⁊ Eadfrið ⁊ ðele geféres.
Is ðerinne mid heom ⁊ [Æ]ðelwold biscop
⁊ breoma bocera Beda ⁊ Boisil abbot,
ðe clene Cuðberte on gecheðe
lerde lustun, ⁊ he his lara wel genom.
Eardræð ⁊ ðem eadige inne ðem minstre
unarimeda reliquia.
ðe monia wundrum gewurðad, ðes ðe writ seogeð
miða ðene drihnes wer, domes bideð.

[t] The only known copy in MS. of this poem is in the Public Library at Cambridge, where it follows the Historia S. Cuthberti, of which, however, it is no part. It is referred to by Symeon in his History of the Church of Durham, iii., cap. vii. The poem has been printed by the learned Hickes in his Thesaurus, Gramm. Anglo-Sax., pp. 178-9, from a MS. in the Cottonian Library, which was most unfortunately destroyed in the fire. It may also be seen in Wright's Reliqq. Antiquæ, i., 159, and in the Preface to the Lindisfarne Gospels, ed. Waring, pp. xxxii, xxxiii.

[SYMEON] DE OBSESSIONE DUNELMI,

ET DE PROBITATE UCHTREDI COMITIS, [ET DE COMITIBUS QUI EI SUCCESSERUNT.][u]

Anno ab incarnatione Domini dcccc.lxix,[v] regnante rege Anglorum Æthelredo, Malcolmus rex Scottorum, filius Kynedi regis, congregato totius Scotiæ exercitu, provinciam Northanhumbrorum cædibus et incendiis devastans, Dunelmum obsidione circumdedit. Quo tempore Alduno episcopatum ibidem regente, Waltheof, qui comes fuerat Northanimbrorum, sese in Beebbanburc incluserat. Fuerat enim nimiæ senectutis, ideoque in hostes nihil virtutis facere poterat. Cujus filio, scilicet Ucthredo, magnæ strenuitatis juveni et militiæ aptissimo, filiam suam nomine Ecgfridam, Aldunus episcopus dederat uxorem, et has villas de terris ecclesiæ Sancti Cuthberti, scilicet, Bermetun, Skirningheim, Eltun, Carltun, Heaclif, Heseldene[w] cum ea sub illa conditione donavit, ut ejus filiam, quamdiu viveret in conjugio, cum honore semper servaret. Videns juvenis præfatus terram ab hostibus devastatam, et Dunelmum obsidione circum-

[u] The words within brackets are additions to the original text, probably by archbishop Parker.

[v] This date is corrupt; the foundations of Durham were not laid till nearly thirty years later. Ethelred did not succeed to the crown of England till A.D. 978, nor Malcolm to that of Scotland till 1003: Aldune's episcopacy did not commence till A.D. 990. The year 969 is probably written in mistake for 999. Even that date was four years before Malcolm's accession to the Scottish throne, but he was already king of Cumbria, and tanist of Scotland, in which capacity he probably commanded the forces of the latter kingdom at the siege of Durham. It is remarkable that we find no notice of this siege in Symeon's History of the Church of Durham. In that work Uchtred is mentioned as earl of Northumberland as early as A.D. 997, when he assisted the bishop in clearing the site of his future city. Probably the title by which he was afterwards known is given him for distinction's sake by anticipation; as the foundation of the city must at all events have preceded the date of the siege, when the earldom was still held by the aged Waltheof.

[w] Barmton and Skerningham, in the parish of Haughton-le-Skerne; Elton, near Stockton; Carleton, in the parish of Redmarshall; Aycliffe, near Darlington; and Monk-Hesleden.

datam, et contra hoc patrem suum nihil agere, adunato exercitu Northymbrorum et Eboracensium non parva manu, Scottorum multitudinem pene totam interfecit, ipso rege vix per fugam cum paucis evadente. Interfectorum vero capita elegantiora, crinibus, sicut tunc temporis mos erat, perplexis, fecit Dunelmum transportari, eaque a quatuor mulieribus perlota per circuitum murorum in stipitibus præfigi; mulieribus autem quæ ea laverant mercedem dederant vaccas, singulis singulas. His auditis, rex Æthelredus, vocato ad se juvene præfato, vivente adhuc patre Waltheof, pro merito suæ strenuitatis et bello quod tam viriliter peregerat, dedit ei comitatum patris sui, adjungens etiam Eboracensium comitatum. Reversus autem Ucthredus domum filiam Alduni episcopi dimisit; et quia eam contra hoc quod promiserat et juraverat abjecit, pater puellæ, videlicet episcopus, terras supradictas ecclesiæ quas cum ea donaverat ab Ucthredo recepit. Dimissa, sicut dictum est, episcopi filia, Ucthredus, civis divitis, nomine Styr filii Vlf,[x] filiam, nomine Sigen, duxit uxorem, quam pater suus ideo ei dedit ut Turbrandum sibi inimicissimum interficeret. Postea vero illo, scilicet Vcthredo, proficiente magis et magis in re militari, rex Æthelredus filiam suam Elfgivam ei copulavit uxorem. Ex qua habuit filiam Aldgitham, quam pater in conjugium dedit Maldredo filio Crinan tein, ex qua Maldredus Cospatricum patrem Dolphini et Walteofi, et Cospatrici. Filiam autem Alduni episcopi quam comes Vcthredus dimiserat, quidam tein in Euervicshire, Kilvert filius Ligulfi, accepit uxorem, de qua genuit filiam nomine Sigridam, quam accepit uxorem Arkil filius Ecgfridæ, ex qua genuit filium nomine Cospatricum. Qui Cospatricus accepit uxorem filiam Dolfini filii Torfini, de qua genuit Cospatricum, qui nuper debuerat pugnare contra Walteof filium Eilsi. Kylvert filius Ligulfi dimisit filiam Alduni episcopi, scilicet Ecgfridam, quam episcopus pater ejus jussit statim Dunelmum venire. Quæ, patris sui jussis obtemperans, cum Bermetun, et Skirningheim, et Eltun, quas in propria manu habebat, rediit, et ecclesiæ et episcopo suas proprias terras secum reddit, et postea velamen accepit, quod et bene servavit usque ad extremum sui diem; et, sepulta in cœmiterio Dunelmensi, diem retributionis expectat.

Ut autem de morte Vcthredi comitis dicatur aliquid, paululum ad superiora redeundum est. Swein rex Danorum, fugato in Normanniam rege Anglorum Ethelredo, regnum ipsius invasit. Sed post breve tempus illo mortuo, rex Ethelredus in

[x] Styr, the son of Ulf, occurs as a benefactor of the church of St. Cuthbert, to which he gave the manor of Darlington, with its appurtenances, and other lands (Hist. Dunelm., iii., 5). The deed of gift is printed in this volume, pp. 150-1.

regnum suum rediit, copulata sibi in conjugium Emma Ricardi comitis Normannorum filia. Post aliquantulum temporis Cnut filius supradicti regis Danorum Swein, cum infinita multitudine veniens in Angliam regnaturus, ad supradictum Comitem misit Vcthredum, rogans, ut ad suum auxilium contra regem Æthelredum cum omnibus quos posset sibi occurreret, totum honorem suum et multo majorem sub ipso habiturus si eum adjuvaret. Erat enim idem Comes magnæ potentiæ, utpote comitatum Eboracensium et Northanhymbrorum habens. At ille, nullo modo id facere volens, respondit, pessimi hominis esse talia contra dominum et generum suum facere. "Nullius rei "gratia," inquit, "hoc agere volo, quia nec debeo; Æthelredo "regi quamdiu vixerit fidem servabo. Est enim dominus meus "et socer, cujus dono divitias et honores satis habeo. Illius "traditor nunquam ero." Itaque Cnut nullum de Vcthredo auxilium habuit. Defuncto autem rege Æthelredo, cum totius Angliæ regnum Cnut arripuisset, ad prædictum Comitem misit, præcipiens ut ad se sicut ad dominum suum veniret. Ille, accepta securitate eundi et redeundi, perrexit. Die statuto cum intrasset ad regem de pace locuturus, per insidias cujusdam potentis nomine Turebrant cognomento Hold, milites regis qui post velum extensum per transversum domus absconditi fuerant, subito prosilientes loricati, in Wiheal, comitem cum suis xl viris principalibus qui secum intraverant obtruncaverunt. Quo occiso, frater ipsius Eadulf, cognomento Cudel, ignavus valde et timidus, ei successit in comitatum. Timens autem ne Scotti mortem suorum quos frater ejus, ut supradictum est, occiderat, in se vindicarent, totum Lodoneium ob satisfactionem et firmam concordiam eis donavit. Hoc modo Lodoneium adjectum est regno Scottorum. Sed Eadulfo post modicum mortuo, Aldredus, quem prædictus comes Vcthredus genuerat ex Ecgfrida Alduni episcopi filia, de qua supradictum est, solius Northumbriæ comitatum suscepit, patrisque sui interfectorem interfecit Turebrandum. Hujus Turebrandi filius Carl et Aldredus comes gravibus exagitati calumniis, dum hinc et inde utrinque insidiarentur, tandem amicorum instantia reducti in concordiam, alterna sese satisfactione mediantibus amicis placabant: atque adeo in amorem alterutrum sunt adunati, ut fratres adjurati Romam simul tenderent. Sed diutina maris tempestate impediti, cœptum iter relinquentes domum sunt reversi. Carl magnifice satis et accurate Comitem suscepit in domum suam, sed post exhibita convivia dum eum nihil mali suspicantem quasi honoris gratia deduceret, in silva quæ Risewde vocatur interfecit, ubi usque hodie locum occisionis ejus parvula de lapide crux ostendit. Interjecto tempore nepos Aldredi comitis comes Waltheof, erat enim filius filiæ illius, missa multa juvenum manu, avi sui interfectionem gravissima clade vindicavit. Erant namque filii Carl convivantes simul in domo fratris sui majoris in Seteringetun non longe ab Eboraco; quos inopinate qui missi fuerant præoccupantes sæva clade simul peremerunt, præter Cnutonem, cui pro insita illi bonitate vitam permiserunt. Sumerlede, qui usque hodie superest, ibi non aderat. Deletis filiis et nepotibus Carli reversi sunt, multa in variis speciebus spolia reportantes.

Sed ut ad superiora redeat stilus. Comes Aldredus genuit quinque filias, quarum tres eodem nomine Ælfledæ vocabantur, quarta Aldgitha, quinta Ætheldritha nominabatur. Ex una Ælfledarum Siwardus comes genuit comitem Waltheofum. Et cum ipsa Ælfleda esset comitissa, quoniam erat filia Aldredi comitis, et ipse filius Vcthredi comitis et filiæ Alduni episcopi, acclamavit ipsa jure hæreditario has supradictas terras, Bernetun, (S)kyrningeim, Eltun, Carltun, Heaclif, Heseldene, quas comes Siwardus, maritus suus, ei donavit, et filio suo Waltheofo comitatum Northymbrorum dedit, sicut ipsius Waltheofi avus, scilicet comes Aldredus, habuerat. Mortuo Siwardo comite et comitissa Ælfleda filia Aldredi comitis, werra surgente, terræ illæ vastatæ sunt. Post multum tempus Arkil filius Ecgfridæ, de quo supra dictum est, qui acceperat uxorem Sigridam filiam Kilverti, et Ecgfridæ filiæ Alduni episcopi, sibi arripuit illas terras jam vastatas et inhabitavit. Uxor vero illius Sigrida moriens, dedit Heseldene Sancto Cuthberto, et Heaclif, et Carltun, quas adhuc ecclesia possidet. Arkil filius Fridegisti, et Eadulf comes, Arkil filius Ecgfrith, hi tres habuerunt Sigridam. Postea Willelmo rege veniente in Angliam, ipse Arkillus fugiens exul factus est. Sicque iterum terra ipsa vastata remansit. His ita peractis, quidam tein in Eoverwicschire, nomine Orm, filius Gamellonis, accepit uxorem unam ex quinque filiabus Aldredi comitis, Ætheldritham, ex qua genuit filiam nomine Ecgfridam, ex qua Eilsi de Teise genuit Waltheof, et duos ejus fratres, et Edam sororem eorum. Et quia illa Ecgfrida erat de genere Aldredi comitis, et filiæ Alduni episcopi, hæreditario jure ipsa Ecgfrida cum marito suo Eilsi arripuit Bermetun et Skirningeim.

HISTORIA TRANSLATIONUM SANCTI CUTHBERTI

AUCTORE ANONYMO.[y]

I.

Quomodo in peregrini habitu a ministro Elfredi panem divisum Cuthbertus accepit, qui postea integer inventus est, et quomodo idem Elfredus ipso adjuvante rex effectus est.[z]

Deus Omnipotens, juste misericors, misericorditerque justus, gentem Anglorum dum pro suis multiplicibus offensis flagellare disponeret, paganarum gentium, Fresonum videlicet atque Danorum, immanitatem illi permisit dominari. Istæ igitur gentes, Vbba duce Frisonum et Halfdene rege Danorum agentibus, in Britanniam, quæ nunc Anglia dicitur, venientes, in tres turmas mox divisæ, tribus in partibus terram pervaserunt. Nam Eboracæ civitatis mænia, una ex his restauravit, regionemque in circuitu incolens ibidem pausavit. At vero reliquæ duæ, multo ab hac[a] ferociores, regnum Merciorum terramque Australium Saxonum mox occupabant, omniaque incendiis, rapinis, atque homicidiis, quaquaversum exterminantes Divina

[y] The first seventeen sections, and a portion of the eighteenth, are transcribed from MS. Cotton, Nero A. ii. The latter part of section xviii, which is wanting in that authority, was copied from MS. Harl., 1924; and the two MSS. were collated throughout. A very minute collation was then made by Mr. Raine of the text so obtained, with MS. Laud 491 in the Bodleian Library, which was found to be superior in accuracy to the others, and has been followed throughout, but the differences are chiefly verbal. Mr. Raine also examined three other MSS. in the Bodleian; Digby 59, Fairfax 6, and Bodley 514; also Cotton MS. Titus A. ii., and Arundel 332, respecting all which see Preface. In the MSS. are two chapters of miracles taken from Beda's Ecclesiastical History, book iv., c. xxxi., xxxii., which it has not been thought necessary to reprint.

[z] This section is derived from the Historia de Sancto Cuthberto at pp. 144-5 in the present volume. The same story is very briefly told by Symeon (Hist. Ecc. Dunelm., c. xxv.), and is repeated by Malmesbury (l. ii., c. iv). Symeon adds, " Quoniam alibi plane per ordinem scriptum habetur, hic non esse repetendum."

[a] *Adhuc*, MS. Harl.

æque ut humana, contagione barbarica contaminabant. Quanti tunc ab eis nobiles et præclari sacerdotes circa ipsa, quibus Dominici corporis et sanguinis sacrosancta mysteria confecerant, altaria trucidabantur, ut propheticum illud recte tunc compleretur, quod dicit, *Effuderunt sanguinem ipsorum tanquam aquam in circuitu Jerusalem*, et illud, *Incenderunt igni sanctuarium tuum, in terra polluerunt tabernaculum nominis tui.*[b] Videres tunc virgines rapi, matronalia jura solvi, infantes ab ipsis matrum uberibus avulsos, ad terram alios elidi, per pedes alios suspendi, inter manus barbarorum alios discerpi; postremo neque sexui, neque ætati, nec ulli quoque gradui, a tam crudelibus parci. Nec sic tamen bestialis illa crudelitas satiari potuit, nisi omnes etiam regii generis, per quos suæ ditioni aliquod timebat periculum, extinxisset; unde illius tempestatis rabiem solus ex omni regio semine pater primi Eaduuardi regis Elfredus vix effugit. Hic, ne simili plecteretur sententia, tres, quibus illa debacchari permissa est barbaries, annos, maxima cum penuria in Glestigiensibus latitabat paludibus. Sed Dei clementia barbarorum illam immanitatem, cum jam cessare suosque post flagella recreare solita miseratione sua judicasset, contigit eumdem Elfredum, cæteris omnibus piscatum missis, solum cum sola conjuge unoque familiari ministro domi resedisse. Aderat interim peregrino habitu quidam, obnixeque petebat elemosinæ compendium, quo famis suæ extingueret incendium; cui mox ipse vultu animoque lætissimus sine mora petenti cibum ut daret ministro præcepit. A quo cum audisset, nihil sibi suisque omnibus ad diurnum remansisse victum, præter panem unum et vini modicum, lætior ex hoc effectus; "Deo," inquit, "gratias, Qui me pauperem "Suum, et tam longe a communi hominum habitatione sejunc-"tum per hunc Suum quoque pauperem visitare dignatur." Et hæc dicens, utriusque medietatem erogari jubet hilariter, Apostolicum illud opere comprobans, *Hilarem datorem diligit Deus.*[c] Quo ille, qui pauper videbatur, accepto, "Domino," inquit, "tuo pro tantæ compassionis affectu sæpius gratificare "ne differas; spero enim, quia hanc illius beneficentiam larga "cælestis misericordia uberius recompensabit." Hæc dixerat ille ministro, hæcque suo minister refert domino. Sed mox ad eum ubi hunc dimiserat locum regressus, pauperem nusquam, panem vero et vinum ita repperit integrum, ut prorsus nec sectionis aliquod videretur habere signum. Quod factum ipse secum stupens, domino quoque suo festinus indicavit. Cujus miraculi novitate percepta, ipse pariter et uxor ejus non

[b] Psalm lxxix. 3; lxxiv. 8. [c] 2 Cor. ix. 7.

minore mentis percelluntur stupore. Et quamvis curiose perquirentes, viam, qua ille venisset vel inde recessisset, omnino non poterant investigare, præsertim quod locus ille aquis palustribus undique inclusus, non nisi cum navi valebat adiri. Interea, ubi nona diei hora venerat, hi, qui piscatum exierant, tres naves piscibus onustas domum reduxerunt, asserentes tantam sibi copiam piscandi non provenisse in totis tribus annis, quibus illis deguerant in paludibus. Tantis itaque Dei beneficiis jocundati, diem illum solito lætiorem deducunt. Venit nox; quisque, post diurnos labores quieturus, suo se reponit in loco. Cumque alto sopore omnes opprimerentur, Elfredus in lecto recubat solus pervigil, labores suos quos barbaricæ persecutionis timore profugus sustinuit mæsto secum corde retractans, simulque de peregrino, ac inopinata piscium multitudine quod hac die sibi evenerat admirans. Et, ecce! lumen, super omnem solis radium[d] splendidius subito refulgens totum in quo jacuit cubiculum cælitus illustrat. Hac visione utpote insolita et tam subita ipse perterritus, priores mox omnes obliviscitur curas, et solum luminis illius fulgorem stupidus contuetur. Tunc quidam in ipso lumine, pontificaliter infulatus, senior, nigro quidem capillo, sed vultu admodum venusto, processit, textumque Evangeliorum auro gemmisque mirifice perornatum dextera prætendens, stupentem illum atque paventem sic dictis promulcet amicis, "Non te, dilecte mi Elfrede, subitus hic mei "adventus splendor perturbet; non te barbarici furoris timor "diutius sollicitet; Deus enim, Qui pauperum suorum gemitus "non spernit, jamjam tuis finem ponet laboribus. Ego tibi "deinceps quoque adjutor ero promptissimus." His protinus ille confortatus affatibus, quis esset, quid appellaretur, aut quare venisset sibi ut panderet rogat obnixius. Tunc senior subridens, "Ille," inquit, "ego sum, cui tantæ humanitatis con-"descensu cibum hodie dari jusseras; sed non tantum pro pane "et vino, quæ mihi dato delectabar, *(sic)* quantum pro interna "mentis tuæ devotione congratulabar. Quod autem quid appellar "interrogas, servum Dei Cuthbertum me pro certo nominari "scias, ideoque huc modo veni ut per me familiarius instruaris "qualiter a persecutionibus diu te affligentibus expediaris. "Ergo misericordiam et justitiam præcipue diligas moneo, "eademque filios tuos servare præ omnibus semper doceto; "quoniam, me impetrante Deoque donante, totius Britanniæ "imperium vobis concedetur disponendum. Si autem Deo "mihique fideles exstiteritis, me posthac ad conterendum robur "omne inimicorum inexpugnabile defensionis scutum habebitis.

[d] Acts xxvi. 13.

"Quare nunc omnem tristitiæ postpone torporem, atque cum "crastina primum aurora rutilaverit, ad proximum naviga littus, "cornuque tuo tribus fortiter intona vicibus. Sicut enim cera "diffluit ab ignis calore, sic tuorum superbia inimicorum dis-"solvetur ab hujus tubæ clangore. Sed quantum in majus "adversariorum dejicietur pertinacia, tantum ad ejusdem clan-"goris auditionem tuorum erigetur amicorum audacia. Quod "enim piis misericordiæ cælestis ad exaltationis confert gloriam, "hoc impiis jure permittit provenire ad dejectionis ingloriam. "Hujus quoque diei horam circiter nonam, de carioribus amicis "et melioribus, quingenti ad te convenient, omnes bene armati. "Et hoc signo credas, quod, septem transactis diebus, apud "montem Assandune totius terræ hujus concurret exercitus, te "velut regem suum in adversis simul et prosperis ubique sequi "paratissimus; ubi cum hostibus dum conflixeris, triumphi "palma proculdubio coronaberis." Hæc Sanctus ubi disseruit, mirantis ab oculis ipso cum lumine disparuit. Ille autem omnium, quæ audierat, complendorum certissimus, illius se patrocinio commendabat attentius. Interea magnis expectata desideriis aurora exoritur. Ille, solito agilior, somno lectoque excutitur; et, ad littus usque perveniens, jussa quæ nocte audierat nil moratus exequitur. Et his quid diu immoramur? Tubæ ipsius clangorem inimici pariter et amici audiunt: illi nutu Divino pavore confusi, subito viribus enervantur: isti, cælitus exultatione perfusi, continuo virtutibus roborantur. Jam quoque die in nonam declinante horam, ipsi de quibus complendæ promissionis signum planius caperet, amicorum cariores et meliores quingenti omnes armis bene muniti ad ipsum conveniunt. Quibus ille, nocturnæ visionis ordinem pandens, "Nunc," inquit, "quanta parentes nostri, qui omnes "jam interierunt, barbarorum tormenta pro suis nostrisque "offensis justo Dei judicio pertulerint vidimus; et nos ipsi, "qui die noctuque ad similia per eosdem exquirimur, quomodo "nullum habeamus jam tutum fugæ locum, videmus, immo "miserabiliter profugi sustinemus. Unde rogo monitis Sancti "Cuthberti, defensoris nostri, attente obediamus, Deo sibique "fideles existamus, vitiorum voragines fugiamus, atque vir-"tutum exercitia diligamus, sic profecto, et promissum cæ-"lestis gratiæ auxilium, et suæ defensionis experiemur ubique "patrocinium." Promissus igitur totius terræ exercitus cum rege suo eodem Elfredo ad prædictum montem prædicta die convenit; nec minus ex adverso feralis illa barbarorum turba, infinitæ suæ multitudini prioribusque confisa eventibus, accurrit velocius. Fit statim ad præliandum conventus, sed dispar pug-nantium eventus. Hinc enim Christianus quam salubre sit in cælesti fidere auxilio comprobat interficiendo; illinc Paganus quam detestabile sit humana præsumere superbia experitur cadendo. Hoc itaque prælio absque detrimento sui exercitus confecto, Elfredus totius Britanniæ imperium obtinuit; et quoniam sancti Confessoris præcepta, quæ susceperat in penuria, memoriter servabat in curia, omnibus semper et ubique adversantium prævaluit moliminibus.

II.

Quomodo, tempestate orta, tres undæ in navim in qua corpus ejus abducebatur cadentes in sanguinem convertebantur.[e]

Per ejusdem quoque persecutionis tempora, intollerabilis tribulatio Northanhumbrorum finibus subito emergens, ecclesias Dei tempestuoso turbine graviter concussit. Tunc quidem magni vir meriti, nomine Eardulfus, episcopatum Lindispharnensis ecclesiæ, qua tunc beatissimus Dei confessor Cuthbertus corpore quiescebat, probabiliter coram Deo et coram hominibus disponebat. Hic dictorum prædicti patris, quæ ultima ipse ab hac vita migraturus suis contradiderat, recordans, loco magis cedere quam reprobis subdi elegit. Sic enim ipse, inter alia quæ de conservanda pacis ac dilectionis concordia satis tunc utiliter admonuit, paterno more suis consuluit, dicens, "Si vos "unum e duobus adversis eligere necessitas coegerit, multo plus "diligo ut eruentes de tumulo tollentesque vobiscum mea ossa "recedatis ab his locis, et, ubicumque Deus providerit, incolæ "maneatis, quam ut ulla ratione consentientes iniquitati, schis-"maticorum jugo colla subdatis."

Erat quoque tunc abbas quidam, Eadradus nomine, et ipse apud Deum miræ sanctitatis, nec exiguæ apud homines nobilitatis, qui ejusdem cum episcopo erga beatissimum Dei confessorem semper extitit devotionis. Igitur, hac tribulationis aura intonante, ecclesiamque Dei fortiter quassante, memorati duo, sumptis secum religiosæ conversationis quibusdam aliis, incorruptum venerandi patris corpus de Lindispharnensi monasterio discedentes asportaverunt. Hoc populus ipsius postquam audivit, domibus cum tota supellectili relictis, cum uxoribus et parvulis continuo subsequitur. Est enim huic, (qui suus proprie dicitur populus, quoniam speciali quadam provisione ab eo

[e] The particulars of this miracle are derived from the Historia de Sancto Cuthberto, and are transferred to Symeon's History of the Church of Durham (c. xxvii). The account of the loss of the copy of the Gospels, and its miraculous recovery, which is given by Symeon in that and the following chapter, is neither furnished by the History of St. Cuthbert nor the work before us.

servatur, nec alibi nisi sub eo vivere valet, sicut aliæ gentes, quæ in extraneis æque ut in propriis degere sciunt terris,) tanta in eo tuitionis securitas, ut nullas adversitatum pene pertimescat injurias. Hoc tamen quod tanta eos pietate ad se confugientes ab adversariis sæpe vindicaverit, de quo in sequentibus quædam dicemus, ipsorum meritis, cum præter paucos pravorum actuum homines sint, nullus applicet; sed in hoc quantum fidendi firmitas valeat, magnopere quisque consideret. Tunc namque per Dei providentiam et sanctissimi Confessoris voluntatem contigit, quatinus cum pretiosissimo sacri corporis sui thesauro longo tempore migrantes, totam pene pervagarentur terram. Episcopus autem et abbas, propter diuturnum laborem nimis tandem confecti tædio, ut suis finem laboribus et sancto corpori sedem in Hibernia quærerent, mutuo inter se diu consilio ventilabant; præsertim quia nullam in tota hac terra remanendi spem habebant. Proinde adhibitis ad hoc quoque de omnibus qui sapientiores erant et ætate provectiores, sui secreta consilii eis pandebant. Placuit itaque illis hoc consilium, et "Evidenter," inquiunt, "in terra peregrina requie-
"scendi locum quærere monemur, quia nisi hoc Dei fuisset
"voluntas ipsiusque Sancti, proculdubio jampridem et suæ sanc-
"titati locus ad requiescendum condignus, et nobis ad manendum
"opportunus fuisset provisus." Hæc illi; sed incomprehensibilis Dei sapientia et ineffabilis misericordia, jam quidem labores eorum determinare, Suique confessoris lætius merita declarare voluit, sed altiori et Sui solius consilio hæc facere disposuit. Ergo ad ostium fluminis, qui Dirwenta vulgo dicitur, omnes simul episcopus, abbas, et populus conveniunt. Ab hoc enim maris portu facilior ac brevior patet transitus in Hiberniam tendentibus. Ibi navis ad transponendum paratur, venerabile patris corpus imponitur, cum episcopo et abbate pauci, quibus hoc innotuerat consilium, ingrediuntur, cæteris omnibus quid agere vellent ignorantibus. Sed quid moramur? Sociis a littore se spectantibus vale dicunt, secundis vela flatibus expediunt, recto versus Hiberniam ductu proram dirigunt. Tunc quis putas mæror fuerit residentium? quis planctus mærentium? Quis luctus dolentium? In terram corruunt, pulvere capita respergunt, vestes scindunt, pectora lapidibus pugnisque contundunt, et in hujusmodi voces tandem simul omnes erumpunt.
"Heu miseri, nos in tempora hæc infelicia cur nati sumus?
"Tu, pater et patrone noster, en tanquam captivus in exilium
"duceris; nos, tanquam oves luporum dentibus, ita miseri et
"captivi adversariis exponimur sævientibus." Nec illi plura. Continuo venti mutantur, fluctus intumescentes elevantur, et quod nunc erat tranquillum atque serenissimum mare fit tem-

pestuosum et obscurissimum; navisque, jam non valens gubernari, huc et illuc inter fluctivagas jactabatur undas; qui enim intus erant velut mortui obriguerant. Interea tres miræ magnitudinis undæ[f] horrifico cum murmure supervenientes, navim medias pene usque ad tabulas impleverunt, atque terribili miraculo, postque Ægipti plagas inaudito, protinus in sanguinem convertebantur. O conditoris nostri stupenda majestas! O nimium amplectenda pietas, quæ suorum corpora Sanctorum quantum a nobis sint formidanda atque veneranda tam horrificis tamque mirificis declarat signorum ostentis! Ergo postquam, sensu aliquantulum recepto, semetipsos qui vel ubi essent recordantur, tantique miraculi magnitudinem ipsi quoque per totum sanguine perfusi contemplantur. Continuo gemunt, lugent, genua flectunt, veniamque stulti ausus toto corpore ad pedes sancti corporis prostrati petunt.[g] Arrepto itaque gubernaculo navim ad litus et ad socios retorquent, et continuo, flantibus a tergo ventis, illuc sine aliqua difficultate perveniunt. Tunc qui prius fleverant dolendo versa vice plus jam flebant gaudendo. Episcopus vero cum sociis suis, pudore simul et dolore non minus lacrimans toto corpore in terram prosternitur, sibique indulgeri precatur obnoxius.[g] His ita gestis, omnibusque laudabiliter concordatis, ad monasterium quod in villa vocabulo Creca fuit illud venerabile corpus deferunt, ibique ab abbate, cui nomen erat Geve, benignissime suscepti, velut in proprio quatuor mensibus residebant. Interim, Divina dispensante gratia, quæ suos ad hoc permittit laborare, ne in bonorum operum exercitatione torpeant, ad hoc iterum novit recreare, ne in caritatis delectatione frigeant, sedes episcopalis, quam superius in insula Lindisfarnensi esse diximus, in Cunceceastre restauratur. Translato igitur illic de Creca beatissimi patris corpore, tamdiu ibi permansit, quousque, non paucis revolutis annis, in Dunhelmo una cum sede pontificali decentissime transponebatur, ubi usque in præsens ejus sanctitas miraculis continuis declaratur.

[f] After the word *undæ*, a hiatus occurred in the MS. from which the text of this work in the *Acta Sanctorum* was taken. The portion wanting has been in part supplied in that and subsequent editions from the corresponding text of Symeon, many pages being introduced which are not to be found in any MS. of the work.

[g] This forms the concluding passage of the twenty-sixth chapter of the History of the Church of Durham. The following sentence occurs in chapter xxviii. of the same work, and is followed by the vision of Abbat Eadred, in which he receives directions from St. Cuthbert as to the redemption of Guthred from slavery, and placing him on the throne of Northumberland.

III.

Quomodo paganus quidam, vocabulo Onalafbald, contra Dei confessorem injurias dixisset, in ingressu ecclesiæ confixus interierit.[h]

Ordinatis deinde omnibus, atque decenter, utpote ad sedem episcopalem, compositis, regulari quoque sub disciplina qui Deo coram sanctissimi confessoris Sui corpore jugiter servirent ibidem constitutis, episcopus ille supra memoratus Eardulfus senectute bona laborum præmia suorum recepturus ab hac vita migravit. Nec multo post ipsius excessum exacto tempore, Cuthardus et ipse, coram Deo et hominibus vita probabili commendatus; omnium electione cathedram episcopalem ejus loco regendam suscepit. Quam quidem, quamvis laboriose (nam multas sæpe ac graves barbarorum sustinuit pervasiones et injurias) sancto tamen Cuthberto se specialiter vindicante atque evidenter adjuvante, doctrinis et exemplis strenue decoravit. Ipsius namque temporibus rex quidam paganus, nomine Reginwaldus, multa cum classe illis in partibus improvise applicuit, universosque meliores vel in bello stravit, vel extra patriam fugavit. Occupavit quoque totam mox terram Sancti Cuthberti, villasque ipsius duobus suis militibus ad sæculum potentibus æqua divisione distribuit, quorum unus Scula vulgariter vocabatur, alter vero, secundum suæ gentis proprietatem, Onalafbald appellabatur. Ambo crudeles et barbari, ambo dæmoniorum cultibus mancipati, ambo veræ religionis et propriæ salutis ignari, temporalis potentiæ nomen affectabant, atque ad interminabilis miseriæ lamenta æternique cruciatus tormenta cæco corde festinabant. Talibus enim Sacra comminatur Scriptura dicens, "*Potentes potenter tormenta patiuntur.*"[i] Hi quamvis, ut diximus, ambo fuissent barbari et crudeles, ille tamen, quem posteriorem nominavimus, immaniorem multo atque crudeliorem, ac prorsus inhumanum, ad suam perniciem se omnibus exhibebat. Non sacrorum ordinum dignitas, non natalium nobilitas ferinum ejus animum ad cujusquam inclinabat reverentiam, sed, tanquam indomabilis bellua, quo quemquam gradu digniorem vel genere considerat nobiliorem, eo contra hunc furorem exacuabat immaniorem. Hic dum multis sæpe injuriis episcopum, congregationem, atque populum Sancti Cuthberti molestaret, prædiaque ad episcopum jure attinentia suæ potestati pertinaciter usurparet, episcopus cum Deo volens

[h] This miracle occurs in the Historia de Sancto Cuthberto and also in Symeon (Hist. Eccl. Dunelm., c. xxxi).

[i] Sap., vi., 7.

lucrari, sedulo corripiebat, atque de suæ profectu animæ commonebat, dicens, "Tantum quæso pertinacis animi deponas rigo-"rem, atque abdicato dæmonum cultu tuum recognoscas Crea-"torem; necnon et ab illicita rerum pervasione ecclesiasticarum "jam te cohibere non renuas. Nam si monita mea hæc sper-"nenda esse putaveris, sanctissimum Dei confessorem suas suo-"rumque injurias, per te totiens irrogatas, cito ac graviter vin-"dicaturum esse non dubites." At ille, quamvis hominibus apparet vivus, occulto tamen Dei judicio jam mortuus, de correptionis verbo quantum poterat meliorari, tantum inde cœperat deteriorari. Dum enim hæc et hujusmodi ab episcopo frequentius audisset, improbæ mentis furia instigatus, ecclesiam die quadam ingreditur, et, episcopo cum tota congregatione coram stante atque audiente, contumeliose proclamans in hæc verba extollitur. "Quid hujus hominis mortui minas mihi quotidie objicitis? Quid "putatis contra me vobis valebit ipsius in quo speratis auxilium? "Deorum meorum omnipotentiam contestor, ipsorumque per "excellentem gloriam juro, quod tam ipsi mortuo quam vobis "omnibus deinceps inimicissimus ero, ut ex hoc aperte discatis, "quam nihil aut ipse aut vos mihi resistere valeatis." Et, his dictis, cum maximæ indignationis arrogantia pedem ut egrederetur avertit. At episcopus omnesque simul fratres in terram mox prostrati, a Deo et sancto Confessore superbas illius minas annullari multum suspirando, et ubertim lacrimando flagitabant. Jam miser ille ad ostium venerat, jam alterum intra limen, alterum extra pedem posuerat, et ibi tanquam clavis per utrumque pedem confixus nec egredi nec regredi valebat, sed immobilis prorsus ibi hærebat. Cœpit quoque mox pallescere et contremiscere, oculisque sanguineis et torvis circumspicere, atque diversis membrorum motibus dolorem quem intus perpetiebatur foras ostendere. Ubi autem, concurrente atque spectante populo innumerabili tam suorum quam Christianorum, ita diutius torquebatur, tandem horribiliter exclamans, beatissimi Confessoris sanctitatem palam confitebatur, sicque impiam suam animam eodem in loco reddere compellebatur. Sed hæc sera ipsius confessio, quamvis sibimet omnino nil prodesset, aliis tamen, ipsis etiam Paganis, plurimum profuit; qui, hoc exemplo conterriti, neque terras neque aliud quid quod ecclesiæ jure competebat, quoquomodo ulterius pervadere præsumebant.

IV.

Quomodo Scotici, qui terram Sancti Cuthberti et Lindisfarnense monasterium pervaserant, subito terræ hiatu absorpti sunt.[j]

Scriptum est, *Ibunt Sancti de virtute in virtutem; videbitur Deus deorum in Syon.*[k] Quod quia hic Deo dilectus Confessor in hac carnis infirmitate processu mentis sedulus agebat, ab illa superna qua Deus deorum videtur specula miraculis nunc coruscando declarat. Nam quantum de virtute in virtutem eundo mente tunc proficiebat, tamen ascensu miraculorum procedendo mirandis primoribus plus miranda nunc exhibet posteriora. Mirandum namque et timendum est de barbari peremptione quod diximus, sed multo plus mirandum atque stupendum de repentina Scottorum dimersione quod dicemus. Temporibus itaque non multis postea transactis, gens Scottorum, coadunato innumerabili exercitu, fluvium Tuyda, qui terminus aquilonalis est[l] terræ Sancti Cuthberti, transgreditur, omniaque homicidiis, incendiis atque rapinis depopulatur. Non gradui, non ætati, non sexui parcebat, sed velut pecudes pari cunctos et inaudita crudelitate prosternebat. Et, hæc agens, nondum suam exsatiavit crudelitatem, quin inmo Lindisfarnense monasterium, nullorum præsumptione antea temeratum, simili crudelitate pervasit. Hæc tanti facinoris fama, postquam ad illius qui tunc rex extitit Guthredi aures pervenit, contra illos cum admodum parva manu festinavit; non enim congregari exercitum brevitas temporis permittebat. Occurrit utique illis in loco qui Anglorum lingua Mundingedene usque ad præsens nuncupatur. Sed quoniam incumbentis tenebræ noctis obstabant, venerat enim illuc vesperascente jam die; bello eos aggredi continuo non potuit, verum ut summo mane imparatos occuparet disposuit. Sed nec consilium ejus ipsos latuit, ideoque semper parati existentes, ipsum, si etiam ab eis declinare temptasset, quia paucos eum habere se autem plurimos esse considerabant, insequi cogitabant. Cum vero rex tantum conspexisset exercitum, et non solum resistere, sed etiam insequi paratum attendisset, nimio timore sollicitabatur eo quod nec ad pugnandum vires habebat, et ab eis fugere pudor et locus prohibebat. Talibus ergo tantisque curarum æstibus variarum molestatus, præ nimietate angustiarum somno prægravatur. Et ecce! egregius Christi miles Cuthbertus mani-

[j] This miracle is recorded at the end of the Historia de Sancto Cuthberto. Symeon adverts to it very briefly at the end of chapter xxviii. of the History of the Church of Durham, adding, "Qualiter autem gestum sit alibi constat esse scriptum."

[k] Psalm lxxxiii. 8.

[l] Australis erat. MS. Harl.

festa visione illi astitit, verbisque consolatoriis exanimatum confortavit, ita exorsus. "Quid tanto maceraris timore? Ne diffidas tuorum paucitati militum cum Dei meumque habeas "auxilium; Deo enim nequaquam est impossibile sive in multis "sive in paucis salvare. Hostes quippe tuos, magis autem meos, "quia pacem meam, nec a Paganis prius violatam, temerare non "formidabant, in sua nunc multitudine gloriantes coram te in "brevi ut lutum platearum delebo. Nam quamvis hominibus "adhuc vivi appareant, in conspectu Dei omnes mortui sunt "computati, unde tuis ut sine mora sint parati præcipere ma-"tures, ut, cum aurora diei primum exoritur, facto impetu super "eos irruas, quoniam in primo congressu terra dehiscente, in "baratrum vivi corruent, et sine tuorum detrimento ipsi omnes "simul disperient." Talia ubi dixerat, visionis illius species disparebat. Rex vero, per hæc multum confortatus, somnum excussit, lecto exiluit, suos convocavit, et quæ viderit vel audierit palam omnibus enarravit. Quibus auditis, quantum prius timore fuerant exanimati, tantum mox regis sui consolatione sunt confortati. Facto igitur mane in hostes irruunt, sed, mirabile dictu, quos modo contra se jacula mittere conspiciunt, in eodem statim momento nusquam nec unum ex his inveniunt. Quod enim vir Dei prædixerat, coram eis terra vivos omnes absorbuerat. Et hic quoque antiquum renovatur miraculum, quando *aperta est terra et deglutivit Dathan, et operuit super congregationem Abiron.*[m]

V.

Quomodo miles Comitis Tostii, nomine Barcwith, dum januas monasterii ejus infringere cupit subito percussus interierit.[n]

Nec silentio prætereundum quanta nostris quoque temporibus ejusdem beatissimi patris fulserint miracula. Regnante nuper piissimo rege Eadwardo miraculum contigit prioribus simile, per quod in unius præsumptoris peremptione multi deinceps correcti sunt a tali præsumptione. Dum igitur Tostius, Comes ille cunctis notissimus, in partibus Northanumbranis comitatum administraret, quidam pravæ actionis vir, nomine Aldan-hamal, ab eo comprehensus, compedibus artissime constringitur. Multa enim mala fecerat: furtis atque rapinis, homicidiis atque incendiis Comitem sæpe offenderat, nec un-

[m] Psalm cv. 17.

[n] Symeon briefly refers to the miracle of Barcwid at the end of chapter xlvi., "quod alibi plenius legitur." The reference in this case is unquestionably to the present work, as this miracle does not occur in the Historia de Sancto Cuthberto.

quam prius comprehendi poterat. Cujus parentes et amici, compassionis affectu permoti, multa pro eo ne capite plecteretur Comiti offerebant, et plura promittebant. At ille, quia totiens tantisque malefactis eum irritaverat, nullum se pro vita ipsius auri vel argenti, aut cujusquam alterius rei commodum vel respicere velle juravit. Tunc ille animo consternatus, solum sibi cogitabat esse remedium si, quoquomodo vinculis expeditus, beatissimi patris Cuthberti confugisset ad monasterium. In eadem quippe villa qua ipse corpore requiescit, hoc est in Dunelmo, tunc custodiebatur. Adhibitis ergo omnibus ingenii ac virium suarum conatibus, ab his quibus constringebatur compedibus se quærebat expedire. Sed quamvis diu multumque in hoc laboraret parum profecit, quoniam timor, qui ex præcepto Comitis imminebat, ut arctissime custodiretur custodes urgebat. Unde suis se conatibus liberari non posse considerans, scelerum suorum conscientia se torquente, graviter ingemuit, atque Deo dilectum Confessorem quo sibi subveniret indigno magna cordis contritione rogavit. Non enim jam quod a Comite sibi minabatur, tam corporis supplicium quam anima formidabat periculum. Interea dum malorum suorum emendationem, si modo evaderet, promittit, subito compedes solutos sibique liberum abeundi locum patuisse conspicit. O magna Dei clementia! Ecce! quod prius insonuit per Prophetarum oraculo, nobis nunc per ipsa loquitur opera. Peccator qua die conversus fuerit et ingemuerit, omnia peccata ejus non recordabuntur. Lætus itaque quod se solutum senserat, sed sollicitus quomodo custodum vigilantiam evaderet, omnem salutis suæ confidentiam beati patris Cuthberti commisit patrocinio. Nec mora. Custodibus ad alia occupatis, et nil tale suspicantibus, fugæ locum sibi permissum esse prospexit, compedes quantocitius excussit, atque cursu rapidissimo monasterium intravit, oppositisque seris, januas omnes ipse solus ab intro firmavit. Casu quidem evenerat, cum post Primam egressis fratribus, illo veniret, ut nullum intus inveniret. Quod inter milites Comitis, nam et ipse in eadem villa tunc erat, ubi auditum est, continuo quidam, Barwith nomine, qui omnes in curia potestate præcessit, usque ad monasterii januas illum insequebatur. Quas cum obseratas illumque intus esse advertit, nimio mox furore accensus "Quid," inquit, "moramur? Quare "januas non infringimus? Neque enim hujus hominis mortui "pax a Deo est tenenda, ut fures, raptores, et homicidæ, huc si "confugerint, nobis insultent quod impuniti evaserint." Sic miser ille ore loquebatur contumelioso; furoris enim magnitudo effecerat, ut quid loqueretur ipse ignoraret. Sed vix verba compleverat, ecce! subito quasi sagitta desuper veniens, caputque sibi transverberans ad cor usque suum pertingeret, sibi visum esse protestabatur. Nec plura locutus, in terram corruens volutabatur; sicque gemendo, ululando, dentibusque stridendo quam graviter cruciaretur, tam audientibus quam intuentibus patefecit. Denique a suis ad hospitium deportatur, nec unum postea verbum proloquens, in eisdem tormentis ad diei tertii eandem usque horam supervixit. Sed et illo tandem ita defuncto atque sepulto, talis tantusque de tumulo ipsius fætor per dimidium spatium anni exhalavit, ut viæ transitum per id loci omnes fugerent. Hoc ergo exemplo Comes ipse cum cæteris omnibus, quibus hæc longe lateque tunc innotuerant, perterritus, non hunc ulterius capere præsumebat, sed postea non parum honorare incipiebat. Tum quoque omnes qui ut a monasterio abstraherentur se vel saltem consensisse meminerunt, similem sibi metuentes ultionem, collata de rebus suis auri et argenti gemmarumque non modica quantitate, super beatissimi Confessoris sepulcrum offerebant, multis cum lacrimis veniam implorantes, et nil tale ulterius se præsumpturos jurantes. Mox itaque ex hac ipsarum oblatione mirifici operis crux, et incomparandi pretii textus Evangeliorum auro gemmisque perornantur, quæ in eodem monasterio ad hujus facti monumentum usque in præsens servantur. Hæc quoque sic gesta fuisse ut scribimus, a fratrum qui videre et ipsius ore qui sic evaserat non semel audivimus.

VI.

Quomodo, corpore ipsius ad Lindisfarnensem insulam propinquante, fluctus expectaverint quousque omnes siccis pedibus transirent.[o]

Exacto deinde paucorum numero annorum, cum excellentissimus rex primus Willelmus regnare cœpisset, Comitem quendam, Rodbertum vocabulo, Northamumbranæ regioni præfecit. Hic, cum in Dunelmum venisset, ab his quibus dominari debuerat circumventus, mox cum suis omnibus crudeliter ob suam occiditur crudelitatem. Non enim ut rectores et defensores se regionis exhibebant, sed rapinis et stupris etiam in legitima sæviebant matrimonia: unde rex indignatus, ut præsumptores illi digna ultione plecterentur, exercitum illuc direxit. Quod ubi eorum auribus rumor ingesserat, innocentes æque ut nocentes fugam parant, isti ne quod meruerant occiderentur, illi ne dum innocentes esse nescirentur pro nocentibus punirentur.

[o] This miracle is detailed by Symeon in chapter l.

Tunc quidem habito inter se consilio, episcopus cum congregatione, cunctique in terra meliores venerabile patris corpus secum asportaverunt, invicem conferentes incomparabiliter sibi melius fore una die omnes interire, quam sine ipso fugam inire. Est insula quæ Lindisfarnea dicitur, cujus supra quoque meminimus, ubi cum in hac carnis infirmitate degeret, ipse monachus monachorum cætui præpositi prioratu prælatus, ac deinde pontificali sede sullimatus, ad postremum quoque, decurso hujus vitæ termino, fuerat tumulatus. Hæc quippe insula, recedentibus et accedentibus oceani æstibus, bis quaque die adiri valet itinere terreno, totiensque non nisi navali ingreditur vehiculo. Ad quam circa vesperam, qua videlicet hora tunc secundum naturæ suæ qualitatem circumquaque plenum erat mare, ipsius cum corpore sanctissimo innumera cleri et populi utriusque sexus et ætatis multitudo cum appropinquaret, nam in ea, quousque quid ageret exercitus scirent, expectare decreverant, ad invicem conferebant. "Modo quid faciemus, "qui ne insulam intremus fluctuum altitudine prohibemur, nec "quo tantam frigoris asperitatem declinemus manendi locum "habemus." Erat enim tunc hiemis frigus acerrimum, velut fieri solet circa Natale Dominicum. Hæc dicentes, ad ipsum insulæ aditum pervenerant, ubi sexui infirmiori et ætati teneriori, ne frigore tam aspero pariter omnes periclitarentur, maxime condolentes; donec circa mane secundum consuetudinem suam mare recessisset, se pernoctare timebant. Sed ecce! inæstimabilis Dei clementia, magis magisque volens declarare quanti pensaret Confessoris Sui merita, illic quoque antiqua pietatis suæ renovavit mirabilia. Nam subito, quod nec ipsi sperare noverant, sic cum introeundi aditum illo tantum loco mare permiserat; cum, sicut diximus, circumquaque fluctuaret plenissimum. Perpendat, quæso, legentium caritas, quanta potuerit esse omnium illorum lætitia qui nunc per ipsa legerunt opera, quod nobis antiquitus gestum Mosaici pandit cantici littera. Dicit enim, *Stetit unda fluens, congregatæ sunt abissi in medio mari.*[p] Et in subsequentibus, *Filii autem Israel ambulaverunt per siccum in medio mari.*[q] Quod mox omnes ingressi, de tanto supernæ pietatis miraculo et stupebant et gaudebant, laudesque Divinæ miserationi et beatissimo confessori decantantes, siccis pedibus insulæ littus attingebant. Sed et dilectio fratrum, qui et ad sæculum nobiles et morum gravitate nobiliores in militari habitu tunc feretrum portabant, nunc autem nobiscum in ejusdem patris monasterio, hoc est in Dunelmo professi, veri sunt actu et habitu monachi: dulcissima nobis

[p] Exod. xv. 8. [q] Ibid., xv. 19.

relatione magnaque cordis compunctione sæpius solet attestari, quomodo se præcedentes fluctus marini post vestigia continuo sequerentur, ita ut nec paulatim euntibus præcurrerent, nec concitæ pergentibus diutius remanerent.

VII.

Quomodo quidam furtum quod in monasterio ejus perpetraverat, ipse prodidit, sicque ibidem miserabiliter interiit.[r]

Superius qualiter quendam pro latrociniis, homicidiis, furtis atque rapinis comprehensum hic Dei confessor liberaverit, atque a persecutore suo vindicaverit posuimus: nunc autem quomodo alter pro furto quod in ipsius perpetraverat monasterio, a dæmone diu graviterque tortus, ibidem interiit, ponemus. Post detestabilem omnibusque notissimam Walcheri Dunelmensis episcopi occisionem, cum rex gloriosus idem Willelmus ad vindicandam tanti facinoris immanitatem exercitum direxisset, omnes mox illi præsumptores et homicidæ silvis se ac montibus abdiderunt. At vero vulgus omne in sua confidens innocentia, sicut scriptum est ut leo justus confidit,[s] solitum sibi cunctisque probatum angustiis beatissimi confessoris petiit patrocinium, et consueto sibi more res suas in ipsius conportavit monasterium. Interea quidam ex his qui erant in castello, genere quidem Francigena, cum tot inibi arcas nullo custodiente conspiceret, (custodes enim in interioribus monasterii quæ sui erant ministerii non ista curabant, nec etiam quamvis alibi rapientes et furantes aliqui regionis illius indigenæ templa Dei temerare præsumunt) spiritu deceptorio mox actus, aptum ibi furandi locum tunc se repperisse arbitrabatur. Igitur notata nocte quadam qua hoc opportune perageret, a custodibus monasterii, ut secundum morem patriæ inibi vigilandi licentia sibi concederetur, eo quod hoc Deo vovisset, rogavit. At illi nil mali in eo suspicantes, quod omnibus conceditur devotis, ipsius quoque, quam simulabat, devotioni libentissime annuunt. Ille autem accepta licentia, per intempestæ noctis silentia, quando gravior est somnus, cum custodes dormire prospiceret, furtum quod improba mente conceperat, malæ devotus operæ adimplebat. Sed paucis inde revolutis diebus, cum nec alicujus furti loco

[r] This miracle is not noticed by Symeon, nor do any of the succeeding ones find a place in his narrative, although it is brought down to a lower period than the date assigned to several of them. This and the succeeding miracles are also wanting in Harleian MS. 1924, in which the account of the translation of St. Cuthbert's body, A.D. 1104, immediately succeeds the narrative in the previous section.

[s] Prov. xxviii. 1.

illo perpetrati vel saltem suspicio haberetur; nam, ut diximus, in ecclesia furtum facere nullus ibi præsumit, ægritudine gravissima et repentina ille corripitur, et tanquam igne ferventissimo decoquitur. Hac ille ardoris magnitudine in mentis insaniam versus, lecto exilivit, et ut in sola erat camisia cursu rapidissimo campum adiit, suumque illic qui pascebatur equum ascendens, in monasterium ante ipsum crucifixum cum impetu magno venit, ululans horribiliterque proclamans, "Miserere "mei, et parce, Sancte Cuthberte, sed quoniam non vis scio, "quia hæc et hæc (nominavit enim ea quæ tulerat) in mo-"nasterio tuo furari præsumpsi." Talia in monasterio huc et illuc discurrendo atque insaniendo dum sine intermissione vociferaret, invitus inde ad hospitium abducitur, lorisque fortibus constringitur, quoniam quicquid ore vel manibus apprehendere poterat velut canis dilacerabat. Qui cum tres sive quatuor noctes in tali tormento agens ab hora in horam magis magisque insaniret, tandem qualiter nescio a vinculis erumpens, in monasterium furiis agitatus cucurrit. Corruit quoque mox coram dilecti Deo Confessoris tumba, et dum chorus Te Deum Laudamus (nam nocturnæ Laudes interim agebantur) personaret, ille, ululando et horribiliter clamando, eadem quæ supra posuimus frequenter iteravit; his quoque alia quædam superadjiciens. Nam cum clamaret "Miserere mei, Sancte Cuthberte," adjecit, "sed quia non vis scio postquam tuo baculo me tam graviter "impulisti." Fatebatur enim hunc sanctissimum Confessorem nocturna visione ad se venisse, magnaque indignatione tres sibi graves inflixisse ictus, quorum dolore ad cor suum jam ingrediente, ad mortem torqueretur. Hæc atque hujusmodi plura dum vesanis motibus atque clamoribus frequentaret, in eodem loco mox toto corpore contrahitur, miseraque illius anima æternaliter arsura inde abstrahitur.

VIII.

Quomodo equus cujusdam, dum ex frugibus ecclesiæ Sancti Cuthberti comederet, subito interierit.

Mirabilia Dei opera scrutans in Psalmis Propheta, licet ubique creaturarum mirandum inveniat, præ cæteris tamen quadam ineffabilis excellentiæ prærogativa, mirabilem Deum in Sanctis[t] prædicat. Proinde, ut laudem Domini loquatur Os nostrum,[u] quid quæso ei dignius quam mirabilia Ejus dicantur, quæ in Sanctis Suis, eos mirificans, Ipse mirabilis operatur. Plane quan-

[t] Psalm lxvii. 36. [u] Psalm cxliv. 21.

tum in Sancto Cuthberto Deus quantumque in Deo Cuthbertus existat mirabilis, miraculorum quotidie declaratur judiciis. Quorum pauca quidem ex his quæ regnante Guillelmo Juniore contigerunt, non utique minora his quæ jam scripta legimus, illius per quem facta sunt ope nitentes scribendo explicabimus. Sanctissimi patris annua translationis festivitas, quæ jam proxima imminebat, populorum undecumque frequentiam Dunelmum, sicut est moris, invitabat. Sed non eadem cunctis fuit intentio devotionis. Isti quidem maxime vel etiam sola tanti patris patrocinia desiderabant; illi vero non tam Sancti suffragia quam mercandi, quæ tunc præcipue sunt studia, cogitabant. Horum numero quidam qui facto quod ei contigerat plurimis jam notior existit, equum adducens secum valentem plurisque pendendum, Dunelmi vendere disposuit. Itaque, cum comitans alios iter agit, videt cominus a latere maturas dudum fruges ecclesiæ, quas, collectis nuper in acervos manipulis, hi qui messuerant, sparsim, ut solet per agros, reliquerant. Huc relicto comitatu solus divertit, nulloque justitiæ respectu ex alienis jumento pabulum præbuit. Quod concite famulus monasterii, cui fuerat ibi cura rerum delegata, dum prohibere studuit, hæc Sancto Cuthberto servientium victui fore profutura indicavit; sed a pertinacia hominem revocare non valuit. Deinde ubi monitis nihil profecit, increpans quoque ac obsecrans, casso labore deficiens, post omnia quæ poterat derisus tacuit. Stomachando quippe contra graves in illum contumelias et maledicta retorsit, neque aliquantisper a præsumptione sese temperavit. Stabat itaque tumens ac rigidus, nullo metu Sancti vel reverentia se inflectens, quin potius fruge hinc et inde disjecta, cœptis multo quam cœperat vehementius insistens; cum, ecce! jumentum, quod modo sanum et incolume pascebatur, repente in terram corruens, statim emoritur, ut putares ipsum tam inopinatæ mortis celeritate non triticum, sed pro eo mortiferum quid sumpsisse. Ita contumacia repressa per quod maxime Sancti reverentiam contempsit, hoc ipsum Sancto vindictam exigente, justissime perdidit. Coactus itaque damno quod pertulit, injuriæ pœnitens et obstinationis, vehementer expavit. Videres hominem pallere ac corpore toto contremiscere, quid ageret præ favore, quove diverteret nescire. Damnum equi jam prorsus nihili reputare, sed ne et ipse simili plecteretur sententia nimium formidare. Itaque irruens solo sternitur, pugnisque se pariter et dictis diverberans, "O me," ait, "miserum, miserationis forsitan indignum! Ecce! quo peccata pertrahunt infelicem. Quid agam? Periturus huc veni. Nec enim aliud locus et meritum mihi promittunt. Hic locus et hæc hora viæ simul et vitæ, ut suspicor, afferent finem." Paululum deinde respirans, in spem veniæ, beatum Cuthbertum precibus et lacrimarum imbribus invocat, et ut miseri misereatur sedulus efflagitat, remittendo culpam simul et in reliquum quam meruisset pœnam. Tandem surrexit, et nudis pedibus toto quod supererat itinere confecto, ad ecclesiæ januam substitit. Neque enim prius intrare præsumpserat, quam eos quos se offendisse putaverat, fratres monasterii, ut pro se apud Sanctum intercessuros sibi reconciliasset. Cujus rei gratia monachum quendam jam intro præmiserat, qui sui merito et familiaritate quam inibi habuerat postulanti veniam facilius impetraret. Ad hoc egresso qui nunc usque superest monasterii præposito, pavens ille ac tremens ad pedes procidit, multisque astantibus ordinem rei prosecutus, misericordiam et judicium in se factum demonstravit; judicium, quod damno perculsus; misericordiam vero, quod non et ipse morte sit mulctatus. Ut videlicet vivens culpam agnosceret agnoscens, defleret deflens, correctiorem se deinceps exhiberet. Unde nunc humiliter pœnitentiam requisivit, sed super eam quam Divinitus pertulit, aliam pœnitentiæ vindictam imponere præpositus ipse cum fratribus nimis inhumanum duxit. Quem ipse injecta manu, non enim aliter ingredi audebat, velut mediator quidam usque ipsam sacratissimi corporis tumbam pallentem paventemque perducebat. Hic quoque corpore prostratus et corde, culpam temeritatis satisfaciendo deflevit, dumque modo veniam mereatur, tale quid se de cætero minime præsumpturum promittit. Sicque ex jumento quod perdidit, emendationem sui lucratus, melior simul et lætior ad sua rediit. Nec ipsum solum, sed et omnes quibus hoc factum innotuit, ad reverentiam venerandi Confessoris pluris habendam etiam in minimis quibusque coegit.

IX.

Quomodo populus in Dunelmo conclusus a duobus exercitibus liberatus fuerit.

Interea præfatus Anglorum rex, et Scottorum Malcolmus, obortis invicem causarum tumultibus, regni utriusque incommodo graves exercebant inimicitias; unde Malcolmus, exercitu producto, fugæ præsidia Northumbranos quærere compulit. Quorum quidam silvarum montiumque sese latebris occulunt. Plures autem, et præcipue qui proprie Sancti Cuthberti populus dicuntur, in Dunelmum sua secum transferunt, hic enim semper in periculis locum habent certum refugii, non tam loci quam pacis, propter sanctissimi corporis præsentiam, munimine confisi. Huc cum tota suppellectili greges universos compellunt, vixque tot et tantis hominum pecorumque turbis oppidi spatia sufficiunt. Inter hæc haud procul inde ad septentrionem suas copias Malcolmus collocat, ibique aliquot diebus demoratur. Interea civitatum quæ proximæ fuerant proceres, numerosæ juventutis constipati militia, hostium conatus præpedire maturabant, jamque et ipsi in vicinia Dunelmi ad austrum castra posuerant. Sed uterque populus, dum sui utrique metu aut pacem alterius aut fugam animo promittit, aliquantulum temporis ibidem transigit. Ita neuter hostium alteri quidem formidabilis, inclusis vero uterque ex otio fuit intolerabilis. Nam simul hominum et promiscui generis animalium multitudo, quæ in angustias compulsa fuerat, vix sese, alio alium premente, ferebat. Nec facile progredi, nec pecora in pasturam ejicere quisquam audebat, cum gladiis undique circumsepti, hinc et inde prædationes mortemque timebant. Quid dicam cimiterium constipatione gregum quorumque occupari, cum ab his vix immunis vel sola potuisset ecclesia servari? His admixtæ infantum, puerorum, mulierumque turbæ parietes ecclesiæ circumvallant, ubi confusis continue clamoribus psallentium in ecclesia voces perturbant. Murmur illorum miseriæ miseria erat etiam audire. Videres, urgente quæ cogit omnia fame, caballum alterius caudam morsu decerpere, alia aliis visu et auditu horrenda facere, plura quoque in mortem usque deficere. Tempus etiam æstatis fervidum periclitantibus mali fuerat incrementum. Quid plura? ut multa paucis absolvam, ubique per oppidum gemitus et

"*plurima mortis imago.*"[v]

Itaque miseris ubi res pene spes, vero penitus humani adjutorii defecerat, ad piissimi confessoris Cuthberti confugiunt patrocinium, cujus in adversis ante crebro jam ceperant experimentum. Concione namque habita, eadem omnes in unum adduxit sententia; scilicet ut solitum patris auxilium ab omnibus in commune precibus et secundum vires invocetur muneribus. Igitur unanimes ad ecclesiam conveniunt, ex contritione cordis preces et lacrimas, ex facultate dona gratuito singuli offerunt, Confessoris opem sibi suisque, nisi mature succurrat perituris, implorant. O clementem Dei justitiam! O justam Ipsius clementiam! *Visitavit in virga iniquitates populi Sui, et in verberibus peccata eorum.*[w] Misericordiam autem Suam, Cuthberto interveniente, non dispersit ab eis. Hic sane, ut legitur, factus est dominus refugium pauperum adjutor in opportunitatibus, in tribulatione. Nec dum crastina lux in aurora proruperat, cum ecce! subito nescio quo terrore Scottorum exercitus

[v] Æn., ii., 370. [w] Psalm lxxxviii. 3.

omnis in fugam compellitur. Horum discessus ubi castris Anglorum fama percrebuit, mox et ille in sua discedendi licentiam contulit. Haud aliter propulsis circumquaque hostibus, votiva exultationis dies oritur, qua in sui libertatem de loci et animi angustiis plebs tota redimitur. Dies, inquam, exultationis, qua, multo largior quam sperare quisquam poterat, eis gratia consolationis exuberat. Solam enim hostium fugam exoptaverant, et, ecce! gemina Dei gratia respirant. Denique, cum hostes discessisse lætantur, eadem hora, quod nec speraverant, suum sibi antistitem de exilio reversum congratulantur. Nam cum portis reseratis plebs exitura festinaret, ecce! obvii officiales episcopi ingrediuntur, et sui ubique jura ovilis episcopo restituuntur. Magna deinde lætitia magnas gratiarum actiones, quas jam hostilis fuga pepererat, gratior universis restitutio præsulis cumulabat. Et hoc in facto cujus sit meriti beatus Cuthbertus quisque prudens intelligit, per quem miserator et misericors Dominus tantas bonitatis Suæ divitias et indignis exhibuit, quia *Suavis Dominus universis et miserationes Ejus super omnia opera Ejus.*[x]

X.

Quomodo quidam, dum furens equos monachorum Sancti Cuthberti de hospitio suo expellere voluisset, ut mortuus ceciderit.

Fluxerat non multum temporis, cum, ecce! per merita sancti Confessoris res item contigit memorabilis. Præpositus monasterii præfatus, ubi ecclesiæ et totius populi communis utilitas expetiit, comitantibus eum e populo non paucis, Australium Anglorum in partes devenit. Erant cum eo et duo e monasterio fratres, quorum uno jam defuncto, alter cum præposito superstes, rei, quam nunc narrandam incipimus, testis accedit indubius. Igitur per gentes, cum jam declinans in vesperam dies et frigus hibernum ad hospitia compellunt, in vicum juxta-positum festinantes, monachis tardius sequentibus, alii alios præveniunt. Quibus per totam villam hospitantibus, angusta quædam domuncula monachis remanet; quæ quidem eis solis, non autem et equis eorum sufficere potuisset. Unde exorata in vicina domo domina, (non enim maritus affuit,) locum jumentis benigne concessit. Quod ille rediens impatienter tulit, qui, et unde essent qui in sua domo equos locare præsumpsissent requisivit. Cognito itaque quod de longinquo venissent, eo magis benevolentiam humanitatis amittit, furensque vociferando, quantocitius equos expelli præcipit. Quem frater a præposito missus quibus potuit blanditiis mitigare studuit,

[x] Psalm cxliv. 9.

deprecans ut Sancto Cuthberto in suis angulum suæ domus permitteret, quoniam aliud jam hospitium aliorum ubique hospitum multitudo illis prohiberet. At ille, quem mentis impotem furor effecerat, precibus contumelias reddit, et in Dei confessorem loquens indigna, omnesque deterrens, horrendis clamoribus insanit; jamque ligamina præcisurus equorum furibundus accurrit. Igitur dum animo, ore, et manu implacabilis sævit, subito ante equos, quasi jam moriturus, immo, ut videbatur, jam moriens, decidit. Cum enim sine voce et motu sensibus exutus haberetur, velut jam exspirans animam in medium exponitur. Tota illa domus se repente in luctum transmutat, actura illius exequias, quem paulo ante furentem et vociferantem vix toleraverat. Audito, præpositus, quod contigit, misso quasi ad morientem fratre, cum alio remanens, intentius precibus instat, et pro miseri salute beati Cuthberti auxilium sedulus implorat. Post aliquod intervallum, vita paulatim redeunte, oculos aperiens, videt fratrem sibi assidere, et "O tuum Sanc-"tum," inquit, "illum precor pro me deprecare." Paulo post, vigore spiritus et corporis recepto, secundum illud Sapientis *Stulto flagellato insipiens sapientior erit,*[y] quibus angulum ante negaverat, cum tota domo sua omnia supplex offerre festinat. Verum id monachorum meritis accidisse nemo putet, sed Dei confessoris reverentia quanti fuerit habenda, nescientem pia docuerunt flagella. Nec mora. Gestum in domo pauperis palatio innotuit regis. Relatum namque ab uno eorum qui interfuit, regem et ipsius primates in Dei laudem et ipsius famuli laudanda merita sustulit.

XI.

Quomodo egestatem patientibus, meritis Sancti Cuthberti, multitudinem piscium mare recedens reliquerit.

Nec multo post, idem pene quod in carne vivens quondam ostenderat,[z] nostris quoque temporibus Confessor venerandus miraculum renovat. Erat omnium præcipua Paschalis festivitas in proximo futura. Sed quia rerum angustia mensis fratrum sufficientiam minus videbatur promittere, minus forte in tantæ sollemnitatis gaudio poterant ipsi gaudere. Unde præpositus memoratus, et alii, quorum id erat officii, fratres pia cura sollicitabantur, ut, post observantias Quadragesimæ uberiori quocunque solatio imbecilles recrearentur. At indies penuria

[y] Prov. xix. 25.
[z] See chapter xi. of Beda's Life of Cuthbert.

crescens frustra sollicitos vehementius angustabat, nec jam spes quidem humani solatii ulla relevabat. Sed, contra hoc quod ipsi sperare noverant, subita Divinæ largitatis benedictione respirant. Siquidem apud Lindisfarnensem insulam oceano secundum tempus recedente, ingentia quædam piscium corpora passim per arenas relicta palpitabant; magnumque intuentibus stuporem et gaudium numero simul et mole præstabant. Quinque enim et sexaginta fuerant; tantæque granditatis ut singulis abstrahendis non nisi boum paria sufficerent. Verum quia locus ipse juris alterius extitit, ex his nec portiuncula quidem fratribus contigit. Aderat enim illorum quidam qui ex tanta Divini muneris abundantia saltem decimas, quod legis et provinciæ antiqua consuetudo exigebat, ecclesiæ requisivit; sed, omnibus negatis, rubore simul et dolore confusus discessit. Et quid moror? Mox superba tenacitas confunditur, et postulantis humilitas mirabilis erigitur. Prospicit eminus frater memoratus multitudinem piscium huc illucque vagari, sed fluctuum adhuc altitudine ad ipsos accessum prohiberi. Spe itaque alacrior factus, patrem Cuthbertum exorabat attentius, quatinus ex tanta copia suorum relevaretur indigentia. Interea undis sensim relabentibus, dum vagi velut errantes feruntur, paulatim recessu maris pariter in sicco relinquuntur. Et cum late per circuitum loca juris essent aliorum, solam quæ monachorum fuerat loci angustiam larga Dei benedictio replet, ut ne unus quidem piscis eam excederet. Pares genere et granditate prioribus, numerum vero superavere duobus. Pulchrum sane, non solum ipsi fratri, sed et indigentibus quibusque res illa spectaculum præbuit, quibus quod a Deo largius accepit, largiter ipse communicavit.[a] Celeriter itaque beneficii cælestis abundantiam fratribus domum transmittit, omnesque in stuporem et laudem Dei res insperata convertit. Taliter animis recreati et corporibus, solito lætius festa Paschalia transigebant, multoque post tempore his epulis abundabant, Illum non cessantes benedicere, *Qui dat escam in tempore opportuno; Qui aperit manum suam, et implet omne animal benedictione.*[b] Nec dubium hanc Dei munificentiam ipsius nunc meritis servulis procuratam, qui maris quondam tempestate præclusus, dum jam nil ciborum habuisset, precibus a Deo quæsivit. Nec mora. Quæ sibi sociisque sufficerent, delfininas in littore carnes invenit. Hæc sane per omnia, sicut narravimus, et ipsius qui interfuerat, quem præfati sumus, actu et habitu monachi, et aliorum qui videre relatione quam frequenter audivimus.

[a] St. Matt. x. 8. [b] Psalm civ. 27; cxlv. 16.

XII.

Quomodo Paulus abbas et Robertus Comes, in loco quem Sancto Cuthberto abstulerant, injuriæ pœnam receperint.[c]

Deum et miracula Dei cum in Sancto Cuthberto laudantes consideramus, misericordiam et judicium cum Psalmista Domino cantamus;[d] Meritis namque magnifici præsulis *Deus, justus judex,*[e] *hunc humiliat et hunc exaltat;*[f] *quia suscipit mansuetos Dominus, humiliat autem peccatores usque ad terram.*[g] Horum experimenta in his quæ jam scripta sunt comprobavimus, et in illis quæ adhuc scribenda sunt comprobavimus. Rem igitur haud in obscuro gestam referemus, de qua, ne quis dubitandum putaverit, pene totius Northanhumbriæ populus testis assistit.

Rodbertus de Mubreio, animo vehemens et armis strenuus, ubi Comitatus honore potiebatur, in honoris detrimentum adversus ecclesiam Sancti odiis exagitatur. Id enim in primis studii quam maxime habuit, ut calumniis fatigatam et injuriis opprimeret. Quacumque res illius vexare et jura contendit dissipare; quicquid adversi poterat facere, plusquam poterat se facturum minari. Unde et ecclesiam in Tinemuthe, proprii videlicet juris ecclesiæ patris Cuthberti, ut tota provincia novit, primam violentiæ suæ prædam efficit. Hinc denique ipsi qui diu inhabitaverant monachi, immo in monachis ipse Sanctus cum contumelia expellitur, et in Pauli cujusdam abbatis, in longinquo degentis, dominium ea transfertur. Quem tamen abbatem, ne rapinam suscipiens ecclesiæ proposito et gradui injuriam faceret, monachi Dunelmenses litteris legatariis per seipsos, per quosque religiosos, monendo, obsecrando, prohibendo, satis quidem, sed frustra, studuerant revocare. Non illum gratia cujusquam inflectebat, non denique venerandi Confessoris, non ordinis reverentia, quominus rapinam susciperet, retinebat. Verum non inpune. Ut enim rerum exitus edocuit, uterque, scilicet rapiens et rapinam possidens, temeritatem pœna vindice persolvit. Abbas enim, præmissis jamdudum monachis, ubi post ipse sequens ecclesiam ipsam primum viderat, subita infirmitate corripitur; et qui sanus et incolumis advenerat, mortuus domum revehitur. At Comes, interjecto tempore, malis, offenso sibi rege, circumvallatus, dum circumfuso quaquaversum hoste procedendi et redeundi via obstruitur, Tinemutham pro

[c] Symeon relates very briefly (chapter lxiii.) the particulars of the loss of the church of Tynemouth, the death of abbat Paul, and the misfortunes of Robert de Moubray, but it is the independent narrative of a contemporary, and not derived from this work, although tinged to some extent by the same prejudices.

[d] Psalm ci. 1.

[e] Psalm vii. 12.

[f] Psalm lxxv. 8.

[g] Psalm cxlvii. 6.

loci firmitate ingreditur. Hic enim locus ab orientis plaga et septentrionis altissima supra oceanum rupe se inaccessibilem præbet, alibi vero situ altiori facili defensione indiget. Hoc ille præsidio et probata militum manu confisus, longe alium quam res habitura erat sibi et hostibus finem promittebat. Biduo enim obsidione facta, hostes, aut vincendi aut cadendi animo, desuper pugnantes ferro et flammis aggrediuntur. Nec mora. Locum difficilem sed non difficile capiunt. Nullo enim sui detrimento irrumpentes, alios obtruncant, alios vulnerando debilitant, rapiunt, trahunt, ipsumque Comitem, vulneratum et jam vitæ diffidentem, in ecclesiam compellunt. O justum Dei judicium! Ecce, ut Scriptura canit, *In operibus manuum suarum comprehensus est peccator.*[h] Et, *Lacum aperuit et effodit eum.* Et, *Incidit in foveam quam fecit.*[i] In eadem certe ecclesia Comes ipse nunc præda efficitur hostibus quam ipsius in Sanctum Cuthbertum præsumptionis prædam supradiximus. In ipsa, inquam, quam superbiens Sancto rapuerat, nunc miserabilis ipse rapitur, trahitur, et ad regem, cujus mortem vita cariorem haberet, perducitur; hodieque in vinculis custodiæ mancipatur. His ita gestis, considerantibus idem locus in utroque manifestat causam pœnæ; ubi enim Sancto injuriam fecerunt, ibi et injuriæ mercedem utrique receperunt. Ibi uni morbus mortis, ibi alteri damnum occurrit totius honoris. Ita una ecclesiola beato Cuthberto ablata: alter vitam, alter non solum divitias et honores, sed etiam, quod his omnibus pluris habuit, corporis libertatem amisit.

XIII.

Quomodo clericus febricitans ad tumbam Beati Cuthberti sanatus fuerit.

Ante non multum temporis, de sepulcro illo, quod depositum servat thesauri cælestis, solitum emanavit miraculum sanitatis. Siquidem apud Australes Anglos quidam ex ordine cleri multos honore præcellens gravissima febre corripitur, quæ diuturno exhaustum cruciatu miserum corpus depascitur. Nec sollicita illi medicorum cura deerat, quæ, spe præmiorum invitata, nihil suæ artis curationi non impendebat. Verum nulla medicandi specie vel leniri aliquatenus molestia poterat, cui per contrarium medicina per dies augmentum præbebat. Cum igitur desperatis medicis nullum remedii genus excogitare quivisset, solam spem salutis habuit, si tumbam incorrupti corporis beati Cuthberti

[h] Psalm ix. 16. [i] Psalm vii. 16.

invisere potuisset, fama namque divulgante compererat ibidem crebro miracula fieri, crebro quocunque incommodo detentos curando relevari. Itaque, tametsi longa molestia tabefactus, longi laborem itineris aggreditur, perveniensque Dunelmum quo decuit honore suscipitur. Ibi quoque solito laborans incommodo, febrium valetudine aliquamdiu concutitur, sed repente meritis Sancti Cuthberti ad integrum saluti redditur. Denique ante sepulcrum ejus dum pervigil in precibus noctem transsigeret, quasi præsentia Sancti corporis exterrita, pestis aufugit, nec ultra hominem tangere aliquatenus præsumpsit. Cui rei tot testes esse noscimur, quot ipsi pretioso Confessoris corpori, licet indigni, deservimus; qui et, orante ad tumbam illius infirmo, Nocturnæ Laudis officia persolvimus, et, post, cum eodem illius sanitati congaudentes, Deo gratias in Sancto Cuthberto decantavimus. Paucis post diebus resumens iter, suos, quos infirmus reliquit, in suæ sanitatis miraculum stupentes et congratulantes reddit.

XIV.

Quomodo quidam qui asinario ecclesiæ Sancti Cuthberti cingulum tulerat repente oculos doluerit.

Aliud quoque sed non alio tempore, in ipsius admirandæ sanctitatis præconium, subito accidit miraculum. Puer ecclesiæ, qui asinis custodiam adhibebat, profuturam pabulo illorum herbam desecuerat. Quo labore et æstu fatigatus meridiano, mollibus in pratis ac suave olentibus in somnum citius resolvitur. Interea extraneus quidam, qui cum aliis socius operis aderat, admota leniter manu, dormienti cingulum solvit, eoque ablato quod ceperat, libere opus repetit. Nec enim sceleri impedimento esse poterat, quem sopor gravis sensibus abduxerat. Evigilans tandem rem quam non parvi pendebat, quasi magnum quid perdidisse se indoluit. Ubi circumquaque requirens nusquam invenerat, mox furti suspicio animum agitat. Postremo crimen quidem non suspicione sed certo in se factum agnovit, sed cui ex pluribus id imponeret incertum habuit. Interea dum sollicitus ab universis requireret cingulum, signis evidentibus accipit furis indicium. Quem suppliciter ut suum sibi reddat expetit, sed, contemptus, nil præter verborum contumelias recipit. Nec sic quidem ille a prece desistens; "Quandoqui-"dem," inquit, "nec misericordia nec justitia te movet, quæso "vel Sancti Cuthberti reverentia mihi meum a te impetret. "Per ipsum ne mihi rapinam facias obsecro, cujus ecclesiæ "servitiis quotidie debitum mei laboris impendo." At ille, qui multum parvo lucro deliquit, ex contemptu pretiosissimi Confessoris gravius quam ex furto crimen incurrit. Ferocius enim quam ante maledictis et conviciis obsecrantem aggreditur, et jam, si denuo inde os aperire præsumpserit, inferendam illi pœnam minatur. Quem puer abeuntem prosequens, hac voce imprecatur, "Quia," inquit, "ego non possum, Sanctus Cuthbertus "injuriam meam ulciscatur." Dixerat, et dicta ultionis sequitur pœna. Nam cum paulo ante integros haberet, subitus oculos dolor et infusa caligo pererrat, ut jam non facile, nisi manum alter porrigeret, pedibus offendiculum ipse præcaveret. Quo in facto secundum meritum ordinante Deo flagellum, ibi recipit effectum dolendi unde processerat causa delinquendi. Qui enim injuriam fecerat illicientibus oculis, injuriæ pœnam recipit dolentibus oculis. Ita qui alteri furando cingulum solvit, ipse se funiculus peccati et pœna peccatum vindicante fortius constringit. Itaque subito ex vidente pene cæcum stupentes sui, dum causam sciscitantes diligentius perscrutantur, ipse nullius mali se conscium, nisi quod asinario ecclesiæ cingulum tulisset, fatetur. Hanc illi solam infelicitatis illius causam intelligentes, illico puerum requirentes, vix tandem inveniunt; postulantesque secum proficisci, ad infirmum deducunt. Igitur versa vice violentiam passus lætatur, qui fecerat contristatur. Stat iste de vindicta gratulans, jacet ille crimen et vindictam deplorans. Stat jam non curans poscere quod reddendum sibi pœnam videt exigere. Jam ut suum recipere dignaretur, humilius quam ante postulaverat, nunc ipse postulatur. Tandem recepto quod ablatum fuerat, dum jam ipsius lacrimis et astantium precibus flecteretur, remittendo injuriam ore et animo illi placatur. Quo facto etsi non ad integram sanitatem, videndi tamen usum recipit, ut rediens cum domino duce itineris non egeret, sine quo paulo ante nec ad ostium accederet. Nec jam mirabatur hanc sibi plagam evenisse, qui in precibus pueri beatum Cuthbertum, per quem adjuratus fuerat, se contemptui meminit habuisse.

XV.

Quomodo de Lindisfarne fugienti cum furto subito mare occurrens iter obstruxerit.

Fugientibus quondam in Lindisfarnensem insulam, mare cum esset plenum, meritis Sancti Cuthberti siccum iter præbuisse subito legimus;[j] nunc, e diverso, ex ea cum furto fugientem repente undas contra morem præpedisse dicemus. Northumbrani cujusdam equus forma, cursu, et cætera sui valitudine pluris

[j] See Section vi.

erat, propter quod ad violentiam vel furtum facile quemlibet illicere poterat. Nam id locorum habitantibus moris esse solet, alterutrum sese furtis et latrociniis affligere, ut quippiam rerum adipiscendo, non tam sibi quam raptoribus quisquam videatur elaborasse. Sed hæc licet invicem sibi quasi licenter faciant, in præfata tamen insula qua beatus Confessor conversatus et tumulatus fuerat, ista velut repentini interitus causas formidant. Igitur illo jumentum suum homo traducit, ubi propter pacis firmitatem, quam ibidem et barbari observant, damnum non metuit. At quidam, diabolico spiritu exagitatus, temeritate sacrilega furtum meditatur, idque perficiendi tempus opportunum præstolatur. Tandem, quam mente male concepit, opere pejus iniquitatem peperit. Denique, beati Cuthberti postponens reverentiam, pacem illius violat, raptoque equo quam citissime abire festinat. Erat enim tempus quo recessus maris insulam renudato littore contiguam terræ reddiderat. Itaque dum sedens equo veloci fuga per arenas ferretur, ecce! subito maris occursu præpeditur, undisque in altum tumescentibus, fugiendi aditus obstruitur. Ille novitatem rei nimio cum stupore pavet, querensque secum, "Quid hic," ait, "miraculi apparet? "Nunc a sæculo præfixam mare transgreditur legem, sui temporis prævenit ordinem. Non enim ordini statuto nunc obtemperat, quando sui recessu liberum pedibus iter jam relinquere "debuerat." Qui tamen quoquo modo posset pertransire cum furto nititur, sed obviis undarum voluminibus ne procedat retunditur. Interea cum hinc et inde maris altitudo circumlueret, nec progrediendi facultatem habebat nec regrediendi, jam equus, sedente desuper fure, fluctibus innatat, dumque undis impellentibus fertur et refertur, conscius facinoris fur ipse salutem desperat. Cælestis ergo misericordiæ opem clamoribus invocat, "Sancte," inquiens, "Cuthberte, miserere, licet indigni. Miserere, inquam, mei. Respice miserando miserum, jam jamque, "nisi succurrere tu digneris, periturum; periturum, inquam, "utraque, corporis videlicet et animæ, perditione. Ecce! humanius me victurum tibi promitto, si, te nunc propitio, mortem "evasero." Nulla in medium mora. Cum se ad ulteriora pervehi jam putaret; ecce! illo nesciente qualiter actum fuerit, in insulam equo sedens quem furatus erat se relatum videt, ultra nil prævalens, velit nolit, ibi malitiæ limitem invenit. Mirandis miranda succedunt. Ubi enim equum dimissurus desiliit, ecce! quas sibi obvians unda contexerat, nudas subito arenas conspicit. Rediens itaque, ubi equitare prius nequiverat perversus, siccis pedibus incedebat correctus. Igitur plenus gaudii de sua ereptione, et stuporis de miraculi novitate, totum ordine quo gestum fuit, cuidam nostræ, id est Dunelmensis ecclesiæ monacho suo relatu patefecit, ne si quod tam magnifice in gloriam Dei factum noverat silentio tegeret, offensam apud Deum incurreret; quia, ut ait Scriptura, *Sacramentum regis abscondere bonum est; opera autem Dei revelare et confiteri honorificum est.*[k]

XVI.

Qualiter infantulus sub trabe bobus eam trahentibus volutatus, nec tamen fuerit læsus.

Loquitur per Prophetam Dominus, *Quicunque honoraverit Me, glorificabo illum.*[l] Proinde quoniam beatus pater Cuthbertus in carne, non secundum carnem vivens, Deum super omnia et in omnibus honorare non destitit, Deus illum et in cælo gloriæ suæ beata contemplatione, et in terra quotidie miraculorum glorificat ostensione. Digna sane omnium admiratione quædam, indigno licet sermone, jam exposuimus; nec minus his mirandum, quiddam subjungere temptabimus. Nec dum annus agitur, ex quo ad ecclesiam, quæ nunc in illius honorem venusto admodum opere fabricatur, profuturum structuræ de longe lignum advehebatur. Tantæ autem granditatis fuisse perhibetur, ut non minus quam octo boum toto conamine adhibito traheretur. Ventum erat prope januam urbis, ubi fatigati boves paululum respirare sinuntur, ut reparatis viribus contra clivum facilius eniterentur, Interea puerorum turba circumfluebat, seque ludendi levitate circa et super ligni machinam varie ferebat. At ubi stimulato bove trabes moveri cœperat, forte cadente infantulo crus ipsius molis pondere et terra intercipitur, diuque ille impulsu ligni stridente rotatur. Ductores enim boum curam habentes non horum quippiam viderant, donec puer fletu et ejulatu præcedentes ad se liberandum revocaret. Accurritur statim; facta difficultate non minima, vix sexdecim virorum toto conatu tantæ molis magnitudo paululum quandoque levatur. Mirabile dictu, lignum quod solo pondere etiam saxa conterere poterat, tenerum os infantis frangere non valebat! Cum enim quasi jam contrito in pulverem crure exspirans crederetur, integer non solum osse sed et carne illæsa recipitur. O res omnium stupore digna! Impetu molis circumactus dolere quidem potuit ut clamaret, non ut salutem amitteret. Sola cutis parumper dilacerata videbatur, sed ob hoc quin statim cursus et ludorum certamina repeteret omnino non impediebatur. Nec dubium quin patris Cuthberti protectio

[k] Tob. xii. 7.

[l] 1 Reg. ii. 30.

sub tormento mortis a morte puerum servaverit, ne quid ecclesiæ ipsius profuturum esse potuisset, infantis innocentiæ nocere debuisset.

XVII.

Quomodo piratas, cum navem cum rebus ecclesiæ abducerent, in ejusdem ecclesiæ juris, insulam Lindisfarnensem, subita tempestas ejecerit.

His et hujusmodi, scilicet novis, nova quotidie succedunt miracula, et stupentibus prima plus addunt stuporis sequentia. Quorum melius plurima silentio, ne incredibilia videantur, quam sermone honoramus infimo. Sed ne omnino prætermissa nos mirabilibus Dei velut ingratos ostendant, paucis, quæ præmisimus, pauca non tam efficaciter quam veraciter enarrando subnectimus. Navis quædam, ecclesiæ negotiis inserviens, loca diversa mercandi gratia inviserat, nec parum exinde usibus monasterii ipsa præstabat. Quadam vice onus expositura cum domum revertitur, cum rebus cunctis ipsa insidiantium præda capitur. Quippe manus navigantium, numero infirma et pugnandi imperitia, pluribus et navali prælio exercitatis haud difficile succubuit victa. Quibus, quia non longe fuerant, ad terram pervectis, præter solam animam nil truculentus reliquit pirata. Æqua deinde sui numeri parte in navem quam ceperant transposita, vela ventis committere properant; et, terrente conscientia, plus terras quam maria formidant. Vere nihil infelicius mali conscientia, quæ dum se ipsam hostem tolerat, et quem non patitur hostem deputat. Ecce! quos nemo persecutus fuerat, in ventos et pelagi profunda mens male conscia fugat. Sed qui Dominum terræ ac maris offendere non metuerant, Ejus nec in terra nec in mari judicium effugere valebant. Denique cum jam velut rapina saturati ad propria redirent, ecce! ab Africo subito turbine oborta, fera illis undique surgit hyems, et verso concitat æquore fluctus, ventisque furentibus et undis feruntur quo tempestas impulit. Quo autem impellantur non norunt, nec boni quippiam usquam sperare poterant, qui malitiæ testem conscientiam habuerant. Aër flatibus, mare persequitur fluctibus, terra propellit metu. Sicque, amissa securitate conscientiæ, ubique amiserunt securitatem vitæ. Inter quæ nec ad momentum quidem ulla vel requie vel spe refocillantur, quibus per dies continue et noctes mortem cuncta minantur. Itaque cum labore mortis et metu gravius quam morte agitarentur, eos, inedia et periculis partim ægrotantes, pariter vero omnes viribus exhaustos, in Lindisfarnensium insulam ejicit tempestas. De quibus nec dum quales fuissent agnitis, meliora satis quam veriora ficta componebat calliditas; fidemque mentientibus vera præbebat calamitas. Habitus miserabilis et sermo lugubris ad miserandum potius quam suspicandum provocabat intuentes. Aderat forte sæpe-memoratus ecclesiæ præpositus. Gerens ille diligentiam recreandis, etiam mensæ suæ participes adhibuit. In aliis quoque se liberalem satis et humanum exhibuit. Fluxerant dies non pauci, cum, ecce! secundis acta flatibus, oneraria, et ipsa ecclesiæ propria navis, illuc allabitur, ubi nautas ipsos in stuporem et lætitiam res inopinata convertit. Quos enim fama crudelitatis cognitos diu multumque sibi timuerant, illuc præmissos metuentes magis quam metuendos inveniunt. Cum deinde salutantes præpositus ipse resalutasset, "Domine" inquiunt, "ecce! piratas, et ecclesiæ cujus es mi-"nister suscipis, foves, et amplecteris hostes! Ecce! navis illius "et omnium quas navis vobis advehebat rerum prædones. Ipsa "vita indignos indigne tanta humanitate dignaris. Horum "sceleris socios, ut ipsi oculis probavimus, ferro cædente ab-"sumpsit interitus. Isti ad hoc ipsum ubique perquiruntur. "Non ergo injustum videatur, ut mortis nunc socientur sen-"tentia, quos eadem sociaverat malitia." His illi quid contrahiscerent non habentes, diriguerunt metu, suorum gementes et suum mox interitum suspicantes; et jam cervicibus ultor gladius impendisset, nisi loci ipsius reverentia, præterea et ipsius præpositi præsentia, id prohibuisset. Illi, quod solam spem salutis habebant, ejus pedibus advoluti, vitam sibi donari flebiles implorant. His omnibus, ille, cognitis, mirandi patris miranda considerans merita, vindictam et vindictæ modum pavens, stupet, et stupens pavet. Miratur plane prius ultionem injuriæ factam, quam injuriam fuisse cognitam; prius coactos velut ad suum judicium reos, quam se nosse reatum. Cogebatur interim advertere, cur per tanta spatia non nisi ad id loci noxios impulerit mare; videlicet, ut cujus ecclesiæ propria abripuerant, diverso exitu in ejus ecclesiæ potestatem ipsi et sua transirent. Hanc quippe ecclesiam Confessor egregius, in carne cælesti vivens, conversatione et sui præsulatus apice, postremo sui incorrupti corporis sibi sepultura consecravit. His igitur subtiliter inspectis, anxius æstuabat, quia e duobus quid potissimum eligeret incertus fluctuabat, Hinc enim prædonum spectat nequitiam, illinc eorumdem afflictorum miseriam. Hinc ecclesiæ injuriam, illinc pensat injuriæ vindictam. In uno justitia severitatem, in altero pietas suadebat lenitatem. Utrumque causa exigebat, sed simul utrumque difficile putabat. Vicit tamen super-exaltans se judicio misericordia, quia quos maria, venti, rerum damna, labores, Deo vindicante, afflixerant, affligi ulterius ab homine furoris esse videbatur non justitiæ. Quos per ecclesiæ villas securitati opportunas dispositos et securos, et rerum necessariarum sufficientes reddidit; donec, sopito qui mortem eis intentaverat rumore, repatriarent, nave propria cum toto apparatu ultro ecclesiæ relicta.

XVIII.

Quomodo post cccc.x *et* viij *annos corpus beati Cuthberti incorruptum sit inventum, et in novam ecclesiam translatum.*

Inter hæc tam frequentium miraculorum opera non eadem apud omnes tam de præsentia sacri corporis beati Cuthberti, quam de incorruptione habebatur opinio. Alii namque illud multo ante hanc ætatem vi quadam occulta alio translatum vanis sibi conjecturis somniabant; atque sepulcrum, licet nunc talis depositi careat commendato, non tamen evacuari virtutum gloria; sed, ad indicium pristini inhabitatoris, nunc quoque celebriter effulgere miraculis. Alii autem sacras quidem reliquias ibidem contineri, sed humani corporis compagem per tot sæculorum volumina indissolutam permanere jura dicebant excedere naturæ. Et, licet virtus Divina omnibus quod vult et quomodo vult imperet naturis, hanc tamen in hujus corporis incorruptione nullius qui vel manu vel visu explorasset testimonio sibi patere. Atque ideo difficile sibi de hoc, quamlibet sancto corpore, credere inexpertum, quod raro paucissimis aliorum Sanctorum corporibus noverant concessum. Taliter his ablationem sancti corporis conjectantibus, illis incorruptionem non admittentibus, affirmantium illud et adesse et incorruptum perdurare fratrum fidei detrahebatur, ideoque pudor aliquantisper anxius ingerebatur. Quapropter ipsi fratres, mentibus ad Deum ac precibus conversi, orabant ut Qui est *mirabilis in sanctis suis,*[m] Hic Sese, ostensione tantæ virtutis, mirabilem ostenderet, et dubium in dubiis indiciis nomini Suo dans gloriam excluderet.

Interea ecclesia, quam quondam Guillelmus episcopus fundaverat, non parva ex parte perfecta, venerabile patris Cuthberti corpus in hanc fuerat transferendum, et dignæ venerationis gratia in loco, quem studiosa manus artificum adaptaverat, decenter recondendum. Imminente itaque iiij kal. Septembris, die scilicet qui ad sollemnem Translationem fuerat præfinitus, inierunt consilium fratres, ut, quoniam nemo supererat qui per experimentum edoceret, ipsi, quantum Deo permittente liceret, qualiter circa corpus sanctum singula composita, qualiter ordi-

[m] Psalm lxvii. 36.

nata essent explorarent; atque ad id die venturo transportandum quæque digna et convenientia viderentur, maturius præpararent. Ne videlicet, cum hora festivæ processionis institerit, aliqua ex improvidentia difficultas impedimentum faciat; atque ita, ex mora exspectationi universorum qui advenerint ingrata, agendis sollemnibus obsequiis fiat injuria. Jussi ergo fratres, numero novem, adjuncto sibi Priore ipsius ecclesiæ, Turgoto, qui jejuniis et obsecrationibus ad hoc sese præparaverant, ix kal. Septembris noctis initio, ante venerabilem sepulcrum prosternuntur, effusisque lacrimis et precibus, manus non sine timore ac tremore apponunt, ut illud aperiant. Quo tandem instrumentis ferralibus patefacto, inveniunt stupentes arcam, quam ex omni parte diligenter parata clavisque affixa ferreis coria totam obduxerant. Quæ videlicet arca, pondere sui et magnitudine, aliis quoque quibusdam indiciis facile dabat intelligi, intra sua claustra loculi alterius depositum contineri. Sed hanc aperire cum diu timore impediente dubitarent, supra-nominato Priore bis terque jubente, confisi obedientiæ virtute, inceptum opus repetunt, ac, dissolutis ferreis ligaminibus, arcam quandoque aperiunt. Vident introrsus positum loculum de ligno, quem grossior de lino triplicis texturæ pannus undique circumdederat, ad mensuram staturæ virilis longum, ejusdemque generis tabula coopertum. Hærebant diu; non enim satis elucebat utrum ipsum sancti corporis hospitium esset, an et aliud adhuc sacras continens reliquias intra se domicilium contineret. Tandem in se reversi, memores dictorum Bedæ, qui corpus beati Cuthberti a fratribus quondam Lindisfarnensis ecclesiæ post xj sepulturæ annos incorruptum inventum, atque supra pavimentum dignæ venerationis gratia reconditum describit;[n] horum, inquam, dictorum reminiscentes, hanc eandem esse arcam animadvertunt, quæ per tot annos tantum cælestis depositi thesaurum conservasset.

Pariter ergo corruentes in terram, orabant suppliciter, ut sua beatus Cuthbertus intercessione iram a se Omnipotentis Dei averteret, si hanc aliquatenus ex præsumptione meruissent. Inerat eis gaudium mixtim cum pavore, quia etsi ex audacia timuissent offensam, ex certitudine tamen tanti muneris ingentem conceperant lætitiam. Agente itaque gaudio resolvuntur in lacrimas, et, gratiarum actione Domino reddita, desiderio suo satisfactum reputabant. Unde ad ipsa sacri corporis secreta altius perscrutanda manus admovere videbatur temeritatis, quam, ut putabant, secutura Divinitus ultio nullo modo relinqueret impunitam. Remissa ergo intentione ulterius quicquam perquirendi, tractabant vicissim, quo et quam congruo

[n] See Beda's Life of S. Cuthbert, chapter xlii.

apparatu futuræ Translationis die corpus debuisset asportari. Porro inter alios ibidem aderat quidam magnæ in Christo constantiæ frater, qui eam, quam nomine prætendebat, per effectum gratiæ caritatem consecutus fuerat. Vocabatur enim Leofwinus, quod Anglorum lingua dicitur Carus Amicus;[o] ipse utique carus Deo, amicus et Deus illi. Patrem namque illius Se fuisse Deus ostendit, continua illum infirmitate castigando: ille filium Dei se fuisse ostendit, flagella Dei patienter tolerando, et gratias semper agendo. Cujus conversationem vitæ quicumque noverat Sanctum in illius pectore Spiritum requiescere dubitare non poterat. Is cum videret fratres trepidantes inventum aperire loculum, et quid gratiæ cælestis, quid novæ exultationis sibi offerret introspicere, accedens in medium, et ferventiori quam solitus fuerat spiritu proloquens, "Quid agitis," inquit, "fratres? "Quid timetis? Bonum illa semper actio finem merebitur, quæ "Deo auctore inspirata inchoatur. Dat nobis spem inveniendi, "Qui dedit voluntatem inquirendi. Atque ea quæ hucusque sine "difficultate peregimus, indicio sunt quid boni de hoc quod restat "agendum sperare debeamus. Nunquam tam prospere nobis "cessissent initia, si hæc usque finem perducere dispositio nollet "Divina. Nec unquam a Deo arguetur temeritatis, quod pro-"cedit ex animo devotionis. Neque enim ex contemptu vel ex "diffidentia sanctitatis ejus aggredimur illius explorare reliquias, "sed ut virtutum Dominus, ipse Rex Gloriæ, eo devotius ab om-"nibus glorificetur quo his temporibus sullimius ex Ejus virtute "miraculum monstretur. Proinde sacri hospitii videamus in-"riora, quatinus de hoc *Quod viderimus oculis nostris, quod per-"spexerimus, quod manus nostræ tractaverint,*[p] nobis constanter "attestantibus, nullum detrahentibus nobis relinquamus argu-"mentum, quo id, quod asserimus, deinceps possit esse ambi-"guum." Hac viri Deo devoti admonitione, fratres, resumpta fiducia, venerandum corpus de post altare, ubi eatenus jacuerat, in medium chori detulerunt, ubi largioris loci spatio quod res posceret licentius agere valerent. Ibi, ablato quod locellum obtexerat velamine, non statim ausi sunt aperire, sed, cum candelis circumeuntes, diligenter explorarunt, si per aliquas forte rimulas vel aliud quodlibet indicium, quid intrinsecus lateret deprehendere potuissent. Sed cum hæc agentibus nil certum pateret, tandem amoto, licet paventes, operculo, vident librum Evangeliorum ad caput supra tabulam positum, ipsamque tabulam tribus per transversum positis sustentari ligneolis, quæ ad

[o] In the margin of MS. Digby there is the following curious note: "Sic dicimus vulgariter *Nother kyn nor wyn*, id est neque cognatum neque amicum." The annotator says elsewhere that Aldunus means Vetus amicus.

[p] John i. 1.

mensuram loculi in latum et longum sese extendens, ea quæ subter erant universa cooperuerat. Habuerat autem immissos sibi duos, unum a capitis, et alterum a parte pedum ex ferro circulos, per quos hanc levantibus nullum difficultas faceret impedimentum. Certum erat sub manibus esse quod quærebant, sed, utrum id inter manus tractarent, incertum habebant. Inerat namque illis ex amore desiderium videndi atque tractandi quod dilexerant, sed ex conscientia peccatorum timor illos ne id auderent repellebat. Ita inter hæc duo dubii pendebant, ut pene nescirent quid magis vellent. Qui taliter titubantes, jussione Prioris et hortatione fratris prædicti roborati, tabulam quandoque levant; ablatoque quod proxime post tabulam sacras cooperuerat reliquias lintheamine, suavissimi odoris fragrantiam naribus trahunt. Et, ecce! beati patris venerabile corpus, scilicet fructum desiderii sui, reperiunt, quod, in dextro latere jacens, tota sui integritate artuumque flexibilitate dormientem magis repræsentabat quam mortuum. Quo viso, pavore percelluntur ingenti, et paulo longius recedentes, non ausi sunt quod patebat intueri miraculum. Cœperunt flexis crebro genibus pectora pugnis tundere, et, oculis cum manibus in altum levatis, sæpius inclamare "Miserere nostri, Domine, miserere." Interdum id quod singuli viderant, ac si non vidissent, sibi vicissim nuntiare. Prostrati toto tandem corpore, lacrimis ubertim fluentibus, septem Pœnitentialibus Psalmis supplicant Dominum, ne in furore Suo eos argueret, neque in ira Sua illos corriperet.[q] Quibus finitis, genibus ac manibus potius reptando quam pedibus incedendo accedentes, tot Sanctorum reliquias ibidem conspiciunt, ut eas illius loculi angustia capere non potuisset, nisi sanctum patris corpus in latus, ut dictum est, decumbens, largius eis una secum quiescendi spatium hinc et inde permitteret. Quas profecto reliquias, ut in veteribus libris legitur, constat esse caput gloriosi regis et martyris Oswaldi, ossa quoque venerabilium confessorum Christi ac sacerdotum, Aidani videlicet, et successorum ipsius venerandi patris Cuthberti, scilicet Eadberti, Eadfridi, et Ethelwoldi. Præterea et ossa Venerabilis Bedæ, qui Vitam beati Cuthberti dilucide conscripserat, una cum illius corpore hospitium quietis habuerant, quæ pariter continebat sacculus de lino. A quo autem de Giruum, ubi post illius obitum sepulta fuerant, illuc translata sint, alibi plane habetur scriptum. Qui enim ossa beati Boisili ipse et doctoris Bedæ sibi revelata in Dunelmensem ecclesiam comportavit, sed diversis in locis ejusdem ecclesiæ ea collocavit. Aliorum quoque Sanctorum plurimæ ibidem reliquiæ sunt

[q] Psalm vi. 2.

repertæ. Voluerunt ergo sacrum corpus patris ex latere versum resupinare; sed quia hoc, propter circumpositarum multitudinem reliquiarum, commode non poterant, placuit, ut, amoto inde paululum sancto corpore, Sanctorum reliquias pariter congregarent, eisque seorsum repositis, suam deinceps singulariter quietis sedem corpus incorruptum servaret. Sed cum ad illud contingendum manus formidarent apponere, orationibus fratris supranominati animos resumunt, ut, ad omne quod majores jusserint, prompti obedire assistant. Cum ergo duo quibus jussum fuerat, unus a capite, alter a pedibus venerabile corpus de loco suæ dormitionis elevarent, cœpit illud quasi adhuc vivens per medium inflecti, carneque solidum et ossibus pondere naturali ad ima demergi. Protinus ex præcepto accurrens tertius, brachiis complexus est medium, sicque illud, substratis tapetiis ac palliis, reverenter in pavimentum deponunt. Quæ tunc illorum omnium lacrimæ quas magnitudo effuderat lætitiæ! Quæ voces gratulationis! Quæ laudes exultationis, cum jam ante oculos hunc gratiæ cælestis haberent thesaurum, in cujus comparatione omne illis viluit aurum! Jam sibi nihil defuturum reputabant, cum inpræsentiarum quasi viventem cernerent, per quem sibi largitas Divina et præsentis vitæ subsidia et futuræ gaudia conferret. Interea, reliquiis Sanctorum ablatis, suam in thecam patris corpus reposuerunt, ventura nocte condignius illud ac decentius locaturi, pro eo quod, jam tunc instante hora Nocturnæ Laudis, angustia temporis non patiebatur eos his diutius immorari. Quapropter decantato humili voce, *Te Deum laudamus*, corpus sanctum illo unde transtulerant, in Psalmis jubilantes Domino, retulerunt. Cum autem mane facto in cœtu fratrum collecto memoriam facerent mirabilium Dei, illi ex novitate rei primo in quendam quasi stuporem versi, postea magis lacrimis quam vocibus conceptum ex hoc suæ mentis gaudium sunt attestati, flexisque in terram genibus, gratias reddiderunt Jhesu Christo, Qui eis et cujus meriti esset quem patronum habebant ostendere, et quid sibi de meritis illius sperare potuissent dignatus sit edocere. At episcopus, non facile his accommodans fidem, omnino judicabat incredibile, corpus, quamlibet sanctum, tamen humanum, per tantum temporis, id est per quadringentos, decem et octo annos, ab omni corruptionis labe intactum perdurare. Cui vix aliquando satisfacere illi jurejurando poterant, qui etiam non jurando non verum dicere crimen ducebant. Nocte vero secuta idem qui ante affuerant fratres, in spiritu humilitatis et in animo contrito delatum rursus in medium chori venerabile corpus, super pallia per pavimentum strata et tapetia deponunt, quod primo extrinsecus pretiosi generis pallium, et post hoc ex purpura dalmatica, deinde lintheamina obvolverant; quæ omnia sine ulla corruptionis macula, integra et candida priscam sui novitatem reservabant. Casula autem, quam per undecim annos habuerat in sepulcro, jam a fratribus tunc inde ablata, alibi pro ostendendo incorruptionis signo nunc servatur in ecclesia. Cum ergo nervis solidum et ex integro incorruptum corpus visu et manibus tractando, levando, ac deponendo certo percepissent, atque sollemni apparatu curatum vidissent, ad ea quibus ante fuerat involutum ex abundanti, pallium quod cæteris pretiosius in ecclesia poterat inveniri, et subtilissimam superaddiderunt sindonem. Quibus magna cum diligentia circumdatum, in suæ quietis placidæ habitaculum cum multa precum et multa dulcium lacrimarum devotione reposuerunt. Sed et alia, sicut fuerant inventa cum illo, recondiderunt, pectinem scilicet eburneum et forpices, suæ adhuc novitatis gratiam retinentes; et, quæ sacerdotem decebant, altare videlicet argenteum, et corporalia, et cum patena calicem, parvum quidem sed materia et opere pretiosum; cujus inferior pars figura leonis ex auro purissimo gestat dorso lapidem onichinum arte pulcherrima cavatum, qui ex studio artificis ita inhæret leoni, ut manu facile possit in gyrum verti, nec tamen auferri. Porro reliquiarum sanctarum quas ejusdem loculi cum illo incluserat hospitium, solum caput beati regis Oswaldi juxta caput gloriosi pontificis, sicut et ante fuerat, locarunt. Nam cæteræ, sicut prædictum est, inde elatæ, alibi sollemniter compositæ in ecclesia, celebriter reservantur reliquiæ. Clauso ergo in suam thecam beati patris corpore, eam panno ex lino grossiore, quem totum cera infuderat, undique circumdatam, usque post altare, ubi prius requieverat, retulerunt, Dominum virtutum benedicentes in operibus Suis; Qui facit mirabilia solus; Cujus magna opera exquisita in omnes voluntates Ejus.[r] Interea promulgato longe lateque venturæ Translationis die, ingens fit undecumque Dunelmum usque populorum concursus; sicut diversæ dignitatis et ætatis, ita et professionis, sæcularis videlicet vitæ et spiritualis, personæ perplures, qui, agnito incorrupti tam longo tempore corporis miraculo, plurimum in Domino lætantur; Eique laudis et gratiarum actione reddita, sua exultant tempora tantæ virtutis ostensione visitari. Inter hos quidam, ex numero abbatum qui advenerant, in his quæ facta fuerant injuriam sibi calumniabatur illatam; arguens improvidæ temeritatis fratres ecclesiæ, qui, se inconsulto nec adhibito, tale tamque insolitum opus per se ausi fuissent aggredi. Oportere namque aiebat se, cum vicinus esset, futurum hujus facti participem advocari; cujus assertione testimonium veritatis pos-

[r] An adaptation from several passages in the Psalms.

set comprobari. Fratres namque qui his secretis nullum ex alia ecclesia testem voluerant assistere, verisimile esse dixit, non tam verum de suo Sancto dicere, quam fingere. Unde, ait, ratio videtur exposcere tam incredibilis rei veritatem etiam ab aliis indagandam, ut populo qui tam frequens accurrit, id nostro testimonio affirmare possimus, quod etiam nos ipsi oculis perspeximus. Hæc in auribus illorum qui cum eo venerant sæpius replicans, animos quorumdam in suum inclinavit assensum. Jam denunciata Translationis dies instabat, et, calumnia abbatis in conventum fratrum delata, gravi mentes illorum concutiuntur scandalo; quo et mendacii notabantur infamia, et iteranda sancti corporis appetebatur revelatio, quam nec extraneis permittere, nec ipsi ulterius ausi sunt iterare. Fit ergo partium magna contentio, abbate obtendente solam fratrum ipsius ecclesiæ non esse admittendam de suo Sancto attestationem; fratribus ex suspecta fide sua confusis et reclamantibus, vel loci desolationem vel suam de loco expulsionem eum moliri; qui cum illorum cum juramento testimonium quasi fictum repellat, sacrilegos eos et omnibus detestandos judicat. "Quapropter absit," inquiunt, "ut ad sacra contuenda huic concedatur aditus, quo agente in suspicionem gravis mendacii pervenimus. Qui enim heri nobiscum exultantes *Gloria in excelsis Deo* cantaverant, hodie nonnulli eorum, calumniante abbate, ex mendacio nos suspectos habent." His ita contendentibus, cum contentioni nullus potuisset finis imponi, utriusque partis se mediatorem interposuit venerabilis memoriæ Radulfus, tunc quidem abbas Sagiensis monasterii, sed postea Cantuariorum archiepiscopus.[s] Is, cum multæ mansuetudinis esset et religionis, in Scripturis quoque Sanctis nobiliter eruditus, cupiens inter dissidentes reformare pacem, "Verum est," ait, quod Scriptura dicit, '*In ore duorum vel trium testium stabit omne verbum*;'[t] quanto magis in ore plurimorum et tam probabilium, ut de illorum testimonio nulla quemquam ratio permittat dubitare. Credimus plane Divinæ virtutis opus vobis in beati Cuthberti corpore revelatum; credimus, inquam, propter quod '*Laudem Domini loquitur os meum, et benedicit anima mea Domino*.'[u] Cum autem tanta sit hujus miraculi evidentia, temerarius forte videbor, si vobis ostensam corporis Sancti incorruptionem, etiam nobis ostendendam postulavero. Et tamen in hac postulatione nec temerarius videri debeo nec superfluus, quia cum '*Perfecta caritas foras*

[s] Radulfus was consecrated bishop of Rochester in 1108, translated to Canterbury in 1114, and died Sept. 19th, 1122. From the expression here made use of, "venerabilis memoriæ," this passage must have been written after his death.

[t] Deut. xvii. 6. [u] Tob. xiii. 19.

"*mittat timorem*,"[v] id ex multa caritate postulandum præsumo, "quod ex dilectione præsumendum postulo, adjuvat preces "nostras, etiam quæ inpræsentiarum accidit causa, ista scilicet "fratris nostri abbatis dubietas, quæ nisi et aliorum testimonio "a corde illius fuerit exclusa, justas contra vos sibi videbitur "movisse calumnias: et in has in futurum plures sibi contrahet "consentaneos. Sed, ut video, ex Dei providentia facta est illi "hæc dubitatio, ut unde vos æstimatis grave fieri scandalum; "inde, ordinante Deo, cumulatior huic loco proveniet gloria. "Nam prosequente preces nostras gratiæ vestræ favore, cum jam "sicut audivimus, ita etiam nos ipsi viderimus, tanto citius "obmutescet obtrectantium calumnia, quanto et vestrum et "nostrum testimonium eadem corroboraverit experientia. Tan- "toque latius in beato Cuthberto gloria Dei prædicabitur, quanto "magis nos, qui hanc oculis probavimus, per diversas longius "partes hinc remeantes dispersi, ea omnibus pandere institeri- "mus." His venerandi abbatis precibus jam episcopus præbuisset assensum, nisi fratribus videretur non statim ei consentiendum, qui grave sibi ex judicio Dei periculum imminere formidabant, si sanctum corpus denuo cuiquam ostendendum inconsulte per- mitterent. Sed prudentium amicorum flexi consilio, tandem, licet difficillime, in hoc consentiunt, ut, amoto abbate qui eis non credendum censuerat, humilis ac religiosus petitor cum aliis qui digni viderentur, ad novam miraculi inspectionem ad- mittatur. Quandoque tamen a consulentibus persuasum est eis, ut etiam illum quam maxime huic rei interesse concederent, qui ipsorum testimonii dubius dubitare et alios fecerat, quatenus ejus miraculi contemplator assisteret, quod eis attestantibus ipse credere noluisset. Taliter contentione sedata, ducente Priore, ingrediuntur oratorium, albis induti, prædictus abbas Sagiensis, et Ricardus abbas monasterii S. Albani, et Stephanus abbas S. Mariæ Eboraci, et Hugo abbas S. Germani in Selebi. Post quos Alexander frater regis Scottorum Ædgari, paulo post ejusdem fratris sui futurus in regnum successor, et Guillelmus tunc Dunelmensis episcopi clericus, sed post sæpedictum Ra- dulfum ecclesiæ Cantuariensis archiepiscopus; deinde et alii qui designati fuerant religiosæ vitæ, tam monachi quam clerici, numero quadraginta, sequuntur. Præterea et plures ejusdem ecclesiæ fratres, nam cæteri episcopo assistebant, jam tunc in ecclesia altare dedicanti. Præmissa itaque suppliciter ab omni- bus oratione, sanctum corpus defertur in chorum, ubi, loculo qui prius concluserant a fratribus patefacto, Prior, elata manu, gravi prohibuit interdicto, ne vel ad corpus vel ad aliquid eorum

[v] 1 John iv. 18.

quæ circa illud fuerant contingendum quisquam præter abbatem de Sagio manu admoveret. Cæteros jubet propius assistere, et visu potius quam contactu veritatem rei experiendo capere: fratres quoque monasterii præcepit indesinenter adesse et vigilanti semper obtutu observare, ne vel particulam fili indumentorum quæ corpus obvolverant, ullo modo aliquis auferret. Fiunt quæ jussa fuerant. Memoratus abbas, uno ejusdem ecclesiæ fratre se juvante, involuta explicans vestimenta circa venerandum caput, utraque illud manu cunctis aspicientibus paululum erexit, et in diversas reflectendo partes integra omnibus juncturis colli compage reliquo id corpori cohærere invenit. Deinde, manu admota, firmius aurem trahens et retrahens, et post hoc alias quoque corporis partes manu perscrutante explorans, solidum nervis et ossibus, cum carnis mollitie repperit corpus. Id etiam per caput tenendo concutiens, adeo in sublime erexit, ut in habitaculo suæ quietis pene sedere visum fuerit. Et ne quid diligentiæ inquirentis deesset, circa pedes quoque et crura eandem studuit experiri integritatem. Fuerant autem nonnulli qui hoc aliquanto diutius intueri paventes, positis super oculos manibus exclamarent eum plusquam res postularet veritatis exequi probationem, cujus tam evidenter ipse tenuisset certitudinem. Cum ergo incorruptionis miraculum satis superque pius inquisitor explorasset, elevata in medium voce proclamavit, "Ecce!" inquiens, "fratres, hoc corpus jacet hic quidem exanime, sed ita sanum "et integrum, sicut ea die qua, cælestia petens, id sancta "reliquerat anima." Diligenter deinde compositis, sicut ante fuerant, omnibus, fratres monasterii veraces et fide digni ab omnibus prædicantur; et ille qui eis non credendum judicaverat, simul cum aliis hoc, quod ante abnuerat, credendum, sive volens sive nolens, affirmabat. Jamque *Te Deum Laudamus* exultantibus cunctis solemniter decantato, omnibusque quæ res poposcerat decenter dispositis, corpus patris humeris portantium excipitur, et in honorem Omnipotentis Dei cantantium voces hymnis late concrepant cælestibus. Præcedentibus cum aliorum reliquiis Sanctorum scriniis, cum ad ultimum venerabile beati Cuthberti corpus cum festivioris obsequii apparatu efferretur ostio, frequens qui foris exspectaverat populus, in lacrimas præ gaudio resolutus, totus obviam ruit, ut portitores sancti corporis vix in tanta constipatione procedere potuissent, et tanto clamore commixtim orantium, exultantium, et exultando flentium, voces premerentur cantantium. Circumeuntes autem novam extrinsecus ecclesiam, ad orientalem ejus plagam stationem fecerunt, ubi, sermonem faciente episcopo, astabant et ipsi, qui miraculum incorruptionis inventæ, quæ jam per quadringentos decem et octo annos in humano corpore perduraverat, se et vidisse et contrectasse omnibus qui advenerant populis pandebant. Nova illi exultatione ad agendas Deo gratias accenduntur qui suæ devotionem mentis dignatus est remunerare tanta gratiæ cælestis manifestatione. Jam dies in altum processerat et episcopus, multa quæ præsentis negotii non postulaverat causa interserens, longioris multos sermonis fecerat tædere. Sed cum tanta esset cæli serenitas ut nullum venturæ puviæ signum in aëre appareret, tanta cœperunt inundatione subito imbres ruere, ut confestim interrupto sermone loculum sancti corporis fratres corriperent, et ecclesiæ concite inferre festinarent. Quo illato, pluvia continuo cessavit, ut hinc nimirum daretur intelligi, Deo non esse placitum famuli sui sacrum corpus aliquanto diutius extra sancta loca detineri. Sed et hoc nullatenus silentio prætereundum videtur, quod cum tanta esset effusio pluviæ inundantis, non tamen vel ornamenta ecclesiæ, quæ tunc omnia fuerant exposita, vel vestes quorumlibet, qui tunc cultius procedebant, ullam ex pluvia vel decoris sui vel usus contraxerint læsionem. Collocato ergo ubi decenter paratum fuerat corpore beati pontificis, resultante laudibus Dei ecclesia, sollemnis celebratur missa, peractisque in salutem fidelium sacro-sanctis mysteriis, *ad propria remearunt cum gaudio, glorificantes et laudantes Deum in omnibus quæ viderant et audierant.*[v] Facta est hæc incorrupti corporis manifestatio sive Translatio post annos depositionis ejus quadringentos decem et octo, et quinque menses, et duodecim dies: hoc est anno ab incarnatione Domini millesimo centesimo quarto, qui est quintus annus regni Henrici; episcopatus vero Rannulfi sextus. Ab origine vero mundi fuerant tunc anni transacti sex millia trecenti tres.

XIX.

Quomodo, ipso die Translationis ejus, tactu loculi corporis ipsius, abbas devotus ab infirmitate diutina manus suæ sit curatus.

Venerat inter alios supradictos abbas monasterii Sancti Albani,[w] suprascriptæ Translationis minister devotus, qui beatum Cuthbertum multo semper excoluit amore, ejusque sepulcrum sæpius fuerat solitus invisere. Is per multum temporis sinistræ manus gravi tenebatur incommodo, ut nec missas celebrare, nec aliud quippiam operis facile sine alterius auxilio posset peragere. Cui medicorum quidem sedula aderat sollicitudo, sed nullius industria quicquam remedii poterat conferre. Itaque collecto

[v] S. Luke ii. 20.
[w] In MSS. Arundel and Gale, the abbat's name, Ricardus, is inserted.

fratrum cætu, ante horam Translationis humiliter ille toto prostratus corpore petiit, ut compatiens sibi fraterna caritas a beato Cuthberto postularet, quatinus suo ipse interventu, a Salvatore omnium salutis ei donum impetraret. Annuit petenti prompta fratrum devotio, et oratione indicta precabantur ut non sua peccata sed fidem petentis aspiceret, et ad gloriam nominis Dei a Deo gratiam ei sanitatis obtineret. Auditi sunt et exauditi utrique; ille per fidem, *Omnia enim possibilia credenti*;[x] illi per caritatem, quæ quanto magis inclinatur proximo tanto magis appropinquat Deo. Peracta, ut supradictum est, sollemni processione, loculus incorrupti corporis sullimius post altare elevandus fuerat super lapidem, quem gratia tanti oneris sustinendi, diligenter manu artificum præparatum, novem pro sui magnitudine altius a terra sustentant columnæ. Ascendit ergo lapidem sæpe-memoratus Prior, ubi, cum ad suscipiendum a portantibus corpus indigeret adjutorio, conversus ad abbatem. "Domine," inquit, "abbas, ascende citius et adjuva me." Ascendit ille, et, oblitus infirmitatis, thecam sancti corporis suscipiendo et recondendo contingens cooperator insistebat studiosus. Quam cum suo in loco reposuissent, tunc demum ad memoriam rediit manus infirma: sed hanc ita firmam sensit ac si in illa nihil unquam molestiæ pertulerit; factumque in se miraculum facili digitorum inflexione, quam ante non poterat, tota die jactando pandere non cessavit. Quo facto in se beneficio, ad laudandum Deum, et ad mirandam beati Cuthberti sanctitatem multorum animos sustulit; domumque reversus, continuo in honorem sancti Confessoris oratorio constructo, tanto eum devotius deinceps excoluit, quanto illius opem sibi celerius adesse sensit.

XX.

Quomodo quidam pro furto fili ablati de loculo codicis Sancti Cuthberti sit punitus ac postea pænitens reparatus.

Legitur in Vita beati Cuthberti[y] quod adolescens ipse adhuc in monasterio, cum beati Boysili dictis pariter et exemplis Dei servitio informaretur, ab eodem ægrotante et jam jamque ascensuro cælestia Evangelium Sancti Johannis didicerit, quod in codice septem quaternionum septem diebus invicem simpliciter conferendo compleverit. Hunc codicem, cum pro merito utriusque, videlicet docentis et discentis, priscæ adhuc novitatis reti-

[x] S. Mark ix. 23.
[y] See the Life by Beda, cap. viii.

neat gratiam, inter alias sacræ venerationis reliquias honesto hæc, scilicet Dunelmensis, ecclesia reservat loco. Est autem huic in quo ponitur ex pelle rubricata in modum peræ loculus, habens ex serico, quod jam vetustas dissolvit in fila, suspendiculum quo per colla, ut dicitur, Sanctorum, videlicet beati magistri et post eum discipuli sui pii hæredis, liber circumferebatur pendulus. Hunc episcopus inter sermonem quem in Translatione, ut supradictum est, ad populum faciebat, cum elata manu omnibus ostenderet, portitore interim paulo negligentius peram vacuam inter compressas turbas tenente, quidam ex officialibus episcopi filum de suspendiculo furatus inter caligas et calciamenta sibi abscondit; ibique donec iret cubitum irreverenter tale servavit furtum. Nocte vero secuta tam gravi cruris ipsius, cui filum illud fuerat appositum, torquebatur dolore, ut non solum nullam dormiendo posset habere quietem, verum etiam cum augmento doloris tumore groscescente cruris, non jam alium hujus molestiæ finem putaret eventurum quam mortem. Tremens ergo ac pavens accersiri fecit presbiterum, cui temerariæ præsumptionis confitens reatum, id consilii accepit ab illo ut sanctarum reliquiarum quam indigne tulerat portione restituta, fratrum in ecclesia sibi reformaret gratiam; quorum intercessione beatus Confessor placatus, veniam sibi stulti ausus impetraret; hocque modo Deo sibi propitio sanitatem recipere valeret. Annuit ille salubri consilio, baculoque ac ministris sustentatus perducitur ad Priorem, et filum quod furtim abstulerat coram reddidit, pœnitendo satisfaciens et lacrimis pro se apud Sanctum Cuthbertum orari, cujus meritis et temeritatis perpetratæ veniam et sanitatis mereretur gratiam. Cui Prior, "Quem," inquit, "offendisti, ei reconciliare, reposito super ejus "sepulcrum quod abstulisti." At ille, per se non audens illuc accedere, comitantibus quandoque fratribus adducitur, ubi, eis pariter orantibus, dolor omnis infirmanti mitescere, et inflatio deformis cœpit detumescere. Nec multo post, sanitate ad perfectum redintegrata, unde corpus illius ad tempus a salute deficiebat, inde animus ad suam salutem vires reparabat, experimento tenens illud *Stulto flagellato, insipiens sapientior erit.*[1]

XXI.

Qualiter juvenis oppressus sub ingenti pondere signi meritis beati Cuthberti illæsus evaserit.

Elapso dehinc tempore memoratus Prior, ductus devotione beati patris Cuthberti, ad honorem ecclesiæ quam suo illustrat

[1] Prov. xix. 25.

corpore, campanam ingentis ponderis fieri præceperat, quam Lundoniæ paratam Dunelmum adduci oporteret. Igitur in officina conflatoria vehiculo imposita magnis exinde modo juvenum, modo boum, modo pariter omnium trahebatur viribus. Porro vehiculum, lignis licet fortibus et arte diligenter compositis adaptatum fuisset, ad tantæ tamen gravedinis molem sustinendam minus sufficiebat. Crebro namque dissolutis compagibus robur pene totum dissiluit. Quod magna cum difficultate quoquo modo reparatum magnum itinerantibus impedimentum attulit. Per planitiem viarum aliquantisper liber erat transitus; ubi vero se in altum terra sustulerat, gravis in ascensu, gravior in descensu cum ingenti timore difficultas, ne scilicet ex alto vel recurrendo vel proruendo campana impetu sui et trahentium faceret læsionem. Aderat frater e monasterio fidelis, cui magna curæ sollertis incumbebat diligentia, ut quoniam infusio campanæ ad votum cesserat, eam salvo incolumem conductu ad beatum Cuthbertum afferret. Qui difficultate hujuscemodi transvectionis sæpe tædio affectus, ex recordatione beati patris resumptis viribus respirabat, sperans indubie illum in rebus difficilibus solito sibi more famulantibus affuturum. Interea cum boum viginti duorum toto campana traheretur conamine, quidam improvidæ temeritatis juvenis, cum quippiam in anterioribus curriculi emendaret, stridens hunc rota valido impetu arripiens per tunicam quæ illi pedes usque longa pertrahebatur, et retinens, pronum in terram stravit, eumque a renibus usque humerum et brachium conquassando percurrens, exanimem, ut putabatur, reliquit. Quis enim nisi mortuum crederet quem sub tantæ molis oppressum machina, sine voce, sine motu, sine sensu jacentem videret? Videns frater auxiliatorem laboris mortuum, præ angustia cordis spiritu ei pene deficiente, quid ageret, quo se verteret nesciebat. Exclamans ergo cum ingenti gemitu, "O, Sancte," inquit, "Cuthberte, ubi "es? Quid agis? Hanc tibi devotis vicem rependis? Non "te talem nunc invenimus qualem sæpe experiendo didicimus." Nec plura impediente gemitu locutus, juvenem paululum a terra jussit erigi. Qui, redeunte paulatim spiritu, inter manus tenentium sedens, "O," inquit, "quam gravis est hæc campana!" Interrogatus a fratre an vivere posset, nihil se sentire fatebatur. Exuta dehinc tunica ut videret an ossa cohærerent ossibus, invenit hominem, quem omnibus contritum membris suspicabatur, non solum ossibus et artuum compagibus integris, sed etiam carne illæsa, nullum prorsus habere signum læsionis: sola quæ proxima carni adhæserat camisia, illo tantum in loco ubi se fervens rotæ currentis præcipitaverat impetus, detrita videbatur et interrupta; tunica tamen quæ forinsecus erat nullum suæ integritatis damnum præferente. Statutus dehinc in pedibus cum equo subvehi non posset, baculo cœpit nutante gressu attemptare incessum, atque ita progrediendo, depulsa paulatim membrorum tabetudine, vultu vivacior, totoque fit corpore vegetior. Post modicum solidiori incessu sine adminiculo sustentantis baculi longiuscule procedens, recepto tandem ad integrum omnium vigore membrorum, sociis laboris atque itineris sese alacris adjutor adjunxit, omnino laborans ne campanæ, quæ sibi opprimendo nocuerat, aliquid forte in ducendo nocivum accideret. Tunc frater ex tam insperata rei mutatione conversus in gaudium, multo uberius tantum Dei beneficium experiendo exultat quam prius per periculum desperando doluerat. Intellexit namque Dei auxilium per beati Cuthberti merita celeriter adesse, ubi humana virtus et industria nil poterat prodesse. Fit itaque lætus ex jam facta miraculi novitate; fit etiam securus de itineris quod supererat prosperitate. Reddita ergo Omnipotenti Deo gratiarum actione, cœpto itinere proficiscitur, habens gaudentem comitem viæ quem ad inopinatam salutem a summo receperat periculo vitæ; qui ipsa die a loco ubi in confinium mortis pervenit, decem miliaria corpore integer et viribus pedes ipse peregit. Sponte namque se ad laborem ingerens, campanam longo usque Dunelmum itinere comitatur, ubi ad sui sepulcrum ereptoris suppliciter prostratus, Salvatori omnium Christo gratias reddidit, Qui eum per interventum Sui sancti Confessoris, cum in mortem cecidit, ad vitam revocavit.

DE PRIMO SAXONUM ADVENTU,

SIVE DE EORUMDEM REGIBUS LIBELLUS.[a]

Voden[b] genuit Vectam, qui genuit Wittam, qui genuit Wichtgils, qui genuit Horsam et Hengest.

Voden genuit Feolthulgeat, qui genuit Waga, qui genuit Wichtleig, qui genuit Wermundum, qui genuit Offam, qui genuit Ongeltheon, qui genuit Edmerum, qui genuit Icel, qui genuit Cnibbam, qui genuit Kinewaldum, qui genuit Crydam, qui genuit Pibbam, qui genuit Pendam.

Voden genuit Beldeig, qui genuit Brond, qui genuit Freothegarum, qui genuit Freowinum, qui genuit Wittam, qui genuit Gewisse, qui genuit Eslam, qui genuit Elesam, qui genuit Cerdic.

Voden genuit Beldeig, qui genuit Brond, qui genuit Benoc, qui genuit Aloc, qui genuit Angenwiti, qui genuit Ingenui, qui genuit Esam, qui genuit Eoppam, qui genuit Idam, a quo reges Northanhymbrorum ceperunt originem.

[a] This title is taken from the colophon at the end of the work in MS. Cott. Caligula, A. viii. The rubric at the commencement, which attributes the authorship to Symeon of Durham, is in a hand of the seventeenth century, probably that of Sir Robert Cotton, who has written his own name on the same page; and is as follows, "Chronicon Symeonis, monachi Dunelmensis, de primis Angliæ gentis regibus; sive a primo Saxonum adventu, h. e. ab anno 449 ad annum 1119, cum nominibus archiepiscoporum Cantuar. et Eborac., et episcoporum Dunelmensium." In this MS., as well as in Domitian viii., and the MS. in Magdalen College Library, 53, 11, the Anglo-Saxon narrative is preceded by a long extract from Nennius, which is here omitted. A portion of it is also in the Durham MS. B., ii., 35.

[b] Respecting the arrangement of these genealogies, see the account in the Preface, from Mr. Walbran's notes. The Magdalen MS. differs from MS. Caligula in the spelling of some of the proper names. In each case the spelling has been adopted which approaches most closely to other authentic lists. Vecta in C. is Ve*t*ta in M., Ve*h*ta in Florence. Wichtgils is spelt without the final *s* in C. Ongeltheo*n* in C. is Ongletheo*u* in M.: in Florence it is Angengeat. Edmer in C. is E*o*dmer in M. Icel in M. is Ic*h*el in C. *P*ibba is in both erro-

Voden genuit Wegdam, qui genuit Sigegarum, qui genuit Sweabdeegum, qui genuit Sigegeat, qui genuit Scabaldum, qui genuit Seafugel, qui genuit Westerfalene, qui genuit Wigilf, qui genuit Vscfrea, qui genuit Yffa, qui genuit Ella.

Prænotata serie generationum, ex qua primi Anglici generis reges prodierant, subnotatur, qui, et ubi, et quoto incarnationis Dominicæ anno regnaverint, post illorum adventum in Brytanniam.

Anno ab incarnatione Domini cccc^{mo}xl^{o}ix^{o},[c] Anglorum, sive Saxonum, gens, invitata a rege Wurtigerno, tribus longis navibus Brytanniam advehitur, apud locum qui dicitur Ypwinesfleot, quasi pro patria pugnatura, re autem vera hanc expugnatura suscepit. Advenerat autem de tribus Germaniæ populis fortioribus, id est Saxonibus, Anglis, Jutis. De Jutarum origine sunt Cantuarii et Vectuarii; hoc est, ea gens quæ Vectam tenet insulam; et ea gens quæ usque hodie in provincia Occidentalium Saxonum, Jutarum natio nominatur, posita contra insulam Vectam. De Saxonibus, id est, ea regione quæ nunc Antiquorum Saxonum cognominatur, venere Orientales Saxones, Meridiani Saxones, Occidui Saxones. Porro de Anglis, hoc est, de illa patria quæ Angulus dicitur, et ab eo tempore manere usque hodie desertus inter provincias Jutarum et Saxonum perhibetur, Orientales Angli, Mediterranei Angli, Merci, tota Northanhimbrorum progenies, cæterique populi Anglorum sunt exorti. Duces eorum fuerunt Hengest et Horsa. Deinde et alii duces advenerunt, qui quas sibi sedes occupaverint, subter annotatur.

DE REGIBUS CANCIÆ.[d]

Primus rex Anglorum, Hengest, qui regnavit xxiiij annis. Post quem filius ejus Oisic xxiiij annis. Post hunc regnavit Octa. Huic in regnum successit Eormenric. Cui filius Eathel-

neously *B*ibba. Beldei*g* in C. wants the final *g*. Fre*othe*gar and Fre*ow*ine in C. are Fre*de*gar and Fre*auv*ene in M. Ele*s*a in M. is Ele*i*a in C. Us*c*frea in M. is Us*e*frea in C.; *Y*ffa in C. is *I*ffa in M. *W*itta, *W*aga, and *W*ermund have the initial v for w in M. Northanh*y*mbri is here spelt Northanh*i*mbri, but elsewhere, throughout, Northanh*u*mbri in M. Occasionally another form, Northanhymbrenses, is used in C., and in these places also Northanhumbri occurs in M.

[c] In the Magdalen MS. Brytanniam, in this section and elsewhere throughout the work, is spelt Br*i*ttanniam; Jutæ and Jutarum have a second *t*, and Ypwinesfleot has a second *p*. Hengest in this and the following section is spelt Hingest.

[d] The Magdalen MS. has no rubric to this section. Here, as elsewhere in the narrative, there are frequent alterations in the arrangement of sentences, and occasional substitutions of one word for another of similar significance, as *post hoc* for *dehinc*, *hunc* for *illum*, *ejus* for *suum*, *et* for *ac*, and such like, but in no case is the sense affected, except occasionally by the alteration of numerals,

bertus successit, qui et primus regum Canciæ extitit Christianus, annis liiij regnavit. Post quem filius ejus Eadbaldus regnavit. Dehinc Erconbertus, frater ejus, xxiiij annis regnavit. Post illum filius ejus Ecgbertus ix annis. Cui frater suus Hlothere successit, xij annis. Post illum Edricus, filius Egberti regis, j anno ac dimidio.[e] Post quem Wichtredus regnavit, filius Egberti, xxxiiij et semianno. Qui moriens, tres filios Eathelbertum, Eadbertum et Alricum reliquit hæredes. Quorum Eathelbertus post patrem regnavit, et Eadbertus in locum fratris successit. Hunc Eadbertum, vastata Cancia, rex Merciorum Kinewulf cepit; et, effossis oculis ejus ac præcisis manibus, regnum Cantuariorum suo adjecit. Deinde ibidem regnavit Cuthred. Post hunc Baldredus rex erat Cantuariorum. Sed hunc Egbertus, rex Occidentalium Saxonum, misso filio cum multa manu, ultra Tamisiam pepulit; moxque Cantuarii, totaque Suthrige, Suthseaxa quoque et Eastseaxa sponte se conferunt ad regem Occidentalium Saxonum: atque ab illo tempore ita regnum Canciæ cessit sub ditione regum Occidentalium Saxonum.

DE REGIBUS ORIENTALIUM ANGLORUM.[f]

Reoduuald. Eorpwald filius ejus. Sigbertus frater illius, bonus ac religiosus monachus vitam terminavit. Egric, cognatus ejus. Anna filius Eani, pater Sanctæ Etheldrithæ, qui occisus est a Penda duce Merciorum. Eathelhere frater Annæ

and this appears to be accidental. In all cases it is pointed out in the notes. On the other hand, the Magdalen MS. furnishes several readings, which restore sense to vitiated passages which are quite unintelligible in MS. Caligula.

With regard to the spelling of names beginning with *Ea* and *Eo* in C., as *Ea*thelbert, *Eo*rconbert, M. has very generally Æ and Œ, sometimes A or E, as *A*thelred and *E*lfleda for *Ea*thelred and *Ea*lfleda in C. In such names as Ea*th*elbert, again, M. has very generally *d* for *th*, but not invariably, even when the same name recurs within a few lines. Words beginning with *Eg* in C. are frequently written *Ecg* in M., as E*cg*bert or E*cg*bricht for Egbert. In Suths*ea*xa, Wests*ea*xa, and similar words, in the middle of which *ea* occur in conjunction, *a* is generally omitted in M. In spelling words such as Kinewulf, Ethelwulf, etc., C. generally employs *wu*, M. generally *w* only, but the practice of neither is uniform. In this section O*i*sic in M. is O*r*sic in C.; and in this section, and generally throughout, Can*t*ia in M. is Can*ci*a in C. As regards the difference of numerals, the reign of Eathelbert in this section is 24 years in C., 23 years in M. The reign of Hengist in M. is 23 years.

[e] Wallingford copies the Kentish genealogy to this point.

[f] The Magdalen MS. has no rubric here. In MS. Caligula, *Saxonum* is written instead of *Anglorum*, and the genealogies of East Anglia and Essex are both placed under it without any separation, and are so copied by Wallingford. Reodwald is written by mistake Trodwald in MS. Caligula, and is corrected from MS. Magd. The latter has E*o*gric for Egric, *Æd*heldri*dæ* for *Eth*eldri*th*æ, *Æ*thelwold for *Ea*thelwold, *E*dmundus for *Ea*dmundus, Guthu*m* for Guthu*n*, *Æd*elstano for Aethelstano.

regis. Eathelwold frater. Aldulf, filius sororis Hyldæ, nomine Hereswith. Eadmundus. Guthun, qui ex pagano conversus ad fidem a rege Eathelstano suceptus de fonte baptismatis, post occisionem Eadmundi in East Anglia regnavit, donante rege Eathelstano.

REGES ORIENTALIUM SAXONUM.[g]

Ethelbertus, qui et Cantuariorum rex, fecerat ecclesiam Sancti Pauli Lundoniæ. Sigebertus, baptizatus a Finano episcopo. Swithelmus. Sibbi, postea monachus. Sigheardus; et frater ejus, Swefredus, filii Sibbi. Swebertus.

DE REGIBUS MERCIORUM.[h]

Penda filius Pibbæ regnavit xix annis.[i] Quo in bello occiso, interfector ejus Oswi, rex Northanhymbrorum, tenuit regnum Merciorum tribus annis. Peada filius Pendæ ibidem regnavit, sed brevi tempore; sed Wuferi filius Pendæ, rebellans contra Oswium, legitimum recepit regnum. Cui filius ejus Ethelredus succedens, regnavit xxix annis. Iste filiam regis Oswi, Ostridam, duxerat uxorem. Tandem, relicto regno, monachus vitam finivit: sepultus est in Bardanige.[j] Post quem Coenredus regnavit. Qui, regno relicto, Romæ factus monachus obiit. Cui successit in regnum Ceolred filius Eathelredi. Post hunc regnavit super Merciam Eathelbaldus xxxix annis. Cui armis valde strenuo pene omnes provinciæ australes, ad confinium usque Humbræ fluminis, cum suis regibus subjectæ fuerunt. Quo interfecto, Bernredus loco illius regnavit. Post quem Offa, potentissimus rex, regnavit xxxix annis. Cui filius suus Egred succedens, parvo tempore regnavit. Deinde Kynewulf regnavit; qui, ut antedictum est, Eadberto, Cantuariorum rege, capto, Canciam sibi subegit. Hic Kynewulfus, vel Koenwulfus, est pater Kenelmi martyris, ut invenitur. Post Koenwulfum tenuit

[g] This rubric is from the Magdalen MS. In that MS. the sections are differently arranged. After the East Anglian kings come the archbishops, then the kings of Mercia, of the East Saxons, the bishops of Durham, and kings of Wessex. The arrangement of MS. Caligula is followed throughout in the text. *Eth*elbertus in this section, is written *Æd*elbertus in the Magdalen MS.

[h] Sibbæ in MS. Caligula; Bibbæ in the Magdalen MS. This name is variously written Wibba and Pibba, or, more frequently, Wybba and Pybba. In this section the Magdalen MS. has Osw*iu* for Osw*i*, *Æ*thelredus for *E*thelredus, *Æ*thelredi for *Ea*theldredi, K*o*ne*w*lf, K*oe*nwlf, K*oi*newlf for K*y*new*u*lf and K*oe*nw*u*lf, Coel*w*lfus for C*e*lw*u*lfus, Burnwlf for Burnulf, Winglaf for Wiglaf, Bur*r*edus for Bur*thr*edus, Judecan for Ludecan.

[i] The Magdalen MS. gives the length of this reign thirty years.

[j] Wallingford copies the genealogy of the kings of Mercia to this point.

regnum Merciorum Celwulfus duobus annis. Deinde Bernulf regnum illud tenuit, sed ab East Anglis occisus interiit. Cui successit Ludecan, et post eum Wiglaf ibidem regnavit. Ultimus Merciorum gentis rex fuit Burthredus. Quo regnante, Dani, qui jam alias Brytanniæ provincias occupaverant, intrantes Merciam, Burthredum regno privaverunt, et cuidam Celwulfo illud regnum sub se disponendum committunt. Rex vero Buthredus, Romam expetens, optimo ibidem fine vitam conclusit. Regnum vero Merciorum reges Occidentalium Saxonum, paulatim expugnantes Danos, in sui ditionem, sicut et alia quarumcunque provinciarum regna Britanniæ, habuerunt.

DE REGIBUS OCCIDENTALIUM SAXONUM.[k]

Anno ab incarnatione Domini ccccºxcºvº Cerdic et filius ejus Cynric, cum v navibus Britanniam venientes, ad ostium fluminis, quod e nomine eorum Cerdicis ora dicitur, applicuerunt. Qui cum debellassent illius loci Britones, post xxiij annos adventus eorum, adepti sunt armis regnum Gewissiorum, sive West Saxonum: regnavitque primus ex Anglis in West Saxonia Cerdic prædictus xv annis. Deinde filius suus Kynric, xxvj annis. Dederant autem duobus nepotibus suis Stufo et Wichtgaro Vectam insulam. Post hunc Ceaulin, filius ejus, xxx et j annis regnavit. Huic successit Ceolric, vj annis. Deinde frater ipsius Celwulf regnavit xiiij annis. Post hunc Kynegils, frater ipsius Celwulfi. Hic primus Occidentalium Saxonum baptizatus est, prædicante ibidem verbum Sancto Birino episcopo,[l] misso ad prædicandum ab Honorio papa. Hunc Kynegilsum de baptismo exeuntem suscepit rex Northanhymbrorum Oswaldus, cujus ipse Oswaldus filiam accepturus erat in conjugem. Post Kynegilsum Kenwalch filius ejus regnavit xxxjº annis. Post hunc Sexburga regina anno uno tenuit regnum. Deinde Eascwine regnavit ij annis. Post illum Kentwine filius

[k] The Magdalen MS. has C*i*nric for C*y*nric, Cerdic-ora for Cerdicis-ora, Gewissorum for Gewiss*i*orum, Wi*th*garo for Wi*cht*garo, Celwlf for Celw*u*lf, Northanh*u*mbrorum for Northanh*y*mbrorum, and so throughout; Kenwalc for Kenwalc*h*, Escwine for E*a*scwine, C*otti*berti for C*oen*berti, Ceaulani for Cealini, *I*ne for Yne, *Ke*nredi for C*oe*nredi, *A*thelheard for *E*thelheard, Sigeb*ri*cht for Sigeb*ir*cht, Brictricum for Bri*th*tricum, *Ecg*bri*ch*tus for Eg*ber*tus, Su*r*reie for Sureie, Suthsexe for Suthse*a*x*a*, *A*thelwlfus and Æthelwlfus for *Ea*thelwlfus, Alcmundi for Alc*h*mundi, Ea*f*i for Ea*s*i, *Æ*thelbaldus for *Ead*thelbaldus, *Æ*thelbrichtus for *Ead*thelbrichtus, *Æ*thelredus for Eathelredus, *Ælf*redus for *Ealur*edus, *Æ*dwardus for *Ea*dwardus, *Æ*thelstanus for *Ea*thelstanus, *E*dredus for *Ea*dredus, Edwi*n*us for Edwius, K*i*nodus for K*y*nodus, *Æ*thelred for *E*thelred, Nor*r*eganorum for Nor*w*eganorum, Hardecnu*t* for Hardecnu*d*, A*thel*redo for Al*dr*edo, Willelmus for Guillelmus.

[l] In margine MS. Caligula—*De sancto Birino episcopo.*

Kynegilsi ix annis. Cui successit Ceadwalla filius Coenberti, filii Cadi, filii Cuthæ, filii Ceaulini, filii Kynrici, filii Cerdici. Regnavit autem Ceadwalla annis ij. Dehinc Romam venit devotus, ibique baptizatus, et, adhuc in albis positus, vitam terminavit, pontificante Sergio papa.[m] Ceadwallo autem successit Yne, de stirpe regia; fuit enim filius Coenredi, qui fuit filius Ceolwoldi. Ceolwold autem fuit frater Kynegilsi regis. Post xxxvij annos regni sui Yne Romæ finivit vitam, relicto regno. Qui etiam dicitur denarium ex singulis domibus regni sui beato Petro Romam unoquoque anno dedisse. Quod diu a successoribus suis observatum est. Post Yne Ethelheard regnavit xiij annis. Cui successit Cuthred, et xvj annis regnavit. Deinde Sigebircht regnavit j anno. Post hunc Kynewulf regnavit xxix[n] annis. Huic Brichtricus succedens, regnavit xvj annis. Quo regnante, Dani primum venerunt in Angliam tribus navibus. Post Brithtricum, suscepit Egbertus regnum, et regnavit xxxv annis, et vij mensibus; multaque regna suo subegit imperio, scilicet Canciam, Sureie, Suthseaxa, et Eastseaxa, et East Angla, et Merciam. Post quem Eathelwlfus filius ejus regnavit; Eathelwlfus filius Egberti, qui fuit Alchmundi, qui fuit Eafi, qui fuit Eoppæ, qui fuit Ingildi, qui fuit frater Yne regis supradicti. Regnavit autem Eathelwulf xviij annis et dimidio. Reliquit autem iiij filios, quorum quisque, alter post alterum, reges fuerunt, viriliter dimicantes contra Paganos, scilicet Danos. Quorum primus Eadthelbaldus post patrem regnavit v annis. Post quem frater suus Eadthelbrichtus vj annis regnavit. Deinde Eathelredus, ejusdem frater, v annis regnavit. Post hunc frater eorum Ealuredus regnavit xxix annis, et vj mensibus, magnamque partem Britanniæ, expugnatis Danis, obtinuit. Excepto isto solo omnes ad australem plagam Humbre fluminis defecerant. Ealuredo mortuo, successit filius ejus Eadwardus, potentia major patre. Multo enim latius quam pater fines regni sui dilatavit. Regnavit autem xxiiij annis. Reliquit autem post se iij filios, quorum quisque, alter post alterum, regnabat. Post patrem primus regnavit Eathelstanus,[o] qui primus regum ex Anglis totius Britanniæ monarchiam tenuit. Nam et Scotiam et Cumbreland et alias insularum sibi provincias subjugavit. Regnavit autem xvj annis. Huic successit frater ejus Eadmundus, regnans vj annis et vij mensibus. Hujus filio Eadgaro jam nato, audivit

[m] Wallingford transcribes the genealogy of the kings of Wessex to this point.

[n] xxx, Magdalen MS.

[o] In margine MS. Caligula—*De Adthelestano primo sceptrigero rege Anglorum.*

beatus Dunstanus in sublimi voces dicentium. "Pax Anglorum ecclesiæ! exorti nunc pueri nostrique Dunstani tempore." Post Eadmundum frater ejus Eadredus regnavit ix annis, et vj ebdomadis. Deinde Edwius filius Eadmundi iij annis et xxxvj ebdomadis, duobus diebus minus, regnavit. Post hunc frater ejus Eadgarus, filius Eadmundi, cui vij reges,[p] scilicet Kynodus rex Scottorum, et Malcolm rex Cumbrorum, et Maccus plurimarum rex Insularum, et alii v subjecti fuerant. Regnavit autem xvj annis et ix ebdomadis. Cui successit filius ejus Eadwardus, iiij annis regnavit. Quo innocenter occiso dolo suæ novercæ, frater ejus Ethelred suscipit regnum, regnavitque in multis periculis xxx et ix[q] annis. Anno autem regni ejus xvj° Onlaf rex Norweganorum et Swein rex Danorum cum magna classe veniunt Lundoniam. Sed, magna vi civium repulsi, alia quæque loca crudeliter depopulantur. Tandem Onlaf, repacificatus regi Ethelredo, baptizatus, recipitur ab illo de fonte. Et revertens patriam, nunquam postea rediit. Swein vero remansit, loca quæ poterat devastans. Anno vero regni sui xx°iiij° Ethelredus rex accepit uxorem filiam ducis Northmannorum Ricardi Primi, ex qua habuit filios Eadwardum et Ealuredum. Anno autem regni Ethelredi xxxvj°, mortuo Swein rege Danorum, Cnut filius ejus cum omnibus Danis pellitur ab Anglia. Sed anno sequenti, cum valida classe, Sandwicum portum intravit. Post Ethelredum filius ejus, Eadmundus Ferreum Latus, ix fere menses regnavit, in quibus quinquies contra regem Danorum Cnutonem acerrime pugnavit; peractoque ultimo bello, concordiam inter se fecerunt reges Eadmundus et Cnut, dividentes inter se regnum Anglorum ea conditione, ut qui superstes fieret totius Brytanniæ monarchiam susciperet. Qua conventione facta, et ab omnibus primalibus firmata, post unum mensem Eadmundus moritur, susceptoque toto Anglorum regno, Cnut regnavit fere xix annis. Cui successit Haroldus, ejus ex concubina filius, regnans v annis. Post quem Hardecnud, filius Cnutonis et Emmæ, frater Eadwardi ex matre, qui regnavit ij annis, xv diebus minus. Huic successit Eadwardus frater ejus, sed filius Ethelredi regis, iiij nonas Aprilis, die Dominico Paschali consecratus; regnavitque pacifice xxiij annis. Illo vero nonas Januarii obeunte, Haroldus dux, filius Godwini comitis, in regnum sublimatur, sicut idem rex Eadwardus moriturus præcepit. Sed ipso eodem anno Haroldus a Guillelmo duce Normannorum pridie idus Octobris cum multo Anglorum exercitu occiditur. Guillelmus postmodum rex Anglorum factus, in die Natalis Domini unguitur in regem ab

[p] viii, MS. Magdalen. [q] viii, MS. Magdalen.

Aldredo Eboracensium archiepiscopo apud Westmonasterium, regnavitque fere xx et j annis. Quo mortuo v idus Septembris, Guillelmus filius ejus successit, regnavitque xiij annis minus xxxviij diebus.

DE NORHYMB' REGIBUS.

Anno ab incarnatione Domini quingentesimo xl° vij°, ab adventu vero Anglorum in Brytanniam anno xc° et viij°, Ida primus rex ex Anglis cœpit regnare in Northanhymbrorum provincia, a quo tota ejusdem provinciæ regum cœpit origo. Habuit autem ex regina vj filios hos, Adda, Ethelricum,[r] Theodericum, Ethricum, Theuthere, Osmerum : et alios vj ex concubina, hos scilicet, Ogg, Alricum, Eccam, Osbaldum, Scor, Sceotheri. Venerat autem Ida, comite patre Eoppa, cum lx navibus ad Flemaburch,[s] indeque boriales plagas occupans, ibidem regnavit xij annis. Quo defuncto, regnum Northanhymbrorum divisum est in duo; Elle namque regnavit in Deira, Adda vero successit Idæ patri in Bernicia, ubi regnavit viij annis. Cui successit Glappa, j anno. Post quem Hussa regnavit vij annis. Post illum Frithewlf vij annis. Huic successit Theodericus, vij annis, post eum. Eathelricus regnavit iiij annis.[t] Huic successit Eathelfridus et regnavit xxiiij annis. Habuit autem vij filios, Eanfridum, et ex sorore regis Edwini (filia Elle)[u] Acca, Oswaldum, Oswium, Oslac, Oswudu, Osa, Offa. Mortuo autem Elle, Eathelfridus expulit filium Elle, Eadwinum, fratrem uxoris suæ, de regno Deirorum. Qui, exulans apud regem Redwallum, ab eodem reductus est in regnum omnium provinciarum Northanhymbrorum. Qui, primus regum Northanhymbrorum effec-

[r] Spelt *Hel*ricum in C., and corrected in the text from M. The several classes of variation in the spelling of names, before explained, continue in this section, besides which Theuthere in C. is spelt Theuteri in M., Flemaburch in C. is Flemabirig in M., Acca is Acha, Red*wall*um is Red*ald*um, Oswi*us*, Osiwi*u*, Alcfridus is Alfridus, Wince*n*hale is Wince*h*hale, and Eborac*u*m is twice spelt Eborac*e*m.

[s] This is the earliest mention of Flamborough as the place of Ida's landing, which is not noticed as such elsewhere by any historian prior to Roger of Wendover.

[t] This list of the successors of Ida to the time of Ethelfrith contains the same names which are enumerated in the Northumbrian chronicle appended to Beda, the genealogies appended to Nennius, and that prefixed to the Historia de Gestis Regum. In the three last the names are arranged apparently according to their propinquity to Ida, but in this list they are arranged chronologically; Ethelric, who occurs early in the others as a son of Ida, being placed last in this, which we know to have been his true position, as he is described as the immediate predecessor of Ethelfrith both in the Saxon Chronicle, and by Malmesbury.

[u] The words within brackets are inserted from the Magdalen MS., where they occur in the margin.

tus Christianus, regnavit xvij annis. Quo regnante, filii Ethelfridi exulaverunt inter Scottos, fugientes patriam propter timorem Edwini; sed, eo interfecto, redierunt. Quorum primus, scilicet Eanfridus, regnavit in Bernica j anno. Quo interfecto, frater ipsius Oswaldus Bernicæ gentis simul et Deiræ adeptus est regnum, atque ex duobus unum populum compaginavit. Regnavit autem ix annis, cui successit frater ipsius, Oswius, primo quidem in sola Bernica, sed, paulo post interfecto Oswino, regnans simul et in Deira. A quo tempore utræque provinciæ unum semper habuere regem. Defuncto Oswio post xxviij annos regni sui, Ecgfridus filius ejus regnavit xv annis. Iste Sanctum Cuthbertum constituit episcopum.[v] Cujus regni anno vij natus est Venerabilis Beda, et traditur septennis abbati Benedicto,[w] cognomento Biscop, in monasterio beati Petri apud Weramuthe, quod paulo ante, hoc est iiij^{to} anno regni[x] Ecgfridi, inceptum fuerat.[y] Post Ecgfridum, frater ejus Alcfridus tenuit regnum xix annis. Cui filius suus Osredus succedens regnavit xi annis. Quo interfecto, Coenredus regnavit ij annis. Post quem Osricus regnavit xi annis. Deinde Ceolwulfus, frater Coenredi, qui regnaverat ante Osricum, ij annis. Ad hunc Ceolwulfum, Beda scribit Hystoriam Anglorum. Erat iste Ceolwulfus filius Cuthe,[z] qui filius Cuthwini, qui Ledwaldi, qui Ecgwaldi, qui Aldelmi, qui Ogge, qui fuit Idæ, primi regis Northanhymbrorum. Ceolwulfus, ubi viij regnaverat annis, relicto regno, monasterium intravit Lindisfarnense, ibique optimo fine in monachatu vitam conclusit. Reliquerat autem successorem regni filium patrui sui Eatæ, Eadbertum, cujus frater erat Ecgbertus archiepiscopus Eboracensis, qui primus post Paulinum accepto pallio confirmatus est in archiepiscopatum. At rex Eadbertus, cum regnasset xxj annis, contempto regno assumptaque tonsura, in ecclesia Eboracensi, quam frater ejus prædictus tunc gubernabat, in clericatu vitam terminavit. Tradiderat autem regnum suum Osulfo filio suo. Quod per unum annum tenens, occisus est nequiter a sua familia juxta Methil-Wongtune.[a] Cui successit in regno Eadthelwold cognomento Moll, et regnavit vj annis. Dehinc, amisso regno in Wincenhale, Alchredum, ex prosapia Idæ, habuit successorem. Qui, cum ix annis regnasset, pellitur de regno in exilium. Post quem Eathel-

[v] *Ordinatio Sancti Cuthberti*, MS. Caligula, in margine.

[w] MS. Magdalen has *Sancto* Benedicto for *abbati* Benedicto, and *Sancti* instead of *beati* Petri. Cognomento Biscop is omitted in M.

[x] vij^{o}, M.

[y] Here Wallingford's genealogy of the kings of Northumberland ends.

[z] *De Sancto Ceolwulfo rege*, MS. Caligula, in margine.

[a] *Methil Wontune* in MS. Magdalen; *i. e.*, *Mithiltune* in margine MS. Calig.

red, filius Ethelwoldi Moll, regnavit v annis.[b] Quo dehinc pulso in exilium, filius Osulfi, quondam regis, supradicti, paternum recepit regnum Elfwoldus.[c] Quod per x annos tenens pie ac religiose, facta a suis conjuratione occiditur in Scidescestre[d] juxta Murum; sed sepultus est honorifice in ecclesia Sancti Andreæ in Hagusteldesham. In loco vero ubi interfectus est, lux cælitus emissa videri sæpius dicitur. In cujus locum successit Osredus, filius Alchredi regis supradicti, regnans uno anno. Quo per dolum interfecto, Eathelredus, de quo supradictum est, de exilio rediens recepit regnum, quod jam secunda vice per vij tenuit annos. Quo apud Corebrygge[e] occiso, Osbaldus per xxvij dies regnavit. Illo vero projecto et in exilium fugato, Eardulfus, ex semine regio, de Comite provehitur in regnum, quod per x annos tenuit.[f] Cui successit Elfwoldus Secundus, ij annis. Post quem Eanredus regnavit xxxij annis. Deinde Eathelredus regnavit ix annis. Post hunc Osberht, xiij annis. Quem Northhymbrorum populus pellens de regno, Ellam, alienum, regii seminis, in ejus locum substituunt. Sed Danis eo tempore Eboracum irrumpentibus necessitas fecit concordiam regum. Uterque enim rex, adunatis viribus, Eboracum tendunt. Et primo quidem in fugam vertunt hostes, compellendo in civitatem illos. Quo cum illos insequerentur, Danis atrociter repugnantibus, cæsi sunt ambo reges cum suo exercitu. His qui superfuerant Northymbris præfecerunt Dani Egbertum, qui regnavit v annis. Deinde Richsi ij annis. Post hunc Egbertus ij annis. Deinde Guthredus, quem, Hardecnuti filium, regium puerum, vendiderant in servum, sed Sanctus Cuthbertus hunc ex servitio promovit in regnum. Regnavit autem xiiij annis. Post hunc Sichtricus ex Danico genere. Huic Eathelstanus rex, monarcha totius Angliæ, regnanti sub se, sororem suam dederat uxorem. Cui defuncto, filius suus Guthferth successit. Quo, Eathelstanus, expulso de regno, sibi deinceps retinuit Northymbriam. Sed post Eathelstanum fratre ejus Eadmundo regnante, Northymbrenses, postponentes fidem quam Eadmundo juraverant, Onlavum, regem Normannorum,[g] sibi

[b] vi annis, MS. Magdalen.

[c] *De Sancto rege Elfwoldo*, MS. Caligula, in margine.

[d] Written more correctly Scithlesceastre in the Magdalen MS.

[e] Correbr*ig*e in the Magdalen MS.; Corbridge, written in a contracted form Cobre in the *Historia de Gestis Regum*.

[f] Up to this point the old chronicle in the Historia de Gestis Regum is the authority followed, but it breaks off in the Historia in the reign of Eardulf. The author of the present work seems to have possessed a more perfect copy, as he carries on his narrative without interruption, and gives information which he could not, so far as we are aware, have obtained from any other source.

[g] *Nota Normannorum* in margine. MS. Caligula.

præfecerunt regem. Qui, cum non posset resistere Eadmundo, tandem repacificatus manum dedit illi, et baptizatus, ab ipso rege inde susceptus, multis est muneribus oneratus. Post hunc Onlaf filius Sichtrici supradicti præficitur rex Norhymbris, qui habuit socium regni Reinoldum, filium Guthferti supradicti. Quibus, Eadmundus, expulsis, Northymbriam sibi subegit. Sed cum post Eadmundum frater ejus Edredus regnaret, contra fidelitatem quam illi juraverant, Northymbrenses expulsum ab Eadmundo rege Onlafum in regnum sibi reduxerunt. Unde rex Edredus offensus Northymbriam depopulatur, expulso Onlafo. Dum vero rex rediret ad Suthengle, Northymbrenses adunati, multos de extrema parte exercitus illius interfecerunt, et quendam Ericum filium Haroldi sibi regem constituerunt. Quamobrem rex redire, totamque Northanhymbrorum gentem in nihilum redigere disposuit. Unde illi perterriti Ericum, quem sibi præfecerant, expellentes, regem Edredum subjectione perpetua et muneribus sibi placaverunt. Ab hoc tempore Northanhymbrorum provincia proprium regem habere cessavit. Deinceps namque per Comitum procurationem, una cum omnibus totius Angliæ provinciis, regi subjecta servivit.

DE NORTHYMBRORUM COMITIBUS.[h]

Primus Comitum post Ericum, quem ultimum regem habuerunt Northymbrenses, Osulf, provincias omnes Northanhymbrorum sub Edrido rege procuravit. Deinde sub Eadgaro rege Oslac præficitur Comes Eboraco, et locis ei pertinentibus; et Eadulf, cognomento Yvelcild, a Teisa usque Myreforth[i] præponitur Northymbris. Isti duo Comites cum Elfsio, qui apud Sanctum Cuthbertum episcopus fuerat, perduxerunt Kyneth regem Scottorum ad regem Eadgarum. Qui, cum illi fecisset hominium, dedit ei rex Eadgarus Lodoneium, et multo cum honore remisit ad propria. His Comitibus successit in comi-

[h] The rubric is wanting in the Magdalen MS. There can be no doubt that this account of the earls of Northumberland, and that which is given in the Historia de Gestis Regum at p. 90, are derived from a common source, the particulars being generally the same, and the phraseology in many cases identical, whilst each contains many details which are wanting in the other. There is one remarkable discrepancy between them, namely, the omission from the series of earls in the Historia of the first Eadulf, the predecessor of Waltheof the elder. This omission is adverted to in the Preface, in connection with the disputed date of the cession of Lothian to Scotland. In this section, *E*ric is written *I*ric in M., Uctred, Uc*h*tred, Carl, Carl*l*, Mor*k*ar, Mor*ch*ar, Niweburn, Niueburn, Ald*u*nus, Ald*wi*nus.

[i] In MS. Magdalen Myrcfor*d*, but the reading in the text seems the correct one, at all events as regards the final letters, if the boundary indicated be the Frith of Forth. The former portion of the word should probably be M*a*re.

tatum Walthef ille Senior, regnante Ethelredo. Deinde Uchtredus filius Walthefi administravit comitatum omnium Northanhymbrorum provinciarum. Huic rex Eathelredus suam filiam Elfgevam dederat uxorem. Ex qua filiam habens Aldgitham, dedit in conjugium prædiviti cuidam, Maldredo filio Crinani; de qua habuit Cospatricum Comitem, patrem Dolphini, Walthefi, et Cospatrici. Occiso autem Uchtredo a Turebrando cognomine Hold per voluntatem Cnutonis regis, frater ejus Eadulf Cudel administravit comitatum: et, post eum, Ealdredus, filius Uchtredi præfati, quem habuerat ex filia Alduni episcopi, antequam duceret filiam regis Eathelredi. Habuit et alios filios ex alio conjugio, Cospatricum et Eadulfum. Cospatrici erat filius Uchtredus, de quo genitus est Eadulfus, qui princeps erat et auctor illorum qui interfecerunt Walcherum episcopum. Interfecto vero Ealdredo Comite a Carl, cujus patrem, scilicet Turebrandum prædictum, ipse Ældredus occiderat, in ultionem sui patris Uchtredi Comitis, ab ipso Turebrando interfecti; successit illi frater suus junior, Eadulfus. Qui postmodum, regnante Eadwardo, occisus est a Siwardo, qui post illum totius Northanhymbrorum provinciæ, hoc est, ab Humbra usque Tweodam suscepit comitatum. Mortuo autem Siwardo, rex Eadwardus comitatum tradidit Tostio fratri Haroldi regis. Dehinc ipso Tostio ab universis sui comitatus, propter nimiam ejus violentiam, projecto de comitatu et exlegato, Edwinus et Morkarus, quibus rex Edwardus comitatus ipsius curam delegaverat, filio Eadulfi Comitis, fratris Aldredi Comitis, nomine Osulfo, comitatum a Tina usque ad Tweodam commiserunt. Sed post ea Copsi a Guillelmo rege suscipiens præposituram comitatus, expulit de comitatu Osulfum. At ille, collectis postmodum viribus, eundem Copsi in introitum ecclesiæ de Niweburne interfecit. Ipse quoque post paucos menses, dum impetu equi currentis ferretur, in lanceam obviantis sibi latronis delatus, statim moritur. Deinde Cospatricus, ex nepte regis Ethelredi progenitus, ut supradictum est, a rege Guillelmo comitatum emptum administravit. Quem postea idem rex ei auferens, dedit Walthevo filio Siwardi Comitis, quem ipse habuerat ex Ealfleda filia Aldredi Comitis. Walthevo vero capto et occiso, commisit rex comitatum Walchero episcopo. Quo occiso, dedit comitatum Albrio. Illo vero relinquente comitatum, datus est cuidam Rodberto de Mulbreio. A quo rex Guillelmus Junior offensus, dum eum vi cepisset, ipse in sua manu retinuit comitatum,[j] hodieque frater ejus, Henricus rex, retinet.

[j] The Magdalen MS. has the following additional and later particulars:— Post mortem Willelmi regis, frater ejus, Henricus rex, comitatum Northanhumbrorum in proprio dominio tota vita sua retinuit, Comitem vero, Rodbertum de

DE REGIBUS DEIRORUM.

Anno ab incarnatione Domini D.lx., Elle cœpit regnare in provincia Northanhymbrorum, scilicet in Deira, et ipse trahens originem unde et alii reges Anglorum. Istius Elle mentio fit in Vita beati Papæ Gregorii. Regnavit autem xxx annis. Cui mortuo filius ejus Eadwinus successit. Sed cum rex Berniciorum Ethelfridus, cum gloriæ esset cupidissimus, quamvis sororem Eadwini duceret uxorem, eum regno pepulit: quem tamen rex Redwaldus restituit regno, rege Ethelfrido occiso. Regnavit super Berniciam simul et Deiram xvij annis. Quo interfecto in pugna a Cedwalla rege Britonum et Penda rege Merciorum, suscepit pro illo regnum Deirorum, unde ipse Eadwinus generis prosapiam duxerat, Osricus, filius patrui sui, qui Ealuricus vocabatur; qui regnans j anno, occisus est a Ceadwalla rege Brytonum. Deinde Oswaldus utriusque provinciæ regnum ix annis tenuit. Illo occiso, Oswinus, de stirpe regis Eadwini, regnavit in Deira. Erat enim filius Osrici supradicti. Eo interfecto, Oswius regnum Deirorum simul et Berniciorum gubernabat. Eathelwaldus tamen filius Oswaldi, qui in Deirorum partibus regnabat, patruum suum Oswium sæpe cum gente Merciorum, et cum Ceadwalla rege Brytonum acriter impugnabat. Verumtamen deinceps Berniciorum provincia et Deirorum unum habent regem.

REGNUM ANGLIÆ ITA DIVIDEBATUR ANTIQUITUS.

Rex Cantiæ, Hengest.

Rex Merciorum, Penda.

Rex Occidentalium Saxonum, Cerdic.

Rex Orientalium Saxonum, Eathelbrich.

Rex Orientalium Anglorum, Reodwald, et postea Eadmundus.

Primus regum Northamhymbrorum, Ida.

Rex Deirorum, Ella, pater Eadwini.

Rex Berniciorum, Eathelbertus, pater S. Oswaldi.

Rex Britonum Ceadwald, i.e Cadwalla.

Rex Australium Saxonum.[k]

In his præscriptis regibus dividebatur antiquitus Angliæ totius regnum ab incarnatione Domini anno cccc°.xl°.ix°, usque

Molbræio, qui captus fuerat a fratre suo Willelmo, ipse in eadem custodia diutissime detinuit. Tandem, rogatu baronum suorum eundem resolvens, concessit illi mutare vitam habitumque sæcularem. Qui, ingressus monasterium Sancti Albani sub professione monachica, ibidem vitam finivit. Post obitum Henrici regis nepos ipsius, Stephanus, qui ei successit in regnum.

[k] Not in MS. Magd.

ad regem Eathelstanum, qui primus monarchiam regni Anglorum obtinuit.[l]

NOMINA ARCHIEPISCOPORUM CANTUARIENSIUM.[m]

Augustinus. Laurentius. Mellitus. Justus. Honorius. Deusdedit. Theodorus. Berchtwaldus. Tatwinus. Nothelmus. Cuthbertus. Bregowinus. Lambertus. Adelardus. Wuluredus. Swiredus. Celnothus. Ethelredus. Plegemundus. Athelmundus. Wulfhelmus. Odo. Dunstanus. Eathelgarus. Sigericus. Elfricus. Elfegus. Livingus. Eagelnothus. Eadfinus. Rodbertus. Stigandus. Landfrancus. Anselmus. Eadulfus. Guillelmus. Teobaldus. Thomas, iiij kal. Januarii martirizatus, anno incarnationis . . . . clxx.[n]

NOMINA ARCHIEPISCOPORUM EBORACENSIUM.

Paulinus. Ceadda. Wilfridus. Bosa. Johannes. Wilfridus. Ecgbertus. Ethelbertus. Eanbaldus. Wulsige. Wimundus. Wulfhere. Ethelbaldus. Lothewardus. Wulstanus. Oscytel. Oswaldus. Aldulfus. Wulstanus. Eluricus. Kynsi. Aldred. Thomas. Girardus. Thomas. Turstinus. Guilelmus. Henricus Morduc. Rogerus de Ponte.

NOMINA EPISCOPORUM DUNELMENSIUM.

Anno ab incarnatione Domini DC.XXXV.[o] Aidanus. Finanus.[p] Colmannus. Tuda. Eata. Cuthbertus. Eadbertus. Eadfridus. Ethelwoldus. Kynewlfus. Higbaldus. Egbertus. Eadredus.[q] Egredus. Lambertus.[r] Hardulfus. (Istius tempore devastata est tota Anglia a Paganis, et corpus S. Cuthberti cum multis Sanctorum reliquiis ab insula Lindisfarnensi exportatum per vij annos hac illacque discursantibus Paganis incertis ferebatur sedibus. Dehinc perlatum est in Cestre, ubi per centum et xv annos requievit.) Cuthardus. Tilredus. Wigredus. Uchtredus. Sexhelmus. Alsius.[s] Aldunus. (Iste transtulit corpus S. Cuthberti in Dunelmum.) Eadmundus. Edredus. Egelricus. Egelwinus. Walcherus. Guillelmus. Ranulfus. Gaufridus. Guillelmus. Hugo de Pused.[t]

[l] The six last words are omitted in MS. Magd.

[m] M. has Cantuariorum instead of Cantuariensium.

[n] The original list of these archbishops of Canterbury in C. ends with Guillelmus. Theobaldus and Thomas are added in a more recent hand. To hem are added in M. Ricardus, Hubertus Walter; all, as well as Thomas, in a ater hand than the rest of the work.

[o] This date is not in M.

[p] M. has Finanus. The text Afinan.

[q] Hudredus, M.

[r] Eanbertus, M.

[s] Æfsius, M.

[t] The text in M. ends with Gaufridus.

APPENDIX.

EXCERPTA HISTORICA ET TOPOGRAPHICA,

IN CODICE SYMEONIS DE HISTORIA ECCLESIÆ DUNELMENSIS IN BIBLIOTHECA PUBLICA CANTABRIGIENSI INSERTA.[a]

I.—A GULIELMO MALMESBURIENSI.

Ab hoc (Ethelwlfo scilicet) Anglorum chronica sursum versus usque ad Adam lineam generationis regum texunt, etc.[b]

II.—A VARIIS DE REGIBUS NORTHANHYMBRORUM.

Anno ab incarnatione Domini dxlvij Ida regnare cœpit, a quo regalis Northanhymbrorum prosapia tenet originem. Eoppa genuit Idam. Pater Eoppæ fuit Esa, pater Esæ Ingui, pater Ingui Angenwi, pater Angenwi Aloth, pater Alothi Benoc, pater Benoci Brond, pater Brondi Beldeg, pater Beldegi Woden, pater Wodeni Freodhlas, pater Freodhlæ Freodhwlf, pater Freodhwlfi Finn, pater Finni Godewlf, pater Godewlfi

[a] These extracts are inserted in the Cambridge MS. of Symeon's History of the Church of Durham, between the table of contents and the body of the work. They bear internal evidence of having been thrown together by the transcriber in the reign of Henry II., and not by Symeon in the reign of Henry I.

[b] This extract is from William of Malmesbury's History of the Kings of England, book ii., chapters ii. and iii., and contains the genealogy of the West-Saxon kings from Ethelwlf upwards to Woden, and so to Noah through his fourth son Stref, who is said to have been born in the Ark; also an account of the division of the kingdom on the death of Ethelwlf between his sons Ethelbald and Ethelbert, and of the death of the former. It ends abruptly in the midst of the account of the Danish invasion in the reign of Ethelbert. See the History of William of Malmesbury as published by the English Historical Society, vol. i., p. 172.

Geota.[c] Ida genuït xii filios, sex legitimo connubio, sex[e] concubinis, Adda, Ethelric, Edric, Teudheri, Osmer, Theoderic; hi filii reginæ: Ocga, Alric, Ecca, Osbald, Scor, Sceotheri; hi filii concubinarum.[d]

Ida regnavit xii annos.

Adda filius Idæ viii annos.

Ethelric filius Idæ vii annos.[e]

Theoderic filius Idæ vii annos.

Ethelfrid filius Ethelrici, filii Idæ, xxiiij annos.

Ethelfrid vii filios habuit; Eanfridum, Oswaldum, Oswinum, Oslac, Oswidu, Oslaf, Offa.

Post Ethelfridum regnavit Edwinus xvij. Edwinus erat filius Ellæ, qui Ella non erat de stirpe Idæ. Iste est Ella, de cujus nomine Sanctus Gregorius alludens, "Bene," inquit, "vocatur "Ella, Alleluia enim oportet ibi ad laudem Dei cantari."

Interfecto Edwino, regnum Northanhymbrorum divisum est. Osricus, qui fuit filius patrui Edwini, Elfrici vocabulo, tenuit provinciam Deirorum j annum. Porro Eanfridus, filius Ethelfridi nepotis Idæ, regnum Berniciorum tenuit j annum.

Oswaldus filius Ethelfridi ix annos.

Oswiu filius Ethelfridi xxviij annos. Iste Oswiu inprimis regni socium habuit Oswinum de stirpe regis Edwini, hoc est filium Osrici, de quo supradictum est. Præfuit Oswinus provinciæ Deirorum vii annis. Post Oswiu regnavit filius ejus Ecgfridus, qui Sanctum Cuthbertum constituit episcopum, Regnavit xv annos.

Alfrid frater Ecgfridi xviii annos.

Osred filius Alfridi xi.

Coenred consanguineus ii.

Osric filius Alfridi xi.

Ceolwlf viij. Iste Ceolwlf fuit filius Cudwine, Cudwine filius Liodwaldi, Liodwald filius Ecgwaldi, Ecgwald filius Aldelmi, Aldelm filius Ocgæ, Ocga filius Idæ regis. Iste Ceolwlf, dimisso regno, monachus factus est in Lindisfarne.[f]

[c] This paragraph is translated from the Saxon Chronicle. The proper names are very inaccurately printed by Twysden, as Fum for Finn, Beoda for Geota, but the MS. is not answerable for these errors.

[d] The names of the sons of Ida seem to have been taken from the Hist. Eccl. Dunelm., l. i., c. xiii. Other lists differing materially in the orthography of some of the names occur in the Nennian genealogies, Florence of Worcester, Alured of Beverley, Roger of Wendover, and in the Saxon genealogies in the present volume (p. 209). Twysden has misprinted one of the names *Tendhi* for *Teudheri*.

[e] Written Aedlric in the Nennian genealogies, where he is called, apparently in error, the son of *Adda*, to whom, as in the present list, he is represented as the immediate successor. After Theoderic, according to the same authority, Frithwald reigned seven years, and Hussa seven, both of whom are here omitted.

[f] From the reign of Ethelfrith to that of Ceolwlf the authorities relied on

Post Ceolfum Eadbert, filius patrui Ceolwlfi, tenuit regnum xx annos. Oswlf filius Eadberti j annum.

Ethelwold Moll vj annos.

Alcred de prosapia Idæ ix annos.

Ethelred filius Ethelwoldi iiij annos.

Elfwold filius Oswlfi regis, nepos Eadberti regis, expulso Ethelredo tenuit regnum x annos.

Iste Ethelwold, injuste a suis occisus, requiescit in Hextildesham, sed in loco quo est occisus lux cælitus sæpe visa est.

Osred filius Alchredi j annum. Iste Osred post annum expulsus est de regno, dolo circumventus.

Postea Ethelred filius Ethelwoldi, de exilio liberatus, regnavit iterum vij. Iste Ethelred filios Elfwoldi ab Eboraco extractos peremit.

Osbaldus regnavit xxvij dies.

Eardulfus x annos.[g]

Elfwold ij annos.

Eanred xxxiij annos.

Ethelred filius Eanredi ix annos.

Illo occiso regnum tenuit Osbryht xiij, quo postea de regno expulso, Northumbrani constituerunt sibi regem non de regia stirpe, vocabulo Ella, quo tempore Danis oppugnantibus Eboracum, Northymbri, reducentes Osbrihtum in regnum, simul cum illo et cum Ella, duobus regibus, contra Danos pugnant. Sed ambo reges occisi sunt. Qui Sancto Cuthberto suas terras abstulerunt, Werkeworth, Tillemuthe, Billingaham, Ileclif et Wigeclif.

Postea regnavit Ecgbert vj annos.

Ricsi ij annos.

Ecgbert ij annos.

Guthred rex, ex servo xiiij annos.

Postea Reignwold occupavit terram Sancti Cuthberti per Sculam, et Onlafbal.

Tunc xxij annos regnavit Eadwardus filius Elfredi regis.

Post Eadwardum regem regnavit Ethelstanus, qui primus totius Angliæ regnum obtinuit xx annos.

Post eum frater ejus Eadmundus regnavit ix annos.

Post Eadmundum, frater ejus Eadred regnavit x annos.

Post Eadredum Eadwi, filius Eadmundi regis, j annum.

are Beda, and the brief Northumbrian Chronology appended to his History. The genealogy of Ceolwlf is given in the Saxon Chronicle, and also in Symeon's History of the Church of Durham, book i., c. xiii.

[g] The ancient *Historia de Gestis Regum* breaks off abruptly in this reign. The authorities now followed are the Libellus de Saxonum adventu, etc., in the present volume, pp. 202-15, and the Historia de Sancto Cuthberto.

Post Eadwi Eadgar, frater ejus, xviij annos.

Post Eadgarum filius ejus, Edvardus, in Scheftesbiri, v.

Post Eadvardum frater ejus, Etheldredus, xxxix.[h]

Post eum Cnut xix annos. Post Cnut Heraldus, filius ejus, v annos.

Post eum Hardicnut, iij annos: post hunc Eadwardus, xxiiij.

Post hunc Herald ad Epiphaniam (et usque ad festum Sancti Calixti).[i]

Willelmus Major, xxj annos: Willelmus Minor, xiij annos.

Henricus anno ætatis suæ lxviij obiit. Regnavit gloriose annos xxxv et menses iiij.

III.—DE PARTITIONE ANGLIÆ IN SCHIRAS ET EPISCOPATUS.[j]

Anglia habet in longitudine DCCC[ta] miliaria a loco Penwithstert vocato, qui situs est xv leugis ultra Michaelstoue in Cornewalas, usque ad Cathenes trans Scotiam. In latitudine habet CCC miliaria a Depiestowe usque Dofre. Habet sedes metropolitanas duas, Cantuariam, et Eboracam; sedes episcopales xv,[k] Rovecestriam; Lundoniam; Northwic; (qui de duobus unus factus est, nam una sedes erat apud Helmam vel Thetford, secunda apud Domnach,)[l] Cicestriam; Wincestriam; Searibi, quam Heremannus episcopus, permittente rege Eadwardo, de duobus episcopatubus, Ramesbiri et Scireburn, unam fecit; Execeastre, quam Leofricus episcopus, permittente rege Eadwardo, de duobus episcopatubus, in Cornewale, ad Sanctum Germanum, et Bridport,[m] unam fecit; Bathun, cujus sedes fuit apud Welle usque ad dies Willelmi regis Secundi et episcopi Johannis; Wirecestre; Hereford; Ceastria, cujus sedes fuit apud Lichfield (vel Coventriam)[n] usque ad dies Willelmi Primi,

[h] After Ethelred Twysden inserts the nine months' reign of Edmund Ironside, but it is not noticed in the MS.

[i] The words between brackets are inserted in a very minute, but apparently contemporaneous, hand in the MS.

[j] There is no title prefixed to this little tract in the MS., but another copy exists in the Arundel MS., Norfolk, 222, which has been published by Gale (Oxford, 1691, p. 560), under the title, "De partitione provinciæ in schiras et episcopatus, *et regna*." Besides what occurs in our MS., the Arundel text contains the list of kingdoms with the bishoprics in each, which are given by Malmesbury (Gesta Regum Anglorum, i., 6), which accounts for the addition of the last clause of the title, "et regna," which does not apply to the tract as now printed. The same extract from Malmesbury occurs also in another part of the Cambridge volume (folio 215), but not in connection with any work of Symeon.

[k] Arundel MS., xx. (including the Welsh sees and Whitherne).

[l] The words within brackets are added from the Arundel MS.

[m] Arundel MS. has Crediton instead of Bridport.

[n] The words within brackets are from the Arundel MS.

et Lanfranci archiepiscopi, et Petri episcopi; Lincolnia, cujus sedes fuit apud Dorkacestre (sed Remigius episcopus transtulit sedem Lincolniæ),[o] fuitque dudum divisa in tres[p] episcopatus; sunt enim in eo viij sciræ et dimidium; Heli, quam Henricus rex Primus fecit, sumpta parte de episcopatu Lincolniæ;[q] Dunelmum, cujus sedes fuit apud Hagustaldensem ecclesiam, et alia sedes apud Halieland; Karliol, cui rex Henricus Primus et Turstinus archiepiscopus Aldulfum episcopum præfecerunt.[r]

Anglia habet xxxij sciras extra Cumberland et Cornewalas.[s] In Cornewalas sunt sex[t] parvæ sciræ. Scotland, Bretland, Wict[u] excipiunter.

Sunt hæ sciræ divisæ per tres leges, WESTSEXENELAGA, DENELAGA, MERCHENELAGA. WESTSEXANELAGA habet ix sciras, Sudsexa, Suderrei, Kent, Berrocscire, Wiltescire, in qua sunt iiij^{m}.DCCC hydæ, Sudhamptescire, Sumersetescire, Dorsetescire, Devenascire. DENELAGA habet xv sciras, Eboraciscira, Snotinghamscira, Deorbiscira, Leorcestrescira, Lincolnescira, Northamptunscira, Huntedunescira, Grantebridgescire, Northfolc, Sudfolc, Eastsaxe, Bedefordescira, Hertfordscira, Middleseaxa, Buckingehamscira.[v] MERCHENELAGA habet viij sciras, Herefordscira (in qua sunt m. hidæ), Gloucestrescira (MM.CCC) Wirecestrescira (MMM.CC), Scrobscira, Cestrescira, Steadfordscira (quingenta) Warewicscira (M.CC), Oxenfordscira (MM.CCCC).[w]

[o] The words within brackets are from the Arundel MS.

[p] duos, MS. Arundel.

[q] MS. Arundel proceeds as follows:—In Wallia vero quatuor episcopatus similiter subjecti Cantuariensi archiepiscopo, unus apud Sanctum David, qui vocatur Menensis; alius apud Bangor; tertius apud Clamorgan, modo Landaff; quartus apud Asaph.

[r] In place of the above account of the sees of Durham and Carlisle, MS. Arundel has the following remarkable statement:—Archiepiscopatus Eboracensis olim in quinque episcopatus fuit divisus, scilicet in unum archiepiscopatum et quatuor episcopatus. Unus fuit ex parte fluminis Usæ; alter apud Ripun; tertius apud Witeby; quartus apud Beverlacum; modo habet sub se tres episcopatus, scilicet Dunelmensem, videlicet Durem, cujus sedes erat apud Lindisfarnensam ecclesiam; alterum Cardolensum, scilicet Carduel vel Carlel, qui fuit subtractus ab Eboracensi, non tamen demptus ab episcopatu; tertium Candidæcasæ, qui vocatur Galaweyæ.

[s] Exceptis Northumberland, Westmerland, Cumberland, in qua continentur vij sciræ. MS. Arundel.

[t] vij erased in the MS., and *sex* written above.

[u] Wallia, Scotia, et Insula de Wiks. MS. Arundel.

[v] MS. Arundel omits Bedfordshire, Lincolnshire, and Norfolk, and inserts "Stanufordiæscira."

[w] The hidage of certain counties in Merchenelaga which is inserted between brackets is from the Arundel MS. The following list of counties, which differs materially in their distribution from our text, is from MS. Cotton, Domitian A. viii., where it is appended to the *Libellus de regibus Saxonum*, printed in this volume *(note continued on next page)*:—

Anglica[x] Britannia, oceani insula, climatis occidui, extremo pene situ ab orbe seclusa, in frigida plaga aquilonis posita, in ultima ferme orbis margine sita, inter omnes vel prima vel maxima,[y] a quibusdam, quia oceano circumgirata est, alter orbis appellatur. Insula singulari amplitudine, omniumque aliarum decus et gloria, quam olim Carolus Magnus provinciam, omnium bonorum fertilitate et copia, cameram suam vocabat.

Danelaga.	*Mercenelaga.*	*West-Saxenelaga.*
Suthfolcscire	Easexa	Kent-scire
Northfolcscire	Middleseaxa	Surreie
Grantbrugescire	Heorteforde	Suthseaxa
Lincolnascire	Huntedun	Hamtune
Everwic	Bedeford	Wiltunescira
Snotingeham	Bukyngham	Sumersetascire
Deorbiscire	Oxenford	Dorsetascire
Stafford	Norhamtune	Devenascire
Seaster	Legercester	Berchscire
Screobescire	Warwicscire	
	Glousesterscire	

Worcestershire and Herefordshire are omitted. Stafford, Chester, and Shropshire are transferred from Merchenelaga to Denelaga, and Essex, Middlesex, Hertfordshire, Huntingdonshire, Bedfordshire, Buckinghamshire, Oxfordshire, Northamptonshire, and Leicestershire are transferred from Denelaga to Merchenelaga.

[x] This paragraph is not in the Arundel MS.

[y] Inter omnes oceani insulas Britannia vel prima vel præcipua est—*Alured Beverlac.*, l. i., sect. iv.

BREVIS RELATIO DE SANCTO CUTHBERTO,

ET QUOMODO CORPUS EJUS DUNELMUM VENERIT, ET EXCERPTA DE VITA ET MIRACULIS SANCTI CUTHBERTI.[z]

I.—QUOMODO IPSE OCTENNIS PUER PER TRIMUM INFANTEM DE CONSTANTIA ANIMI ET EPISCOPATU SIT PRÆMONITUS.

[a]VENERABILIS igitur Domini famulus Cuthbertus octavo suæ ætatis anno, qui post infantiam pueritiæ primus est, per trimum infantem de constantia animi ammonitus, relicta continuo ludendi vanitate, ad stabilitatem et maturitatem conversus est. Crescensque per dies animoque adolescentior, in Divinæ religionis cultu existens, nocte quadam, dormientibus sociis, cum ipse juxta morem pervigil in oratione duraret, vidit animam Sancti Aidani Lindisfarnensis episcopi, inter cælestium choros agminum ad cælum deferri. Compunctus hoc visu Deo dilectus adolescens renuntiat sæculo rebusque sæcularibus, et monasticam mox properat subire disciplinam. Intrans autem Mailrosense monasterium monachus, ut de ipso canitur, venerabilis et per cuncta laudabilis digne efficitur, ac corpore, mente habitu, factisque probabilibus castris Dominicis associatur.

II.—HIC CORPORE, MENTE, ET HABITU FACTUS EST MONACHUS.

Anno Dominicæ incarnationis sexcentesimo quinquagesimo

[z] This compilation follows the tract, De Translationibus S. Cuthberti, in Cotton MS., Nero, A. ii., in Laud, 491, in Cotton MS., Titus, A. xi., and, in part, in MS. Gale, Trin. Coll., Camb., O. iii., 55. It appears to have occupied the same position in the MS. from whence the text in the Acta Benedictorum has been derived, the copy being an imperfect one, as regarded the latter portion of the first work and the earlier portion of the second. The fragments have been treated by the editor of the Liber de Translationibus as parts of the same work, and have been united by the insertion of a long extract from Symeon's History of the Church of Durham, so as to present the appearance of an integral history. The first eight sections are epitomized from Beda and the anonymous monk of Lindisfarne, the remainder are from Symeon, and in two or three cases from the Liber de Translationibus, with the exception of the last, which is compiled from various sources.

[a] The initial letter is handsomely illuminated in MS. Laud.

primo, ab adventu Sancti Augustini in Angliam quinquagesimo quinto, ex quo autem gens Northanimbrorum per Sanctum Oswaldum et Aidanum fidem Christi suscepit septimo decimo, anno regni Oswiu nono, ubi sub disciplina Boisili, sublimium virtutum sacerdotis et monachi, et ejusdem ecclesiæ præpositi, degens, omni se monasticæ institutionis observantia, vigilando videlicet, jejunando, orando, et cætera quæ regulæ sunt sedulo exequendo exercebat, et formam exempli se cunctis præbebat.

III.—HIC PRIOR.

Defuncto autem Boisilo ipse pro eo ibidem præpositus ordinatus est. Peractis vero ibi felici conversatione tredecim annis, transtulit eum reverentissimus ipsius abbas, Eata, in Lindisfarnense monasterium, quod tunc, ut Mailrosense, abbatis jure regebat; ut ibi, sicut et in Mailros post obitum beati Boisili fecerat, regulam monasticæ perfectionis, præpositi auctoritate, doceret, anno Dominicæ incarnationis sexcentesimo sexagesimo quarto. Qui, qualis, quantusve in eodem monasterio vixerit, vel quibus se studiis ad cælestia promerenda exercuerit, vel signis claruerit, vel quomodo, ut omnes lucrifaceret, omnibus omnia factus sit,[b] legat librum de vita et virtutibus beati viri qui scire voluerit.

IV.—HIC HEREMITA.

Cumque in eodem monasterio duodecim annorum curricula complesset, ut Domino Deo suo secretius militaret, insulam Farne, comitante abbatis sui et fratrum gratia, multum lætabundus ingreditur, ante ipsum cunctis pene inhabitabilem propter demorantium ibi fantasias dæmonum. In hac tantum sui erat negligens, tantum cælestibus ardebat desideriis, tanta animi perfectione Divinis invigilabat mandatis, et tanta Divinæ contemplationis puritate supernam suspirabat patriam, ut merito multum confidenter cum Apostolo dicere posset, *Nostra conversatio in cœlis est.*[c]

V.—HIC ELIGITUR IN EPISCOPUM.

Anno Dominicæ incarnationis sexcentesimo septuagesimo sexto, anno regni Egfridi sexto, monachatus sui vicesimo sexto, intravit insulam Farne vir Domini Cuthbertus, per novem annos mira animi alacritate Domino militabat. Postea congregata

[b] Ep. ad Romanos, ix. 22.
[c] Ep. ad Philipp., iii. 20.

synodo non parva sub præsentia piissimi regis Egfridi et beatæ memoriæ Theodori, Cantuariensis archiepiscopi, in loco qui dicitur Twiford juxta fluvium Alne, unanimo omnium consensu ad episcopatum Lindisfarnensem electus est. Qui, cum, multis legatariis pro se missis et litteris, nequaquam suo loco posset erui, rex præfatus, et Trumwine episcopus, cum pluribus religiosis et potentibus, veniunt, genu flectunt, et per Dominum adjurant, lacrymas fundunt, obsecrant, donec et ipsum lacrymis plenum ad synodum pertrahunt. Quo perveniens, licet plurimum renitens, compellitur ab omnibus episcopali officio collum submittere.

VI.—HIC ORDINATUS EST.

Ordinatus est autem Eboraci a Theodoro Dorobernensi archiepiscopo, septimo kalendas Aprilis, ipso die Paschæ, convenientibus ad consecrationem ejus vij[tem] episcopis, præsente rege Egfrido, quintodecimo anno regni ipsius, sexcentesimo octogesimo quinto incarnationis Dominicæ. Suscepto igitur episcopatu episcopalem curam episcopaliter per omnia ministrabat, in omnibus, et in turbis existens monachus.

VII.—DEPOSITIO EJUS.

Duobus vero annis in regimine episcopali transactis, sciens in spiritu appropinquare diem sui transitus, repetiit insulam mansionemque suam. Prima igitur ebdomada Quadragesimæ, feria quarta, cœpit ægrotare; et reversus quarta feria post mediam Quadragesimam, tribus continuis ebdomadibus infirmitate decoctus, instante nocturnæ orationis tempore, perceptis sacramentis salutaribus, tertiodecimo kalendas Aprilis migravit ad Dominum, luna prima.

Anno Dominicæ incarnationis, videlicet, sexcentesimo octogesimo septimo, episcopatus sui tertio, anachoreseos tertiodecimo, monachatus tricesimo septimo,[d] ex quo autem rex Oswaldus et Aidanus episcopus pontificalem sedem in Lindisfarnea insula instituerunt quinquagesimo tertio, corpus illius ad beati Petri Apostoli ecclesiam, quæ in insula Lindisfarnensi est, delatum est, ibique ad dexteram altaris petrino in sarcophago repositum.

VIII.—QUOMODO INTEGER INVENTUS EST POST UNDECIM ANNOS.

Transactis sepulturæ ejus annis undecim, die depositionis

[d] The words from episcopatus are omitted in MS. A.

illius, quæ est tertiodecimo kalendas Aprilis, aperientes sepulchrum ejus fratres, ut ossa illius, quæ jam sicca invenienda putabant, supra pavimentum dignæ venerationis gratia locarent, invenerunt corpus totum, quasi adhuc viveret, integrum, et flexibilibus artuum compagibus, multo dormienti quam mortuo similius. Vestimenta quoque quibus indutum erat, intemerata et prisca novitate et claritate miranda. Extremam partem indumentorum ejus pro ostendendo incorruptionis signo tollentes, novo involutum amictu corpus, levique in theca reconditum, supra pavimentum sanctuarii composuerunt.

IX.—QUOMODO DESTRUCTA EST EJUS ECCLESIA.

Anno ab incarnatione Domini DCC.xciii., etc. (Symeonis Hist. Dunelm., II., v.)

X.—QUOMODO AQUA IN SANGUINEM CONVERSA EST.

Anno ab incarnatione Domini DCCC.lxxv., etc. (Hist Dunelm., II., vi., xi.)

XI.—DE TEXTO EVANGELIORUM.

Hac tempestate dum navis, etc. (Hist. Dunelm., II., xi., xii.)

XII.—DE CRECA. XIII.—DE CUNCHECESTER. XIV.—DE SCOTTIS.

Cum etiam corpori suo, etc. (Hist. Dunelm., II., xiii.)

XV.—DE RHIPUM.

Anno Dominicæ incarnationis CM.xcv, ab obitu Sancti Cuthberti ccc.ix, regni vero Æthelredi xvii, pontificatus sui sexto, Aldunus episcopus, cælesti præmonitus oraculo ut cum incorrupto sanctissimi patris corpore quantocitius fugiens superventuram pyratarum rabiem declinaret, tulit illud cxiii. anno, ex quo in Cunchecestre locatum fuerat, et cum omni qui ejus dicitur populo in Hripum transportavit, tempore veris: in qua fuga illud memorabile fertur, quod in tanta multitudine nemo a minimo ad maximum ulla infirmitatis molestia affligebatur, sed sine ullo labore et incommodo viam gradiendo incedebant. Animalia etiam tenera[e] et nuper nata, sana et incolumia, sine aliqua

[e] The imperfect MS. used by the editors of the Acta Sanctorum became available at this point, the hiatus extending beyond the word *tenera*. This and the following section together form section xx. of the Liber de Translationibus in the printed copies.

difficultate et vexatione toto itinere gradiebantur. (Hist. Dunelm., III., i.)

XVI.—DE WARDELAU.

Post tres autem vel quatuor menses, etc. (Hist. Dunelm., III., i.)

XVII.—QUOMODO SANCTUM CORPUS IN DUNELMO LOCATUM EST.

Præfatus autem antistes cum sanctissimo corpore Dunelmum veniens, locum quidem natura munitum, etc. (Hist. Dunelm., III., ii., iv., vi.)

XVIII.—DE INVENTIONE SANCTARUM RELIQUIARUM. XIX.—DE SANCTO BEDA.[f]

Sub hoc antistite in ipsa Dunelmensi ecclesia, etc. (Hist. Dunelm., III., vii.)

XX.—DE PRÆSUMPTIONE CUJUSDAM PRESBYTERI.[g]

Post Edmundi obitum, pontificatum Dunelmensis ecclesiam Egelrico regente, inusitata res facta, etc. (Hist. Dunelm., III., x.)

XXI.—QUOMODO SERPENS COLLUM CUJUSDAM STRINXIT.[h]

Fuit et alius quidam pravæ actionis vir, Osulfus vocabulo. (Hist. Dunelm., III., xii.)

XXII.—DE FURTO OBLATIONIS AD SEPULCRUM.[i]

Eodem tempore quidam ad sollemne, etc. (Hist. Dunelm., III., xiii.)

[f] These two sections, with the two preceding, form sections xxi., xxii., xxiii., and conclude chapter v. (containing sections xv.-xxiii.) in the printed copies.

[g] Section xxiv., being the commencement of chapter v. in the printed copies. Then follows section xxv., containing the story of the Countess Judith and her maid, which forms section xxviii. of the Cotton MS.; and sections xxvi. and xxvii., in which are related the legends of Aldanhamel and Barcwid, as printed in the present volume, pp. 168-170.

[h] Section xxvi. of the printed copies.

[i] Section xxix. of the printed copies.

XXIII.—QUOMODO OCCISI SUNT NORMANNI IN DUNELMO.[j]

Anno ab incarnatione Domini M.lxix, ex quo corpus beati Cuthberti Dunelmum ab Alduno est perlatum lxxiv, tertio regni sui, Willelmus rex Anglorum quendam Rodbertum, cognomine Cumin, etc. (Hist. Dunelm., III., xv.)

XXIV.—DE QUADAM FUGA CUM SANCTO CORPORE.[k]

Rege autem Willelmo eodem anno Eboracum veniente, etc. (Hist. Dunelm., III., xv.)

XXV.—QUARE FEMINÆ NON INTRANT ECCLESIAM SANCTI CUTHBERTI.

In nullam ecclesiarum pene, etc. (Hist. Dunelm., II., vii.)

XXVI.—DE EODEM.

Quarum quædam vocabulo Sungive, etc. (Hist. Dunelm., II., viii.)

XXVII.—ITEM DE EODEM.

Erat et alia quædam uxor cujusdam divitis, etc. (Hist. Dunelm., II., ix.)

XXVIII.—ITEM DE EODEM. XXIX.—DE CRUCE ET DE IMAGINE CRUCIFIXI ET S. MARIÆ ET S. JOHANNIS EVANGELISTÆ.[l]

Pontificante post Ægelwinum Ægelrico, Judith filia comitis Flandrensium Baldwini, honesta valde et religiosa, etc. (Hist. Dunelm., III., xi.)

XXX.—QUOMODO SANCTUS OSWALDUS ET SANCTUS CUTHBERTUS PER VISUM CUIDAM APPARUERUNT IN PRÆSCRIPTA FUGA.[m]

In fuga memorata quidam ultra amnem Tynam præpotens, Gillo-Michael.[n] (Hist. Dunelm., III., xvi.)

[j] Section xxx. of the printed copies.

[k] Section xxxi., being the conclusion of chapter v. of the printed copies of the Liber de Translationibus.

[l] These two sections occur earlier in the printed copies, of which they form section xxv. The three previous sections are not included in the printed copies.

[m] Sections xxii., xxxiii., xxxiv., being the commencement of chapter vi. of the printed text of the Liber de Translationibus Sancti Cuthberti.

[n] This legend of Gillo-Michael is related by Symeon on the authority of the

XXXI.—DE FRAUDE EGELWINI EPISCOPI.[o]

Reportato in Dunelmum, etc. (Hist. Dunelm., III., xvii.)

XXXII.—QUOMODO REX WILLELMUS, MUTATO PROPOSITO ET DECRETO, SANCTO CUTHBERTO SUOS PROTEGENTE, FUGAM INIIT.[p]

Tempore Walcheri episcopi, primi ex ordine clericali Dunelmensis ecclesiæ episcopi, excepto quodam simoniaco, post aliquot menses mortuo, rex prædictus Willelmus de Scotia, etc. (Hist. Dunelm., III., xix.)

XXXIII.—QUOMODO SANCTUS CUTHBERTUS QUENDAM RANDULFUM CASTIGAVERAT, ET SUOS A TRIBUTO LIBERAVIT.[q]

Post tempus aliquot, etc. (Hist. Dunelm., III., xx.)

XXXIV.—QUOMODO SANCTUS CUTHBERTUS SEXELMUM, EPISCOPUM SIMONIACUM, PEPULIT, ET DE TERRA SUA FUGAVERIT.

Defuncto autem Uhtredo episcopo, etc. (Hist. Dunelm., II., xix.)

XXXV.—MORS REGIS IMPII HALFDENI.

Cum ergo et corpore suo. (Hist. Dunelm., II., xiii.)

XXXVI.—QUOMODO SANCTUS CUTHBERTUS PRÆBUIT EXEMPLUM SUCCESSORIBUS SUIS.[r]

Venerabilis autem Cuthbertus. (Hist. Dunelm., I., x.)

individual who saw the vision, the particulars of which he had frequently heard from his own lips. The author of the compilation before us copies Symeon's narrative *verbatim*, giving as his authority the testimony of the same party, from whom, however, he does not say that he had himself heard it, but that *very many* had heard it, thus confirming the impression which we derive from the perusal of the compilation throughout, that the author epitomized Symeon at no very great interval, when some of the very many auditors of the second-sighted monk were still alive to testify to the accuracy of the report of his narrative.

[o] Section xxxv. of the printed copies.

[p] Section xxxvi. of the printed copies.

[q] Section xxxvii. of the printed copies. Two other sections occur in the printed text, viz., section xxxviii., which forms the seventh section of our MSS. of the Liber de Translationibus, p. 172 of this volume; and section xxxix., which forms the third chapter of the third book of Symeon's History of the Church of Durham. Symeon relates the miracle on the authority of certain religious and aged priests from whom he had repeatedly heard it. In the printed text his statement on this head is adopted without alteration.

[r] Not in MSS. A. or N.

XXXVII.—VISIO BOSONIS.

In tempore Willelmi quidam militum ejus vocabulo Boso. (Hist. Dunelm., IV., ix.)

XXXVIII.—QUO ANNO SANCTUS CUTHBERTUS ORDINATUS EST, ET QUANTUM AMABATUR ET VENERABATUR AB ANTIQUIS REGIBUS.[s]

Anno Dominicæ incarnationis DC.lxxxv, ordinatus est beatus pater Cuthbertus in ipsa sollemnitate Paschali, id est, septimo kalendas Aprilis, ad Lindisfarnensem ecclesiam, ipso rege præsente, et vij ad ejus consecrationem venientibus episcopis, in quibus Theodorus primatum tenuit. In die ordinationis Sancti Cuthberti commutaverunt ipse et Eata sedes episcopales communi consilio Egfridi regis, et Theodori archiepiscopi, et aliorum, scilicet Ceadæ et Ceddæ, et aliorum v episcoporum et omnium majorum: sicque Eata apud Hesteldesham sedit, Sanctus vero Cuthbertus Lindisfarnensem cathedram obtinuit. Hujus Lindisfarniæ terminus est a fluvio Tuoda usque ad Warnedmuda, et inde superius usque ad locum ubi aqua Warned oritur juxta montem Hiberdune, et inde usque ad fluvium Bromwic, et inde usque ad fluvium Tyl. Et illam terram ultra Tuydam a fluvio Edre, ab aquilone usque ad locum quo cadit in Tuoda; et totam terram quæ jacet inter istum fluvium Eddre, et alterum qui vocatur Leder; et totam terram quæ pertinet ad monasterium Sancti Balteri, quod est in Tiniggcham, a Lambre-more usque ad Escemude. Et dederunt rex Egfridus et archiepiscopus Theodorus terram in Eboraco Sancto Cuthberto a muro Sancti Petri, usque ad magnam portam occidentalem, et usque ad murum civitatis versus austrum. Et dederunt ei villam quæ dicitur Creic, et tria miliaria in circuitu, ut ibi posset manere in eundo et redeundo de Eboraco. Ibi Sanctus Cuthbertus congregationem monachorum et abbatem nomine Geve, ut quidam dicunt, statuit. Huic adjecerunt civitatem Luel, id est Carlel, et in circuitu xv miliaria, et ibi Sanctus Cuthbertus congregationem sanctimonialium et abbatissam ordinavit, et scolas ibi

[s] This section has been printed by Mr. Longstaffe in the Archæologia Æliana, vol. ii. (8vo series), p. 6, from the Lawson MS. As a record of the possessions of the church of St. Cuthbert, it is neither complete nor altogether accurate; nor does it furnish us with any reliable information which we do not already possess from authentic sources. It has, however, been thought expedient to print it *in extenso*, for the sake of comparison with the Historia de Sancto Cuthberto, the Historia de Gestis Regum, and Symeon's History of the Church of Durham. The text is taken from MS. Gale, O. iii., 55; the chapter does not occur either in MS. Laud or Cotton, Nero, A. ii.

constituit. Postquam vero Sanctus Cuthbertus suscitavit puerum a mortuis in villa quæ dicitur Exanforda, dedit ei rex Egfrid terram quæ vocatur Ceartmel et omnes Britanni *(sic)* cum eo, et villam quæ dicitur Suth-gedling, et quicquid ad eam pertinet. Hæc omnia bonus abbas Cyneverdus sub Sancto Cuthberto ordinavit sapienter ut voluit. Ea tempestate pugnavit rex Egfridus contra regem Merciorum Wulfere filium Pendici, et, cæso exercitu ejus, fugavit eum. Postea dedit Egfridus rex Sancto Cuthberto Mailros et Carrum, et quicquid ad eam pertinet. Non multum post hunc Egfridum successit in regnum Ceolfus filius Cudwining, seque Sancto Cuthberto subdidit; et, dimisso regno cum uxore pro amore Dei, se cum magno thesauro ad Lindisfarnense monasterium contulit, barbam deposuit, coronam accepit, et Sancto Cuthberto villam dedit nomine Werchewurde cum suis appenditiis. Sed post hæc quidam rex, nomine Osbertus, Werchewurde abstulit Sancto, sed post annum vitam cum regno perdidit. Post eum regnavit Elle, qui bene promisit sed male egit; abstulit enim Sancto duas villas, Billingeham et Ileclif; sed cito per Hubbam ducem Fresonum fugatus et cæsus, vitam dedecorose finivit. Statim post Ceolfwulfum factum monachum obiit Sanctus Cuthbertus; et successit Eddred episcopus, qui reædificavit ecclesiam in Northam, et transportavit illuc corpus Ceolfi regis, ipsamque villam dedit Sancto Cuthberto et Gedewrde, et alteram Gedewurde, et ædificavit villam Geinford, deditque eam Sancto Cuthberto; et postea ædificavit Billingeham, et Ileclif, et Wigeclif, deditque Sancto. Quando Sanctus Cuthbertus factus est monachus regnavit Oswigius, et alii dicunt quod iste fuit Oswiu frater Oswaldi regis, et interfecit Oswinum regem Berniciorum, filium Osrici regis Edwini filii. Ante Oswigium regnavit Penda rex. Mortuo Oswigio, regnavit Egfridus filius ejus. Post eum Ceolfridus; et post hunc Gudredus qui per Sanctum Cuthbertum apparentem per visionem abbati Edredo in Luercestre factus fuit rex, Erdulfo episcopante, anno ab incarnatione Domini DCCC.XC°. Post hunc Ælfredus qui dedit Sancto totam terram inter Tesam et Tinam. Isti Gudredus et Ælfredus reges adjecerunt Dunelmensi episcopatui omnia quæ ad episcopatum Haugustaldensem pertinuerunt. Per l enim et iiij annos ante devastationem Northumbriæ sedes episcopalis ibi cessaverat. Æelfredo defuncto regnavit filius ejus Ædwardus; et post hunc Edelstanus filius ejus, et post, Ædmundus frater Adelstani. Quo mortuo, anno Dominicæ incarnationis nongentesimo quadragesimo octavo, Edredum fratrem hæredem regni reliquit.

Hi omnes cultores Sancti Cuthberti leges ejus et privilegia

confirmaverunt, et servaverunt, et terras cum multis aliis donariis Sancto contulerunt. Sed Edred moriens reliquit hæredem filium fratris sui Edmundi, nomine Edwi, malignæ mentis hominem, omnibus odiosum. Hic a finibus totius Angliæ expulit Sanctum Dunstanum de incestu eum corripientem. Unde omnes ab Humbre usque ad Tamisiam, contra Edwinum offensi, ultra Tamisiam eum fugaverunt, et juniorem fratrem suum regem fecerunt, nomine Ædgarum. Qui cum multos annos feliciter regnasset, filio suo Edwardo, qui jacet in Sceftesbiri, regnum moriens reliquit. Qui in brevi novercali fraude occisus, Edelredum fratrem hæredem habuit. Deinde Cnud regno Anglorum potitus, et ad Dunelmum veniens, per v miliaria, a loco qui Garmundi Via dicitur, nudis pedibus incedens, ad sepulcrum Sancti Cuthberti venit; et ibi ei obtulit, et dedit liberam et quietam, Steindrop, cum omnibus appenditiis suis. Post hunc regnavit Edwardus filius Ethelredi et Emmæ, Qui primo anno regni sui monachum quendam, nomine Egelricum, de Burc, episcopum præfecit ecclesiæ Dunelmensi; sed eam regere non valens ad proprium monasterium rediit, sicque sine episcopatu vitam finivit. Postea anno Dominicæ incarnationis M.lxxiij, sui regni anno viij, Willelmus rex, post Haroldum occisum potentissimus, versus Scotiam regnum suum visurus, et si qui rebelles ei essent subditurus, ad Sanctum Cuthbertum oraturus venit. Cui sciscitanti de vita et miraculis Sancti, et de antiquitate et origine episcopatus, prudentiores ecclesiæ dixerunt ei Sanctum Oswaldum regem, ascito Sancto Aidano de Scotia, sedem episcopalem in Lindifarnensi insula primitus instituisse, et ei dedisse. Dixerunt etiam quomodo rex Egfridus et Theodorus archiepiscopus invitum, de solitaria vita extractum, episcopum fecerunt; et quanta veneratione ab eodem rege dum vixit semper habebatur, et a subsequentibus Christianis regibus post mortem quantum diligebatur, et honorabatur; et quomodo omnia ad eum pertinentia semper augmentabant, et sua auctoritate confirmabant, ut in perpetua libertate, et quietitudine permanerent, et cum omnibus consuetudinibus, ut ipsi in sua manu habuerant.

Hæc cum rex et alia multa audisset, propria manu cum auro et pallio imperpetuum servanda tribuit libere et quiete Deo et Sancto Cuthberto et Walchero episcopo, Waltham, cum omnibus appenditiis suis; dedit et l mansiones in Lindesei; et adjecit postea Willelmo episcopo Welletunam et Hovedene, cum omnibus suis appenditiis, cum saca et socna et omnibus legibus, sicut et ipse in propria manu habuit. Isto eodem rege Willelmo laudante et concedente, Ædgarus rex Scotiæ donavit et reddidit Sancto Cuthberto et Willelmo episcopo in Lodoneio Berewic cum omnibus suis appenditiis; Et monachis in ecclesia Dunelmi Deo et Sancto Cuthberto servientibus Coldingham, cum suis omnibus appenditiis, sicut in carta continetur; quam ipse et fratres sui propria manu signaverunt et firmaverunt.[t]

[t] This section concludes the Relatio de Sancto Cuthberto, but in the Lawson MS. it is followed by some curious particulars relative to the lordship and church of Hexham, which are printed with it in the Archæologia Æliana by Mr. Longstaffe. They will also be found in the Memorials of the Church of Hexham, edited by Mr. Raine for the Surtees Society, vol. i., p. vii. of Appendix.

[VITA S. MARGARETÆ SCOTORUM REGINÆ,

AUCTORE, UT QUIBUSDAM VIDETUR, TURGOTO MONACHO DUNELMENSI.]

[PROLOGUS.]

[u]EXCELLENTER honorabili, et honorabiliter excellenti, reginæ Anglorum, Mathildæ, T.,[v] servorum S. Cuthberti servus, in præsenti, pacis et salutis bonum; et, in futuro, bonorum omnium bonum.

Venerandæ memoriæ matris vestræ placitam Deo conversationem, quam consona multorum laude sæpius prædicari audieratis, ut litteris traditam vobis offerrem, et postulando jussistis, et jubendo postulastis. Scilicet mihi præcipue in hoc credendum dicebatis, quem, gratia magnæ apud illam familiaritatis, magna ex parte secretorum illius conscium esse audieratis. Hæc jussa et hæc vota ego libens amplector; amplectens, multum veneror; venerans, vobis congratulor, quæ a Rege Angelorum constituta regina Anglorum, vitam matris reginæ, quæ semper ad regnum anhelabat Angelorum, non solum audire, sed etiam litteris impressam desideratis jugiter inspicere; ut qui faciem matris parum noveratis, virtutum ejus notitiam plenius habeatis. Et quidem mihi imperata perficiendi prona est voluntas; sed, fateor, deest facultas: major est quippe hujus negotii materia, quam mihi sit vel scribendi vel loquendi efficacia. Duo namque sunt quæ patior, quibus hinc et inde trahor. Propter magnitudinem rei, obedire formido; propter jubentis auctoritatem, et illius de qua dicendum est memoriam, contradicere non audeo. Sed quamvis, sicut dignum esset, tantam rem explicare non valeo; quantum tamen possum (quia

[u] The initial E in colours, red, green, and blue; square.

[v] *Theodericus* in the Acta Sanctorum, and in Pinkerton's edition. At the end of the paragraph there are added in a hand of the seventeenth century, *Per Turgotum Dunelmensem.* On the question of the authorship of this work, see the Preface.

hoc et ejus dilectio et vestra exigit jussio) intimare debeo. Gratia namque Sancti Spiritus, quæ illi dederat efficaciam virtutum, mihi, ut spero, enarrandi eas sumministrabit auxilium. *Dominus dabit verbum evangelizantibus*:[w] et iterum, *Aperi os tuum, et ego adimplebo illud.*[x] Neque enim poterit deficere Verbo, qui credit in Verbo: *In principio enim erat Verbum.*[y] In primis igitur cupio, et vos, et alios scire per vos, quod si omnia, quæ de illa novi prædicanda, dicere conabor, vobis, propter regiæ dignitatis apicem, in matris laude adulari putabor. Sed procul absit a mea canicie, virtutibus tantæ feminæ mendacii crimen admiscere. In quibus exponendis, Deo teste ac judice, profiteor me nihil, supra id quod est, addere; sed, ne incredibilia videantur, multa silentio supprimere; ne, juxta illud Oratoris, cornicem dicar cignæis coloribus adornare.[z]

(CAPITULA.)[a]

I. *Quod Margarita regina effectu operis servaverit decorem nominis.*
II. *Quam nobili prosapia genealogiam duxerit.*
III. *Qualiter in prima ætate cœperit, et in honorem sullimata honore non delectata fuerit.*
IV. *Quod in loco nuptiarum ecclesiam erexerit, et ecclesiarum ornamenta quam studiose præparari fecerit, quantoque moderamine se suosque gubernaverit.*
V. [*Quomodo*] *filii honeste* [*nutriti sint*].
VI. [*Quam*] *studiosa fuerit in lectione* [*quær*]*endo in hac non solum suam, sed etiam aliorum salutem.*
VII. *Quantum decoris et gloriæ regno Scottorum contulerit.*
VIII. *Quomodo* [*correxerit*] *ea quæ contra fidem et sanctæ ecclesiæ consuetudinem agebant, et ad regulam* [*celebrare*] *con*[*sueverit*].
IX. *Quantum compunctioni et orationi, jejuniæ quoque et misericordiæ dedita fuerit operibus.*
X. *Qualiter ante Dominicum Natale et in Quadragesima vitam consueverit ducere.*
XI. *Quod in testimonium sanctæ conversationis ejus quiddam Dominus ostenderit.*

[w] Psalm lxvii. 12. [x] Psalm lxxxvii. 10. [y] S. Joh. i. 1.
[z] I cannot verify this reference.
[a] The sections to which these capitula refer, have each in the MS. a coloured initial letter. In the printed text Roman numerals have been prefixed. In three other places similar coloured letters are placed at the commencement of sentences, as specified in the notes. The blanks in the capitula are supplied (within brackets) from corresponding passages in the sections to which they refer.

XII. *Quod obitum suum præscierit, et quædam futura prædixerit.*

XIII. *Qualiter de hac vita migraverit.*

I.

Quod Margarita regina effectu operis servaverit decorem nominis.[b]

[c]Multi, ut legimus, a qualitate mentis originem traxerunt nominis; ut in illis vocabulum prætenderet, quod gratiæ, quam acceperunt, conveniret. Sic denique Petrus a petra Christo, ob fidei firmitatem; sic Johannes, quod est Dei gratia, ob Divinitatis contemplationem et Divini amoris privilegium; et filii Zebedæi, (Boanerges) id est Filii Tonitrui sunt dicti, propter evangelicæ prædicationis tonitruum. Quod in hac virtutis femina invenitur: quæ decorem, quem homine præferebat, majori animæ pulchritudine vincebat. Namque Margarita vocabatur, et ipsa in conspectu Dei fide atque opere ut pretiosa Margarita habebatur. Itaque Margarita vestra, mea, nostra, immo Christi, et quia Christi idcirco plus nostra, jam nos reliquit ad Dominum assumpta. Assumpta est, inquam, Margarita de mundi hujus sterquilinio, et rutilat nunc in [æterni Regis posita ornamento. Inde] enim ne[mo, ut reor, dubi]tabit, cum ejus vitam et vitæ [finem][d] paulo post audierit. Cujus mecum colloquia, sale sapientiæ condita, dum recolo; dum lacrymas, quas compunctio cordis excusserat, considero; dum sobrietatem et morum compositionem intueor; dum affabilitatis et prudentiæ reminiscor; lugens gaudeo, et gaudens lugeo. Gaudeo, quia ad Deum, quem suspiraverat, transiit; lugeo, quia cum illa in cælestibus non gaudeo. Illi, inquam, gaudeo; quia quæ crediderat, jam nunc videt *bona Domini in terra viventium:*[e] mihi autem lugeo, quoniam in terra mortuorum, dum mortalis vitæ miserias patior, quotidie clamare compellor, *Infelix ego homo, quis me liberabit de corpore mortis hujus?*[f]

[b] These special headings are not in the MS., but are inserted from the list of chapters which has just been given.

[c] The initial letter is again ornamented in red, green, and blue.

[d] The portions of the text which are rendered illegible in consequence of the partial destruction of the MS. by fire are enclosed within brackets. They are taken from Pinkerton.

[e] Psalm xxvii. 13.

[f] Ep. at Rom., vii. 24.

II.

Quam nobili prosapia genealogiam duxerit.

[[g]Quoniam igitur de illius,] quam in Christo habuerat, mentis nobilitate, mihi est dicendum, de illa quoque, quo secundum sæculum claruerat, videtur aliquid præmittendum. Ejus avus extiterat rex Ædmundus, qui pro eo quod pugnandi strenuus et invincibilis erat hostibus, ab excellentia virtutis contraxerat insigne nominis; nam quod Latine dicitur Ferreum-Latus, Anglorum lingua est appellatus *(blank)*. Cujus frater ex patre, non autem ex matre, piissimus ille atque mansuetissimus fuerat Edwardus, qui se patrem patriæ exhibuerat; et alter quodammodo Salomon, id est pacificus, magis pace quam armis regnum protexerat. Gerebat animum iræ victorem, avaritiæ contemptorem, superbiæ prorsus expertem. Nec mirum: nam sicut a majoribus gloriam dignitatis, ita vitam quoque honestatis quodam quasi hæreditario jure est assecutus: Rege Anglorum Ædgaro, et Comite Normannorum Ricardo, avis, non solum nobilissimis, sed etiam religiosissimis, progenitus. Quorum Eadgarus, ut quantus in sæculo, qualisque fuerit in Christo breviter agnoscatur, rex simul et justitiæ ac pacis amator futurus præsignabatur. Nato enim illo, audivit beatus Dunstanus beatos in cælo Angelos gratulantes, et cum magna gratulatione psallentes; "Sit pax, sit magna Anglorum "ecclesiæ lætitia, quamdiu puer natus regnum tenuerit, et Dun-"stanus mortalis vitæ viam concurrerit." Ricardus quoque, genitor genitricis ipsius Edwardi, Emmæ, tanto nepote dignus effulserat, vir per omnia strenuus, omnique præconio laudandus. Nemo etenim de suis progenitoribus, vel in Comitatus honore felicior, vel in religionis amore ferventior. In summis divitiis positus, spiritu, velut alter David, erat pauperrimus; dominus populorum constitutus, servorum Christi servus fuit humillimus. Inter alia quæ, in suæ religiosæ devotionis monumentum, fecerat, nobile illud Fiscannense monasterium pius Christicola contruxerat; in quo ipse, sæcularis quidem habitu, sed monachus actu, sæpe cum monachis conversari, eisque inter manducandum cibos cum silentio apponere, et potum consueverat ministrare; ut, secundum Scripturam, quanto magnus erat, tanto se in omnibus humiliaret.[h] Cujus magnificentiæ ac virtutum opera qui plenius nosse desiderat, Gesta Normannorum,[i] quæ etiam ipsius acta continent, legat. Ab his tantæ claritudinis et excellentiæ progenitoribus, nepos Edwardus in nullo

[g] Small red initial. [h] Eccl. iii. 20.
[i] See Duchesne.

degeneravit; ex solo, ut antedictum est, patre frater Eadmundi regis; cujus filius, Margarita exorta, claritate meritorum claram perornat seriem progenitorum.

III.

Qualiter in prima ætate cæperit, et in honorem sullimata honore non delectata fuerit.

[j]Cum ergo in primæva adhuc floreret ætate, vitam sobrietatis ducere, ac Deum super omnia cœpit diligere, in Divinarum lectionum studio sese occupare, et in his animum delectabiliter exercere. Inerat ei ad intelligendum quamlibet rem acuta ingenii subtilitas, ad retinendum multa memoriæ tenacitas, ad proferendum gratiosa verborum facilitas. Cum ergo in lege Domini die ac nocte meditaretur, et, tanquam altera Maria secus pedes Domini sedens, audire verbum illius delectaretur; suorum magis quam sua voluntate, immo Dei ordinatione, potentissimo regi Scottorum Malcolmo, regis Dunecani filio, in conjugium copulatur. Sed quamvis ea quæ sunt mundi compelleretur agere, mundi tamen rebus ex desiderio contempsit inhærere: plus enim delectabatur bono opere, quam divitiarum possessione. De temporalibus æternas sibi mercedes parabat, quoniam in cælo, ubi erat thesaurus ejus, cor suum locarat. Et quia præcipue regnum Dei et justitiam Ejus[k] quærebat, larga Omnipotentis gratia honores ei et divitias affluenter adjiciebat. Omnia quæ dicebantur prudentis reginæ imperio agebantur. Ejus consilio regni jura disponebantur; illius industria religio Divina augebatur; rerum prosperitate populus lætabatur. Nihil illius fide firmius, vultu constantius, patientia tolerabilius, consilio gravius, sententia justius, colloquio jucundius.

IV.

Quod in loco nuptiarum ecclesiam erexerit, et ecclesiarum ornamenta quam studiose præparari fecerit, quantoque moderamine se suosque gubernaverit.

[l]Postquam culmen ascenderat honoris, mox in loco ubi ejus nuptiæ fuerant celebratæ, æternum sui nominis et religiositatis erexit monumentum. Triplici enim salutis intentio(ne), nobilem ibi ecclesiam in Sanctæ Trinitatis ædificavit honorem;

[j] A small green letter. [k] S. Matt. vi. 33.
[l] Red letter.

ob animæ videlicet regis et suæ redemptionem, atque ad obtinendam suæ soboli vitæ præsentis et futuræ prosperitatem. Quam ecclesiam diversa ornamentorum specie decoravit; inter quæ, ad ipsum sacrosanctum altaris ministerium, non pauca ex solido ac puro auro vasa fuisse noscuntur, quæ tanto certius nosse poteram, quanto cuncta, jubente regina, ego ipse diutius ibidem servanda susceperam. Crucem quoque, incomparabilis pretii, imaginem Salvatoris habentem, quam auro purissimo et argento interlucentibus gemmis vestiri fecerat, ibidem collocavit, quæ intuentibus palam fidei ejus devotionem hodieque demonstrat. Similiter et in aliis quibusque ecclesiis sacræ devotionis et fidei sig[na reliquit: quod ecclesia S. Andreæ contesta]ta, cruci[fixi venustissimam, quam ibidem] ipsa erexerat, sicut hodie [cernitur, serv]at imaginem. His rebus, id est quæ ad Divinæ servitutis cultum pertinebant, numquam vacua erat illius camera; quæ, ut ita dicam, quædam cælestis artificii videbatur esse officina. Ibi cappæ cantorum, casulæ, stolæ, altaris pallia, alia quoque vestimenta sacerdotalia et ecclesiæ semper videbantur ornamenta. Alia manu [artificum parabantur; alia], jam parata, admiratione digna habebantur. His operibus feminæ deputabantur, quæ natu nobiles, et sobriis moribus probabiles, interesse reginæ obsequiis dignæ judicabantur. Nullus ad eas virorum introitus erat, nisi quos ipsa, cum interdum ad illas intraret, secum introire permittebat. Nulla eis inhonesta cum viris familiaritas, nulla unquam cum petulantia levitas. Inerat enim reginæ tanta cum jocunditate severitas, tanta cum severitate jocunditas, ut omnes qui erant in ejus obsequio, viri et feminæ, illam et timendo diligerent, et diligendo timerent. Quare in præsentia ejus non solum nihil execrandum facere, sed ne turpe quidem verbum quisquam ausus fuerat proferre. Ipsa enim universa in se reprimens vitia, cum magna gravitate lætabatur, cum magna honestate irascebatur. Nunquam hilaritate nimia in cachinnum soluta, nunquam irascendo fuerat in furorem effusa. Interdum aliorum peccatis, suis vero semper, irascebatur, ira illa laudanda, et justitiæ semper amica, quam habendam præcepit Psalmista, *Irascimini,* inquit, *et nolite peccare.*[m] Omnis vita ejus, summo discretionis moderamine composita, quædam erat virtutum forma. Sermo ejus sale sapientiæ conditus, silentium erat plenum bonis cogitationibus. Sobrietati morum ita ejus persona conveniebat, ut ad solam vitæ honestatem nata credi potuisset. Ut [autem multa breviter dicam, in omnibus quæ

[m] Ep. ad Ephes. iv. 26. The words are those of St. Paul, not of the Psalmist.

loquebatur, in omnibus] quæ agebat, [cælestia se cogitare] ostendebat.

V.

Quomodo filii honeste [nutriti sint].

[n]Nec minorem quam sibimet, filiis curam impendebat; ut, videlicet, cum omni diligentia nutrirentur, et quam maxime honestis moribus instituerentur. Unde quia sciebat scriptum, *Qui parcit virgæ odit filium,*[o] familiari ministro injunxerat, ut quoties infantili lascivia delinquerent, sicut ætas illa solet, eos ipse minis et verberibus coerceret. Quo religioso matris studio, multos qui provectiores ætate fuerant morum honestate infantes transcendebant: semper inter se benevoli existebant et pacifici, et minor ubique honorem exhibebat majori. Unde et inter missarum sollemnia, cum post parentes ad offerendum procederent, junior majorem prævenire nullo modo præsumpsit, sed secundum ætatis ordinem major juniorem præcedere consuevit. Quos sæpius ante se ductos, Christum et fidem Christi, juxta quod ætas illa capere poterat, docere; et, ut Eum semper timerent, diligenter studebat admonere. "Timete," inquit, "O "filii, Dominum, *Quoniam non erit inopia timentibus Eum*;[p] et si "Eum dilexeritis, Ipse vobis, o viscera mea, et præsentis vitæ "prosperitatem, et cum Sanctis omnibus æternam reddet felici- "tatem." Hæc matris desideria, hæc admonitio, hæc pro sua sobole die noctuque cum lacrymis oratio, ut suum Creatorem *in fide quæ per dilectionem operatur*[q] agnoscerent, agnoscendo colerent, colendo in omnibus et super omnia diligerent, et diligendo ad cælestis regni felicem gloriam pervenirent.

VI.

[Quam] studiosa fuerit in lectione, [quæ]rendo in hac non solum suam sed etiam aliorum salutem.

[r]Nec mirandum quod sapiens regina tanto se suosque regimine moderabatur, quæ sapientissimo sacræ semper Scripturæ magisterio regebatur. Nam, quod ego in illa multum admirari solebam, inter causarum tumultus, inter multiplices regni curas, miro studio Divinæ lectioni operam dabat; de qua cum doctissimis assidentibus viris etiam subtiles sæpius quæs-

[n] Blue and red letter.
[o] Prov. xiii. 24.
[p] Psalm xxxiii. 10.
[q] Ep. ad. Gal. v. 6.
[r] Red letter.

tiones conserebat. Sed sicut inter eos nemo illa ingenio profundior, ita nemo aderat eloquio clarior. Evenit itaque sæpius, ut ab ea ipsi doctores, multo quam advenerant, abcederent doctiores. Plane sacrorum voluminum religiosa, nec parva illi aviditas inerat; in quibus sibi acquirendis familiaris ejus caritas, et caritativa familiaritas, meipsum me fatigare plerumque cogebat. Nec in his solummodo suam, sed etiam aliorum quæsivit salutem: primoque omnium ipsum regem, ad justitiæ, misericordiæ, eleemosynarum, aliarumque opera virtutum, ipsa, cooperante sibi Deo, fecerat obtemperantissimum. Didicit ille ab ea etiam vigilias noctis frequenter orando producere; didicit, ejus hortatu et exemplo, cum gemitu cordis et lacrymarum profusione Deum orare. Fateor, magnum misericordiæ Dei mirabar miraculum, cum viderem interdum tantam orandi regis intentionem, tantam inter orandum in pectore viri sæcularis compunctionem. Ipsam tam venerabilis vitæ reginam, quoniam in ejus corde Christum veraciter habitare perspexerat, ille quoquomodo offendere formidabat; sed potius votis ejus et prudentibus consiliis celerius per omnia obedire properabat. Quæ ipsa respuerat, eadem et ipse respuere; et quæ amaverat, amore amoris illius amare. Unde et libros, in quibus ipsa vel orare consueverat, vel legere, ille, ignarus licet literarum, sæpe manu versare solebat et inspicere: et dum ab ea quis illorum esset ei carior audisset, hunc et ipse cariorem habere, deosculari, sæpius contrectare. Aliquando etiam advocato aurifice ipsum codicem auro gemmisque perornari præcepit, atque perornatum ipse rex ad reginam, quasi suæ devotionis indicium, referre consuevit.

VII.

Quantum decoris et gloriæ regno Scottorum contulerit.[s]

Hæc quoque regiæ stirpis nobilissima gemma, regii honoris magnificentiam regi multo magnificentiorem effecit, cunctisque regni primatibus, et illorum ministris, plurimum gloriæ ac decoris ipsa contulit. Fecerat enim ut mercatores, terra marique de diversis regionibus venientes, rerum venalium complures et pretiosas species, quæ ibidem adhuc ignotæ fuerant, adveherent: inter quas cum diversis coloribus vestes, variaque vestium ornamenta, indigenæ, compellente regina, emerent; ita ejus instantia diversis vestium cultibus deinceps incedebant compositi, ut tali decore quodammodo crederentur

[s] There is no break in the MS. to shew that this chapter begins here. The sense, however, requires it.

esse renovati. Obsequia etiam regis sublimiora constituit, ut eum procedentem sive equitantem multa eum grandi honore agmina constiparent; et hoc cum tanta censura, ut quocumque devenissent, nulli eorum cuiquam aliquid liceret rapere; nec rusticos aut pauperes quoslibet quolibet modo quisquam illorum opprimere auderet vel lædere. Regalis quoque aulæ ornamenta multiplicavit, ut non tantum diverso palliorum decore niteret, sed etiam auro argentoque domus tota resplenderet. Aut enim aurea vel argentea, aut deaurata sive deargentata fuerunt vasa, quibus regi et regni proceribus dapes inferebantur et potus. Et hæc quidem illa fecerat, non quia mundi honore delectabatur, sed, quod regia dignitas ab ea exigebat, persolvere cogebatur. Nam cum pretioso, ut reginam decebat, cultu induta procederet, omnia ornamenta velut altera Esther mente calcavit; seque sub gemmis et auro nil aliud quam pulverem et cinerem consideravit. ·Denique in tanta celsitudine dignitatis maximam semper habuit servandæ curam humilitatis. Tanto enim facilius omnem ex mundiali honore superbiæ tumorem reprimebat, quanto fragilis vitæ transitura conditio mentem illius nunquam fugerat. Illius enim sententiæ semper recordabatur, qua instabilis humanæ vi[tæ status sic discribitur: *Homo natus de*] *muliere brevi vivens* [*tempore repletur*] *multis miseriis, qui quasi flos egreditur et conteritur, et fugit velut umbra, et nunquam in eodem statu permanet.*[t] Illud quoque beati Jacobi Apostoli semper in mente versabat, *Quæ est*, inquit, *vita nostra? Vapor est ad modicum patens, deinceps exterminabitur.*[u] Et quia, ut Scriptura loquitur, *Beatus homo qui semper est pavidus;*[v] tanto facilius peccata venerabilis regina devitabat, quanto tremens et pavens districtum judicii diem indesinenter ante mentis oculos sibi præsentabat. Unde crebro me rogabat, ut quicquid in ejus vel verbo vel facto reprehendendum perviderem, id reprehendens secreto illi indicare non dubitarem. Quod dum rarius et tepidius quam vellet facerem, importunam se mihi ingerebat; dormientem et velut sui negligentem me arguebat: "*Corripiat,*" inquit, "*me justus in misericordia et* "*increpet me: oleum, autem,* id est adulatio, *peccatoris non* "*impinguat caput meum;*[w] meliora enim sunt vulnera diligentis, "quam inimici blandientis oscula." Hæc dicens, reprehensionem sui, quam quilibet alius deputare poterat ad opprobrium, ipsa ad virtutis appetebat profectum.

[t] Job xiv. 1, 2.
[u] S. Jac. iv. 14.
[v] Prov. xxviii. 14.
[w] Psalm cxl. 5.

VIII.

Quomodo ea quæ contra fidem et sanctæ ecclesiæ consuetudinem agebant [eradicaverit], et ad regulam [reducere] con[sueverit].

[x]Religiosa, et Deo digna regina, cum mente, verbo, et factis ad cælestem patriam tenderet, etiam alios secum in via immaculata invitabat ire, quo secum possent ad veram beatitudinem pervenire. Malum cum videret, admonuit ut bonus fieret; bonum, ut melior existeret; meliorem, ut optimus esse studeret. Quam fide Apostolica ferventem zelus domus Dei, quæ est ecclesia, comedit: unde quoque illicita, quæ in ea pullulaverant, eradicare penitus laboravit. Cum enim contra rectæ fidei regulam et sanctam universalis ecclesiæ consuetudinem, multa in [gente illa fieri perspexisset, crebra Concilia statuit ut, quoquomodo] valeret, ad veritatis viam errantes, Christo donante, reduceret. Quorum Conciliorum illud cæteris principalius esse constat, in quo sola, cum paucissimis suorum, contra perversa consuetudinis assertores, *gladio Spiritus, quod est verbum Dei,*[y] triduo dimicabat. Crederes alteram ibi Helenam residere, quia, sicut illa quondam Scripturarum sententiis Judæos, similiter nunc et hæc regina convicerat erroneos. Sed in hoc conflictu rex ipse adjutor [et præcipuus residebat; quodcumque in hac] causa illa jussisset, [dicere paratissimus] et facere. Qui, quoniam perfecte Anglorum linguam æque ac propriam noverat, vigilantissimus in hoc Concilio utriusque partis interpres extiterat. Igitur regina, præfatione præmissa, ut qui cum catholica ecclesia in una fide uni Deo servirent, ab eadem ecclesia novis quibusdam et peregrinis institutionibus discrepare non deberent, primum proposuit, Quadragesimale jejunium non legitime observare, quia hoc non cum sancta ubique ecclesia . . . . in capite jejunii, scilicet . . . . . septimana, feria secunda, consueverant inchoare. Contra illi; "Jejunium," inquiunt, "quod agimus Evangelica auctoritate, quæ Christi "narrat jejunium, per sex ebdomadas observamus." At illa, "Longe," ait, "in hoc Evangelio discordatis: legitur enim "ibi, Dominum quadraginta diebus jejunasse, quod manifestum "est vos non facere. Nam cum per sex ebdomadas sex Do-"nici dies a jejunio abstrahuntur, triginta tantum et sex dies "ad jejunandum remanere noscuntur. Non ergo Evangelica "auctoritate quadraginta, sed triginta et sex dierum constat "vos observare jejunium. Restat itaque ut quatuor diebus ante "Quadragesimæ initium jejunare nobiscum incipiatis, si Do-

[x] Red letter.

[y] Ep. ad Ephes. vi. 17.

"minico exemplo xl dierum numero abstinentiam observare "volueritis: a[lioquin] contra ipsius Domini auctoritatem, et "totius sanctæ ecclesiæ vos soli repugnabitis traditionem." Hac illi perspicua veritatis [x]ratione convicti, deinceps, sicut sancta ubique solet ecclesia, sacrorum jejuniorum cœperunt inchoare sollemnia.

[x]Aliud quoque proponens regina, jussit ut ostenderent qua ratione die sancto Paschæ, secundum morem sanctæ et Apostolicæ ecclesiæ, sacramenta corporis et sanguinis Christi sumere negligerent. Respondentes illi: "Apostolus," inquiunt, "de "his loquens, ait: *Qui manducat et bibit indigne, judicium sibi "manducat et bibit.*[a] Unde quia nos peccatores recognoscimus, "ne judicium nobis manducemus et bibamus, ad illud myste- "rium accedere formidamus." Quibus regina, "Quid igitur?" inquit, "omnes qui peccatores sunt sacrosanctum mysterium "non gustabunt? Nemo ergo illud sumere debet, quia nemo "sine sorde peccati, nec infans cujus est unius diei vita super "terram. Si autem nemo illud percipere debet, cur Domino "dicente clamat Evangelium, *Nisi manducaveritis carnem Filii "Hominis, et biberitis Ejus sanguinem, non habebitis vitam in "vobis?*[b] Sed plane sententiam, quam de Apostolo profertis, "secundum Patrum intellectum aliter necesse est intelligatis; "non enim omnes peccatores sacramenta salutis indigne sumere "deputat. Cum enim dixisset, judicium sibi manducat et "bibit, addidit, non dejudicans corpus Domini (hoc est non "separans illud in fide ab escis corporalibus) judicium sibi "manducat et bibit. Sed et ille qui absque confessione et "pœnitentia, cum suorum inquinamentis scelerum, ad sacra "mysteria accedere præsumpserit, ille, inquam, judicium sibi "manducat, et bibit. At nos, qui, multis ante diebus, facta "peccatorum confessione, pœnitentia castigamur, jejuniis atte- "nuamur, eleemosynis et lacrymis a peccatorum sordibus ab- "luimur, in die resurrectionis Dominicæ, ad Ejus mensam in "catholica fide accedentes, carnem et sanguinem Agni imma- "culati, Jhesu Christi, non ad judicium, sed ad peccatorum "sumimus remissionem, et salutarem percipiendæ beatitudinis "æternæ præparationem." His ab ea perceptis, respondere nihil potuerunt, atque agnita deinceps ecclesiæ instituta in mysterii salutaris perceptione observaverunt.

[c]Præterea in aliquibus locis Scottorum quidam fuerant, qui, contra totius ecclesiæ consuetudinem, nescio quo ritu barbaro, Missas celebrare consueverant: quod regina, zelo Dei accensa,

[x] A blue letter. [a] 1 Cor. xi. 29. [b] S. Joh. vi. 53.

[c] A red letter occurs here, and a green letter at the commencement of the next sentence.

ita destruere atque annihilare studuit, ut deinceps qui tale quid præsumeret, nemo in tota Scottorum gente appareret. Solebant quoque, neglecta Dominicorum dierum reverentia, ita illis, sicut et aliis diebus, quibusque terreni operis insistere laboribus; quod non licere, ratione pariter et auctoritate, ipsa ostendebat. "Dominicum," inquit, "diem, propter Dominicam quæ in eo "facta est resurrectionem, in veneratione habemus, ut in eo "servilia opera jam non faciamus, in quo nos a servitute diaboli "redemptos novimus. Hoc et beatus papa Gregorius affirmans "dicit, Dominicorum die a labore terreno cessandum est, atque "omnino orationibus insistendum; ut si quid negligentiæ per "sex dies agitur, per diem resurrectionis Dominicæ precibus "expietur.[d] Idem quoque pater Gregorius, quendam propter "opus terrenum, quod die Dominico fecerat, districta increpatione feriens, eos, quorum hoc consiliis egerat, duobus mensibus excommunicatos esse decrevit." His sapientis reginæ rationibus contrăire non valentes, ita postmodum reverentiam Dominicorum dierum ejus instantia observarunt, ut nec onera quælibet his [diebus quisquam portare, nec alius alium] ad hoc auderet comp[ellere.

I]llicita etiam novercarum conjugia, similiter et uxorem fratris defuncti fratrem superstitem ducere, quæ ibi antea fiebant, nimis ostendit execranda, et a fidelibus velut ipsam mortem devitanda. Multa quoque alia, quæ contra fidei regulam et ecclesiasticarum observationum instituta inoleverant, ipsa in eodem Concilio damnare, et de regni sui finibus curavit proturbare. Universa enim quæ proposuerat, ita sanctæ Scripturæ testimoniis, atque sanctorum Patrum corroboravit sententiis, ut contra hæc nil omnino respondere valerent; quin potius deposita pertinacia, rationi acquiescentes, universa libenter implenda susciperent.

IX.

Quantum compunctioni et orationi, jejuniæ quoque et misericordiæ dedita fuerit operibus.

[e]Venerabilis itaque regina, quæ domum Dei, Deo se adjuvante, sordibus atque erroribus purgare studuerat, ipsa, Spiritu Sancto cor ejus irradiante, dignius de die in diem Dei templum fieri meruit; quod eam veraciter esse optime novi, quia et exteriora ejus opera vidi, et conscientiam, ipsa mihi manifestante, cognovi. Mihi namque familiarissime loqui,

[d] I cannot verify the references.

[e] A red letter.

suaque pandere secreta dignabatur, non quia bonum aliquid in me erat, sed quia inesse putaverat. Cum enim mihi de animæ salute, et de perennis vitæ loqueretur dulcedine, verba omnis gratiæ plena proferebat, quæ vere inhabitator cordis ejus, Spiritus Sanctus, per os illius sonabat. Tantum vero inter loquendum compungebatur, ut tota in lacrymas resolvenda putaretur, atque, illius compunctione, mens mea in fletus compungeretur. Præ cunctis vero quos ego nunc novi mortalibus, orationi et jejuniorum studiis, misericordiæ ac eleemosynarum dedita erat operibus. Ut ergo primum de oratione dicam, in ecclesia nemo illa silendo quietior, sed orando nemo aderat intentior. Nihil enim unquam in domo Dei sæculare loqui, nihil terrenum agere, sed [tantum consueverat orare, orans lacrymas fundere; solo quidem] corpore in terra, sed mente Deo proxima: nam præter Deum, et quæ Dei erant, nil ejus pura quæsivit oratio. De jejunio autem quid dicam? nisi quod per nimiam abstinentiam gravissimæ infirmitatis incurreret molestiam. His duobus, id est orationi et abstinentiæ, beneficia copulavit misericordiæ. Quid enim illius pectore clementius? Quid erga egentes benignius? Non solum sua, sed etiam seipsam, si liceret, pauperi libenter impenderet. Omnibus suis pauperibus erat ipsa pauperior: illi enim non habentes habere cupiebant: ista vero quæ habuerat dispergere studebat. Cum in publicum procederet vel equitaret, miserorum, orphanorum, viduarum greges quasi ad matrem piissimam confluxerunt; quorum nulli ab ea sine consolatione abcesserunt. Et cum omnia, quæ secum ad usus egentium circumtulerat, distribuisset, vestes, vel quascumque res, quas tunc habebant qui ei divites vel ministri aderant, pauperibus dandas accipere solebat, ne aliquando egenus tristis abiret. Nec hoc illi moleste ferebant, quin potius sua illi offerre certabant, quoniam omnia sibi ab illa duplo reddenda pro certo sciebant. Interdum etiam quodcumque illud esset regis proprium, egeno tribuendum tulit, quam ille pietatis rapinam omnino acceptam semper et gratam habuit. Nam quoniam ipse ad mandatum suum in cœna Domini, et ad Missarum sollemnia nummos aureos offerre consueverat, ex his aliquos ipsa sæpius pie furari, et pauperi qui eam inclamaverat solita erat largiri. Et sæpe quidem cum rex ipse sciret, nescire tamen se simulans, hujusmodi furto plurimum delectabatur; nonnunquam vero manu illius cum nummis comprehensa, adductam, meo judicio, ream esse jocabatur. Nec solum indigenis egentibus, verum etiam de omnibus pene nationibus, ad illius misericordiæ famam properantibus, cum hilaritate cordis munificentiam exhibebat largitatis. Licet profecto nobis de illa dicere, *Dispersit, dedit pauperibus; ideo justitia ejus manet in sæculum sæculi.*[f] Quis autem enumerando explicare poterit quot et quantos dato pretio libertati restituerit, quos de gente Anglorum abducens captivos violentia hostilis redegerat in servos? Nam et occultos exploratores quaquaversum per provincias Scottorum miserat, ut, videlicet, qui captivorum duriori premerentur servitute, et inhumanius tractarentur, ubique perquirerent, eique subtiliter, ubi, et a quibus affligerentur, renuntiarent: talibus ipsa ex intimis visceribus compatiens, celeriter subvenire, et redemptos ad libertatem festinavit renovare.

Quo tempore in regno Scottorum plurimi, per diversa loca separatis inclusi cellulis, per magnam vitæ districtionem, in carne, non secundum carnem, vivebant: Angelicam enim in terris conversationem ducebant. In his regina Christum venerari, diligere, suoque crebrius adventu et alloquio visitare, atque illorum se precibus satagebat commendare. Et cum non impetrare posset, ut ab ea terrenum aliquid vellent accipere, petebat obnoxius, ut ei aliquid eleemosynæ vel misericordiæ faciendum dignarentur præcipere. Nec mora: quicquid illorum voluntatis erat devota implevit, vel pauperes ab egestate recreando, vel quosque afflictos a miseriis quibus oppressi fuerant relevando. Et quoniam Sancti Andreæ ecclesiam advenientium undique populorum religiosa frequentat devotio, super utraque littora maris, quod Lodoneiam dividit et Scotiam, habitacula construxerat; ut, post laborem itineris, peregrini ac pauperes illuc requieturi divertere possent; ibique omnia, quæ reficiendi corporis necessitas exposceret, parata invenirent. Siquidem ministros ad hoc solum ibidem constituerat, ut quæque advenientibus necessaria fuissent parata semper haberent, eisque cum magna sollicitudine ministrarent. Quibus etiam naves delegaverat, ut euntes et redeuntes transferrent, nec aliquod transvectionis suæ pretium ab his qui transferendi fuerant unquam exigerent.

X.

Qualiter ante Dominicum Natale et in Quadragesima vitam consueverit ducere.

[g]De venerabilis reginæ quotidiana conversatione, de quotidianis ejus misericordiæ operibus aliqua jam dixi; nunc qualiter ante Dominicum Natale quadraginta dies, et totum Quadragesimæ tempus solita fuerit ducere, breviter temptabo dicere. Cum principio noctis paululum requievisset, ecclesiam ingressa,

[f] 2 Cor. ix. 9. [g] A red letter.

primum Matutinas de Sancta Trinitate, de Sancta Cruce, postmodum de Sancta Maria ipsa sola complevit; hisque finitis Officia Mortuorum incepit: post quæ Psalterium inchoavit, nec, quousque ad finem perduceret, cessavit. Celebrantibus hora congrua presbyteris Laudes Matutinas, interim ipsa Psalterium vel inceptum finivit, vel uno finito alterum jam incepit. Peracto autem Matutinæ Laudis officio, rediens in cameram, sex pauperum pedes cum rege ipsa lavare, et aliquid, quo paupertatem suam solarentur, solebat erogare. Summa quippe cura fuerat camerario, ut, ante introitum reginæ, per singulas noctes pauperes introduceret, quatenus, ad serviendum eis ingrediens, ipsa paratos inveniret. His peractis, quieti se ac sopori contulit. Cum vero mane facto lecto surrexisset, precibus et psalmis diu insistebat, et inter psallendum misericordiæ opus peragebat. Novem enim infantulos orphanos, omni auxilio destitutos, prima diei hora ad se introduci fecit reficiendos. Jusserat namque cibos molliores, quibus infantilis ætas delectatur, illis quotidie præparari; quos allatos illa flexis genibus apponere, sorbitiunculas eis facere, et, quibus ipsamet utebatur coclearibus, cibos illis in ora dignabatur mittere. Ita regina, quæ ab omnibus populis hono[rabatur pro Christo, et ministræ et matris pi]issimæ officio fun[gebatur. Poterat sa]tis congrue illud beati Job dicere, *Ab infantia mea crevit mecum miseratio, et de utero matris meo egressa est mecum.*[h] Inter hæc trecentos pauperes in regiam aulam consuetudo erat introduci; quibus per ordinem circumsedentibus, cum rex et regina ingrederentur, a ministris ostia claudebantur; exceptis enim capellanis quibusdam religiosis et aliquibus ministris, illorum eleemosynæ operibus interesse nulli licuerat. Rex ex una, regina vero ex altera parte, Christo in pauperibus servierunt, magnaque cum devotione cibos et potum, specialiter ad hoc præparatos, obtulerunt. Quo facto, ecclesiam regina consuevit intrare, ibique prolixis precibus, et lacrymarum gemitibus, semetipsam Deo sacrificium immolare. Exceptis enim Horis de Sancta Trinitate, de Sancta Cruce, de Sancta Maria, intra diei et noctis spatium duo vel tria his sanctis diebus Psalteria complevit; atque, ante publicæ celebrationem Missæ, quinque vel sex privatim sibi Missas decantari fecit.

His expletis, cum reficiendi tempus instaret, viginti quatuor pauperes ante refectionem suam ipsa humiliter ministrando refecit. Exceptis enim omnibus, quas superius dixi, eleemosynis, istius numeri pauperes, id est viginti quatuor, quamdiu vixit, per totius anni circulum sustentaverat; quos ipsa quocumque

[h] Job xxxi. 18.

in loco maneret, juxta se manere; et, quocumque pergeret, illos se comitari statuerat.

Quæ, postquam in illis Christo devote ministraverat, suum quoque corpusculum reficere consuevit. In qua refectione, cum curam carnis, secundum Apostolum, non faceret in concupiscentiis,[i] vix habuit in vitæ necessariis. Comedebat enim ut tantum vitam servaret, non ut delectationi acquiesceret. Refectio tenuis et sobria [incitabat esuriem magis quam restinguebat. Gustare videbatur] cibum, non sumere. Hinc, rogo, hinc perpendatur, quanta et qualis ejus continentia fuerit jejunando, cujus tanta extiterat abstinentia convivando. Et quamvis totam in magna con[tinentia vitam duxerit,] his tamen, id est quadraginta ante Pascha et Natale Domini diebus, incredibili abstinentia se affligere consuevit. Unde, propter nimium rigorem jejunandi, acerrimum usque finem vitæ passa est stomachi dolorem, nec tamen infirmitas corporis virtutem debilitavit boni operis. In sacra lectione studens, in orationibus persistens, in eleemosynis indeficiens, prorsus in omnibus quæ Dei erant se vigilanter exercens. Et quia sciebat scriptum, *Quem diligit Dominus corripit, flagellat autem omnem filium quem recipit*;[j] suæ carnis dolores, quasi clementissimi patris flagellum, cum patientia et gratiarum actione libens amplectitur.

XI.

Quod in testimonium sanctæ conversationis ejus quiddam Dominus ostenderit.

[k]Cum ergo his et hujusmodi dedita esset operibus, et continuis laboraret infirmitatibus, ut, juxta Apostolum, virtus in infirmitate perficeretur,[l] de virtute [transiens] in virtutem, de die in diem melior reddebatur. Terrena omnia mente deserens, toto desiderio ardebat, cælestia sitiens; "*Sitivit anima mea ad Deum, fontem vivum; quando veniam et apparebo ante faciem Dei?*[m] Mirentur alii in aliis signa miraculorum, ego in Margarita multo magis admiror opera misericordiarum: nam signa bonis et malis sunt communia; opera autem veræ pietatis et caritatis bonorum propria. Illa sanctitatem interdum ostendunt, ista etiam faciunt. Dignius, inquam, miremur in Margarita facta, quæ illam Sanctam faciebant, quam signa, si aliqua fecisset, quæ hominibus sanctam tantum ostenderent. Dignius illam obstupescamus, in qua per justitiæ, pietatis, misericordiæ et

[i] 1 Thess. iv. 5. [j] Heb. xii. 6. [k] A red letter.
[l] 2 Cor. xii. 9. [m] Psalm xlii. 2.

caritatis studia, antiquorum Patrum facta magis quam signa consideramus. Quiddam tamen narrabo, quod ad religiosæ vitæ illius indicium pertinere non inconvenienter dixerim, ut puto. Habuerat librum Evangeliorum, gemmis et auro perornatum, in quo quatuor Evangelistarum imagines pictura auro admixta decorabat, sed et capitalis quæque littera auro tota rutilabat. Hunc codicem, præ cæteris, in quibus legendo studere consueverat, carius semper amplexata fuerat. Quem quidem deferens, dum forte per vadum transiret, liber, qui minus caute pannis fuerat obvolutus, in medias aquas cecidit; quod ignorans portitor, iter quod inceperat securus peregit; cum vero postea librum proferre vellet, tum primum quod perdiderat agnovit. Quærebatur diu nec inveniebatur. Tandem in profundo fluminis apertus jacere reperitur, ita ut illius folia impetu aquæ sine cessatione agitarentur, et panniculi de serico violentia fluminis abstraherentur, qui litteras aureas, ne foliorum contactu obfuscarentur, contexerant. Quis ulterius librum valere putaret? Quis in eo vel unam litteram parere crederet? Certe integer, incorruptus, illæsus, de medio fluminis extrahitur, ita ut minime ab aqua tactus videretur. Candor enim foliorum, et integra in omnibus formula litterarum ita permansit, sicut erat antequam in fluvium cecidisset; nisi quod in extremis foliis, in parte, vix aliquod humoris signum videri poterat. Liber simul et miraculum ad reginam refertur, quæ, reddita Christo gratiarum actione, multo carius quam ante codicem amplectitur. Quare alii videant quid inde sentiant; ego, propter reginæ venerabilis dilectionem, hoc signum a Domino non ambigo.

XII.

Quod obitum suum præscierit, et quædam futura prædixerit.

Interea cum Omnipotens Deus piis ejus operibus æterna jam reddere præmia pararet, ipsa se ad introitum vitæ alterius, multo quam consueverat studiosius, præparabat. Nam, sicut paulo post ex ipsius verbis manifestabitur, suum de hac vita exitum, et alia quædam futura, longe ante præscîsse videbatur. Itaque secretius me alloquens, suam mihi ex ordine vitam cœpit replicare, et ad singula verba lacrymarum fluvios effundere. Tanta denique inter colloquendum ejus erat compunctio, tanta ex compunctione proruperat fletuum profusio, ut (sicut mihi videbatur) nihil proculdubio esset, quod a Christo tunc impetrare non posset. Flente ipsa, flevi et ego: diu flentes, interdum tacuimus, quoniam singultu prorumpente verba proferre nequivimus. Flamma quippe compunctionis, quæ cor illius concremaverat, ex verbis ejus spiritualibus meam quoque mentem attigerat. Cujus per linguam dum verba Sancti Spiritus audirem, et per verba conscientiam ejus perviderem, tanta ejus familiaritatis gratia me indignum judicabam.[n] Cum de necessariis sermonem finisset, rursus ita me alloqui cœpit. "Vale," inquit. "Ego posthac in hac vita diu non subsistam; tu autem "non parvo post me tempore vives. Duo ergo sunt quæ a te "postulo: unum, ut, quamdiu vixeris, animæ meæ in Missis et "Orationibus tuis memineris; aliud, ut filiorum meorum ac "filiarum curam habeas, amorem impendas, præcipue Deum "timere et amare doceas, et ab eis docendis nunquam desistas: "et cum in culmen terrenæ dignitatis quemlibet ex eis exaltari "videris, illius maxime pater simul ac magister accedas; scilicet "admonendo, et, cum res exegerit, arguendo; ne propter mo"mentaneum honorem in superbiam tumeat, nedum per avari"tiam offendet, ne per mundi prosperitatem æternæ vitæ neg"li[gat felicitatem. Hæc sunt," inquit, "quæ] ut sollicite "fa[cias, sub Dei præsentia], Qui nunc nobis tertius assistit, "mihi quæso promittas." Quibus ego verbis iterum prorumpens in fletum, omnia quæ rogaverat diligenter me promisi facturum; non enim illi contradicere audebam, quam sic indubitanter futura prædicere audieram. Quæ, ut prædixerat, ita nunc et res ipsa comprobat; quia et ego post illius mortem vivo, et ejus sobolem in dignitatem honoris sublimatam aspicio. Expleta itaque collocutione domum rediturus, re[ginæ ultimum vale dixi:] non enim ejus faciem unquam postea vidi.

XIII.

Qualiter de hac vita migraverit.

[o]Nec multo post acriori quam ante consueverat infirmitate corripitur, et, ante suæ evocationis diem, longæ ægritudinis igne decoquitur. Cujus obitum ita, sicut ab ejus presbytero didici, narrabo; quem ipsa propter ejus simplicitatem, innocentiam, castitatem, præ cæteris familiarius dilexerat: qui post

[n] Instead of the above paragraph, Capgrave's abridgment of this biography, printed also by Surius, has as follows:—Habebet confessarium Turgotum, secundum Priorem Dunelmiæ. Illo ergo ad se accersito, vitam suam replicare cœpit, et ad singula verba lachrymarum flumina profundere; tantaque erat sub ejus sermonibus compunctio, tantus lachrymarum imber, ut nihil proculdubio esse videretur, quod tunc a Christo impetrare non posset. This is copied by Pinkerton, p. 381.

[o] A red letter.

mortem reginæ, pro ipsius anima perpetuo se Christi servitio tradidit; et ad sepulchrum incorrupti corporis sanctissimi patris Cuthberti suscipiens habitum monachi, seipsum pro ea hostiam obtulit. Hic ergo reginæ in extremis vitæ inseparabiliter aderat, et egredientem de corpore animam illius ipse precibus Christo commendaverat. Cujus exitum ita sicut viderat per ordinem, cum sæpius inde a me quæreretur, ita referre cum lacrymis solet.

Per dimidium, inquit, annum et aliquanto plus, nunquam equo sedere, raro autem de lecto valuit surgere. Quarta ante suum obitum die, cum rex in expeditione esset, atque illa longo terrarum intervallo, quid erga ipsum ea die ageretur, nullius nuntii celeritate scire potuisset, tristior solito effecta, hoc nobis sibi assidentibus dixit: "Forte hodie tantum mali regno Scot-"torum [accidit, quantum multis retro temporibus non pro-"venit." Nos vero hæc] audientes, ejus [dicta tunc qui]dem negligenter accepimus; [sed, post] aliquot dies veniente nuntio, eodem die quo hæc regina dixerat, regem fuisse occisum intelleximus. Quem quidem ipsa, quasi futurorum præscia, multum prohibuerat ne quoquam cum exercitu iret; sed nescio qua de causa contigit, ne tunc illius monitis obediret. Cum ergo quartus post regis occisionem dies instaret, illa, paulisper levigata infirmitate, Missam auditura oratorium intravit; ibique suum exitum, qui jam imminebat, sacrosanctum, Dominici corporis et sanguinis viatico præmunire curavit. Quorum salutari gustu refecta, prioribus mox aggravata doloribus, lecto prosternitur, et ad exitum, crescente molestia, vehementius urgetur. "Et quid faciam? quid morer? Quasi mortem, Domine mee, ulterius possim differre, et vitam longiorem facere, sic timeo ad ultimum ejus pervenire. *Sed omnis caro fænum, et omnis gloria ejus quasi flos fæni: exaruit fænum, et decidit flos.*[p] Facies ejus jam in mortem palluerat, cum ipsa me atque alios mecum, sacri altaris ministros, sibi astare, suamque animam psallentes Christo jubet commendare. Ipsa quoque illam, quam Nigram Crucem[q] nominare, quamque in maxima semper veneratione habere consuevit, sibi afferri præcepit. Sed cum loculus, in quo fuerat inclusa, citius aperiri non posset, regina graviter ingemiscens, ait: "O nos miseros! "O culpabiles! ulterius sanctæ crucis non merebimur as-"pectum." Quandoque tamen de loculo prolatam, eique allatam cum reverentia suscepit, complecti, deosculari, oculos, faciem illa significare crebrius studuit.

[p] 1 S. Petr. i. 24.
[q] "Crucem Scotiæ nigram." Tiberius, E. i., 186 *a*.

Jamque, frigescente toto corpore, nihilominus tamen ipsa semper orabat; et quinquagesimum Psalmum ex ordine decantans, crucem interim sibi ante oculos statuens, utraque manu tenebat.

Interea filius ejus,[r] qui post patrem regni gubernacula jam nunc in præsenti tenet, rediens de exercitio, cubiculum reginæ intravit. Quæ illi tunc angustiæ! Quis animi cruciatus! Stetit ibi adversis undique rebus angustatus; quo se verteret nesciebat. Patrem namque cum fratre peremptum matri nunciaturus advenit; matrem, quam præcipue amaverat, jam jamque morituram invenit. Quem primum plangeret ignorabat. Dulcissimæ tamen matris abscessus acriore dolore cor illius pungebat, quam ante oculos suos pene mortuam jacere videbat. Super hæc omnia eum cura de statu regni sollicitabat, quod morte patris perturbandum pro certo noverat. Undique mœrorem, undique contraxerat ipse dolorem. Regina, cum velut in agonia jacens a præsentibus rapta putaretur, subito collectis viribus filium alloquitur. Interrogatur enim ab ea de patre et fratre. Sed ille quod verum erat dicere noluit, ne audita morte illorum continuo et ipsa moreretur: nam respondebat, eos benevalere. At illa graviter suspirans, "Scio," inquit, "fili, scio. "Per hanc sanctam crucem, per nostræ consanguinitatis pro-"pinquitatem te adjuro, ut quod verum nosti edicas." Ille coactus, rem, sicut erat gesta, exposuit. Quid eam putares acturam? Quis in tot adversitatibus contra Deum non murmuraturam crederet? Eodem quippe tempore conjugem amiserat, filium perdiderat, seipsam infirmitas ad mortem usque cruciaverat. Sed in omnibus his non peccavit labiis suis, neque stultum quid contra Deum locuta est; quin potius oculos et manus ad cælum dirigens, in laudem et gratiarum actionem prorupit, dicens: "Laudes et gratias tibi, Omnipotens Deus, "refero, Qui me tantas in meo exitu angustias tolerare, hasque "tolerantem ab aliquibus peccati maculis, ut spero, voluisti "mundare." Senserat illa mortem adesse, moxque orationem, quæ post perceptionem Dominici corporis et sanguinis a sacerdote dici solet, incepit: "Domine," inquiens, "Jhesu Christe, "qui ex voluntate Patris, cooperante Spiritu Sancto, per "mortem Tuam mundum vivificasti, libera me." Cum diceret, "Libera me," liberata vinculis corporis anima, ad veræ libertatis, Quem semper dilexerat, auctorem Christum migravit, particeps effecta eorum felicitatis, quorum secuta est exempla virtutis. Tanta enim cum tranquillitate, tanta cum quiete illius fuerat exitus, ut, ad æternæ quietis et pacis regionem animam

[r] Filius suus Edgarus. Tiberius, E. i., 186.

illam migrasse dubium esse non debeat. Et, quod mirum est, faciem ejus, quæ more morientium tota in morte palluerat, ita post mortem rubor cum candore permixtus perfuderat, ut non mortua sed dormiens credi potuisset.[s] Igitur corpus ipsius honorabiliter, ut reginam decebat, involutum, ad Sanctæ Trinitatis, quam ipsa construxerat, ecclesiam deportavimus; ibique, sicut ipsa jusserat, contra altare et sanctæ crucis (quod ibidem erexerat) venerabile signum, sepulturæ tradidimus. Atque ita corpus ejus illo in loco nunc requiescit, ubi illud in vigiliis, orationibus; lacrymarum fnsionibus, genuum flexionibus, affligere consuevit.

Explicit Translatio Sanctæ Margaretæ Scottorum reginæ. Incipit prologus in Vita Sancti Niniani episcopi.

[s] Obiit enim quarto idus Junii, et in ecclesia Sanctæ Trinitatis (quam) ipsa construxerat contra altare sepelitur .... autem David filius Sanctæ Margaretæ .... Angliæ Henrici primi moraretur nocte .... tore sua Matilde regina qua Mat .... (MS. Cotton, Tiberius E. i. here ends abruptly). The words after *sepelitus*, "[Cum] autem David filius," etc., are taken by Capgrave from *Aelred of Rievaulx's Genealogy of the Kings of England.* They are also printed with slight verbal alterations by Surius, and reprinted by Pinkerton, *Vitæ Sanctorum Scotiæ*, p. 383. The narrative is also copied by Fordun (l. v., c. 40), as he alleges, from Turgot, and will be found amongst the extracts ascribed to Turgot, reprinted from the Scotichronicon in the present volume. See Extract X.

EXCERPTA E SCRIPTIS TURGOTI,

ECCLESIÆ DUNELMENSIS PRIORIS,

APUD SCOTICHRONICON JOHANNIS FORDUN.

I.

De[t] rege Scotorum, Malcolmo Canmore magnanimo, dignum aliquid dicendum duximus, ut, cujus fuerit cordis, quanti vel animi, unum ejus opus hic exaratum legentibus declarabit. Relatum est aliquando sibi, de suis quendam summis proceribus illum occidendum cum suis hostibus convenisse. Imperat rex hæc nuntianti silentium: siluit et ipse, proditoris, qui forte tunc aberat, expectans adventum. Qui cum ad curiam cum apparatu magno regi venisset insidiaturus, rex ei suisque vultum solitum atque jocundum prætendens, finxit se nihil audisse vel scivisse, quæ mente cordetenus recolebat. Quid plura? Jubet ipse rex omnes venatores suos summo mane cum canibus convenire. Et jam noctem aurora abegerat, cum rex, vocatis ad se cunctis proceribus et militibus, in venando spatiatum ire festinat. Venit interim ad quandam planitiem latam, quam in modum coronæ densissima silva cingebat; in cujus medio colliculus unus quasi turgescere videbatur, qui diversorum colorum floribus, pulchra quadam varietate, depictus, fatigatis quandoque militibus ex venatu gratum præbebat accubitum. In quo cum rex cæteris superior constitisset, secundum legem venandi, quam Tristram vulgus vocat, singulis cum canibus et sociis singula loca delegat, et obsessa undique bestia, ubicunque eligeret exitum, mortis inveniret exitum. Ipse vero rex seorsum ab aliis solus abscessit cum solo, suum secum retinens proditorem.

Ab omni autem aspectu et auditu remoti, rex subsistit, et vultu torvo volvente pugnam, in hæc verba prorupit. "Ecce," inquit, "ego et tu mecum, solus cum solo, similibus armis pro-"tecti: Non est qui mihi, licet regi, assistat, nec tibi sub-

[t] Fordun, v., 11, 12. This extract is taken *verbatim* from the *Genealogy of the Kings of England*, by Aelred of Rievaulx.

"veniat; nec est qui videat aut audiat, nisi arbiter Deus. "Nunc ergo si valeas, si audeas, si cor habeas, imple quidem "opere quod corde concepisti, et redde hostibus meis quod "promisisti. Si me occidendum putas, quando melius, quando "securius, quando liberius, quando tandem virilius? An vene- "num parasti? sed hoc muliercularum esse quis nesciat? An "insidiaris lectulo? hoc possunt et adulteri. An ferrum, ut "occulte ferias, occultasti? hoc sicarii, non militis esse, nemo "qui dubitet. Age potius quod militis, et non proditoris; age "quod est viri et non mulieris; atque solus cum solo con- "gredere, ut saltem proditio tua turpitudine videatur carere, "quæ nunquam infidelitate carere potest." Hactenus vir ille nequissimus hæc vix sustinuit, et mox verbis ejus, quasi gravi fulmine, percussus, de equo cui insidebat citissime descendit, projectisque armis, ad pedes regis corruit, cum lacrymis atque tremore cordis ita dixit; "Domine mi rex, ignoscat mihi ad "præsens hoc meum velle iniquum tua regia potestas; et si "usque modo aliquid super hujuscemodi traditione tui corporis "cor meum malignum conceperit, amodo delebitur, et in fu- "turum contra omnes me tibi fidelissimum, Deo cum Sua "genetrice teste, promitto." Cui rex ait, "Noli, amice, timere; "noli pavere: nihil a me, nec per me mali, pro re ista susti- "nebis. Obsides tamen in pignore jubeo quod mihi nomines, "atque adducas." Quibus nominatis, et statim postmodo adductis, rex inquit, "In regis verbo tibi dico, res ante pro- "missa stabit." Ille vero proditor regis voluntati, in his quæ præmisimus opportuno tempore satisfaciens; sic revertuntur ad socios, de his quæ fecerant vel dixerant nemini loquentes.

II.

"Rex[u] Eadwardus, pronus in senium, eo quod ipse non "susceperat liberos, misit ad" Imperatorem,[v] "ut filium patris "sui Eadmundi Irneside, Eadwardum, cum omni sua familia "mitteret," etc.[w]

III.

Cernens[x] autem Eadgarus Etheling res Anglorum undique

[u] Fordun, v., 13. This extract, so far as it is included in inverted commas, is from Malmesbury, and is properly ascribed to him by Fordun; but he attributes the substitution of "Imperatorem" for "regem Hunnorum" to Turgot, whereas it occurs in Aelred, and in Aelred only of extant authorities.

[v] Regem Hunnorum—Malmesbury.

[w] Fordun continues the narrative from Malmesbury.

[x] Fordun, v., 16. The commencement of this extract is from the Genealogy of the Kings of England, and it is probable that the details are from some other

perturbari, ascensa navi, cum matre et sororibus in patriam reverti, qua natus fuerat, conabatur: sed Summus Imperator, Qui ventis imperat et mari, mare commovit, et in spiritu procellarum exaltati sunt fluctus ejus. Sæviente vero tempestate, omnes, in desperatione vitæ positi, sese Deo commendant, et puppim pelago committunt. Igitur, post plurima pericula et immanes labores, misertus est Dominus desolatæ familiæ Suæ; quia, ubi humanum deesse videtur auxilium, ad Dominum necesse est recurrendum. Innumeris tandem quassati pelago periculis, coacti sunt in Scotiam applicare. Applicuit igitur illa sancta familia quodam loco qui sinus Sanctæ Margaretæ ab incolis deinceps appellatur; nec hoc casu contigisse sed eam Summi Dei providentia credimus ibi advenisse. Igitur in dicto sinu præfata commorante familia, cunctisque rei finem cum timore exspectantibus, nuntiatum est regi Malcolmo suum adventum; qui tunc ab eodem loco haud procul cum suis manebat, et ad navem nuntios dirigens rem inde veram sciscitabatur. Nuntii autem illuc venientes, et magnitudinem navis præter solitum admirantes, regi quæ viderant festinant quantocitius indicare. Quibus auditis, rex plures et prudentiores prioribus, de summis suis proceribus, illac direxit. At illi, sicut nuntii regiæ majestatis suscepti, virorum proceritatem, mulierum venustatem, et familiæ totius industriam, non sine admiratione diligentius considerantes, gratum apud semetipsos inde colloquium conferunt. Quid plura? eventum rei, et rerum seriem et causam, nuntii ad hoc destinati dulci alloquio et eloquenti dulcedine investigant. Illi autem, ut novi hospites et advenæ, causam et modum suorum applicatuum verbis plica carentibus eis humiliter exponunt et eloquenter. Reversi autem nuntii, cum seniorum reverentiam, juvenum vero prudentiam, matronarum maturitatem, et juvencularum venustatem suo regi nuntiassent, quidam subintulit dicens; "Vidimus ibi quandam domi-"nam, quam ob formæ incomparatam speciem, et eloquentiæ "jocundæ facunditatem, cum ob cæterarum fæcunditatem vir-"tutum, illius familiæ judicio meo dominam suspicans, tibi, rex, "annuncio; de, cujus mirabili venustate et moralitate mirandum "magis sentio quam narrandum." Nec mirum si illam dominam crediderint, quam dominam non solum illius familiæ, sed etiam,

work of Aelred, not now extant, to which he refers in these words: "Hac occasione actum est, ut Margareta regis Malcolmi nuptiis traderetur, cujus laudabilem vitam et mortem pretiosam liber inde editus satis insinuat." He may indeed refer to the life of St. Margaret which immediately precedes these extracts in the present publication, but the words appear rather to indicate a work of his own, and Aelred has been credited by all our bibliographers with the authorship of a life of Queen Margaret.

post fratrem, Angliæ totius hæredem, immo regni sui participem, futuramque reginam, Divina prædestinaverit providentia. Rex autem audiens illos Anglos et ibidem adesse, propria persona illos visitat et alloquitur, et unde venerunt, aut quo vadant plenius explorat: Anglicam enim linguam simul et Romanam, æque ut propriam plene didicerat, cum post patris sui mortem quatuordecim annis in Anglia mansisset, ubi forte de cognitione hujus sanctæ familiæ aliquid audierat, quare cum eis mitius ageret, et benignius se haberet.

IV.

Rex[y] igitur utcumque Margaretam viderat, eamque de regio semine simul et imperiali genitam esse didicerat, ut eam in uxorem duceret petiit et obtinuit, decimo quarto regnationis suæ anno, tradente eam Eadgaro Etheling, fratre suo, "magis "suorum quam sua voluntate, immo Dei ordinatione."[z] Nam sicut olim Esther Assuero regi pro suorum salute concivium Divina providentia, ita et hac "illustrissimo regi Malcolmo "copulata fuit in conjugium;"[z] nec tamen quasi captiva, immo multis abundans divitiis, quas patri suo Eadwardo, tanquam hæredi, rex Angliæ suus patruus prius dederat; (quem etiam ipse Romanus imperator Henricus, sicut ante paulo prædiximus, non minimis muneribus oneratum in Angliam misit;) quarum partem permaximam hæc sancta regina secum in Scotiam transtulit. Attulit etiam plurimas Sanctorum reliquias, omni lapide vel auro pretiosiores; inter quas fuit illa sancta crux, quam nigram vocant, omni genti Scotorum non minus terribilem quam amabilem pro suæ reverentia sanctitatis. Nuptiæ quidem factæ sunt non procul a sinu maris quo applicuit, et magnifice celebratæ, anno Domini millesimo septuagesimo, loco qui dicitur Dumfermelyn, quem tunc temporis rex habebat pro oppido.

[y] Fordun, v., 17. After this extract follows a passage from William of Malmesbury, after which Fordun proceeds as follows:—"In Vetusta Chronica sic reperi scriptum. Anno Dom. millesimo septuagessimo rex Malcolmus Angliam usque Diveland sive Cliveland vastavit, et tunc clitoni Eadgaro et sororibus Margaretæ et Christinæ, ubi eas invenit regem Angliæ fugientes, ut in Scotiam irent in reditu pacem suam donavit, et Margaretam postea sibi in matrimonium junxit." The old chronicle here cited is the Historia de Gestis Regum, which does not appear to have been known to Fordun as a work of Symeon, but to have been regarded as an anonymous authority.

[z] The words within inverted commas are taken, with slight verbal alteration, from Turgot's Life of Queen Margaret, printed above, Section VI. "Suorum magis quam sua voluntate, immo Dei ordinatione, potentissimo regi Scotorum Malcolmo in conjugium copulatur."

Erat enim locus ille naturaliter in se munitissimus, densissima silva circumdatus, præruptis rupibus præmunitus: in cujus medio erat venusta planities, etiam rupibus et rivulis munita, ita quod de ea dictum esse putaretur,

Non homini facilis, vix adeunda feris.

V.

De[a] illorum, magnifici videlicet regis Malcolmi et celebris reginæ, virtutum operibus, et eleemosinarum largitione, sicut in Legenda vitæ beatæ reginæ[b] Turgotus testatur, hic aliqua breviter recitabo, Sicut enim David propheta in Psalmo cecinit, *Cum sancto sanctus eris*;[c] sic et ipse rex a sancta regina sanctis operibus frui, et animum ab iniquis, ejus hortatu, ut verificetur quod dixerat Paulus, *Per mulierem fidelem sanctificabitur vir infidelis*,[d] didicit refrænare. Nimirum "ipsam tam venerabilis vitæ "reginam, quoniam in ejus corde Christum inhabitare prospex- "erat, ille quodammodo formidabat offendere, sed potius votis "ejus et prudentibus consiliis per omnia celerius obedire pro- "perabat. Quæ etiam ipsa respuerat, eadem et ipse respuere; "et quæ amabat, amore illius amare. Unde et libros, in quibus "ipsa vel orare consueverat vel legere, ille, licet ignarus lite- "rarum, sæpe manu versare solebat et inspicere. Et dum ab "ea quis eorum esset carior audisset, hunc et ipse cariorem "habere cœpit, et sæpius deosculari et contrectare: quandoque "etiam advocato aurifice, ipsum codicem auro gemmisque "perornari præcepit, atque perornatum ipse rex ad reginam, "quasi suæ devotionis indicium, referre consuevit."[e]

"Didicit et ejus exemplo vigilias noctis frequenter orando "producere, et cum gemitu cordis et lacrymis devotissime Deum "orare. Fateor," inquit Turgotus, "fateor magnum miseri- "cordiæ Dei miraculum mirabar, cum viderem interdum tantam "orandi regis intentionem, tantam inter orandum in pectore "viri sæcularis compunctionem."[f]

"In Quadragesimali tempore, et diebus Adventus ante Do- "minicum natale," nisi major sæcularis occupatio impediret,

[a] Fordun, v., 23, 24.

[b] The legend here referred to is the Life of Queen Margaret, which is printed in the present volume, from which the passages denoted by inverted commas are extracted.

[c] Psalm xvii. 26.

[d] 1 Cor. vii. 14.

[e] p. 241 of this volume.

[f] p. 241.

"peracto Matutinali officio, et auroræ Missarum sollemniis celebratis, rediens in cameram rex, pedes sex pauperum cum regina lavare, et aliquid, quo paupertas consolaretur, solebat erogare, Summa quippe cura fuit camerario, ut, ante introitum reginæ, per singulas noctes pauperes introduceret, qualiter ad serviendum eis, immo Christo in eis, ingrediens ipsa paratos inveniret. His peractis, quieti se ac sopori contulit."[g]

"Cum vero, mane facto, de lecto surrexit, precibus et psalmis diu insistebat, et inter psallendum misericordiæ opus peragebat. Novem enim infantulos orphanos, omni auxilio destitutos, prima diei hora ad se fecit reficiendos introduci: jusserat namque cibos molliores, quibus infantilis ætas delectatur, illis quotidie præparari, quos allatos ipsamet, flexis genibus, illis apposuit, sorbitiunculas eis fecit, et cochlearibus cibos in ora eorum mittere dignabatur. Ita regina, quæ ab omnibus populis honorabatur, pro Christo et ministræ officio sollicitæ, et matris dulcissimæ fungebatur pietate. Potuit satis congrue illud beati Job dicere; *Ab infantia mecum crevit miseratio, et de utero matris meæ egressa est mecum.*[h] Inter hæc trecentos pauperes in regiam aulam consuetudo erat introduci, quibus per ordinem circumsedentibus, cum rex et regina ingrederentur, a ministris ostia claudebantur: exceptis enim capellanis quibusdam religiosis et aliquibus ministris, illorum eleemosinarum operibus interesse nulli licuerat. Rex, ex una, regina vero ex altera parte, Christo in pauperibus servierunt, magnaque cum devotione cibos et potum, ad hoc specialiter præparatos, obtulerunt. Fuerunt autem rex et regina charitatis operibus ambo pares, ambo cultu pietatis insignes. Quo facto," rex pro temporalibus et regni sui negotiis sese sollicitus occupare, "regina solebat ecclesiam intrare, ibique prolixis precibus et lacrymarum gemitibus seipsam Deo sacrificium corditer immolare: exceptis enim horis de Sancta Trinitate, de Sancta Cruce, et de Sanctâ Maria, intra diei et noctis spatium, duo vel tria his sanctis diebus psalteria complevit; atque ante publicæ celebrationem missæ, quinque vel sex privatim sibi missas decantari fecit."[i]

"His expletis, cum reficiendi tempus instaret, viginti quatuor pauperes, ante refectionem suam, ipsa humiliter ministrando refecit."[j]

[g] Abridged from the Life of St. Margaret in this volume, p. 248.
[h] Job xxxi. 18. [i] p. 248. [j] p. 248.

VI.

Anno[k] Domini millesimo nonagesimo tertio — tertio idus Augusti, rex Malcolmus novam Dunelmensem ecclesiam fundare cœpit et ædificare,[l] ponentibus eodem rege Malcolmo, Willelmo ejusdem ecclesiæ episcopo, et Turgoto Priore, primos lapides in fundamento. Fundavit itaque ecclesiam S. Trinitatis de Dumfermelyn ante diu, quam multis ditavit donariis et redditibus. Cumque maximam prædam ex Anglia, more solito, ultra flumen These, de Clefeland, Richemond, et alibi sæpius adduceret, castrumque de Aylnwick, sive Murealden,[m] quod idem est, obsideret, obsessosque sibi rebellantes oppido affligeret, hi, qui inclusi fuerant, ab omni humano excludebantur auxilio. Et cum tam forti et impetuoso exercitui vires eorum desse, nec ad resistendum valere cognoscerent, inito consilio, novo proditionis ingenio usi sunt, in hunc modum: Unus autem præ cæteris peritior, fortis robore, et audax in opere, se discrimini mortis obtulit, ut vel se morti traderet, aut socios a morte liberaret. Nam regis prudenter adiit exercitum, et, ubinam esset rex, et quis, benigne interrogans, quærentibus causam inquisitionis dixit, se castrum regi traditurum, et in argumentum fidei claves ejusdem in hasta sua coram omnibus portavit oblaturus. Quo audito rex, doli nescius, incaute a tentorio inermis exiliens et minus provide, occurrit proditori; at ille, quæsita opportunitate, inermem regem armatus transfixit, et, latibula silvæ vicinæ festinanter ingressus, eorum manus evasit. Sicque rex idem strenuus obiit die Sancti Bricii anno Domini M.XCIII. Turbato igitur exercitu, dolor dolorem accumulat: nam Eadwardus regis primogenitus a Northumbris lethaliter vulneratur, qui decimo

[k] Fordun, v., 25.

[l] It is scarcely necessary to say that Malcolm has no claim to be considered as the "founder" and "builder" of the church of Durham. He is mentioned indeed in the *Historia Regum* in the present volume as having assisted at the ceremony of laying the foundation stones, but this statement is unsupported by the authority of Symeon's History of the Church of Durham.

[m] This account of the siege of the castle at Alnwick occurs nowhere else, nor is there any reason to believe that there was a castle at all at Alnwick at this date. All that we know on reliable authority is that Malcolm was surprised and slain in the vicinity of the river Alne by Morel, the lieutenant of Robert de Mowbray, earl of Northumberland, whose name seems to be incorporated in the appellation furnished in the text to the scene of his achievement, Murialden quasi Morelden, or Moreldun, the Hill of Morel.

The ridiculous tale of the person who pierced the king's eye, receiving from that exploit the designation of "Piercy, quod Anglice sonat perforare oculum," is interpolated in some MSS. of Fordun. This story must necessarily have been invented after the Percy family became the possessors of Alnwick, and so gave point, if not probability, to the fiction.

septimo kal. Decembris, anno prænotato, tertia die post patrem, apud Eardwardisle foresta de Jedwood fatis cessit, et sepultus est in ecclesia Sanctæ Trinitatis de Dumfermelyn juxta patrem ante altare Sanctæ Crucis.

VII.

Quod[n] ut audivit regina, multis ante infirmitatibus ad mortem pene cruciata, immo, quod verius est, Spiritu Sancto præscivit, confessione facta, et in ecclesia communione devote percepta, Deo se precibus commendans, animam sanctam cælo reddidit, decimo sexto kal. Decembris, die quarto post mortem regis, anno quo supra, in Castro Puellarum. Itaque cum adhuc corpus reginæ esset in castro, ubi illius felix anima ad Christum, Quem semper dilexerat, migravit, Donaldus Banus, frater regis, ejus audita morte, auxilio regis Norwagiæ, regnum, multorum manu vallatus, invasit, et prædictum castrum, ubi regis justos et legales sciebat hæredes, hostiliter obsedit. Sed quia locus ille natura sui in se valde munitus est, portas solummodo credidit custodiendas, eo quod introitus aut exitus aliunde non de facili pateat. Quod intelligentes qui intus erant, docti a Deo, meritis ut credimus sanctæ reginæ, per posticum ex occidentali plaga sanctum corpus deferebant. Ferunt autem quidam in toto itinere illo nebulam subnubilam omnem familiam illam circumdedisse, et ab aspectibus hostium miraculose protexisse, ut itinerantibus in terra vel mari nihil obfuit, sed ad optatum prospere locum, ecclesiam scilicet de Dumfermelyn, ubi nunc in Christo requiescit, sicut ipsa prius jusserat, pervenientes deportarunt. Sic quidem Dovenaldus regnum obtinuit, veris hæredibus, adhuc in minoritate constitutis, effugatis. De inclito rege Malcolmo habentur hæc metra

Ter deca quinque valens annis, et mensibus octo,
  Malcolmus sanctus rex erat in Scotia.
Anglorum gladiis in bello sternitur heros,
  Hic rex in Scotia primus humatus erat.

Interea Eadgarus Etheling, frater jam dictæ reginæ, timens illud Lucani, quod generaliter dictum est, evenire posse suis nepotibus, *Nulla fides regni sociis*, etc., ideo tutius eos ad tempus esse credidit subtrahere, quam avunculo secum regnaturos committere. Omnis enim in errore consortem sibi quærit, in regno nullus. Quamobrem filios et filias regis et sororis suæ reginæ congregatos, in Angliam secum secretius

[n] Fordun, v., 26.

transduxit, et eos per cognatos et cognitos, non manifeste, sed quasi in occulto, nutriendos destinavit. Timuit enim ne Normanni, qui tunc temporis Angliam invaserant, sibi vel suis malum molirentur, eo quod Angliæ regnum eis hæreditaro jure debebatur. Et licet ibidem, quasi secreto, tempore parvo mansisset, tamen divulgatum est apud regem quod ejus assisteret traditioni: sicque, quod verebatur, accidit in hunc modum.

VIII.

Eodem[o] tempore, regnante Willelmo II., miles quidam de genere Anglico, Orgarus nomine, gratum exhibere se regi volens, convenit, calumnians eundem clitonem, Eadgarum, viz., genere gloriosum, nam sic ipsum nominabant, de regis Willelmi prædicti traditione. Causa autem coram rege super hoc prolata, quia Eadgarus de regia stirpe fuerat progenitus, et regno, jure Anglico, proximus; rem causam esse veram, ut sibi præcaveret, autumans, auctorem vi et protectione regia tuebatur: nec incerta de Eadgaro jam poterat esse sententia, si crimen impositum probari potuisset. Hinc anxius effectus Eadgarus cœpit diligentius inquirere, si quis vel verbo vel consilio causæ partis suæ auderet favere. Verumtamen timor regis eum præmia pollicentem prævenerat, quia se non impune optimates illi favere posse credebant, qui pro ejus defensione regis odium incurrissent. Fluctuanti igitur et nimia anxietate dejecto, miles de Wintonia, Anglicus natione, genere non ignobilis, nomine Godwinus, veteris parentelæ ipsius non immemor, opem se præstiturum in hac re tam difficili compromisit. Instabat jam dies hujus causæ diffinitioni præfixus. Affuit continuo actoris superciliosa persona, qui, quoniam corporis viribus præstare videbatur, et propter peritiam bellandi, quam satis noverat, nullum sibi certamine parem æstimabat: sed et huic æstimationi favor regis accessit. Quibus elatus, facile probaturum se credebat quicquid alteri imposuisset. Eo igitur sic calumniante, compellitur Eadgarus se duello defendere, vel alterum pro se bello subrogare; sic enim lata sententia rei veritatem exspectabat. Godwinus igitur, Eadgari causam in se capiens, interposito, ut moris est, utrimque juramento, Eadgarum se defensurum exponit. Fit mox hinc inde magnus armorum apparatus. Pugnaturi conveniunt: Orgarus favore regis elatus, regiis satellitibus

[o] Fordun, v., 27.

hinc inde vallatus, insignibus etiam armorum ornamentis splendidus procedit. Godwinus e contra, licet non æquali ducum favore regi faventium, non minori tamen confidentia animi, locum certaminis est ingressus: qui, etsi regis iram pro partis adversæ tuitione formidaret, jure tamen hanc naturæ vicem rependendam arbitrabatur, ut illius causam ageret, quem justius sibi cæterisque actorem natura dominari debuisse cognoverat. Hinc etiam calumniatorem cum justa animadversione increpat, qui Anglicus genere existens, naturæ videretur impugnator: quem enim ut dominum venerari debuerat, utpote de jure generis existens, cui se et omnia sua debuisset. Silentio namque per præconem omnibus imposito, et vadiis utrorumque a judice in certaminis locum projectis, ut Deus, secretorum cognitor, hujus causæ veritatem ostenderet, proclamante, postremo res armis, et causa superno Judici committitur.

IX.

Nec[p] mora, insurgit alter in alterum, actor in defensorem. Mox ictus hinc geminantur et inde. Orgarus, impetu facto, dum alter scuto ictum accepit, partem scuti non modicam amputat. Nec segnius Godwinus, ictu gravissimo accensis animis, in ictum consurgit, et dum alter flectit scutum incautius inter caput et humerum, ictu vibrato os illud cum loricæ nodis prorumpit, quod cervici humerum conjungit sinistrum. Sed hoc ictu capulus solvitur et manum ferientis fefellit, et gladius de manu tenentis labitur. Hoc hostis comperto, licet vulnere graviter affectus, manuque læva debilitatus, gravius tamen in adversarium consurgit, eumque tanto facilius debilitaturum esse se existimans, quod eo caruisset adjumento quo præcipue pugnare debuisset: spes tamen ipsa dominum suum fefellit. Nam Godwinus, licet adversario pro posse toto obsistente, scuto protenso, inter immanes ferientis ictus gladium jamdiu elapsum sustulit de terra. Quem cum firmiter ob capuli diminutionem tenere nequivisset, duobus digitis anterioribus aciem gladii complexus, etsi absque læsione adversarium suum lædere feriendo non posset, in pugnando tamen, et ictus funestos jaciendo, non adversario suo videbatur esse inferior Non enim aut incursioni hostis cessit, aut ab ictibus ille cessavit. Uno quidem ictu cum capitis diminutione adversarii sui oculum eruens, ictu iterato partem reliquam hostis fraudu-

[p] Fordun, v., 28.

lenti corporis adeo inutilem vulnerando effecit, quod pedes non ultra subsistere Orgarus nisus est, sed pene mortuus terræ prosternitur. Jamque cum magno fragore armorum, hosti prostrato ille non piger pedem imposuit, et subito fraus et calliditas hostis jam evacuata detegitur, et reus perjurii palam arguitur. Abstracto namque cultro, qui caliga latebat, ipsum perfodere conatur; cum ante initum congressum juraverat se nihil, nisi arma decentia militem, in hoc duello gestaturum. Mox tamen perjurii pœnas persolvit: cultro siquidem erepto, cum spes reum desereret, crimen protinus confitetur. Attamen hæc confessio nihil ad vitam illi profuit elongandam; undique vero, vulnere succedente vulneri, perfodebatur, donec animam impiam vis doloris et magnitudo vulnerum expelleret. His itaque peractis, hujus duelli casus omnes mirantur, et justum Dei judicium sunt laudantes, eo quod, calumniatore expugnato, is qui veritatis fuerat et innocentiæ defensor, nec unum quidem vulnus ab impetente fuerat perpessus. Nam exinde tam regi quam ducibus, ob insigne virtutis indicium, acceptissimus exitit: adeoque superati hostis terras et possessiones hæreditario jure rex ei concederet possidendas. Sed et Eadgarus Etheling, dum regi probatur fidelissimus, factus est etiam ei amicissimus, insuper et eum donis ditavit multis et honoribus.

X.

De[q] dictorum regum Eadgari et Alexandri, simul et David, de quo dicetur, sororis reginæ Matildis bonæ admirabili gloria animique virtute, quamque fuerit in officiis Divinis sacrisque vigiliis assidua et devota; in tanta insuper potestate quam humilis, qui scribere voluerit, alteram sibi Hesther nostris temporibus declarabit. Quod facere nos omisimus, tum propter materiæ magnitudinem, tum propter harum rerum minorem adhuc cognitionem. Unum tamen illius referam opus, quod ex ore nominandi et nunquam obliviscendi David regis audivi; per quod qualis fuerit circa pauperes Christi satis, ut arbitror, elucescet. Cum, inquit, adolescens adhuc in curia regis servirem, nocte quadam in hospitio meo cum sociis meis, nescio quid agens, ad thalamum reginæ, ab ipsa vocatus, accessi: et ecce! domus plena leprosis, et regina in medio stans, deposi-

[q] Fordun, v., 40. This also is from Aelred, who cites the authority of David *Rex*, which is quite consistent with the date at which he wrote, but not so with Turgot, who died nine years before David came to the throne.

toque pallio, cum se linteo præcinxisset, posita in pelvi aqua, cœpit lavare pedes eorum et extergere, extersosque utrisque constringere manibus, et devotissime osculari. Cui ego; "Quid "agis, inquam, o domina? Certe si rex sciret ista, nunquam "os tuum, tabe tali pollutum, suis dignaretur tangere labiis." Tunc illa subridens, "Pedes," ait, "Regis Æterni quis nesciat "labiis regis morituri esse præferendos? Ergo certe, frater "carissime, idcirco vocavi te, ut exemplo meo talia discas "operari." Sumpta deinde pelvi, "Fac," ait, "quod me facere "intueris." Ad hanc vocem vehementer expavi, et nullo modo id me pati posse respondi: nec dum enim sciebam Dominum, nec revelatus fuerat mihi Spiritus Ejus. Illa igitur cœptis insistente, ego mea culpa ridens, remeavi ad socios meos.[r]

[r] Besides the extracts given above, the following passage, which occurs in chapter xviii., is ascribed in some MSS. to Turgot:—Anno Domini M.lxvii. Sancta Margareta copulata fuit matrimonialiter regi Malcolmo anno regni sui decimo quarto. Hic Angliam usque Cleveland vastavit, et rediens per Wervicam, quæ est ostium Weri fluminis, intravit Scotiam, et invenit ante se Eadgarum Etheling et sorores suas Margaretam et Christinam in nave latitantes prope Culros; et Margaretam matrimonio copulavit. Christina vero soror ejus in Christi sponsam benedicitur. Malcolmus rex genuit ex Margareta sex inclitos filios, scilicet Eadwardum, Eadmundum, Æthelredum, Eadgarum, Alexandrum, et omnium regum strenuissimum David; et duas filias, Matildem scilicet, postea reginam Angliæ, cognomento Bonam, et Mariam comitissam Bononiæ: de quibus singulis postea suo loco dicetur. Qualis vero, vel quanti meriti fuerat illa beata regina Margareta apud Deum et homines, vitam ejus laudabilem et mortem, ac miracula, liber inde confectus legentibus declarabit. It will be seen that the first part of this extract, although it has a general resemblance to the parallel narrative in the Historia Regum, differs materially from it. In the latter work the first casual meeting of Malcolm with Edgar Atheling and his mother and sisters is said to have been at Wearmouth.

INDEX NOMINUM.

B

C

D

E

F

G

H

L

O

P

R

S

T

INDEX LOCORUM.

D

H

Q

R

S

T

ADDENDA ET CORRIGENDA.

p. 9, note, line 29. For *two*, read *three*.
p. 13, note *f*. For *Litchfield*, read *Lichfield*.
p. 18, note *q*. For *Hereford*, read *Rochester*.
p. 21, note *m*. For *Ouuini*, read *Osuuini*.
p. 55, note *l*, line 2. For *m*, read *w*.

p. 63, line 8. For *Cuthbertus*, read *Cutheardus*. In the notes to the same page alter the following references:—Reference *k* should be after the word *interiit* at the end of line 24. Reference *l* should be substituted for *k* after the word "Sihtrico" at the end of line 29. Reference *m* for *l* at the end of line 31.

p. 64, line 5, substitute reference *n* for *m* after "Ethelstano." At the end of line 11, *n* may remain, as this and the preceding reference are both of them to the Saxon Chronicle.

p. 65. Reference *s* at the end of line 12 should be placed after the word "occiderunt" in the preceding line: *s* in lines 12 and 15 should be *t*.

p. 77, note *d*. The annotator is right. Taddenes-scylf is Tanshelf or Pontefract. See the Domesday book.

p. 107, line 4 from foot of page. Honorius VI. ought, no doubt, to be in the MS. II. There has been no Honorius VI.

In the History of the Translations of St. Cuthbert the Gale MS. was not examined before the first nine chapters had been printed off. It supplies the following corrections, and a few misprints are also put right.

p. 159, line 27, remove the comma after "audisset."
p. 160, line 2, for *ille*, MS. Gale reads *illo*.
p. 160, line 23, for *promulcet*, MS. Gale reads *permulcet*.
p. 160, line 33, for *et vino quæ*, read, with MS. Gale, *vinoque*, and omit the (*sic*).
p. 161, line 5. For *in majus*, MS. Gale reads *immanis*.
p. 161, line 18. After *audierat* MS. Gale adds *ita ut audierat*.
p. 162, line 2. After *sit* add *in*.
p. 163, line 13. For *nimis*, MS. Gale reads *nimio*.
p. 164, line 21. For *obnoxius*, MS. Gale reads *obnixius*.
p. 167, line 9. For *tamen*, read *tantum*. In the next line, for *primoribus*, MS. Gale reads *prioribus*.
p. 168, line 16. For *exiluit*, MS. Gale reads *exilivit*.
p. 169, line 7. For *quoquomodo*, read *quoquo modo*; line 20, for *anima*, read *animæ*; line 24, for *oraculo*, read *oracula*.
p. 170, l. 14. For *abstraherentur*, read *abstraheretur*.
p. 171, last line. Omit the colon after *monachi*.
p. 174, line 2. For *judiciis*, read *indiciis*; line 11, for *sunt*, read *fiunt*; line 37, for *favore*, read *pavore*.
p. 175, line 16. Stop this line thus, "*agnosceret, agnoscens defleret, deflens correctiorem*," etc.
p. 176, last line but one. Read *in auroram*.
p. 194, line 7. For *cum eo venerant*, MS. Gale reads *convenerant*.
p. 197. MS. Gale omits the last sentence of chapter xviii.
p. 205, line 3. For *suceptus*, read *susceptus*.
p. 207, line 21. For *Eafi*, read *Easi*.

Mitchell and Hughes, Printers, 24 Wardour Street, London.

THE SURTEES SOCIETY.

REPORT FOR THE YEAR MD.CCC.LXVII.

WITH regard to the progress of the Surtees Society during the past year, it is almost superfluous to say that it enjoys its customary prosperity. Our finances are in a satisfactory condition. Our list of members is full, and the candidates for admission are more numerous than the vacancies.

In consequence of the unexpected bulk of the two volumes for 1866, the Society has resolved to issue one only for the current year. This is the first part of the writings ascribed to an ancient northern chronicler, Symeon of Durham. Hitherto the chief work of this well-known author has been overlaid with a vast and unnecessary series of extracts from earlier writers. One of the main objects of the editor of the Surtees edition has been to throw these aside, and to present nothing to the reader with which the name of Symeon cannot be intimately connected, whether these materials appear as the production of his own pen, or as the handiwork of others of which he has availed himself. In an appendix several valuable tractates have been given, the most interesting of which is the account of the Translations of the body of St. Cuthbert, the greater portion of which has never been in print before. The best thanks of the Society are due to the editor, not merely for his labour, but for the pecuniary assistance he has given to enable the Society to ensure the completeness of the volume.

Several volumes are at the present time in a state of preparation. The first is the Correspondence of John Cosin, the well-known Bishop of Durham. Recent and careful investigations have added largely to the information we possess about this famous prelate. Numerous letters to and from him have been discovered; and the present volume will contain a remarkable and hitherto unknown body of correspondence between him and Richard Montague, before they were raised to the bench.

The Society has taken up another subject which is an interesting one at all times, more especially at the present. The Articles and Injunctions of the heads of the church within the northern province have never appeared in a collected form. Some of them are known through the valuable although ponderous work of Wilkins, and others are to be met with in other publications, but a complete edition of these curious and important codes of local ecclesiastical rules has never been made. This it will be the object of the Society to supply.

A third work, which is being prepared for publication, may be briefly mentioned. It is the Ephemeris or Diurnal of Abraham De la Pryme, a Yorkshire antiquary in the time of William III. and Queen Anne. The manuscript collections of this scholar are widely scattered and are little known, but the appearance of his Diary will give a fair insight into the character and feelings of one of those topographical labourers whose exertions have done honour to the county of York.

THE SURTEES SOCIETY,

ESTABLISHED IN THE YEAR 1834,

In honour of the late Robert Surtees, of Mainsforth, Esquire, the Author of the History of the County Palatine of Durham, and in accordance with his pursuits and plans; having for its object the publication of inedited Manuscripts, illustrative of the intellectual, the moral, the religious, and the social condition of those parts of England and Scotland, included on the east between the Humber and the Frith of Forth, and on the west between the Mersey and the Clyde, a region which constituted the ancient Kingdom of Northumberland.

NEW RULES AGREED UPON IN 1849; REVISED 1863.

I.—The Society shall consist of not more than three hundred and fifty members.

II.—There shall be a patron of the Society, who shall be President.

III.—There shall be twenty-four Vice-Presidents, a Secretary, and two Treasurers.

IV.—The Patron, the Vice-Presidents, the Secretary, and the Treasurers, shall form the Council; any five of whom, including the Secretary and a Treasurer, shall be a quorum competent to transact the business of the Society.

V.—The twenty-four Vice-Presidents, the Secretary, and the Treasurers, shall be elected at a general meeting, to continue in office for three years, and be capable of re-election.

VI.—Any vacancies in the offices of Secretary or Treasurers shall be provisionally filled up by the Council, subject to the approbation of the next general meeting.

VII.—Three meetings of the Council shall be held in every year, on the first Tuesday in the months of March, June, and December; and the place and hour of meeting shall be fixed by the Council, and communicated by the Secretary to the members of the Council.

VIII.—The meeting in June shall be the anniversary, to which all the members of the Society shall be convened by the Secretary.

IX.—The Secretary shall convene extraordinary meetings of the Council, on a requisition to that effect, signed by not less than five members of the Council, being presented to him.

X.—Members may be elected by ballot at any of the ordinary meetings, according to priority of application, upon being proposed in writing by three existing members. One black ball in ten shall exclude.

XI.—Each member shall pay in advance to the Treasurer the annual sum of one guinea. If any member's subscription shall be in arrear for two years, and he shall neglect to pay his subscription after having been reminded by the Treasurer, he shall be regarded as having ceased to be a member of the Society.

XII.—The money raised by the Society shall be expended in publishing such compositions, in their original language, or in a translated form, as come within the scope of this Society, without limitation of time with reference to the period of their respective authors. All editorial and other expenses to be defrayed by the Society.

XIII.—One volume, at least, in a closely printed octavo form, shall be supplied to each member of the Society every year, free of expense.

XIV.—If the funds of the Society in any year will permit, the Council shall be at liberty to print and furnish to the members, free of expense, any other volume or volumes of the same character, in the same or a different form.

XV.—The number of copies of each publication, and the selection of a printer and publisher, shall be left to the Council, who shall also fix the price at which the copies not furnished to members shall be sold to the public.

XVI.—The armorial bearings of Mr. Surtees and some other characteristic decoration connecting the Society with his name, shall be used in each publication.

XVII.—A list of the officers and members, together with an account of the receipts and expenses of the Society, shall be made up every year to the time of the annual meeting, and shall be submitted to the Society to be printed and published with the next succeeding volume.

XVIII.—No alteration shall be made in these rules except at an annual meeting. Notice of any such alteration shall be given at least as early as the ordinary meeting of the Council immediately preceding, to be communicated to each member of the Society.

PUBLICATIONS OF THE SURTEES SOCIETY,

WITH THEIR RESPECTIVE SALE PRICES.

N.B.—Of several of these volumes the number of copies on hand is very small; some will not be sold except to members of the Society under certain conditions, and all applications for them must be made to the Secretary.

1. Reginaldi Monachi Dunelmensis Libellus de Admirandis Beati Cuthberti Virtutibus. 15s. Edited by Dr. Raine.
2. Wills and Inventories, illustrative of the History, Manners, Language, Statistics, &c., of the Northern Counties of England, from the Eleventh Century downwards. (Chiefly from the Registry at Durham.) Vol. I. 15s. Edited by Dr. Raine. *(Only sold in a set.)*
3. The Towneley Mysteries; or, Miracle Plays. 15s. Edited by James Gordon, Esq. The Preface by Joseph Hunter, F.S.A.
4. Testamenta Eboracensia; Wills illustrative of the History, Manners, Language, Statistics, &c., of the Province of York, from 1300 downwards. Vol. I. 30s. Edited by Dr. Raine.
5. Sanctuarium Dunelmense et Sanctuarium Beverlacense; or, Registers of the Sanctuaries of Durham and Beverley. 15s. Edited by Dr. Raine. The Preface by the Rev. T. Chevallier.
6. The Charters of Endowment, Inventories, and Account Rolls of the Priory of Finchale, in the County of Durham. 15s. Edited by Dr. Raine.
7. Catalogi Veteres Librorum Ecclesiæ Cathedralis Dunelm. Catalogues of the Library of Durham Cathedral at various periods, from the Conquest to the Dissolution; including Catalogues of the Library of the Abbey of Hulne, and of the MSS. preserved in the Library of Bishop Cosin at Durham. 10s. Edited by Dr. Raine. The Preface by Beriah Botfield, Esq.
8. Miscellanea Biographica; a Life of Oswin, King of Northumberland; Two Lives of Cuthbert, Bishop of Lindisfarne; and a Life of Eata, Bishop of Hexham. 10s. Edited by Dr. Raine.
9. Historiæ Dunelmensis Scriptores Tres, Gaufridus de Coldingham, Robertus de Greystanes, et Willelmus de Chambre, with the omissions and mistakes in Wharton's Edition supplied and corrected, and an Appendix of 665 original Documents, in illustration of the Text. 15s. Edited by Dr. Raine.
10. Rituale Ecclesiæ Dunelmensis; a Latin Ritual of the Ninth Century, with an interlinear Northumbro-Saxon Translation. 15s. Edited by the Rev. J. Stevenson.
11. Jordan Fantosme's Anglo-Norman Chronicle of the War between the English and the Scots, in 1173 and 1174. Edited, with a Translation, Notes, &c., by Francisque Michel, F.S.A. 15s.
12. The Correspondence, Inventories, Account Rolls and Law Proceedings of the Priory of Coldingham. 15s. Edited by Dr. Raine.
13. Liber Vitæ Ecclesiæ Dunelmensis: necnon Obituaria duo ejusdem Ecclesiæ. 10s. Edited by Rev. J. Stevenson.
14. The Correspondence of Robert Bowes, of Aske, Esq., Ambassador of Queen Elizabeth to the Court of Scotland. 15s. Edited by Rev. J. Stevenson.
15. A Description or Briefe Declaration of all the Ancient Monuments, Rites, and Customs belonging to, or being within, the Monastical Church of Durham, before the Suppression. Written in 1593. 10s. Edited by Dr. Raine.
16. Anglo-Saxon and Early-English Psalter, now first published from MSS. in the British Museum. Vol. I. 15s. Edited by Rev. J. Stevenson.
17. The Correspondence of Dr. Matthew Hutton, Archbishop of York. With a selection from the Letters of Sir Timothy Hutton, Knt., his Son, and Matthew Hutton, Esq., his Grandson. 15s. Edited by Dr. Raine.
18. The Durham Household Book; or, the Accounts of the Bursar of the Monastery of Durham from 1530 to 1534. 15s. Edited by Dr. Raine.
19. Anglo-Saxon and Early-English Psalter. Vol. II. 15s. Edited by Rev. J. Stevenson.
20. Libellus de Vita et Miraculis S. Godrici, Heremitæ de Finchale, auctore Reginaldo, Monacho Dunelmensi. 15s. Edited by Rev. J. Stevenson.
21. Depositions respecting the Rebellion of 1569, Witchcraft, and other Ecclesiastical Proceedings, from the Court of Durham, extending from 1311 to the reign of Elizabeth. 15s. Edited by Dr. Raine.*

* *Members have the privilege of purchasing the first twenty-one volumes, or any of them, except No. 2, at half-price.*

22. The Injunctions and other Ecclesiastical Proceedings of Richard Barnes, Bishop of Durham (1577-87.) 15s. Edited by Dr. Raine.

23. The Anglo-Saxon Hymnarium, from MSS. of the Eleventh Century, in Durham, the British Museum, &c. 16s. Edited by Rev. J. Stevenson.

24. The Memoir of Mr. Surtees, by the late George Taylor, Esq. Reprinted from the Fourth Vol. of the History of Durham, with additional Notes and Illustrations, together with an Appendix, comprising some of Mr. Surtees' Correspondence, Poetry, &c. Edited by Dr. Raine. (*Only sold in a set and to a Member.*)

25. The Boldon Book, or Survey of Durham in 1183. 10s. 6d. Edited by Rev. W. Greenwell.

26. Wills and Inventories, illustrative of the History, Manners, Language, Statistics, &c., of the Counties of York, Westmerland, and Lancaster, from the Fourteenth Century downwards. From the Registry at Richmond. 14s. Edited by Rev. J. Raine.

27. The Pontifical of Egbert, Archbishop of York (731-67), from a MS. of the Ninth or Tenth Century in the Imperial Library in Paris. 11s. Edited by Rev. William Greenwell.

28. The Gospel of St. Matthew, from the Northumbrian Interlinear Gloss to the Gospels, contained in the MS. Nero D. IV., among the Cottonian MSS. in the British Museum, commonly known as the Lindisfarne Gospels, collated with the Rushworth MS. 14s. Edited by Rev. J. Stevenson.

29. The Inventories and Account Rolls of the Monasteries of Jarrow and Monkwearmouth, from their commencement in 1303, till the Dissolution. 12s. Edited by Dr. Raine.

30. Testamenta Eboracensia, or Wills illustrative of the History, Manners, Language, Statistics, &c., of the Province of York, from 1429 to 1467. Vol. II. 25s. Edited by Rev. J. Raine.

31. The Bede Roll of John Burnaby, Prior of Durham (1456-64.) With illustrative documents. 12s. Edited by Dr. Raine.

32. The Survey of the Palatinate of Durham, compiled during the Episcopate of Thomas Hatfield (1345-1382.) 15s. Edited by Rev. W. Greenwell.

33. The Farming Book of Henry Best, of Elmswell, E.R.Y. 12s. Edited by Rev. C. B. Robinson.

34. The Proceedings of the High Court of Commission for Durham and Northumberland. 14s. Edited by Mr. W. H. D. Longstaffe.

35. The Fabric Rolls of York Minster. 25s. Edited by Rev. J. Raine.

36. The Heraldic Visitation of Yorkshire, by Sir William Dugdale, in 1665. Edited by Robert Davies, F.S.A. (*Only sold in a set and to a member.*)

37. A Volume of Miscellanea, comprising the Letters of Dean Granville, the Account of the Siege of Pontefract by Nathan Drake, and Extracts from the Rokeby Correspondence. Edited by Rev. George Ornsby, Mr. W. H. D. Longstaffe, and Rev. J. Raine. (*Only sold in a set and to a member.*)

38. A Volume of Wills from the Registry at Durham; a continuation of No. 2. Edited by Rev. W. Greenwell. (*Only sold in a set and to a member.*)

39. The Gospel of St. Mark, from the Northumbrian Interlinear Gloss to the Gospels contained in the MS. Nero D. IV., among the Cottonian MSS. in the British Museum, commonly known as the Lindisfarne Gospels, collated with the Rushworth MS.; a continuation of No. 28. 10s. Edited by Mr. George Waring.

40. A Selection from the Depositions in Criminal Cases taken before the Northern Magistrates, from the originals preserved in York Castle. Sæc. XVII. Edited by Rev. J. Raine. (*Sold only in a set and to a member.*)

41. The Heraldic Visitation of the North of England, made in 1530, by Thomas Tonge, with an Appendix of Genealogical MSS. Edited by Mr. W. H. D. Longstaffe. (*Only sold in a set and to a member.*)

42. Memorials of Fountains Abbey. Vol. I. Comprising the Chronicle relating to the Foundation of the House, written by Hugh de Kirkstall; the Chronicle of Abbats, &c., and an historical description of the Abbey, with illustrations. Edited by Mr. J. R. Walbran. (*Only sold in a set and to a member.*)

43. The Gospel of St. Luke, from the Northumbrian Interlinear Gloss to the Gospels contained in the MS. Nero D. IV., among the Cottonian MSS. in the British Museum, commonly known as the Lindisfarne Gospels, collated with the Rushworth MS.; a continuation of Nos. 28 and 39. 14s. Edited by Mr. George Waring.

44. The Priory of Hexham, its Chronicles, Endowments, and Annals. Vol. I. Containing the Chronicles, &c., of John and Richard, Priors of Hexham, and Aelred Abbat of Rievaux, with an Appendix of documents, and a Preface illustrated with engravings, pp. 604. £2 2s. Edited by Rev. J. Raine.

45. Testamenta Eboracensia, or Wills illustrative of the History, Manners, Language, Statistics, &c., of the Province of York, from 1467 to 1485. Vol. III. 25s. Edited by Rev. J. Raine.

46. The Priory of Hexham. Vol. II. Containing the Liber Niger, with Charters and other Documents, and a Preface illustrated with engravings. 16s. Edited by Rev. J. Raine.

47. The Letters, &c., of Dennis Granville, D.D., Dean of Durham, from the originals recently discovered in the Bodleian Library. Part II. 16s. Edited by Rev. George Ornsby.

48. The Gospel of St. John, from the Northumbrian Interlinear Gloss to the Gospels in the MS. Nero D. IV. (A continuation of Nos. 28, 39, and 43.) 14s. With Preface and Prolegomena. Edited by Mr. George Waring.

49. The Survey of the County of York, taken by John de Kirkby, commonly called Kirkby's Inquest. Also Inquisitions of Knights' Fees, The Nomina Villarum for Yorkshire, and an Appendix of illustrative documents, pp. 570. 25s. Edited by Mr. R. H. Skaife.

50. Memoirs of the Life of Mr. Ambrose Barnes, late Merchant and sometime Alderman of Newcastle-upon-Tyne. 21s. Edited by Mr. W. H. D. Longstaffe.

51. Symeon of Durham. The whole of the works ascribed to him except the History of the Church of Durham. To which are added the History of the Translations of St. Cuthbert, the Life of S. Margaret Queen of Scotland, by Turgot, Prior of Durham, &c. Edited by Mr. John Hodgson Hinde. 25s.

The Council propose to select their future volumes out of the following manuscripts or materials, or from others of a similar description.

1. The Correspondence of John Cosin, Bishop of Durham. Gathered together for the first time from the original MSS.; now being prepared by the Rev. George Ornsby for 1868.

2. The Articles and Injunctions issued by the Bishops and Archdeacons within the Province of York, from the earliest period to 1662. Now being prepared by the Hon. and Rev. Stephen Lawley.

3. The Ephemeris or Diary of the Rev. Abraham De la Pryme, the Yorkshire Antiquary, in the latter part of the 17th century. Now being prepared by Mr. Charles Jackson.

4. The Memorials of Fountains Abbey. Vol. II. To contain the Papal Bulls, the Royal Charters of Privilege, and a portion of the Title Deeds of the Monastery relating to its property in the North of England. With engravings of seals, &c. Five sheets have already been printed under the editorial care of Mr. J. R. Walbran.

5. Symeon of Durham. Vol. II. To contain the History of the Church of Durham, with an Appendix consisting of several historical tractates, illustrative of Symeon's work.

6. The Account Rolls, Charters, &c., of Durham (Trinity) College, Oxford, with lists of its early members, and other authentic and original information relating to it.

7. The Lords of the Soil of the County of Durham from the earliest period to the Reformation, comprising the descent of the estates and various other particulars, genealogical and heraldic, relating to their owners, largely illustrated with engravings of seals, etc. To be prepared by Mr. W. H. D. Longstaffe and the Rev. William Greenwell.

8. The Letters, Despatches, Extracts from the Household Books, and other works and papers of Lord William Howard of Naworth, from the originals at Castle-Howard, Naworth Castle, and London. To be prepared by Mr. Robert Davies.

9. The Lives of S. Wilfrid by Eddi, Eadmer, and Fridegodus, with other Biographical and Historical Documents relating to the Church of York and its rulers. To be prepared by Rev. William Stubbs, M.A.

10. A Volume of Early Rituals, supplementary to those already published by the Society, to contain as many of the unpublished Pontificals as the Society can obtain access to, including that of St. Dunstan in the Imperial Library at Paris. To be prepared by Rev. Dr. Henderson.

11. A Volume of Documents relating to the Ancient Guilds in the City of York; to contain especially, the Register of the Guild of the Corpus Christi, which is preserved in the British Museum. To be prepared by Mr. Robert Skaife.

12. The Inquisitions Post Mortem for the North of England, from the originals at London and Durham.

13. A Volume of Extracts from the Depositions preserved in the Ecclesiastical Court at York, from the fourteenth century downwards.

14. The Visitation of the County of York in 1584, by William Flower.

15. A Volume of Wills relating to the Counties of Cumberland and Westmerland, principally from the Registry at Carlisle.

16. A Collection of Letters and Papers relating to the Dissolution of the Northern Monasteries, the proceedings of the Visitors, and the opposition of the Monks.

17. The Annals of the Pilgrimage of Grace, derived from unpublished documents of the greatest interest and curiosity in the State Paper Office and the British Museum.

18. A Volume of Extracts from the Proceedings of the Court of Chancery at Durham, relating to cases in the Counties of Durham and Northumberland in the sixteenth and seventeenth Centuries.

19. A Concluding Volume of Extracts from the Proceedings of the Ecclesiastical Court of Durham.

20. A Continuation of the Testamenta Eboracensia.

21. Cardinal Langley's Survey of the Palatinate of Durham, together with Extracts from the contemporaneous Bailiff's Rolls.

22. Memorials of Kirkstall Abbey; The History of its Foundation; the Chronicle of Kirkstall; and Extracts from the Charter Books of that ancient house.

23. Selections from the yearly Rolls of the Bursar of the Monastery of Durham, beginning in 1270.

24. The Charters and Account Rolls of the Cells of Lytham and Stamford.

25. The Chartularies of Holm Cultram, and other documents relating to that Monastery.

26. The Chartulary of Whitby Abbey, and the Chronicle of that house.

27. St. Mary's Abbey, York, its Annals, by Abbat Simon de Warwick; with Extracts from the Chartularies.

28. The Charter Book of St. Leonard's Hospital at York, with several of the early Account Rolls, Wills of Benefactors, etc.

29. The Evidences of the ancient Family of Calverley, from the originals in the possession of Sir Walter Calverley Trevelyan, Bart.

30. Letters, hitherto inedited, relating to the Outrages, Feuds, etc., on the borders of England and Scotland.

31. The Autobiography of Anne Countess of Pembroke, Dorset and Montgomery, with other Documents relating to the house of Clifford.

32. The Correspondence of Thomas Baker (the "Coll. Jo. socius ejectus") with the Literary Men of his day.

33. The Correspondence of Dr. George Hickes and Hilkiah Bedford, the celebrated Non-jurors and Antiquaries.

34. The Correspondence of Adam Baines, the first M.P. for Leeds.

35. A Glossary of Ancient North Country Words to illustrate and explain, especially, the Works already published by this Society.

List of Officers and Members, June, 1867.

PATRON AND PRESIDENT.

His Grace the Duke of Buccleuch and Queensberry, K.G., etc.

VICE PRESIDENTS.

Edward Akroyd, Esq., M.P., Bank Field, Halifax.
Robert Henry Allan, F.S.A., Blackwell Grange, Darlington.
John Booth, jun., Durham.
Rev. Canon Chevallier, B.D., Durham.
Rev. John Dixon Clarke, M.A., Belford Hall.
James Crossley, F.S.A., President of the Chetham Society, Manchester.
Rev. John Cundill, B.D., Durham.
Robert Davies, F.S.A., York.
John F. Elliot, Elvet Hill, Durham.
John Fawcett, Durham.
Rev. William Greenwell, M.A., Durham.
Edwin Guest, LL.D., Master of Caius College, Cambridge.
Thomas Duffus Hardy, Her Majesty's Deputy-keeper of Records, London.
William Henderson, Durham.
John Hodgson Hinde, Stelling Hall, Gateshead.
W. H. D. Longstaffe, F.S.A., Gateshead.
Richard Lawrence Pemberton, The Barnes, Sunderland.
Rev. Daniel Rock, D.D., F.S.A., 17, Essex Villas, Kensington, London.
Sir Walter Calverley Trevelyan, Bart., F.S.A., Wallington, Newcastle-on-Tyne.
The Very Rev. George Waddington, D.D., Dean of Durham.
John Richard Walbran, F.S.A., Fallcroft, Ripon.
Albert Way, F.S.A., Wonham Manor, Reigate.
Rev. C. T. Whitley, M.A., Bedlington, Newcastle-on-Tyne.
Sir C. G. Young, F.S.A., Garter King-at-Arms.

SECRETARY.

Rev. James Raine, M.A., York.

TREASURERS.

John Gough Nichols, F.S.A., 25, Parliament Street, Westminster.
Samuel Rowlandson, Durham.

MEMBERS, WITH THE DATES OF THEIR ADMISSION.*

Richard Abbay, Great Ouseburn, Boroughbridge, 13th December, 1861.
Sir John Dalberg Acton, Bart., Aldenham Park, Bridgenorth. 17th June, 1861.
George E. Adams, Rouge Dragon Pursuivant of Arms, Heralds' College, London. 13th December, 1862.
Rev. E. H. Adamson, M.A., St. Alban's Parsonage, Gateshead. 14th December, 1860.
The Advocates' Library, Edinburgh. 13th March, 1851.
Edward Akroyd, M.P., F.S.A., Bank Field, Halifax. 15th December, 1859. (*Vice-President* 1866-7.)
William Aldam, Frickley Hall, Doncaster. 13th December, 1862.
Robert Henry Allan, F.S.A., Blackwell Grange, Darlington. (*Treasurer*, 1834-1844. *Vice-President*, 1844-1867.)†

* The number of three hundred and fifty members, to which the Society is limited, is now full. Judging from past experience, there will be ten or twelve vacancies every year, and these will be regularly filled up. New members will be elected by the Council according to priority of application, unless the son or the representative of a deceased member wishes to be chosen in his place.

William Anderson, Stonegate, York. 13th December, 1861.
The Society of Antiquaries, London. 1st March, 1864.
The Society of Antiquaries, Newcastle-on-Tyne. 24th September, 1853.
John Reed Appleton, F.S.A., Western Hills, Durham. 15th December, 1859.
The Library of the Athenæum Club, Waterloo Place, London. 13th December, 1861.
J. H. Aveling, M.D., Sheffield. 14th December, 1860.
John Harrison Aylmer, Walworth Castle, Darlington, 12th July, 1836.
J. H. Backhouse, Darlington. 5th June, 1866.
Rev. William Baird, Vicar of Dymoke, Gloucestershire. Dec. 6th, 1864.
Charles Baker, F.S.A., 11, Sackville Street, London. 13th December, 1861.
E. B. Wheatley Balme, Cote Walls, Mirfield, Normanton. 8th December, 1863.
J. W. Barnes, Durham. 7th March, 1865.
Thomas H. Bates, Wolsingham. 7th June, 1864.
Rev. Thomas Bayly, B.A., Sub-chantor of York Minster, and Treasurer of the Yorkshire Architectural Society. 14th December, 1860.
William Beamont, Warrington. 28th September, 1843,
Wentworth B. Beaumont, M.P., Bretton Hall, Wakefield. 14th March, 1862.
George S. Beecroft, M.P., Abbey Lodge, Kirkstall, Leeds. 8th December, 1863.
Alfred Bell, 49, Lincoln's Inn Fields, London. 31st March, 1849.
George Bell, York Street, Covent Garden, London. 1st March, 1864.
The Royal Library at Berlin. 14th March, 1863.
Rev. Dr. Besley, Long Benton, Newcastle-on-Tyne. 16th March, 1861.
Sir Edward Blackett, Bart., Matfen, Newcastle-on-Tyne. 15th December, 1859.
Robert Willis Blencowe, Secretary of the Sussex Archæological Society, The Hooke, Lewes. 13th March, 1851.
John Booth, jun., Durham. 18th June, 1862. (*Vice-President* and *Local Secretary*, 1864-7.)
Rev. Joseph Bosworth, LL.D., F.R.S., Professor of Anglo-Saxon in the University of Oxford, Water-Stratford, Bucks. 14th December, 1861.
E. C. Boville, Willington, Burton-on-Trent. 15th March, 1860.
John Bowes, Streatlam Castle, Durham.†
Richard Bowser, Bishop Auckland. 14th March, 1863.
Rev. Canon Boyd, M.A., Rector of Arncliffe, Skipton-in-Craven. 7th March, 1865.
The Viscount Boyne, Brancepeth Castle, Durham. 15th December, 1852,
William Boyne, F.S.A., 4, Lindsay Row, Chelsea, London. 13th Dec., 1862.
Rev. J. S. Brewer, M.A., Reader at the Rolls, and Professor of English Literature, King's College, London. 13th December, 1862.
Thomas Brooke, Armitage Bridge, Huddersfield. 14th December, 1860.
Douglas Brown, 15, Hertford Street, Mayfair, London. 11th March, 1858.
James Brown, M.P., Rossington Hall, Bawtry. 13th December, 1862.
Alfred Hall Browne, 5, West Hills, Highgate, London. 13th December, 1861.
Rev. John Collingwood Bruce, LL.D., F.S.A., &c., Secretary of the Society of Antiquaries, Newcastle-on-Tyne. 6th June, 1856.
The Duke of Buccleuch and Queensberry, K.G., &c., Dalkeith. (*The first President of the Society*, 1834-1837. *President* 1865-7.)†
Rev. W. E. Buckley, M.A., Middleton Cheney, Banbury. 13th March, 1851.
Robert Anthony Burrell, Durham. 17th June, 1861.
Thomas Burton, Turnham Hall, Selby. December, 1857.
Rev. William Bury, Chapel-house, Kilnsey, Skipton-in-Craven. 14th December, 1860.
C. H. Cadogan, Brinkburn Priory, Morpeth. June 4th, 1867.*

† Those gentlemen to whose names a cross is appended have been members of the Society since its foundation in 1834.

* Those gentlemen to whose names an asterisk is attached have become members during the past year.

Rev. Thomas Calvert, B.A., Dinnington, Newcastle-on-Tyne. 13th December, 1862.
The Lord Archbishop of Canterbury. 13th March, 1857.
Ralph Carr, Hedgeley, Alnwick. 26th September, 1844.
Rev. T. W. Carr, Barming Rectory, Maidstone. 13th December, 1861.
William Carr, Little Gomersal, Leeds. 5th December, 1865.
Edward Cayley, Wydale, Scarborough. 13th December, 1861.
Rev. Reginald Arthur Cayley, Rector of Scampston, Lincoln. 13th December, 1861.
William Chadwick, Arksey, Doncaster. 5th December, 1865.
John Barff Charlesworth, Hatfeild Hall, Wakefield. 14th March, 1862.
Edward Charlton, M.D., Secretary of the Society of Antiquaries, Newcastle-on-Tyne. 6th June, 1856.
Rev. James Allen Charlton, Gosforth, Newcastle-on-Tyne. 8th December, 1853.
William Henry Charlton, Hesleyside, Hexham. 31st May, 1849.
Joseph Chester, 14, St. George's Terrace, Blue Anchor Road, Bermondsey, London. 5th December, 1865.
The Chetham Library, Manchester. December, 1857.
Rev. Temple Chevallier, B.D., Canon of Durham, Professor of Mathematics and Astronomy in the University of Durham. 12th July, 1836. (*Vice-President*, 1836-1867.)
The Library of Christ's College, Cambridge. 13th December, 1862.
Rev. John Dixon Clarke, Belford Hall. 1st June, 1853. (*Vice-President*, 1855-1867.)
Rev. John Haldenby Clarke, M.A., Hilgay, Downham, Norfolk. 5th December, 1865.
J. W. Clarke, M.A., Trinity College, Cambridge.. December, 1857. (*Local Secretary*, 1858-1867.)
Thomas K. Clarke, jun., John William Street, Huddersfield. 8th December, 1863. (*Local Secretary*, 1864-1867.)
Edward Clayton, New Walk Terrace, York. 7th June, 1864.
John Clayton, Newcastle-on-Tyne. 8th December, 1853.
The Duke of Cleveland, Raby Castle, Staindrop. September, 1841.
Alexander Cockburn, 12, Walker Street, Edinburgh. 6th June, 1854.
Rev. William Collins, M.A., St. Mary's, Ramsey, Huntingdon. 15th December, 1859.
John Cookson, Meldon Park, Morpeth. 15th December, 1852.
The Royal Library at Copenhagen. 14th March, 1863.
Sir Joseph William Copley, Bart., Sprotborough, Doncaster. 13th December, 1862.
Rev. G. E. Corrie, D.D., Master of Jesus College, Cambridge. 28th December, 1837.
Rev. Thomas Corser, M.A., F.S.A., Rector of Stand, Manchester. 28th September, 1837.
Christopher Croft, Richmond, Yorkshire. 8th December, 1853.
R. Cross, Bottoms Lodge, Tintwistle, Manchester. 6th December, 1864.
James Crossley, F.S.A., President of the Chetham Society, Booth Street, Manchester. 11th March, 1858. (*Vice-President*, 1861-1867.)
Matthew T. Culley, Copeland Castle, Wooller. 13th December, 1861.
Rev. John Cundill, B.D., Perpetual Curate of St. Margaret's, Durham. 31st May, 1849. (*Vice-President*, 1849-1867.)
Rev. J. W. Darnbrough, M.A., Rector of South Otterington, Thirsk. 6th Dec., 1864.
Robert Darnell, jun., Mount Villas, York. 16th March, 1861.
Rev. William Darnell, Bambro', Belford. 5th December, 1865.
The Lord Bishop of St. David's, Abergwili Palace, Caermarthen. 13th March, 1851.

Robert Davies, F.S.A., The Mount, York. 13th March, 1851. (*Vice-President*, 1861-1867.)
Rev. Thomas Dean, M.A., Warton, Lancaster. 16th March, 1861.
Robert Richardson Dees, Wallsend, Newcastle-on-Tyne. 15th December, 1859.
Rev. Stephen Poyntz Donning, M.A., St. Andrew's College, Bradfield, Reading. 14th March, 1850.
Rev. William Denton, M.A., 48, Finsbury Circus, London. 17th June, 1861. (*Local Secretary*, 1862-1867.)
William Dickon, F.S.A., Alnwick. 12th July, 1836.
Rev. James F. Dimock, Barnburgh Rectory, Doncaster. 8th December, 1863.
George Dodsworth, Clifton, York. 13th December, 1862.
Rev. W. W. Douglas, M.A., Rector of Salwarpe, Worcester. 7th Nov., 1865.
The Hon. and Very Rev. Augustus Duncombe, D.D., Dean of York. 15th December, 1859.
The Right Hon. Sir David Dundas, Inner Temple, London. 30th December, 1858.
The Lord Bishop of Durham, Auckland Castle. 13th December, 1861.
The Library of the University of Durham. 16th June, 1858.
Rev. John Edleston, D.C.L., Vicar of Gainford, Darlington. 8th Dec., 1863.
Rev. J. H. Eld, B.D., Fellow of St. John's College, Oxford, Fyfield, Berks. 14th March, 1863.
John F. Elliot, Elvet Hill, Durham. 12th July, 1836. (*Vice-President*, 1849-1867.)
Edmund Viner Ellis, Gloucester. 17th June, 1861.
William Viner Ellis, Gloucester. 30th December, 1858.
Charles Elsley, Mill Mount, York. 5th December, 1865.
Rev. Richard Elwyn, M.A., Head Master of St. Peter's School, York. 5th December, 1865.
Rev. Dr. English, Warley House, Brentwood. 14th March, 1862.
John Errington, High Warden, Hexham. 14th March, 1862.
The Lord Bishop of Exeter. 5th December, 1853.
The Very Rev. Monsignore Eyre, Newcastle-on-Tyne. 11th December, 1856.
Rev. W. K. Farmery, 18, Bank Street, Leeds. 7th March, 1865.
James Farrer, Inglebro', Lancaster. 31st May, 1849.
Miss ffarrington, Worden Hall, Preston. 14th December, 1860.
G. W. J. Farsyde, Fylingdales, Whitby. 8th December, 1863.
John Fawcett, Durham. 29th September, 1842. (*Vice-President*, 1843-1867.)
The Lord Feversham, Duncombe Park, Helmsley. 4th June, 1867.*
John Fisher, Masham. 14th March, 1862.
Matthew Ford, 8, Lincoln's Inn Fields, London. 5th December, 1865.
Charles Forrest, Lofthouse, Wakefield. 1st March, 1864.
The Viscount Galway, M.P., Serlby Hall, Bawtry. 15th December, 1859.
Henry H. Gibbs, St. Dunstan's, Regent's Park, London. 15th December, 1859.
William Sidney Gibson, F.S.A., Tynemouth. 26th September, 1844.
The University of Göettingen. 8th December, 1863.
Nicholas Charles Gold, Whitefriars Street, Fleet Street, London. 8th December, 1863.
The Very Rev. William Goode, D.D., F.S.A., Dean of Ripon. 8th Dec., 1863.
John Edward Thorley Graham, Scarbro'. 5th December, 1865.
William Grainge, Harrogate. 25th February, 1859.
William Gray, York. 15th March, 1860.
Rev. William Greenwell, M.A., Librarian of the Dean and Chapter of Durham. 28th September, 1843. (*Treasurer*, 1843-1849. *Vice-President*, 1849-1867.)
John Beswicke Greenwood, Dewsbury Moor House, Dewsbury. 14th December, 1860.
The Earl de Grey and Ripon, Studley Royal, Ripon. 15th December, 1859.
Edwin Guest, LL.D., F.S.A., &c., Master of Caius College, Cambridge. (*Vice-President*, 1856-1867.)†

Edward Hailstone, F.S.A., Horton Hall, Bradford. May, 1846.
The Ven. W. Hale Hale, M.A., Archdeacon of London, Canon Residentiary of St. Paul's, and Master of the Charter House. 26th September, 1839.
The University of Halle. 8th December, 1863.
John Hammond, East Burton, Bedale. 7th June, 1864.
Rev. William Vernon Harcourt, M.A., Canon of York, Nuneham Park, Abingdon. 14th March, 1862.
Philip Charles Hardwick, F.S.A., 21, Cavendish Square, London. 14th March, 1850.
Thomas Duffus Hardy, H.M. Deputy Keeper of Records, The Rolls, London. 13th December, 1862. (*Vice-President*, 1865-1867.)
John Harland, F.S.A., 13, Union Terrace, Cheetham Hill, Manchester. 17th June, 1861.
William Harrison, Ripon. 30th December, 1858.
William Harrison, F.S.A., &c., Samlesbury Hall, Blackburn. 17th June, 1861.
Rev. W. Estcourt Harrison, M.A., Clifton, York. 13th December, 1861.
The Right Hon. T. E. Headlam, M.P., Chancellor of the Dioceses of Durham and Ripon, 20, Ashley Place, Victoria Street, London. 13th December, 1855.
Henry Healey, Smallbridge, Rochdale. 14th December, 1860.
William Henderson, Durham. 27th May, 1847. (*Treasurer*, 1847-1858. *Vice-President*, 1858-1867.)
Rev. W. G. Henderson, D.C.L., Head Master of Leeds Grammar School, 31st May, 1849. (*Secretary*, 1849-1852.)
The Lord Herries, Everingham Park, Hayton, Yorkshire. 15th December, 1859.
Rev. William Hey, M.A., Canon Residentiary of York. 14th March, 1862.
Rev. William Hildyard, M.A., Market Deeping, Lincolnshire. 14th March, 1862.
John Hodgson Hinde, F.S.A., &c., Stelling Hall, Stocksfield-on-Tyne.† (*Vice-President*, 1843-1867.)
Rev. James F. Hodgson, Staindrop, Darlington. 6th December, 1864.
Richard Wellington Hodgson, North Dene, Gateshead. 11th December, 1856.
Rev. Henry Holden, D.D., Head Master of Durham Grammar School, 16th June, 1858.
John Dickonson Holmes, Barnardcastle. 4th June, 1867.*
The Very Rev. W. F. Hook, D.D., F.R.S., &c., Dean of Chichester. 14th March, 1862.
A. J. Beresford Hope, M.P., F.S.A., &c., Connaught Place, Hyde Park, London. 15th December, 1859.
The Lord Houghton, Fryston Hall, Ferrybridge. 30th December, 1858.
Fretwell W. Hoyle, F.G.H.S., Eastwood Lodge, Rotherham. 14th December, 1860.
Henry Arthur Hudson, Bootham, York. 7th March, 1865.
William Hughes, 24, Wardour Street, London. 7th March, 1865.
Rev. Thomas Hugo, M.A., F.S.A., The Chestnuts, Clapton, London. 14th March, 1862.
The Hull Subscription Library. 14th March, 1862.
Rev. Henry Humble, M.A., Canon of St. Ninian's, Perth. 31st May, 1849.
William D. Husband, York. 13th December, 1862.
Richard Charles Hussey, F.S.A., 16, King William Street, Strand, London. 12th July, 1836.
Joseph Hutchinson, Durham. 6th December, 1864.
Rev. Dr. Hymers, Brandesburton, Beverley. 30th December, 1858.
Rev. H. D. Ingilby, M.A., Ripley Castle, Ripley. 15th December, 1859.
Robert Henry Ingham, M.P., Westow, South Shields.†
C. J. D. Ingledew, M.A., Ph.D., F.G.H.S., Tyddyn-y-Sais, Caernarvon. 13th December, 1855.
Henry Ingledew, Newcastle-on-Tyne. 1st March, 1864.
Charles Jackson, Doncaster. 14th December, 1860. (*Local Secretary*, 1863-67.)

Henry Jackson, St. James' Row, Sheffield. 15th December, 1859.
William Jackson, Fleatham House, St. Bees, Whitehaven. 7th March, 1865.
Sir Walter James, Bart., Betteshanger, Sandwich. 5th December, 1865.
Rev. Joseph Jameson, B.D., Precentor of Ripon Minster, Ripon. 8th December, 1863.
Rev. Henry Jenkyns, D.D., Canon of Durham. September, 1838.
Rev. J. F. Johnson, Gateshead Fell, Durham. 11th December, 1856.
Rev. J. W. Kemp, M.A., New Elvet, Durham. 8th December, 1853.
Rev. John Kenrick, F.S.A., York. 15th December, 1859.
John Henry Le Keux, Durham. 13th December, 1861.
W. W. King, 28, Queen's Square, Cannon Street, London. 8th December, 1863.
Rev. Francis Kirsopp, Hexham. 7th March, 1865.
Rev. William Knight, Hartlepool, Durham. 13th December, 1862.
John Bailey Langhorne, Wakefield. 31st May, 1849. (*Local Secretary*, 1858-1867.)
The Hon. and Rev. Stephen Willoughby Lawley, M.A., Trevayler, Penzance. 8th December, 1863.
George Lawton, Nunthorpe, York. 12th July, 1836.
The Leeds Library. 11th December, 1856.
Octavius Leefe, 61, Lincoln's Inn Fields, London. 13th December, 1861.
Joseph Lees, Clarksfield Lees, Manchester. 17th June, 1861.
Rev. H. G. Liddell, M.A., Charlton King's, Cheltenham. 26th September, 1837.
The Library of Lincoln's Inn, London. 13th March, 1851.
William Linskill, Ellenbank, Blairgowrie, N.B. 13th December, 1855.
The Liverpool Athenæum. 6th June, 1855.
William Hugh Logan, Berwick-on-Tweed. 18th June, 1862.
The London Library, 12, St. James' Square, London. 13th March, 1851.
William Hylton Dyer Longstaffe, F.S.A., Gateshead. 17th March, 1855. (*Vice-President*, 1859-1867. *Local Secretary*, 1858-1867.)
Rev. J. L. Low, M.A., The Forest, Middleton-in-Teesdale, Durham. 16th June, 1858.
Rev. Henry Richards Luard, M.A., Registrar of the University of Cambridge. 24th June, 1859.
John James Lundy, F.G.S., Assembly Street, Leith. 16th March, 1861.
David Macbeath, 48, Mark Lane, London. 15th March, 1860.
Rev. E. M. Macfarlane, M.A., Dorchester, Wallingford. 7th June, 1864.
John Whitefoord Mackenzie, W.S., Vice-President S.A. Scotland, and M.R.S.N.A. Cop., 16, Royal Circus, Edinburgh. 14th July, 1835.
Messrs. Macmillan and Co., 16, Bedford Street, Covent Garden, London. 7th March, 1865.
The Library of Magdalen College, Oxford. 18th June, 1862.
The Lord Bishop of Manchester, F.R.S., &c., Mauldeth Hall, Manchester. 11th December, 1856.
James Meek, Middlethorpe Lodge, York. Lord Mayor of York, 1867. 6th December, 1864.
Walter Charles Metcalfe, Epping, Essex. 13th December, 1862.
Robert Mills, F.S.A., Shawclough, Rochdale. 16th March, 1861.
John Mitchell, 24, Wardour Street, London. 24th June, 1859.
E. J. Monk, Mus. Doc., York. 6th December, 1864.
C. T. J. Moore, Frampton Hall, Boston. 25th February, 1859.
M. T. Morrall, Balmoral House, Matlock Bank, Derbyshire. 16th March, 1861.
Walter Morrison, M.P., Malham Tarn, Skipton-in-Craven. 1st March, 1864.
George Gill Mounsey, Castletown, Carlisle. 17th March, 1855. (*Local Secretary*, 1858-1867.)
The Royal Library at Munich. 14th March, 1863.
Charles Scott Murray, F.S.A., Danesfield Park, Great Marlow. 15th December, 1859.
W. Magson Nelson, High Royd, Leeds. 4th June, 1867.*

The Literary and Philosophical Society, Newcastle-on-Tyne. 17th March, 1855.
Edward Hotham Newton, Westwood, Scarbro'. 13th December, 1862.
John Gough Nichols, F.S.A., 25, Parliament Street, Westminster.† (*Treasurer from the Foundation of the Society.)*
Thomas S. Noble, York. 5th December, 1865.
Rev. Charles Best Norcliffe, M.A., York. 12th March, 1852.
The Duke of Northumberland, Alnwick Castle. 6th June, 1865.
John Openshaw, Bur House, Bakewell. 15th June, 1863.
John R. Ord, Darlington. 30th December, 1858.
Rev. George Ornsby, Fishlake, Doncaster. 24th June, 1859.
Rev. Sir F. G. Ouseley, Bart., M.A., Precentor of Hereford, and Professor of Music in the University of Oxford, St. Michael's, Tenbury, Worcestershire. 11th December, 1856.
The Right Hon. Sir Roundell Palmer, M.P., 6, Portland Place, London. 8th December, 1863.
Thomas William Parker, Northfield House, Rotherham. 6th June, 1865.
Edward Peacock, F.S.A., Bottesford Manor, Brigg. 10th June, 1857.
Albert Pearson, Knebworth Rectory, Stevenage. 4th June, 1867.*
Joseph Pease, Darlington. 19th December, 1854.
George Peile, jun., Greenwood, Shotley Bridge. 7th March, 1865.
Richard Lawrence Pemberton, The Barnes, Sunderland. 13th December, 1855. (*Vice-President*, 1857-1867.)
Hugh Penfold, Library Chambers, Middle Temple, London. 14th March, 1862.
James Stovin Pennyman, Ormesby Hall, Middlesbro'. 8th December, 1853.
The Imperial Library at St. Petersburgh. 14th March, 1863.
Rev. Gilbert H. Phillips, M.A., Brodsworth, Doncaster. 30th December, 1858.
Rev. Ralph Platt, Durham. 30th December, 1858.
Francis S. Powell, M.P., Old Horton Hall, Bradford. 7th June, 1864.
The Ven. Archdeacon Prest, Rector of Gateshead, The College, Durham. 7th June, 1864.
James Pulleine, Clifton Castle, Bedale. 14th December, 1860.
Bernard Quaritch, 15, Piccadilly, London. 24th September, 1853.
Rev. James Raine, M.A., Canon of York, York. 12th March, 1852. (*Secretary*, 1854-1867.)
Rev. John Raine, M.A., Blyth Vicarage, Worksop. 18th June, 1862.
Rev. Canon Raines, M.A., F.S.A., the Vice-President of the Chetham Society, Milnrow, Rochdale. 14th December. 1860.
J. R. Raines, Burton Pidsea, Hull. 14th December, 1860.
Stephen Ram, Ramsfort, Goree, Ireland. 6th June, 1856.
Sir John William Ramsden, Bart., Byram Hall, South Milford, Yorkshire. 14th March, 1862.
The Lord Ravensworth, President of the Society of Antiquaries, Newcastle-on-Tyne. 6th June, 1856.
W. F. Rawdon, Bootham, York. 14th December, 1860.
Arnold W. Reinold, 4, Kingston Square, Hull. 8th December, 1863.
Godfrey Rhodes, Rawdon Hill, Otley. 1st March, 1864.
Charles H. Rickards, Manchester. 13th March, 1851.
The Proprietors of the Ripon Public Rooms. 14th December, 1860.
William Rivington, Hampstead Heath, London. 15th December, 1859.
T. W. U. Robinson, Houghton-le-Spring, Durham. 14th December, 1860.
The Very Rev. Daniel Rock, D.D., 17, Essex Villas, Kensington. 14th March, 1850. (*Vice-President*, 1851-1867. *Local Secretary*, 1858-1867.)
Rev. H. R. Rokeby, Arthingworth Manor, Northants. 14th March, 1862.
John Roper, Clifton Croft, York. 13th December, 1862.
Rev. George Rowe, M.A., Principal of the Training College, York. 7th June, 1864.
Samuel Rowlandson, Durham. September, 1841. (*Treasurer*, 1858-1867.)
J. B. Rudd, Tollesby Hall, Guisbrough, 13th March, 1857.

John Sampson, York. December, 1857.
George Gilbert Scott, Spring Gardens, London. 4th June, 1867.*
Simon Thomas Scrope, jun., Danby Hall, Bedale. 16th June, 1858.
The Trustees of Dr. Shepherd's Library, Preston. 6th December, 1864.
Thomas Shields, Scarborough. 8th December, 1863.
Rev. E. H. Shipperdson, M.A., The Hermitage, Chester-le-Street. 6th June, 1856.
The Signet Library, Edinburgh. 6th December, 1864.
Henry Silvertop, Minsteracres, Gateshead. 21st May, 1849.
The Library of Sion College, London. December, 1857.
R. H. Skaife, The Mount, York. 6th December, 1864.
Rev. Richard Skipsey, M.A., Bishopwearmouth.†
Rev. Alfred Fowler Smith, M.A., Rector of St. Mary's, Thetford. 6th December, 1864.
John Smith, Her Majesty's Keeper of Records, Doctors' Commons, London. 13th December, 1861.
John George Smythe, Heath Hall, Wakefield. 13th December, 1862.
George Smurthwaite, Richmond, Yorkshire. 8th December, 1863.
The Statistical Society, 12, St. James' Square, London. 30th December, 1858.
George Stephens, Professor of English Literature in the University of Copenhagen. 24th September, 1853.
The Royal Library at Stockholm. 14th March, 1863.
John Storey, 71, Albion Street, Leeds. 6th June, 1865.
John Stuart, New Mills, Currie, Edinburgh. Secretary the of Spalding Club, and of the Society of Antiquaries, Scotland. 24th February, 1853. (*Local Secretary*, 1862-1867.)
Rev. William Stubbs, M.A., Professor of Modern History in the University of Oxford, Librarian to the Archbishop of Canterbury. 13th March, 1851. (*Local Secretary*, 1862-1867.)
Charles Freville Surtees, M.P., Army and Navy Club, St. James' Square, London. 15th December, 1859.
Henry Edward Surtees, M.P., Dane End, Ware, Herts. 10th June, 1857.
Sir S. Villiers Surtees, Chief Justice of the Island of Mauritius, Silkmore House, Stafford. 8th December, 1853.
Rev. Scott F. Surtees, M.A., Sprotborough Rectory, Doncaster. 14th December, 1860.
William Edward Surtees, M,A., Seaton Carew, Durham. 15th March, 1860.
Sir John Swinburne, Bart., Capheaton, Morpeth. 5th June, 1866.
G. E. Swithinbank, Newcastle-on-Tyne. 14th December, 1860.
Christopher Sykes, M.P., Brantingham Thorpe, Hull. 15th December, 1859.
John Sykes, M.D., Doncaster. 24th June, 1859.
Rev. Francis Tait, M.A., Prebendary of Exeter, and Vicar of Axminster. 6th December, 1864.
Henry Taylor, the Colonial Office, London. 6th June, 1852.
Thomas Greenwood Teale, Leeds. 8th December, 1853. (*Local Secretary*, 1862-1867.)
Wilfred Tempest, Ackworth Grange, Pontefract. 4th December, 1866.*
Christopher Temple, Q.C., Temporal Chancellor of Durham, 15, Upper Bedford Place, London. 6th June, 1856.
Rev. Francis Thompson, Durham. 7th March, 1865.
Leonard Thompson, Sheriffhutton Park, York. 13th December, 1862.
Sir Nicholas William Throckmorton, Bart., Coughton Court, Bromsgrove. 13th December, 1862.
William Thwaites, Ripon. 7th June, 1864.
John Tiplady, Durham. 6th June, 1865.
Sir Walter Calverley Trevelyan, Bart., F.S.A., &c., Wallington, Newcastle-on-Tyne.† (*Vice-President from the Foundation of the Society.*)

The Library of Trinity College, Cambridge. June 5th, 1866.
H. J. Trotter, Bishop Auckland. 4th June, 1867.*
Charles Tucker, F.S.A., Secretary of the Archæological Institute, Marlands, Heavitree, Exeter. 15th December, 1852.
E. P. Turnbull, Fellow of Trinity College, Cambridge. 7th June, 1864.
Henry Turner, Low Heaton Haugh, Newcastle-on-Tyne. 12th July, 1836.
Rev. James Francis Turner, North Tidworth, Marlborough. 14th March, 1850.
Edmund H. Turton, Larpool Hall, Whitby. 13th December, 1861.
George Markham Tweddell, West Villas, Stokesley. 6th December, 1864.
The President of St. Cuthbert's College, Ushaw, Durham. September, 1838.
The Earl Vane, Winyard, Durham. 17th March, 1855.
The Library at the Vatican. 14th March, 1863.
Rev. C. J. Vaughan, D.D., Vicar of Doncaster, Chancellor of York, and Chaplain in Ordinary to the Queen. 13th December, 1862.
Rev. Philip Vavasour, Ripon. 8th December, 1862.
The Imperial Library at Vienna. 14th March, 1863.
The Very Rev. George Waddington, D.D., &c., Dean of Durham. September, 1841. (*Vice-President*, 1843-1867.)
Rev. George Wade, Fulford Grange, York. 18th June, 1862.
John Richard Walbran, F.S.A., Fallcroft, Ripon. 15th December, 1859. (*Vice-President*, 1860-1867.)
Rev. William Walbran, B.A., Radcliffe, Manchester. 6th December, 1864.
John Hope Wallace, Featherstone Castle, Haltwhistle. 14th March, 1863.
The Library of St. Edmund's College, Old Hall Green, Ware. 8th December, 1863.
George Waring, M.A., 2, Park Terrace, The Parks, Oxford. 14th Dec., 1860.
Albert, Way, F.S.A., &c., Secretary of the Archæological Institute, Wonham Manor, Reigate. 15th December, 1852. (*Vice-President*, 1859-1867.)
Christopher M. Webster, Pallion, Bishopwearmouth. 15th December, 1859.
His Excellency M. Van de Weyer, the Belgian Ambassador, 50, Portland Place, London. September, 1841.
W. W. Whitaker, 32, St. Ann's Street, Manchester. 16th March, 1861.
Robert White, Claremont Place, Newcastle-on-Tyne. 12th December, 1851.
Rev. C. T. Whitley, M.A., Vicar of Bedlington, Newcastle-on-Tyne.† (*Vice-President*, 1836-1867.)
John Whitwell, Kendall. 1st March, 1864.
Rev. W. A. Wightman, Vicar Choral of York Minster, St. Mary's, York. 6th December, 1864.
Joseph Wilkinson, Town Clerk, York. 14th March, 1862.
John Wilson, Bootham, York. 14th December, 1860.
Basil Thomas Woodd, M.P., Conyngham Hall, Knaresbro'. 8th December, 1863.
William Woodman, Town Clerk, Morpeth. 31st May, 1849.
The Lord Archbishop of York. 15th June, 1863.
The Library of the Dean and Chapter of York. 13th March, 1857.
The York Subscription Library. 16th March, 1861.
Sir Charles George Young, F.S.A., &c., Garter King at Arms, Heralds' College, London.† (*Vice-President*, 1836-1867.)
The Earl of Zetland, K.T., Aske Hall, Richmond. 13th March, 1851.

ACCOUNT OF SAMUEL ROWLANDSON, ESQ., AS TREASURER OF THE SURTEES SOCIETY.

From 1st January, 1865, *to 31st December*, 1866.

Date		£	s.	d.
1865.				
Jan. 1.	To Balance in hands of Treasurer on last account	116	9	4
Dec. 5.	To received of Edward Akroyd, Esq., towards the Printing and Illustrating 2nd vol. of Fountains Abbey	180	0	0
1866.				
Mar. 6.	To amount received of Messrs. Andrews and Co., for balance of sale of books (after deducting expenses) for 1865	78	4	4
Dec. 31.	To amount of Subscriptions received by Samuel Rowlandson, Esq., and J. G. Nichols, Esq., from 1st January, 1865, to 31st December, 1866	771	15	0
1867.				
May 24.	To amount received of Messrs. Andrews and Co., for balance of sale of books (after deducting expenses) for 1866	25	5	5
		£1171	14	1

Date		£	s.	d.	£	s.	d.
1865.	FOUNTAINS, VOL. II. :—						
May 26.	By paid J. R. Walbran, Esq., on account				49	10	0
1866.	YORK WILLS :—						
December.							
	By paid Leighton, Son, and Hodge, for binding	16	12	8			
	By paid Rev. James Raine, for editing	55	13	0			
	By paid J. B. Nichols and Son, for printing	119	18	0	192	3	8
	DEAN GRANVILLE :—						
	By paid Rev. Geo. Ornsby, for editing, etc.	54	15	0			
	By paid Leighton, Son, and Hodge, for binding	14	8	0			
	By paid Gilbert and Rivington, for printing	81	6	0	150	9	0
	THE LINDISFARNE GOSPELS, PART IV. :—						
	By paid Combe, Hall, Latham, and Co., for printing	89	10	6			
	By paid Leighton, Son, and Hodge, for binding	16	19	1			
	By paid George Waring, Esq., for editing	49	16	6			
	By paid Day and Son, for Chromo-Lithographing	13	7	9	169	13	10
	HEXHAM, VOL. II. :—						
	By paid Monkhouse and Co., for lithographed plan	3	9	6			
	By paid Mitchell and Hughes, for printing	81	1	0			
	By paid Leighton, Son, and Hodge, for binding	16	19	10			
	By paid W. H. D. Longstaffe, Esq., for expenses	2	8	6			
	By paid Rev. James Raine, for editing	43	0	0	146	18	10
	MISCELLANEOUS EXPENSES :—						
	By paid Rev. James Raine, Secretary's allowance for 1865 and 1866				60	0	0
	By paid Messrs. A. Johnson and Co., for printing Reports for ditto				15	15	0
	By paid Durham Advertiser, for printing Circulars				0	14	0
	By paid for Postage Stamps, &c., for Treasurer, 1865 and 1866				5	0	0
	By paid Assistant Treasurer, two years' salary				4	4	0
					794	8	4
	Balance in hand of Treasurer on this account				377	5	9
					£1171	14	1

We, the Auditors, appointed to credit the Accounts of the Surtees Society, report to the Society that the Treasurers have exhibited to us their Accounts from the 1st January, 1865, to the 31st December, 1866, and that we have examined the said Accounts and find the same to be correct, and we further report that the above is an accurate Abstract of the Receipts and Expenditure of the Society during the period to which we have referred. As witness our hands this 2nd day of September, 1867.

RALPH PLATT, D.D.
JOS. HUTCHINSON.

www.ingramcontent.com/pod-product-compliance
Lightning Source LLC
LaVergne TN
LVHW020110110826
845151LV00001B/117

* 9 7 8 1 4 2 5 5 4 4 1 6 4 *